Political Justice

POLITICAL JUSTICE

The Use
of Legal Procedure
for Political Ends

✦

BY OTTO KIRCHHEIMER

PRINCETON, NEW JERSEY
PRINCETON UNIVERSITY PRESS
1961

Chapter VII, " 'Democratic Centralism' and Political Integration of the Judiciary," appeared originally as an article in the *Yale Law Journal*, *68*, 705,
copyright © 1959 by the *Yale Law Journal*, and
in *Archiv des Öffentlichen Rechts*, *85*, Heft 1,
1960; Chapter IX, "Asylum," in the *American Political Science Review*, *53*, copyright ©
1959, by the *American Political Science Review*,
and in *Westdeutscher Verlag*, Heft 82 of the
Arbeitsgemeinschaft für Forschung des Landes
Nordrhein-Westfalen, 1959; and section 1
of Chapter X, "The Quality of Mercy,"
in *Social Research*, *28*, 151-70,
copyright © 1961 by
Social Research.

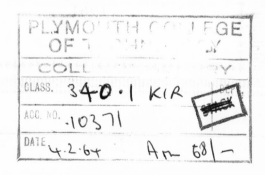

TO THE PAST,
PRESENT,
AND FUTURE VICTIMS
OF POLITICAL
JUSTICE

PREFACE

✦✦

THE title of this book needs an explanation, particularly for the American reader. The term Political Justice is usually taken to reflect the search for an ideal order in which all members will communicate and interact with the body politic to assure its highest perfection. Is it, then, gross linguistic abuse and utter cynicism to apply this term, as European writers have traditionally done, to the most dubious segment of the administration of justice, that segment which uses the devices of justice to bolster or create new power positions? The opposite is nearer the truth. The Greek ideal grows sharper in profile precisely because justice in political matters is more tenuous than in any other field of jurisprudence, because it can so easily become a mere farce. By utilizing the devices of justice, politics contracts some ill-defined and spurious obligations. Circumstantial and contradictory, the linkage of politics and justice is characterized by both promise and blasphemy.

What follows is an attempt to explain and elucidate this many-sided problem. It is neither a history of political justice nor a collection of its most noteworthy incidents and cases; rather than giving a panorama of the major political contests which have passed across the legal stage, it tries to relate the political content to the juridical form under which cases take place. I have, for example, omitted recital of the Dreyfus case, still commonly regarded as the *cause célèbre* of political justice in modern times. Dreyfus was an ordinary careerist, insensitive to the conflicts and contradictions of his age, who became innocently enmeshed in the labyrinth of political justice, a *statist* in his own play.

In the great drama of all times and therewith of our times—the limits of obedience to established powers by those who discount those powers' moral title and foresight—the players may be sometimes brave and heroic, at other times frightened and confused. But none of them, whether they are styled politicians or opinion molders, officials or judges, lawyers, conspirators, or revolutionaries, are innocent.[1] Wyshin-

---

[1] I have not dealt explicitly with the problem of the death penalty. For whatever they are worth, here are my personal thoughts as they relate to the problem of political justice. (A) The right to kill a human being in the pursuance of a political claim or in defense of a political system presupposes a high degree of conviction as to the superior quality of such a system. (B) If there exists a system on our planet to which I would be willing to grant such tremendous power, I have not, perhaps a sign of my

sky and Bukharin, Judge Medina and his Communist foes, the French
military tribunals, their FLN prisoners, and the latter's supporters among
the French community—all knew that behind the charge and the
answer to the charge were the images of past, present, and future
political orders whose record each of them tried to defend or to build
up. As it suits their momentary purposes, both the defense and the
authorities might either push into the foreground or contrive to hide
what connects the charge and the rebuttal sheet to their wider political
meaning. Defendants may be certain of eventual victory, busy putting
themselves into the right position for posterity, or desperately trying
to efface the memory of their past thoughts and actions. All we can
do here is to check on all their respective credentials and performances,
inquire into their methods and assumptions, their claims and counterclaims.

The literature on political justice is immense. Any new trial against
a real or imaginary enemy of the realm conducted somewhere on the
globe opens the floodgates of literary polemics and fills the bookshelves
to the brim. All those with an ax to grind add to the literature, be it
on the individualized basis of the West or in the more standardized
form of Communist martyrology and official vituperation. In addition,
there are the productions of civil liberties organizations and Western
and Eastern international lawyers' groups. The latter representatives
scurry over the earth, glaring at one another's deficiencies. They are
busily preparing protests and mapping questionnaires and answer
sheets, trying to determine how far the various nations have carried
that elusive rule of law which they all profess to have rendered prominent in their societal arrangements.

Then there are the learned commentators and the respected guild
of opinion writers. The former have relented a bit on their previous
self-assertiveness in legal exegesis. Having abandoned the pretension
of being able to deduct rules from a rational analysis of the texts, they
now simply make serviceable interpretations more or less coherent. The

---

ignorance, come across it. A world union might be in line for such a prerogative mainly
because—possibly an illusion—it would not need to make use of it. Until a more permanent world system can be established, an inclusive power syndicate, including at
least the two major antagonistic power groupings of our times, might become a
strictly temporary recipient of such powers. (c) Political systems of all persuasions
often raise the claim that they have killed or are prepared to kill their foes as a matter
of self-defense. Frequently the claim is patently fraudulent: the more serious it is, the
more it is beyond possible scrutiny.

judge, the main oracle of the law, might sometimes seem to be veering toward abandoning altogether the business of harmonizing various interpretations; in the shifty business of state protection he is at least tempted to play it by ear and follow the needs of the day. Finally there are the legal theorists, whose intellectual efforts stand in inverse ratio to their influence on actual practice.

I have drawn in varying degree on the output of all these individuals. Thus the reader will find in the following pages a sort of guide through substantive problems rather than a bibliographical beacon.

I am grateful to Dr. Kenneth Thompson and the Rockefeller Foundation for their continued support of my work. In its early stages my manuscript benefited greatly from the interest and advice of Dr. A. R. L. Gurland. I am also indebted to Professor Karl Loewenstein for his exhaustive criticism of the original manuscript. Mr. Bernard Morris, Miss Elizabeth Todd, and above all Miss Judy Walton of the Princeton University Press provided much appreciated editorial guidance. Professor Ernst Friesenhahn, judge at the German Federal Constitutional Court, was kind enough to provide me with not easily accessible material. The unfailing courtesy of Dr. Edmond Jann and many other members of the legal staff at the Library of Congress made my forays through their treasures both pleasant and successful. My thanks go also to the Busch-Reisinger Museum in Cambridge, Massachusetts for their kindness in allowing me to use the Grosz print, and to Suhrkamp Verlag in Frankfurt, for their permission to quote from Bertolt Brecht in Ch. VII.

I am grateful to Mrs. Heinz Heinemann, who prepared the index. And for the time-consuming and burdensome technical job involved in producing a book, my appreciation goes to my suffering spouse, to Mrs. Anne Walker, and to the staff of the Princeton University Press.

Preliminary versions of several chapters have appeared in the following journals: Ch. VII in the *Yale Law Journal*, Vol. 68 (1959), and in *Archiv des Öffentlichen Rechts*, Vol. 85 (1960); Ch. IX in the *American Political Science Review*, Vol. 53 (1959), and as Heft 82 of the Arbeitsgemeinschaft für Forschung des Landes Nordrhein-Westfalen, *Westdeutscher Verlag*, 1959; and part of Ch. XX in *Social Research*, Vol. 28 (1961).

August 1961
Freiburg, Breisgan

CONTENTS

xi

PART TWO

The Judge, the Defendant, and the State

PART THREE

Political Justice Modified:
Asylum and Clemency

CONTENTS

Political Justice

CHAPTER I

INTRODUCTION

++

C'est une chose surprenante que la puissance d'opinion accordée en général par les hommes, à l'intervention des tribunaux. Cette puissance est si grande, qu'elle s'attache encore à la forme judiciaire quand la substance n'existe plus, elle donne un corps à l'ombre.
—ALEXIS DE TOCQUEVILLE, *De la Démocratie en Amérique*, I, 8*

++

EVERY political regime has its foes or in due time creates them. If in its structure[1] and in the ground rules for the circulation of its elites the regime bore the hallmark of Plato's philosopher-king, it might be able to distribute ideological and material goods according to some preconceived pattern. But any regime is more likely to represent the joint product of tradition, the accident of history, plus an accretion of responses to the pressures of its time. Thus the merits of claims presented for validation to the powers-that-be are always bound to provoke controversial reaction. The resulting struggles between the established power holders and their foes, and generally between competitors for political power, assume a great variety of forms. Resort to courts is neither the most incisive nor the most frequent form. Dramatic changes in the composition of elites, the rank order of social classes, the authority of political systems, styled

* "It is a strange thing what authority the opinion of mankind generally grants to the intervention of courts. It clings even to the mere appearance of justice long after the substance has evaporated; it lends bodily form to the shadow of the law."

[1] The words *regime* and *government* connote *inter alia* a different magnitude of change. France's Third Republic, Pétain, the Fourth and Fifth Republics are all regimes. Premier Tardieu and Leon Blum under the Third Republic, Darlan and Laval under Pétain, Laniel and Mendès-France under the Fourth Republic are governments within the same regime. Yet the difference might at times get blurred. If there is no doubt that the chancellorships of Herman Müller and Stresemann correspond to two different governments under the single Weimar Republic, Chancellor Brüning, though in form representing a government under Weimar, may be said to have presided over a different regime. And whether Chancellor Adenauer will be found to have headed a government in the Federal Republic, or whether his reign will have been a regime distinct from that of his successors, only the future will tell. In spite of this difficulty, which is grounded in the nuances of political reality rather than in semantics, an attempt will be made to use the concepts along the lines explained above.

(Compared with the properties of a "political system," however, both regimes and governments are on a lower level of abstraction, connoting greater degrees of concretization.)

3

revolutions, or equally dramatic reconfirmation of the old order, such as the defeat of a peasant revolt or an attempted establishment of the earthly reign of a spiritual community that is hostile to traditional belief systems—all to a large extent bypass the courts. At best, the courts will be cast into the somewhat placid role of confirming results reached elsewhere. The courts' regular jobs confine them to the middle ranges. They operate in the zone of seemingly endless thrusts and counterthrusts through which power positions are strengthened and the incumbent regime's authority is impressed on friend and waverer; but often, at the same time, new images and myths are pressed forward by foes of the regime who try to expose and erode established authority. Even in these middle ranges, however, the courts function as little as any other official agency, as an exclusive staging area for clashes between conflicting political claims. The battle is likely to be joined simultaneously in the parliament and administrative office, the newspaper and the factory, the school and the church.

The fight for political domination may thus range over wide fields. Yet as long as the territorial state wields final authority, formalized political decisions are bound to be channelled through parliament, executive authority, and the courts. Of the three, the courts' share in the making of decisions is most limited. Parliament creates the law and, at least theoretically, supervises an all-important executive, handling the making of policy decisions as well as being prime mover for administrative chores. The courts' part in the public business consists less in advancing their own substantive solutions of issues of public concern than in holding themselves in readiness for settling a great number of conflict situations. Among these situations, the clash between the authorities of the day and their foes is significant.

It is true that over extended periods of time and in many lines of business the state has refused and is still refusing—though only for a diminishing number of categories—to submit to court adjudication its actions and the private party's claims against its agencies. Moreover, when likely to face enforcement difficulties for their prospective decisions, courts might, to preserve the prestige of the institution, embrace doctrines of abstentionism in regard to what they then label "political questions." In contradistinction, state organizations operating under constitutional regimes generally do not refuse to submit the fate of their foes to court recognizance as a means of restricting the latter's movement or personal liberty. Also, and increasingly since the nineteenth century, foes of the established order may even take their complaints to the courts through defamation suits against reigning politicians, damage suits against agencies or persons who have interfered with their freedom of movement, and habeas corpus actions; and the courts will put them all on their dockets.

What does such apparent liberality mean? Does it mean that the state organization is willing to entrust its protection against and its quarrel with its foes to an agency outside its immediate control? Is the prestige advantage it draws from the validation of its claims by such agency worth the corresponding loss of discretion in dealing with its foes? Does the impossibility of differentiating clearly between a foolproof private sphere and the cautionary realm of public concern give personal security such a high priority that it vanquishes all resistance to effective protective measures for individual and group? Or is the whole judicial apparatus a mirage? Do the needs of the state apparatus bear down so heavily on court practices that they make its supervision of repressive programs a mere ritual? If it is equally extreme to call courts the palladium of political liberty or mere registrars of decisions that are made elsewhere, what is their actual role in political struggle?

The answers to this intricate problem are far from clear and uniform. The historical and contemporary record of regimes' attitudes toward their actual and potential foes is a checkered one. In most periods of history, the political action of the group or individual coming into conflict with the goals of power holders has not been afforded some guaranteed sphere of impunity. Factions and persons might be interlocked in battle for the possession and direction of the official apparatus of coercion, but each of the contending parties would take it for granted that whoever comes out on top also commands the citizens' energies and loyalties. To put it in terms of Plutarch's interpretation of Solon's energetic legislative efforts to reject an epicurean interpretation of man's behavior: "He [Solon] did not like the idea that some individual remains indifferent in the face of public danger and, securing his private affairs, glory that he has no feeling of the distempers of his country. He thought it only right that from the onset of public trouble he attach himself to the juster cause. Instead of waiting to see who would be victorious, he should assist the honest cause and venture with them."[2] To the extent that political deviations were tolerated, such benefice was due largely to the respective weakness or strength of established power positions. It resulted from a possibly nonrepetitive configuration of political forces. During the nineteenth century, in what were called, perhaps prematurely, the civilized nations, a measure of

[2] *Lives* xx.

constitutionally sanctioned protection was granted with some consistency to the political foe of the established order. During the twentieth century, this sphere of unofficially sanctioned political behavior has shrivelled; while by no means extinct, it has now become problematic in the majority of places on the globe. What, then, is the function of courts in political strife? In the simplest and crudest terms, disregarding for a moment the embellishments, enlargements of function, and safeguards of the age of constitutionalism: the courts eliminate a political foe of the regime according to some prearranged rules.

Of the manifold devices to rid the regime of political foes, the judicial inquest obtains neither the quickest nor by any means the most certain results. The desired goal—elimination of a political foe from political competition, or seizure of his worldly goods—may be performed by other agencies. Some of them involve informal violence and are highly irregular. Others form the stock-in-trade of politics: the ballot, a recent and partial substitute for the bullet; the pulpit, now partly replaced by its modern equivalent, the media of communications, working the full range of psychological pressures; and last but not least, Philip of Macedonia's ass with sacks of gold, noiseless and leaving behind them few traces. All do similar and, considering the proximate aim, possibly superior service. Do judicial proceedings belong altogether in this same category? Are they nothing but another device in the continuous process of stabilizing or changing power relations? Where rests the qualitatively different element, transcending the level of proximate result?

Judicial proceedings serve to authenticate and thus to limit political action. Power holders may have an infinite number of security interests. Some of them, though perhaps far-fetched, are arrived at rationally; others are the product of imagination. By agreeing to a yardstick, however nebulous or refined, to cut down the number of occasions for the elimination of actual or potential foes, those in power stand to gain as much as their subjects. Authentication removes the fear of reprisals or liquidation from multitudes of possible victims, and encourages a friendly and understanding disposition toward the security needs of the power holders on the part of their subjects. The more elaborate the paraphernalia of authentication, the greater the chance of vicarious popular participation in its conundrums. When proceedings remain largely secretive, the character of those sitting in judgment, whether it rests on magic, tradition, or on the much narrower basis of rational professional qualification, must perforce form the main basis of approval. In proceedings to which the public has some access, authen-

6

tication, the regularizing of the extraordinary, may under favorable circumstances be transformed into a deeper popular understanding and political participation. Modern means of communication do not restrict participation in or reactions to a trial by those present and, with some delay, by a wider educated public. If the participants wish, proceedings may be thrown open to virtually the whole world. The dynamics of such an undertaking—the vicarious participation of a virtually unlimited public in the unfolding of political reality, re-created and severely compressed for trial purposes into categories within easy reach of the public's understanding—fashions a new political weapon. Such mobilization of opinion may remain a mere by-product of judicial proceedings; but it may and in modern times frequently has superseded the original goal of judicial proceedings, authentication. At the same time it may destroy the proceedings' inherent limitations.

What a state organization does with its statutory arsenal, its security blueprints, and blank checks will depend on the state of mind of its leadership and on the amount of concerted hostility in the body politic. These two influences are not necessarily related. The greater the reservoir of public dissatisfaction, the more the regime's political effectiveness will depend on a planned and discerning use of its legal weapons. If it allowed its administration of justice to run after every incident that could be worked up into a case, it would soon lose breath as well as face. Seeking the spontaneous assent of foes is at best difficult and long-term. To instill in potential foes the habit of prudence and a measure of obedience requires the tracking down of the significant rather than the available foe. Attempts to enforce universal compliance may end up in universal lawlessness, heralding the breakdown rather than the strengthening of the existing order. To develop rational criteria rather than emotional slogans for dealing with political foes, the regime must be able to differentiate between the isolated and occasional foe and the organized group and, within the group, between the leader and his followers. Failing the latter, the regime may incur political risks in inverse proportion to the likelihood of its success. Importuning the isolated foe may be a cautionary device, a seemingly harmless popular pastime—a matter of flexing muscles in self-confirmation. Yet such a move may prove costly if it implants the seed which starts communion with the martyr.

Where the allegiance of masses rather than the action of selected individuals becomes the focal point of contention, formal obeisance rather than retribution seems the more logical goal. The official system has to be kept going and possibly reinforced by its depriving the mass

7

of dissenters of easy incentives to challenge the regime, by allowing the average camp follower to stay on the sideline, by a policy of graduated disqualifications and rewards, and by strategic individual acts of submission. Transferring loyalty conflicts from the ranks of the regime into those of the foe might, other factors being equal, help to hold the outer defense perimeter and obtain outward conformity rather than multiplying the opportunities for martyrdom; the more spectacular task of reclaiming lost souls would be left as the penultimate hope and aim. The reservoir of potential followers of the foe of the regime fills and empties in accordance with the tidings of the battle. If the right kind of key is used, these followers are rarely locked completely from either side.[3]

The differentiation between followers and leaders, facilities for which are found in criminal codes, enforces a certain amount of passive obedience and keeps the machinery of enforcement from breaking down or becoming a mere apparatus of registration. If it does not help a regime on the downgrade to survive catastrophes due to deeper and more encompassing causes, it saves it from wasted motion and embarrassment. If this differentiation, which permits followers to move to the sidelines, is dismissed without simultaneous resort to crude, sweeping, and often bestial forms of "disqualification," such as deportation or execution, according to "objective" criteria of race, social status, religion or nationality, the regime is confronted by a dilemma. Mass prosecutions follow unavoidably from the failure to differentiate between leaders and followers in a politically hostile organization.[4]

[3] See Appendix A.

[4] It was this type of dilemma which the American occupation authorities conjured up in their quixotic insistence on making their German charges initiate denazification proceedings against a potential 3,669,230 people. This vast multitude became theoretically liable to the proceedings—a sort of cross between a criminal court and an administrative agency. After a trial equipped with the customary safeguards, they were to be classified into one of five categories, according to their involvement in NS politics, and thereafter to be visited with corresponding sanctions.

This attempt to institute bona fide court proceedings on a conveyor belt system (which was imitated by the other allies only with extreme prudence and so long as it fit their political plans and interests) was from the outset destined to bog down under its own weight and become a meaningless paper shuffling. Far from isolating major National Socialist figures, it created a firm bond among the disparate crowd of potential victims of denazification, from the master brains who had directed the political and economic sectors of national life to the last village teacher and postal clerk. In due course, its originators had to smother their own brain child in a cascade of scarcely face-saving "amnesties," and with it any serious attempt to expose the responsibility for the regime's culpability. This culpability arose from the peculiar association between many of the upper strata of German society and its déclassé elements.

This inept attempt at proceedings against whole segments of the population shows

These cursory remarks on the differences between prosecuting deviant leadership and containing their followers point up two major problem areas. The first concerns the institutional patterns of relations between a regime and its political foes, viewing the foes as a movement rather than as obstreperous and dangerous individuals. In our period hostility to an existing regime is rarely any longer the isolated expression of loosely joined individuals or an inchoate sentiment among the upper echelons of society. Nor, if hostility is organized, is it restricted to upholding a particular segment (religion, property) against the encroachment of today's rulers who would be willing to compromise on almost anything else. Since the nineteenth century, the days of Irish Nationalists, English Chartists, and the German Social Democrats, the fine art of loyalty-absorbing counterorganizations has been developed parallel to the growth of state power. Whenever such full-fledged counterorganizations fuse the ideological and material interests of larger groups, any state organization which does not want to turn to the Fascist or Communist pattern of total repression of political deviation may face major problems of political mass control.

Another problem put into bold relief by the accelerated rate of political change in our time concerns the feasibility of trial by fiat of a successor regime. Keeping a present political foe at bay is one thing, prosecuting him once he has been vanquished another. Considerations governing both situations are not all necessarily identical. Reversals of political fortunes have not been uncommon and many a Hydra supposedly slain by its foes has raised a head again. The very possibility and danger of a reversal points up many a successor regime's preoccupa-

---

the continued wisdom of having a sharp dividing line between actual proceedings and some automatic disqualifications or a formal purgatory oath. This distinction is at least an arguable, if problematic, means of controlling a mass of camp followers and the criminal trial of the selected few. Its aim is to eventually disorganize the enemy camp and to convert the established fact of defeat into the image of its historical and moral necessity.

The literature on this episode is considerable. The official document speaks for itself: The Office of the US High Commissioner, Fifth Quarterly Report, October 1-December 31, 1950, pp. 46-55. For an early but quite realistic glimpse at denazification in the legal field, see Karl Loewenstein, "Reconstruction of the Administration of Justice in American Occupied Germany," *Harvard Law Review*, Vol. 61 (1948), pp. 419-67, esp. pp. 442ff. John Gimbel, *A German Community under American Occupation, Marburg, 1945-1952* (Stanford, 1961), chs. 9, 10, provides a vivid local analysis. The farce of denazification is now being brought home rather disagreeably to the Federal Republic by their cynical DDR competitors, through the unearthing of some unsavory records on the past behavior of incumbent West German judges. Germany's embarrassment at having to deal with the record of these judges after fifteen years becomes evident from Max Güde, *Justiz im Schatten von Gestern*, Hamburg, 1960.

tion (the last in the long procession being the 1960 Turkish and South Korean regimes) with delving into its predecessor's record, holding it up to contempt, and instilling into the public feelings of loyalty and gratitude toward those who have delivered them from the evil. In doing so, however, the regime faces the ticklish problem of casting its pedagogical goal into a suitable legal form. It must attempt to minimize the partisan element which inevitably mars such proceedings and to differentiate between accountability for mere political misjudgment and responsibility for criminal and inhuman behavior committed during such political action.

The more inclusive and the less clearly definable are the rules which separate licit from illicit political behavior, the more important is it who guards such rules.[5] The history of political jurisprudence turns to some extent on the principles affecting the selection of those who will render judgment. The wide variation in the character of jurisdiction shows that in perfecting their legal tools, those in power are subject to everchanging momentary preoccupations. But larger considerations

[5] The state's interest being everybody's interest, could every citizen, in case of danger, act on his own to secure the survival of the state? An ancient doctrine translated into a legal enactment in Athens as early as 410 B.C. vindicates as everybody's right the slaying of one who is about to change or has already changed the political status of the polis. (See Arthur Bonner-Smith, *The Administration of Justice from Homer to Aristotle*, Chicago, 1938, Vol. 2, p. 47; for Lord Mansfield's espousal of the doctrine, justifying the military suppression of the Gordon rioters without previous authorization from civilian magistrates, see S. Maccoby, *English Radicalism, 1762-1785*, London, 1955, p. 329.)

The mere act of rising against the regime extinguishes one's citizen status and makes him into an enemy. This doctrine, which has had a sturdy life, has meaning and justification when the attack actually rather than theoretically prevents the competent authorities from functioning; this is the pristine core of any martial law doctrine. If extended far beyond this situation, it invites an unwarranted shift in the constitutional distribution of functions in favor of the executive at a time when safeguards against such shifts are most needed. The classic case is Cicero's ordering the execution of Catilina's friends without waiting for the exercise of the right of *provocatio* to the Centuriate Assembly. This doctrine may also open the door altogether to political anarchy, serving as cloak for partisan murder in the reputed interest of the fatherland; this happened, for example, in the Weimar Republic in the early 1920's.

It is a test of a functioning state organization that it be equipped to handle its foes according to previously determined lines of jurisdiction, without being swamped by the problematic support of uninvited partisans, thus maximally excluding the merging of partisan advantage and public necessity. In analyzing the types of political jurisdiction, we shall therefore exclude the outright partisan in search of a title. This incident is more frequent in rudimentary public organizations (such as the barbarian kingdoms of the early middle ages), which approach a mere sanctioning of the results of a never-ending stream of private feuds. But we shall also exclude the modern executive acting without any title but its own certificate of necessity and convenience; this was the style of Hitler during the so-called Röhm Putsch in the spring of 1934.

cause recurrent patterns in their reactions to the needs of the moment. There are three main ways in which those who carry out the business of authentication exercise their authority:

1. The charisma of a single person: a tribal leader, a priest (in theory and, to a greatly varying degree, also in practice) the ruler of antiquity, the medieval king, or the monarch of the absolutist era. Rendered by the fountainhead of justice, each decision rests on the pre-eminence of its source and derives its intrinsic merits from that source;

2. The political assembly, whether of aristocratic or democratic origin: in the aristocratic line, the *Areopag* of Athens, to a more limited extent the Roman *Senatus*, the House of Lords, or the French *Sénat*; in the democratic line, the Athenian Assembly, the Roman Centuriate Assembly, the bodies sitting in judgment on Charles I or Louis XVI, or, in a more diminutive form, the Athenian *Helia*, or the Anglo-American assizes. While the source of authority rests on the community's pre-eminent and possibly representative position (or at least on its "cross section" claim), the individual decision rests on an evaluation of community standards and needs arrived at through a mixture of intuitive, emotional, and rational considerations of benefit or loss for the community and for the individual affected by the decision;

3. The professional: the Roman *Quaestor* of republican times, the member of an imperial council of the later Empire, the member of a continental court who has studied at Padua or Bologna, the British judge appointed on the basis of his experience at the bar, or the full-time member of a present-day judicial organization. The agency in whose name the decision is rendered, the ruler or the people, recedes behind the *substantive* rationality, the purposes which a judgment serves, and the *formal* rationality, the network of prescribed rules through which the judgment has been reached.

In some instances the authority or, for short intervals, the naked physical power of coercion of the single person and the assembly may have been strong enough to carry the judgment of execution. But whether it was a Roman or Byzantine emperor, or a French king during the emergence of the national state, his own immediate interest in the political case was never completely in harmony with the theorem of the fountainhead of justice. This was true even if the need for unity and continuity formed a much travelled bridge between the results of the process of justice and its rationalization. Moreover, the more vague the authority, the more doubtful the likelihood of executing judgment.

Of these three primary forms of jurisdiction, there are four main combinations. The first, now part of history, is a balance between monarchic and aristocratic and monarchic and professional elements. The medieval balance between the monarch and his principal vassals required that the vassals participate in the king's council to give the judgment a chance of execution. The later professional and bureaucratic balance between the king and his learned judges—attenuated in later absolutism into the prince's right of confirming judgments—became a prerequisite to the effective functioning of the territorial state.

The second combination, a balance between the jurisdiction of the territorial state and the church, also belongs to history. But in our present era of the decline of the territorial state, the corresponding rise of supranational functional authorities, and the persistent though unrecognized claims for loyalty by worldwide movements, this attempted balance should hold more than perfunctory interest. Its checkered history seems to show that it was easier in theory than in practice to lay out areas of exclusive jurisdiction and to arrange necessary cooperation in heresy proceedings. From Pope Martin's captivity (A.D. 653-656) to the days of Joan of Arc, divergence of interests and the changing strength of the two parties led to frequent transgressions of jurisdictional boundaries. At times it was an open contest, at others only slightly veiled by a network of transparent fictions.

The third combination is the balance between the aristocratic and the democratic elements, faint traces of which still exist. To this balance belongs the *provocatio* of the Roman Republic in which every Roman citizen was allowed to bring a capital sentence by any authority before the Centuriate Assembly.[6] The impeachment proceedings under English, French, or present American law, instituted by the popular assembly before the upper house, rest on the need for cooperation of a popular element in a body that was originally under aristocratic and now under a remoter form of popular control. This cooperation is a *sine qua non* for passing a major political judgment. It might break down in decisive instances, indicating a shift of political balance.[7]

---

[6] In form, the authority sentencing the political foe might have been a political official, such as the consul; but in reality, this official would not have acted without having the *auctoritas* of the *senatus* behind him. See Gustav Geib, *Geschichte des römischen Kriminalprozesses*, Leipzig, 1842, p. 41.

[7] Tiberius and Gaius Gracchus as well as Catilina's friends were entitled to have their case brought before the people of Rome. If, unlike their Greek counterparts, the Centuriate Assembly could not discuss the case, they had the right to vote on it. The argument from emergency (*perduellio* automatically taking away the citizen quality —the cardinal theorem of the aristocratic party, as Theodor Mommsen called it [*Römisches Strafrecht*, Leipzig, 1899, p. 258]) involved a change of the constitutional

The fourth, the balancing principle of our present-day society, starts from the omnipresence of the professional, the learned judge, who brings special education and experience to his job. Professionalization, specialization, tenure privileges, and invocation of the law—a seemingly neutral point of reference that produces a counterdemand for political, meaning today democratic, controls. The first echelon of democratic control is the association of selected members of the public with some parts of the decision-finding process.[8] The popular element is weaker than the professional in this mixed popular-professional type of jurisdiction; this is so because of the juror's lack of professional training and the jury's attenuated representative character. In contrast to the assembly type of political jurisdiction, this specially selected cross-section of the people assisting the professional judiciary expresses opinions current among the people. But it has not the opinion-absorbing character of the full-fledged political representative.

In special political jurisdictions (whether instituted for special political offenses, whoever commits them, or only for political offenses by exalted political dignitaries), either the political or the professional element might predominate. At one end of the spectrum is the French-style revolutionary tribunal of 1793, comprising five professional judges and twelve jurors, all appointed by the same Convention. At the other is the contemporary Western European constitutional or supreme (federal) court, where the political element dwindles to some parliamentary participation in the process of cooptation of professional judges. Between these two extremes there have been many intermediary forms.

On the surface, the constant see-saw battle seems to have ended temporarily with something like victory of the bureaucratic-professional over the democratic-political element. The professionals staff the courts, either excluding the nonprofessional or, at best, leaving the lay members in a marginal position. Yet, despite the triumph of the professional in personal and staffing terms, changes which have intervened during the last century and a half have put a different inter-

---

balance in favor of the aristocracy—a change soon to be replaced by the *principatus*. In both Strafford's and Laud's case, the reverse was true: the lower house substituted a bill of attainder after the Lords had refused to act on the impeachments as proposed to them by the Commons. This revolutionary action indicated the passing of the traditional balance in favor of political justice by fiat of the democratic assembly.

[8] Continental practice excludes the jury from pretrial judicial investigations and by now associates the professionals with the laymen in the findings of all elements of the judgment. Both continental and Anglo-American practice leave the direction of the trial in the hands of the professional judge. Anglo-American law leaves questions of law as well as sentencing to the professional.

pretation on the role of the professional; in a somewhat larger sense, they have provided countervailing political elements to professionalism.

Until late in the eighteenth century, the professional on the bench was a retainer of the prince, appointed by him for a general line of legal jobs and possibly also put (French style) on an extraordinary commission to do a specific job concerning important affairs of state which the prince did not wish to entrust to his regulars. The prince was his employer who might even be able to cashier him[9] and to whom he would look for preferment. With his newly gained immovability, however, he acquired somewhere between 1701 and 1848 a new master: public opinion. In his most immediate if intermittent capacity as member of the jury, the new democratic master, often inexperienced in political affairs, was neither too demanding nor always able to size up all the implications of the case before him. But behind the juror was a figure less precise and massive than his old master, the prince, but generally much more ubiquitous and persevering: the critic in parliament and the newspaper, his eye and ear.

The transition to the judge of the postabsolutist era worked most easily under Anglo-American conditions. Coming traditionally from the ranks of the more successful lawyers and politicians, the judge continued to listen closely to the prevailing opinion trends. This type of receptivity might work occasional hardship for the cause of some small but vigorous and obstinate minority which came into conflict with the rest of society. Yet the wide margin of personal freedom granted by a nonchalant and successful commercial society, together with the habitual inclination of the judges to consider the effect of their own demeanor on all strata, come election day, reduced the likelihood of such occurrences. What clashes did occur—the Haymarket trial, for example—instantly reveal that impartiality beyond the most superficial, technical level is difficult in an opinion-governed society and that the modern trial, conducted under the glaring lights of worldwide publicity, has an image-creating capacity.

In the constitutional monarchies of continental Europe the judge became a kind of buffer between public opinion and the bureaucratic establishment. With one foot in the official establishment and the other in the moderately liberal camp of the day, he eyed skeptically both the demeanor of the incipient mass parties and the official attempts to suppress or, when that failed, to needle them. Often trying to reduce to its legal form the political content of the conflict between authorities

[9] Though not in France: see Chapter VIII, introduction.

and mass organizations, the judge stayed strictly within the limits of his job. In doing so he fulfilled the expectations of neither the official-dom, who wanted him to help domesticate the Hydra of what today is called subversion, nor of the regime's foes, who wanted him to help expose what they called the baseness and depravity of those in power.

In the dynamics of the nineteenth century domestic power struggles, the judge, who was just escaping the political tutelage of the executive establishment, might have considered himself acting at times as an arbiter between the official establishment and society at large.[10] When he administered the state's law, he did so under the watchful eye of public opinion which had itself outgrown the role of mouthpiece of the authorities and was now becoming the voice of the community, directed toward the educated minority. Some of the most intelligent organs of public opinion believed ardently in the perfectibility of human institutions. Consequently, they wanted to restrict coercion to its very minimum and were quick to criticize existing institutions, including the courts, for any attempt to silence discordant voices. Others, anxious about the need to uphold traditional values against the onrush of the disorderly and covetous masses, felt that everlasting political and social progress was a delusion. They looked at the courts as an integral part of the defense system of traditional society, a kind of second line of defense with orders to protect the first line, the officialdom and especially the army, against intellectual and political foes.

When the various skirmishes between the authorities and their foes merged and submerged into a conflict of such depth and such clearly drawn lines—a sort of legal Armageddon to make the reduction of the conflict to its lowest legal denominator impossible—the judiciary found itself in difficulties; any position it took made it appear partisan in the eyes of many in the community. Under such circumstances, the courts might suffer in their own ranks the contretemps of the deep division of public opinion (witness the Dreyfus affair). Even with the modest and very provisional degree of social, as distinct from legal, finality which a court's judgment in a political case is usually able to

---

[10] The French *magistrat* of the Third Republic was from the outset in a somewhat less favorable position than his brethren working under the conditions of the constitutional monarchy. When society and official establishment merge completely, as they did under the conditions of the parliamentary republic, the judge will bear down with redoubled energy on the "enemies of society" (an attitude which became especially apparent during the various anarchist trials), with the latter paid back in kind. See, for example, Elisée Réclus, *L'Évolution, la Révolution et l'Idéal Anarchique*, Paris, 1898, p. 101.

provide, the government may lose the ability to enforce the judgment on the recalcitrant individual and his group. The judgment may then become nothing but a mere incident in a reappraisal and rearranging of the country's scale of values and institutional arrangements.

Many of the major intrasociety conflicts of the turn of the century have subsided, leaving ripples in place of tidal waves. But others have moved from intrastate to worldwide concern. The political and ideological struggle, first between Fascism and democracy, lately between Communism and the older types of political arrangements (mass democracy, semi-authoritarianism, and so on), moves both within the individual state and between states, producing exclusive clientele and friendship-enmity relations. The judiciary cannot but be engulfed by these conflicts, which, whatever the traditional formulas in use, have wrought basic changes in its presuppositions and methods of work. These changes may be characterized as follows:

1. The generalization of the political-ideological conflict with the attendant military and political risks have caused all regimes to reinforce police and informal institutional controls over their subjects' associations and political activities. They have acted with particular intensity toward those whose activity may be construed to have any bearing on national preparedness, ideological or material. Since these controls function to a large extent in the societal, economic, and parapolitical sphere, they are removed from the area of direct political coercion; thus they come only tangentially and interstitially under court scrutiny.

2. Such controls, far from being resented by the great majority of the population, parallel major opinion trends in mass society.

3. In contrast to nineteenth century public opinion, public opinion today rests on a much broader basis, drawing into its sphere the great majority of the population. This change in audience structure and the corresponding orientation of the media have made opinion more uniform, less alert, and more uncritical; politics, of no primary interest to the majority, is only incidental to the enjoyment of mass consumer goods. To the extent that politics injects a strange and disorderly world with new demands, reactions are both defensive and sharply ethnocentric: people are prepared to view their time- and situation-bound institutions as universal models. The internal deviant and potential foreign foe are considered *hostis generis humani*.

4. For a multiplicity of reasons that lie in the traditional structures and cleavages of societies and in the different stages of their social

development, nineteenth century ideologies not only persist to some degree (in Italy, Greece, and to some extent France), but have by now been merged into and superimposed by the new worldwide cleavages. This has prevented the rise of a uniform opinion and has led to domestic political polarization, mitigated only by the general contemporary trend toward depoliticization in mass society.

How do these changes affect judicial participation in the national political scene? As *de facto* control and attempted isolation of potentially hostile elements are carried out by informal police and, more important, by internal organizational devices (self-control in labor unions, opinion factories, political parties, civil service and affiliated and controlled ancillary contract and research establishments), the need to resort to courts arises where (a) formal restriction of freedom may become necessary for successful police and security operations; (b) control measures have passed the dividing line between informal restraints (usually fully effective) and actual coercion, and the victim therefore seeks formal adjudication; (c) the regime in question has decided on a policy of either totally repressing its foes or of wearing them down, restricting their political availability by continuous judicial proceedings against them; and (d) where carefully chosen segments of deviant political activity are submitted to court scrutiny, less for direct repressive effect than for dramatizing the struggle with the foe and rallying public support.

These four are merely a check list of possible occasions for court action in connection with repressive programs in contemporary non-totalitarian society. The prevailing domestic situation will determine to what extent such issues need to be referred to the court. From British latitudinarianism, which restricts the need for court intervention to the very minimum, to the fully repressive policy of the Federal Republic of Germany, national variants remain considerable.

In the face of these drastic changes in the courts' operating conditions and, concomitantly, in the structure of national consciousness, the limits have narrowed within which courts today may decide political issues. By the same token, the possible effect of their action has widened. Beyond their power to authenticate official action (which, for the above reasons, may actually have declined), the courts have become a new dimension through which many types of political regimes, as well as their foes, can affirm their policies and integrate the population into their political goals.

During the nineteenth century, with the beginnings of mass organizations, it was the defendant's friends rather than the authorities who profited from the chance to create beneficial images and give their campaign a new *élan* at a time when it was most needed. And most authorities were relieved at being able to steer the case through the courts without giving rise to new agitation. The defendant's propagandist talent and journalistic invective might outrun his organizational power. But Armand Carrel's National during the trial of the 1834 conspirators before the Pairs, Feargus O'Connor's Northern Star in Jack Frost's 1840 trial, and Karl Marx, the pamphleteer, commenting on the trial of the Kommunistenbund before the Cologne assizes in 1852—all these, even when they could only turn momentary defeats into positions of moral strength, were not without their effect on the public.

In the twentieth century mass society, public authorities are endangered by the long-run effects of sagging public morale and political apathy; in totalitarian states the danger is not so much revolutionary attempts at the existing regime as a split in internal ranks. Thus public authorities today have made a more conscious effort to use the trial form for purposes of internal mobilization. From the closing days of World War I to Ben Gurion's desire to use the full account of the extermination of the Jews, uniquely provided in an Eichmann trial, as the focal point for Israel's self-assertion before continuing threats to its existence, there has been a neverending effort to enlarge the effectiveness of political action by resort to the courts.

In the ideological fight for dominion over people's minds, the courts are agencies closely connected with public affairs. At least in non-totalitarian countries they remain outside the direct control of the executive establishment. Yet their particular public position of trust has made the courts' conduct of politically tinged trials a crucial element in the political process. At the same time, it has sharply increased what is the inevitable danger in all such trials: deformation through partiality of underlying assumptions and procedures. It has also increased all the techniques of indirect pressure which form part of the transformation from the limited public opinion of the nineteenth century to the directed mass opinion of today.

If a judiciary operates with a margin of tolerance that is set by its own interpretation of opinion trends and political and moral requirements, rather than by the commands of an identified sovereign, how can it be organizationally and intellectually equipped to face such contingencies? This is a major theme of our inquiry. We must therefore differentiate between a judiciary seeking its own adjustments and answers to the pressures of the times and a judiciary which has been fully integrated with the goals and objectives of the political authorities. To the Western judge, for example, opinion trends are reminders that, to be able to serve as norms of community behavior, decisions must move within the penumbra of present-day contingencies. The Eastern judicial functionary, on the other hand, develops the details of a political line regarding which a political command structure has established fixed yardsticks of responsibility for action taken or omitted. Even under the contingencies and pressures of modern society, there remains an appreciable difference between the presuppositions and methods of the traditional opinion-directed judiciary and the more recent party-directed one.

To some extent, the action of a judge is conditioned by the behavior of the defendant. In the average defendant's case, reversal of the roles of defendant and judge remains in the realm of day-dreaming; as people are apt to do, the defendant will rearrange his accidental rencontre in the most pleasing fashion. With the political defendant, though, reversal of the roles becomes real; whatever adjustments he is likely to make to the necessities of the situation are of a tactical and narrow nature. They may depend *inter alia* on his attitude toward the psychological skill of a lawyer who can bridge the considerable gap between proximate advantage and the maintenance of the fixed star, the political goals of the defendant. But in essence his justification must perforce remain the identification with his cause. Moves and counter-moves of all trial participants, therefore, relate to this basic constellation of the political trial.

Does political justice find its ultimate justification in the unfathomable purposes of history, where yesterday's defeats, abuses, and sufferings may be the promise of tomorrow's greater glory? The worth of such expectation in terms of lives maimed and destroyed is completely insecure and conjectural. How many people who do not, or no longer, identify meaningfully with a political cause have been drawn into the maelstrom of political justice? How many causes must remain, through no fault of their promoters, forever abortive? Or should one abandon the quest for an ultimate meaning and simply fall back on the need for upholding the authority of the existing regime and using the court's verdict as proof that the action taken was necessary and legitimate? But a court has, at least officially, little business with the actual need for political prosecutions which are within the discretionary province of the government; it deals only with their admissibility and the sufficiency of proof under the existing law. More important, who will ever be able to guarantee that the cause of the regime invoking the court's support has been worth upholding?

It is seldom recognized that asylum and clemency form an integral part of political justice. They belong to it by identity of style: the same haphazardness and irregularity of performance. But beyond these formal characteristics there is an inner logic and necessity which tie them both firmly to the chariot of political justice. The more remote the practices of political justice from even the palest image of justice, the more imperative are the existence and operation of these extraordinary and apparently unrelated remedies. Asylum is an accident, for it depends both on the good luck of a foe of a regime and on the policies of a bystander, a third country, willing to grant it. The reason for granting or refusing asylum, the rules or the absence of rules governing its grant, the study of actions and motivations, become integral to the radiations of political justice.

If asylum is an accident, possibly enlarged into a beneficial policy, clemency is an abandonment of claims, possibly not admitted. Under what circumstances will a political system make such a gesture? How much of it is sheer weariness with the seemingly indeterminable consequences of its own past action? Is it senseless to try systematizing what an existing power holder might be willing to grant? And if it can be systematized, will it not again show a pattern of profit to those who put the machinery of political justice in motion, as if they had redoubled the interest on a dubious investment? Is this, then, the point where all attempts at rationalization must stop? Are we merely facing a safety valve which operates as disconcertingly as political justice itself?

But if all political justice is shrouded in indefiniteness and in what our friends further to the east call, somewhat depreciatively, practicism, then why bother? Indefiniteness in the absence of a clearcut rule may have its hidden advantages: the political defendant and his friends will draw as much spiritual satisfaction from the abjectness and the fitful working of a system which downed them as will the prosecutor and judge mutually congratulating each other for their rectitude and spirit of patriotic devotion. History might decide their eternal conflict. But I rather doubt it. The phrase is too round and serviceable to be true. The historical process, throwing uninterruptedly on the dungheap thousands of political solutions without regard for the personal worth and the quality of those who personify them, cannot qualify as a satisfactory yardstick of political justice. The device of submitting some choice morsels of political conflicts to courts must exist by its own wits.

In the following pages we shall narrate and speculate upon how the device works, what the various parties might expect by repairing to courts, with what degree of justification courts are styled as such, under what terms the conflicts are submitted, sidetracked, or washed out, and how their projected, expected, or unexpected outcome affects their respective enterprises.

PART ONE

Political Justice:
Cases, Causes, Methods

CHAPTER II

CHANGES IN THE STRUCTURE OF STATE PROTECTION

++

THERE are no universally valid criteria for what constitutes political action as distinct from other types of social action. Something is called political if it is thought to relate in a particularly intensive way to the interests of the community. According to its own estimate of its needs (which does not always coincide with its "objective" needs), each dominant group, class, or individual will develop criteria by which reprehensible acts, when grave enough, will necessitate public action. Correspondingly, infinite numbers of "political" things might in the course of time enter, leave, and re-enter the sphere of formalized public reaction. Under many Roman emperors, the slightest act or omission that might be construed as a sign of disrespect—the omitted obeisance before the likeness of the ruler, the query to the fortuneteller about the emperor's health prospects —was frequently brought under the *majestas* nomenclature.[1]

Our contemporary Western civilization would, by and large, consider some measure of abuse of the supreme authorities of the day a confirmation of the reign of political freedom; to many authorities, therefore, such abuse would be a psychologically beneficial concession to the spirit of the age. Some other territorial authorities, however, might get busy quickly and fill the statute book anew with provisions to defend the patrimony against its detractors. Jurisdictional fights which for Henry II (Plantagenet) and Thomas à Becket signified the quintessence of their political struggle, the respective jurisdictions of state and church, are in our age and political climate fought with subsidy votes rather than with criminal sanctions.[2] Reversely, if in Justice Mansfield's time private business transactions between nationals of warring countries

---

[1] Tacitus, *Annals* I, 72.

[2] At worst, in Catholic lands they might become the subject of defamation suits loaded with political overtones; witness the Bishop of Prado's indignation when his clergy's right to publicly denounce from the pulpit the demeanor of individual members of the community was challenged in civil court. See Fiordelli, Appeal Court Firenze, March 1, 1958, Foro Italiano, II (1958), p. 741. It is symptomatic, however, that the appeal court in quashing the verdict of the lower court which had convicted the clergyman, did not deny the jurisdiction of the state court; instead, it fell back on the least offensive and least controllable of all categories: lack of *mens rea*.

were still tolerated, our era considers them treasonous enterprises. In the constitutional role of the modern party of "friendly" persuasion regularly participating in the game of official politics, it may seem logical that documents of a political party be included in the protection granted to state secrets;[3] such a protection would have seemed meaningless and pointless in the nineteenth century, when parties were at best the mouthpieces of vague multitudes who were seeking entrance into the citadel of the establishment.

The distinction between *inimicus*, the private adversary, and *hostis*, the foe of the commonweal, holds true for our civilization up to a point. As guidepost for action separating private animosity from reprehensible political action, it has about the same value as the dividing line between the objective characteristics and tendencies of capitalist developments and the personal qualities of individual entrepreneurs. In actual practice, their elements may mingle and mutually reinforce each other. Menelaos' private quarrels with Paris have often been built up into a mighty expedition against Troy. The public consequences of personal animosities do not invariably remain as circumscribed as in the case of Bismarck's anger against his too independent Ambassador Harry von Arnim: there the result was an obscure addendum to the German Penal Code.[4] Henry VIII (Tudor) even penalized as treason his spouse's neglect to communicate to him her premarital lack of chastity.[5] The ratiocinations of ancient rulers and modern political personnel acting under the psychological conditions of the one-party state have a tendency to quickly cross, recross, and efface the partition between private consideration and public needs, merging them, Hermann Goering style, beyond recognition.

1. The Early Setting

The history of state protection enactments mirrors the variety and

[3] Entscheidung des Bundergerichtshofs StE 4/59 of November 27, 1959. The curious decision does not mean what it says. It denies that the defendant has been convicted exclusively for what she did: furnish information on personalities, meetings, and so on, of a political party in which she held a clerical appointment. It asserts that the conviction rests on the potential danger arising from what she could have done had her position developed into one that gave her access to state secrets proper. In point of fact, the judgment does extend the protective screen provided for state secrets to the collection of sundry information on party affairs.

[4] Par. 353a of the Penal Code, inserted in 1876. Karl Binding (*Lehrbuch des gemeinen deutschen Strafrechts*, Leipzig, 1905, Vol. II, 2, p. 495) calls it "odious and still-born."

[5] 33 Henry VIII, Statutes of the Realm, Vol. 3, Ch. 21, Parts 8, 9, p. 859.

multiplicity of protective needs.[6] Where there appear at an early time what we might call substantive provisions, they are concerned with the need to verbalize specific harmful situations: the attempt of the king's sons to reach out for their father's job, the unauthorized killing of a hostage, the complicity in the enemy's subjugation of a fortress. Since it was taken over by the tribuni plebis, the early Roman concept of *perduellio* has been largely a reaction against behavior in a specific situation: the reprehensible attitude of the aristocracy against the plebes and their representatives.[7] If the definition of *perduellio* as it entered the language of the late Roman codifications (Dig. 48.4.11) emphasizes its subjective element, the *animus* against the *res publica*, the concept of *crimen laesae majestatis* (abbr. *majestas*), which partly superseded the former, becomes the prototype of indefiniteness: it is any reprehensible attitude publicly evinced against the *res publica* and its security. No wonder it has easily survived the centuries, implemented but not superseded by innumerable specifications. Thus the specific needs of power holders who want a remedy for a local or transient situation vie with the vaguest general formulas that allow for all future contingencies. To call political offense every action which offends the vital interests of the community is a blank check for the power holder who actually determines where these needs begin and end. In contrast to the tangible and more concise object of such offenses as property relations and especially bodily security, danger to the realm often consists in more or less subtle interference with interpersonal relations that happens to run counter to the needs of established authority. But there must be at least some allegation of a duty to act or refrain from action that has gone unfulfilled.

Within the "vague circumference"[8] of the offenses against the power holders, the historical core would seem to be in the attitude toward the enemy. This is a situation where actual behavior can be checked against a fairly self-evident and unambiguous code of what constitutes loyalty. But beyond the original element of *proditio*, the nonpermissible action or nonaction in face of an external foe, the picture gets easily blurred. Which psychological and political gestures of possible remote

[6] The word *state* here is only shorthand for a great many forms of public organizations. The polis, the Roman *res publica*, the feudal king, the estates, absolute monarchy, eighteenth and nineteenth century constitutional governments, mass democracy, and mass totalitarian society—all entertain different ideas about their relation with the population, and this is mirrored in the shape and form of their protective legislation.

[7] C. H. Brecht, *Perduellio*, Munich, 1938, pp. 191-98.

[8] F. Pollock and F. W. Maitland, *History of English Law*, Cambridge, 1923, Vol. 2, p. 503.

or indefinable consequences are liable to be repressed as damaging to the fortunes of the power holders? The expected degree of loyalty will depend on the kind of relationship between the man or institution entitled to receive loyalty and the one from whom loyalty is expected, which again may be a function of the looseness or compactness, definiteness or indeterminateness of the particular political organization. At times, the operation involved in determining the debt of loyalty might well appear to be circular. The chance to repress some unwelcome behavior might cause the nomenclature to be tagged on it. Thus protective need and protective capacity may show an inverse ratio. The baron who challenged his king to battle may be almost endlessly appeased, while the simple subject, who predicted that come ascension John will no more be king, will lose his life.[9]

Is loyalty compatible with the advocacy of political change? Mommsen, for example, thought that political change as such was permissible in Republican Rome, even though this freedom did not extend to the re-establishment of hereditary kingship, which remained specifically prohibited.[10] It may well be that, compared to loyalty to a specific person, loyalty to an impersonal institution embracing a number of subinstitutions leaves theoretically more leeway to work changes in the subinstitutions. In loyalty to a person there may exist a very hazardous dividing line between merely modifying the ruler's prerogatives and trying to dispossess him entirely. But it is one thing for the historian to discern the interstices of particular religious, social, and political structures through which political change has come about; it is another thing for a regime to allow its subjects to argue and insist on change. Moreover, the quest for change may have been clothed for a long time in exactly the opposite form: stipulations on the permissible range of remonstrance against major power holders' violations of acquired political positions, or organization of the forever unorganizable right of resistance.

Trying to differentiate between the principle of permissible change and the motley prohibitions against some specific ways to perfect it is more a mental operation of the age of constitutionalism, the second half of the eighteenth century and the nineteenth century. Previous

---

[9] *Ibid.*, p. 506. See also Heinrich Mitteis, *Politische Prozesse des frühen Mittelalters in Deutschland und Frankreich*, Heidelberg, 1927, especially the story of the trial of Markgraf Ekbert v. Meissen, p. 41; the indefiniteness of the Frankish *infidelitas* concept is extolled in Victor Ehrenberg, *Commendation und Huldigung nach fränkischem Recht*, Weimar, 1877, pp. 116, 117.

[10] Mommsen, *Römisches Strafrecht*, p. 550.

official utterances had managed to smother consideration of the inevitability and permissibility of change under the feint horror over the ways and means to carry it out. From the days of the Greeks to the eighteenth century, the offenses against the state were left in the most indeterminate form, encompassing whatever the power holders saw fit and were able to bring under it. It might include any personal or service-connected squabble between the sovereign and his advisers, as well as any injury to the state's fiscal interests. It was accompanied by a strong belief that the heinousness of such an offense, far from requiring special caution in establishing the facts in the situation, justified otherwise inadmissible procedures for ferreting them out. Cardinal Richelieu only expressed what was widespread practice when he said: "In normal affairs the administration of justice requires authentic proof; but it is not the same in affairs of state. . . . There urgent conjecture must sometimes take the place of proof; the loss of the particular is not comparable with the salvation of the state."[11]

In the *majestas* category, the Roman Republic had allowed the admission of the testimony of a slave—who could be tortured—in favor of as well as against his master. And from the time of Tiberius, torture of a citizen was admitted in the *majestas* line of cases. From the formative period of the Western state in the thirteenth century until the middle of the eighteenth century, both the court of the territorial sovereign and the ecclesiastical court would officially admit torture as an integral part of inquisitive procedure. (Today, such practices are more spotty, or at least unofficial.) The development of inquisition was advanced considerably by the church's ardent interest in combatting heterodox beliefs.

There was, then, a minimum of restraint and a clearcut tendency not to forego any advantage, both in the framing and the application of norms, when the power holder's own interests were in jeopardy. Exaggerated notions about the handling of political cases, arising from the mental climate of the nineteenth century, are misleading. Unless there was some special reason deriving from political tactics, the political position of the defendant, and the relations of strength among the trial participants, proceedings might be quickly disposed of—until the eighteenth century, when there was little chance for effective interference by a defense lawyer, and when facilities for producing witnesses for the defense were sometimes severely restricted. In many countries the case would be dealt with in secret, as an affair of state; even when

[11] *Testament Politique Paris*, 1764, Vol. 2, p. 27.

there was a special interest in publicity, interrogations of possibly prolonged nature would all be in private. Whether the adversary of the
powers-that-be was a nobleman, suspect of having schemed for some
change in the composition of the government personnel, an office holder
who had fallen from grace, or a common citizen who dabbled in organizing religious dissent from the established ways, his trial was an affair
of state more than a case in court. The defendant might as a rule have
a better chance by throwing himself at the mercy of the authorities
rather than by trying to make his own interpretations of his attitude
prevail.

2. *The Era of Constitutionalism*

Change came on a broad front during the eighteenth century.
The English Revolution somehow established the admissibility of the
citizen's standing up for his professional, property, and, more dubious,
religious interests. When in 1688 Justice Allibone in the Seven Bishops'
libel case, curtainraiser to the Glorious Revolution, summed up for the
jury, he tried hard to hold to the dividing line between the legitimate
interest of the private individual and the matters of government, which
are not his concern:

"No man can take upon himself to write against the actual exercise
of the government, unless he has leave of the government, but he makes
a libel, be what he writes true or false. No private man can take upon
him to write concerning the government, for if once we come to
impeach the government by way of argument, it is the argument which
makes it the government or not the government. . . . For what has a
private man to do with government if his interest be not stirred or
shaken? . . . If the government does come to shake my particular
interests, the law is open for me and I may redress myself by law. . . .
It is the business of government to manage matters relating to government, it is the business of subjects to mind only their properties and
interests."[12]

The jury disavowed him. However, outside the precinct of Parliament
the right to political dissension still remained a matter of controversy.
As late as 1773 Boswell's oracle could proclaim: "No member of society
has a right to teach any doctrine contrary to what the society holds to
be true. The magistrate, I say, may be wrong in what he thinks; but

[12] *State Trials* (Howell), Vol. 12, p. 427. See also the account of this decisive political trial in Macaulay's *History of England*, Vol. 2, Ch. VIII.

while he thinks himself right he may and ought to enforce what he thinks."[13]

Though the limits of political dissent were still controversial, another property had been snatched from the vast and formless domain of the *majestas* offenses. English legislators and juries, the immortal Beccaria, and German academic luminaries all recognized that there should be a more precise dividing line between fundamental enmity to the established political organization and the numerous minor violations of the state's authority, including its general interest in the maintenance of public order.[14] Yet while the French Revolution liberated the political individual by vindicating for him full participation in the political process, it also bound him to be loyal to the momentary majority's political visions and to their concomitant estimate of the state's security needs. There needed to be some distance, however small, from the cauldron of the revolution before some sort of balance could be found between political freedom and the security claims of the state. This opportunity presented itself during the various trials that were part of the English backwash of the French Revolution.

Thomas Hardy was hailed into court in 1794 for his share in the public agitation caused by suggestions to remodel Britain's political system after the pattern of revolutionary France. His counsel, Thomas Erskine, invoked the right of men to revamp the institutions under which they lived. In summing up the proceedings, Sir James Eyre tried to refute the argument of defense counsel and set forth the following principle: "The observation has been repeated that people have a right to alter their government. That proposition under certain circumstances might be true, but it should not have been introduced into a court of justice, bound to administer the law of existing governments and suffering no innovation of it. It tends to unsettle man's mind, to bring on a thirst of innovation, and to shake all the foundations of government."[15] The 1794 judge seems not too sure of his ground. The jury rejected his somewhat illogical differentiation between the general justifiability of advocating political change and the court's inability to entertain such notions. Hardy was acquitted.

[13] *Life of Johnson*, ed. G. B. Hill and L. F. Powell, Oxford, 1934, Vol. II, p. 249.

[14] Farinaccus, writing in 1610, had an inkling of the distinction but he never tried to put it to systematic use. See J. M. Ritter, *Verrat und Untreue an Volk, Reich und Staat*, Berlin, 1942, p. 244, n. 142.

[15] *State Trials* (Howell), Vol. 24, p. 1371. Hardy was acquitted of treason. He might have been convicted had the prosecution shown restraint and charged him with sedition. See William H. Holdsworth, *History of English Law*, London, 1952, Vol. 13, p. 164.

Although it was ushered in by fearsome reactions to the French Revolution, the nineteenth century showed increasing indulgence to those who strayed from the accepted political and social norm. This did not happen furtively or underhandedly. Gradually, if fitfully, man's right to cast doubt on the foundations of established political patterns came to be openly recognized.

In this respect, the surface landscape of substantive criminal law may well be deceptive. In England, for example, Edward III's treason law remained on the statute books, vying with later statutory interpretations and a new body of antisedition legislation that was less wieldy for political prosecution than the arquebuse of treason charges. And both in England and the United States, where at the turn of the eighteenth century revived sedition legislation[16] had but an abridged life span on the federal level, penalization of treason and sedition was based on an unconscionably broad definition of the offenses.[17] In actual practice, however, Anglo-American legal thought and court usage throughout the one hundred years from Waterloo to the battle of the Marne concentrated on more promising and rewarding areas.[18]

In continental Europe, nineteenth century legal thought harnessed its energies to dismantle the traditional concepts of *perduellio* and *majestas*. Deeply affected by Enlightenment currents, it took pains to sunder different provinces enclosed by the complex of "crimes against

[16] The sorry course of this short-lived prelude to later American antisedition legislation has been comprehensively narrated in James M. Smith, *Freedom's Fetters*, Ithaca, 1956.

[17] The treason law has found an appraisal, interesting enough to be rendered in full, by a practitioner and outstanding student of nineteenth century British criminal law, James Stephen, *History of Criminal Law*, London, 1883, Vol. II, p. 283:

"The general effect of the whole is that the statute, which has been so much praised, is really a crude, clumsy performance, which has raised as many questions as it can have settled, and which has been successful only when it was not required to be put in force. It has been praised by one party because it does not in terms relate to treasonable conspiracies, and by another because they approved of the artificial construction of which they saw it was capable. The fact that it has been in force for 530 years seems to me to show only the extreme indifference of the public to the manner in which their laws are worded, and the attachment of the legal profession to phrases which have been long in use and to which an artificial meaning has been attached. If, however, we turn from the mode by which the present result has been arrived at, to the result itself, I do not think it can be said to be a bad one, except in so far as the levying of war has been interpreted to extend to the great riots for a political object."

[18] For United States treason law developments, see Willard Hurst, "Treason in the United States," *Harvard Law Review*, Vol. 58 (1945), pp. 226-72, 395-444, and 806-57. Even in extremis during the Civil War did American jurisprudence develop a certain dexterity in avoiding the use of treason constructions; cf. James Randall, *Constitutional Problems under Lincoln*, rev. ed.; Urbana, 1951, p. 91.

the state," where previously the listing of individual situations had served to exemplify rather than limit the offense area.[19] It tended to distinguish sharply the violent overthrow of the constitutional order (offenses against internal security)[20] from attacks on the nation's external security that caused damage to its military or diplomatic armor. Moreover, these two types of offenses were separated from the residual content of the *majestas* concept, viz. verbal or physical injury to the person of the monarch, sometimes extended to include members of the ruling family and government officials.

Foreshadowed in Prussia's Allgemeines Landrecht of 1786 (put into force in 1794), the separation of offenses against the prince from other political crimes was effected in the Code Napoléon, which put the finishing touch on the revolutionary legislation of 1791. The new principle was further elaborated in the writings of Anselm Feuerbach. The sorting out of the various categories of political offenses, as undertaken in these codifications, was followed by campaigns to restrict governments' rushing to the courts as a means to arrest the spread of "subversive" ideas. It was François Guizot, historian, civil servant, and later minister of Louis Philippe, who, in his widely-read "Dès Conspirateurs et de la Justice Politique" (1821) and "De La Peine de Mort en Matière Politique" (1822), strongly counseled against intermingling the government's job of leading public opinion with the judicial job of examining specific allegations relating to reprehensible acts rather than to objectionable opinions. The constitutional order regulated exercise of political power. An act was deemed reprehensible if it was a violent attack directed at the total structure of this order.

Change in the constitutional order is now considered a legitimate objective, provided that only legitimate means serve the intended ends. During the nineteenth century political groups became freer to contemplate complete remodeling of the existing order. So long as they kept to prescribed ways of change and did not become involved in the circuit of violence, translation of thought into propaganda enjoyed some measure of license. Inherent in the contractual aspect of the constitution which had come to Feuerbach via Kant and Rousseau, the new approach to political offenses was scarcely contested.

As government becomes increasingly the legitimate concern of the polity at large, courts will try to differentiate permissible modes of

---

[19] Part of the development may be followed in Ritter, *op.cit.*

[20] Designated, from the end of the eighteenth century on, as *high* treason and thus, at least in German-speaking countries, set off even terminologically from betrayal of the nation's external security.

opposition from reprehensible action and language bordering on violence. Even a justice full of prejudice against the cause of the defendants (as was Pennefather presiding over the 1843 Irish trial of David O'Connell and his associates for seditious conspiracy) would not deny in principle the defendant's right of freely discussing and, through addresses to the Queen and Parliament, pushing for major political changes.[21] What remains controversial, as it did to some extent in the case of the Chartist propaganda, are the boundary lines between lawful propaganda and nonviolent attempts to erect subsidiary systems of government that both push and subvert the established order.[22] Today the boundary lines of the nineteenth century seem unconsciously generous.

A more serious matter was treason conceived as a threat to external security. When committed by noncitizens, it was often, though not consistently, termed espionage. Treason did not hit at a specific constitutional order conceivably subject to change at a turn of political fortune or at a new stage of social development. Treason imperiled the very existence of the political organization, the national state rather than its evanescent and changing form, and remained exposed to correspondingly severe treatment.[23]

With the national state as society's definitive form, intelligence with the enemy assumed the features of the deadliest of all sins—witness Dreyfus. Contrariwise, a Boulanger or a Déroulède, who only plotted to hoist himself into power, was dealt with as a character from an *opéra bouffe*.[24] Two complementary partners, nineteenth century liber-

[21] Cf. Pennefather's summing up: *State Trials*, new series, Vol. 5, esp. p. 622. See also K. B. McDowell, *Public Opinion and Policy in Ireland, 1801-1846*, London, 1952.

[22] In the House of Lords, O'Connell's conviction was quashed by the three Liberal lawlords, as against the vote of their two Conservative brethren; the absence of "specific offenses" was emphasized (*ibid.*, p. 94), together with tampering with the jury register. The Chartists could not hold as much discipline among their motley crowd, and the ambiguities in which their program was couched—outcome of both intellectual bewilderment and tactical choice (cf. Mark Hovell, *The Chartist Movement*, Manchester, 1918)—were therefore not much help to the defendants in court; see the famous 1839 Birmingham Bullring case, Queens v. Collins, *State Trials*, new series, Vol. 3, p. 1150. From the vantage point of the twentieth century, however, the most remarkable features are the patience and forbearance with which the contemporary British governments faced the Chartist agitation and unrest; see F. C. Matter, "The Government and the Chartists," in *Chartist Studies*, ed. by Asa Briggs, London, 1959, pp. 372-404, esp. pp. 384, 395.

[23] The Italian Penal Code of 1888, the codice Zanardelli, underscores the difference by clearly separating *Delitti contro la patria*, the first title of the special part, from *Delitti contro i poteri dello stato*, its second title.

[24] When in 1899 Déroulède, leader of the League des Patriotes," tried to incite

alism and nationalism, gave birth to the only conceivable form of political existence: the finite national state. Freedom became the leeway to move within the confines of the national order.

As long as penal provisions against vilification of the prince were retained, or provisions to protect the uncrowned head of state introduced, attention focused on the public function for which protection was granted. What the law now shielded was the personified authority of the state, not the image of majesty anointed by representatives of divine power.[25] During the nineteenth century this minor part in the protective armor of governmental authority suffered more and severer assaults than any other; this was because of the weakness of the institution it guarded, viz. constitutional monarchy.

Criminal prosecution for insult to the ruler remained plentiful in countries ruled by constitutional monarchs; in Germany, for example, 622 such cases were prosecuted in 1894, and as many as 275 in 1904.[26] The reason lay in the constitutional setup. Attacks on cabinets not responsible to parliament and not expressive of the will of a parliamentary majority were *ipso facto* directed at the person or institution exercising the power of appointment. And the prestige of the monarchy took a beating every time it was defended in court. It did not matter that proof of offensive allegations practically was not permissible,[27] or that considerable effort was made to evade trial by jury.[28] Regardless

General Roget to march on the Elysée, the government put him before the assizes for a mere misdemeanor. To no avail did Déroulède protest against this jurisdiction, clamoring to be put before the High Court for having tried to overthrow the regime. Only after the assizes had acquitted him did the government invoke the jurisdiction of the High Court—but in vain. See P. Fabreguettes, *Traité des délits politiques et des infractions*, Paris, 1901, Vol. 2, p. 745.

[25] A. F. Berner, *Lehrbuch des deutschen Strafrechts*, 14th ed.; Leipzig, 1886, p. 346. Both the extraordinary sharpness of the very personal attacks on French presidents and minister presidents of the 1890's and the ineffectiveness of resorting to the court of assizes as a way of protecting them are narrated in some detail in Maurice Garçon, *Histoire de la Justice sous la troisième Republique*, Paris, 1957, Vol. 3. By now, however, the whole subject of defamation and the legal control of publications in general has been withdrawn from the jurisdiction of the assizes and shifted to the tribunal correctionel, which sits without any lay members. See Roger Pinto, *La liberté d'opinion et d'information*, Paris, 1955.

[26] *Vergleichende Darstellung des deutschen und auslaendischen Strafrechts. Besonderer Teil*. Berlin, 1906, Vol. 1, p. 587.

[27] Olshausen, *Kommentar zum Strafgesetzbuch*, 7th ed.; Leipzig, 1905, comment on Para. 95.

[28] The Austrian emperor's minister of justice, a reputed university teacher of criminal law, Julius Glaser, argued in all seriousness (*Kleine Schriften zum Strafrecht*, 2nd ed.; Vienna, 1882, p. 805) that offenses of *lèse majesté*, like those against religion, were not to be considered political offenses and hence were exempt from the jurisdiction of courts of assizes.

of the makeup of the court, public trial permitted widely publicized criticism of the government, which would have been no more effective had it been made in parliament.

At first sign an anomaly when compared to the receding tide of offenses against the state, the torrent of prosecutions for offenses against the ruler merely recorded the political community's reaction—a mild and almost playful one at that—to the shortcomings of central Europe's constitutional systems.

3. State Protection in Contemporary Society

On the whole, the restricted system of hesitant and conscience-stricken state protection during the nineteenth century did not outlast the war of 1914 to 1918, symbolic dividing line between the dying age of constitutional liberalism and the turbulent new era of mass democracy and totalitarianism. Unlike its eighteenth century French predecessor, the Russian Revolution did not usher in a half century of consolidation, restoration, and pacification. Whether triumphant or defeated, whether uneasily tolerated or savagely hit by violent counterthrusts of Fascism and National Socialism, the revolution and its aftermath imprinted an indelible mark on the epoch's legislative endeavors to protect governmental structures. There were other no less characteristic birthmarks. Protective legislation today bears distinct traces of the changing fortunes which affected the concept of the national state, its ultimate maturation, and its decline and progressing disintegration.

What had made the eighteenth century's *raison d'état* an effective maxim of political action was the universally accepted fact that populations of individual states were, and had to remain, nearly completely insulated against each other. To the aristocratic governments of the time, which felt secure in their respective areas of domination, interstate relations were calculable and by definition out of reach of internal conflict; there was no danger of popular elements' invading the government's preserve.[29] Spreading communication across state frontiers, hallmark of the industrial age, foreshadowed change at a time when national states emerged and consolidated. Still, this did not immediately affect the citizens' loyalty to the national structures, products of bureaucracy's toil, the middle-class community's ideological and material needs, and the not yet fully integrated masses' aspirations. Not until late in the nineteenth century did the disciples of Marx and Bakunin begin to

[29] See Friedrich Meinecke, *Die Idee der Staatsräson*, Munich/Berlin, 1924, Ch. 2, 5, "Friedrich der Grosse."

challenge the very existence of the national state; the Second International's pathetic failure unmasked the futility of their threatening gestures.

World War I marked the zenith of the national state. Ever since the 1920's its road has been paved with doubts and apprehensions. The new universe of communications allows worldwide interest groups and political movements to escape the impact of national law. Organized interests erode national loyalties on only a limited, mostly economic, range; and save for letterhead projects, they have refrained from shaping new, global loyalties. The international party or movement reaches out for more ambitious aims.

The Fascist pattern of conquest with its "New Order" labels, which did not hide admittedly ethnocentric imperialism, damaged beyond repair the national state's specific restrictions and monopoly on patriotic allegiance; biological race, with demarcation lines redrawn if need be to meet operational requirements of empire-building strategy, transcended state-confined nationhood. With far greater destructive power did the Communists' universality claim hit at the national state's sovereign jurisdiction.

Movements of this kind, once installed in power, exact unconditional obedience. And although they tend to do away with the confining features of the national state, their very expansionism has produced, inside and outside their sphere of domination, powerful counterstimuli reinforcing the citizens' allegiance to their respective states regardless of whether or not these conform to the "nation" concept of nineteenth century political philosophy. Today the state structure as such is the national entity to which the individual owes patriotic devotion; this goes for the totalitarian empire in which one master nation lords it over a number of others, as well as for a multinational federation or surviving specimens of the old nation-state type.

Of course the picture is far from uniform. The greater the scope of remaining independent national action, the more national loyalty retains its influence over thoughts and individual movements, and the less it is relegated to represent merely a traditional device of territorial organization in the stage of drastic reshaping. But even where, as in Western Europe, national loyalty is declining because of the rise of new centers of functional organization and the concomitant refocusing of interest, it has not yet been sufficiently replaced by new symbols.[30]

[30] The ambivalence of a situation where old values are vanishing yet new ones are not sufficiently established is excellently brought out in Ernst Haas, *The Uniting of Europe*, Stanford, 1958, esp. pp. 352ff.

The result is a strange period of transition as difficult for those in search of new durable attachments as for those charged with upholding fading traditional ones.

Although the state today is the citizen's point of reference, increasing numbers of individual citizens cross state frontiers on business, for family reasons, or as tourists; and diplomatic, commercial, or technical agents of international good-will or subversion must work on a global scale. But these are tiny groups. In addition, the international operators are frequently assigned to the supranational realm, not to generate new, international loyalties, but for the specific purpose of formulating, propagandizing, or representing national ones. In turn, the popular masses, to the extent that they are drawn at all into the sphere of political action, have in a roundabout way developed stronger patriotic loyalty. By identifying themselves with the national cause, their organizations transmit mass pressure to the national government structure while at the same time they cement their members' cohesion. This enhances their own and the masses' prestige. National pride and national aspirations serve as a convenient leverage to exert influence on personnel and on the continuously growing national services provided by government agencies.[31]

International compacts regulating production and distribution of numerous commodities, from armaments to entertainment, may increasingly impoverish the substance of national life, particularly in smaller countries of lesser political rank. But it is through the nation that international influences are brought home to the last consumer and taxpayer. While patriotism no longer means too much as the mainspring of political action, it still offers anchorage to legislative action for the protection of the state. Meeting the challenge of the new global foci of loyalty, such state action has been widening its scope by leaps and bounds.[32]

Whatever the state's pattern, its protective armor thickens and stiffens.[33] As a first consequence, nineteenth century dualism in dealing

[31] See Morton Grodzins, *The Loyal and the Disloyal*, Chicago, Ill., 1956. In Ch. 2 the author probes the components of national loyalty.

[32] Allegiance to the Catholic Church, which in earlier times often outweighed patriotic commitments, has undergone considerable change. The Church's supranational orientation has weakened, to the extent that national hierarchies now have an interest in adjusting to democratic conditions of organized action. As long as the Church does not consider a governmental system antagonistic to the sum total of its belief system and ways of organization, its national units operate within a framework akin to, if not identical with, that of interest-motivated pressure groups.

[33] To appraise the change in tempo and repressive urge, one has only to compare

with external and internal security loses its impact. Particularly those traditional provisions which once safeguarded internal security are today, though still on the statute books, being increasingly submerged by a flow of new legislation. Internal and external aspects fuse in concepts such as "demoralization" of army or nation, or "danger" to the independence of federation or state.[34] In one of the more recent enactments, the rewriting of the permanent French security legislation (to be distinguished from the numerous Algerian war accretions), the notion of "external security" itself disappears even from the captions and merges into an all-embracing security concept.[35] In the wake of the new political constellation and its refashioned security concept, a long drawn out conflict finds in many lands its legislative if not its intellectual solution. Should individual freedom be given the greatest leeway, and prohibitions and punishments restricted to clearly definable acts which characterize an advanced stage in the endeavor—usually referred to as *undertaking* or *Attentat*—to overthrow the political order by force? Or should the hostile attitudes' earliest manifestations, possibly inconsequential in themselves, be nipped in the bud? For the time being, the latter approach has gained predominance.

Judicial practice had long anticipated the legislative innovation. During the 1920's in France, for example, extensive interpretation came to prevail, if intermittently, when the 1883-1884 laws which had been framed to cope with the anarchism of that period (laws which an

---

the leisurely pre-World War I bureaucratic discussions on never-enacted new legislation against mounting socialist agitation—now available in the collection of official documents of that period published in the DDR (*Die Auswirkungen der ersten Russischen Revolution von 1905-1907 auf Deutschland*, ed. Leo Stern, [East] Berlin, 1954, Vol. 2/1, pp. 260-77)—with any contemporary action patterns.

[34] France, Code Pénal, Art. 76.3, enacted April 9, 1940, and 76.3(d), enacted March 11, 1950 (consolidated into Art. 70.4 in June 1960). For the extensive interpretations of these notions by military courts, see Pinto, *op.cit.*, and the abundant polemic literature around the Henri Martin case; cf. *L'Affaire Henri Martin*, with comments by Jean Paul Sartre, Paris, 1953. For a criticism of the impreciseness of the incriminations and of the excessive grant of jurisdiction to military tribunals, see Émile Garçon, *Code Pénal Annoté*, Paris, 1952, Vol. 1, notes 126-130 to Article 76; Switzerland Strafgesetzbuch, Art. 266, enacted August 30, 1951. New protective legislation is dealt with in Pierre A. Papadatos, *Le Délit Politique*, Geneva, 1955, Ch. 3; his survey, however, dwells mainly on Swiss and Greek penal provisions.

Recent French ad hoc legislation, the stretching of permanent concepts such as endangering the integrity of the territory, and their varying use by administration and courts have recently been dealt with in a well-informed comparative civil liberties handbook, which covers France, the United States, and the German Federal Republic: Frede Castberg, *Freedom of Speech in the West*, Oslo/New York, 1960.

[35] Decree of June 4, 1960, *Journal Officiel*, June 8, 1960, p. 507.

irreverent public had christened "les lois scélérates") were applied to Communist propaganda efforts, especially those concentrating on the army. In Germany the same objective was served within a considerably broader area by the courts' giving a new meaning to the term *under-taking*. In the early days of the Weimar Republic[36] courts had already ruled that an antigovernment undertaking, at least when set up by Communists, was punishable even though the specific insurrectionist purpose had not been established and chances of success were remote.[37] It is the same pattern which had been enshrined in the crop of sedition and criminal syndicalism laws enacted by American state legislatures in the years succeeding the Russian Revolution. Much later, and in a world now shaped by and attuned to the consolidation and expansion of the Bolshevist Revolution, this doctrine is taken up by Judge Learned Hand in his gloss on "clear and present danger."[38]

This changed attitude shows up equally in a closely related subject. From the thirties of the last century until the eve of World War I, in the halcyon days of receding absolutism, constitutional monarchies, and liberal democratic regimes, public opinion and, in their van and under their pressure, constituted authorities acknowledged rather than contested the differences between political and common offenses. The state, it was reasoned, had to safeguard itself against its foes, but this did not necessarily imply a need to stamp one's foe as a dishonorable man and a scoundrel.[39] Whatever part psychological and sociological optimism and romanticism played in this attitude,[40] where it obtained it induced the granting of special privileges to the political offender: a scale of so-called parallel punishments, including at times the abolition of the death penalty and the creation of some form of *custodia honesta*, lacking any dishonorable connotation, was worked out; and there was minimum special treatment under ordinary prison conditions and nonimposition of loss of civil rights. Since World War I such magnanimity has almost everywhere receded. The new enactments show haste to assimilate the political offender maximally to the common criminal in many particulars, except perhaps in extradition.[41] There

[36] See below, Ch. V.

[37] This practice was criticized severely, but unsuccessfully, by the Hamburg professor Moritz Liepmann, in his *Kommunistenprozesse*, Hamburg, 1928.

[38] See below, Ch. IV.

[39] For the classic nineteenth century view, see Joseph Ortolan, *Eléments du droit pénal*, 5th ed.; Paris, 1886, pp. 707-09.

[40] For a discussion of related problems, see Ch. VI, Sec. 4.

[41] The change is described in M. Ancel, Le Crime Politique et le Droit Pénal du Ving-tième Siècle," *Revue d'Histoire Politique et Constitutionelle*, Vol. 2 (1938), pp. 82ff.

may be some protests and hesitations when deprivation of privileges hits strategic strata among the population (as in the aftermath of the postwar collaboration trials in Western European countries);[42] but few protests are heard when the victims belong to small and consistently unpopular marginal groups.[43]

In the democratic government systems, the new legislation, consolidating and enlarging older restrictive and punitive patterns, came in two waves. The first swept Western Europe on the eve and through the early stages of World War II. The second followed the postwar onrush of Communist expansion; it took definite shape in the 1950's, extending now particularly to countries which had been in or close to the Fascist orbit before facing the Communist assault. All these legislative innovations have one thing in common: they do not limit punishable action to direct participation in attempts to destroy by violence the established governmental system. Reducing external and internal security needs to a common denominator, they seek to protect the political order from any intellectual, propagandist, and especially organizing activity directed ultimately toward revolution.[44] In examining the relationship between ends and means, courts are no longer required to weigh the gravity of the danger to governmental structures, or to assess the relevance of incriminated acts. Such considerations do not seem to matter in the face of the major predicament, viz. that the democratic process does not prevent political enemies from using democratic guarantees to destroy legality and freedom.

This is why limiting criteria fail to dispel the vagueness of the new subversion concept, and why far greater attention is paid to the general attitude of the offender group than to actual, often trifling manifesta-

[42] See the cautious criticism in E. Garçon, *op.cit.*, Vol. 1, note 163, before comment to Art. 75. The decree of June 4, 1960, Arts. 18 and 19, has reintroduced the differentiation between a political punishment called *détention* and a criminal punishment called *réclusion*. Only the implementing regulations and their actual application will show whether the device belongs in the field of publicity or penal policy.

[43] During the discussion of the new legislation against political foes during the 1951 Bonn Bundestag session, one member drew his colleagues' attention to the problem, but found no response: Ewers in Verhandlungen des Deutschen Bundestages, 1. Wahlperiode 1949, 160. Sitzung of July 11, 1951, Stenographische Berichte, p. 6481. Since then, the legal representatives of the victims of this now-established policy have, quite naturally, raised their voices. See Heinemann-Posser, "Kritische Bemerkungen zum politischen Strafrecht *der Bundesrepublik in Neue Juristische Wochenschrift*, Vol. 12 (1959), pp. 721-27, which criticizes legislation and court practices.

[44] This was clearly brought out in the parliamentary debate on the first bill to amend the German Criminal Code. See 158 Sitzung (July 9, 1951), Stenographischer Bericht, p. 6304.

tions of hypothetically revolutionary action. At times an attempt is made to describe the exact boundary lines between loyal and disloyal opposition.[45] Moreover, there are detailed specific provisions which spell out what makes propaganda relations between individuals and groups at home and individuals abroad illicit and subject to criminal prosecution.

Because the substance of authority is under constant attack, its purveyor must watch closely the protection of its institutions and adornments. A multitude of new provisions battle the disrespectful, the malevolent, and the opponent who spreads lies. The latter species is not infrequent; instead of accepting reality at its face value and taking advantage of hostile interpretations, groups basically opposed to the established order feed their clientele a radically distorted version of reality: either they don't know better or care only about the calculated effect. Those at or near the summit of public power are protected by a higher tariff of penalties, though retribution might be circumscribed by the opportunity granted the offender to prove his case.[46] The mere fact of vituperation of the constitutional order, or of its symbol or exponents, is penalized as a calculated expression of ill-will toward constituted authority. If abuse of existing institutions carried on by a publication can be construed to endanger the state, correspondingly higher punishments may apply.[47]

[45] As in the new Art. 88.2 of the German Criminal Code. Under these provisions, centrally directed propaganda and campaigns for a plebiscite against rearmament and for the speedy demise of the Adenauer regime have, even before the banning of the Communist Party, been penalized as enterprises hostile to the constitution. See the judgment of the Federal Court of August 2, 1954, in "Hochverrat und Staatsgefährdung," Urteile des Bundesgerichtshofes, Karlsruhe, 1957, Vol. 1, pp. 19-73. Incidentally, the new provisions make it now unnecessary to stretch the "undertaking of treason concept." As a full-fledged substitute has been furnished by the legislator, the court may now concede—a pyrrhic victory for the defense—that the undertaking of high treason rests on a definite plan tied to realization in the foreseeable future, and connotes something more than just hostile propaganda campaigns. *Ibid.*, pp. 55-60.

[46] The German Criminal Code, Art. 187(a), as amended in 1951; France, decree of May 6, 1944, Arts. 26-35; Art. 35(c), however, excludes proof if the assertion refers to facts that concern the private life of the person in question, or else relate to happenings of more than 10 years ago. The latter limitation gives rise to any number of interpretative difficulties.

[47] Art. 93, German Criminal Code, as amended 1951. The decision of the Federal Court of September 11, 1957 ("Hochverrat und Staatsgefährdung"), Urteile, Vol. 2, pp. 159-85, deals with the case of an unaffiliated individual who wrote and sold pamphlets that defended and glorified NS policies, especially in regard to the Jews. He was sent to prison for two years for the production and spreading of state-endangering literature. Under the conditions of constitutional government such utterances and writings, especially if produced by isolated individuals, would more often than not be considered

Alleged fact disseminated from hostile intentions may be malignant even if exposed as mendacious; proved to be true, it often turns into high explosives. Vituperation meant to destroy the prestige of those in power often reduces the distance between the powerless detractors and the prized target power. Hedged between the two, the area of genuine political criticism is overhung by clouds which hide the light separating fact, fancy, and wish. It is not easy to disentangle the components and isolate the maliciously slanderous contribution. Many a recent statute has ignored the difficulty, subjecting legitimate criticism to punitive provisions.[48]

Speedup production of legislative weapons does not necessarily mean they will be put to use. It expresses anxieties of the moment, and in a

---

a regrettable price to be paid for the freedom of speech. German sensitivity to oral and written utterances of extreme anti-Semitic character—especially if they seem to praise the Hitler record—is a product of historical experience and of the present near-unanimous agreement to stamp out the slightest attempt at a repeat performance.

[48] For example, the new Art. 109(d) of the German Criminal Code extends special protection from defamation to the armed forces (Bundeswehr) of the Federal Republic of Germany. Prison terms now threaten those who "make false or grossly distorted factual allegations which, if disseminated, would be apt to disrupt Bundeswehr operations." Prison also awaits individuals spreading such allegations while aware of their falsehood and of the damage caused to the Bundeswehr in the performance of its duties. Because of its inclusive vagueness, the provision was criticized from the Bundestag floor and strongly denounced by the Social Democratic spokesman, Adolf Arndt, attorney and erstwhile judge and prosecutor. See also Verhandlungen (n. 44, above), 2. Wahlperiode, 191. Sitzung (February 7, 1957), pp. 10911-10920. However, what might have become a severe clash between deep-seated pacifism and official policies was avoided when the Frankfurt prosecutor entered a *nol pros* in the defamation suit initiated by the military authorities against Martin Niemöller, who had called the professional formation for which the army was preparing "training for professional criminals." The prosecutor found that Niemöller had not put forth factual statements of an untrue nature, but had uttered a libelous value judgment for which he could invoke a legitimate interest. The interesting text of the *nol pros* decision is reprinted in *Frankfurter Allgemeine Zeitung*, May 27, 1959, p. 9.

The most recent German enactment penalizes attack on human dignity by the incitement to hatred against segments of the population. It also enters the difficult business of trying to stamp out publications or any other external signs of a banned party. See 6th Penal Law Amendment Act of June 30, 1960, BGBL, 1, p. 478. Also relevant are the terms of the new Art. 226 of the French Penal Code (December 1958). The article contains a sweeping contempt of court protection directed against any criticism —outside the purely technical area—"which tries to bring miscredit to any legal decision under conditions which might affect the authority or independence of the judicial apparatus." Maurice Garçon, "De l'Infaillibilité de la Justice," *Le Monde Hebdomadaire*, 25-31 December 1958, p. 5, remarks that the eighteenth century, which allowed Voltaire to work toward the rehabilitation of the memory of Calas by furiously attacking his judges, was more liberal, not to speak of the first stages of the campaign to liberate Dreyfus. The campaign had to be undertaken long before the technical material for the revision of the judgment could ever be assembled.

purely mechanical way meets a need for reassurance. A blueprint has been made available and specifications will be inserted if and when required. A survey of the legislation is like a stock inventory: it does not control sales prospects. State protection is highly malleable. In no other field is there a greater gap between the potential and the actual; in no other field is the shape of practice more subject to the requirements of the hour, bureaucratic proclivities, and assessment of profit and loss expressed in popular sensitivity and reactions of groups exposed to sanctions.

Democratically-poised Britain may feel she can afford to be lackadaisical toward both enactment and enforcement; she may restrict protective action to situations of espionage and exclude more far-reaching interference with the political process. In France the bureaucratic machine is safely protected against parliamentary interference through wide delegations of power. Recently it has even been unmindful of the respectful advisory objections of the Conseil d'Etat against some of its efforts to establish discretionary control of obnoxious political behavior.[49] In addition to the recent total revamping of the security legislation, it has more and more been turning out mounting heaps of sometimes loosely worded substantive security provisions and procedural rearrangements. Application used to come in fits and spells; lately it has been intensified by the regime's efforts to reach not only its North African foes but their many supporters in the French body politic.

As early as 1951 the Federal Republic of Germany had come up with an all-embracing body of statutory security legislation, ceaselessly perfected to catch any detractor and rabble rouser (shades of Hitler) who might veer outside the zone of temperate criticism. So far it has been used predominantly for stamping out, unemotionally, steadily, and in businesslike way, the glimmer of Communist political activities. In the United States today, following the development of atomic energy exploitation and adaptation, there is a body of new statutory law; grafted on the previous espionage provisions; none of them carries the constitutional treason safeguards of two witnesses to the overt act, even though, at least for citizens, betrayal of the nation's trust forms part of the rationale for the severity of punishment. But application of treason and espionage provisions, especially after settlement of the batch of World War II incidents—among them the cases of United States' born propagandists stationed in enemy territory—has been rare. In addition,

[49] For a survey of the whole corps of ad hoc legislation, see Paul Thibaud, "Les Atteintes à la Sûreté des Français," *Esprit*, March 1961, pp. 353-80.

there is the constitutional twilight zone of sedition legislation of the last decades; here are the problematic and sporadic attempts of state politicians to enforce such legislation, and the inquisitorial machines for the production of contempt citations against uncooperative political deviants.[50] Application has depended on the trade winds of domestic political competition and pressures and on the corresponding see-saw battles in the higher federal courts.[51]

What problems the application of security legislation creates for the political style and how it affects the universe of political discourse in different countries will be discussed in the next chapter.

[50] After some earlier hesitations, the following five cases have given a new lease on life to inquisitorial expeditions followed by contempt citations: Watkins v. United States, 354 U.S. 178 (1957); Sweezey v. New Hampshire, 354 U.S. 234 (1957); a series of recent 5:4 Supreme Court decisions: Braden v. United States, 5 L ed 2d 653 (1961), and Wilkinson v. United States, 5 L ed 2d 633 (1961). This lease, which applies to both the federal and the state level, will hold at least until the next change in court personnel or atmospheric conditions.

[51] The vast literature on United States practices may easily be followed in the elaborate notes and extensive bibliographies of Thomas I. Emerson and David Haber, *Political and Civil Rights in the United States*, 2nd ed.; Buffalo, 1958.

CHAPTER III
THE POLITICAL TRIAL

✦✦✦

Let us lay the evils of the city on the friar
and rid ourselves of them all.
—BERNARDO RUCELLAI ON SAVONAROLA

✦✦✦

THIS chapter first introduces the essential difference between the average criminal trial and the political trial. It then uses three case studies to portray the main categories of political trials. These are:

A. The trial involving a common crime committed for political purposes and conducted with a view to the political benefits which might ultimately accrue from successful prosecution;

B. The classic political trial: a regime's attempt to incriminate its foe's public behavior with a view to evicting him from the political scene; and

C. The derivative political trial, where the weapons of defamation, perjury, and contempt are manipulated in an effort to bring disrepute upon a political foe.

Then, on the basis of recent Swiss and West German cases, we shall discuss problems arising from the creation of numerous new types of offenses, which rest on both the alleged need for more extended state protection and on the continuing effacement of the distinction between the internal and external foe, mainstay of nineteenth century political jurisprudence. The traditional trial, beyond the pale of constitutionalism, riding roughshod over the defendant's procedural rights, and trying to squeeze propaganda value from possible distortions of actual events, is differentiated from some contemporary versions of the extremist show trial. The latter uses actual events as a small peg, at best, on which to hang an all-inclusive educational tale. This will be illustrated by the NS Grynszpan trial project, as well as by analysis of the extended use of the trial form for creating a new, alternative reality in line with the momentary needs of the political regime during the Stalin period.

In conclusion we shall ask what determines the chances of attaining political effects beyond the elimination of a foe. We shall also take up the limited usefulness of political trials in establishing meaningful interpretations of the past.

1. The Political and the Criminal Trial

Throughout the modern era, whatever the dominant legal system, both governments and private groups have tried to enlist the support of the courts for upholding or shifting the balance of political power. With or without disguise, political issues are brought before the courts; they must be faced and weighed on the scales of law, much though the judges may be inclined to evade them. Political trials are inescapable.

A truism, is it not? And yet many a jurist is likely to deny that there is such a thing as a political trial; to say that the thing exists and often entails consequences of importance is, in the eyes of such men of Law Immaculate, equivalent to questioning the integrity of the courts, the morals of the legal profession. These standard-bearers of innocence are apt to contend that where there is respect for law, only those who have committed offenses punishable under existing statutes are prosecuted; that alleged offenders are tried under specific rules determining how to tell truth from falsehood in the charges preferred; and that intercession of political motivations or aspirations is ruled out by time-honored and generally recognized trial standards, which guide administration of justice among civilized or, to use a now more popular term, free nations.[1]

In this view there is no basic difference between a murder trial involving the demise, under odd circumstances, of a doctor's wife in Cleveland, and one concerned with the shooting, following a hotly contested election, of a politician in Kentucky; between a perjury trial dealing with testimony in alimony proceedings, and one that revolves around statements made under oath before a congressional committee probing into the membership of groups hostile to the established order; between a libel suit prosecuting a competitor's derogatory statements about the solvency of a business concern, and one based on a campaign speech by a cabinet minister in which a member of the opposition was alleged to have taken money from a foreign government; or between

---

[1] The ambiguity of such basic definitions of present-day political systems has not escaped the attention of students of opinion formation and political semantics. Originally meant to characterize the democratic structure of the political community, the term "free nations" has come to denote freedom from subservience to the Soviet bloc only; it no longer refers to absence of domestic despotism or to *any* foreign chains. On the other side of the fence, the term "people's democracy," a tautology, has but a negative relationship to meaningful protection of popular rights or democratic freedoms.

proceedings concerning abuse of police powers in the case of a raided mobster meeting, and such as relate to a suspended clandestine session of a party driven underground.

Whatever the political background of the individual case, those who hold this view insist, once the public prosecutor has found the evidence sufficient to warrant conviction and has succeeded in taking the hurdle of grand jury, committing magistrate, or *chambre des mises en accusation,* the trial court will sift the evidence and apply the law; the difference in the subject matter, the stature of the individuals or groups involved, the degree of public interest, or the possible widespread implications of the verdict will not matter. Thanks to the lawyers' technique and the protected position of the court, such individual features will be reduced to purely circumstantial matters.

Some trials may figure in the annals of political history and others be recorded by the history of morals or the history of insurance frauds. Differences in subject matter will not change the judicial trial's nature and aim, viz. to bring out the facts and apply to them the law on the statute books. From this point of view, there is no reason why the term *political trial* should not be discarded altogether as cheap stock in trade of a sensationalist newspaper or a disgruntled loser's gratuitous self-indulgence.

The self-appointed defenders of the court's honor protest too much. Fascinated by the seemingly identical methods which allow the courts to arrive at judicial conclusions, they are inclined to disregard possible differences in objectives.[2] What were the interests involved in identifying the killer of the doctor's wife? Murder had been committed, attracting inordinate attention because of the social position of the victim and the only traceable murder suspect. Regardless of the uproar, police and prosecution (assumed to be honest and efficient) could have had but one aim: to track down the culprit. They were out, first, to collect data sufficient for an indictment and, second, to marshal enough evidence in court to enhance the chances of a verdict of guilt.

As far as the community and the public at large were concerned, police and prosecution did a good job: the presumptive murderer had been caught without undue delay and brought to trial; each side had its day in court; and a final verdict was reached. The public order was vindicated. The habitual feeling of security, shaken by an unusual killing

[2] Henry Cockburn, a nineteenth century Scottish lawyer handling political trials and later a judge used the following characterization: "To see no difference between political and other offenses is the sure mark of an excited or stupid head" (*An Examination of the Trials for Sedition in Scotland,* Edinburgh, 1888 [written in 1853], Vol. 1, p. 68).

and uneasily undermined by an unidentified murderer's escape, was restored.

Aside from the usual gruesome thrills and their exploitation by mass media—byproducts in our civilization of any big court affair—what counts, then, is affirmation of the public order through the instrumentality of the trial. From the vantage point of the prosecutor who represents the government, it is of little consequence whether X was tried and convicted or whether a hypothetical Y or Z would have faced the court in his stead. The immediate effect of the trial-conviction of X blends with the less tangible but more durable one of restored confidence. This is all that the guardians of the public order can and usually do expect of a criminal trial.

Conversely, all that matters to the accused is acquittal. To him the stakes are high: it is his neck, his freedom, his family's fate. Victory or defeat is his alone. Even though this or that special facet of his motives or circumstances, as it emerges at the trial, may mean a great deal more to the social historian and psychologist and help them focus the problems of a generation or a social class, the trial takes place at his own personal and private level. The case before the court is at the end of a chain of circumstances which are important here only to the extent that they bear on the personal history of the defendant. To the political community these happenings, fatal to the *dramatis personae*, are merely police-blotter items. Sometimes they are immensely interesting; sometimes they suddenly disclose or expose hidden aspects and dimensions of contemporary civilization. Withal, they are memorable and important as cases rather than causes.

In a political trial all this has a different complexion. The judicial machinery and its trial mechanics are set into motion to attain political objectives which transcend both the bystanders' curiosity and the governmental custodian's satisfaction in the vindication of the political order. Court action is called upon to exert influence on the distribution of political power. The objectives may be to upset—fray, undermine, or destroy—existing power positions, or to strengthen efforts directed at their preservation. Again, efforts to maintain the *status quo* may be essentially symbolic, or they may specifically hit at potential or full-grown existing adversaries. Sometimes it may be doubtful whether such court action really does consolidate the established structure; it may even weaken it. Yet that it is in both cases aimed at affecting power relations in one way or another denotes the essence of a political trial.

Now one might protest that we are applying a somewhat too narrow power concept: that judicial action may be invoked as a means to affect changes in power relations on a much broader front. Any civil suit concerning either relations between major business enterprises or relations of such enterprises with public agencies involves an attempt to reach or frustrate changes in special power relations. Moreover, many a nonpolitical criminal trial may have decidedly political effects—for example, in relation to the political career prospects of the district attorney or the internal power structure of a labor union. All this may be readily admitted. But it is the direct involvement in the struggle for political power, rather than the long-range political effect of socioeconomic power contests, or the derivative political effect of the confirmation or destruction of personal power positions, which gives the political trial proper its particular color and intensity and marks its peculiar problem areas.

Under the aura of constitutionalism, the number of those who may invoke court action to influence power relations is theoretically unlimited. What is limited and subject to specific rules is the procedure that will permit the power contest to enter judicial channels. Only government institutions may bring a public action.[3] Individuals or groups not in power will follow a different course of action, such as filing suits in defamation or provoking others to sue them, a weapon usually easy to wield against any political competitor in or out of government. By means of an action in defamation, any individual in power or, more important, any aspirant for power may bring attitudes and acts of his rivals and enemies, even those abroad, under judicial scrutiny, indirectly subjecting such attitudes and actions to judicial determination. Of course, this type of court review of political conduct is precluded by totalitarian government structures, which do not permit problems of power distribution within the ruling group or caste to be aired in public. Only politically tinged action in defamation that serves indoctrination purposes will reach the courtroom. Generally, the totalitarian courtroom is available for overt political action only at the rulers' behest. Where tradition remains powerful enough to preserve a minimum of procedural guarantees, the political trial today remains a contest, rather than a unilateral reaffirmation of unassailable power positions. It need not be, and most frequently indeed is not, a contest of equals. As a contest it bears no resemblance to the political trial of the Middle Ages, to which vassals overextending their domain were summoned to be stripped of their fief or at least cut down to a size that no longer

[3] Public action is contingent on a number of formal requirements and must pass a special bureaucratic area, the prosecutor's office; sometimes, at least in the United States, it must also pass a grand jury. Some aspects of this problem are treated below in Ch. V, Sec. 2.

threatened the supremacy of the overlord.[4] Intended to reestablish and consolidate the overlord's legal title to domination, the medieval trial directly threatened safety and possessions of the defendant who was trusting enough to appear in court; he had a better chance when he stayed away and prepared for the risk of open warfare. The defendant in the modern political trial is likely to be present in court, not only because of the government's unequaled coercive power, sufficient to compel his presence without major military or police action, but also because it gives him a fighting chance he dare not forego.

The political opponent against whom court action has been taken by the powers-that-be may well have the chance to flee the jurisdiction of the court or even escape abroad. But if he does he runs the risk of helping the cause of his detractors rather than of his own or his group. It is not only totalitarian organizations that require their leaders and officers to stay on the job and hold the fort in the face of criminal prosecution, and that impose disciplinary sanctions upon those who escape on their own. Flight abroad need not preclude continuation of political action, nor even substantially limit its effectiveness; yet the fugitive may have to make deals and engage in transactions with foreign groups or governments. Even under favorable circumstances this may embarrass his group, limit its freedom of action, or involve undesirable political or ideological commitments. (General de Gaulle's and his Free French Government's awkward position in wartime England is a case in point.)

Persecuted totalitarian parties stand a better chance to move their personnel at will. Their machines keep active personnel under rigorous control, are used to reshuffle staffs even under normal conditions, and have greater facilities for assigning large groups of people to posts in different countries, without irrevocably committing the party to a specific course of action in the future. But even they cannot prevent the individual fugitive from suffering considerable loss of prestige, as reflected, for example, in the career of the French Communist leader Maurice Thorez.[5]

Nontotalitarian defendants have even more reason to prefer appearance in court to lengthy exile. This applies no less to defamation or perjury trials. While the defendant may sometimes have a chance to escape damaging publicity or court trial by resigning official positions or signing admissions that do not involve criminal sanctions, he will

---

[4] See Heinrich Mitteis, *op.cit.*

[5] What kind of criminal action threatened or initiated against a clergyman by the DDR authorities would constitute a legitimate reason for his abandoning his flock and fleeing to the Federal Republic? This question has become the object of both public and intraorganizational discussion since the mid-fifties.

frequently prefer to fight it out in court on the off-chance of rebutting the charges or at least salvaging, or possibly enhancing, his political reputation as an intrepid victim of a hostile political course.

Generally characterized by the dramatic configuration of a contest, the nature of which indicates the proceedings' political importance and public effect, modern political trials show variations in subject matter, legal issues, and procedure. In regard to these criteria, a few clear categories may be observed.

As we pointed out above, political issues may well pervade trials involving common crimes, that is, offenses which may have been committed by any member of the community for any one of a multitude of possible motives. Political coloring would be imparted to such a garden-variety criminal trial by the motives or objectives of the prosecution, or by the political background, affiliation, or standing of the defendant. Depending on political climate, judicial tradition, and general mores, the trial may specifically serve egotistic purposes of the groups in power by eliciting or publicly recording information that sheds unfavorable light on political opponents. While giving maximum publicity outside the courtroom to whatever evidence damaging to the political foe should appear at the trial, governmental authorities or influential political groups will also have the chance to advertise strict adherence to the standards of law equally impartial to all, and to play down the political element within the framework of highly regular proceedings deserving of universal recognition.

In another category are offenses so construed in the penal codes as to protect the established governmental system from activity specifically directed against it and conducted in a generally disapproved manner—treason, sedition, and so on, with all kinds of modern derivatives (discussed in Chapter II).

When courts are called upon more and more frequently to curb or suppress political conduct deemed harmful to the public order, artificial legal devices acquire special importance. Reprehensible political action is no longer limited to the two traditional types, the criminal offense as a political tool and the political offense proper. More and more, the courts have to deal with offense artifacts. No law can impose sanctions upon all types of action which in some future situation may be taken to be criminally harmful. Often enough, the specific act which to the government seems the reprehensible expression of a prejudicial political attitude or action pattern is not punishable under the law, or is technically so elusive that it defies prosecution. Instead of the act itself, then, a substitute act is brought before the bar, viz. the verbalization—pinned down as perjured or defamatory—of a suspect pattern of attitude which may or may not have crystallized in a pertinent criminal offense. Action in perjury or defamation brings forth this prototype of the modern political trial. There is also a geographically limited subspecies: through the agency of contempt proceedings the political foe in America today is penalized for nonverbalization.[6]

In the following pages, these categories of political trials will be shown as specific cases, and discussed with an eye to historical background and political implications.

2. *The Homicide Trial as Political Weapon*

A criminal trial can be useful in political conflicts. Frequently, the opportunity to make political capital out of it may present itself, in the person of the alleged or actual perpetrators, as a natural consequence of an incontestably committed offense. In other cases—in those involving corruption charges, for example—the trial may have been brought about by painstaking efforts of rival political groups, the muckraking of a newspaper in quest of larger circulation, or the tenacious pursuit of an individual with a personal grudge.

Or a new elite, helped into power by vitriolic attacks on the predecessors' integrity, may find it profitable to probe into the record of the vanquished and dig up enough dirt to drag men of the deposed regime into the courtroom. Newly established rulers of totalitarian persuasion may also be tempted to discredit groups linked to the old order and not usually exposed to the hazards of political prosecution; for example, they may heap upon the clergy charges of homosexual practices, tax evasion, or currency law violations. This offers the chance to emphasize minor blots on the enemy's escutcheon (often overshadowed by darker blemishes on that of the new masters), creating a scandalizing cinerama of a society doomed to degeneracy and decay but miraculously saved in the nick of time.

Whether the setting be an everyday occurrence under normal conditions, a deliberate assault by a rival group, or a systematic campaign of character assassination, there is hardly a type of common offense—not barring the picayune and outlandish—which could not be used to kindle political passion. The show can be made sensational when the charge is murder, the victim a party leader, and the defendant a prominent

---

[6] The strategic position of this category has recently been brought out clearly in the dissenting opinion of Justice Douglas in Hannah v. Larche, 363 U.S. 420, 493, 501 (1960).

exponent of the rival party. It is this type of fireworks that showered Kentucky's political scene on the threshold of this century.

For the first time since 1859, the Republicans in 1895 managed to win a Kentucky gubernatorial election. The business slump and the Democratic split over silver sent William O. Bradley to Frankfort with a margin of 8,912 votes. However, the legislature continued to be controlled by the Democrats. After the purge of the solid bloc of gold-Democrats in 1897, the Democrats were operating under the firm grip of Senate Majority Leader William Goebel (1856-1900). He had risen to prominence in a series of bitter fights. No "Bourbon" or standard-bearer of the Confederate veteran, he was linked with the party machine of the more industrialized northern and western counties and had made his career as foe of special interests, notably the railroads and their Republican spokesmen. Democratic success in the 1897 legislative and the 1898 congressional elections showed that control of the state remained in the balance. It encouraged Democratic allegations that voting frauds by Republicans and gold-Democrats had tilted the scales in 1895.[7] Goebel therefore became instrumental in quickly pushing through the 1898 legislature a revised election law. It centralized the machinery of election supervision and gave powers to election commissioners, to be elected by the legislature, who in turn were to appoint county commissioners who would select officers to preside at the polling places. General Assembly committees drawn by lot, without mandatory minority representation, were to pass on contested returns.[8]

This maneuver was, in Republican interpretation, plainly a "ripper," designed in passing to take from the newly elected Republican governor all power to influence election machinery and place it in the hands of assured Democratic partisans.[9] "Goebel's election law" was a menace to Republicans, who denounced it far and wide as an insidious assault

[7] Looking back four decades later, one of Goebel's principal lieutenants, founder and publisher of the *Owensboro Messenger*, spokesman for West Kentucky's miners, and advocate of social reform, was still to write, full of indignation: "It was notorious that in counties like Jefferson (Louisville) and in the mountains, where the goldmen with the Republicans had the appointive power of election officers, in many precincts Bryan had no representation whatever in election officers, inspectors, or official challengers." See Urey Woodson, *The First New Dealer. William Goebel, His Origin, Ambitions, Achievements, His Assassination, Loss to the State and Nation*, Louisville, Kentucky, 1939.

[8] While this was amended in 1900 to ensure bipartisan representation, the main features of the much maligned law were retained. Its constitutionality was upheld by the Kentucky Court of Appeals.

[9] Lucien Beckner, "Drifting Sand of Politics, 1900-1944," in Frederick A. Wallis and Hambleton Tapp, eds., *A Sesqui-Centennial History of Kentucky*, Hopkinsville and Louisville, Kentucky, and Little Rock, Arkansas, 1945, Vol. 2, p. 722.

on democratic institutions. And it threatened dissenting Democrats, particularly the "gold men" defending industrial interests, who had a foothold in some of the local machines.[10]

The controversial election law was but one of the flaws in Goebel's armor. Both Bourbons and gold men still wielded strong influence on local party machines. At the Democratic nominating convention Goebel had started out with a mere 168½ out of 1,092 votes. Hush-hush deals, tricky floor maneuvers, and steamroller tactics persuaded a worn-out and befuddled convention to nominate him on the twenty sixth ballot by 561 to 529 votes, but lost him the trust and respect of many a friend. Not only did party ranks split, producing an "Honest Election Democrat," but the Populists, too, after an eight-year interval, nominated a candidate of their own. As usual, the Democrats won the legislative election,[11] but Goebel, their gubernatorial candidate who was to unseat the first Republican governor, lost out to William S. Taylor, prominent Republican and financier.

The Republican candidate received only 48.4 per cent of the popular vote, compared to McKinley's 50.1 per cent in 1896, but he led Goebel by 2,383 votes, with almost four per cent of the votes cast going to dissenter tickets. The returns, as certified by the state commissioners, were: Taylor, 193,714; Goebel, 191,331; Brown, 12,140; Blair, 3,038.[12] Besides his election law, which deterred potentially Democratic voters, Goebel's roughshod tactics cost him over 15,000 votes of declared political sympathizers.

In a puerile challenge, Goebel had boasted: "You cannot outvote me, and you cannot count me out; you Republicans will do the voting, but we Democrats will do the counting."[13] The counting, despite the county and state commissioners' party loyalty, let him down. What remained was recourse to the legislature under "Goebel's law." When the legislature convened on January 2, 1900, the Democratic State Committee

[10] The most widely listened-to prophet of industrialization, Henry W. Watterson, editor for half a century of the *Louisville Courier-Journal*, branded the law a "monstrous usurpation of power by a few unscrupulous men." See Thomas D. Clark, *A History of Kentucky*, New York, 1937, p. 609.

[11] County commissioners had certified 54 Democrats and 46 Republicans as elected to the General Assembly; the assembly's contest committees subsequently turned over four Republican seats to Democrats. The composition of the State Senate after the 1899 election was: Democrats 26; Republicans 12.

[12] County board returns had given slightly higher totals to both leading contenders (195, 150 and 192, 850, respectively). The state commissioners invalidated roughly equal numbers of votes on both tickets.

[13] Recalled by the *Louisville Evening Post* (Republican), July 18, 1900. The Democratic press did not deny that such had been the gist of many campaign speeches.

voted, reportedly against Goebel's advice, to contest the returns for governorship and lieutenant governorship, alleging undue pressure, company coercion of railroad employees, intimidation by troops stationed in cities to quell disorder, and considerable irregularities (such as violation of secrecy through use of transparent ballots) in a number of counties.[14] In spite of the hazards of the lot, the contest committees included Republicans, but were nonetheless dominated by intransigent Democrats. The decision seemed a foregone conclusion.

The Republican leadership, by then installed in state office, decided to act. On January 25 the strong man of the Republican machine, Secretary of State Caleb Powers, former West Pointer and professional pro-union sermonizer from the hills, brought to Frankfort 1,200 armed mountaineers; 17 railroad cars had been supplied for this purpose by courtesy of the Louisville and Nashville Railroad. Moral pressure was to be exerted on public opinion—and through it on the legislature—in a "peaceful" manner; part of the guns the men had brought were stacked in the offices of the adjutant general and the commissioner of agriculture. The city had become a military encampment. Republican officials impeded the decisive meeting of the legislature by barring the premises. On January 30 William Goebel, on his way to the state capitol in company of other Democratic politicians, was shot. The shots had been fired from a window in the office of the secretary of state, who had left town an hour earlier.

The contest committees meanwhile had submitted their reports. Without recount of votes, the contentions of the Democratic State Committee were accepted in full; the legislature was invited to invalidate the election of Republican Governor-elect Taylor and his running mate. On January 31 the General Assembly at last met in official session and voted to adopt the reports, declaring Goebel elected governor, and J. Cripps Wickliffe Beckham lieutenant governor. The same day, Goebel, surrounded by doctors, was sworn in as head of the Commonwealth; on February 3 he was dead. With both parties claiming legal possession of the state executive, the situation bordered on civil war. On February 1 Lieutenant Governor Beckham, sworn in as acting governor, issued an order removing the Republican adjutant general from the command of the National Guard and appointing in his stead John B. Castleman, a Democrat. An armed clash seemed unavoidable.

The outbreak of hostilities was prevented by the negotiations of more sober party leaders. Impressed with the refusal of the banks to honor

---

[14] The allegations are set out on the margin of Taylor and Marshall v. Beckham, 178 U.S. 548, 552, 557 (1899).

checks signed by either office claimant, they arrived at an agreement on February 6. Over the signatures of, among others, Beckham and Republican Lieutenant Governor John Marshall, it stipulated acceptance, pending judicial decision, of the General Assembly's vote as binding upon both parties.[15] The armistice was there, notwithstanding Governor Taylor's refusal to endorse it or abide by its terms. On April 6 the Kentucky Court of Appeals—three Democrats and two Republicans (of whom only one dissented)—ruled that the legislature had acted within its constitutional powers; the court must not look further than that.[16] On May 21 the United States Supreme Court agreed and, with only Justice John M. Harlan dissenting, dismissed the case for want of jurisdiction.[17] The Democrats had won the first round.

Already the second round was coming up. Gubernatorial elections for the remainder of Goebel's unexpired term were slated for November 1900. It was essential for the Democratic leadership to deflect the public's interest from the election law that had infuriated so many and from the subsequent election grab by the legislature. How better obtain this objective than by proving the Republican Party's complicity in Goebel's assassination? "The Republicans said, 'They stole one election,' and the Democrats answered, 'They killed our Governor.'"[18] Through the six months that followed, all efforts of "Goebelized Democracy" (the Republican campaigners' favorite term) concentrated on pillorying the Republicans' guilt. The then fantastic amount of $100,000 was appropriated by the legislature for the apprehension and prosecution of the killers.

By the standards of nineteenth century Kentucky mores, shooting to kill was neither unusually sensational nor particularly upsetting. What made the Goebel killing an inordinate affair was the unique chance to

[15] Spade work was done by the two rival holders of the adjutant general's office, who found a common ground in Masonic loyalties; the story has been told in stilted narrative by John B. Castleman, *Active Service*, Louisville, Kentucky, 1917, p. 235.

[16] Taylor v. Beckham, 108 Kentucky 278 (1900); 56 Southwestern Reports 177 (1900).

[17] Taylor v. Beckham (see n. 14 above), p. 549. Viewing the right to office as a property right, and applying the "due process" construction then in vogue, Justice Harlan would have accepted jurisdiction and reversed the decision, invoking the Fourteenth Amendment. He contended (*op.cit.*, pp. 602, 606) that the Kentucky legislature had acted "outside of all law, and in utter contempt of the constitutional right of free men to select their rulers." Harlan was a Republican from Kentucky and had been prominent in state politics. A rabid "conservative" in Republican ranks, he had defended state rights against federal encroachments, and in 1865 launched a violent press campaign against the Thirteenth Amendment, which he termed "a flagrant invasion of the right of self-government" (E. M. Coulter, *The Civil War and Readjustment in Kentucky*, Chapel Hill, N.C., 1926, pp. 279ff). Harlan ran twice for governor, but was defeated. He was Kentucky's attorney general from 1863 to 1867.

[18] Clark, *op.cit.*, p. 609.

link an assassination to a plot said to have been hatched by one of the major parties.

The prosecution got hold of one Henry E. Youtsey, law-trained clerk in the state auditor's office, who claimed to have been present, as an accomplice, at the actual shooting on the premises of the secretary of state. Youtsey named James B. Howard, a participant in the mountaineers' invasion of the state capital, as the man who had fired the shots. He alleged that the shooting had been agreed upon at previous meetings; he said that Governor Taylor and Secretary of State Powers had taken part in the meetings and helped set afoot the assassination plan. Other equally questionable testimony implicated a score of Republican party hacks and lawyer-politicians.

The stories fitted perfectly—too perfectly—the purpose of the Democratic machine. True, Taylor gave up the fight for the governorship after the Supreme Court ruling and escaped to Indianapolis. Indiana refused extradition, charging the Commonwealth of Kentucky with political abuse of justice. But Powers was seized when preparing to flee. The top Republican leaders' efforts to elude trial were widely advertised as pointing to their guilt. And the fact that Powers, when caught, was carrying a document signed by Taylor and granting him gubernatorial pardon for alleged complicity in the killing, was taken to implicate rather than absolve him.

Howard, the man accused of having pulled the trigger, bluntly and consistently denied participation in the killing and any knowledge of a conspiracy; so did Powers; and so did Taylor, who was never questioned in court but supplied a written deposition. Apart from Youtsey, no eyewitnesses of the shooting came forward. There was even serious doubt as to whether the shots actually had come from Powers' office. Evidence implicating Powers, dubious from the outset, was shaken on cross-examination. Yet most of the testimony was muddled and contradictory.[19] Important witnesses had been implicated in one way or another and were thus at the mercy of the prosecution, which held out the promise of *nol pros.* Powers was tried by an all-Democratic jury, and the presiding judge was a Democratic politician, formerly lieutenant governor of the Commonwealth.

The responsibility of the Republican leadership could have been

[19] The testimony is now readily available in Francis X. Busch, *They Escaped the Hangman*, Indianapolis, 1953. The book also includes a comprehensive account of the consecutive trials—with appeals and reversed sentences—in which the case against Powers was considered and reconsidered from 1900 through 1908.

established only if there had been incontrovertible evidence for why the men from the hills had been brought to Frankfort. Had Powers commandeered their services as hatchetmen to kill off Democratic politicians? Or had the men merely come to town to petition the legislature so that the will of the electorate should triumph? Refusing to accede to most of the instructions asked for by the defense, the presiding judge, in summing up the evidence, did his utmost to de-emphasize this highly pertinent, if not crucial, issue.[20] Convictions had to be secured prior to the November election. After the Powers trial had dragged on for six weeks, it took the jury all of twenty minutes, on August 17, 1900, to bring in a verdict of guilty. The sentence was imprisonment for life.

Party leaders and opinion molders reacted as would be expected. In the Democrats' minds there was no doubt that the Republican Party in its entirety stood convicted of murder. To the Republicans the verdict revealed, like a "flash of lightening," mortal danger to the Commonwealth; the state, they said, was on the verge of a precipice.[21] Still, the campaign job had not yet been completed. Two more convictions were to follow. On September 5 a life sentence was meted out to Howard.[22] In October Youtsey was tried and also sentenced to prison for life. The

[20] The instructions to the jury, as requested by the defense and as issued by the court at the 1900 trial, may be found in Caleb Powers, *My Own Story. An Account of the Conditions in Kentucky Leading to the Assassination of William Goebel, Who Was Declared Governor of the State, and My Indictment and Conviction on the Charge of Complicity in His Murder*, Indianapolis, 1905. A shattering criticism was delivered in the majority opinion of the Kentucky Court of Appeals reversing the first judgment. See Powers v. Commonwealth, 110 Kentucky 386, 399 (1901); 61 Southwestern Reports, 735, 745 (1901).

[21] See comment on August 19, 1900 in the rival Louisville papers, *Courier-Journal* (Democratic) and *Evening Post* (Republican).

[22] Criticism of defense tactics, as seen through the trial lawyer's lenses and based on rather cynical appraisal of the jurors' susceptibility to propaganda arguments, has been supplied by a well-versed member of the Frankfort bar, L. F. Johnson, *Famous Kentucky Tragedies and Trials. A Collection of Important and Interesting Tragedies and Criminal Trials which Have Taken Place in Kentucky*, Louisville, 1916, pp. 308ff. As Johnson points out, the first trial in the series, which preceded the Powers trial, ended in the acquittal of the defendant, Garnett D. Ripley, who had been indicted as an accessory. This was a glorious feat of lawyers who had joined the prosecution in denouncing the Republican leaders' conspiracy. Similar tactics could have prevented Howard's conviction and spared him years in jail. But when at the second trial his lawyers, well-known Democrats, embarked upon this road, too much damage had already been done by their Republican predecessors, who had battled for the party leadership's honor in the 1900 proceedings. Of course, to defend Powers "was almost a hopeless task" because of his political prominence. Crudely put, but not unconvincing.

fact that he refused to appeal, and in consecutive trials heaped more damaging evidence upon other defendants, supported belief in his guilt. The whole truth has never been established.[23]

The election campaign meanwhile moved toward the climax. By October the Democrats had modified the election law, removing one of the main points of contention. And as the state contest remained in the foreground, overshadowing by far the national Bryan v. McKinley fight, they applied themselves all the more zealously to stigmatizing the Republicans as helpers of assassins. They insisted that election of a Republican governor would secure a pardon for those already convicted and for the governor-elect who had escaped;[24] they warned the voters against a state administration that would "overhaul" for false imprisonment the Franklin county jury responsible for the Goebel murder convictions. Governor Beckham, running for re-election, made refusal of pardons one of his main platform planks.

The Republicans' case was not as simple to state. They of course dissociated themselves from the murder and stated that the real culprits must be punished. Emphatically denying the guilt of their leading men, they recalled cruel miscarriages of justice that had victimized men like Titus Oates and Alfred Dreyfus. The association of ideas this evoked stressed the blatant injustice of the Goebel murder trials and make executive clemency appear the only way to right the wrong; the mournful image of the bleeding frame of liberty provided the background.[25]

Whether campaign oratory bore down on assassins and the men behind them, or whether it exhorted efforts to save freedom from "Goebelized Democracy," the Goebel case thoroughly pervaded the electoral battle. When the votes were counted, the Democrats were in the lead, though victory was far from overwhelming. Governor Beckham won re-election by the slim margin of 3,700 votes; the Republicans had

[23] From whatever evidence had appeared, Youtsey's character did not appear overly attractive. However, there was no evidence of a deal with the prosecution. Whereas Powers and Howard were pardoned by a Republican governor in 1908, Youtsey was to remain in jail until 1917, when he was finally granted executive clemency by a Democratic governor.

[24] See the *Courier-Journal*, August 23 and October 27, 1900. At the 1900 Republican national convention, William S. Taylor, fugitive from Kentucky courts, headed the Kentucky delegation and was greeted by an ovation when he took his seat. It seemed likely that the unseated governor would re-enter Kentucky politics if his party won the gubernatorial election.

[25] See the *Evening Post* write-ups of campaign speeches delivered by the temporary chairman of the Republican state committee ex-Governor Bradley on July 18, and by gubernatorial candidate Yerkes on September 26, 1900.

topped 1899 returns by a few hundred votes; the Democrats recouped only part of the vote they had lost to the "Honest Election" and Populist tickets.

With Beckham back in office, pardon for the Goebel murder defendants was out of the question. The defendants filed appeals and the court fight dragged on for years. Howard appealed twice and obtained two reversals, only to see the life sentence confirmed at a third trial in 1902. Powers' second appeal brought a third trial in 1903, which ended in a death sentence. One more appeal followed. The protracted fourth trial, with bipartisan jurors and a more balanced judge, resulted in 1908 in a hung jury, ten jurors voting for acquittal and recommending pardon.

The pardon actually came under the Republican administration which had been swept into office in 1907. Released from jail, Powers obtained the congressional nomination in a traditionally Republican district, and embarked on an uneventful four-term career in Washington.

The Goebel affair had lost public significance long before. It had no bearing on the state elections in 1903, when Beckham was re-elected governor for a full term by a considerably larger plurality (26,450) than any recorded in Kentucky in ten years. And it was only a dim memory in 1907, when tobacco tenants unfurled the banner of mutiny. Other murders and other pardons appeared fleetingly on the political scene, but none was enlaced any more in that unique web of political and legal strategy; none became the focal point of an all-out struggle for power.

The story has been told here in great detail because of its exceptional transparency. The political and the criminal issue fused uniquely in the fierce conflict that in 1900 swept Kentucky. If there had been definite proof that the Republicans' leaders did not shun murder to retain and reinforce their hold on the state, it is quite likely that the combined weight of political interest, legal opprobrium, and moral indignation would have crushed the Republican Party. As things went, however, the 1900 series of trials blurred the issues and left the uncommitted public utterly confused. Testimony was contradictory, many a witness came out of the proceedings thoroughly discredited, and the facts remained veiled.

Widespread disgust with organized politics and loss of confidence in the administration of justice would have been a natural reaction. But the 1900 election evinced little change in popular attitudes. Abstention, on a minor scale, affected the Democratic rather than the Republican camp. The rift in Democratic ranks had been patched up, if only superficially; this was enough to restore to their party a narrow margin of victory. Campaign concentration on the criminal issue had hardly swayed a substantial number of voters. Characteristically enough, the broader national issues, which both Kentucky parties had sought to keep out of the campaign, were heeded more attentively at the polls than in emotional public debate. Bryan carried the state with 8,000 votes over McKinley, more than double the margin Beckham had in the gubernatorial contest.

The Democrats' role as prosecutors obviously had some boomerang effect. Recapture of the 1899 dissident silver vote should have swelled the Democratic state totals noticeably beyond the 200,000 and some votes actually cast for Bryan. It would seem, moreover, that the criminal indictment of the Republican leadership failed to deprive the Republicans of more votes than they may have lost the day Goebel was murdered and most likely sacrificed through the year on the altar topped by the "cross of gold."

3. Case Studies in the Meaning of Treason

The first two cases to be discussed belong to what was still the transitional period of the early 1920's. Both relate to political episodes originating in World War I. Though still adjudicated under the legal concepts of the prewar period, they appear, in retrospect, to have been already fully engulfed by the political habits and thought patterns of a later time.

The roots of both trials rest in attempts to tear down the wall, erected by nineteenth century jurisprudence, between opposition to governmental policies and treason; between differences of opinion about the pursuit of national policies and making common cause with the external foe. The judicial machine was used as a support position or as an integral part of concomitant political action on the enlarged political stage of mass democracy. Revolutionary explosions, set off in the muddy trenches of World War I, smashed whatever remained of the separation between opposition and treason—*pièce de résistance* of nineteenth century political jurisprudence. With it went its essentially limiting element, which had helped protect the individual from governmental or private political abuse of power.

The first case will show how the heavy weapon of the treason trial is used by the government of the day for eliminating a domestic political foe, while, at the same time, the initiation of proceedings serves to better integrate the population into the war effort. The second case shows how the strategy of the derivative political trial can destroy the career of a political foe and produce and solidify harmful political images. In this strategy a specific segment of the political record of a highly placed politician is attacked by his foes. Becoming plaintiff, the politician must then stand on his interpretation of the record, as chosen by the defendant, in order to safeguard his reputation.

A. OPPOSITION AS TREASON: L'AFFAIRE CAILLAUX

After three war years, France by the fall of 1917 was in poor shape. The morale of home front and army was badly shaken. Losses in human lives, deterioration of living conditions, disorganized economy, and wide-range maladministration had undermined enthusiasm for carrying the war to a victorious end. After the stalemate of the Marne, the government, largely under British pressure, had ordered a costly offensive under General Robert Nivelle (1856-1924), made commander-in-chief of the northern and northeastern armies in December 1916. Launched in April, the offensive achieved nothing but a speedup in the already planned retrenchment of German troops. Nivelle was removed in May.

Revolution in Russia was no help; rather, it encouraged the craving for an early peace. Unrest among the troops swelled. By the end of the summer open mutiny was recorded in the French near east army, followed by a flareup of the long smoldering conflict between French and British war chiefs. Inter-Allied friction increased in spite of the United States' entry into the war; Woodrow Wilson was by no means committed to the pursuit of a crushing victory.

Mounting political tension multiplied the French government's domestic problems. The all-party "Sacred Union," which at the beginning of the world conflagration had permitted the formation of a war government removed from normal pressures of the parliamentary process, had virtually fallen apart. The cabinet responsible for the Nivelle offensive was torpedoed on the inside by left-of-center War Minister Paul Painlevé (1863-1933), who urged the inclusion of Socialists, and on the outside by victory apostle Georges Clemenceau (1841-1929), whose long career as the standard-bearer of the left, dedicated to breaking conservative governments, smashing right-wing politicians, and exposing military conspiracies against the Republic, had culminated in an alliance with the military and in frantic efforts to cover up monarchist and ultranationalist subversion.

In August Clemenceau succeeded in ousting Minister of the Interior Louis Malvy (1875-1949), who was guilty of overzealous investigation of monarchist activities and of lack of zeal for the national issues; Malvy was later to be tried for treason. By September the cabinet was without a majority. Painlevé, who took over (without Socialist participation), had not learned the lesson; he uncovered a monarchist plot among army officers. Further disclosures would be bad for national morale, Clemenceau concluded; in November he contrived the ouster of the Painlevé cabinet.

Leading political groups disagreed widely about the course of action to take. There was general consensus that police and judicial proceedings should nip in the bud defeatist campaigns that were emanating, with German backing, from shady journalists and financial operators. But opinions clashed fiercely on the subject of war and peace. What was to be done about peace feelers, which kept coming from both neutral governments and the weaker links in the enemy coalition, particularly Austria? The war-to-the-victorious-end party, galvanized by Clemenceau's dynamic and unscrupulous drive, had the support of Raymond Poincaré (1860-1934), president of the Republic; the military command was now safely in the hands of Ferdinand Foch (1851-1929) and there was a loose coalition of center and right-of-center groups in parliament. The party emphasized commitments to the Allies and the importance of inter-Allied agreement; its stand against peace initiatives was buttressed by the Austrian government's reluctance to cut loose irreparably from the German ally.

At the other pole, particularly among left-of-center groups, growing disappointment over the seemingly-endless stalemate war, combined with pent-up resentment of British tutelage and army primacy. Lenin had just seized power and pulled Russia out of the war. Wilson seemed agreeable to diplomatic action for peace. Amidst the uncertainties of 1917, year of depressing procrastination, negotiated peace seemed a desirable solution.

But groups amenable to this approach were neither united nor determined to embark upon a course which all along had been branded as treasonable. Concerted action required forceful guidance by a leader of stature and popular appeal. Circumspect mathematician Painlevé was not the man of the hour; nor was mellifluous Aristide Briand (1862-1932), a great orator who had served as premier and director of foreign policy. One man only, Joseph Caillaux, could become the rallying point for a peace coalition. When the Painlevé cabinet capsized, the alternative presented itself to many as inescapable. The new helmsman, they thought, would be either Clemenceau, high priest of victory, or Caillaux, political leader in semiretirement, critic of the futility of war, prewar partisan of Franco-German rapprochement, and man of many political and high-finance contacts in the capitals of the world.

Was the alternative ever a real one? Did Caillaux stand a chance to win parliament and the public for a radical reversal of the political course? Poincaré seems to have contributed a great deal toward making the choice appear ineluctable,[26] for a purpose; once Caillaux was turned into a bogeyman, it would be so much easier to let "Tiger" Clemenceau, target of many fears and age-old resentments, take the reins, block the "appeaser's" way, and save France from disaster.

Old enemies, Poincaré and Clemenceau, buried the hatchet, at least for a while, in a common endeavor. The Tiger was made head of the government, and plans were laid not merely to defeat Caillaux in the parliamentary arena but actually to destroy him. He would stand trial and be ignominiously exposed as a man lacking in patriotic devotion, a traitor to the nation. Thus a mortal blow would be dealt to peace initiatives and defeatist leanings.[27] On November 20 Clemenceau, acquainting parliament with his government program, announced the cabinet's resolve to prosecute. On December 11 the Chamber was requested to lift Caillaux's immunity. On January 14, 1918, Caillaux was arrested.

It took some doing to charge Caillaux with treason. Preliminary investigation had been entrusted to military justice. The evidence—*ramassis de ragots* [trashpile of gossip], Caillaux sneered[28]—changed its aspect from one day to the next. Poincaré, a lawyer of no small repute, knew it was flimsy; and he was not overly impressed with the case built up by the under secretary in charge. All the more important was it to convict Caillaux in the eyes of public opinion even before he faced a court of law.[29] No effort was too much for Poincaré and Clemenceau.

26 Raymond Poincaré, *Au Service de la France*, Paris, 1932, Vol. 9, p. 370.

27 Highly skeptical of realistic chances for political action at the time, Caillaux was willing to withdraw from the political scene and go into exile, if only temporarily. This would have thwarted the Poincaré-Clemenceau plan. But the offer was rejected. Two decades later, Georges Mandel, Clemenceau's political heir, let Caillaux have documents from Clemenceau's files which indicated that the character assassination plot had been primarily of Poincaré's making, not Clemenceau's. Poincaré's hatred of Caillaux had long been a matter of common knowledge.

28 The defendant's own account and analysis of the case, with many excursions into the historical and political background, are found in Joseph Caillaux, *Devant l'Histoire: Mes Prisons*, Paris, 1921.

29 A running commentary in Poincaré, *op.cit.*, Vols. 9 (1932) and 10 (1933), reflects his continuous preoccupation with the staging of the case.

And there were things in Caillaux's past which made him vulnerable.

Born to politics and big-business pursuits, Joseph-Marie-Auguste Caillaux (1863-1944) had held office of the highest rank in government and business. A rather conservative rural constituency elected him to the Chamber when he was 35. Two years later he was finance minister in a militantly left-wing cabinet.

This was not a turncoat's exploit. Caillaux had entered politics with a farsighted program, which he stuck to. His political philosophy called for fiscal reform, new orientation in foreign policy, and reduction of armaments—illusory objectives unless sought by a fighting alliance of the left. Concrete action in this direction, however, was much in line with the economic interest of the smallest investors, that is, the mass of farmers and urban real estate owners. Through the four decades in which Caillaux was to remain in the front row of French politics, left-of-center coalitions were indeed successful at the polls whenever their specific proposals made sense in sober cash terms to large sections of the small coupon-clipping proprietors. Caillaux's basically conservative voters never failed to re-elect him.[30]

The secret of this appeal was in the peculiar tie between politics and economics, whose stranglehold on the Third Republic became marked at the turn of the century. Since the days of the Second Empire the bulk of the small property holders had been prone to invest savings in gilt-edged bonds. Government spending had come to depend largely on steady increases in the national debt; increasingly, too, a considerable part of the savings went into loans raised in France by foreign governments, particularly czarist Russia. The small holders' foreign investment was not without a measure of influence on the conduct of foreign affairs. The ensuing system of alliances entailed a greatly enlarged military establishment, which imposed an added burden on the government budget. The drain on the capital market practically cut off capital supply to the industrial economy, save in one privileged sector. "Munitionmakers" were the ones to profit by stepped-up armament orders

[30] For an appraisal of Caillaux's role as viewed by his constituents, who after his comeback in the 1920's made him a senator and speaker of the conseil général, see Emile Roche, *Caillaux que J'ai connu*, Paris, 1949.

Since this chapter was written, Caillaux's political record has been investigated in great detail in Rudolph Binion's *Defeated Leaders: The Political Fate of Caillaux, Jouvenel and Tardieu*, Columbia University Press, 1960, pp. 18-116. The larger narrative, rather than perceiving a "grand design" merging Caillaux's thoughts on foreign and domestic issues, stresses the often contradictory interplay of day-to-day pressures and tactics in Caillaux's moves in the period immediately preceding World War I.

paid for out of French or foreign bonds sold primarily to small investors. Perennial budget difficulties and the growing power of the armament industry (and of the steel and iron tycoons behind it) heavily increased conservative pressure in the political arena. Repeatedly the reaction of the voters showed disquiet over this constellation.

Caillaux's way out of the maze was in a combination of financial and political steps. He fought for high-income taxation, for it would reduce budgetary loan requirements. He was instrumental in channeling savings into (a) industrial stocks[31] and (b) bonds of foreign corporations engaged in opening up underdeveloped areas. This tied in with his insistence on Franco-German economic cooperation and political rapprochement. The far-reaching foreign policy objectives were interconnected. France would be in a position to sever financial and military ties with Russia's Balkan ventures. Urgent heavy-industry demands for reconquest of Lorraine iron ores would no longer dictate foreign and domestic strategy. The "global metallurgy combine" would cease to be overlord. Durable peace at the eastern border would permit an incisive cut in armed forces and armaments. Joint operations of French finance and German industry in underdeveloped zones would de-emphasize military aggrandizement, keep down purely military and administrative interest in colonial possessions, and substantially reduce dependence on Britain's naval supremacy and Empire strategy.

This was no abstract theorizing. For the first time in French history, a progressive income tax, which fully exempted incomes in low and medium-low brackets, was introduced under Caillaux's premiership in 1911-1912. During the same period Caillaux succeeded in settling the Franco-German dispute over Morocco, thus laying the groundwork for common economic pursuits in Africa.[32] Chief author of the 1911 Franco-German treaty, Caillaux encountered bitter opposition in the government majority's ranks and, disavowed by his foreign minister, saw his cabinet tumble.

His financial operations became more intensive. He worked hard at draining off investment in Russian bonds into agricultural and industrial development of areas outside French colonial territory. He enlisted French capital in the German-initiated infiltration campaign in spheres of British financial supremacy. Elected leader of the Radical Party in

[31] In later years Caillaux was to be furiously attacked for his excess of zeal in furthering stock promotion and, more specifically, for having permitted during his tenure as head of the financial administration issue of fraudulent stock. This was said to have engulfed huge amounts of small investors' savings.

[32] For his own presentation of the revolutionary attempt to secure peace on the Continent, see Joseph Caillaux, *Agadir. Ma Politique Extérieure*, Paris, 1919.

1913, and back in cabinet office as finance minister the same year,[33] Caillaux inspired a broad popular movement against army expansion, especially the three-year conscription law. Once more an aggressive left-wing coalition was on the march. Radicals and Socialists were on the point of winning the March 1914 general election. A peace and reform government headed by Caillaux, supported by Jean Jaurès, the great Socialist tribune, was in the making.[34]

Then, in a weird imbroglio of politics and personalities, tragedy struck. Caillaux's activities had generated ire and raging fury in many quarters. Industry magnates, generals, newspaper publishers whose venality he had helped expose, royalists around vitriolic *Action Française*, and scores of right-wing politicians—in short, all those who for years had persecuted Dreyfus—spouted concentrated venom at Caillaux. Seemingly unperturbed, Caillaux sneered at his detractors and goaded them. One of the most brilliant minds in French parliamentary annals, and a persuasive political writer, Caillaux was self-assertive to the extreme and not above flaunting his intellectual superiority and political astuteness. Haughtily he displayed contempt for public reactions, disdaining with nonchalance elementary caution and reserve in private life and personal contacts. He had been divorced and had remarried a divorcée. Private correspondence, frank in the discussion of marital tangles and amorous sentiment, and alluding with levity and cynicism to relevant matters of public concern, had been left floating around. *Figaro*, the paper that hounded him most, had got hold of the letters. It printed some and announced salacious revelations to follow. On March 17, 1914, Mme. Caillaux, frantic with worry, walked into the *Figaro* office and fired a volley of shots at Calmette, the editor, killing him on the spot.

The shots abruptly halted Caillaux's political activity. Convention required self-effacement pending judicial decision; Caillaux resigned from the cabinet and withdrew from public life to prepare his wife's defense. He stayed out of the political arena through the crucial summer months of 1914.[35] A Paris jury acquitted Mme. Caillaux.

[33] Caillaux insisted, in *Devant l'Histoire*, that by rallying the cabinet to his policy in 1913-1914, he had incurred the undying hatred of Poincaré, then newly installed in presidential office. Poincaré was quoted at the time as denouncing *urbi et orbi* the weaknesses of the policy he attributed to Caillaux, who, he said, had been forced upon him as the true policymaker under the nominal premiership of Gaston Doumergue (1863-1937).

[34] ". . . The will of the country ushers in a Caillaux-Jaurès cabinet," wrote the Belgian envoy in a despatch from Paris on March 10, 1914 (*ibid.*).

[35] The cabinet had not asked Caillaux to step down, and might not ever have

The outbreak of the war shattered the hope for a left-wing coalition. Jaurès had been assassinated, and Caillaux, practically isolated, was out of touch with government affairs. He still was feared. He had not given up his views on foreign policy, nor did he conceal the fact that early termination of hostilities was more important to him than victory. But he kept aloof from political activity, made no public statements. He joined the army and began to quarrel with his superiors. The government offered him a supply mission assignment overseas. He accepted, and later was praised for the services he had rendered.

The winter of 1914-1915 he spent in Latin America. He was bitter and talked freely. In Rio de Janeiro he made the acquaintance of a Count Minotto, representative of the Guaranty Trust Company of New York, who was there on a semiofficial trip. Minotto, as Caillaux knew, was seeing Count Luxburg, German ambassador to Argentina. But unknown to Caillaux, tales of his remarks reached Berlin. One of Luxburg's reports, for example, said that Caillaux had made remarks about the stupidity of the German press, which praised him lavishly and thus made him suspect to French opinion.[36] Luxburg's reports were intercepted, and French prosecutors were later to say that Caillaux had requested the Berlin government not to jeopardize his services to the German cause.[37]

Back in France, Caillaux was as imprudent and careless as he had always been about the company he kept. He had contacts with one Bolo, shady financial promoter who turned out to be a German agent assigned to buying French newspapers. He contributed articles to the newspaper *Bonnet Rouge*, which had switched from prewar support of Caillaux's policies to victory propaganda to peace campaigns; the paper's manager Duval was caught cashing Swiss checks traceable to the German government. He consorted with the editor Almereyda, in turn a semianarchist, war propagandist, and antiwar government critic, who

dared suggest that he should. The resignation came before the president of the Republic had had a chance to exert pressure.

[36] Caillaux had no illusions about the German press. He assumed that it was doing a job for the government and industry magnates interested in a long war; their designs would not have been served by a powerful peace movement in France. But he had failed to enlighten Minotto on the subject.

[37] Minotto's role in the affair was never cleared up. He returned to New York and married a meatpacking heiress. In 1917 he was interned as an enemy alien, allegedly because his mother had been a German. As late as 1921, Caillaux publicly stated that Minotto's internment had been requested by the French government to prevent him from interfering with the prosecution's case against Caillaux. Although referred to as a German agent in French court proceedings, Minotto was not prosecuted for espionage in the United States.

likewise was accused of working for the German government. Caillaux's unfortunate weakness for this kind of shady company resulted from his gratitude for their help at the critical period of his wife's trial. At that time they had acted as his bodyguards, claque, and publicity agents. What is more, he failed to report to the proper authorities transparent attempts of German agents to get in touch with him by correspondence or through go-betweens. Bolo and Duval eventually were convicted and executed; Almereyda committed suicide in prison; and the police got hold of the subagent who had approached Caillaux.

Early in 1917 Caillaux and his wife, after being manhandled by a nationalist mob, took off on a vacation trip to Italy. There Caillaux moved in circles critical of their government's war policy and into which what later proved to be an enemy agent had found entrance. In a conversation with the one Italian politician of "correct" political persuasion he was able to get hold of, Caillaux made no bones about his stand. The conversations, along with the defeatist propositions he developed before the Pullman porter on his return trip, were reported with customary distortions to Paris authorities.

Back home he remained inactive. He did not take the floor in parliament, nor was the one recorded address he delivered before his constituents different from any other politician's routine pep talk. He had not even been sure how soon he would return to France. Contemplating a prolonged stay in Italy, he had taken along voluminous files; he left them in a bank vault in Florence, blissfully unaware that he was sowing suspicion in his vigilant enemies' minds.

When the case against him was launched by the end of the year, the "secret papers" in Italy caused a sensation. The French authorities obtained Italian assistance in opening the safe deposit box. The press was fed the story that stocks worth millions of francs had been found; headlines screamed about the enormous fortune that Caillaux had taken out of the country to hurt the nation's economic armor. (Subsequently, a barely visible news item retracted the gross exaggeration.)

Actually, the Florence "caché" contained mostly manuscripts, which were to attract the prosecutor's special attention. One of these summarized the development that had led to the outbreak of the war. The parts played by a number of French politicians were appraised and no quarter was given; the writing was by no means complimentary to Poincaré. Was this not disparaging the nation's leadership at a time of crisis? Another piece of writing, labeled "Rubicon," was made up of cursory notes which Caillaux had at an earlier date jotted down to clarify his ideas about what he would do if recalled to office. He had contemplated a ten-month parliament recess, during which the cabinet would enjoy emergency powers; he had envisaged High Court proceedings against *Action Française* monarchists, enemies of old. Was this not attempted treasonable usurpation of power?

When at last in 1920 Caillaux faced the High Court, the public prosecutor, dutybound to salvage the prestige of the wartime president and his serviceable parliamentary majority, had the bizarre inspiration to liken the content of the Florence papers to a *crime de lèse-majesté*. Caillaux merely retorted that basing a criminal prosecution on unpublished notes simply would not do one hundred and some years after the French Revolution.[38] (He could have added that more than three hundred years had elapsed since the Peacham case of 1609, when this kind of argument was clearly rejected.)[39] Not even senators loyal to the Poincaré-Clemenceau regime, who sat as High Court judges, could conceive that the political records of wartime rulers were protected from criticism by the Penal Code. The judgment only mentioned the Florence papers as indicative of the motives behind the defendant's actions.[40]

It takes time to weave even this kind of fabric. Procrastination in the Caillaux case was doubly revealing, for no serious political obstacles had to be overcome. To lift Caillaux's parliamentary immunity presented no problem; Caillaux himself had insisted on a full-fledged trial. The December 1917 immunity debate on the floor of the Chamber gave him a chance, however, to state his case, and he made the best of it. It was one of the most effective speeches of his long career. He did not deny lack of discretion in dealing with suspicious characters, but he dwelt all the more emphatically on the fundamental issues the nation must face beyond the mere prosecution of the war. Nor did he fail to contrast journalist Clemenceau, courageous champion of Dreyfus's cause, with Premier Clemenceau, stage architect for another Dreyfus affair. This did not alter the predetermined decision. Just a month before, the Clemenceau cabinet had obtained his investiture by the Chamber. Even though there was a decrease in government votes,[41] the Chamber was not going to disavow the cabinet on the immunity issue.

[38] Session of the High Court of February 24, 1920, as reported in *Le Temps* of February 25, 1920.

[39] *State Trials* (Howell), Vol. 2, p. 869.

[40] Text of judgment in Dalloz, *Répertoire de Législation, de Doctrine et de Jurisprudence*, 1923, II, 34.

[41] According to *Journal Officiel*, 1917, p. 3,078, voting on the confidence motion on November 20 was as follows: ayes, 418; nos, 65; abstaining, 41. The resolution lifting Caillaux's immunity (*ibid.*, p. 3,660) was passed as follows: ayes, 396; nos, 2; abstaining,

The slow progress of the investigation, during which Caillaux was questioned again and again by the examining military judge, government-inspired adverse publicity around the Florence incident, and some rumors about government endeavors to bring the case before an amenable judge, rather than the competent one, caused opposition criticism. Twice, in January and February 1918, the government's handling of the case was brought before the Chamber by the Socialists, who insisted on a committee investigation. But Clemenceau's majority held, and no parliamentary inquiry was permitted to interfere with the military examiners.[42]

Who was to try the case? The idea of a military tribunal seems to have repelled Clemenceau from the start. "I am a politician, and I prosecute a politician," he is reported to have said.[43] Was he impressed with Caillaux's allusion to his Dreyfusard past? Or was he afraid that a military tribunal would impose the death sentence[44] and give an immeasurably unfavorable turn to what was for him a fight for political prestige? Whatever it was, a decree transferring the case to the political jurisdiction proper, that is, the Senate sitting as High Court, was issued on October 13, 1918, and a Senate-elected commission of inquiry took up where the military examiners had left off.

It took the commissioners sixteen months to prepare the case for trial. When the High Court convened in February 1920, the war had long been over and the initiators of the proceedings had withdrawn from active politics—Poincaré temporarily, and Clemenceau for good. But their disciples had won the first postwar elections of November 11, 1919, and their overwhelming majority in the *Chambre bleu-horizon*[45] was paralleled by a solid bloc in the Senate.

The evidence before the High Court portrayed Caillaux in few pleasing colors: a man less than circumspect in personal contacts; a man still choosing his loyalties in the light of bitter enmities and resentments of the summer of 1914, poisoned months of the Calmette drama; and a man still imbued with his own superiority and haughtily contemptuous

---

140. As Caillaux had welcomed the resolution, the opposition indicated its disapproval of the cabinet by casting abstention ballots.

[42] The vote for the cabinet on January 15 was 369 to 105, and on February 8 it was 374 to 99, as recorded in *Journal Officiel*, 1918, p. 6,386.

[43] Thus Poincaré, *op.cit.*, Vol. 9, p. 399.

[44] Joseph Caillaux, *Mes Mémoires*, Paris, 1947, Vol. III (1912-1930), p. 203, cites evidence—not too well substantiated, though—that judges of the military tribunal had favored capital punishment.

[45] "Sky-blue Chamber": sky-blue, World War I French equivalent of field-gray, symbolized extreme nationalism or, in terms of political topography, a right-wing coalition of emphatically conservative leanings.

in his criticism of government policy. He neither radiated nor attracted warmth.

Neither Malvy, friend and protégé, acquitted of treason but convicted instead of culpable malfeasance in office, nor Briand, oldtime rival and still a man of great influence, supplied exonerating testimony. Neither remembered having been semiofficially told by Caillaux, as the latter claimed, that he had rebuffed the advances of that very same German agent with whom the prosecution said he had been "in correspondence." Censuring Caillaux for wanting frankness and circumspection, Briand, himself out of office for three years, would not, in behalf of the accused, go beyond moral disapproval of the dog-eat-dog atmosphere which drove men of politics to regrettable conduct.[46]

As viewed by the prosecutor, Caillaux's activity and thought coalesced in a picture of treason, committed by means of intelligence with the enemy. The underlying reasoning, wherein political considerations outweighed those of legal construction, was based on three propositions: (1) to achieve victory it is imperative to believe in it, and to uphold confidence in the army; (2) no person or institution but the informed and responsible government is entitled to determine the proper way to fight a war; (3) any kind of assistance to the enemy, direct or indirect, is a crime.[47]

No doubt there was ample evidence that Caillaux had neither believed in victory nor had ever intended to help the army keep the confidence of the people. There was little evidence to prove that Caillaux had usurped the government's power to determine war policy. That the Germans indefatigably advertised him as a true statesman and the only Frenchman with political sense was psychological warfare and not to be held against him, the victim. And assistance to the enemy? The proposition was involved and knotty.

Assuming that the government and the prosecutor were right in claiming that compromise peace necessarily implied Germany's hegemony, had advocacy of such peace been tantamount to assisting, aiding, and comforting the enemy? Was it not, contrary to the prosecutor's opinion, essential to prove that the defendant had been of a guilty mind,

[46] Testifying before the High Court on March 17, 1920, as reported in Le Temps of March 18, 1920. Le Temps carried full-size trial reports, including exhaustive coverage of testimony. Briand's words were: ". . . When they [men of politics] are out of government, it is assumed that they would do anything to get in again. The frightful thing is that there is no closeness between men of public affairs. It is as though they were out to tear each other to pieces when, instead, whatever the divergent political views, strong ties of solidarity ought to bind them together."

[47] High Court session of April 14, 1920, as reported in Le Temps of April 15, 1920.

had intended, be it hesitantly, to strengthen the German cause, and had been aware of so doing? Was the charge not spuriously founded on the momentary, purely coincidental convergence of what was good for the Germans and what the defendant deemed conducive to a durable peace?

The prosecution's argument ignored an elementary fact, viz. that efforts of opposite sides may once in a while run parallel without concurring in motives and objectives. The defense made the most of this weakness in the argument. The evidence was interpreted at length by Marius Moutet, fencemaster of parliamentary tactics, and Vincent de Moro-Giafferi, high priest of courtroom drama. The real post-mortem on the reasoning of the prosecution was done by a veteran of the bar, Charles-Gabriel-Edgar Demange (1841-1925), a highly skilled if old-fashioned craftsman in legal analysis. He had the full attention of the elderly gentlemen of the Senate when he showed that the subjective element of the crime had been skipped by the prosecution. The audience was impressed.

Political single-mindedness rather than legal logic marked the defendant's concluding statement. Caillaux was hardly adroit in defending his actions from the blame of the law, but there was no denying the consistency of his political argument. "The initiators of war are in iron and steel," he had proclaimed in the course of the proceedings,"[48] and to this he reverted time and again. The charge of having sought a Franco-German peace in 1916-1917, without consideration of inter-Allied commitments, he countered with a claim to praise. His peace effort in 1911, he said, had delayed the coming of war by three years and had given France, very much in contrast to the overnight disaster of 1870, enough time to mend her fences. History's inescapable equivocation was Caillaux's shield: one who has evaded war may claim to have secured a chance to prepare better for future contingencies. In its outlook, too, the defendant's plea was irrefutable. His central objective, United States of Europe, had not lost its urgent appeal since prewar days.

The High Court's judgment was a compromise. Recalling an episode of the French Revolution, Caillaux called it *une mésure*, a political act rather than a manifestation of justice.[49] The court said that an inten-

[48] High Court session of February 25, 1920, as reported in *Le Monde*, February 26, 1920.

[49] See Caillaux, *Mes Mémoires*, Vol. III, p. 130. The reference was to Robespierre's judicial annihilation of Danton. A juror had been heard to observe: "This is not a trial; this is a political act. . . . We are not jurors; we are statesmen. . . . There can't be two [men at the helm]. One must be destroyed."

tion on the part of the accused to support the enemy cause had not been established; however, because of the defendant's correspondence with the enemy, damaging political and military information had been furnished to the enemy coalition, and the defendant was punishable under the terms of Article 78 of the Penal Code.[50] In vain did Demange submit that the defendant, indicted for violations of Article 71 (conspiracy to undermine external security) and Article 77 (intelligence with the enemy), was being convicted of a crime he had not been accused of nor had he defended. The sentence was imprisonment for three years, restricted domicile for five years, and ten years' forfeiture of civic rights.[51] The prison term had been calculated to permit immediate release—Caillaux had been held for over two years in preventive detention. Clemency arithmetics, however, had failed to sway a strong opposition group; 150 senators had voted for conviction, but 98 had cast their votes for full acquittal.[52]

The judgment aroused widespread criticism. Criminal intent had been established no more by correspondence with enemy agents than by the charges of which the Senate had acquitted Caillaux. The one letter he wrote to an enemy agent contained his refusal to have any truck with him. At the trial, Henri de Jouvenel testified that Caillaux was guilty, not of intelligence with the enemy, but of lack of intelligence with Allies.[53] This perhaps best summed up the government's case.

What was the long delayed trial's effect? Its importance certainly was not in the verdict. Once the new cartel of the left had defeated the conservative coalition at the elections of May 11, 1924, the High Court sentence was stricken from the record; Caillaux was elected

[50] Art. 78 then in force read: "When correspondence with nationals of any enemy power, albeit not for the purpose of committing one of the crimes designated in the preceding article, will nonetheless have resulted in furnishing to the enemy information prejudicial to the military or political situation of France, or her allies, those having conducted such correspondence shall be punished."

[51] Dalloz, *op.cit.*

[52] Lack of precision in the correspondence-with-the-enemy provision had been pointed out before in R. Garraud, *Droit Pénal Français*, 3rd ed.; Paris, 1916, Vol. III, Para. 119.3. Inadequate caution in handling such corespondence, the authoritative commentator said, was a mistake rather than a crime. In contrast to the old Art. 78, the provision now in force—new Art. 79.4 (Art. 81 since June 1960)—imposes punishment on offenders who entertain, without government permission, relations with subjects or agents of the enemy. There is no need to prove damage suffered by the state through the information which has been furnished. Moreover, the burden of proof is reversed: the defendant has to establish that he acted in accord with the government. See E. Garçon, *Code Pénal Annoté*, Comment to Art. 79.4, nos. 88-89.

[53] Related in A. Fabre-Luce, *Caillaux*, Paris, 1933, p. 179.

senator, and by April 1925 once again held office as minister of finance.[54] The important and outstanding fact is that a chain of circumstances had permitted Poincaré and Clemenceau to launch the case, remove Caillaux from the political battlefield at the last stages of the war, and not only expose him to public opprobrium as a man unpatriotic enough to disrupt national unity, but also drag him through the mud as a traitor and enemy agent.

The slandered man's conviction was no longer of essence in 1920 when the High Court finally arrived at its decision. Caillaux's elimination had been of inordinate importance, though, in the somber winter days of 1917-1918. And the cliché *Caillaux in Jail on Suspicion of Treason* had added immensely to the government's image-producing capacity, so badly needed at this critical time.

Wartime imagery faded quickly. It was all gone when a left-of-center coalition under Briand came to power after a ten-year delay—to face the disenchanting political reality of the 1920's.

B. THE LIBEL SUIT OF THE PRESIDENT

If a treason indictment constitutes the heaviest and most cumbersome weapon in the fight for political power, provoking a political adversary into initiating a suit for defamation constitutes a more volatile, ambiguous, and—due to the opportunities it opens for those momentarily excluded from the fruits of political power—an infinitely more widespread device. Its effectiveness as a weapon will vary from country to country, depending both on the particularities of legislation and on the attitude of the general public and the judge toward defamation in politics.[55]

One of the countries in which defamation in politics and ensuing defamation suits became a regular stock-in-trade was the Weimar Republic. As early as 1920 were the German Nationalists able to utilize this weapon with good success against the most versatile and ingenuous, if not the most conscientious, politician of the period, then Reich Minister of Finance, the Center Party member Matthias Erz-

---

[54] See Ch. X, Sec. 4. He resigned the following year because of disagreement with the Socialists on matters of financial and economic policy. From then until the dying days of the Third Republic, he served as chairman of the Senate's finance committee. Malvy, another amnestied "criminal," held the same office in the Chamber through about the same period.

[55] David Riesman has offered an excellent comparative study on the subject in "Democracy and Defamation," *Columbia Law Review*, Vol. 42 (1942), pp. 1085-1123, 1282-1318.

berger (1875-1921). From the vast array of cases which his foe and im-perial predecessor Karl Helfferich produced as evidence for Erzberger's illicit intermingling of politics and the pursuit of private gain, most proved to be above board. Yet the few cases in which Helfferich was able to make his accusations stick were enough to constitute some measure of moral victory for the defendant, leading to the plaintiff's resignation from office.[56]

In the 1924 defamation suit of the Reich President Friedrich Ebert (1871-1925) the stakes were infinitely higher. Transcending the issues of private and public morality, they involved the legitimacy of the new republican establishment itself and, with it, the historical role played by its first president during what one might call the incubation period of the Republic, the January days of 1918. The contest in court promised to become all the more important as Ebert's period of office was now, autumn 1924, drawing to its close. Both his preparedness and his chances to become the standard-bearer of a republican coalition for the June 1925 election, the first popular election to the office, seemed to depend on the handling and outcome of the trial.

Ebert's record, not unlike that of the other European political leader of the twenties who rose from the ranks of the labor movement, Ramsay MacDonald (1866-1937), is beclouded. His life work is marred by the failure of the enterprises with which he was intimately connected, the Social Democratic Party and the Weimar Republic. As things worked out, he first presided over and then, through his attitude during the war, deepened the fatal split of the German working class, in order to become during his presidency the middle man between the generals and the old-time bureaucrats, who used him as a shield and pawn, and the Republic's politicians. But this may be an unduly harsh view of his ability to keep the Weimar Republic a going concern. Had he been more fortunate, had he lived in the England of the 1940's, he might have filled with distinction the role of an Ernest Bevin (1881-1951), becoming both agent and symbol of the permanent and coequal asso-ciation of the popular masses with the affairs of the state. What history easily forgives and smiles at indulgently in the Bevin success story—his mannerism, his being hoodwinked and bamboozled by the staff over which he presided, the whole difficult process by which a politician arisen from the lower ranks of society becomes a coequal associate of

[56] Klaus E. Epstein, *Matthias Erzberger and the Dilemma of German Democracy,* Princeton, 1959, contains in Ch. 15 an exhaustive survey of the trial.

the older ruling strata, whose approval he covets the more eagerly as it seems necessary to him to fulfill his historical role—turns into tragedy where the outcome is utter failure.

But whatever the historian's judgment of Ebert's role, few denied that he was what one would commonly call a German patriot, in the meaning used in the first two decades of this century. He was foremost among those labor politicians who, without ulterior motives, wished for the victory of the German cause. Only relatively late, in early summer 1917, was he, in common with the majority of German middle class politicians, made to realize that a compromise peace, one which would at the very best safeguard a kind of *status quo*, was the maximum to be hoped for. But this insight by no means detracted from his zeal in trying to keep the home front on an even keel. For that purpose he used to the hilt his position as chairman of the Social Democratic Party and as one of its most influential parliamentary representatives. He did so even though this policy increased the danger of alienating larger working class strata from the policies of the Social Democratic Executive Committee. Thus Ebert played directly into the hands of those of his former party colleagues who had cut loose from the official party discipline and were engaged in organizing a rival Independent Social Democratic group, energetically bent on mobilizing support toward ending the war as speedily as possible. Nevertheless, before the ink on the peace treaty of 1919 was dry, the propaganda of the extreme right and sections of the moderate right began asserting that the war could have been won but for the treacherous riots, strikes, and wholesale defeatism leading to revolution and loss of the war; for these the whole political left was made responsible.

The historical episode connected with this trial formed one of the more important of the links serving to build up the legend of a German army: invincible on the field of honor, but forced to abandon the fight because of the stab in the back it suffered from treacherous foes at home. In late January 1918, strikes broke out simultaneously in a great number of metallurgical plants and other war industries in many major industrial centers of Austria and Germany. The strikers set up committees of their own, with neither trade union help nor approval, formulating both political and economic grievances. At one end of the scale they demanded peace without annexation, with working class representatives to participate in peace negotiations—an especially popular point in the days when the public spotlight was on the wrangling going on at Brest-Litovsk over scarcely veiled German demands for annexation of large parts of formerly Russian territory. At the other end they demanded improvements in the food situation, protested against the power of the military both over the country at large and the factories in particular, and requested thoroughgoing democratization of public life. The latter point was still a burning public issue, given the spectacle of Prussian ruling groups doggedly resisting any idea of scrapping Prussia's iniquitous electoral system.

Those most active in the committees were in contact with the dissident elements of the left. Yet their demands only expressed what had by that time become generally accepted thought patterns among the majority of the population. The Executive Committee of the Social Democratic Party, as much as the trade union leadership, was surprised and overwhelmed by the outbreak of the strike on January 29; when invited, the party's Executive Committee resolved to have its delegates join the strike committee of eleven.

This invitation had not come easy. Georg Ledebour (1850-1947), leader of the dissident Independent Socialists whose group had already joined up, battled furiously against extending the invitation, foreseeing correctly that such enlargement would emphasize the search for an early compromise with the authorities. But the majority of the committee, trying to create the widest possible political support for their movement, decided against him. One of the three members delegated by the SPD Executive Committee was Friedrich Ebert. After lasting five days, and involving in Berlin alone in its last stages over half a million men, the strike had to be called off. The Imperial Government, under pressure from Ludendorff's High Command and advised by the Berlin police officials, clamped down martial law, instituted courts-martial, and refused to make the slightest concessions to the strikers.

Both Ebert's and his party's motives in joining the strike, and especially Ebert's attitude during the strike, became the object of an action in defamation in 1924. The trial actually came off twice. It started when, on an official visit by Ebert in Munich, 1922, a National-Socialist agitator called him a traitor to his face. Ebert's lawyers advised him to withdraw his action when the Munich court insisted on his personal appearance in court. Meanwhile, however, the law had been changed, allowing for the president's testimony to be taken at his official residence. Thus when the same agitator repeated his line, the public prosecutor, joined by Ebert as private party, hauled into court an editor of a small nationalist paper that had reprinted the agitator's account with some insulting embellishments of its own. The case came up for trial at the local court in Magdeburg in December 1924. The court sat with two judges (German nationalists to the bone, as it was later learned) and two lay assessors.[57]

The testimony, ranging far afield, focused on two interrelated questions: what were the motives of the SPD Executive Committee in joining the strike committee, and what was Ebert's attitude while on the committee, especially on the occasion of his speech at the open air mass meeting of January 31, 1918? The large array of witnesses fell into four sharply distinguished categories. The first were the solid phalanx of SPD functionaries, including the former Independent Socialist parliamentarian and member of the strike committee Wilhelm Dittmann (1874-1954), who at that same meeting had tried to address the crowd after Ebert, but was seized by the police, hauled before a court-martial, and given a five-year sentence of *custodia honesta.* Their testimony followed a simple line: after the party's Executive Committee initially refused to have anything to do with the strike, Ebert executed party orders in joining the committee as the only effective way to quickly kill it. They also enlarged on the generally patriotic role of the SPD, recognized by all and sundry authorities of the year 1917-1918. Ebert's own interrogation was in line with the testimony of this group.

The second were a band of former or present leftists, all more or less hostile to the SPD, who had in some form or other been mixed up in the strike. They included the present chairman of the eleven-man strike committee. They stressed that the SPD executive joined the committee in self-interest, as a way to improve the party's standing among the working class; during the last years the party had grievously suffered through its all-out patriotism. Except for one witness, who had meanwhile switched to the extreme right, this group was quite willing to admit that Ebert tried, albeit in vain, to mitigate the strikers' demands; from their viewpoint this was another point to be chalked up against him. This version would accord with the testimony of the

---

[57] Trial and judgment have been reported in full in Karl Brammer, *Der Prozess des Reichspraesidenten,* Berlin, 1925. To evaluate the testimony the exhaustive trial reports in the *Berliner Tageblatt* were also used; Friedrich Karl Kaul, "Justiz wird zum Verbrechen," [East] Berlin, 1953, pp. 153-189, gives the narrative, as seen through the eyes of the principal German Communist lawyer of the fifties. Otto Landsberg, "Der Prozess Rothardt" (the defendant journalist), *Die Justiz,* Vol. 1 (1925), p. 124, contains the evaluations of one of Ebert's lawyers, especially interesting for the private utterances of the judges. Later disciplinary action against one of these judges, based on a 1921 derogatory remark about Ebert and leading to a "reprimand," is discussed in Otto Landsberg, "In Eigener Sache," *Die Justiz,* Vol. III (1927), p. 211.

one uncommitted witness who, in the pursuit of his job as a journalist, had listened to Ebert's speech. He described Ebert's dilemma in trying to retain the confidence of a severely critical audience and yet not make too many concessions which would get him out of line with his own policy: to affirm the need for continuing national defense until an honorable peace with the enemy could be reached.

The third group, which received the largest amount of public attention, were what one might call "organized witnesses." Once the political potentialities of the trial became clear to nationalist politicians, a local Berlin politician and clergyman undertook to systematically collect witnesses who could produce "interesting" testimony. The focus shifts from the elusive question of motivation and goals to Ebert's utterances at the January 31 meeting. Assertions now crop up that Ebert was handed a slip of paper asking him how workers should respond when called up for military service—a burning problem, as the authorities tried to silence agitators by calling them to the colors. Ebert supposedly replied that the orders were to be disregarded. His own recollection on this point is somewhat fuzzy at best. This organized testimony not only did not fit in with his previous known behavior patterns, but was out of harmony with the tenor of the discussions that had taken place on that specific point in the party executive. Moreover, the main find among those chance witnesses, a man whose line fitted in well with the political needs of the nationalists, was so thoroughly discredited that the judgment discarded his testimony altogether.

The fourth category consisted of officials of that period, among them generals or police officers who were no friends of the Social Democrats. The police reports on the strike contained nothing unfavorable to Ebert. The utterances of the generals, officials, and politicians varied, according to their present frame of mind. Some insisted on the lack of munition possibly caused by the strikes, or implied that the SPD did not help them enough in the pursuit of the war. Others recognized the unqualifiedly patriotic merits of the SPD. The defense was even able to produce a Hindenburg letter of December 1918 in which he apostrophized the plaintiff as a "patriotic man who loves his fatherland."

In their zeal to have their client appear a good patriot, however, Ebert's lawyers had to contend with one major difficulty: the interpretation of the SPD's attitude, which would arise from reading the party's official mouthpiece, the Berlin daily, *Der Vorwärts*. Without being too convincing, the lawyers had to deny the paper's representative character. Evaluation of the editorials during the critical period clearly shows two points: (1) the strike came as a complete surprise to the SPD, the party had nothing to do with its outbreak; (2) however, the SPD could not think of taking any position against it. As the paper said in its review after the strike had been broken, "Circumstances are often stronger than men."[58] Perhaps the paper somewhat overplayed the initial joy of the SPD executive in being able to join the strike. But it surely went out of its way to emphasize that the SPD would stand with the strikers, come what may, while at the same time it uttered the fervent hope that the SPD would succeed in its attempt to play honest broker between the government and the workers.[59] After the failure the paper chided the government for having precluded a compromise, thus creating a situation where it had to describe the SPD executive's role as a choice between the "Scylla" of committing treason against the workers and the "Charybdis" of committing treason against the state.[60]

But Ebert had lost his case long before judgment day. Caillaux, though he faced a purely political jurisdiction sitting and argued in the same constitutional and political system under which his alleged offense had occurred, had dared counterattack, pitting his political ideas against those of his adversaries. Ebert's lawyers and friends had a much easier case: a change of regime had since occurred, produced by the very circumstances which were at the basis of the reproaches against Ebert—the increasing popular rejection of policies and methods used by the old imperial government. But Ebert and his lawyers accepted battle on the terms of their enemies. They did not insist, as one witness calls it, that their action at that time was saving the fatherland,[61] that it was nothing but an historical incident in the inevitable and necessary breakdown of the old order. Instead, they decided—as a device to refute the stab-in-the-back myth—to defend themselves against not having been valiant enough protagonists of the old order and therewith having undermined the (nonexistent) chances of holding out much longer.

To the SPD's 1924 clientele, and even to the prospective customers for whom, after merger with the Independent Socialists, they now had to compete with the Communists, this approach was either meaningless or else a mark of distinction. To their adversaries, the ambiguities of

[58] *Vorwärts*, editorial of February 6, 1918.

[59] *Ibid.*, editorial of January 31, 1919. Richard Mueller, *Vom Kaiserreich zur Republik*, Berlin, 1924 (written by the head of the eleven-man strike committee before the inception of the Ebert trial), would confirm this interpretation of the SPD attitude.

[60] *Vorwärts*, editorial of February 3, 1918.

[61] Testimony of former member of the Council of People's delegates, Emil Barth, December 10, 1924.

their attitude in January 1918—an attitude grounded in the discrepancy between the policies of official Germany, Ludendorff's Germany, and the feelings and expectations of the majority of the German population, which the SPD reflected—had convicted Ebert in advance. Yet it may well be that Ebert and his lawyers acted not only from conviction but also from a lack of choice. As president and possible candidate for popular re-election, Ebert had to cater to that middling part of public opinion which emphasized the continuity between imperial and republican Germany and therefore wanted to gloss over the circumstances leading to the breakdown of the old regime.

The presiding judge and his colleague, however, were among the more rabid of these adversaries of the republican establishment. In his carefully worked-out judgment, the judge neatly dodged the historical and moral issue—which according to one of the critics was the real issue of the case[62]—by saying it was outside his province. Though they might have been perfectly patriotic, Ebert's motivations were, according to the judge, irrelevant. He had committed treason by his participation in the strike committee and his speaking engagement, causing damage to the national defense effort. Having thus found that the defendant had established proof for his major contentions, the court sentenced him to three months' prison for the insulting language he had used.

The next day the government, including its Nationalist Party members, sent the president a testimonial letter exalting his patriotism, with the right-wing press and many of the prominent right-wing politicians taking exception to the cabinet's action.

As Ebert died in February 1925, we shall never know whether the outcome of the trial would have destroyed his chances of becoming a candidate for the popular election to the presidency to be held in June. While the case was pending on appeal, an amnesty intervened and terminated proceedings against the defendant without the judgment ever becoming final. Most of the academic lawyers of the period criticized the judgment, either denying that Ebert had intended to cause damage to the interests of the empire or applying the old principle of *compensatio lucri cum damno*.[63] The latter construction would not only exclude the element of guilt, but would deny the existence of the objective factors constituting a treasonable undertaking. However, the opposite opinion found a spirited defense. It held that the need

[62] See the opinion of Hugo Sinzheimer, in Brammer, *op.cit.*, p. 184.
[63] Graf Dohna, "Vorsatz bei Landesverrat," *Deutsche Juristenzeitung*, 1925, p. 146; Gustav Radbruch in Brammer, p. 169.

to disregard ulterior motives or remote goals, in the face of the proximate intention to defy the public order, rested in the need for unified political command.[64]

Six years later the Supreme Court went out of its way to make amends for its straying Magdeburg brethren. In a different case of defamation, but one based on the same old allegations, it unearthed an old-world wartime case where a German industrialist had been acquitted of the charge of treason. He had continued to make raw materials available to his factory in Russia, because the factory's facilities would otherwise have been sequestered by the enemy and made part of the enemy war effort.[65] In applying the same principle *compensatio lucri cum damno,* the court vindicated Ebert's memory. It warmed the hearts of Ebert's political friends, but it had not the slightest effect on the torrential nationalist and National-Socialist campaign, which had long since played up the story of the Magdeburg trial and the verdict in an indefatigable effort to identify the Weimar Republic and its first president with treason to the fatherland.

The Ebert trial shows that the magnifying effect of political propaganda via courtroom proceedings is a general quality of the enlarged political stage in a society that is becoming a mass democracy. Whoever can grab and use its potentialities can run away with it, turning the results against his political foe.

4. Enlarging the Area of Prohibited Activity

In contrast to the Caillaux and Ebert cases, which both date back to events of World War I, the Swiss and German cases took place in the fifties, under the far wider terms of the post-World War II state protection legislation. But as previously emphasized, legal enactments do not necessarily control judicial policy. The two cases we shall narrate were staged in a period that mirrored both fear of the onrush of Communism and concern over previous and current exaggerations of political justice under totalitarian conditions. They therefore show an uneasy balance between a regime's holding tightly to the advanced legal position of fully controlling its citizens' suspicious foreign contacts, and its avoiding, or at least being apprehensive about, drawing all the logical consequences from cutting the last piece of ground from under the political freelance and marginal foe.

[64] Träger, "Rechtsgutachten betreffend den Prozess des Reichspräsidenten Ebert," *Der Gerichtssaal,* Vol. 91 (1925), pp. 434, 438.
[65] Entscheidungen des Reichsgerichts in Strafsachen, Vol. 65 (1931), pp. 423, 431.

A. THE LIMITS OF FACT-FINDING

The position of a small state in a world of giants and far-flung political movements is at best uncomfortable. When war breaks out and the pygmy insists on staying neutral and independent, things are bound to get worse. A nearby giant may easily use organized sympathies across the border to double the pressure on and enforce obedience from the still neutral dwarf state. Maneuvering between physical and moral survival, statesmen of the small neutral country will have to make compromises and submit to humiliations.

It is easier for the historian than for the political leader to say what the limits of adaptation should be. The leader who must make the decisions has a hard time of it. Under obvious pressure, the Swiss government, for example, refrained at the beginning of World War II from disbanding the National Socialist Party, which would have served the Reich as a spearhead had Hitler ever made up his mind to place Switzerland within the orbit of his "New Order." How was this self-restraint justified? Says an official Swiss publication: "The head of the Federal Department referred in his statement before the National Council to the fact that decisions at German headquarters were not taken solely on the merits of the matter at hand, but that they often resulted from the irate mood or the situation of the hour. Disbandment of German organizations in Switzerland could have incited the making of such impulse-triggered decisions."[66]

National sensitivity sharpens when such tightrope-walking, with all the humiliation it involves, becomes the only means of self-preservation. Indignant censure hits those at home who have a part in bringing about or exploiting such a barely tolerable situation. It was only natural that supporters of National Socialism who had carried on pro-Hitlerite activities in Switzerland should have been brought to trial once immediate danger to national security was over.[67]

Patriotic conduct had been the normal thing throughout the war for the great majority of the Swiss people. But there remained fringe groups, which grew under pressure among those to whom adaptation was a matter of convenience rather than principle. So long as the danger of invasion was imminent, much could hardly have been done about such obvious inclination to seek cover before approaching disaster.

[66] "Bericht des Bundesrates betr. anti-demokratischer Umtriebe," *Bundesblatt*, Vol. I (1946), p. 39.

[67] For a survey of prosecutions of Nazi sympathizers, see *Bundesblatt*, Vol. III (1948), p. 198. 112 proceedings were carried out from 1946 through 1948.

All the more did specific action impose itself after the war; part of patriotism's moral norm was to be translated into law by legislative effort rather than emergency decrees of the executive. In a way, Switzerland's urge to keep out of foreign entanglements combined with the moral impetus to uphold patriotic rules of conduct.

Traditionally, the Swiss had been averse to reinforcing state protection. In the 1920's and 1930's, protective legislation had repeatedly been defeated by popular vote. Wartime experience contributed decisively toward breaking down this age-hallowed resistance. In 1950 a number of emergency decrees that had been issued piecemeal in the late 1930's and 1940's were consolidated in an integrated body of statutory criminal law.[68]

One of the most far-reaching provisions, Article 272, as amended by federal law of October 5, 1950, aimed at political intelligence serving foreign interests. Unlike other parts of the new legislation, penalization here was not made conditional upon untruthful information or intent to support anti-Swiss aspirations. Prosecution was permissible whenever transmission of information to foreign recipients resulted in damage to Swiss interests. The provision was applied in a few unreported cases; one concerned a Swiss businessman who had informed United States consular authorities about a competitor's NS record; another involved information supplied to Senator McCarthy's office about left-wing individuals and groups in Switzerland.[69]

The first major test came in 1952 when the Federal Council gave its consent—required by statute—to criminal proceedings before the Federal Court against André Bonnard, professor of philology at the University of Lausanne. Not an enrolled member of the (Communist) Swiss Workers Party, Bonnard had been active for some time in numerous Communist-sponsored affairs. Among other things, he served on the executive board of the World Peace Congress. On March 2, 1952, he received a letter from the secretary of the World Peace Congress president, Joliot-Curie, the physicist, in which information was requested on the International Red Cross. The letter expressed special interest in data which would disclose the background of the International Red Cross as a private Swiss group, show close connections between its leading men and banking and industrial interests,

[68] See Jean-Claude Wenger, *Gefährdung der verfassungsmaessigen Ordnung*, Aarau, 1954.
[69] See the survey by the official in charge of enforcing statutes protecting national security: Federal Attorney W. Lüthi, "Zur neueren Rechtsprechung Über Delikte gegen den Staat," *Schweizer Zeitschrift für Strafrecht*, Vol. 69 (1955), pp. 298-334.

and indicate the extent of Anglo-American contributions. The reason was obvious. The Red Cross had offered impartially to investigate North Korean complaints about alleged American use of bacteriological warfare. North Korea, supported by the USSR, had rejected the offer, and it was now imperative to prove that she had been fully justified in so doing.

Part of the requested evidence was not too difficult to collect. Red Cross headquarters obligingly provided one of Bonnard's two collaborators with available official documentation. For the rest, having discarded his female assistant's fragmentary, hardly relevant data, Bonnard went in for some digging. From Red Cross handbooks, corporation directories, and polemical writings by Socialist authors, he established important financial and economic offices held and interests represented by prominent Red Cross officers; he also found that during World War II contributions had been received from Germany and Japan.

He mailed the results of his study and set out on a trip to a Peace Congress meeting. On June 30, while waiting for an airplane, Bonnard was searched by the Swiss police. They seized notes for a speech on rearmament, European union, the state of Swiss opinion, and connections between the Red Cross and Geneva's financial aristocracy. In a completed draft of introductory remarks, Bonnard stated that for a long time he had admired the Red Cross but thorough study had led him to agree with the attitude taken by the North Koreans.

The case was not brought up for trial until April 1954, after an investigation of 21 months. The facts were hardly in doubt. Witnesses for the defense—French and Belgian colleagues of Bonnard's from the WPC executive board—exalted the group's great work for peace; so did the defendant, insisting that nothing in his attitude or conduct justified the least criticism. The prosecutor asked for a three-month prison sentence against Bonnard, eight days for the latter's male assistant, and acquittal, but prorate defrayment of costs, for the less effective female assistant.

The court did not fully concur. It brushed aside whatever information Bonnard had collected for his Berlin address, but it held that transmission of the requested research data to Joliot-Curie constituted a punishable offense. From Switzerland's point of view, the court argued, the defendant's efforts to show the Red Cross executives' financial connections held no significance; his actions had been made reprehensible because of the purpose attached to his report by those for whom it had been prepared. The same kind of data, collected by a newspaperman for the general reader, would not have entailed judicial consequences. What made collection of data a reprehensible act of political intelligence on behalf of foreign principals was the fact that the job had been done for the purpose of justifying North Korean rejection of a Red Cross investigation. There was no need to prove actual damage to Swiss interests, inasmuch as the defendant's action had been directed against an organization domiciled in Switzerland, exclusively directed and operated by Swiss citizens.[70]

Extreme though the court was in determining what constituted an act of intelligence, it displayed remarkable caution in fixing the penalty: fifteen days in prison for the principal and eight days for his male assistant; the female researcher, in accordance with the prosecutor's request, was merely sentenced to defray part of the cost of the proceedings. Moreover, the sentence against Bonnard was suspended. The court emphasized that Bonnard had shown no sign of regret. If he had, the court said, he would have exploded his defense, viz. that he had been within his lawful rights when acting as he did. The court, however, saw no reason to assume that the defendant would resume his wrongdoing; convicted, he would possibly sit in judgment over himself and mend his ways. The court's wistful comment did not say that the law it had to apply was absurd. It cannot even be taken for granted that the judges knew it was. A different conclusion, however, was difficult to draw.

Public reaction was mixed. There was visible uneasiness over a law so vague that it permitted prosecution for acts clearly within the limits of legitimate political criticism.[71]

No articulate reference, however, laid bare the core of the security enforcement issue as it affects tiny Switzerland. Neutrality may work as a comfortable rule-of-thumb in everyday affairs, and a government may even be able to uphold it in an emergency. But the principle of neutrality—the neutrality of the official state organization—will not necessarily restrain the mind of the individual citizen. The urge to take sides according to one's political lights may be stronger than caution. Men will act as their convictions tell them to act and, if it should suit their purpose, allow the products of their thoughts to cross state fron-

---

[70] Entscheidungen des Schweizerischen Bundesgerichts Strafsachen, Vol. 80 (1954), Part IV, p. 71.

[71] The judgment found unenthusiastic approval in "Der ehrbare Agent," *Neue Zürcher Zeitung* (April 23, 1954), Sec. 7, p. 1. Other papers, mostly in Western Switzerland or in the Socialist camp, were moderately critical.

tiers. Calling such crossings "an act of political intelligence" is not likely to prevent it.[72]

B. THE DEFINITION OF AN INDEPENDENT POLITICAL OPERATOR

Compared with the loyalty problems of postwar Germany, those of Switzerland have an air of benign simplicity. Because Switzerland has developed over a long period one of the most successful national communities, competition for loyalty involves mainly the degree of recognition which citizens ought to grant to somewhat extensively conceived priority claims of the confederation. In contrast, the loyalty problems of postwar Germany already seemed a hopeless jungle between 1945 and 1949. With the unified Reich a victim of the lost war, and with sovereignty passed into the hands of four foreign powers overlording various local governments, the individual German's relations with his new, temporary sovereigns were not determined by any fixed norm of behavior. Fear and expectation, private advantage and corresponding servility vied with a high sense of public responsibility and a resolute will to seek a new, independent national existence. An occasional defamation suit still evokes this troubled period and the antagonists as often as not agree to drop the whole affair. Using today's standards to measure the haphazard pursuits of a time when there was no recognized or recognizable national norm, there is no profit in calling on the law.

In 1949 came the consolidation into two antagonistic new states, the Federal Republic and the German Democratic Republic (DDR). Consolidation, however, could not efface many of the effects of this externally imposed separation. Innumerable conflicts arose from this subdued political warfare[73] going hand in hand with some form of practi-

---

[72] There is also a somewhat earlier decision concerning a Swiss Communist who in 1951 went on a "political pilgrimage" to Budapest to attend the executive meeting of the Communist International of Journalists. Among other things while addressing that body, he called Switzerland the center of United States espionage and made exaggerated and inexact, though not baseless, statements on Swiss budgetary expenses for armament purposes and the sending of weapons experts to Formosa. In sending him to prison, the court applied the new Art. 266 bis, which, in the understanding of the court, would make it unnecessary to prove that the defendant supported an already existing enterprise hostile to Switzerland, if it only clearly inferred from the facts that his machinations intended to provoke such an outcome. *Arnold,* Entscheidungen des Schweizerischen Bundesgerichts, Vol. 80 (1953), Part IV, p. 24.

[73] There are iniquities resulting from an extensive interpretation of Art. 100(e) 1 of the Penal Code, allowing anyone who has been forced into even a simulated agent relation by the DDR authorities to be prosecuted in the Federal Republic. These are vividly described in H. W. Ruhrmann, "Verfassungsfeindliche und Landesverräterische Beziehungen," *Neue Juristische Wochenschrift,* Vol. 12 (1959), pp. 1,201-06.

cal accommodation, a situation of mutual nonrecognition but compulsory sharing of the former Reich territory.

The problems of the agent and the double-agent or news vendor, living simply on buying, selling, or fabricating news—the whole army of those on both sides of the fence who make a living from spying, reporting, and creating real or fictitious diversions—need not detain us here. Their diversified activities have either been anticipated or followed by an extensive body of legislation and jurisprudence, trying to cover the widest range of action. Treason, with its derivatives, was formerly considered the most heinous of all crimes; it is still this serious in many countries where the patriotic norm has not been eroded, as happened in Germany under the impact of its policies and its fate in the thirties and forties. But to the public consciousness today, treason is just one of many shady business pursuits in a marginal, rather insecure existence.[74]

Due both to the split of the country and the intelligence interests of a great many nations, this type of service trade in Germany has enlarged manifoldly, by comparison with its growth in other states. Its main impact is probably less its questionable achievements than its effect on

[74] In 1957 there were treason and treason-derivative court proceedings against 269 persons. However, the number of cases noted by the police, which includes all types of antistate activities, was 8,761. Unfortunately, the German agencies do not convey to the outside specific enough material to show how many cases handled by the prosecutor's office terminated with some kind of *nol pros*. (See Statistisches Jahrbuch 1959, p. 102; Bundeskriminalamt; Polizeikriminalstatistik fuer 1957; the latter should be compared with the handful of treason and espionage cases prosecuted in 1957 in the United States. Cf. Annual Report of the Attorney General for 1957, pp. 50-54.)

Recent official figures published in *Frankfurter Allgemeine Zeitung*, July 29, 1960, show 799 convictions "of agents of the Soviet bloc" in West Germany from August 1951 to December 31, 1959. 1,650 agents were not prosecuted, for they surrendered voluntarily to the authorities. As it may be assumed that the Western powers show a similar interest in Eastern Germany and, moreover, as a good-sized number of agents pursue their trade without either being caught or surrendering to the authorities, one arrives at totals which would confirm the impression that espionage has, at least in Germany, become a well-established minor business. The equally official estimate of 16,000 hostile agents busy throughout a single year in Western Germany, though probably somewhat exaggerated for pedagogical purposes, and also problematic because of the difficulty of sorting out intelligence operators from subversives, would generally confirm this impression. If one adds the corps of Western operators in Eastern Germany, the figure may easily surpass 25,000. Of course, in contrast to their brethren of "the official intelligence communities," these clandestine operators are not invariably working full time. Yet, adding up the legitimate and the illegitimate operators, their total will certainly surpass the number of professional politicians (in a few individual instances the categories have been known to overlap) on both sides of the Elbe. This is quite a symptomatic and revealing novelty, rather telling in regard to the present-day style of German politics.

the style of German politics. It contributes more than its full share to the veil of secretiveness, the general dearth of spontaneous political life, and the all-pervasive officialism. But just because of this decreasing spontaneity in political life, it becomes of major significance where to draw the line between an independent political operator and an agent acting on the instructions and in the interest of a foreign principal. Most of those working in the field of "contacts" have such a principal, sometimes a variety of principals, whose orders they discharge in a more or less ambiguous way.

In the last years the West German Federal Court has confronted a few cases where the exact line between an agent and an independent operator has raised both difficult and interesting questions. We might mention the first case somewhat more briefly, as its interest lies more in its personal than its political aspects. It concerns the first president of the West German Office for Constitutional Protection, Otto John. Finding himself under rather mysterious circumstances in East Berlin, John entered a period of limited cooperation with the DDR authorities. He espoused those Eastern official propaganda lines which coincided with his own known beliefs and fears, without, however, otherwise accepting Communist terminologies and ideologies. He also made some factual statements (which he later admitted to be incorrect) on the secret work of the Gehlen organization in France and on secret protocols to the European Community treaty. After having spent about a year under Eastern auspices, he escaped and returned voluntarily to the Federal Republic. Indicted for various forms of treasonous activities, he was tried before the Federal Court in December 1956.

We need not enter into his system of defense. It involved claims, rejected by the court, of his having been abducted to East Germany; his cooperation with Eastern propaganda organs he excused by referring to threats on his life and security. His case reveals a complete alienation from the political style as it had evolved in the Federal Republic, without his having been converted at all to the competing patterns of the East. Caught in the split politics of his country, he was a wanderer in a political no man's land. His unprepared flight to East Berlin, executed on the spur of the moment, his limited amount of cooperation and disenchantment with the DDR authorities, and his carefully planned return flight into the Federal Republic—he might have escaped to another country—reveal more the tragedy of an unstable and unpolitical person than a politically conscious design and pattern. His punishment, four years of penal servitude, is overly harsh, according to the opinion of many observers and critics, presumably including the federal attorney who had asked for a two-year prison sentence.[75]

This case reveals some of the difficulties which the application of the new penal provisions creates in serious cases of loyalty conflicts. The new Para. 100(d) penalizes relations with a government that is outside the territorial application of the law (the cumbersome language was selected to include the DDR government which, from the viewpoint of the Federal Republic, is neither a recognized nor a foreign government). But, as the reporter of the bill at the 1951 Bundestag discussion made quite clear, such relations must have been established with the intention to support endeavors or actions directed against the security of the Federal Republic. The reporter explicitly added, "The mere fact that these endeavors or acts are in contradiction to the political interests of the Federal Republic is not sufficient."[76]

But did John really want to undermine the existence of the Federal Republic in establishing his East German contact, or did the condemnation of the federal government's military policy, with all its domestic repercussions, not exactly correspond with the opinions long held by John? Was the invocation of the special duties incumbent on him in his official position, emphasized in the judgment of the court, enough to dispel the argument that parallel interests need not necessarily connote treasonable intent.[77] But inasmuch as John was guilty anyhow of having made distorted factual statements revealing fake state secrets, doubts about his intention to undermine the West German establishment did not matter too much.

The difference between an agent and an independent political operator whose thoughts and programs deviate strongly from those officially acceptable became decisive in the case of Dr. Heinrich Agartz, tried before the same court in November and December 1957. Agartz had been the director of the Economic Research Institute of the Trade Unions (WWI) and, through 1954, their main advisor in matters of theory and program. But his way of visualizing German developments from the angle of Marxist analysis of class forces, though never decisively rebuffed by the trade union headquarters, was often a hindrance to accommodation and compromise within the ranks of the far-flung organization. Moreover, political adversaries had built him up into a

[75] See the criticism Politische Strafjustiz in *Deutsche Universitaets Zeitung*, 1957, p. 5.

[76] Neumayer, in Verhandlungen, 1. Wahlperiode 158. Sitzung, July 9, 1951, p. 6,323.

[77] See judgment of December 22, 1956 of the Federal Court in Hochverrat und Staatsgefaehrdung, Vol. II, pp. 77, 133-37.

kind of scarecrow symbol. Dismissed from his trade union job in December 1955 as a result of interoffice rivalries and dissensions in which he operated with neither skill nor loyalty, he took to publishing a biweekly sheet of his own: the Economic and Social Correspondence. Supported by colleagues, some of them also ousted from the Trade Union Institute, he submitted both trade union policies and all of West Germany's social and economic institutions to a trenchant Marxist analysis.

As the 400-odd copies which it sold did not provide a sufficient financial basis, he accepted some East German help, granted in the form of subscriptions to 2,000 copies. A lower level East German functionary, acting as chauffeur and courier, brought the money to West Germany in lump sums. It was then paid in smaller amounts and under various fictitious names via postal money orders to Agartz's account, to create before the world at large and especially before his unsuspecting collaborators the impression that these amounts had come in from bona fide subscriptions. The story broke when an anonymous caller—strongly suspected of being an East German official—tipped off the West German police, putting them on the trail of the car and the chauffeur who carried a 21,000 DM. installment.

Unlike Otto John, who in court took a decided anti-Communist stand, Agartz took full responsibility for his actions and remained strictly in the role of a Marxist critic. The judges fastened their questioning on black and white images of freedom and suppression; these never produced any satisfactory response from the defendant, for in measuring societal performance in both East and West Agartz was using different yardsticks from those his judges tried to elicit from him. In addition, the testimony of the witnesses as well as the defendant's correspondence file tallied to some extent with his contention that the financial support and contact with the East had not in the least influenced his political independence. The prosecution attempted to build the subsidies and the destructive criticism of the correspondence into a picture of a Western support position built for and in the interest of the Communist Party. It thus tried to bring the case in line with the John decision, where some knowledge by John of the possible political consequences of his action, rather than his political motivations, was declared the decisive element.

The prosecution, asking for a prison sentence of one year, tried to extrapolate from some of the obiter dicta of the Constitutional Court's opinion in the case against the Communist Party.[78] Their purpose was

[78] See Ch. IV, Sec. 3.

to raise doubts as to whether such a Marxist critique of present-day Western society was constitutionally permissible. But the main question was whether keeping contact with and taking subsidies from DDR authorities for publishing a Marxist sheet was treasonable if the proof of the defendant's conformity with Eastern attitudes could be rendered only by a haphazard, incomplete parallelism of policies—a parallelism based on some shared theoretical assumption rather than on any concrete agreement on policies and actions. Agartz was acquitted for lack of proof, his secretary for lack of guilt, the chauffeur and go-between for Agartz and the East Berlin trade union authorities received an eight-month prison sentence as a paid agent.

It may well be that the judges pondered over some points which the defendant's lawyers took good care to bring up during the trial. One of his lawyers, Dr. Gustav Heinemann, a member of the executive board of the Evangelical Church, was especially qualified to draw the court's attention to the subsidies flowing from Western Protestant sources to their brethren in the DDR. To the authorities of the DDR these subsidies must have looked at least as obnoxious, if not more so, than DDR support for Agartz's publication did in Western eyes.[79]

If the judges considered this point, their opinion showed no trace of it. Yet in pondering the riddle of the mysterious phone call, which put the West German security organs on the track of the go-between, they showed that they were very conscious of another possible trap: that the East German authorities might want to make propagandist capital out of a conviction of Agartz, using it as evidence for the West German determination to suppress the independent left.[80] But otherwise, the judges were intent on avoiding anything that would constitute a precedent narrowing down their controversial interpretation, previously worked out. According to that interpretation, the main motivation and goal of the perpetrator need not be directed toward undermining the constitution; he is guilty merely by consciously giving some support to hostile anticonstitutional elements.

Fully upholding this construction,[81] they still acquitted Agartz, for they did not know whether he had intended to become an integral part of the hostile enterprise. In other words, a fool—namely, one who believes that he will not be forced in the last analysis to pay the price for favors rendered—may also be a knave, but this equation is no more than a presumption. And a debatable presumption, leaving open a

[79] See the trial report in *Der Spiegel*, December 11, 1957.
[80] See the judgment of December 13, 1957, reprinted in Hochverrat und Staatsgefaehrdung, Vol. II, pp. 186, 213.
[81] *Ibid.*, pp. 213-21.

narrow channel for those who insist on swimming against the current even when the ambiguity of their situation, or at least the reputedly bad company, should discourage them from doing so.

What looks at first like some subtle juggling of abstractions among the various compartments of *mens rea* only mirrors the profound ambiguity of the objective situation: casting out for some outside succors to work changes in the internal structure of the Federal Republic necessarily implies some sort of opening for the foes of the establishment itself, even if this opening was unintended by and unwelcome to the actor. The court might well have wanted to protect the freedom of any West German to establish contact and discuss with official East German authorities; it did this again recently when it acquitted the so-called abductor of Otto John, Dr. Wolfgang Wohlgemuth, who arranged for John to meet his official East German discussion partners.[82] The mere fact that resort to a court is needed to establish the limits between sympathetic contact—partial parallelism of thought patterns— and integration into and subordination to hostile designs shows the obnoxious, but inevitable, consequences of narrowing the realm of what is considered legitimate political activity.

Logically, such consequences would stand out clearly in the politics and courts of a divided country, where there are still common concerns that transcend purely technical contacts. Yet existing differences in the grant of political freedom provide an additional lever for mischief to the state organization that can manipulate its antagonist's definition of political freedom to the latter's disadvantage. To whittle down the structural disadvantage, without in the process making the dissenter perforce a captive, looks like attempting to square the circle. But it might be an enterprise as necessary as it is difficult, once it has been decided that the circulation of doctrines must be dependent on a certificate of origin.

5. Trial Practice Beyond the Constitutional Pale

Constitutional governments have many times been able to curtail drastically the activities of their adversaries. But if they want by death or imprisonment to eliminate them altogether from the community, they must utilize the agency of a court, with all the previously described hazards such action incurs.[82a]

[82] The Wohlgemuth judgment of January 1959 has been reprinted in *Frankfurter Allgemeine Zeitung*, January 7, 1959, p. 7.

[82a] The terms "beyond the constitutional pale" and "nonconstitutional conditions" are used here exclusively as a nonpolemic shorthand, indicating (1) a high degree of

Under nonconstitutional conditions, the trial is not a necessary means of disposing of political adversaries, those active as well as formerly active, or of people who are adversaries only in an objective sense, that is, are members of groups which, not by any specific reproach addressed to them, but on the basis of certain characteristics, are deemed hostile to the established regime. By purely administrative procedures —ranging from death and purely arbitrary periods of incarceration or banishment to confinement or banishment for definite periods—may such a regime dispose of its foes. The criteria governing the choice between administrative and judicial disposal seem never to have been hard and fast.[83]

But judicial determination requires the assertion of an element of personal fault, and this narrows down the choice between administrative and judicial determination of a case. While the purely objective criteria of choice can be refashioned, with some help from the arrested person, to resemble determination of personal responsibility for specific acts, purely practical considerations limit the number of cases where such refashioning is feasible. Purely administrative procedures become almost mandatory where, for example, huge numbers of people are involved and the operation must occur with great speed; this was the case with *dekulakisation* (deportation of members of ethnical or national groups from the USSR) and, more recently, when great numbers of the Algerian population were assigned compulsory residences. In the practice of the Third Reich the time of hostile contact with the regime or its adherents may often have been the main determinant of the choice; an old adversary of the regime, one who was not necessarily recently active, may have been shoved into a concentration camp while a recently active one may have had to face a court—at least as a prelude to a later sojourn in a concentration camp. But none are exclusive criteria; moreover, the criteria themselves are constantly modified, according to shifting political and administrative situations.

---

subordination of the judicial apparatus to the political command structure of a given society; and (2) the ensuing absence or minimization of the court's role in balancing the individual's interest against that of the official order.

[83] Jerzy G. Gliksman, "Social Prophylaxis as a Form of Soviet Terror," in *Totalitarianism*, ed. C. J. Friedrich, Harvard University Press, 1954, p. 66. See also *Trotsky's Diary in Exile*, Harvard, 1958. The entry of April 9, 1919, p. 80, tells why a trial against the czar, reviewing the sum total of the czarist regime's policies, could not be carried through. There were three reasons: the uncertain course of the civil war; the need to show both friends and foes that there was no way back; and a point emphasized by Lenin, that judicial proceedings would not allow the execution of the family members, who by necessity must fall victim to "the principle of dynastic succession."

Not the exclusive use of courts, nor the exclusive use of purely administrative procedures, nor the ratio of their alternative use, nor the switching back and forth between them suggests the degree of brutality and terror of the regime, inasmuch as both courts and administrative boards may, after a certain transitional period, assume many identical characteristics. But the very nature of a trial and of the objectives pursued in turning over a case to courts establishes a certain difference between the procedures. A bureaucratic handling of an individual's fate is done on the basis of general instructions and suggested "delivery" quotas of disloyal or potentially disloyal elements. But in a court case the prospective victim must be allowed to play a role, however limited, of his own. Rather than constituting a purely statistical incident in a general administrative program, he must become an individual defendant. He must be allowed to face and answer his accusers without physical coercion being applied to his person on account of his behavior in open court.[84] The requirements have intentionally been set this low to cover proceedings in any number of regimes and in those regimes which deviate in any degree from the patterns of constitutionalism. They would, for example, apply to trial techniques before, during, and after the Stalin period.

Not even in Eastern Europe has the Stalin-type trial technique ever pre-empted the field of political trials that deviate from the norm of constitutionalism. A somewhat older political trial practice has continued unabated: the judicial disposal of political adversaries, carried through under severe curtailing of the defendant's procedural rights and by a court somewhat more partisan than in a political trial under constitutional conditions. There is also a preponderance, but not an invariably complete dominance, of partisan witnesses. There is no attempt, however, to make the defendant part of the government plot. Whether he incurs additional risks or not, he may sometimes win a point against the government, occasionally even fortified by the assistance of a lawyer worthy of his name. At any rate, he has a chance to hurl his defiance against the government and measure the abyss separating him from the official doctrine. This type of trial is not a totalitarian invention; it has long been in vogue. In the eighteenth and nineteenth centuries, progress was made—in doctrine if not always in fact—in putting the king's enemy in court on the same level with the king. This progress is one of the more exquisite flowers of our late

[84] This definition would not exclude the possibility that the defendant was tampered with, physically or psychologically, in the pretrial stage.

civilization, ostensibly more endangered and problematic than many others. The older practice is going on right now under our very eyes in many non-Communist countries, such as Spain, Portugal, Greece, Algeria, and, Israel excluded, the countries of the Middle East.[84a]

This model was widely followed during the first postrevolutionary period in the USSR, at the time when the revolution was endangered by the triad of internal discontent, economic chaos, and foreign intervention. In some cases the charges brought before the courts—as distinct from terroristic reprisals carried through with a minimum of formality —were drummed up. In a number of cases of terrorism, where the individuals responsible had connections with the government's opponent parties, the government tried to fix responsibility on the leaders of those parties. The trials had a double goal: they could both justify a policy of suppression of these parties and underline the possible rewards, even in the postconviction stage, for those willing to come to terms with the government.

The most memorable of these trials was the one carried through in June and July 1922 against the Social Revolutionary Party. In its initial stage, Western European socialist lawyers participated in the trial on the basis of an accord, reached between members of the Second and Third International, on the guarantees both for the conduct of the trial and for the exclusion of the pronouncement of death sentences. The fact that the government carried on two parallel trials—one, the real trial, against the recalcitrant social revolutionaries, the second against repentant and cooperative social revolutionaries—underlined heavily the educational role the trial was to play. But their parallelism also emphasizes that these trials were still within the precinct of the older political trial tradition. The defendant faced many difficulties: a party court, many zealous witnesses for the prosecution, curtailment of their defense, organized "spontaneous" pressure on the court. But still the trial did not bring the government full satisfaction. The shifting tactical attitudes of the individual defendants, the degree of their withdrawal from or isolated participation in resistance against the regime stood out in full; but what also stood out was the lack of any evidence on the single charge that would have made the party suspect in the eyes of their own adherents and the population at large: their asserted cooperation with Denikin.[85]

[84a] From the abundant literature on methods of judicial repression outside the USSR orbit, we mention only a recent entry: "La Répression en Espagne," *Esprit*, Février 1961, pp. 309-24.

[85] See E. Vandervelde et A. Wauters, *Le Procès des Socialistes-Révolutionaires à*

There is evidence that the Yugoslav regime is following essentially the same pattern, in trials against both dissident members of the ruling elite and against adversaries outside its ranks. Of the latter kind, perhaps the most significant trial was that of Cardinal Aloysius Stepinac in summer 1946. Stepinac's position was for many reasons tactically favorable. His trial mirrored more than a national conflict; he was a high dignitary of an international religious organization, the Catholic Church, on whose loyal support he could count.[86] Moreover, the Cardinal had a mortgage on the allegiance of the Croatian people, not only as their acknowledged religious leader, but as the steadfast protagonist of their claim for a separate national existence. Tito might not have brought him to trial at all had Stepinac only obliged the government by relinquishing his office and removing himself from the country.[87] Tito's strong point, on the other hand, was the degree of the church's identification with the oppressive Ustaschi regime, under the leadership of Ante Pavelic, governing under joint Italian and Nazi sponsorship, and especially its policy of forcing great masses of orthodox people to convert to Catholicism.

The defense suffered many disadvantages. It had only six days between the indictment and the trial to prepare its case. While the prosecution had a seemingly inexhaustible reservoir of witnesses at hand, the court severely restricted the number of defense witnesses it was prepared to hear. It excluded much of the available documentary evidence offered by the defense. Moreover, Tito resorted to the well-known device of the "amalgam": intentionally blurring the picture, he joined Stepinac—indicted only for his political conduct during the Ustaschi regime and for his failure to disengage himself completely from contact with adherents of the former regime—with a number of defendants accused of terroristic acts. Yet in some fashion the defendant and his two lawyers were allowed to make their points. As to the most ticklish and explosive point, the compulsory conversions,

---

Moscou, Brussels, 1922, which gives the account of some of the Western lawyers who participated for about two weeks in the defense. The lawyers then withdrew, at the request of the defendants, for nonfulfillment of the above-mentioned engagements entered into by the Communist authorities. See also the accounts in L. Schapiro *The Origin of the Communist Autocracy*, Harvard University Press, 1955, pp. 166-67, and E. H. Carr, *The Bolshevist Revolution, 1917-1923*, London, 1950, Vol. I, pp. 181-83.

[86] Material on the proceedings, the background of the trial, and a great number of documents pertaining to the basic conflicts underlying the trial have been published in George Pattee, *The Case of Cardinal Aloysius Stepinac*, Milwaukee, 1953. While the book is favorable to Stepinac's cause, it also includes the most important arguments and documents of the other side.

[87] *Ibid.*, p. 56.

his lawyer tried to point to the need for the lesser evil to obtain the greater good, the salvation of human beings who would otherwise certainly be slaughtered.[88]

Exactly as in Ebert's defamation case, while the argument is plausible, it does not eliminate the ambiguity that the salvage job might at the same time be intended to pay dividends to those who undertake it. Stepinac himself refused to enter into the conversion question; with his conscience clear, as he asserted, he left the point to the judgment of history.[89] Instead he immediately counterattacked, taking the role of a legitimate spokesman of his nation, determining his relations to today's and yesterday's regimes, and invoking Yalta and the Atlantic Charter against the present regime. He rejected Tito's claim to invoke his personal responsibility for anything done before his accession. Given the conflicting claims of three regimes, the exiles in London, Tito's "in the woods," and Pavelić's in Zagreb, Stepinac alleged that his duty was to find the best ways of protecting the nation. Attacking the religious and educational policy of the regime, he offered a compromise, but only on the level of negotiations from sovereign to sovereign, and taunted the regime to make him a martyr. The court avoided this trap, sending him to prison for sixteen years, later changed by government fiat to compulsory residence.

This type of trial leaves the parties essentially where they were before. It does not change the fundamental position of either the present regime or its foes. With the regime in administrative control it will not fail to mark its points, but because of chivalry, nonchalance, or the certitude of its own superiority, it will allow its adversary the satisfaction of appealing to history. Moreover, both sides will use all the available propaganda outlets—the regime monopolizes the home market and the adversary often the foreign markets—to carry their side of the story exclusively.

But such trials retain many traditional concepts. Though they will take care of the regime's security needs, this somehow remains a mechanical and unsatisfactory solution. Unless the regime can drive home a point of undisputed moral relevance, its dominion becomes neither more nor less legitimate by such proceedings. The obstacle, it is easy to see, is the defendant. If he could be assigned a specific role within an action pattern planned around an objective situation, a trial might be better utilized for the making of history, in the sense that it would create desirable concepts corresponding to official needs. The

[88] Ibid., p. 237.   [89] Ibid., p. 239.

trial as an educational enterprise might come closer to the goal of creating reality in the image of those in power.

How such an educational enterprise would look has been revealed to us in the Grynszpan case. The case stands out for the simple reason that there is no need to reconstruct from the actual course of the trial the strategy and goals of those guiding the prosecution, for the memos and protocols of discussion of those in charge are available. Hershel Grynszpan killed the German diplomat Ernst vom Rath on November 7, 1938. Imprisoned and medically examined, but not yet tried by the French authorities, he was delivered to the Germans for the asking in the summer of 1940.[90] In the summer of 1941 Grynszpan was moved from a German concentration camp to the regular Berlin prison for persons awaiting trial. The federal attorney's office was asked to draw up the indictment before the People's Court; the murder of vom Rath was construed to be indirectly aimed at the German political leadership, thus constituting a case of treason coming under the jurisdiction of the court. But aside from the question of regularity of rendition by France, and the tenuousness of German jurisdiction, the legal authorities faced a more substantial practical difficulty. In 1942 at the very latest, and probably even earlier, Grynszpan abandoned the theory that he had committed the murder as a protest against Hitler's barbarous actions, especially the expulsion of his parents from Germany to their native Poland. He alleged that his action was the outcome of homosexual relations.

But all these were minor difficulties, as minor as the role of Grynszpan in the whole affair. The greatest difficulties came from jurisdictional conflicts over the responsibility for the conduct of the trial and, concomitantly, the question of its political orientation. A first draft of the indictment was made by an official of the Ministry of Justice. But Goebbels, the minister of propaganda, rejected it as completely insufficient, an apolitical murder which did not show up Grynszpan as an exponent of an all-Jewish conspiracy. Based on this argument, Goebbels tried to assume the leading role in the conduct of the trial.

---

[90] Helmut Heiber, "Der Fall Grünspan," *Vierteljahreshefte für Zeitgeschichte*, Vol. 5 (1957), pp. 134-72, contains a detailed account based on German official and unofficial files, as well as interviews with those who had a hand in the preparation of the German case. I am also grateful to Mr. Gerald Schwab of the State Department, who was kind enough to put at my disposal his unpublished George Washington University M.A. thesis on the case, resting on the examination of a great number of additional documents; needless to say, he bears no responsibility for my conclusions. A conversation in 1958 with Dr. Friedrich Grimm, NS foreign trial expert (see Ch. VI, Sec. 4), however, failed to elicit any further information.

According to him, Hitler followed his suggestion and handed over the juridical direction of the trial to Georg Thierack, president of the People's Court. As Goebbels outranked Thierack, he arrogated for himself a right of general control of the enterprise. But this arrangement offended Joachim von Ribbentrop, the minister of foreign affairs. He protested against the disregard shown toward the foreign policy angle. To his mind, the murder was an act of sabotage against the policy of Franco-German reconciliation that he had inaugurated. In addition, the fundamental plan of "World Jewry" to draw the Western world into a war with Germany seemed neglected. With Thierack presiding, a great number of conferences took place between the representatives of the three ministries to reconcile the various viewpoints. Diligent search, however, did not reveal direct relations between Grynszpan and the plans and activities of World Jewry. The formula under which the trial was to take place was therefore conceived as "the intellectual authorship of World Jewry."

Seven days were to be provided for the trial. The first day would be devoted to the facts in the case. Thereupon would follow the story of the humane methods by which the expulsion of Polish Jews from Germany was carried out. Next would come the narration of the murder itself. But all this would not take long. Fully three and a half days would be devoted exclusively to the search for intellectual responsibilities. The whole supply of anti-Semitism and pseudo-science would be enlisted for that purpose. Star of the trial was to be Georges Bonnet, former French Minister of Foreign Affairs; he would show how the murder torpedoed Franco-German reconciliation. From the outset, Thierack entertained doubts as to the tenor of Bonnet's testimony, emphasizing the key role of a translator who could "remedy difficult situations." Following Bonnet was to be a reading of French and Jewish newspapers and other documents. Then there would be a lecture on the intellectual authorship of World Jewry in the crime by the renowned Dr. Friedrich Grimm, perennial German rightist lawyer and at that time the Third Reich's expert on foreign trials, who had already been active in the first stages of the case. On the sixth day the speeches for the defense would take place, including that of an official defense lawyer who, as his attitude in future cases would show, was a reliable addition to the prosecution staff. Nothing was left to accident: the minutes of the coordinating committee show that he was to be oriented by Thierack on the appropriate forms for his intervention. On the seventh day the nominal director of the show, the vice president of the People's Court, who *pro forma* would preside at the trial, would read the verdict.

The plan, laid out in the minutest detail, came to naught. Jurisdictional squabbles were by no means solved. The Ministry of Justice showed its displeasure at being shoved into the background; it asked that it be clarified whether Hitler, when giving orders to proceed with the trial, was aware of Grynszpan's statements concerning his homosexual relations with vom Rath. Ribbentrop wanted more lectures on the relationship between World Jewry and foreign policy. Goebbels did not think that the story of the expulsion of the Jews in 1938 would be good propaganda copy. General interest in the trial ebbed somewhat when it became clear that Bonnet would not be willing to put in an appearance. And there remained the unsolved problem of the homosexual tale.

Thus on April 18, 1942, despite Ribbentrop's intervention, the trial date was postponed for the time being, and, as it turned out, sine die. Hitler's uncertainty as to whether Grynszpan's homosexual tale would not destroy the effect of the well-designed plot figured in his decision to abandon a show trial.[91] But there was another consideration: by April 1942 Hitler had for a number of reasons become markedly cooler toward France; this made it impolitic to carry on a show which, by concentrating on the all-Jewish conspiracy, was bound to make the sins of France's prewar conduct appear milder.

Grynszpan's trial, which never came off, was to be a stage show tailored to fit specific propaganda needs. The formal object of the trial, to mete out retribution for Grynszpan's crime, served only as a peg on which to hang the educational tale. "The trial thus offers a possibility to prove to the whole world the decisive participation of world-Jewry

[91] It must remain conjectural whether the tenacious zeal of both Ribbentrop and Thierack to revive the show for their own benefit saved Grynszpan's life. There are conflicting reports about his fate. But Grynszpan's father and brother, testifying at the Eichmann trial on April 25, 1961, asserted that they had no communication from him after 1939 (*Frankfurter Allgemeine Zeitung*, April 26, 1961). In November 1936 the Munich District Court started to try an action for the defamation of the memory of the assassinated Ernst vom Rath. The defendant was a journalist who had repeated the allegations of previous homosexual relations between vom Rath and Grynszpan. As Grynszpan was unavailable, the veracity of the homosexual tale could not be substantiated; however, the testimony of Ernst Lautz, former Chief Attorney at the People's Court, and of Goebbels's former Secretary of State L. Gutterer, confirmed still further the propagandist nature of the planned proceedings; see esp. the trial report in *Frankfurter Allgemeine Zeitung*, November 15, 1960, p. 5.

in the outbreak of the present war," wrote Goebbels to Hitler.[92] Consequently, the implications of this tale could be shaped at will. If there were any difficulties in crystallizing the proper trial objects, they arose only from the need to find a common denominator for the ambitions and objectives of the various competing bureaucracies, or from a dearth of convincing or compliant enough yes-men.

But the preparations revealed one major flaw beyond the possible counterproducing implications of the homosexual tale.[93] Their most severe shortcoming and their greatest advantage were one and the same. The enterprise was nothing but an educational show, drawn from an imaginary situation which existed only in the NS mind. Grynszpan, whether viewed as a personality or as an event, was too marginal to adequately symbolize the dangers of a Jewish conspiracy. Between the NS and their accidental victim the gap of noncommunication was too large to allow Grynszpan's action to be translated into the major danger for Germany's future.[94]

[92] See the entry in Goebbels's diary under April 7, 1942 (microfilm, p. 1,747), where the correct psychological arrangements and the need to achieve a positive political effect are stressed.

[93] While it may seem strange that Grynszpan was never made to see the light about abandoning the homosexual tale, the explanation is simple. In Hitler Germany the judicial administration, which included the handling of pretrial investigations and the prison bureaucracy, did not on its own partake in the physical violence that was engulfing so many aspects of national life. For that the intervention of the security services would have been needed; yet, given the controversy over the handling of the case among so many interested agencies, these services would have been reticent about proceeding on their own. The general reason why the country never experienced Stalin-type trials seems to lie in the following: at least since 1938, dissension in the upper ranks of society was so widely diffused that there was no need to provide an alternative reality with which adversaries had to be carefully identified for prosecution purposes.

[94] In contrast, the Reichstags fire trial, the most famous German political trial of the thirties, was only on the threshold of totalitarian trials, for the Supreme Court bench in winter 1933-1934 was not yet fully integrated into the Hitler system. It was a trial carried through by a totalitarian regime in the process of consolidation and conducted before an old-line jurisdiction working in a totalitarian atmosphere to which it had not yet fully adjusted. The government's intention to "make" the March 1933 election—by burning the Reichstag themselves and charging it to the Communists, or, according to a more plausible interpretation, turning the deed of a completely isolated individual into a Communist conspiracy—had been carried through according to plans. Everything else was an afterthought, a bravado attempt, not too well synchronized, to put up an alternative reality in court. The judges were intimidated or credulous enough not to probe into the mysteries of the Van der Lubbe story, especially his behavior in court, thus allowing the hapless victim to be railroaded to his death. But they deprived the Hitler government of the *post festum* confirmation of its built-up alternative reality: they acquitted the German and Bulgarian Communists, for which feat the court was promptly relieved of any further jurisdiction over political cases.

Thus the NS failed to achieve what had become the arch point of the political trials of the middle and later Stalin era: to fuse the mechanical elements of the political trial outside the atmosphere of constitutional government—the comfortable but unproductive certainty of the result—with the creation of a political imagery appropriate for present needs. The Stalin era had tried to overcome the difficulties of the purely educational show: lack of focus on the unique historical event. By making the defendant in his particular historical role into an organ of confirmation of the trial producers' image of reality, one also eliminated the clash of interpretations, which both marks and mars the traditional political trial.

Although varying in many details, the major pre-World War II Russian trials as well as the postwar Eastern European trials—the Rajk trial in Hungary in September 1949, the Kostoff trial in Bulgaria in December 1949, and the Slansky trial in Czechoslovakia in November 1952—all follow a set formula.[95] They all turn on some objective situation whose major concern is the political leadership. In the prewar trials in the USSR, the concern was related to the probability of a German attack; in the Eastern European trials it was concern over the possible effects of Tito's defiance of the USSR authorities. The defendants were individuals who presumably wanted or at least were able—should objective conditions show a change in policy—to substitute for the present leadership. The presumption was based on their former record of opposition within the party, in some instances on a more recent dissension, but often exclusively on their official position. Many of these individuals, especially in the USSR, had long been eliminated from positions of influence.

But to show the justifiability of the official course of action, from the viewpoint of dramatizing the impending dangers and also of substantiating the convergence between foreign threats and inimical domestic tendencies, a number of victims who had indicated some willingness to cooperate were made to stand trial. The motivations and the possible terms of cooperation need not concern us. Suffice it to say now that with two exceptions—Krestinsky in the USSR trial of 1938 and Kostoff in the Bulgarian trial of 1949—the defendants generally stayed within the agreed terms.[96]

[95] The variations are dealt with in detail in Nathan Leites and Elias Bernaut, *Ritual of Liquidation*, Glencoe, Ill., 1954, Epilogue. These trials, all except the Czech one, have been public. Official transcripts have been published of all trials, though the Czech one is not complete.

[96] As regards Krestinsky, see *The Case of the Anti-Soviet Bloc of Rights and Trotsky-*

What the defendants admitted to was a prefabricated and alternative reality. The prosecution put up a collection of motley facts in which real occurrences were inextricably bound up with purely fictitious happenings. But their admixture pointed to an alternative reality, consisting of dangers which would have come to pass but for the vigilance of the official hierarchy. The factual occurrences were taken from any number of political activities and decisions with which the defendants had been associated during their political and professional careers. At times they referred to positions on questions where defendants had been in the minority regarding the line of action ultimately taken. In other cases they referred to negotiations with foreign officials which when they occurred were not only perfectly within the scope of the defendants' official duties but were in many cases fully approved in advance by competent party authorities.[97] In other cases the defendants were charged with a domestic course of action which had at the time been the generally acknowledged party line but had meanwhile undergone changes.[98] To arrive at a criminal qualification of such actions, the prosecution set forth an endless series of espionage activities and betrayals which, they showed, were carried through in the service of both the police of preceding regimes and of foreign countries to which the defendants were recruited for various reasons.

Thus occurrences which denote at worst internal dissension in party ranks, or more or less abortive and hesitant attempts to establish contact with others who were working toward a change of policy and personnel, were made to appear completely different. Entirely fictitious espionage connections were utilized as motivations to explain the defendant's willingness and attempts to carry through extreme acts. These acts as charged would include wrecking, sabotage, murder of political leaders, and opening the way to foreign invasion by agreement with potentially hostile powers. In each instance the framework of charges fitted some expectations of future events which, had they come

---

ites, Moscow, 1938, pp. 54-59. See also *Traitscho Kostoff und seine Gruppe,* Leipzig, 1951, pp. 74-81, 639. (In the latter work the trial record is manifestly incomplete. For an attempt to refute Kostoff's repudiation of his previous confessions, see pp. 385-400.)

[97] This was especially true in regard to Krestinsky's dealings with German military officials. *Ibid.,* pp. 259-64. For corresponding situations from the Czech trial, see *Prozess gegen die Leitung des Staatsfeindlichen Verschwörerzentrums mit Rudolf Slansky an der Spitze,* Prague, 1953, p. 193. A critical evaluation of the Slansky trial may be found in Marcel Peju, "Hièr et Aujourd'hui: le Sens du Procès Slansky," *Les Temps Modernes,* May, June, and July 1953.

[98] For a discussion of this, see Leites and Bernaut, *op.cit.,* p. 388.

to pass, would have brought disadvantage to the country and displacement to its now ruling elite while they improved the defendants' chances to stage a comeback at a moment of crisis. The prewar USSR charges dovetailed with estimated German plans in regard to the USSR, while the Eastern European trials might have fitted into some possibly emerging Balkan federation as a possible counterweight to direct USSR overlordship of the local governments.[99]

To obtain the alternative reality, the proceedings followed what have been called "rules of translation."[100] Under the defendants' sometimes willing, sometimes grudging cooperation, certain of their thought and discussion patterns were translated into the realm of action and debited to the hypothetical consequences of these nonexistent actions. Thus Vishinsky in his prosecutions and, with much less skill and vigor, some of his satellite successors led their victims close to admitting that foreseeing certain contingencies is tantamount to supporting them. They took the defendants through the remotest possible situations that could arise from what they made them admit were consequences of their political action. They always forced on them interpretations that were in line with the prosecution's theory of how the defendants would have acted had these situations arisen. The difficulty of the prosecution's enterprise was that proof rested more or less exclusively on the confessions of defendants and testimony of codefendants, but without any independent corroboration by witnesses outside the scope of the prosecution's power. Whenever independent checks could be made on those in foreign countries who were implicated in the tales of the prosecution and the defendants, these persons not only vigorously denied all the factual allegations but in many instances proved the physical or logical impossibility of the events admitted at the trial.[101] Attempts by the prosecution to provide a greater amount of concreteness and verisimilitude—when, for example, they called on witnesses unconnected with the major events and made them describe the circumstances and physical location where treasonous conduct had taken place—could not substitute for these major shortcomings. Such witnesses could testify to true, but in themselves neutral, facts, but could give no independent corroboration of the treasonous nature of such contacts.[102]

[99] See the corresponding testimony in *Laszlo Raijk und Komplicen vor dem Volksgericht*, East Berlin, 1950, pp. 84, 153, and *Traitscho Kostoff*, pp. 151, 158.

[100] See Leites and Bernaut, *op.cit.*

[101] This has been done systematically in *Not Guilty. Commission of Inquiry into the Charges Made against Leon Trotsky in the Moscow Trials*, New York, 1938.

[102] See, for example, *Laszlo Raijk*, pp. 273-78.

Confessions to heinous crimes part committed, part contemplated, in the service of an alternative course of political action were used to dramatize the existing dangers to prevailing policies. The prosecution pinpointed these dangers by associating them with a nucleus of people working actively to bring about the very situations which all loyal citizens would want to avoid. We can only conjecture to what extent during the trial the majority of the population or even of party members became aware of the often subtle qualifications contained in the defendants' testimony and pleas.

The technique of confession as a sign of repentance and unity in extremes is an alternative to the open assertion and even dramatization of an irreducible and lasting conflict. Both policies have equally advantageous and harmful implications. The policy of confessions, working through the defendant's admitting to a series of fictitious crimes, may by the very extremeness of the admitted forfeitures produce negative popular reactions. The present setup, of which the defendants were for a long time an integral part, must be shot through with corruption and be weak enough to fall at the slightest provocation. On the other hand, the very admission might be enough to shock the population into closing ranks, or at least into carefully avoiding linking specific dissatisfaction with more inclusive political goals. At the same time, by showing the adversaries in all their baseness and abjectness, confession prevents them, even if they survive, from ever becoming again a rallying point for opposition. It may be this point which stands out most clearly when the regime compares the relative merits of confessions against the adversary's being allowed to take his stand at the trial. Even if silenced for good, the myth of his resistance might become a permanent memory or symbol.

In the final analysis, the choice of how to deal with adversaries brought into court under nonconstitutional conditions, especially if the case concerns members of the ruling party, may result from many complex factors. It may derive from the sum of historical experience, particular conditions, and from the makeup of the antagonists on each side. The Polish and the Yugoslav Communist parties and the East German Socialist Unity Party have never adopted the practice of covering the abyss of contradictory policies with the spectacle of prosecution for abject crimes and at least partial confessions in open court. Mrs. Hilde Benjamin, East German Minister of Justice, in defending a turn to harsher policies of repression, explained why such methods had been rejected and even censored by countries that had once practiced them. She quoted from Scholochow's "And Quiet Flows the Don": "This work is dirty, but even in this type of work one has to remain conscious of one's responsibility toward the Party. And one has—please understand me—to preserve some humanity. We destroy by iron necessity, but one should not make a circus of it."[103] In emphasizing that this was said in the midst of civil war and in the face of white atrocities, she made it quite clear that the rule should apply all the more in the absence of such extreme conditions.

In the average political trial outside the confines of constitutionalism, the significance of the acts debited to the defendant may become twisted. Confessions may be encouraged not only by offering rewards—this may also be done under more "civilized" conditions—but also by instilling the fear that those unwilling to play ball may be handled without the benefit and the remnants of protection provided by public proceedings. In short, official energy will be bent on producing and highlighting the desired pedagogical effect. The more the activities of the defendant and the defense lawyer can be circumscribed and the critical public opinion controlled—another major difference from a constitutional climate—then all the more effective can this official energy be. Under such circumstances one segment of reality might be blown up beyond all proportion and the defendant debited with the projections of his action patterns.

But still, even the most imaginative projections depend, however tenuously, on the prosecution's ability to squeeze from them some parcel of reality that can be construed and publicly offered as proof for the grand design against the public weal. The horizon of education by trial remains limited. It is obviously much more limited than where the trial stage is set by the Stalin kind of lore, where the prosecution produces reality afresh, in line with the changing political needs of the moment and with at least some assistance from the defendant. But except for the use of the outward forms, the Stalin-type proceedings retain nothing of what characterizes the political trial as a trial: the battle over the course or the meaning of actual historical happenings.

[103] *Neue Justiz*, Vol. XI (1957), p. 673. Published parts of the judgment of the East German trial against deviating party members (Wolfgang Harich and his group) suggest that the trial was conducted in harmony with the views expressed by Mrs. Benjamin, Vol. XI (1957), p. 166.

6. *Trial as a Political Technique*

The Stalin type of trial form both excelled and was limited by the certitude of prearranged results. However, when the conduct of a political trial approximates normalcy, it takes on more of the properties of all political action: it becomes more aleatory in its immediate and long-term effects.

Political decisions concern the choice of future courses of political action. Ignorant of the indecipherable combination of variants which will determine such a course, men ponder over past performances in order to find a cue for action. The familiar or seemingly familiar is substituted for the unknown. Along with the parliamentary debate, the political trial may serve as one of the techniques of substitution. In the parliamentary debate, past and present intertwine constantly with the contestant's record, which the voters judge according to how skillfully he has manipulated or, in some cases, obliterated the past as a guide to the future. The trial, however, purports to seal off the judgment of the past from the expectations of the future. It tries to isolate some element of the past performance, picking it as a sort of raw material, aimlessly and continuously spit out by Chronos, the factory of time. Having torn the incident from history, the trial turns its strongest spotlights on it, to disclose its minutest detail. The purpose of this concentration is not antiquarian and only incidentally concerned with retribution. The past is reconstructed for the sake of the future as a possible weapon in the battle for political domination. The wall of isolation between the segment of history chosen for dissection and the web from which it was separated remains an artificial one. But to narrow the focus is a recognized method of appreciating a past situation. The smaller the area of reconstruction, the simpler and less complicated its outline and the less complex the judgment which will go into its evaluation. At the same time, the search for concreteness is the search for standards of judgment. The present and the future are full of complexity. No solutions are without conflicting countersolutions and pressing counterclaims.

A trial seems to provide as an object the segment of history, as a yardstick for judgment the law, and as a signpost for the future the verdict. For the object of the trial to be correctly perceived, the chosen segment has to be reconstructed. It is a prerequisite for the judicial decision to debit an individual with the role played within the specific historical context. Only in this way can the judge be made the appropriate person to take a political conflict under advisement. Were the conflict submitted to him in a form that transcended the historical configuration, as a question of principle or policy, he would be out of place in judging it. Whether Democrats or Republicans should take office, whether war should be pursued to the bitter end or compromise peace be concluded, the judge would have neither competence nor aptitude to answer. But unlike his brethren concerned with other branches of the law, the criminal judge cannot withdraw into muteness. He cannot assert the existence of a *political* question or an *act of government*. These concepts, whatever the derivative rationalizations about the nature of such acts, rests on the knowledge that either the government would not want the facts and their implications discussed in public or that the courts would have a hard time enforcing judgments against a seriously recalcitrant government. But fortunately for the criminal judge and the community which he serves, conflict situations have been narrowed down and treated as history before being submitted to him. They pertain to past segments of a still present conflict, allowing him to disregard its present elements and treat it exclusively as a past event.

As the parties naturally differ, the roles played by defendants or plaintiffs must be reconstructed for the benefit of the court, and the testimony of the witnesses may become decisive. But the political trial adds additional complications to the well-known difficulties of trial reconstruction. Witnesses will have been forewarned to re-enact their roles with scrupulous attention to staying within the limits of their past performance. Will they? Even a party in a civil suit will reinterpret the former happenings in the light of his present relations to the party concerned. Even if his relations to the party are a matter of the past, his reliability as a witness will depend on the degree of objectivity he has toward his former experience. Only the innocent bystander— if he is not acting under the impression that he must cover up for some completely unconnected irregularity which could be discovered during the trial—is free from such deformations of his testimony. But he might be rare to come by in a political trial.[103a]

The witness may have a manifold commitment. His first is to the actual role he played during the event itself. Assertions as to the defendant's deeds, words, or motives are necessarily determined by the witness's own position in the historical event. He may have been the

---

[103a] A well-balanced evaluation of the different categories of evidence in a politically-oriented murder trial may be found in David D. Bien, *The Calas Affair: Persecution, Toleration, and Heresy in Eighteenth-Century Toulouse*, Princeton, 1960, Ch. 6.

defendant's or plaintiff's political adversary in terms of their objective, possibly also his competitor in regard to clientele or claim for authority. He may have been his political partner, his close friend, or his political partner and personal competitor. When he is now asked to dissolve the defendant's or plaintiff's role into the cluster of action, attitudes, and relationships from which the event was composed, his own role will be the first determinant in his testimony.

But yesterday's and today's political situations or political commitments of the witness may not be the same, and thus may lead to a more or less perceptible reconstruction of his or the defendant's historical role in the light of present commitments. A minimum of change may have occurred if the witness has since disappeared from the political arena as an active combatant. His opinions and vistas may have frozen at the point where he took off, or was taken off, and every word now uttered may only serve to justify "posthumously" both his previous stand and his present interpretation of history. If the witness is still an active player on a scene where neither his own nor the defendant's future is clearly recognizable, caution may be his watchword. While not interested enough to change the facts, he will avoid throwing harsh lights on them: his leitmotiv will be the clair-obscure, tout comprendre c'est tout pardonner. But if a witness should feel his or his organization's future at stake in his interpretation of the historical event, he will re-edit the script. The ambiguities and openness of every situation that has not yet reached its terminal point are radically eliminated. With hindsight at his disposal, the retouching will seem to show only one possible interpretation.

Finally there are the age-old figures who invariably show up in political trials where testimony rather than confession is the preferred method: the informer and the turncoat. Their trouble as witnesses lies in their degree of perfection. The key they carry to the riddle seems to lead to the most handy and logical reconstruction results. But is it the fundamental key? The most logical solution may not come closer to the real course of the event than the one which could be pieced together from dozens of contradictory items. The most perfect logical result might obscure or hide some revealing stages which form an integral part of an event being re-enacted from a script rather than from life.

Reconstruction undertaken with the help of testimony may thus be unpromising in many respects. The witness's urge both to justify his own role of yesterday and determine the reality of tomorrow via reinterpretation of the past might be too powerful to be withstood. Recollection and reinterpretation become interchangeable. But there is a type of political trial where this observation will apply with less force. Observable fragments of action patterns might not refer to complicated historical events in which interaction of a great number of people was required to create the specific, in itself complicated, historical event. A situation may sometimes be reduced to one simple occurrence of daily life with which every member of the community is familiar by personal experience or from his reading of newspapers' local feature stories. Whether somebody has known somebody else, has received money or documents, or has wounded someone with a gun seems to be no more doubtful or complicated than any ordinary fact of life. If the political trial can be reduced to this level, then the hazards inherent in the witness's double role—as coauthors of past history and as active participants in the making of present history—are not greater than in any other ordinary trial. However, there is one further prerequisite: people at large must have reached common agreement on the meaning of these simple facts in order to allow some universally acknowledged conclusions to be drawn from them.

This point may be illustrated with an example still vivid in our minds. By his own choice, Alger Hiss had eliminated all the questions which loomed so large in other trials we have analyzed: the limits of loyalty or the justification of apparent disloyalty. Given the near-unanimity in the approach to the problem of national policy prevailing in the United States in 1949, Hiss's position doubtless could not have been much different from the one he took. Because he affirmed his full loyalty, questions pertaining to the choice and relevance of the State Department documents, assertedly delivered by him to Chambers, were inapplicable as determinants of his motivations.[104] The very fact that Hiss assumed the mantle of patriotic correctness reduced the case from the level of interpretation and understanding of the defendant's behavior to the gyrations of a popular detective story. If the evidence showed that Hiss saw Chambers after he had joined the State Department, and if there was enough proof—the testimony of one problematic witness supported by some rather important circumstantial evidence—that Hiss did deliver State Department cables to Chambers, the case was at an end in the courts. The rest was the public's concern.

The process of translating and transforming fragmentary acts into a simplified picture of political reality has set in. It is a collective process that takes place simultaneously in millions of minds, and it is more

[104] See Alistair Cooke, *A Generation on Trial—The United States v. Alger Hiss*, New York, 1950, pp. 161-64.

intensive than the more passive reception of the artificial reality pre-fabricated for the purposes of the totalitarian trial. In the minds of millions, the fixed, cinematic episode is totally identified with the political beliefs with which the defendant is presumably identified though not charged.

But the identification between the deed or artifact, distilled for the purpose of the trial, and the political goal with which it is presumed to coordinate does not always succeed so well. The fullness of the image may depend on the confines of the law, its handling by the court, and the interest of the parties in developing the whole story. The latter point is particularly important under Anglo-American criminal procedure which leaves the greatest leeway to the parties in arranging for proof. For entirely opposite reasons the parties might expect a more favorable outcome if the scope of the inquiry were limited, and no more than a truncated picture of reality were reproduced. If truncation causes doubts about the picture's meaningfulness, it does not necessarily mar its political effectiveness. To turn once more to the Hiss case: if, for example, an attempt had been made to find a clue to the process of Hiss's motivation, what would have happened to the political effectiveness of the image of the intellectual as a traitor? The nature of the revealed documents might have weighed against those accessible with equal facility, and without having been pilfered. Or, in which direction did Hiss try to exercise any influence on policy formation? Neither point was ever alluded to during the trial. Of course, by denying any participation in the pilfering, Hiss showed from the outset that he was not in the least interested in this line of inquiry; but what is decisive is that neither was the prosecution. In building an effective image of a traitor, it concentrated, in addition to Chambers' tales, on an elaborate showing of the general character of the pilfered documents. But it carefully shunned any attempt to turn to the quest for motivation, from which something meaningful might have been learned of the defendant's mental process; an attempt to make the image concrete might have led to qualifications limiting the trial's political usefulness.

But the opposite proposition might be equally true: political effectiveness of the image may be increased by complete rather than fragmentary re-enactment. When Kravchenko sued the Communist-controlled *Lettres Françaises* for defamation of character, the area of proof was not restricted to the circumstances of Kravchenko's life, morals, and intellectual abilities. Inasmuch as Kravchenko had interwoven in his book the story of general social and economic conditions in Russia, the proof of his allegation, as well as the facts of his personal life, could be considered part of the test of his veracity. Thus, following the liberal terms of the 1944 ordinance, the Tribunal de la Seine did not act on the defense's suggestion to limit proof to allegations concerning Kravchenko's personality, his record as a party member, administrator, family man, and the sharply contested interpretation of his desertion from the USSR mission in Washington during the war. If the numerous witnesses with first-hand experience could be interpreted as supporting a substantial part of Kravchenko's assertions, his tale could not be styled to be false—even though, as the judgment expressed it, he "overlooked many evolutionary aspects."[105] Soviet conditions as they emerged from the tales of the witnesses showed enough likeness to Kravchenko's picture not to be called "totally erroneous and exaggerated" by the court. Accordingly, Kravchenko should not have been called a liar, despite the emergence of some less than admirable traits in his personality. By allowing the presentation of evidence that went beyond Kravchenko's character and the genesis of his writings, by permitting the picture of USSR society to be developed with all its contradictions, the trial became one of the most powerful agents for substituting the picture of the USSR work day for the Sunday image of the patriotic ally.

At times, both trial and verdict together take the character of an afterthought, a mere footnote to history required by the workings of the legal machinery, as interpreted in Western society. Court action may constitute a validation or an invalidation of an action whose political effect was calculated for and has spent itself at a much earlier period. This is what happened in the Caillaux case, where trial and judgment came more than two years after the precedent-shattering starting of proceedings and the detention of the defendant had created the political effect anticipated and desired by Clemenceau and Poincaré. What seems a huge combined political and judicial effort in the Caillaux case constitutes only a routine practice in other circumstances and on a lower level. A demonstration may be forbidden, a meeting be dispersed as a matter of on-the-spot discretionary administrative judgment. Validation or invalidation a year later by administrative court or incidental criminal court action may cause a small stir, giving some ammunition for a question in parliament or some newspaper polemics, scarcely comparable in effect to the order when issued. In such cases a court merely trails the action. The very time lag between action and scrutiny contributes to the relative freedom but also to the limited effectiveness of the court; it acts

[105] Pour Servir à L'Histoire de ce Temps, No. 9. Le Procès Kravchenko contre les Lettres Française, Paris, 1949, Appendix.

only as examiner of the ultimate justifiability of the administrative action.

It is not unusual for a court to be used as a screen behind which to hide a careful pattern of inaction. More or less veiled assertions might have been made in speech or writing in regard to the antecedents, personality, methods, or goals of a contemporary figure or group. The announcement of a defamation suit, sometimes accompanied by an injunction to prevent repetition, might follow promptly and be given as wide a circulation as possible. But often, inadvertently or by design, the characterization will be a mixture of falsity and truth, which makes it difficult to separate the elements of each. Few persons in public life, especially if well established, will want to run the risk of time, money, and energy; above all, they will not want a multitude of lawyers, past and present adversaries, and personal enemies—attracted, as to a magnet, by the chance to vent their anger on the witness stand—to pry into their affairs.[106] Political outsiders, rabble rousers, unsuccessful strugglers on the road to success, with little to lose and everything to gain, might eagerly grab at what promises to be additional publicity if not much else.

The established politician knows better. Unless the assertions are clearly scurrilous and proof in the jurisdiction strictly kept to the assertion in point, he might try to compromise the issue with as good a statement as he can get from his assailant and withdraw promptly, and possibly very quietly, from the action that began with a fanfare of publicity. The prompt announcement of the action, showing his fearlessness in the moment of maximum attention to his reactions, will be calculated and allowed to have the same public effect as a successfully completed action. The symbolic value of the intrepid march into court will be allowed to stand for the actual battle in court.

Not always, however, will the defamed person feel able to afford such a course. Ebert, as we saw, thought he owed it to his office and reputation to engage in a court action. So did Harold Laski, when faced with a newspaper account of an election meeting which alleged that he had affirmed the necessity of revolutionary action if Labor were unable to reach its goal by consent. The lawyer of the opposite side, Sir Patrick Hastings,[107] professes never to have understood why Laski did not withdraw his action after the 1945 election battle was over, re-

---

[106] Harold Laski has vividly described the ordeal of a libel trial under conditions of modern publicity. His remarks are reprinted in Kingsley Martin, *Harold Laski*, London, 1953, p. 274.

[107] Patrick Hastings, *Cases in Court*, London, 1949, pp. 55, 71.

vealing the Conservative failure to turn the incident into an effective campaign weapon. Thus his opinions conform to the pattern of substituting the symbol of court action for actual determination of the case. Laski probably thought that he owed it to the Labor Party to refute any doubts of his adherence to the tenets of democracy. Yet the jury returned a verdict of not guilty against the *Newark Advertiser*.

The concrete conditions of English political life prevented Laski's defeat from assuming the boomerang effect of the Ebert case. Whatever shock the outcome of the trial might have meant to Laski, the well-established pattern of his limited usefulness to the Labor Party did not change fundamentally because of the trial. If the Conservative Party's use of Laski as a negative symbol did not scare the voters away from the party, even less would a jury verdict confirming that Laski might have conditionally upheld the necessity of a revolutionary course; the practices of the Labor government would seem to make the likelihood of this course more remote every day.

Whether a trial conducted under a constitutional regime will bring political benefits or drawbacks to its instigators seems to be almost as uncertain as the outcome of an election campaign. Prosecution might be planned as an incident to a political campaign. The Powers case was discussed here as the most perfect example of such synchronization. The almost automatic identification of the defendant Powers and the Republican Party seems to make the decision in the case part of the election campaign. Penal action and political action seem to complement each other, with the penal action planned for political results and the consequent political action—the gubernatorial election—necessary to uphold the result of the penal action. But the same case shows that the fructification of such parallelism depends on the credibility of the trial as a whole. Thus there are rather definite limits to the synchronization of penal and political action.

Communist critics have asserted time and again that this parallelism plays a major role in constitutional regimes. Foreign policy factors like the Korean War or the Indochinese defeat, as much as domestic troubles of the government, are responsible for introducing politically motivated prosecutions.[108] Drawing their conclusions from their own practices, Communist authors tend to forget that constitutional governments are subject to some limitations in their arranging of criminal prosecutions, which do not necessarily always prevail under totalitarian regimes. While

[108] Marcel Willard, *La Défense Accuse*, 3rd ed.; Paris, 1953.

policy decisions of constitutional governments might partly determine the conditions under which speech and agitation will be prosecuted, a larceny of secret documents or a politically motivated murder must first happen before it can start its way through the courts. Police organizations all over the world may have a creative mind, with do-it-yourself kits at hand in case their enemies are not willing to oblige.[109] But such devices have only limited usefulness where the emphasis rests on piloting a case successfully through court in which testimony may be freely examined. Synchronization of political and court action may promise greater dividends than are available for distribution.

The instigators of a political trial will face many uncertainties if they want to use the legal form for purposes beyond harassment or elimination of a political foe, and if they want to advance into the territory of image-creating or destroying. The vagaries of the medium they use, legal procedure, are compounded by their need to rely on witnesses who might be living in a political world of their own, not to speak of adversaries who may successfully urge their own interpretation on judge or jury. The narrower the scope of the theme selected for proof, the greater the likelihood that the operation will succeed, but the less chance that the result will do more than serve momentary political purposes. Thus the lasting results of the propaganda trial are likely to be paradoxical. The morality play, after serving the political needs of the day, will survive mainly as a testimony to its initiators' own frame of mind, which may well prove more distorted than that of their victim.

[109] However, it might be comparatively rare to find a police official proudly admitting to such exploits. In his *Souvenirs d'un Préfet de Police*, Paris, 1885, Vol. 1, L. Andrieux, a former Lyon politician, relates how he ordered the dynamiting of the statue of Thiers in Versailles as a means to encourage stiffer repression of anarchism: "Il fallait que l'acte fut consommé, pour que la répression fut possible" (p. 101). See also the tale as narrated by the anarchist writer Jean Grave: *Le mouvement libertaire sous la Troisième République*, Paris, 1930; on p. 193 Grave relates police financing of the anarchist mouthpiece, *Révolution Sociale*.

CHAPTER IV
LEGAL REPRESSION OF POLITICAL
ORGANIZATIONS

+++

Mit allen anderen Parteien kann man sich vertragen und unter Um-
ständen paktieren, mit dieser [Sozialdemokratischen Partei] nicht.
—THEODOR MOMMSEN, 1884

Dem ebenso falschen wie perfiden Köhlerglauben muss ein Ende
gemacht werden, dass die Nation sich teile in Ordnungsparteien und
eine Umsturzpartei. . . . Jede Partei ist eine Umsturzpartei.
——THEODOR MOMMSEN, 1902*

+++

THE present chapter analyzes the forms of treatment applied by
an established regime to hostile groups. Within narrowly
defined limits, both minority regimes and oppressed majority
elements may find a temporary advantage in calculating their
moves so as to remain within the confines of the legal order, iniquitous
though this legal order may be from the viewpoint of the majority
groups. However, the European experience of the nineteenth century
would indicate the futility of trying to suppress major groups with
discriminatory legislation while at the same time upholding parliamentary institutions and basic liberties.

After discussing the attitude of reigning minorities toward majority
elements, we shall take up in detail the behavior of majority governments toward hostile minority groups that form an opposition of principle. For that purpose, we shall deal with the various formulas and
techniques for controlling such hostile minorities—whether small dissident groups or larger movements—as well as the motives guiding their
respective policies.

A discussion of the advantages which the democratic process draws
from limiting defensive measures to the repulsion of tangible and con-

* "One can get along, and possibly even come to terms, with all parties except this one
[the SPD]." From a letter written during the debate on the antisocialist laws, quoted
from L. M. Hartmann, *Theodor Mommsen*, Gotha, 1908, p. 124.
    "We must make an end to the false and perfidious superstition that the nation is
divided into loyal parties and one subversive party. . . . Every party is subversive."
From an article, "Was uns noch retten kann," *Die Nation*, December 13, 1902, reprinted in Hartmann, p. 255.

crete threats against the public order, rather than striving toward ideological conformity, concludes the chapter.

Our subject is the repression of political group activities by regimes subscribing to the rule of law and at least professedly averse to arbitrary suppression of political opponents. Espousing the supremacy of law does not automatically rule out discrimination and inequality of treatment; nor does acceptance of binding legal standards preclude arbitrariness, faithful companion of inequality. However, the emphasis here is on the legal character of the repressive system. Disquieting, perturbing questions are on all our minds. Can repression of political activity be legitimate? In depriving some individuals and associations of rights guaranteed to all, does it not deny the very essence of law? Is it not bound to sap the foundations of democratic government? On the other hand, is not legal repression, with appropriate safeguards, an acceptable price to pay to escape lawless suppression and arbitrary reprisals?

What, within this frame of reference, constitutes legal repression? Establishing lines of jurisdiction and distributing the various chores of repression according to the regime's political needs is but one element of legality. The Hitlerite Reich in some of its division of labor—between the Ministry of Justice, the People's Court, the Special Courts, the Gestapo, and the SS, for example—did not make its repressive system an instrument of law.[1] Something more is involved.

Repression cannot be legal unless there is a framework of substantive and procedural norms binding upon and serviceable to both the government and the governed, a single standard for the public prosecutor and those he hails into court. The state's efforts to penalize opponents must be subject to freely usable control by a third agency that does not take orders from the government, is committed to enforcing an established set of norms, and is exposed to a modicum of public criticism.

No doubt such legal safeguards against the abuse of repressive power may be precarious and lapse into ambiguity. Enough vigor or will power may not be left to either government or court to enforce legality against overwhelming and explosive forces within society. Outbreaks of violence, whether instigated or merely tolerated by the government, may be so widespread, and the authority of the court so feeble, that the fate of those hostile to or victimized by the dominant currents of the

---

[1] An interesting jurisdictional quarrel between various totalitarian repressive institutions is described in Helmut Heiber, "Zur Justiz Im Dritten Reich: Der Fall Elias," *Vierteljahrshefte für Zeitgeschichte*, Vol. 3 (1955), pp. 275-96. It shows how the SS, by snatching jurisdiction from the office of the Reich attorney at the People's Court, and with the help of the president of the People's Court, was able to railroad the Czech Minister President Elias quickly to death in 1941.

day may be settled outside of legal channels. Out of step with the march of events, which has shifted the balance of power, they will rely in vain on the protection given by the law to those who stay within its bounds and use its machinery; the agents of law enforcement will have been made to look the other way.

If such vacations from legality endure and become the rule, legal repression will give way to a different mode of repression. But so long as the protective devices operate, however imperfectly, and so long as it suits the interests and ideological predilections of those in power to accept the authority of the legal order as equally binding upon rulers and ruled, chances are that repression will remain within the legal pattern. It is the possible modifications of this pattern—to the point of self-annihilation—with which the following marginalia are concerned; they are fragmentary remarks that dwell only on the juridical form of deep-rooted political change.

1. Repression by Minority Fiat: Benefits and Limitations of Legality

Legality of repression does not necessarily mean it is effected at the behest of a government that wields power as the representative of a democratic majority. In the long period of transition from absolutism to democratic rule, many a government bound by a constitution and devoted to the principles of supremacy of law tried time and again to prevent progress of democratization by introducing repressive legislation which would curb the activity of democratic movements as reprehensible subversion. In essence this meant that the legal rule of a minority was to be protected by law from legal replacement by the rule of a majority.

Frequent in semiconstitutional monarchies, this practice throughout the nineteenth century was typical in colonial rule. A tiny minority of colonizers would establish itself as the legally constituted body politic, lording it over the vast majority of natives. Deemed underdeveloped and not mature enough to participate in democratic rule, the indigenous population, save perhaps for minor privileged groups, would be denied representation, and any effort to break through the barrier would be repressed by law.

In the second half of the twentieth century, only remnants of colonial rule are left as a memento of legal repression that was devised to perpetuate minority rule. (Totalitarian systems based on one-party rule and total suppression of all deviant political activity do not enter the picture.) But the remnants do exist. And the traditional philosophy of colonial domination has not changed its color. The assertion is still there that the affairs of the overwhelming majority of the population must be handled by the legally enthroned minority if safe and sane conditions for everyone are to be maintained.

Such, for example, is the legal theory of white rule in the Union of South Africa. In an exchange of letters with the South African National Congress in 1952, the prime minister, rejecting the Congress's demand for parliamentary representation and restoration of liberty and democratic rights, contended that compliance with the wishes for gradual development toward a mixed community "must inevitably lead to disaster for all population groups."[2] In particular, it would expose the Bantu to the rigors of full competition and make them lose their landholdings now safe under the prevailing legal system.[3] The rulers claim the role of guardian angel rather than oppressor of the subjugated majority, a claim blandly rejected by the leaders of the two main non-white political organizations, the African National Congress and the South African Indian Congress. Still, the minorities' hold on economy and coercive machinery has so far been strong enough to bar change, while the majority are too apathetic, illiterate, and diffuse to force their way. So far, the legal order at the service of the minority has successfully defied any challenge from the more advanced sections of the majority.

Yet behind transparent power relations, the protective function of the legal order, even a thoroughly iniquitous one, is still in evidence. It is served by procedure rather than substance. True, the fundamental principle of legal equality, not formally abrogated for interracial relations, is constantly infringed upon by legislative enactments. These acts close the last loopholes left by the courts' policy of upholding the principle of legal equality.[4] But here the protective function of the legal order comes in. Enforcement of racial inequality is still not tantamount to arbitrariness. Once brought to light, police brutality may be curbed by the courts. Higher courts try to some extent to control local magistrates who exercise both their administrative and judicial functions un-

[2] The correspondence is reprinted in Leo Kuper, *Passive Resistance in South Africa*, Yale University Press, 1957, p. 237.

[3] For refutation of the argument, see L. Marquard, *The People and Politics of South Africa*, London, 1952, p. 46.

[4] See Rex v. Zihlangu, 3 South African Law Reports 871 (1953); Tayob v. Ermolo Local Road Transportation Co., 4 S.A. 440 (1951). But see Rex v. Sachs, 1 S.A. 393 (1953), which concerns a case decided after the introduction of explicit statutory change. It gives effect to the express will of parliament. See also the discussion in Edgar H. Brookes and J. B. Macaulay, *Civil Liberty in South Africa*, Capetown, 1958, Ch. 4.

der a double handicap: heavy social pressure from the white community and substantial case load caused by vexatious statutes that control the living conditions and movements of the nonwhite population.[5] Appeal judges uphold procedural guarantees and standards. Although this cannot change the basically oppressive features of the social system, violence and brutality are checked in higher court clarification and interpretation of the society's legal concepts. While parliament writes the law in accordance with the government's wishes, the court exerts a modicum of moderating influence when it states what the law should mean.[6]

The spokesmen for the vanguard of the oppressed majority may not be sure how ready the popular masses will be to follow their lead. This is why they preferred for a long time to confine themselves to symbolic breach of rules imposed by the ruling minority. Occasionally they would even advise government agents of their intended transgression; of their plan, for example, to enter a waiting room forbidden to members of non-Caucasian races.[7] Advance notice enabled the police to react promptly and hold the act of disobedience within narrow limits. To the initiators of disobedience this minimized the political risk, for more generalized campaigns of defiance could boomerang. Poor communications, fear, wanting insight into the importance of the action, and the ingrained habit of obeying white authorities could prevent potential adherents from responding to Congress's slogans; on the other hand, un-

[5] For a general appreciation of the effects of courts, see Marquard, *op.cit.*, p. 118. Statistics indicating the incredibly high number of nonwhite prosecutions may be found on p. 1,482 of the Senate Session, March 5, 1956. The figures probably would be still more unfavorable if those who violated the pass laws were not, in cases of noncontradiction, assigned to some form of semicompulsory labor. See James Fairbairn, "The Case of Nelson Langa," *New Statesman*, November 16, 1957, p. 640.

[6] See, for example, Rex v. Tetive, 4 S.A. 298 (1957). The accused native was not given a chance to obtain legal representation; conviction and sentence were set aside, and the case was sent back to a different magistrate. There are many cases limiting the effects of strict administrative controls of native labor organizing activity. See, for example, Rex v. MPeta, 4 S.A. 257 (1956). Rex v. Sibaude, 4 S.A. 23 (1956) tried to limit government harshness in dealing with purely political offenses. A general survey of government practices may be found in Kuper, *op.cit.*, pp. 47-71, and 154-80, and more recently in Brookes and Macaulay, *op.cit., passim.*

In 1955, 75 trade union officials, including 35 Europeans, 21 Natives, 12 Colored, and 7 Asians, were put on the "liquidator's list," that is, were prevented from exercising any public activity. The prohibition included compulsory resignation from any organization in which "the liquidated" had been active. In the same year the corresponding number of nonunion organizers put on the liquidator's list was 529, including 198 Europeans, 237 Natives, 54 Colored, and 40 Asians. House of Assembly Debates, Vol. 90 (1956), p. 182.

[7] See the description in Kuper, *op.cit.*, Ch. 5.

disciplined and uncontrollable masses might heed the appeal only too well, and generalized disobedience would make the police abandon legal repression—individual arrests and trials precluding conviction without specific evidence—in favor of wholesale persecution of actually or potentially hostile individuals and organizations. The legal order protected the "subversive" majority inasmuch as it defined and circumscribed the risk involved in intentional, demonstrative violation of repressive law.

Likewise, the legal system of repression offered definite advantages to the ruling minority. To some extent it permitted the rulers to anticipate the moves of the organized opposition. In exchange for legal protection granted individual members of the majority, the government expected the majority to refrain, for the sake of the broader cause, from instigating, and to do their utmost in preventing, active violence as distinct from passive disobedience.[8]

The advantages of the legal pattern in the South African model also point to the delicate balance that made them possible. The leaders of the majority clung to legality in their actions because they counted on a mass reservoir of potential adherents whom they hoped to turn into reliable and disciplined followers; they wanted to do this by education and by drawing them into the ever-widening campaigns of disobedience directed against selected features of the minority regime. Only this way could they envisage ultimate superiority over the minority's seemingly invincible power—a power resting on organization, technology, education, and so on. Conversely, in tolerating and using the cloak of legality, the leaders of the ruling minority trusted in the durability of prevailing social arrangements; they counted on being able to continue covering with legal forms the proper social and administrative weapon for obstructing the majority's ascent to power.

Under these circumstances, legal repression was not likely to reduce basic tensions between majority and minority. The era of the "war of position" did not foreshadow stable or more effective forms of collaboration in the future. It was as if war were being waged by adversaries whose choice of weapons was limited by existing, essentially transitory disproportion in strength. Weakening the minority's position without being willing to accept compromise would call the turn; the ruling group would feel impelled to scrap legal repression and introduce stronger, more pervasive, and less law-beholden controls; the courts,

[8] Of course, these organizations have little control over the vast amount of unorganized individual violence bred by such an oppressive system. See C. W. de Kiewiet, *The Anatomy of South African Misery*, London, Oxford University Press, 1956, Ch. 3.

perhaps even then speaking for elements not fully in sympathy with the minority's present political leadership, would either be packed or sidetracked and stripped of the residual power which permits them to act as stabilizers.

There are strong indications that this delicate balance, with oppression exercised under the protection of the legal order, is tipping over. The minority has extended immensely the realm of oppressive legislation, engulfing more and more fields of social activities.[9] Further, it tried to deprive the majority of its leaders through the device of protracted, though unsuccessful, treason proceedings.[10] As the oppressed masses familiarize themselves with increasing techniques of resistance,[11] and as more cautious leadership groups are challenged by the emergence of the more aggressive Pan African Congress, repression tends to move swiftly out of the legal channels.[12]

Wielded by minority rule, legal repression frequently amounts to nothing more than barely holding the fort. Daily pursuits may go on without major disruption, insecurity is minimized, repression remains within some limits, and cruelty is reined in on both sides. It may also serve, as the end of British rule in India has shown, to restrain accumulation of resentment and hatred; having extended to the majority a minimum of legal protection in the past, the defeated minority, once its domination has become untenable, will be able to bow out with a minimum of violence and a maximum of orderly process. Certainly in the long run law may mitigate but it cannot abrogate the consequences of social disequilibrium.

2. *Nineteenth Century Record of Repression*

In the course of the nineteenth century struggle for democratization of the political order, the very essence of political action underwent fundamental change. The industrial age completely revolutionized the tools and techniques of political conflict. Legal repression of political

[9] Analysis of the most vital statutes is in Brookes and Macaulay, *passim*. The whole range of discriminatory enactments as well as the practices of the authorities have recently been surveyed in *South Africa and the Rule of Law*, Geneva, 1960, pub. by the International Commission of Jurists.

[10] For a splendid survey of the legal framework and political implications of the trial, see Th. G. Karis, "The South African Treason Trial," in *Political Science Quarterly*, Vol. 76 (1961), pp. 217-40.

[11] The beginning of wider resistance techniques was the Johannesburg bus boycott of 1957; see Joe Rogolly in 5 *Forum*, Johannesburg, March 1957, which emphasizes that here "Africans learned about their strength" (p. 14).

[12] Such is essentially the course of South African events since the Sharpeville tragedy in April 1960.

activity faced breathtaking substitution of targets. In the end it became self-defeating. How this came about is worth recalling.

In the early stages, popular discontent and disaffection seriously threatened the powers-that-be only when it erupted in rebellions, street fights, and physical clashes between badly armed insurgents and better equipped but not always reliable police and army troops. The fighting involved only a few urban centers. On the side of the people, participants were but an infinitesimal fraction of the popular masses whose demands and strivings were at stake. Whenever the rebels were defeated in physical contest, legal repression of kindred pursuits was easy, though it rarely achieved a lasting effect.

All this changed with full-speed urbanization, industrialization, mechanization of transport, substitution of generalized military conscription for armies of hirelings, universal spread of literacy, growth of mass media of communication, and so on. Moreover, every success in the fight against minority rule signaled basic change in the rules of political warfare. As ever-increasing segments of the people gained the right to vote and obtained minimum guarantees of free speech and free assembly, violence as a means of popular political action gradually lapsed into oblivion. Mass organization, wide-range propaganda, mass meetings, use of the ballot, and organized stoppage of work replaced street fights and barricades.

Previously, action had been confined to small groups of conspirators, a few barricade fighters, and emotionally high-strung crowds who emerged sporadically in only a few places, showed little cohesion, were seldom aroused, and easily dispersed. Now organized masses dominated the scene, showing steady discipline and a high degree of cohesion based on common interests and consistently indoctrinated common beliefs, ready to follow a centralized authoritative leadership, and trained to shun disorderly, violent, and unlawful procedure. Aspiring to equal status, unimpaired franchise, and participation in political rule, that is, exchange of minority rule for legally established and guaranteed decision-making by the majority, such mass movements were irrepressible. To hold them down by crude force would have required an immense apparatus of coercion, which in the long run the army of conscripts was not. And the path of legal repression soon proved to be strewn with insuperable obstacles.

Legal repression of a popular majority's political will is inconceivable unless there is a firmly established constitutional order to sanction the minority's dominant position and close up tightly all legal avenues for the majority's nonrevolutionary ascent to power. But constitutional rule makes it impossible to completely bar the people from power. And once the middle classes were given legal access to power through parliamentary representation, points of ingress were bound to multiply.

In nineteenth century constitutional monarchies there were many interconnected ways of arresting popular pressures. These included: more or less severe property and educational ballot restrictions, which drastically scaled down the number of voters; and strict separation of legislation and budget appropriation, common business of the executive and legislative branches from the exercise of executive powers by the monarch, that is, the military and the bureaucracy. But in sharp contrast to the colonial system of ethnocentric rule, nineteenth century constitutional regimes denied neither the essence of equality before the law nor considerable leeway for social mobility and its concomitant, viz. political rights for growing numbers of those rising in the social pyramid.

Even in periods of reaction, restoration of the pre-1789 ancien régime was hardly dreamed of. Chateaubriand expressed a widespread feeling when he said: "L'Europe court à la démocratie. La France est-elle autre chose qu'une république entravée d'un directeur?"[13] The ambiguities of the postrevolutionary setup did not escape the ruling minority. The refashioned nation-centered legitimacy of its rule was not without flaws. While the traditional sanctification of the monarchy had been abandoned, the only alternative source of authority, democratic majority, was rejected; and yet it had become impossible to ignore that in both juridical logic and political reality the fact of equality before the law entailed equal participation in the exercise of political power.

To be sure, revolutionary uprisings were crushed on the spot. Rue Transnonain and Lyons, 1834; Chartist riots, 1839; Berlin and Vienna, 1848; Paris Commune, 1871—these are the milestones of bloody popular defeats. But only the rudimentary form of political action was vanquished. Defeat shattered the early democratic organizations. Here and there it undermined shaky coalitions of labor organization nuclei and loose groupings of liberal political reformers and parliamentary standard-bearers of radical republicanism.[14] When the shooting was over, however, the parliamentary rostrum soon regained its far-reaching importance as the focal point of antigovernment criticism and reformist or revolutionary agitation, and the first precursors of modern mass organizations began to emerge. Still, so long as suffrage remained restricted, popular agitation stayed within manageable limits, unless, as

---

[13] Georges Weill, *Histoire du Parti Républicain en France*, Paris, 1901, p. 135.
[14] P. Thureau-Dangin, *Histoire de la Monarchie de Juillet*, Paris, 1884, Vol. II.

in Ireland, it was reinforced by added discontent growing out of national resentment and starvation.

Eventually, popular suffrage did come: in 1848 in France, where Louis-Philippe's high finance and stock exchange ideas for the management of public affairs had made middle-class claims combine with democratic popular currents; and in 1867 and 1871 in Bismarck's Germany, as a tricky device to neutralize the liberal middle-class vote. By including in the electorate urban labor and the underprivileged strata of the rural population, Bismarck changed the balance of political forces. Could the growing popular movement still be held at bay by means of legal repression? Bismarck did try his best. The weakness of a government system granting suffrage to all and sundry, yet adamant in preventing the popular vote from affecting the exercise of governmental power, was at the base of the 1878 antisocialist legislation. In seeking to destroy incipient democratic mass organizations while retaining the representative system, Bismarck's repressive law sought mutually exclusive objectives. Reenacted successively down to 1890, the law was directed against individuals and groups "actively engaged in destroying the order prevailing in state and society." It empowered government agencies to ban meetings and associations serving such purposes, and to banish agitators. This permitted the disbandment of all organizations of the recently (1875) merged socialist parties. The government's repressive power was severely curtailed from the outset, for election meetings and campaigning were exempt from the statutory ban. Bismarck knew that parliament would not grant him power to tamper (at least on the national level) with the newly-introduced principle of equal representation.

This robbed the repressive legislation of much of its striking power. Repeated interference with the freedom of movement of socialist spokesmen elected to parliament on the platform of the banned party did not seriously handicap their political activity inside parliament chambers, and it left them enough leeway for political agitation outside its precincts. They enjoyed a great deal of publicity, kept up contacts with their voters, and in general availed themselves of an irreducible minimum of propaganda facilities; while serving as the political center of the prohibited organization, they were in permanent liaison with its organizing center and publication headquarters maintained abroad.[15]

[15] The most vivid description of the years of persecution is still August Bebel, *Aus Meinem Leben*, first pub. in 1914, and reissued in 1946 in East Berlin. The third volume deals almost exclusively with the author's experience with the law. The balance sheet is

No matter how zealous police and prosecutors were in ferreting them out, enemies of the state had a fair chance of recourse to the courts. Wherever publications were repressed, the Reich Commission, a special administrative agency set up under the 1878 law, reviewed complaints; at times, especially in the late years of the law's operation, it gave them some satisfaction.[16] A large part of the banned party's prohibited activities escaped control altogether; they were carried out from across the border or under the cloak of parliamentary immunity. In addition, the proscribed popular movement met with increasing sympathy in the lower ranks of the bureaucracy.

More and more, legal repression missed its target. Only for a short while did it check socialist advance. After having dropped at the first election held under the law, socialist votes showed a continuous upward trend. And in 1893, at the first national election held after the abrogation of the law, the Social Democratic Party polled 23 per cent of the popular vote, outdistancing all other groups.

Was another attempt to be made at legal repression, if on a limited scale? A proposal tending to incorporate part of the abandoned anti-socialist legislation into the criminal code was introduced by the government in December 1894. In the debate on the Reichstag floor Freiherr von Stumm-Halberg, the big landowner, industrialist, and confidant of court and army leadership, drew a more logical if admittedly theoretical conclusion: he recommended that socialists and anarchists be deprived of the vote and their agitators deported or interned. This would have been the end of legal repression and a changeover from a constitutional to a police state. No Reichstag majority was to be found to approve of such revolution in reverse.[17] But the Reichstag majority had also lost faith in what limited repression had been applied under the 1878 law. It rejected the government bill and all amendments and restored common penal law; it would have administrative and judicial authorities go on needling the socialists, but it would no longer rely on special repressive techniques to stop the rise of socialist labor. Still

drawn in Paul Kampffmeyer, *Unter dem Sozialistengesetz*, Berlin, 1928. The parliamentary debates are reported in *Die Sozialdemokratie vor dem Deutschen Reichstag*, Hamburg, 1878.

[16] Of a total of 318 complaints filed with the Reich Commission, 69 were decided in favor of the complainants, as recorded in "Der Kampf der Deutschen Sozialdemokratie in der Zeit des Sozialistengesetzes," *Die Tätigkeit der Reichskommission*, ed. Leo Stern, East Berlin, 1956, Vol. I, p. 10.

[17] "Umsturz und Sozialdemokratie," Verhandlungen des Deutschen Reichstags am 17 Dezember 1894 und 8-12 Januar 1895, nach dem offiziellen stenographischen Bericht, Offenbach a.M., 1947, Vols. I and II. Stumm's speech may be found in Vol. I, pp. 68-81.

engaged in an uphill fight for full recognition by the old privileged groups, the representatives of liberal and Catholic middle-class groups shied away from restricting the citizens' free and equal access to the political process, basis of their own claim to legitimacy. No friendly feelings toward the socialists were involved; they deeply distrusted their escape from middle-class tutelage and their advocacy of a program promising not just social improvement but also radical revamping of society's structure. The moderate man of the Reichstag majority simply did not care to give the government more legal weapons for dealing with political opponents. They were not sure that intensified legal repression would not backfire and help rather than curb the socialists; nor were they sure that such weapons might not one day be used against themselves.

Similar feelings of uneasiness in regard to repressive measures shaped the public mood in 1912, in the days of the last major battles fought for the democratization of Europe's political order when the suffragettes waged an all-out war for the women's vote. No mass agitation without parliamentary echo. The imprisonment of the suffragette leader Sylvia Pankhurst provoked angry verbal exchanges on the floor of the Commons between Prime Minister Herbert Asquith and Labor's George Lansbury, defender of the suffragettes. Lansbury even resigned his seat to mobilize opinion against a parliament betraying its trust. His Majesty's (Liberal) Government then had Lansbury arrested for vagrancy (not sedition). Both he and the suffragettes were offered freedom for a promise to behave themselves forthwith; they refused. Renewed agitation and disturbances in London's East End followed. To make things worse, the government showed marked indulgence to Conservatives such as Edward Carson, Andrew Bonar Law, and F. E. Smith (the future Lord Birkenhead), accused of fostering armed resistance to the government's Irish policy. Reluctant to deploy full-dress repression against a campaign which ostensibly had become a fight for more democratic freedom, the government found itself on the defensive and sounded retreat.[18]

Though not necessarily in favor of full equality for women, popular opinion reacted sharply to the use of force and coercion in a political dispute, and Great Britain's mature parliamentary regime proved sensitive to the public mood. Basically no different was the response,

[18] Raymond Postgate, *The Life of George Lansbury*, London, 1952, p. 130. For a later episode where Lansbury used the same tactics with full success—equalization of rates between boroughs—see p. 218.

about the same time, of Prussia's bureaucratic rulers when faced with the Social Democrats' vehement public campaign for an improved election law; not really dependent on the voters' favor, Prussia's strong men did not give in, yet they chose to abstain from setting up a new repressive machinery to halt Social Democratic agitation.[19] It was still legally permissible and well in line with administrative practice to repress moves aimed at democratization; but manifest repression was no longer in harmony with the spirit of the time—in semiautocratic Prussia no more than in parliamentary Britain.

It is conceivable that even in the climate of progressive democratization, severe legal repression, with or without hastily concocted special legislation, could have served one specific purpose: elimination of anarchist violence. This actually occurred in the 1880's and 1890's, but with less of an impact than was officially asserted; and it emanated from small, isolated groups rather than from a dangerously centralized, widespread movement. But the mechanism was not too effective in this respect either. Governmental authorities were not particularly concerned with the anarchist's crimes per se; nor would they pay special attention to differences between broader anarchist propaganda and the narrow realm of anarchist deeds; the anarchist was far more important as a bogeyman. Once the scare was there, it was tempting to make out a case against socialists as disguised anarchist dynamiters and arsonists, and to use it, as Bismarck did in 1878, to justify repressive antisocialist legislation.[20]

In reality, contacts between early democratic and later socialist organizations, on the one hand, and anarchism, on the other, had been few and not exactly friendly. The more advanced and disciplined the socialist organization, the more outspoken, even violent its hostility to both doctrinal and practical anarchy. In fact, governments on the lookout for special instruments of antisocialist actions only rarely

---

[19] The Prussian and imperial bureaucracy prevented any attempt by the army and navy authorities to introduce special legislation in order to protect the armed forces against the kind of revolutionary agitation that occurred in Russia in 1905. This episode may now be followed in *Die Auswirkungen*, ed. Leo Stern (Ch. II, n.33 above).

[20] In 1929 a German professor of history could still try to convince his readers that the Social Democrats had some sort of intellectual responsibility for anarchist actions. See Adalbert Wahl, *Deutsche Geschichte*, Stuttgart, 1926, Vol. II, p. 67. For a correct appreciation, see G. D. H. Cole, *Marxism and Anarchism, 1850-1890*, London, 1957, pp. 336, 340-41. Marius Boisson, *Les Attentats Anarchistes*, Paris, 1931, p. 143, gives some rather telling glimpses of the violent socialist feelings toward anarchists. For the course of French anarchism, see the detailed story in Jean Maîtron, *Histoire du Mouvement Anarchiste en France, 1880-1914*, Paris, 1951.

succeeded in winning parliamentary majorities for such spurious identification of socialism and anarchism. Official propaganda painted a gruesome picture of the dregs of society engulfing civilization. This is where damage was done. Falling for their own propaganda, the governments dealt with a social phenomenon of historic magnitude as they would with matters of police and court routine. In due course, enforcement agencies applying special repressive legislation became the laughing stock of the movement they were to control.

But for a few revolutionary outbreaks of short duration and the lingering sore of Ireland,[21] repression of political enemies throughout the nineteenth century remained by and large within the bounds of legality. If it was occasionally used to excess to counter the rise of new political mass organizations, its extent and effect were checked by the authorities' interest in watching and assimilating the new phenomenon; this in turn supplied the opposition with novel weapons. A lesson had been learned. The conclusion was inescapable that legal repression of political activity directed against the established regime was a gigantic task overtaxing the resources of nineteenth century power holders.

3. Criteria for Repression of Hostile Groups
under Majority Rule

The crushing of the revolutionary Paris Commune in 1871 may be deemed the most savage act of repression in the nineteenth century, and this to a large extent without the mitigating influence of legal procedure. Contrasting sharply with earlier acts of repression, the Paris massacre was the exploit of a government with full title to democratic legitimacy; free elections had swept it into power five months before. A democratically constituted government, it apparently felt free to engage in ferocious reprisals which an old-fashioned minority regime might have shunned.

Repression wielded by men who represented incontestably the majority of the people has an aura of justification different from that of any minority regime. The minority may contest the honesty of the elections, may reproach the majority with having entrenched itself through abuse of popular ignorance, or may claim that it has been deprived of propaganda facilities and resources. This will do the minor-

---

[21] Establishment of rival centers of authority by Irish revolutionary groups goaded the government in London into suspending habeas corpus and making use of other procedural shortcuts. At no time, however, was Ireland's representation in the House of Commons impaired or curtailed.

ity no good. The group once recognized as the majority will benefit psychologically from this very recognition; it will have been legitimized as expressing—perhaps not perfectly, but enough for all practical intents and purposes—the will of the people. In the Socialist v. Communist debate on democracy and dictatorship, inspired by the 1917 Soviet Revolution in Russia, the Bolshevik position was tactically weak not merely because they could not possibly ignore the Marxian authority of Karl Kautsky, chief literary spokesman for the Social Democrats. More important, the Social Democrats were hard to refute in their emphasis on the democratic legitimacy of majority rule. Lenin and Trotski had no way out but to argue that the actually proletarian and socialist majority would have no chance to prevail over the capitalist minority controlling the economy, the coercive machinery of the government, and the making of public opinion; for this reason, a proletarian dictatorship would have to be established temporarily to assure the true majority, who were not necessarily fully represented in "bourgeois" parliaments, of the exercise of power. The Communists would submit to majority decisions, provided that the genuine, revolutionary will of the majority rather than its distorted parliamentary substitute had a chance to express itself. To put it differently, the risk of majority vote against the "proletarian revolution" was to be eliminated before the majority could be permitted to act. The "Leninist" doctrine thus salvaged the majority principle. But the principle was not to be applied until the dictatorship of the proletariat had completed the job of putting the "true" majority in the place of the "false" majority of "bourgeois democracy."[22]

It goes without saying that the "revolutionary vanguard" of the stipulated "true" majority will necessarily lack democratic legitimacy. No matter how stubbornly the ruling "capitalist minorities" may resist the alleged revolutionary rule of the majority, the revolutionary "vanguard's" right to dislodge them rests only on its own belief that a clearly expressed majority will in time legitimatize its action. An oppressed minority may be morally justified in refusing allegiance to the legal authority of a government controlled by an oppressor minority; but unless confirmed by popular decision, its revolutionary claims

[22] Karl Kautsky, *Die Diktatur des Proletariats*, Vienna, 1918, has been answered by V. I. Lenin, *Die Proletarische Revolution und der Renegat Kautsky*, first pub. in 1918 in Moscow; 1951 German ed., East Berlin, cited. See esp. p. 36, where the assumption that in a somewhat more serious revolution the course of events could be decided by the relationship between majority and minority is treated as the greatest idiocy, as betraying the masses, and as withholding from them manifest historical truth.

will never add up to democratic legitimacy. Even the moral title would be lacking if the revolutionary minority were out to overthrow majority rule on the contention that today's majority, when reduced eventually to minority status, will surely refuse to bow out and yield its place to the revolutionary force, which by then has won over the majority of the people.[23]

In order to retain title to democratic legitimacy, the majority must consent to submit to periodic voting decision by an electorate free to choose from a variety of contestants. If dethronement of the majority is not justified by a minority's prediction that the majority of the moment will never abdicate in the face of reversed majority-minority proportions, how far, then, may the majority go—within the framework of democratic legitimacy—in defending its position? Is it entitled to suppress a minority on the mere suspicion that it plans to violently overthrow, whenever feasible, the majority group in power? Or should it guarantee such minority the freedom to pursue its plans? Who is to decide whether the majority's allegations regarding the minority's evil intentions were valid or designed merely to make up for actual loss of power and influence and to weaken the opposition? And of what good is the majority's title to legitimacy if those opponents who might one day be its strongest rivals are excluded from participation in the contest for popular votes and majority status?

This is the problem of how to deal with groups deemed hostile to the established democratic regime, but intent on operating within it a so-called opposition of principle. What does the majority's legal repression of admittedly or allegedly revolutionary minorities imply? Is it permissible? Justifiable? Necessary?

The problem has often been dealt with under the heading free speech. Is protection of free speech an absolute, essential as it is to the democratic process? Or should untrammeled formation of consensus as the source of democratic decision-making be weighed against its own innate tendencies toward self-destruction and protected from such tendencies through restriction of participation and expression? While the questions are pertinent, free speech in this context is but a short-

[23] The opinion was contained, if only in a contingent and hypothetical form (making the use of violence dependent on the future undemocratic attitude of a small majority against a powerful minority) in the 1926 Linz Program of the Social Democratic Party of Austria. History has shown that the minority's hypothesis was correct, though it must be an open question to what extent an element of self-fulfilling prophecy was present. However, the situation has since completely changed, and the 1926 formula has been abandoned.

hand version of a large cluster of manifestations which crystallize in the organizations through and in which modern democracy comes to life.

Within the framework of democratic institutions, three distinct answers have been prominent in recent times: (a) full equality granted hostile groups; (b) formal equality with various kinds of limitations on the groups' participation in public life; and (c) suppression of the groups and prohibition of assimilated activity.

Repression of activity deemed damaging to the established political order is most comprehensive, of course, when the hostile group is made to disband. This may encompass exclusion from the polls, prohibition of public activity for members or former members, and penalization of membership in the dissolved group and its successor organizations.[24] The most important democratically governed countries that have banned or at least tried to ban specific political groups are: the Federal Republic of Germany and—with must less consistency and with a certain fluidity which reflects legal impediments and transitory political factors—the United States. Similar, though abortive, moves have also been made in Australia.[25] As the democratic order is expected to benefit from suppression of hostile groups, the place of such repressive policy within the constitutional framework has doctrinal and practical implications. Compared to older constitutions, such as those of the United States or Australia, those framed in recent years and embodying twentieth century political experience provide a different basis for dealing with specific democratic phenomena of our times. The 1949 German constitution makers, for example, were very specifically concerned with protecting democratic institutions from open or stealthy attack by antidemocratic mass movements. A special

[24] There is no need here to consider temporary suppression that is clearly limited to a well-defined emergency period. Likewise, recapitulation of the South African situation may be dispensed with. There, outlawing of Communism is but a logical by-product of upholding the government's racial policies through legal repression of "any doctrine or scheme which aims at the encouragement of feelings of hostility between the European and non-European races of the Union." The rather fluid situation in a number of Latin American countries—including those where democratic legitimacy of the government in power is not subject to doubt—has been left out intentionally, for discussion of national peculiarities would lead too far afield. The special cases of Algeria and Greece are equally omitted from consideration. For the situation in the thirties, see Karl Loewenstein, "Legislative Control of Political Extremism in European Democracies," 38 *Columbia Law Review* (1938), pp. 591, 726.

[25] See Lester Webb, *Communism and Democracy in Australia*, Melbourne, 1954; there is interesting comment to the effect that the Labour Party showed little interest in amending the bill, for it justifiably expected that the act would be thrown out in court (p. 176).

clause was inserted in the Bonn Basic Law (Article 21) which branded as unconstitutional all "parties which in their objectives or the conduct of their adherents tend to impair the foundations of a free democracy or to imperil the existence of the Federal Republic." Another clause (Article 9) expressly prohibited associations "opposing the constitutional order."[26]

No such specific withdrawal of constitutional protection was envisaged in the Constitution of the United States, and punitive statutes —the so-called sedition laws, for example—have been objected to as violations of freedom of speech guaranteed by the Constitution. More recent repressive legislation, especially the 1954 Communist Control Act, may be legally vulnerable on other grounds, too. A preliminary decision on the validity of sedition legislation was reached in the Dennis case in 1951, the Supreme Court refusing by a 7-2 vote to invalidate Section II of the Smith Act of 1940, which makes it unlawful to advocate or teach overthrow of the government by violence, or to organize groups for such purposes.[27] Without this court decision, the later, more far-reaching security legislation blocking off Communist-inspired activity, and in particular the crowning enactment of 1954, would have been difficult to pass.[28] The German Constitutional Court has had a comparatively easy job. As suppression of parties is a constitutionally sanctioned procedure, the court's authority is invoked only to establish the facts. So far it has made two findings: suppressing the Socialist Reich Party (October 1952) and the Communist Party (August 1956).

In a democratic system the activity of a revolutionary party has its paradoxical aspects. While expressing the very essence of an open society, it is directed at uprooting this society. And yet an open society, even if it is not torn apart by crucial social or racial problems, must give rise to such hostile activity so long as there is no universal agreement on the desirability of structural change; political myths retain their attractiveness, and the distribution of social and political power remains unequal—something which neither free elections nor added pressure groups can make disappear. But then how can democracy, bent like any other political system on self-preservation, permit the unimpeded operation of groups hostile not only to the present govern-

[26] H. von Mangoldt and F. Klein, *Das Bonner Grundgesetz*, 2nd ed.; Berlin-Frankfurt, 1957, vii to Art. 21.

[27] Dennis v. United States, 341 U.S. 494 (1950).

[28] See "The Communist Control Act of 1954," Note, *Yale Law Journal*, Vol. 64 (1955), p. 712.

ment but to the very essence of a system in which change is predicated on majority agreement?

While the man of theory might reason that a basically sound democratic society need not fear the appeal of antidemocratic philosophies, the practical politician is likely to be more impressed with the assumption that those in charge will never tolerate adverse activities that may cause tangible damage. Should inefficiency be the criterion of permissible hostile action? But then, only a soap-box orator would have a fair chance to pass the test. Speaking for no one but himself or for just an esoteric group, and out of touch with major society trends in his notions of evil and salvation, he would hardly kindle a dangerous flame. Political action would not grow out of whatever feelings of compassion, derision, pleasure, or enthusiasm he might evoke. Surely even in the soap-box world a dangerous species may emerge—one that combines religious prophecy with political exploitation of fear, anxiety, and resentment. The prophet's isolation need not prevent his initiating a movement of religious reorientation that has political implications. But so long as this doctrine does not capture the minds of multitudes and become translated into organizing and institutionalized pursuits, he will remain proof personified of political inaction. To the policeman entrusted with public safety, this may be just the ideal measure of permissible political deviation. The police officer's indiscriminate protective urge is not, however, the proper standard for the preservation of a democratic climate. There must be other standards by which to judge the acceptable area of active disagreement.

From the safety officer's ideal of guaranteed ineffectiveness, attention shifts to the horizon of the judge, who is searching for a more adequate gauge of the bearable and unbearable range and nature of revolutionary opposition. He must consider past experience, future expectations, the ends pursued and the means applied by the revolutionary group, the doctrine it subscribes to, and the relation, if any, between doctrine and action patterns.

Lessons of current history were obviously on the minds of American legislators and magistrates, the Bonn constitution makers and the Karlsruhe Court; of less impact between 1949 and 1957 were the experience of the Alien and Sedition Law and the 1918-1920 record of United States persecution of political beliefs, which in retrospect evoke incredulity and shame.[29] A deep imprint on the lawmakers' and

[29] J. M. Smith, *Freedom Fetters*. For the second wave of oppression see R. K. Murray, *Red Scare*, New York, 1955.

judges' minds was left by the establishment in 1948 of Communist rule in Czechoslovakia, model of the seizure of power by a strong minority under the guise of a perfectly legal change of cabinets. And both in and outside Germany vivid memories persisted of the National Socialists' enthronement in 1933—triumph of a party of revolt that enjoyed legal status and used it to form a government in seeming agreement with the constitution doomed to destruction by the new rulers.[30] In recent years all this greatly influenced the thinking of jurists and political leaders. What seemed most pressing was the grave danger inherent in the revolutionary minority's opportunity to use the democratic government itself in setting up a one-party power monopoly that was not restrained by constitutional safeguards or observance of legal norms. But to define the degree of danger requiring defensive action is a political decision rather than a question of law. Understandably, German postwar lawmakers—in both the Basic Law and the Constitutional Court Statute—left to the Federal cabinet the decision of whether to institute proceedings aimed at the suppression of an antidemocratic party.[31] Analogously, enforcement of various types of antisubversive federal legislation in the United States devolves on the executive branch in the person of the attorney general.

This strategic expedient does not, however, solve the pertinent problem. It has to some extent remained with the courts to determine when, how, and under what conditions a political group's purportedly antidemocratic actions, attitudes, or anticipation of future action constitutes sufficient grounds for its suppression. The courts' contribution deserves closer scrutiny.

A. THE ANTICIPATION OF "REMOTE CONSEQUENCES"

To assess how dangerous is an antidemocratic group, the judge will rely on his evaluation of possible future developments even more perhaps than of past experience. His verdict becomes, as Justice Jackson has dubbed it, "a prophecy in the form of a legal decision."[32] When the known facts about a revolutionary group, its goals, structure, and

---

[30] Karl Dietrich-Bracher, *Die Aufloesung der Weimarer Republik*, Stuttgart, 1955.

[31] The Federal Republic's Constitutional Court was quite emphatic when, in its judgment banning the Communist party, it stated that the decision on whether or not to institute action for establishing a party's "unconstitutionality" under Art. 21 of the Basic Law rested exclusively with the executive branch and was within the latter's discretionary power; whether such action was politically advisable was no concern of the court. See *Der KPD Prozess Dokumentarwerk*, ed. Pfeiffer-Strickert, Karlsruhe, 1956, Vol. 3, pp. 583, 606.

[32] Dennis v. U.S., 570 (concurring opinion).

activity, must be balanced against the projected interrelations of countless other determinants of unknown direction and magnitude, the result is not likely to be unequivocal. Only historical examples, of course, are available to corroborate this sceptical view. They may help clarify conjectural thinking.

In 1924 a Bavarian court found Adolf Hitler, an alien, guilty of having organized and directed an attempted *coup d'état*, and sentenced him to a five-year term of confinement. But it refused to order as mandatory the deportation of the convicted alien at the completion of the confinement term, and authorized the release of the prisoner after he had served one tenth of the term imposed by the sentence. Could correct evaluation of Hitler's possible future role have altered the decisions referred to? Or did these decisions indicate the reluctance of sufficiently influential German groups to take decisive action in support of the democratic order?

The latter version would suggest strong emphasis on factors barely susceptible to modification, such as Hitler's bend of mind and will power and the sum total of German conditions in the 1920's; it would mean that the general course of events could not possibly have been turned in the opposite direction by more repression and less leniency and complacency. If, however, one chose to believe that alternative decisions could easily have been arrived at by the Munich court and its supporting cast in the Bavarian administration, the inference would be inescapable that Hitler's early release from prison and nondeportation played an important role in his rise to power. It is practically impossible to determine in retrospect, let alone to anticipate how variations of one element in a complex process affect the total outcome. But it would not seem justified to dismiss the hypothetical possibility that manifold variations of a number of elements could combine to produce a different outcome. If every link in the chain of repressive action at the disposal of the Weimar Republic had been used differently, would the ascent to the summit of power still have been open to Hitler?

In his appeal court opinion in the Dennis case, Judge Learned Hand blazed the intellectual trail for the 1950 majority of the Supreme Court. He held that the law's protective function in behalf of the constitutional order must extend to acts not necessarily reprehensible in themselves but whose remote consequences should be judged injurious, provided that the inherently damaging tendency of the incriminated act could be established and intent to bring about the ultimate effect evidenced.[33] This construct would seem rather tenuous when measured by the infinite variety of factors which may intervene between the act and its "remote consequences," factors of which repression or nonrepression is but one, and not the most important one. Only a slender thread ties together remoteness and probability. Moreover, the reasoning is a bit too close to the concept of ineffectiveness as a criterion of permissible action to give much intellectual comfort. Still, Judge Hand's opinion merits more than passing attention. It reflects growing intellectual discomfort in the face of the judicial attitude prevailing at the time: the propensity to solve all difficulties uncritically, by invoking "clear and present danger" to inhibit undesirable activity. Actually, this threadbare formula contains nothing but "the shorthand statement of those among the mixed or compound utterances which the First Amendment does not protect."[34]

At least with respect to Communist or Communist-inspired activity, considerations revolving around "clear and present danger" are obsolete. The formula aims at specific action in a concrete situation. This is illusory when the acting unit of the purportedly revolutionary organization no longer responds spontaneously to specific stimuli from a concrete local situation or from the emotional rather than intellectual impact of the political climate in general, but instead carries out directives from a national or international center, not knowing their specific purpose nor being able to judge their possible effect. To the extent that the making of decisions moves further away from the lowest level of the organization where action is effected, the individual responsibility of those engaged in action disintegrates; at the same time they lose sight of any possible connection between day-by-day acts in which they participate and the ultimate goals pursued. This is not the concern of the public prosecutor alone. It is a matter of deep concern to the revolutionary party itself. Revolutionary politics deals in future contingencies. There is no chance for revolutionary action unless a clearcut, immediate, elementary connection between the experience and action of the day and the great promise of a "new world" for the future can be implanted in the minds of those whose active support is necessary to the revolutionary cause. How is such connection to be established when actual execution of orders is divorced from policy making? The probable effect of a person's shouting "Fire!" in a crowded theater—Justice Holmes' famous paradigm—is foreseeable

[33] U.S. v. Dennis, 183 F 2d 201, 212, 213 (2d Cir. 1950).
[34] Dennis v. U.S., 517 (concurring opinion).

with near certainty. In the same category belongs John Stuart Mills' differentiation between the permissible rallying cry, "Corn dealers are starvers of the poor," and the punishable attempt to underline this slogan by having an excited mob demonstrate before the house of the corn dealer.[35] When antiwar handbills are distributed among draftees about to leave for the front lines, the possible alternative effects are within narrow limits. Prediction and assessment become guesswork, however, when repercussions of wide-range political manifestations are involved. Proven and tested Soviet endorsement of the teaching that permits a choice between different roads to socialism, for example, could make the Communist cause more palatable to broad popular masses in the Western world. Would it?

The categories of proximity and remoteness scarcely help calculate possible consequence of political acts. Other elements in the concatenation of causes and effects may be far more important in a given historical situation. The chance to foretell with a degree of precision the effect of one single cause is extremely rare. It could have been anticipated, for example, that the 1939 Hitler-Stalin pact would make the French Communist leadership switch from patriotic anti-Hitlerism previously approved by Moscow to a position of neutrality vis-à-vis the belligerents in a war now turned a "conflict of imperialist powers"; what would then follow was hardly predictable. If instant suppression by the government had not relieved the Communist Party of the loathsome job of rationalizing and whitewashing its turncoat performance, it is conceivable, though by no means certain, that its inner cohesion would have been badly shaken and many a party follower would have turned against it.

To a large extent, the effectiveness of party action amidst an array of unforeseeable and immeasurable future contingencies depends on the interrelation of doctrine, goals, and observable action pattern. Doctrine and goals cannot be mysteries revealed in clandestine gatherings to a handful of the faithful and dedicated and divulged in public only through stool pigeons and renegades. While the emphasis on external as against internal consumption may vary, and while tactical considerations may dictate a measure of concealment and disguise, the ever-present imperative need for indoctrinating sympathizers, training active members, and imposing a rigid intellectual discipline upon party officers limits doctrinal shiftiness or interchangeable sets of assorted goals. Communist parties in particular are committed to a system of beliefs

[35] *On Liberty*, Ch. 3.

that forms a fairly coherent body of doctrine; party dogma to them certainly is not an afterthought haphazardly appended to purely behavioral action patterns. It is the specific structure of this dogma—part analytical thought aspiring to absolute knowledge, and part eschatology—which serves to relate everyday action to ultimate goals. Communist teaching gives ample evidence that interdependence of goals, doctrine, and action patterns is the mainstay of Communist Party activity.

Judge Medina in 1949 and the German Constitutional Court in 1955-1956 undoubtedly had a valid reason to focus trial proceedings on this fundamental interdependence. The German court in particular was in a position to pursue the theme with consistency and single-mindedness, as it had but one central question to answer: is the doctrine which the Communist Party teaches and wittingly applies to the German scene compatible or incompatible with the "free democratic" essence of the Federal Republic's system of government? To this extent the trial in Karlsruhe is likely to attract more lasting interest than the one in New York. Judge Medina tried, at least in form, a criminal case; the defendants were accused of specific acts, namely, of having taught a doctrine advocating violence and calculated to incite characteristic action whose specific nature would be determined at a future date. As a consequence, the meaning of the teaching was often lost in court behind the prosecution's effort to pin down the doctrine too literally and narrowly, and to supplement text interpretation by testimony of witnesses of a special, not exactly dispassionate, brand: converts from Communism and infiltrated agents. The defendants in turn produced as witnesses of no less dubious neutrality a galaxy of party stalwarts.

Unencumbered by such peripheral, often unsavory procedures and their attendant fireworks, the German court was satisfied to sift literary evidence and study the interpretation submitted by both the government and the Communist Party, including extensive oral statements by the party's authoritative leaders. With all the chances for doctrinal justification at their disposal, the German defendants were in a difficult position. As the Basic Law of the Federal Republic expressly withholds the guarantees of free speech and free party activity from advocacy of political change affecting the foundations of democratic government, the defendants had to show, for example, that restriction of democratic freedoms was not an integral part of their party doctrine. This indeed was bound to bring the crucial issue to the fore. The issue had to some extent been obscured at the New York trial, for no one knew what criteria would be applied by the higher courts to the contested prohibition of "advocacy" under the Smith Act. As evaluation of undemocratic activity on the basis of inferred consequences seems to bog down in equivocation, and as it is of questionable legal usefulness, the German experiment, undertaken on a firm constitutional basis, in judging a party by its doctrine assumes more far-reaching importance.

B. THE ROLE OF THE PARTY DOCTRINE

In persistently regarding Communist Party doctrine as an indivisible whole, binding upon the conduct of the party organization and every individual party member, the German Constitutional Court did exactly what Leninism demands of his followers, thus putting the Communist Party on the spot. Being evasive and tortuous in their refutation of the unconstitutionality charge, the party's lawyers went to all lengths to obviate discussion of what party doctrine ineluctably implies for party activity.[36] As the court did not oblige, a more complex course was taken. The party's spokesmen insisted that only the immediate objectives pursued in the obtaining historical situation were within the purview of the court and that these must be viewed as independent from and unrelated to revolutionary implications of the party's social theory; these implications, they said, referred solely to an expected future situation.

In concrete terms, this separation of daily objectives from ulterior revolutionary goals, unique in Communist Party history, was translated into a fictitious bisection of party policy according to historical stages sharply set off from one another. During the first stage, which would last until Germany was reunified, the Communist Party in the Federal Republic, accepting the operation of the Basic Law and acknowledging the absence of an objective revolutionary situation,[37] must fight for preservation and extension of democratic rights and freedoms. At the second stage, beginning with the merger of the two separate German states, introduction of "socialist democracy"—no longer by implication hemmed in by the Bonn constitutional order—would be the party's immediate task.

Twisted constructs of this kind had been unnecessary in the defense of American Communists. The problem at the Dennis trial, for example, was different. There the charge to be refuted was more narrow and the rules of evidence determined a more mechanical handling of

[36] *KPD Prozess*, Vol. i, pp. 434, 898, 942.
[37] *Ibid.*, pp. 590, 897.

the question of proof. Attention was focused on two points: the definition of "teaching"; and the elusive difference between permissible exposition of doctrine and illicit advocacy of action that effects specific parts of the doctrine. The defendants were free to admit that it was within the realm of their doctrine to discuss historical situations in which the violent overthrow of the capitalist system was inevitable; but they had to deny having advocated a doctrine requiring the violent overthrow of the government of the United States.[38] It was up to the prosecution to show that, beyond the realm of abstract exposition, advocating overthrow had been not virtually implied[39] but actually committed.

Trial tactics apart, how to separate discussion and exposition of violent overthrow as an abstract theory from actual advocacy of such doctrine may be an interesting object for university seminars, but the difference has no meaning in actual life.[40] In any political organization, whatever its philosophy, to expound the party doctrine is as essential for achieving results as to advocate it. A differentiating criterion may be required by a lawyer advising party officials on a prosecution-proof text, a defense attorney, or an appeal court judge groping for a tangible hallmark in piles of political writings and testimony transcripts on who said what at which meeting. But if there is a dividing line, it should run between exposition of abstract doctrine, including teaching and advocacy, and laying out action patterns however embryonic and indistinct.

Leaders of a newborn, shapeless, and rudimentary organization, such as the Socialist Reich Party, may possibly expect action patterns to evolve spontaneously from a feeling of togetherness cemented by shared experience, tradition, and selectivity in recruitment. They would pay little attention to articulating doctrinal thought, and a court concerned with grasping the living reality of the party would be justified in attributing a minimum of importance to its doctrinal utterances. The Communist Party's doctrinal behavior is altogether a different thing.

[38] The following exchange between Richard Gladstein, counsel for the defense, and Louis B. Budenz, witness for the prosecution, recorded in the trial transcript (United States Supreme Court Record, Vol. 341, pp. 491-532, Part 6, p. 3907) is symptomatic:
  Gladstein: "All the time when you were editor of the *Worker*, did they ever openly come out in so many words that they wanted to advocate overthrowing the government?"
  Budenz: "No—the Marxist-Leninist implication was there."
[39] In Yates v. United States, 354, U.S. 298, 325 (1957), the government insisted in vain that the dividing line be drawn at this very point.
[40] *Ibid.*, Vol. 3, p. 615.

Within the framework of the Marxist-Leninist teaching on the "unity of theory and practice," theory indicates objectives, direction, and methods of action. Theoretical knowledge imposes upon society the replacement of capitalism by socialism; it discloses that this fundamental change must take the shape of a revolutionary transformation; it determines the ways of revolutionary action leading toward this goal; and it teaches the necessity of total permanent mobilization of all "progressive" forces and their subordination to uniform, rigid, and pervasive intellectual and organizational discipline.

The role of violence in this history-ordained revolutionary process appears in two ways. For one, it is inescapable destiny: the dominant class of capitalist society, whose position in the process of production has been slowly undermined over a long period of time, must be dispossessed and suppressed; and as no class in history has ever given up its role without a struggle,[41] the violent clash is inevitable. Secondly, violence is a job necessary for the sake of progress, a duty devolving on the prime movers of the historical process in the present era, that is, the working class, guided by the revolutionary, Marxist-Leninist Communist Party. What is doomed to fall must be given a shove and a thrust to make it fall. Swift, well-planned, violent action will speed up mankind's advance toward harmonious existence.

Obviously, this historical mission of the Communist Party is not easily reconcilable with the observance of the constitutional order in a democratic state. Here Communist interpreters introduce another distinction, equally serviceable in United States courts and at the trial in Karlsruhe. Marxist-Leninist theory commands a thorough, penetrating, examination of the "objective" situation prevailing at any given moment in history. At the present juncture, the interpreters contend, the "objective" situation bars a revolutionary course of action; consequently, only ignorance and malice could impute to the Communists the intention to interfere with the democratic process in Germany, or to advocate violent overthrow of the government in the United States. Does "knowledge of the laws of history" give Communist doctrine a special status in court? Are Communist lawyers the only expert witnesses whose interpretation of Communist teaching must be accepted on faith? Even conceding that under the principle of freedom of scientific inquiry Communist doctrine is no more subject than any other political philos-

---

[41] With noticeable impatience the East German lawyer representing the Communist Party at the Karlsruhe trial, in explaining these fundamentals to his learned audience, barely veiled his irritation at having to tell the facts of life to grown-up and well-educated people; *Der KPD Prozess*, Vol. 1, p. 560.

ophy to verification or invalidation by court decision, why should a court renounce the right to do its own study of the doctrine's implications?

The Karlsruhe court definitely refused to yield to the interpretation monopoly claimed by the Communist Party and its doctrine and law experts; Communist doctrine—to the extent that it had become a determinant of action patterns—was held essential for the court's interpretation and understanding of the party's conduct,[42] and it did a comprehensive analytical job. The procedure seems sensible and legitimate in the light of Article 21 of the Basic Law. If it is the right and duty of a party member to check the correctness of this or that move against the tenets of party doctrine, why indeed should an outside observer refrain from learning the meaning of Communist action from the logic by which each point in doctrine and action must fit into the sum total of official teaching?

Throughout the trial, spokesmen for the Communist Party kept insisting that no action of the party in the postwar period had ever violated the democratic process. There simply could have been no other way for doing the job which history in this situation had imposed upon a party of the German working class; keeping within the framework of the Bonn Basic Law was a matter of course. Party statements before the court evoked again and again the established constitutional order to justify the content of Communist political action in Western Germany: their prime emphasis on reunification; intransigent opposition to a government carrying out a policy of remilitarization while betraying Germany's independence for the benefit of a foreign power; awakening the working class to the threat of a Fascist repeat performance— in short, all facets of the Communist campaign to arouse the people against the Adenauer government, which symbolized the overall style of the prevailing political system.

But the court had little difficulty in upsetting this edifice. It showed that the attempted dissociation of present-day acceptance of the constitutional system from future revolutionary action in reunified Germany was nothing but intellectual gymnastics without any meaning in the daily life of the Communist organization;[43] that every step taken by the party must fit in with its overall revolutionary plan derived from the Leninist concept of the historical process; and that all Communist strategy was, as it were, mapped out on two levels.[44] On the first, the

---

[42] *Ibid.*, Vol. 3, p. 716.   [43] *Ibid.*, p. 720.

[44] The two-level description corresponds in essence to what was referred to at the New York trial as the use of Aesopian language.

use of constitutionally permissible means—coalition governments, governments of national unity, and so on—was envisaged for the achievement of immediate ends; on the second, all such tactical moves were elements of continuous revolutionary advance toward the ultimate aim, establishment of a classless Communist society. While specific party attitudes and activities could be regarded as unaffected by any statutory prohibition, and would not as isolated instances require repressive intervention, they must be viewed differently, as links in a chain of action directed toward ultimate revolutionary change. The sum of all individual elements is an indivisible continuity within which quantitative growth will entail change in quality whenever circumstances will permit.[45]

Called upon to determine whether or not the Communist Party under the terms of Article 21 of the Basic Law remained within the confines of constitutionally permissible action, the Constitutional Court could not possibly evade what was the logical conclusion from the specifically Communist pattern of interdependence of doctrine, ultimate goals, and immediate action. The verdict was total prohibition; enforcement was entrusted to the administration of the states, criminal sanctions, if necessary, to be imposed by the courts.

C. THE WEIGHT OF SPECIFIC ACTS

Both substantive determination of the sphere of permissible revolutionary propaganda and action and uniform enforcement of repressive policies directed against political parties are more problematic in countries whose constitutions are of the older liberal type. In the United States, the June 1957 Supreme Court decision in the Yates case, involving the leadership of California's Communist Party, left the 1951 Dennis ruling theoretically controlling.[46] The Yates decision explicitly approves Judge Medina's charge in the Dennis trial, with its differential treatment of teaching abstract doctrine and using language reasonably calculated to incite to action.[47]

Nonetheless, the range of activities to which the Smith Act may be applied has been cut down remarkably in two ways: (1) the Yates decision restricted the meaning of the term "organizing" in Section 2 (3) to initial activity in the process of setting up an organization; this makes it easier to invoke the statute of limitation. And (2) the Supreme

[45] See Helmut Ridder's review devoted to the judgment in *Neue Politische Literatur*, Vol. 12 (1957), p. 364. To Ridder, the CP's allegiance to the democratic order appears just on the verge of a radically different kind of action.
[46] Yates v. United States, 321.
[47] *Ibid.*, p. 326.

Court refused to follow the German precedent and the opinions of Justices Vinson and especially Jackson in their emphasis on a composite picture of the overall party pattern involved; instead, it insisted on proof of individual steps that realized the advocacy of revolutionary action, such as instruction in sabotage, training for street fighting, or indoctrination of how to move masses of people in times of crisis.[48]

The Yates case shows how the potentiality of a revolutionary party can be evaluated differently, according to whether its general mold and structure are taken into account or whether judgment is based on evidence of specific action. In preparing the Yates case, the government had scraped the bottom and found only crumbs. A new majority group on the court, going over the meager evidence of specific acts of incitement with a finetooth comb, retained very little. Of the fourteen defendants, it acquitted five outright; in returning against the protest of Justices Black and Douglas, nine cases sent to the lower courts, it supplied suggestions as to how the available fragmentary evidence might possibly be handled.

In the light of the Yates decision, however, the government preferred to ask the district court to dismiss the cases of the remaining nine defendants. In another case against seven Hawaiian Communist and labor officials, the Court of Appeal for the Ninth Judicial District, also on the basis of the Yates decision, reversed the convictions on appeal, opining that Yates "leaves the Smith Act, as to any further prosecution under it, a virtual shambles."[49] Since then, the picture may have changed again, because of the long-overdue decisions which contrive to uphold the validity of the 1954 Subversive Activities Control Act and of the membership clause of the Smith Act. However, the 5:4 decisions open at least as many problems as they purport to solve. The majority has, for the moment, refused to tackle the patent issue of self-incrimination which enforcement of the registration provision would engender.[50] Moreover, not only has it reinterpreted membership to mean *active*

---

[48] *Ibid.*, pp. 331-32. For a refutation of the argument that a party per se may constitute a criminal gang, see Justice Black in Barenblatt v. United States, 360 U.S. 109, 135 at 146 (dissenting opinion).

[49] Fujimoto v. United States, 251 Fed. 2 (Ct. Crim. App. 9), 342 (1958). However, the attitude of the appeal courts in then-pending cases has not been uniform. Some have felt that the evidence met the test laid down in Yates, and upheld the convictions. Cf. the cases quoted in Walter Gellhorn, *American Rights*, New York, 1960, Ch. IV, n. 17, p. 211.

[50] "Communism and the First Amendment. The membership clause of the Smith Act," *Northwestern Law Review*, Vol. 52 (1957), pp. 527-42. The note goes into a discussion of lower court prosecutions undertaken before the decision in the Yates

membership,[51] but it has (as a comparison between the Scales and Noto decisions will show) left the question of what would constitute prohibited types of advocacy as wide open as ever.[51a] Under these circumstances, it is too early to say whether attempts to drive the Communist Party completely out of business as an overt institution will be successful, or whether the party will still be able to hold conventions and publish and distribute literature.

Like the various American statutes of the 1950's, the Communist Party Dissolution Act which Australia passed in 1950 was meant to suppress the party and eliminate Communist influence in labor unions. Having in the preamble enumerated as established facts all common grievances against the Communist Party, the act decreed its dissolution and sequestration of its assets; it also set forth administrative rules for two special operations: to disband Communist controlled organizations; and to make Communists and any individual likely to engage in activities prejudicial to the state ineligible for public office in corporate bodies and industrial organizations.

As Australia's central government operates under a constitution which limits federal prerogatives to explicitly stated activities, the framers of anti-Communist Party legislation had taken particular care to tie up provisions of the law with national defense. But six high court judges, with only the chief judge dissenting, parted company with parliament on this issue and invalidated the dissolution act.[52] They argued that the issue was unrelated to national defense unless of manifest emergency.[53] One of the jurists criticized the act's failure to connect the objectionable aims of the Communist Party with specific acts.[54] Two others objected, though not too forcefully, to outlawing a party by an individual piece of legislation that violated the concept of generality inherent in the rule of law; objective standards or tests of liability, they held, should have been established for all.[55] No added basis of the validity of the act was seen in the preamble's statements, considered at best

---

case. It discusses both the legal difficulties arising in the application of the membership clause as well as its missing rationale.

[51] Communist Party v. Subversive Activities Control Board, 6 L ed 2d 625, 694, 731, 735 (1961).

[51a] Scales v. United States, 6 L ed 2d 782, 800 (1961); Noto v. United States, 6 L ed 2d 836 (1961), which reverses a conviction under the same membership clause for insufficiency of evidence of advocacy of action.

[52] Commonwealth Law Reports, Vol. 83 (1950-1951), pp. 1-285.

[53] Thus Justice Dixon, *ibid.*, pp. 195, 202; Fullagar, p. 262; and McThiery, p. 208.

[54] *Ibid.*, p. 192 (Dixon).

[55] *Ibid.*, pp. 192 (Dixon) and 278 (Kitto).

prima facie evidence of facts or a summary of the legislature's motives in passing the law.[56] Australia's voters sided with the six court critics of the experiment in repressive legislation. A constitutional amendment devised to overrule the court was turned down by popular vote, with a plurality of 52,082.[57]

We may summarize the essential differences between a trenchant and a conservative approach to the legal treatment of action directed against the established democratic system of government. Those adopting the more aggressive approach, as exemplified by the Karlsruhe court, insist on considering the suspected group's perennial readiness to take any steps indicated in a given situation by a centrally manipulated body of doctrine, whether such steps be parliamentary activity, propaganda, disguised infiltration, incitement to unlawful action, or organized violence. The more conservative approach, discernible in the above American and Australian court decisions, suggests that under the rule of law more specific acts be made the basis of judgment. Those endorsing this approach are not satisfied with knowing that the group in question proceeds to acquaint the faithful and those recruited for initiation with the rich arsenal of political action; they think that such a hypothetical armory should not be judged before it is unlocked. They contend that the leadership's effort to create a state of psychological readiness for future action is not sufficient to invite overall repression.

Thus the more radical approach tends to culminate in total suppression of the group deemed ready to assault democratic institutions whenever it should suit its purposes. The less radical approach results in less rigid action and requires frequent shifting of positions and repeated relocation, to match the occasion, of battle lines in the conflict between the governmental organization and the hostile group. In choosing one approach or the other, it would seem advisable to give thought to two more elements of the problem: motives prevailing in typical situations, and conceivable alternative solutions.

D. TACTICAL MOTIVATIONS IN SUPPRESSING MARGINAL HOSTILE GROUPS

In recent practice legal suppression of political parties has been something of a puzzle. It has hit Communist or Fascist organizations which lacked influence or were hardly capable of causing damage to national security or political order. Why bother to suppress practically unimportant, if not obscure, groups? Undoubtedly, suppression was made

[56] *Ibid.*, pp. 224 (Williams) and 264 (Fullagar).
[57] L. Webb, *op.cit.*

easy by the groups' insignificance: it would have been a tougher and more complicated job to ban stronger ones. Also, prohibition of smaller groups can be easily handled in a routine way and kept at the level of normal police and court action, without spectacular political repercussions.

The disbandment of the German Communist Party under the August 17, 1956 ruling of the Federal Constitutional Court is a case in point. The government was quite certain that it would manage to put the party out of business without major fireworks, and none were started. Future tangles would have to be anticipated only if the Communist Party was expected to spend a great deal of time, effort, and money in building a vast underground machine. This was not likely. The party enjoys little popular sympathy and cannot count on much outside help for its underground workers; large-scale underground operations could not possibly pay off unless reunification, Eastern style, were in sight.

Still less trouble was expected from the ban of the rightist Socialist Reich Party. Right-wing groups have, at the present moment, no direct line to funds comparable to those which the Communist Party, if it so chose, could allocate to underground work. Without funds, radical groups of the extreme right have no chance to organize clandestine activity in any way menacing the cohesion of the established system of government.

Whatever the difference in potential resources for illicit operations, neither the Communist Party nor the Socialist Reich Party really endangered the Federal Republic's political order. Motives for their suppression must be sought in psychological reactions to past experience and more remote considerations of political strategy.

The Socialist Reich Party was banned at a time when Western Germany's political and economic stability was still in doubt. In those northwestern provinces where the party had its strongholds, unemployment was still considerable because of dismantlement in industry and the presence of innumerable refugees and those expelled from the East. The party, which barely disguised its kinship with National Socialism, made itself particularly conspicuous in the 1951 diet election campaign in Lower Saxony. It revelled in nationalist demagoguery; it attributed widespread misery to "Allied dictates"; it accused all German postwar governments and parties of destroying the nation under orders from foreign conquerors; it besmirched the memory of executed anti-Nazi conspirators as traitors to the Fatherland. In short, the SRP revived ultranationalist philosophies and used Nazi techniques to vilify and denounce the exponents of the democratic system. This "neo-Nazism" not only attracted unwelcome attention abroad, but caused indignation and violent protest on the part of all major political groups in Germany.[58] The press was vehement in its criticism. Concerted counteraction, spearheaded by the labor unions, was launched by democratic organizations. Public opinion was unanimous that the 1949 Basic Law's provisions for outlawing antidemocratic parties be invoked against the SRP.

Vociferous though it was, the SRP actually had neither the organization nor the inner cohesion to imperil democratic institutions.[59] But it provoked clashes reminiscent of the lost battles of the Weimar Republic, it necessitated police action, it created unrest, and it may have caused tumultuous repercussions. Still, the Federal cabinet, averse to providing neo-Nazi tendencies with undeserved publicity, and wary of experiments with constitutional provisions never yet subjected to the test of experience, remained hesitant.[60] It gave way to pressure from militantly democratic groups when it half-heartedly decided, on May 4, 1951, to state that the SRP had run afoul of the Basic Law. However, groups influential in the government camp continued to disapprove of court action.

Two days later, election returns in Lower Saxony confirmed the fears of those who had insisted on repression. The Socialist Reich Party had gathered eleven per cent of the popular vote. What was more, it had made heavy inroads into the electorate of the highly conservative German Party (Deutsche Partei), northwestern Protestant mainstay of the Adenauer government. Pressure on the Federal cabinet increased. Had it still refused to bring the case before the Constitutional Court, judicial action might well have been initiated by the Bundesrat, upper chamber of the federal legislature,[61] where the Social Democrats controlled the majority vote. After another six months' delay, the cabinet finally filed its petition on November 19 and on January 24, 1952 the Constitutional Court decided to start proceedings.

Court action was not rushed. The high tribunal did not announce until July 15 that its findings were unfavorable to the SRP. An injunc-

---

[58] Otto Busch and Peter Fürth, *Rechtsradikalismus in Nachkriegsdeutschland*, Berlin, 1947, esp. p. 192.

[59] *Ibid.*, p. 92, emphasizing the decline of the party that took place before the start of the trial.

[60] *Ibid.*, p. 176.

[61] Para. 43, 1 of the Law on the Constitutional Court of March 12, 1951 (BGBL, II, 243) gives the Federal Council a right to ask for a party ban; Sec. 2 opens the same possibility for a state government, if the party in question operates exclusively on its territory.

tion was issued restraining the party from further propaganda and public action. It took the court three more months to render its judgment. Eleven months had gone by since the government had filed its petition and the court certainly did not argue imminence of danger to the established order. The main emphasis was on the composition and recruitment of the SRP's leadership, which betrayed intent to reconstitute the old Nazi party. This, in the court's view, in conjunction with the party's authoritarian structure, bore out the contention that the party's action was directed against the foundations of the democratic order.[62]

Clearly, what had caused the suppression of the Socialist Reich Party was its well-nigh childish arrogance in flaunting Nazi techniques, Nazi mannerisms, and Nazi personnel, and the unexpected strength of active anti-Nazi sentiment made obvious by the brazen insult to the forbearance of the most mild-mannered and least militant democrats. Genuine danger to the democratic order, if there was one, was peripheral.

Motivations for the banning of the Communist Party are more difficult to establish. The party had been in full decline long before the government, on November 23, 1951, four days after bringing action against the SRP, asked the Constitutional Court to pass on the party's constitutionality. By the time the first federal elections were held in 1949, the Communist vote, considerably stronger in early regional elections, had dropped to 5.7 per cent of the total national vote cast, with only a few industrial districts showing a markedly higher proportion: up to 15 and even 20 per cent in a couple of individual constituencies. Regional elections in 1950 and 1951 revealed further decline at an ever-increasing pace. By 1953 the Communists' share in the national vote had gone down to 2.2 per cent, far below the 5 per cent minimum required for obtaining seats in the federal legislature.

The number of enrolled party members in the early fifties was in the neighborhood of 70,000. It is impossible to guess how many of these were dedicated followers of the party line, but it is an established fact that there were plenty of other kinds among them: pre-1933 oldtimers who kept up nominal allegiance but had no faith in the Eastern high command which directed party activity in the West; opportunists who

---

[62] See *Das Urteil des Bundesverfassungsgerichts vom Oktober 23, 1952 betreffend Feststellung der Verfassungswidrigkeit der sozialistischen Reichspartei*, Tuebingen, 1952, esp. p. 74. On the structure of the party, see Busch and Fürth, *op.cit.*, pp. 264, 276, which emphasizes its exclusive and strict avant-garde character, and comments on its similarities with and differences from the National Socialist leadership concept.

deemed it wise to pay party dues as an insurance premium against future contingencies; and old-style socialists, attracted by the Communists' use of the familiar class-struggle phraseology and distrustful of the Social Democrats' ideological vagueness and unenviable record. Made up of such heterogeneous components, the Communist organization was not strong enough in position or moral cohesion to expect as much as moderate success in domestic affairs. Protection of democratic institutions on the home front cannot conceivably have inspired the government to seek suppression of the unimportant and partly disintegrating party. And neither the general public nor political leadership groups showed sympathy with or interest in the court action.

The government's case against the Communist Party found the high tribunal lacking in judicial zeal. The trial was not started until exactly three years after the government filed its petition. It was repeatedly adjourned for periods of many weeks. It terminated after almost eight months on July 14, 1955, without verdict or temporary injunction. The judgment was withheld for another thirteen months. Altogether it took the court fifty seven months, as compared to eleven months in the SRP case, to arrive at a decision. Even then the judgment was announced not without visible pressure from the government and its majority;[63] the inevitability of the verdict, in terms of the wording of Article 21 of the Basic Law, was as evident as its feasibility was controversial. Even the government had refrained for years from pushing its case too strongly. When at last in 1955 and 1956 it became adamant, it was obvious that no sudden flareup of Communist subversion had provoked this ultimate intransigence. What, then, prompted the government's insistence on a verdict of "unconstitutional"?

In its political and organizational activity the postwar Communist Party in Western Germany was never anything but a fully-owned subsidiary of the SED, Eastern Germany's "Socialist Unity Party," loyal and obedient ally of the Communist Party of the Soviet Union. It goes without saying that the SED and the Bonn government do not see eye to eye on matters of foreign relations and German reunification. Reunification to the SED is but a preliminary stage on the road to Germany's full integration into the Soviet bloc. At the opposite pole,

---

[63] When the law on the Constitutional Court was amended on July 21, 1956 (BGBL, I, 6621), to effect a better distribution of the court's caseload between its two sections, jurisdiction over party bans according to Art. 21 of the Basic Law was shifted to the Second Senate; however, then-pending cases were left with the First Senate, if the proceedings were to terminate before August 31, 1956. Thus the government and its majority virtually forced the hands of the First Senate to pronounce judgment.

the Bonn government envisages complete elimination of the Eastern regime through free elections, to be followed by the Communist-controlled provinces' integration in the West German state.

At the present juncture neither policy has a chance to succeed. Yet the possibility of quadripartite or global negotiations on the German issue—virtually on the international agenda all the time since 1955—has made the men of Bonn, a tactically-minded breed of high intelligence, particularly responsive to considerations of positional strength. The Bonn government clearly does not wish to be encumbered any longer by an Eastern agency operating as a West German party and *ipso facto* acknowledged under the Federal Republic's constitutional law as an operating democratic organization. The government may also have given some thought to the value of a banned Communist Party as a bargaining point.

What is perhaps more important, the government certainly did not spurn the advantage it could gain when equipped, by courtesy of the Constitutional Court, with a special tactical weapon. Intent on barring a "softer" approach to East-West relations, the government would expect to see its domestic position strengthened considerably if it could show that all propaganda favoring a "milder" foreign policy was really an advocacy of unprincipled dealings with the political force convicted by the highest tribunal of the land of active hostility to the democratic order. Entreaties for friendly transactions with the East would be so much easier to reject on the strength of a judicial finding proving that the inevitable result would be enthronement of political forces destructive of the democratic process. Of course it can be affirmed with great logical force that the policy of outlawing the Communist Party is not well reasoned: that it stretches the device of constitutional party suppression far beyond the protective purpose which the constitution makers (with Konrad Adenauer in the chair) had in mind; that it is not worth the inevitable sacrifice of freedom at the outer fringes of the political system; and that it is unwise to help the Communists escape continued defeat at the polls. All this merely lends weight to the contention that the government's reasons had little to do with the urge to safeguard democratic institutions, and a great deal more with the deep-felt need to buttress its foreign policy and fortify its battle lines in a divided country.

How do suppression efforts in the United States look in comparison? The American Communists' political strength is but a fraction of what their German brethren at their weakest can muster. Where is the menace? A recurrent theme has been the Communist Party's readiness and fitness to serve as an espionage center. This is part of the rationale of Supreme Court opinions.[64] (The theme also marks the Preamble to the Australian Dissolution Act.) Is there a one-way connection between espionage and the Communist Party's legal status? If adherents to the Communist doctrine are expected to show no hostility to demands of the Soviet espionage service, in what way would this attitude be affected by the Communist Party's forced switch from active participation in public life to the sterility of clandestine plotting? Is it the chance to expound revolutionary doctrine in broad daylight and to compete with other political groups that makes devotees of the revolution contemptuous of national interests and patriotic allegiance? Does enjoyment of the democratic freedom of political action weaken or strengthen residual ties which may still bind Communist sympathizers to the community at large? These questions must not be discarded as immaterial unless there is sufficient reason to assume that the liquidation of a legally operating Communist Party would also break up its organizational skeleton and so completely destroy all channels of communication between party members as to leave them in a state of utter isolation. This is unlikely.

Another aspect is no less pertinent. By and large, spying has become a full-time occupation requiring vocational training and special skills. In this career the operatives' ideological preferences are of secondary importance, as is a spotless party record. The "apparatus" of Soviet espionage for the United States does not primarily employ American party veterans, and it may be taken for granted that increasing infiltration of government agents into party ranks has made the "apparatus" highly suspicious of party adherents of more recent vintage. Modern, highly bureaucratized intelligence services are not based on the contribution of amateurs from the ranks of specialists in political campaigning, theoretical indoctrination, or union disputes.[65]

From whatever angle the relationship between party activity and espionage is scrutinized, all available evidence points to a marked

[64] Frankfurter concurring in Dennis v. United States, 547-48.

[65] David Dallin, *Soviet Espionage*, New Haven, 1955.

There is an additional consideration which militates against banning an opposition of principle that is suspect of close relations with the enemies of the realm: the importance of secrecy as a necessary means of safeguarding the vital interests of a nation has become questionable. As Henry A. Kissinger forcefully argues (*Nuclear Weapons and Foreign Policy*, New York, 1957, pp. 226, 420), it is one of the paradoxes of the atomic age that survival has come to depend on *lack of secrecy*, that is, on a potential foe's correct information of the weapons readily available to the other side.

decline in the usefulness of legally operating Communist organizations as recruitment channels and relay stations for Soviet espionage. This certainly does not make their activities more dangerous to national security than they were some fifteen or twenty five years ago.

Growing inclination to clamp down on Communist parties has had other, psychologically more compelling reasons. An abrupt change in the international climate occurred at the close of World War II. There was a consolidation of the two antagonistic blocs, which now dominates the global scene; there was in the United States an overpowering feeling of frustration over the course of the Korean war and the re- moteness of any durable solution to the global conflict. It was natural that attention should have focused on the native exponents of pro- Soviet doctrines, obvious symbol and tangible agency of world Com- munism regardless of the adherents' motives or degree of allegiance to Soviet rule.

The spread of such feelings among different social groups combined with genuine fear of domestic Communism and limited knowledge of facts which may justify such fear. Stouffer's inquiry has shed sufficient light on this segment of opinion formation.[66] There was an obvious connection between such emotional patterns and the enactment of more and more stringent repressive legislation whose constitutional validity was at best doubtful. Less thought was given in legislative debates to chances of enforcing the new restrictive rules within the framework of existing legal structures than to the possible reactions of voters. But there is no indication that the voters were as incensed over the issue as had been surmised.[67]

American Communists have long lost any foothold they ever had within the major interest groups; labor unions under Communist con- trol have either disintegrated or been reduced to isolated minor units. As a result, the Communists do not even enjoy as much political pro- tection as groups under attack usually may obtain—in a business way, if in no other—through political go-betweens and their "contacts."[68] They have become political football for politicians and party machines at the local or state level. The legislative fight around the 1954 Com- munist Control Act, for example, revealed clearly that the legislators'

[66] Samuel Stouffer, *Communism, Conformism and Civil Liberties*, New York, 1955.
[67] *Ibid.*, p. 88.
[68] The unfriendly welcome given to Communists or Communist-tainted groups or persons involved in intra-union fights before New York courts is analyzed in detail in Clyde W. Summers, "The Law of Union Discipline: What the Courts do in Fact," *Yale Law Journal*, Vol. 70 (1960), pp. 175, 196.

decisions were not based on preferences for one or the other course of action, or on the merits or demerits of either; they were determined by the need to outdo the other fellow in vociferously rabid anti-Communism.[69] Endorsement of more stringent repressive features meant protection from unfavorable public reaction. It was tempting to prove one's unshakable resolve to fight "subversion" by casting a vote for provisions of dubious usefulness and questionable constitutionality.

The framers of this type of legislation cannot be suspected of political ignorance. They knew that the constitutional system protects, along with the well-intentioned citizens, the followers of extreme groups, however repugnant to public sentiment, so long as these groups are not tainted with criminal fraud or mob violence. They knew that this protection has retained a measure of effectiveness, even though recourse to the constitution's protective devices may be tortuous and time-consuming. It is very conceivable that in drafting the most untraditional clauses of the new laws, legislators may have relied on the corrective effect of constitutional routine and particularly on the courts' skill in pulling emergency brakes.

The making and the early handling of recent American repressive statutes have brought into sharp focus the dual nature of *ad hoc* legislation designed to repress or punish. To condition the political climate and public opinion is one thing; to map out a program of effective legal action is quite another. To combine the two is to introduce a lasting measure of legal uncertainty. There is always the risk that those engaged in enforcing *ad hoc* laws may take them literally, forgetting about the rules of the political game and the intentionally nonenforceable elements of gratuitous demagoguery and propaganda that went into the writings of the legal text.

Notwithstanding the use of different legal techniques, American experience so far has had this in common with German postwar practice: requirements of political tactics, rather than the extent or imminence of specific damage to democratic institutions, has determined the degree and scope of legal repression of antidemocratic groups.

[69] The practical results of competitive pressure to outdo one's colleague in anti-Communism may be seen in Fleming v. Nestor, 326 U.S. 603 (1960). A 5-4 majority under the leadership of Justice Harlan upheld an amendment to the Social Security Act (42 U.S.C. §402 n 1954) that cut off pensions to people deported for membership in the Communist Party (even if this membership applied to the thirties, when the party operated without the statutory disabilities added in the forties and fifties).

4. *Variations in Attitudes toward an Opposition of Principle*

Legal repression by complete or partial majority fiat has been directed so far against small groups of little importance in domestic affairs. No evidence shows how the procedure would work when applied to stronger organizations firmly supported by larger segments of the people. In such cases, frequent practice has been to refrain from formal encroachment upon rights and freedoms of the hostile group while exposing it to a barrage of parliamentary and administrative restrictions, tantamount in some instances to a well-knit system of planned harassment.

Open repression, as was mentioned before,[70] is bound to miss the target and repel friends when the persecuted group assumes the stature of a mass movement, controlling a large section (say, more than twenty per cent) of the popular vote. The movement opposed on principle to the established order may emerge as a rival center of political integration; in the minds of followers as well as some in the population at large, its symbols supplant those of the nation and its leaders constitute an authority competing with that of the legal government (witness the role of August Bebel under the Kaiserreich, or Jean Jaurès under the pre-1914 French Republic).

True, in terms of effective power the range of conflict in pre-1914 continental Europe was limited. But this was primarily because parties as such had not yet become transmission belts of governmental authority, and the international cohesion of the political order's opponents was more ritual than strategic coordination. Bebel and Jaurès were revered popular leaders and prophets of a better world, not heads of shadow cabinets ready to take over; they were spokesmen for international fraternization, rather than national directors of a supranational authority. The position of the parties they represented—part expression of organized mass pressure, and part medium of prophecy and religious dedication—was too ambivalent to result in a genuine contest for power.

This changed for the prodemocratic socialist and labor parties in the period between the wars. But the Communist parties in Italy and France were caught after World War II in an equivocal position reminiscent of the pre-1914 socialist movement. An aura of ambivalence enveloped their participation in national cabinets in the early postwar years (1945-1947). Friends and foes alike expected the Communists to translate popular vote and parliamentary strength into effective power, with the help, or breaking the resistance, of the coalition governments

---

[70] Sec. 2 above.

they had entered. Whatever the strategy they chose, there seemed to be no doubt of their ultimate goal: total domination. And Communist participation in coalitions was regarded as a means toward this end. But obviously the French and Italian Communist parties were not pure action groups following directives in a disciplined way. To a large extent they were merely focal points of mass emotions of dissatisfaction, protest, or hope, which did not necessarily imply organized and directed action. When the Communists were ousted from cabinet position by their erstwhile partners, nothing happened. Western European Communism's onward march had come to an end.

As a result, the Communist parties in both Italy and France were relegated to the position of minority groups excluded from participation in governmental power and opposed not to this or that parliamentary combination, but to the established regime in its entirety. Consolidation of shaky government majorities without Communists was not easy. A decade later, the respective positions of the administration and the Communist opposition of principle in France and Italy appear frozen in accordance with a similar alignment on the international scene. The followers of the Communist parties were, in a way, doomed to wait for some spectacular change that would signal a resumption of the all-out offensive. Meanwhile, they had no choice but to accept and adjust themselves to the survival of the established order and make the best of it. Around the organizational kernel of Communist parties bent on the destruction of the prevailing system, there remained the mass of followers responsive at election time to the party's call; they were perhaps ready to follow its guidance in exceptional situations, but preferred to be left alone in everyday life, not revealing where their loyalties would go in the event of a crucial head-on collision.

Against this background suppression of the Communist Party in either France or Italy would have been an incalculable risk. The democratic legitimacy of the regime could suffer considerably from suspension of the rights and privileges of a political group representing a large segment—one fifth or more—of the voting population. Even if a combination of social and economic pressure and police operations were enough to enforce the ban, there might be enough resistance to throw the judicial machinery out of gear and cancel what is the benefit of limited repression, the chance to preserve intact the legal process and the framework of democratic institutions. Political upheaval could ensue, bringing about radical change in the political system.

Groups opposed on principle to the established system do perform an important function in the body politic. They serve as channels for a more or less orderly expression of basic antagonism to the system, widespread in both France and Italy. Their presence is a weighty factor in the functioning of the mechanisms through which parliamentary parties supporting the regime established popular consensus. Elimination of large groups hostile to the regime could make these mechanisms inoperative or unnecessary. This would affect the primary function of loyal parties, whose legitimation vis-à-vis other power structures— organized interests, bureaucracy, the military, and so on—rests on their performance in integrating and upholding the social order, their special domain.

With the opposition of principle gone, the parties' services might lose importance; the other power structures might become exclusively controlling. To keep in check underground activities of the suppressed group would certainly be a job for the executive's coercive machinery rather than for parliament or parties; and new official organizations in a great variety of fields would have to be built to integrate the suppressed group's homeless clientele. All in all, suppression of the hostile opposition forces would be likely to weaken rather than strengthen the position of parliamentary parties. Further, it would create misrepresentation, be it exaggerating or underrating, of the hostile forces' impact on opinion formation. The implications of that for the country's international standing would be potentially far more damaging than disclosure of the range of popular discontent in the voting strength of unsuppressed opposition ever could be. All this explains why the major political groups, which neither favor nor expect rapid change in the socioeconomic structure, and consequently do not anticipate sweeping victories of the opposition of principle, tend to be greatly apprehensive of the vacuum which complete suppression of the opposition would create.

A. POLITICAL AND ADMINISTRATIVE DISCRIMINATION WITHIN THE CONSTITUTIONAL FRAMEWORK

To the opposition group itself, continued participation in the political process offers substantial advantages. It permits easy communication beyond the confines of the party organization proper with various groups of less committed sympathizers; success or failure of the party machine and its political course can thus be tested at frequent intervals and the risk of sudden shift in popular sympathy minimized. Success at the polls provides party officers with parliamentary seats, emolu-

ments, and immunity from prosecution; legislation and judicial interpretation may curb but not abolish immunity privileges. As antiparlia-
mentarian anarcho-syndicalism no longer influences larger groups, the
fact of being represented in parliament—as an advanced detachment on
enemy territory—gives the opposition group added authority. This may
be a comfort to many followers who, though they dream of revolutionary change, long to be part of a respectable group.

A revolutionary party tightly controlled by an omnipotent leadership
group and looking for broad mass support finds ample rewards as a
legally admitted contender for votes and elected office. The more so
since such a party, if sufficiently versed in Leninist doctrine, will make
use of the benefits of legality without undertaking loyalty commitments
beyond the minimum formalities it must make to qualify.

If this be double-dealing, it has not been without an echo from the
regime under attack. Democratic governments have evolved an ambiguous approach to the legal status of intransigently hostile groups.
Reluctant to take the risk and strain of total suppression, they have
tended to apply partial restrictions to block the enemy progress and
obstruct his activity. One example among many may suffice. In 1953
the French administration requested parliament to suspend the privileges of leading Communists. They were to stand trial before a military
tribunal on charges of having contributed to undermining the morale
of the army in a manner prejudicial to national defense. The request was
denied, for a specific reason. The majority sided with those who felt
that permission to stage the trial would merely becloud the true issue,
namely, whether the Communist Party should not be suppressed altogether.[71]

In the absence of such legislation, the French and Italian governments have exerted administrative and legislative effort to institute as
much of a special regime as possible without sacrificing essential freedoms and equality before the law. Some of the restrictions have affected
the electoral process. Election laws were revised in both France and
Italy in the early fifties with a view to limiting parliamentary representation of extremist parties. For this purpose the principle of proportional representation, generally accepted on the continent in the early
postwar years, was modified so as to permit parties to pool their votes
and award surplus seats or even all seats to combined interparty slates
of candidates holding more than fifty per cent of the departmental
(France) or national (Italy) total. This favored parties that were willing

[71] Assemblée Nationale, Débats, 2 legisl., Vol. 19, November 13, 1953, p. 5,073.

and able to join in an electoral alliance. Three national elections were held under this type of election law: France, 1951 and 1956; and Italy, 1953; but only the first justified the governmental expectations. In Italy a large enough portion of the voters proved reluctant to endorse procedures which seemed unfair and patterned in the Fascist mold; in France many a regional party organization thought it the better part of wisdom not to engage in electoral alliances.

The Italian law, widely called *legal truffa*, the cheat law, was abrogated in 1954, and the election in 1958 was held under the previous system of proportional representation; almost as before, 140 Communist deputies and 59 senators were sent to Monte Cittorio. In France the advent of the authoritarian-bureaucratic Fifth Republic introduced much more severe modifications of the election law. Directed mostly against the Communists was the return to the single-member constituencies of the 1930's, with run-off ballots when no candidate received a majority on the first try; this was combined with a judicious gerrymandering of industrial area election districts. The result justified expectations: with 18.9 per cent of the total votes cast for their lists in the first ballot, the Communists gained exactly 10 seats, while the party with the next highest number of votes cast, the Gaullist catch-all UNR with 17.6 per cent of the vote cast received 188 seats.

However, even as long as bulky Communist groups were entrenched in parliamentary strongholds, other ways were found to make them ineffective: denial of committee chairmanships, refusal of access to classified information, and, above all, exclusion from cabinet formation. In some instances when constitutional provisions made the designation of the head of government dependent on a specific plurality, a prospective candidate for the post of minister president would declare in advance that Communist support, even if preferred, would not be accepted. Free to criticize the government, introduce motions, and participate in legislative debate, the Communists were quite effectively barred from exerting influence on the formation and functioning of the cabinet.

In one country only is the position of the Communist Party, with a sizeable parliamentary group, by and large still comparable to that of the early postwar years in most Western European countries. This is Finland, whose strategic position precludes one-sided commitments in foreign affairs and calls for careful consideration of the slightest Soviet reaction. So long as the Soviet government refrains from subjugating or exerting heavy pressure on the smallish neighbor country, Finland's non-Communist parties will be prepared to pay a price for independence and bow to the necessity of accepting the Communist Party's almost full-fledged participation rather than merely formal attendance in the parliamentary process. Though it has not been represented in any of the coalition governments since 1948, the party enjoys the *de facto* privileges of scrupulously observed political equality, and fully participates in the political process.[72] This is obviously an exception. As a rule, the governmental process today in democratic countries with strong Communist groups works on the principle of giving the Communists only the constitutionally safeguarded minimum privileges.

Below the governmental level, the handling of Communist demands for equal rights is to some extent a matter of administrative discretion. To what extent may discriminatory disadvantages be imposed on hostile groups without flagrant violation of the principle of legal equality? The Italian government, for example, in a release of December 4, 1954, announced that its fight against the Communist Party and associated groups would be conducted throughout on the administrative plane, without recourse to special legislation.[73] Refusal of passports to worker members of the Communist Party who are seeking employment abroad is part of this policy.

In France the removal of some Communists from office or non-admission of alleged Communist sympathizers to the entrance examination for the national school of administration has been quashed by the Conseil D'etat whenever the government failed to supply requested information.[74] Both old and recent cases suggest that practices of

[72] For Finnish readiness to make allowance for new "objective" situations—whether they seem to demand a narrower scope for Communist activity, as in the beginning of the thirties, or whether, as in 1944, they quickly re-establish such activity, with the help of constitutional urgency procedures—see Paavo Kastari, " Constitutional Protection of Civil Rights in Finland," *Democracy in Finland*, Helsinki, 1960 (pub. by the Finnish Political Science Association), pp. 58-73. In 1957, Kastari shows (pp. 69-70), the requirement of a 5/6 majority for initiating these (by now traditional) urgency procedures for a constitutional amendment helped the Communist Party to prevent the adoption of a specific piece of retroactive legislation in the field of social policy; thus the requirement reinforced the tactical position of an opposition of principle.

[73] See Piero Calamandrei, "La Costituzione e le leggi per attuarla," *Dieci Anni Dopo 1945-1955*, Bari, 1955, p. 295. This brilliant article (pp. 214-316) together with the more theoretically oriented piece of Marino Bon Valsassina ("Profilo del opposizione anticonstituzionale nello stato contemperaneo," *Rivista Trimestale di diritto publico*, Vol. 7 [1957], pp. 531-623) constitute the best exposition of the theory and practice of politically motivated discrimination within those Western European constitutional states which do not ban the anticonstitutional opposition as a matter of principle.

[74] The most recent case is Lemaire; see *Revue du droit public*, 1959, p. 804; here, dismissal of an official, grounded exclusively on his opinions, was declared illegal. For

exclusion would be sanctioned if the government provided such material.[75] In other spheres a policy of selective discrimination has been followed, with the government fastening on to particular types of activity or just utilizing discretion where no particular rule prescribes or presupposes a strict equality of treatment. Thus Communist mayors and city councilors have been removed from office as participants in riots; Communist-inspired, mostly propagandistic, resolutions of municipal councils have been vetoed; Communist-controlled labor unions have been excluded from governmental consultations unless prescribed by law; and so on. There is also the practice of barring interest group affiliates of a powerful opposition of principle from access to and representation in official bodies. A double-edged device, this may diminish the influence of the organizations while distorting the actual weight of various organizations in the social process, thus making it more difficult for the bureaucracy to arrive at meaningful, generally acceptable decisions.[76]

Would the entering into function of the Italian Constitutional Court in 1956 make a difference in the policy of administrative disqualifications and disfavors? The early decisions of the court swept away some of the police powers that the government had continued to exercise on the basis of the Fascist Public Security Law of June 18, 1931, which, among other things, made distribution of political propaganda material subject to approval by the police. However, the court's jurisdiction

---

the much overwritten Barel case, concerning admission to the entrance examination for the National School of Administration, see *Revue du droit public*, 1954, pp. 519-38, with a note by Waline that explicitly defines the field of application of the ruling.

[75] Among recent cases, Sieur Grange, *Revue du droit public*, 1959, p. 798, is especially interesting. It concerns the annulment of the forced domicile order against an Algerian lawyer. The case, like the 1954 school case, was decided against the administration, for it refused to furnish any motivation for the order. The decision stated explicitly that if the administration had alleged that Grange belonged to a Communist group, the court would have accepted this allegation as the motivation behind the prefect's measure. A more liberal lower administrative court approach, which puts the burden of proof of nondiscrimination on the administration, is discussed in Réné Bourdoncle, "De l'obligation de réserve qui s'impose au fonctionnaire français," *Rec. Dalloz*, 1960, p. 237.

[76] Some good examples of the French practice of administration discrimination may be found in Jean Meynaud and Alain Lecelot, "Groupes de pression et politique de logement," *Revue Française de Science Politique*, Vol. VIII (1958), pp. 821-60. The Italian practices of barring Socialist and Communist labor associations from representation, and the consequences of these practices, are touched upon in Joseph La Palombara, "The Utility and Limitations of Interest Group Theory in Non-American Field Situations," *The Journal of Politics*, Vol. 22 (1960), p. 45. For the same phenomenon and similar consequences in regard to European organizations, see Ernst Haas, *The Uniting of Europe*, p. 409.

cannot be invoked by political parties. Regional governments which could bring some kinds of cases before the courts have not been set up in sufficient numbers to allow the opposition of principle to utilize this avenue of approach to the court. While particular individuals may allege the unconstitutionality of some law or measure in a pending suit before any court, the court would have to accept the plea as not "manifestly unfounded," or would have to find the decision of the constitutional point a necessary prerequisite for the judgment in the individual case before sending the file on to the Constitutional Court.[77]

If for no other reason than this very narrow line of access to the court, it is not likely that its jurisprudence will seriously affect lower level administrative practices. Moreover, it will be difficult in many instances to prove intentional discrimination because of political affiliation or beliefs; also, time lost in litigation may be as detrimental to victims of administrative discrimination as an unfavorable court decision. In any event, administrative discretion serving to obviate the principle of equality before the law without openly negating it may become one way of introducing consistently differential treatment for parties loyal and hostile to the constitutional order. Whether this will deter the hostile group's followers or make them rally around its standard-bearers is debatable. Especially if the opposition of principle can wage a good part of its fight on the basis of upholding the values of a free society against unconstitutional encroachment (which it presently does in Italy, against the attempts of the combined operation of the traditional alliance between the public powers and the Church), then it will develop sympathies among wider intellectual strata otherwise not easily within its grasp.

As a weapon in the fight between the established government and forces hostile to the political system, legality is a two-edged sword. It lends the appearance of justice and decency to the action of the government, but it reduces the action's range and blunts its striking power. Of course, this applies to the opposition as well. Legality permits the minority to claim the protective shield of the law, but it also instills in the minds of the minority's followers the urge to be protected, and makes them bring pressure on their leaders to stay within the bounds

[77] On the early years of the Italian Constitutional Court and especially the first decision on the unconstitutionality of some parts of the public security law of 1931, see Paolo Biscaretti di Ruffia, "Die Taetigkeit des Italienischen Verfassungsgerichtshofes waehrend der 2 ersten Jahre seines Bestehens," *Schweizer Juristenzeitung*, Vol. 54 (1958), pp. 317-26. On the procedural aspects, see Giovanni Cassandro (judge of the court), "The Italian Constitutional Court," *American Journal of Comparative Law*, Vol. 8 (1959), pp. 1-14, esp. p. 10.

of permissible action so as not to jeopardize the broad range within which protection may be obtained. So long as the law remains in operation, it will narrow down the area of conflicts. These conflicts may occur when the government violates legal equality and oversteps the boundary line between political and administrative discretion; or the opposition may appeal to masses of potential followers to embark on an all-out offensive, turning the war of position, characteristic of the 1947-1959 decade, into a war of movement. The legal order will tend to limit rather than extend the area of explosive friction so long as the conflicting forces, uncertain of future development and shunning the risk of violent conflagrations, exercise a measure of restraint. It is a measure of recognition of the objective factors militating for a policy of watchful accommodation between a regime and its opposition of principle that the coming of the authoritarian-bureaucratic de Gaulle regime has not introduced any fundamental change in this pattern. Although a deliberately vague sentence in Article 4 of the 1958 Constitution—on the respect which parties must render to the principle of national sovereignty and democracy—might have furnished a desired pretext to ban the Communist Party, de Gaulle refrained from doing this. Even when the Communists were still lustily agitating against the official policy toward Algeria, they were left free to sell their line to present and potential customers. The new regime proved unwilling to undertake an additional trial of strength, which might have overtaxed its capacity or at least have forced it to undertake deeper changes in political patterns than it had bargained for.

B. THE POLICY OF EQUAL TREATMENT

There is not much to say about the third way a constitutional democratic system can handle fundamentally hostile groups. It expresses the essence of the constitutional order, equal rights for every man, and of the democratic political system, majority rule with unconditional protection of minority rights, including the right to turn into a majority. Regulation of political life according to these precepts was once the basis from which the other variants—legal suppression of hostile groups and discrimination, with equal rights retained in principle—departed and to which they must return, either partially and temporarily or for good. If they do not return to them, the political system has obviously undergone radical change and, driven by circumstances and the sweet habit of arbitrary exercise of power, abandoned legal in favor of unlimited repression.

In its purest form, the pattern of equal rights and equal treatment has been preserved in Great Britain, parts of the British Commonwealth, and the Scandinavian countries. In legal terms the pattern is based on the traditional separation of a generously inclusive realm of permissible action, with guaranteed freedom of belief, propaganda, and association, from the sphere of illegal acts which include violence, damage to legal institutions, fraud, blackmails, intimidation, and so on, and incitement to commit such acts. Within this framework there can be no urge to extend the concept of action to an organizational or behavioral pattern derived from or tied up with espousal of a specific program of revolutionary change, unless and until such pattern has been translated into specific acts violating the legal order.

A democratic regime retaining this pattern abhors discrimination by administrative fiat, though it may well establish legislative and administrative safeguards against infiltration of hostile elements into sensitive key positions and illicit divulging of information whose secrecy is essential to the protection of the community. The regime might also prevent aggravation of existing cleavages by prohibiting the wearing of uniforms. It grants its adversaries full electoral and parliamentary equality. It has not so far run into major difficulties because of the freedom it protects; it is true, of course, that the hostile groups' participation in the exercise of governmental power has never affected the political balance in countries of unlimited democratic equality, where the anti-democratic parties of either Communist or NS complexion are small.

These countries restrict access only to sensitive positions and secret information; members who are friends and sympathizers of hostile groups are otherwise unimpeded. They are active in many walks of public life, share in public activities, and hold office in universities, labor unions, cooperatives, and so on. They have every opportunity to articulate their programs and to criticize, expose, and denounce, in the light of their doctrines, the tradition, institutions, and prevailing factual conditions. While all accounts may not be in, the record of these countries so far shows no deterioration of democratic institutions nor any damage to national security or international standing traceable to equal treatment of hostile groups.[78]

[78] It is revealing that the informative treatment of British internal security by H. H. Wilson and Harold Glickman (*The Problem of Internal Security in Great Britain, 1948-1953*, New York, 1954) proceeds rather quickly from a general discussion of criminal prosecutions under the heading of sedition or the 1934 Incitement to Disaffection Act—without quoting a single recent case—to the field of the government's moderate security program and the spillover to the educational field, correctly considering in-

To be sure, the antidemocratic parties in these countries are too insignificant to threaten the functioning of the democratic process. For a while, the British Communist Party succeeded in getting a single representative elected to the House of Commons; it has had none for many years. In the Scandinavian countries Communists are somewhat stronger but still of distinctly minor importance. In none of these countries have Communists ever ventured seriously into action disruptive of the democratic process, even if, as in Sweden, they sometimes control the margin of Lower House votes, which can provide the Social Democratic Party with a legislative majority. This is not a miraculous coincidence. The reader may be tempted to dismiss the equal treatment pattern with a shrug of the shoulders and an impatient, "They can well afford it." What matters, however, is not *that* they may still indulge in the luxury of equal treatment, but *why* they may. The absence of a Fascist threat is too elementary to be looked into. And that these countries know of no present or foreseeable future danger of a Communist assault on the political order must in essence be ascribed to two sets of historical conditions: (a) deep-rooted in these countries, democratic legality has become the only conceivable basis of all social and political action. It has become absurd to assume that legally established government could violate the legal order to stay in office indefinitely and prevent changes. Experience has convincingly disproved such notions. (b) And it is precisely the Communists' questionable loyalty to democratic institutions which isolate them from the social strata to which they appeal. British or Scandinavian workers don't need the Communists to tell them how to establish public ownership in industry and transportation, control private investment, plan manpower allocation, satisfy consumer needs through nonprivate outlets (co-ops), industrialize agriculture and dictate its production program, build an all-embracing social security system, or "socialize medicine." To the extent that workers respond to socialist stimuli, the Communist Party cannot sell them wares which they have; to the extent that the Communist Party fails to respond to democratic stimuli and refuses to bow out of existence, it sells out its chance to attract even passing attention.

The proven possibility of farreaching change within the framework of democratic institutions leads to some increase in the average citizen's interest and participation in public life. This in turn insures higher

---

ternal union relations as the main and purely political battleground of Communism. Its interesting concluding section discusses differences between British and United States approaches to the problem, especially emphasizing the missing rewards for an anti-Communist political career.

standards of performance and incorruptibility in administrative services, the judiciary, management of public enterprise, social agencies, labor unions, and so on. Social and economic discrimination against religious or ethnic minorities has practically disappeared. Labor relations look back on a history of increasing recourse to legal procedure; physical coercion from above and destructive violence from below are a dim memory of the dark ages. All this has resulted in general acceptance of an unwritten code of conduct and morality in social and political action which exposes the violator to public opprobrium, if not ostracism. Constant pressure of the "democratic climate" has introduced so high a degree of selectivity into the formation of the political elite that party, cabinet, and legislative offices in all major political groups are reserved for personnel of above-average intellectual, educational, and opinion-molding ability. Given such a situation, the Communist Party has nothing to offer that seems preferable to the prevailing democratic climate and the prospects of social change within the framework of democratic legality.

C. EQUAL TREATMENT AND THE FUTURE OF DEMOCRATIC INSTITUTIONS

It may be argued that only unique historical situations permit such easy, favorable, democratic solutions; and that, in the absence of exceptional conditions, necessity imposes a different approach to a more tangible and imminent antidemocratic menace. But it is hard to see how, for example, complete or partial legal suppression of the American Communist Party would provide a quicker rate of urban renewal, eliminate racketeering, raise the intellectual and educational level of political officeholders, abolish political illiteracy all around, eradicate corruption in public life, obliterate all traces of traditional violence in labor disputes, and banish racism. It would be no less logical to expect it to make good spellers out of the average crop of college students.

If inherited shortcomings of the democratic process in the United States make the threat to democratic institutions appear slightly more menacing than it is in countries that "can afford" to guarantee equal treatment to hostile groups, imposition of new restrictions would hardly be the best way to overcome old weaknesses and correct clearly cherished wrongs.

This is almost too obvious to emphasize. Some judges concede the point when they draw a line between the repressive verdict's legal structure, which they endorse, and its relevance or usefulness in social and political terms, which they refuse to pass on. In confining themselves

to legal exegesis, they evade the crucial issue. Conclusions are ⏐
the outside observer.

It does not require particular sagacity to realize that legal repre
of democratic mass movements is bound to be futile in the long
In specific instances it may nonetheless reduce the danger of unchecked
violence threatening to engulf both oppressor and oppressed; the path
of accommodation and orderly retreat need not be made impassable.
Resorted to by a minority in power, legal repression may benefit the
oppressed majority, leaving the oppressor no choice but to make concessions or forgo the benefit of constitutional government.

There is no need to tap the arsenal of legal repression when groups
hostile to the established order are weak. And there is ample reason
not to do so. The ligaments of democratic institutions are apt to suffer
in a society which concentrates its energies on repressing malcontents
rather than solving essential problems of human living; the degree of
damage will vary with the intensity with which the community lets itself
be saddled with the business of repression.

Needless to say, no democratically patterned society will tolerate unlawful violence as a way of life. The trouble is that totalitarian parties
operating under conditions of modern mass society are organized and
disciplined in such a way as to ensure alternate use of ideological and
propaganda techniques and means of physical coercion. Changeover
from one to the other—on which the party leadership has a tight grip—
is elusive. This clouds the demarcation line which should separate propaganda and teaching from planned organization of violence. Still, if the
democratic process is to be preserved, it would seem best to confine
repression to that provable specific action which clearly oversteps the
line.

Thus circumscribed, repressive action will no doubt display infirmities. It is within reason, however, to expect such infirmities not to be
submerged in undying loyalty to a martyred cause, but to be offset by
fermentation both within the hostile group and, even more, among its
uncommitted sympathizers. The hostile group's decomposition is more
likely to be furthered by improvement of society's conditions than by
sacrificial fanaticism bred in catacombs.

Aimed against sizeable hostile groups with considerable mass following, legal repression entails the perilous prospect that its initiators
and promoters will be taken farther afield than was envisaged. Masses
are not to be forcibly held underground. Unless the following of the
outlawed group retains and avails itself of the chance to infiltrate democratic mass organizations, thus tempting the government increasingly

to widen the scope of repression, millions of would-be revolutionists will be suddenly "on the loose," shorn of traditional organizational ties and loyalties of great cohesive power. Shielded from organized revolutionary assault, society may find itself exposed to unorganized protest, lawlessness, and violence of anarchic dimensions. Any attempt, repulsive per se to a democratic society, to deflect such mass aggressions into government-charted and government-operated channels, would be likely to line up easily maneuverable cohorts of uprooted men under orders— another mortal threat to the democratic process. In postwar Italy and France, where legal repression of Communist organizations of considerable magnitude and radiation loomed on the horizon, such desperate voyage toward an unknown destination was avoided, thanks chiefly to the reluctance of the Communist leaders themselves to embark on a strategy of open clashes with the established authorities. There is no guarantee that their caution will prevail forever. The problem— as the June 1960 Italian riots have shown—may arise anew.

The dilemma confronting a democratic society is whether or not repression should be used to corroborate one's own dogmatic stand. A caveat to those who choose either method. The course of repression in democratic society is paradoxical indeed. When foreseeably effective, repression seems unnecessary; when advisable in the face of a serious threat to democratic institutions, it tends to be of only limited usefulness, and it carries the germs of new, perhaps even more menacing dangers to democracy.

Apart from this sociopolitical paradox, is repression as such, viewed in a broader context, a matter of rational choice? Should it not be regarded as an elaborately rationalized expression of a deep-seated human need for aggression, violence, exercise of power, and aggressive domination? If so, it would seem all the more noteworthy that whoever advises repression in a democratic society should find himself compelled to grope for a rational validation of each repressive act that is contemplated or undertaken. Is this not at least a remarkable testimonial to the merits of constitutional processes rooted in the democratic system?

The Judge, the Defendant, and the State

Part One dealt with the historical and conceptual framework of political justice. It then discussed a number of concrete trial types and configurations, as well as variants of official policies toward obstreperous, dissident groups as a whole. Part Two turns first to some of the *dramatis personae*, especially the judge, and also the defendant and his lawyer. It discusses the organizational and societal framework for judicial action within a constitutional and, exemplified by the DDR, a one-party regime. The section concludes with analysis of a particularly frequent and characteristic subspecies of political justice, trial by fiat of a successor regime. Under discussion here will be the major problem areas of such a trial, the nature and quality of political jurisdiction, the relation of the judge to the regime under which he serves, and the problems of differentiating between political and criminal responsibility. These lead to an evaluation of both the benefits and limitations of the most prominent of the successor trials of our generation: the Nuremberg trial.

CHAPTER V

CONDITIONS OF JUDICIAL ACTION

++

Se défier de la magistrature, est un commencement de dissolution;
détruisez l'institution, réconstruisez là sur d'autres bases . . . mais
y croyez!

—HONORÉ BALZAC, *Splendeurs et Misères*, 3. partie*

++

1. The Job

IN autumn 1933 the British Attorney General Sir Thomas Inskip
(1876-1947) delivered an address from the pulpit of one of the small
London churches around Bloomsbury Square. During the question
period an elderly lady asked, "Sir Thomas, if Jesus our Lord came
back to earth, would we recognize and treat him accordingly?" Sir
Thomas, obviously taken aback, and unmindful that he might minimize
his embarrassment by referring his questioner to Dostoyevsky's answer,
mumbled in a somewhat halting and recalcitrant manner the reply
incumbent on a loyal and honest servant of any established regime.
How could he have done otherwise? How can the representative of an
established order accept the legitimacy of conflicting loyalty claims, even
if they are based on the invocation of the same symbols and values
which the established order invokes? The judge's patent of installation
is at the same time the millstone around his neck.

Claims have to be measured by some yardstick and his yardstick
must be the order which installed him. If the judges were at the same
time Camus' juges-pénitents, knowing that their titles have been disproven and disallowed, they could not fulfill the functions for which
they were chosen. If they are playing their roles, they must assume not
only that the powers which sent and put them there can maintain and
support them, but that their backers' titles can withstand inspection.

The question may not arise every day. Most of their clientele live in
the same universe as the judges do. If they transgress the law, even the
very act of transgression is, as Hegel put it, nothing but its affirmation.
The transgressor's goals are those of the world which surrounds him;

* "To distrust the judiciary marks the beginning of the end of society. Smash the
present patterns of the institution, rebuild it on a different basis . . . but don't stop
believing in it."

he only tries some shortcuts which the judge is wont to disallow in the interest of his competitors, who scramble after the same goals in society's approved ways. If somebody robs a bank because bank robbing is after all his trade, and a highly specialized and uncertain one at that, no question of principle arises between the robber and society. Whatever the penal theory of the individual judge—retribution, the wholesome effect on the offender, or a similar effect on potential offenders—the robber must pay the penalty for his unorthodox methods. If a modern combination of Robin Hood and Saint Elizabeth robs a bank in order to distribute the fruit of his labors among the starving and forgotten, he is classified as a crank—if he does it once. After a repeat performance, he will be styled a specially pernicious criminal; he will be in imminent danger, in the same category with the youthful Stalin who robbed a bank to help finance his revolutionary organization.

The affront to the established order may appear in endless variations. Whether the attack is a frontal or a flanking movement, however, the title of the established power holders may be none the safer for it. Yet under what we have come to know as a constitutional system, the difference between the frontal and the flanking attack may involve subtle questions of legality. And the same judge who represents the existing order has a mandate to distinguish the various shades of attacks.

But despite this unavoidable ambiguity of his position as bonded defender of existing institutions and the guarantor of their fairness, there is not much merit in the often-heard epithet, "soldier of the law."[1] Those who invoke it most consistently never doubt that it refers to the judge's duty to underpin with his authority the action of the existing power holders. But even if maintenance of the public order forms part of his function, his services would become meaningless if he were to act as a soldier. While both the soldier and the judge owe loyalty, the different objects of their loyalty—the hierarchical command and the mandate of the law—condition differential loyalty structures. In the hierarchical chain of command a soldier obeys orders which he may

---

[1] "Eh bien messieurs, ai-je l'air d'avoir peur? Tous ici magistrats nous sommes à notre poste de combat et nous ne le déserterons point. Si l'un tombe, l'autre ramasse le drapeau et marche en avant. Il y aura toujours des soldats et des magistrats tant qu'il aura des lois, un drapeau et une patrie." This is how Quesnay de Beaurepaire, prosecuting Ravarol in 1892, addressed the judges, seeking to overcome their fear that they, like one of their colleagues, might become the butt of anarchist violence. Quoted in Pierre Bouchardon, *Le Magistrat*, Paris, 1926, p. 121. Clemenceau used the same figure of speech when beating down parliamentary opposition to the handling of proceedings in the Caillaux case (see above, Ch. III, 3A). So did Nebelung, one of the judges acquitted in the Justice trial in Nuremberg, when addressing the court. Justice trial transcript, October 12, 1947, p. 10,353.

reject only in extreme and manifest situations of illegality, and then only at his own risk and peril. The law is not a chain of command and knows no soldier to execute its orders. Being a directive toward reasoned investigation, interpretation, and consequent findings, it requires something other than the devotion of an activist. The latter creates a new reality; the judge, acting in most cases on a situation created by others, grants or withholds legitimacy.

The policeman makes an arrest, the administrator refuses a building permit, the executive board of a union expels a member, a wife leaves her husband—the court cannot obliterate the consequences of such actions, regardless of whether the action is later upheld or invalidated. The man arrested by the police will, as a rule, suffer in community esteem even if he is later on released on the basis of an alibi. The man who had to fight for a year or two through boards and courts to get his building permit may meanwhile have lost his chance for a favorable mortgage arrangement. Regardless of what future chances the airing of his case in court may offer him, the union member might have lost his livelihood by expulsion due to union maintenance membership provisions in the contract or simply the hostility of his coworkers. The mere fact of desertion drastically changes the relation between the partners to a marriage, no matter what dramatic and unforeseen turn their relations might take during divorce proceedings. Whatever its power, the court cannot recapture a situation which the very fact of action has changed beyond redemption. At times the irrevocable effect of action may be so strong that the other party resigns itself to its consequences, especially if the actor should be prudent enough to pay a price for the other party's recognition of the new *status quo*. But sometimes either such renunciation will not take place, or, as in an arrest, the legal order will make validation a prerequisite for maintaining the status created by the action. In both circumstances a contest as to the legitimacy of the action will take place. At times the parties concerned may be in a position or, due to practical or legal barriers, may be forced to defer action until a judgment has confirmed their claim; if so, the relation between action and legitimation will be reversed, with legitimation becoming a condition precedent to action. At any rate, it is as a legitimizer or an "illegitimizer" of particular action patterns that the court will be asked to intervene. It is probable that in many of these instances the party, whether a government agency or private party, will, with the help of competent legal advice, model its action so as to fully expect the benefits of legislation and previous court rulings. But whatever the excellence of the party's tactical situation, its conversion into a legally enforceable claim needs confirmation by the one state agency to which such function has been entrusted. If so asked, it becomes the court's particular business to choose which of the many possible claim situations should be legitimized, that is, equipped with a title for enforcement by state organs.[2]

This need for legitimation by some outside, neutral source may not always be self-evident. The actor may reject such a course as incompatible with the meaning, dignity, and self-evident character of his deed; or popular acclaim may seem to make recourse to a different source of legitimacy supererogatory. But such cases of avowedly revolutionary action aside, power wielders are prone to invoke court sanction all the more eagerly if they feel the need to minimize the novelty and shock of new departures by having them assimilated to traditional ways of proceeding. Whether they will always be willing to pay the price of such legitimation is another matter. Governments might try to square the circle, reaping the benefit of recognition of their action patterns while unwilling to take the risks involved in invoking court approval. As we shall see later, this is where the fine dividing line appears between a true legitimizer and a fraudulent one, between a court and a drum court. On the other hand, those who have suffered from the hands of the wielders of official or unofficial power will generally not want to miss whatever chance the resort to court proceedings may open up for them, regardless of whether such resort remains their only weapon or serves only as one among several interconnected means of defense or counterattack.

The legitimizer's authority rests on the community's preparedness to recognize the judge's capacity to lend legitimacy to or withdraw it from an individual's act. Thus the judge's very function presupposes the separation between action and legitimation. Only revealed truth carries legitimacy in the substance of its message. And even then, adversaries and competitors might deny its claim to legitimacy. As Cardinal Bérulle fashioned the counterclaim, "Ces gens [the Protestants] sont sans autorité de la part de Jésus, comme si Dieu (lequel ils disent les envoyer pour des effets si grands et si divins) avait oublié à les pouvoir d'une autorité légitime et à leur donner les marques du ciel, qui ont toujours accompagné ceux qui ont été envoyé de sa part."[3]

The separation between the line of action and the line of legitimation does not necessarily coincide with the other great divide, between norm

---

[2] J. Goldschmidt, *Der Prozess als Rechtslage*, Berlin, 1925, pp. 151, 490ff.

[3] *Correspondence*, Paris-Louvain, 1937, Vol. 1, p. 110.

creation and norm implementation.[4] Both the administrator and the judge derive their formal authority from the norm. Wherever social relations are couched in the language of the law, an administrative act as well as a judicial sentence habitually refer back to the authority of the norm, password and warrant of origin if not necessarily the major determinant of the decision. Which categories from the endless stream of norm-implementing acts are singled out to be submitted to the special legitimizing procedure of the courts? Which are accepted as valid without such placet, as a matter of tradition and political choice? There is no universally accepted rule that a controversy between two parties over what rule should govern their relations must form the subject matter of a judicial decision; nor that an unchallenged petition to competent authorities for a license or a grant is the only proper subject matter for an administrative decision.[5] There are so many intermediary forms of action between a simple request to the authorities and a full-fledged controversy between legal contestants that it would be hard to make an a priori decision on the necessary form of their handling. Also, a hard and fast theoretical dividing line would unduly minimize the element of structural identity. Both the administrative act and the judicial sentence presuppose an identical mental operation: judging the applicability of the norm to the facts of the case and herewith providing a certain amount of discretion for whoever is the official interpreter of the norms.[6]

The difference seems to depend on which aspects of various subjects the community is considering. Speed or the need for special technical competence may lead to an assignment other than emphasis on absolute impartiality or broad experience in interpersonal relations. At times the community might try to combine the advantages of both proceedings, trying to secure both special competence and a knack for the impartial handling of interpersonal relations. But viewed from their difference from rather than their similarity with administrative rulings,

[4] It is becoming generally recognized that the division of state function leads to a bifurcation between norm creation and decision of individual cases, rather than to the traditional division into three powers. The most searching discussion of this complex problem may be found in Hermann Jahreiss, "Die Wesensverschiedenheit der Akte des Herrschens und das Problem der Gewaltenteilung," *Mensch und Staat*, Koeln, 1957, pp. 175-95.

[5] Richard Thoma and Gerhard Anschuetz, eds., *Handbuch des Staatsrechts*, Tübingen, 1932, Vol. 2, p. 133. But see the criticism of E. Friesenhahn, "Über Begriff und Arten der Rechtsprechung," *Festgabe für Richard Thoma*, Tübingen, 1950.

[6] Chester Bernard, *The Function of the Executive*, New York, 1950, p. 280, calls the judicial process a "highly specialized administrative process." See also Hans Kelsen, *Justiz und Verwaltung*, Berlin, 1929. Kelsen, however, overstates the case.

judicial proceedings stand out both by their required degree of formalization and, just as clearly, by the distinctive position of the official handling them. The administrator is a line official whose findings may be superseded, and who himself may be replaced at times by his hierarchical superiors, who can thus carry their viewpoint to victory with a minimum of friction. The judge, whether constitutional, administrative, penal, or civil, has been maximally immunized against governmental and other pressures by rules governing both his tenure and his assurance that the case once put into his hands, according to prearranged rules of caseload distribution, will remain there. He has the additional assurance that his decision, if reviewable at all, may be reopened only before persons and bodies working and deciding under similar conditions. Moreover, there are exceedingly narrow limits within which the judge may transfer part of his business to any substitute, even if the substitute is a member of the judicial body itself. The calling of the judge, in contrast to the holding of an administrative job, is distinctly personal and nontransferable.[7] It is not the policy of the office, but the perception and reasoning of the man directly in charge, that matters. By the judge's person and office being lifted out of the stream of administrative offices and actions, he is kept from giving more than perfunctory attention to matters of feasibility and practicability, presumably examined beforehand. He is invited to concentrate on providing both private and public action alike with a more permanent certificate of legal correctness, conformity, or nonconformity with the law.

Much of the meaning and authority of the judge depends, of course, on the practices governing his selection. In the Western world at present there are, broadly speaking, two bases for recruitment. On the European continent, judicial officeholding has become by and large an official career. Having passed the necessary university courses and qualifying exams, a young man, or, in recent times in some countries, a young woman,[8] may enter into its lower grades and thus open up the ex-

---

[7] For a discussion of the requirements, see Helmut K. J. Ridder, *Empfiehlt es sich, die vollständige Selbstverwaltung aller Gerichte im Rahmen des Grundgesetzes gesetzlich einzuführen?* Verhandlungen des 40. deutschen Juristentages, Öffentlichrechtliche Abteilung, Tübingen, 1953, p. 129.

[8] The professional entrance examination for the judicial career in France has been open to women since 1946. Among the 202 candidates who presented themselves in 1958, 120 were women. (*Pouvoir Judiciaire*, July-August 1958, p. 4). However, the recent (1958/1959) French judicial reform involving substantial salary raises might reverse the trend; the problem of judicial office as a career for women is treated, with some comparative material, in the April 1956 issue of *Pouvoir Judiciaire*. According to Sir Carlton Allen ("The Layman and the Law," *Journal of the International Com-*

pectation for a lifetime job. As against the continental judge, product of a career planned in advance, the office of Anglo-American judge is seen as a crowning of a successful and unblemished career in law, whether in private practice, as prosecutor, and, more recently (and still somewhat suspect), as a government lawyer in the service of an administrative office or agency. In contrast to this attempt at cross-fertilization, the continental judge remains the product of a narrower education. With the exception of a career in the highest specialized courts (conseil d'état, constitutional courts, supreme labor courts, and so on), climbing the steps of the judicial ladder remains the near-monopoly of those who started at the base. Cross-fertilization remains an intraservice affair. It is limited either to mutations from the ranks of the prosecutor's office—the half resigned, half relieved, "Je me fais asseoir" one sometimes hears from a French procureur—or to appointments to the higher courts from the number of those judges, prosecutors, and other officials who have served a stint in the central judicial administration. These appointments are often bitterly resented by those who try to climb their way up through the ranks. As the continental judicial cadres may be quite large,[9] the Achilles heel of the continental judicial system, as Jhering[10] called it, remains the question of the criteria for advancement rather than for the original appointment which, once the necessary prerequisites are fulfilled, is more in the nature of a routine matter. In the Anglo-American system there are fewer judges. They are paid, not like their continental brethren according to civil service schedules, but according to a scale that is comparable to the lower ranks of private executives. The possibility for advancement is correspondingly rare and

mission of Jurists, Vol. 2 [1959], p. 77), a quarter of all English justices of the peace, who handle over 95 per cent of the criminal prosecutions, are now women.

[9] Germany in 1957: 11,360 judges plus 1,554 prosecutors (Deutsche Richterzeitung, Vol. 35 [1957], p. 110). France, as of January 1, 1960: 5,537 judges and prosecutors (Pouvoir Judiciaire, September-October 1960). In both cases, the count includes only those judges who come under the jurisdiction of the Ministry of Justice; this excludes those sitting in administrative and other specialized courts.

A recent inquiry into the social background of the French metropolitan judiciary gives the following picture. Of 1,233 judges, 8 have a working class background; to this group some from the category monde rural—a total of 80—might have to be added. There is a strong professional contingent: 104 whose fathers were judges, 130 in other law jobs, 4 clergymen, 87 school teachers, 56 physicians, 72 in the army, 153 civil servants, 117 business men, 30 industrialists, and 60 in banking and insurance. In 332 cases the father had died, or no indication of professional background was available. (André Sauvageot, "Les origines sociales de la Magistrature d'aujourd'hui," Pouvoir Judiciaire, January 1960.)

[10] R. Jhering, Zweck im Recht, Leipzig, 3rd ed.; 1916, Vol. 1, p. 304.

none too important.[11] In this system it is the criteria for initial appointment which matter.

Emphasis for original selection in Anglo-American practice, and for promotion on the continent, rests on an admixture of elements of co-optation and selection by political authority. Popular election, though still practiced in United States territorial units, is being pushed back into a mere confirmation of the combined co-optation and political selection practices. Co-optation—whether based on the recommendation of the whole legal fraternity, as in the recommendation of the bar, or, as in continental Europe, on those of the senior judges rating their junior colleagues—lays the stress on personal integrity, conformity with prevailing thought patterns, and intelligence in the job. Given the difference in composition and outlook of those consulted, the European emphasis slants more toward seniority, while Anglo-American selection will fasten on personal success and personability, if reached via more or less rigidly defined socially approved paths.[12] As an exclusive principle of selection, co-optation has rarely been accepted, for it would give a self-perpetuating group too exclusive a power over the minds and attitudes of its members, at the same time fastening the group's standards and policies on the country at large. A German observer plastically compared its exclusive practice to an autonomous compass which, obeying its own laws, hangs freely in the belly of the democratic ship of state. Due to its strategic position, it would soon determine the course of the ship without need to follow the order of any helmsman.[13] But to a degree of admixture constantly modified and subject to the vicissitudes of changing political requirements, co-optation has always had an important place in selection practices.

Limited and circumscribed by the necessary regard for the principle of co-optation, final executive decision rests on the following considerations: in a political system still largely personalized, as in the United States, first consideration, within the framework of regional quotas and recognized denominational, national, and racial group claims,[14] goes to

[11] See the interesting recent statement of Judge Charles Wyzanski, declining promotion from the district bench to the Federal Appeal Court, *New York Times*, January 22, 1959, p. 16.

[12] Some useful hints may be found in A. Von Mehren, "The Judicial Process: A Comparative Analysis," *American Journal of Comparative Law*, Vol. 5 (1956), pp. 147-228.

[13] Ridder, *op.cit.*, p. 124.

[14] Of course, distribution quotas are subject to change: appointing authorities might have the perspicacity to recognize a new group claim, which gains them the gratitude of the group members. And once it is recognized, every political competitor will, for future appointments, have to honor the group claim, which has meanwhile become the norm for distribution.

friendship and political debt to those who have furthered and supported the appointer's career. The personal element aside, selection is political in two, not necessarily related, ways. As a rule, appointment will be restricted to members of the majority party who are connected with, working for, or strongly recommended by the party's important regional officeholders.[15] At the same time, selection will fall on those who will be assumed to be in general sympathy with the social and economic outlook of the incumbent administration; this will be at least partly reflected in the distribution of the nominees among the various law jobs (university teachers, members of regulatory commissions, corporation lawyers, and so on). The claims of lame duck politicians will be given sympathetic consideration by their respective political friends. While the recent requirement of a full FBI field investigation adds possible respectability to the political choice, it makes it rather unlikely that personalities as "controversial" in their previous careers as Justices Brandeis or Black would ever ascend to the bench.[16]

Despite these manifest shortcomings of appointment procedures, the mere fact that appointment—which, by the federal government, is almost exclusively for life—often comes at the zenith of a successful legal career is not without its consequences. It allows, and at least on the federal level conduces to, some detachment from former associations, if not necessarily habits of thought. It encourages a concentration on making a name that conforms with the standards of a profession whose traditional prestige is higher than that of the continental European judge, who is considered on a level with other state functionaries. Unperturbed by promotion considerations,[17] which may breed a peculiarly

[15] The rules suffer some exception when, as in the United States in the second half of the fifties, the Republican executive which appoints and the Democratic Senate majority which confirms are beholden to different patronage organizations; the organizations' claims have to be compromised, or a deadlock and a backlog of unfilled jobs will develop.

[16] For the official formulas for the present selection practices, as seen through the eyes of their promoter, see William P. Rogers, "Judicial Appointments Under the Eisenhower Administration," *Journal of the American Judicature Association*, Vol. 41 (1957), pp. 38-42.

[17] Of course, even in the United States promotion may follow what must appear to many as a successful handling of a particular case. To weigh the merits of Judge Medina's promotion we must take into consideration the popular image of his being crucified by the Communist lawyers—a consideration that scarcely stands professional scrutiny (see the dispassionate analysis of Justice Frankfurter in Sacher v. U.S., 343 U.S. 1, 23, 38 [1951], and the U.S. Supreme Court Record, Vols. 341, 494-532, Part 6, pp. 3,863, 8,571). Medina's handling of the trial, his summation and sentencing, as well as the subsequent contempt proceedings against the defense lawyers, were widely applauded by the American public at large. His promotion thus expresses a complete

neurotic state of mind (characterized aptly the search for the learned rather than the just decision),[18] the judge may be more inclined to consider himself the representative of society at large rather than of its momentary political structure.

Before entering into the difficulties of this proposition, some comparison with European practices seems appropriate. Compared with American practices, both English and continental selection seem recently to have veered toward a more conscious emphasis on purely professional qualifications. This is increasingly true for England, where governmental leaders after the war have shown some reserve in espousing previously traditional claims to high judicial office that rest on a political rather than professional basis.[19] However, the office of police court magistrate or justice of the peace, except for forty legally trained magistrates in metropolitan areas, is as much a political reward, if not more (due to the absence of needed professional qualifications provided by his clerk), than its American counterpart. In continental Europe renewed emphasis on professional aptitude has gone hand in hand with closer scrutiny of a candidate's whole record for promotion by a body more representative of the community at large. This has been one of the reasons for taking appointments from the exclusive control of the ministries of justice. While generally keeping in line with promotion selections submitted in more or less formalized way by regional senior judges, the ministries of justice retained enough job control to engage in the time-honored practice of rewarding politically deserving judges and prosecutors and coldshouldering or putting in storage the promotion of judges who had made political enemies.[20] The new appointment committees or judicial councils, composed of members of the ministries of justice, delegates chosen by the judiciary, and members or nominees of parliaments, have led to a blending of the principles of co-optation and political appointments, possibly cutting off some of

---

identity of popular and governmental judgment, pointing to the fallibility of both. For some appropriate comparisons from eighteenth and nineteenth century British cases showing the doubtful meaning of contemporary executive and parliamentary approval of judicial action patterns, see Henry Cockburn, *op.cit.*, Vol. i, p. 90.

[18] P. Calamandrei, *Procedure and Democracy*, New York, 1957, p. 44.

[19] See the excellent and vivid picture drawn by R. M. A. Jackson, *The March of Justice in England*, 3rd ed.; Cambridge, 1960, pp. 236-37.

[20] Pierre Bouchardon, the examining judge who instructed the case against Caillaux (and who, a quarter of a century later, was to head the commission instructing the case against Laval) went to see Camille Chautemps, after Chautemps became minister of justice in the revived 1924 Cartell des Gauches, to complain about his not receiving any promotion. Chautemps' advice was, "Faites-vous oublier." Bouchardon, *Mes Souvenirs*, Paris, 1953, p. 129.)

the rough edges of both.[21] In France only, the advent of the present authoritarian-bureaucratic regime has not only abolished a modicum of parliament-controlled participation in the Council of the Magistracy, but has also emancipated the council completely, re-establishing in only thinly disguised form full executive control of appointments and promotions.[22]

The judge's job consists in individualizing the norm. The cleavage which separates the norm giver from the norm interpreter is construed as a protective device for both. That the judge cannot do what the legislator is doing to establish the general rule, and that the legislator is not supposed to exercise the judge's legitimate duty to ferret out the facts in a case and their relation to the general norm: this is one element of freedom in society.[23] Delightfully simple in theory, the distinction is not always as easy in daily practice. Norms are not meant for eternity. Their existence is geared not only to long-term community needs but also to individual sets of circumstances and specific sociopolitical configurations of the age. Some of these configurations may be so unique, overpowering, complex, and delicate that there is little room for differentiating between the construction of the principle and the rule for the case. Both remain inextricably mixed and the executive may want to remain in command of the situation. Yet what was yesterday's unique case might by tomorrow become a settled way of life, liable to be entrusted to the judiciary under general legal instructions mirroring a new societal equilibrium.

[21] However, these committees in which prosecutors are not represented have somehow narrowed the prosecutors' promotion chances via migration to the ranks of the judiciary. In France, Article 1 of Ordinance 1271 (see n. 22 below) has belatedly rectified this oversight. Usually in France not more than 20 to 40 prosecutors are annually elevated to judicial office; see the interesting discussion, "Siège et Parquet," in *Pouvoir Judiciaire*, May 1959, p. 45.

[22] The ordinances 1270/58 and 1271/58 of December 22, 1958 leave only the nomination of first presidents of appeal courts and councillors of the Cour de Cassation to the Judicial Council (Art. 12 of Ord. 1271). In all other cases the Council may only tender advice. The promotion list is prepared by a commission sitting with six representatives of the judiciary and the service heads of the Ministry of Justice (Art. 35 of Ord. 1270). As to the actual conditions under which the Council was forced to exercise its "right of advice" to hundreds of nominations of the de Gaulle regime, *see* M. Rossignol, *Pouvoir Judiciaire*, March 1959. A recent decree (1380/160, December 21, 1960), which allows the transfer of metropolitan judges to Algeria for six-month periods, endangers the immovability of French judges. The text of the decree, together with a number of protests, has been reprinted in *Pouvoir Judiciaire*, January and February 1961.

[23] Adolf Arndt, *Das Bild des Richters*, Karlsruhe, 1957, p. 16.

At times the legislator might not be satisfied with such general instructions. He may want to impart his energies and his particular and momentary vistas to the work of the judiciary. He may describe in great detail the factual situation which he wants to regulate, so to speak, already anticipating the rule for the case.[24] But if the disguise wears too thin, if the description is ostensibly chosen to deprive the judge of his freedom of appreciation, whether or not an individual case fits the legislative description, the judge will have to apply for a different job description: the legitimizer becoming a registrar, a change expensive not only for those who suffer its consequences, but for the prestige of those who ordered it and of those who must carry it out.

The line of separation between norm creation and its individualization, however, does not necessarily mean, as one might want to conclude, that the judge's job is nonpolitical. The dichotomy of general rule–individual decision does not coincide with a further differentiation between the setting of the community's pace and the implementation of political decisions down the line. The idyllic picture of a strong political leadership making the fundamental decisions of the realm with an elite of judges and civil servants willingly administering within this framework to the daily needs and sorrows of the people at large[25] projects an utopian concept, rather than the reality of nineteenth century constitutional monarchy, into the reality of twentieth century mass democracy. In the real picture of nineteenth century constitutional monarchy, the judge, functioning both as representative of officialdom and interpreter and guarantor of the security needs of civil soicety, had a thoroughly political function.

The distinction between the legal and political functions cannot be grounded in the judge's relation to the antecedent norm or in any possible variation of Montesquieu's famous mouthpiece analogy. Undoubtedly judges are occasionally, sometimes habitually, prone to enter polite doubts of the wisdom of the statute over whose enforcement they

---

[24] The difficulty of differentiating between laws for individual cases—arising from special situations or the absence of general legislation—and iniquitous laws violating the principle of equality before the law, establishing privileges, and granting special dispensations or visiting special punishments on individuals, have often been discussed. For recent discussions, see *Das Gesetz als Norm und Massnahme* (Veroeffentlichungen der Deutschen Staatsrechtslehrer, Heft 15), Berlin, 1957; and, with a wealth of material, Hans Schneider, "Über Einzelfallgesetze," *Festschrift für Carl Schmitt*, Berlin, 1959, p. 159. Few laws are as clearly discriminatory ad personam enactments as the one dealt with in United States v. Lovett, 328 U.S. 303 (1946). For a recent marginal German case, see Chapter VIII, n. 36 below.

[25] See Werner Weber, *Spannungen und Kraefte im Westdeutschen Verfassungssystem*, 2nd ed.; Stuttgart, 1958, pp. 112ff.

have been made to preside, but insisting all the same on applying the law as they find it. But even in countries where no explicit mandate or permission to examine the constitutionality of legal enactment enlarges the discretion of the judge, the half explanatory, half apologetic reference to the judge's subservience to the law is at best a playful protective device; at worst it testifies to his unwillingness to understand his own role in the social process. His job, the decision of individual conflict situations, takes place within the double limits of traditional procedure and statutory enactments. At the same time, it presupposes either open or implied decisions on preferable, possibly conflicting sociopolitical solutions, and the most advantageous or least harmful means of reaching decisions on them.

Whether it is the intrinsic difficulty of the subject matter,[26] the intentional attempt to increase the implementing discretion for narrowing or widening the scope of application, or the momentous political need to wave the big stick of legislative action while smuggling into it the possibility for avoiding its use, it is the character of the implementation which determines the life history of the norm. The validity of a norm does not follow from its existence, but from the fate it suffers in the administrative and judicial process.[27] Even a crystal-clear norm remains meaningless when it meets steadfast administrative and judicial avoidance. Yet the clarity and preciseness of a norm may be in inverse proportion to the importance of its subject matter.

The judge's decision is therefore perforce no less related to the realization of community values than the decisions of other participants in the political process. The difference, if there is one, is elsewhere. It lies in the interstitial character of judicial action. A government, its administrative branches, or a modern political party work around the clock, or at least their publicity agents will work overtime to create such an impression. The unsettled status of international affairs, the military programs contingent on such a state of affairs, and the concomitant need to keep the underlying population in the right mixture of appreciation and apprehensiveness create a neverending stream of govern-

[26] Glenville L. Williams, "Language and the Law," *Law Quarterly Review*, Vol. 61 (1945), p. 62: "It is far easier to make a statute which contains large determinables than limited ones, but if we wish to see clearly . . . we must avoid words like just and reasonable and properly, and similar almost indefinitely extensible terms. The words have so little color of their own, that they can be made to take almost any hue we desire."

[27] "Positive norms can be compared to crystals which are deposited in a saturated solution and continue to be maintained by that solution, but which would break down, if they were placed in a different fluid." Alf Ross, *On Law and Justice*, London, 1958, p. 98.

mental programs and actions. Nevertheless, the day-to-day relations which govern communications between government and individuals and between the individuals themselves are only partially affected by this surfeit of feverish activity. Even in a society like ours, undergoing profound structural changes over relatively short periods, interpersonal relations over wide areas have recognized rules. When innovations are introduced, their mutually beneficial character is stressed by those most interested in their adoption; frequently they are either voluntarily accepted or the sense of community approval may be so obvious, clearcut, and overwhelmingly strong, that potential dissenters are forced into a pattern of resigned toleration. If these conditions are absent, litigation will result. To be sure, there are, as touched upon before, a great many situations where the settled ways of community affairs necessitate court intervention in each and every case without drawing into doubt settled rules or involving the development of new community patterns: divorce, confirmation of a preliminary arrest, disposal of a criminal action come to mind. But the concept of interstitial action refers not to the number of these routine affairs the courts participate in; it refers to the frequency of their exercising the right of overseeing by doubting, checking, remodeling, or forcing changes in the actions of other participants in the political process. Even so, it remains courts' particular prerogative that they may without much notice re-examine any routine action which hitherto passed inspection without difficulty, consider it in a new light, and turn it into a contest over a principle. "Interstitial" thus means that the courts are occasional rather than regular participants in the community's vital policy actions. Only a severely truncated segment of community actions—and not always those that are most urgent—ends up in the courts. The composition of this segment is determined by both the strategy of private parties and the varying needs of public authorities.

Thus interstitial decisions imply above all that the court has to wait until an action is brought before it. The decision on what action to bring or refrain from bringing to the court, under what form or heading to bring it, and when and to some extent where to start it must necessarily be of vast, often determinative influence on the work of the court.

2. Patterns of Prosecution

Among those who might take the initiative for putting the court machinery into motion, the state has a particular place. It maintains a staff of trained lawyers, steeped in doing the ground work for initiating court action; but in our day and age this is a feature of any major private corporation. Unlike the corporation bureaucracy, however, it may not only enter into contests of how to define, maintain, or advance the boundary line of private power positions, but may also move directly toward taking away life or personal freedom indefinitely. Hierarchically organized, those entrusted with this sensitive chore have a dual point of reference: the legal norm and the political leadership of their time and period.

Statutory rules and practice might in theory offer a variety of approaches to the prosecutor's job. One might start from the assumption that whenever a violation of a norm comes to the notice of the authorities, the perpetrator ought to be prosecuted. Or, beginning from the opposite assumption, law enforcement is a matter within the lawful discretion of the authorities, which gives their activities from the outset a permissive and selective look.[28] The differences in practice between the continental legality principle and Anglo-American selectivity (which

---

[28] Modern administrative practices create infinite ways to become liable to criminal prosecution. For example, Form 57, to be filled out by every applicant for a federal job, asks the applicant to list all arrests and charges since he has passed his sixteenth year and the nature of the final disposal of the case, excluding only minor traffic violations. (This, incidentally, throws a curious light on official evaluations of acquittals or a magistrate's reasons for dismissing a case.)

Unlike the European law, the statutory body of the United States and of any of the states will not allow the applicant to pass over those misdemeanors or even felonies of ancient vintage, which time and his consequent good conduct might be deemed to have extinguished, and which, under continental usage, have been consequently expunged from his judicial record. Faced with the alternative of either substantially diminishing his chances of being considered for the job, or having the Damocles sword of discovery and potential prosecution for misstatement hang over his head (18 U.S.C. 1001, 62 Stat. 749 [1948]), the applicant is likely to take whatever course his personal makeup and the circumstances of his life situation command. If the variance is discovered, he becomes not only liable to dismissal, but his case might be sent to the Justice Department for possible prosecution. The latter practice may be the exception rather than the rule, and the administrator might be satisfied with speedy and noiseless removal of the person from his roster. Moreover, the Department of Justice might choose not to prosecute—somewhat different from its practice when misstatements on Form 57 concern the hiding of some former "subversive" connection. (See the Annual Report of the Attorney General of the U.S., 1957, p. 58.)

But the unnecessarily broad formula, coupled with the absence of a mandatory forgiveness statute (the urgent need for such a statute is discussed in Aaron Nussbaum, *First Offenders—A Second Chance,* New York, 1956), increases the number of potential legal traps for the unwary, thus contributing to the feeling of anxiety, apprehension, powerlessness, and consequent subservience to established authority so detrimental to the concept of active citizenship. How the elements of a criminal record may be artificially built up from a defendant's reluctance to lay open small, politically tinged convictions in naturalization proceedings may be seen from the dissenting opinion of Justice Clark in Chaunt v. U.S., 364 U.S. 350, 356 (1960). It is "the jungle panic of the primitive," as a great writer calls the fear of punishment and the attending general anxiety in the face of officialdom. Hermann Broch, *Gesammelte Werke,* Erkennen und Handeln, Vol. 2, Zürich, 1955, p. 237.

is motivated if for no other reason than by the sheer magnitude of the job)[29] are not so radical as their theoretical differences might suggest. First, the continental system has been forced to make explicit allowance for some measure of selectivity, both in minor offenses and in the political field.[30] Second, under both systems the private party with a vested interest to see the prosecution get started retains some right, however ineffective, to complain via judicial channels, with the ultimate goal of browbeating the prosecution into initiating criminal proceedings. But vastly more important, under either system the evaluation of the chances of the prosecution, especially the scrutiny of the character and sufficiency of available testimony, reopens wide areas of legitimate discretion. As a rule, this discretion will not be misplaced in a case without political connotation. The robber, murderer or arsonist will go to trial whenever the evidence warrants an indictment. And the fact that the prosecution may be theoretically at the bidding of the political authorities will make no difference. Trouble becomes more frequent when either the person or the connections of the suspect person, or the nature of the offense to be charged, or both, produce uncertainties, recrimina-

[29] A concise and realistic statement of the functions of the American prosecutor has been made by Attorney General, later Justice Robert H. Jackson, in "The Federal Prosecution," an address reprinted in *Journal of the American Judicature Society*, Vol. 24 (1940), pp. 18-20. Some comparative hints are given in J. C. Smith, "Personnel of Criminal Law in England and U.S.," *Cambridge Law Journal*, 1955, pp. 80-100. Some dissatisfaction with the working of the legality system in political cases pervades the instructive little book of the German Chief Federal Prosecutor, Max Güde, *Probleme des politischen Strafrechts*, Hamburg, 1957, esp. pp. 13, 23. (For recent changes, see n. 30 below.)

[30] The most recent German legislative effort in this field (Par. 153[c] of the Code of Criminal Procedure) allows the Federal Attorney, with the permission of the Federal Court, to *nol pros* a political case. This is done not only for timely repentance and to assist in preventing harmful effects, etc., but also "if the carrying through of the prosecution would endanger the security of the realm"—a consideration which obviously has no relation to the guilt of the defendant, but rests entirely on an evaluation of political circumstances. The Federal Attorney, in defending this novelty (Güde, "Legalitätsbegriff und Rechtsstaat," *Monatschrift für Deutsches Recht*, Vol. 12 [1958], p. 285), remarked correctly that with this development the principle of legality loses its "sharp-edged antithetical character."

Even a recent decision of the Federal Court, September 23, 1960 (3 StR 2/60), which exalts the legality principle in political cases, is forced to admit the existence of these statutory exceptions, which for all practical purposes do away with the principle itself.

Despite the ambiguous wording of Art. 1 of her Code of Criminal Procedure, France follows strictly the "opportunity" principle (A. Vitu, *Procédure Pénal*, Paris, 1957, pp. 242-43); so does Italy. For a comparative survey of the fields of application of the principles of "opportunity" and "legality," see F. Clerc, *Actes du 5. Congrès International de Droit Pénal*, Geneva, 1947, pp. 212ff.

tions, and various pressures. If it is the person concerned who evokes political interest—the faulty income tax return of a politician, the fraudulent contract of a politically well-connected person, or, what has become more frequent, the conflict of interest of a strategic officeholder —the balance of advantages and disadvantages of either course of action might be a delicate matter. Professionals and politicians share in this decision.

Much depends on the personality of the man who forms the link between the hierarchy of the professionals and the wider arena of politics, the attorney general or continental minister of justice. A lawyer by profession (even Hitler had in some fashion to bow to this prerogative of the legal profession), and usually a lawyer-politician by formation, he might, in America and to some extent in England, entertain legitimate hopes that his services will be rewarded by a choice judicial appointment. But even if his standing in politics is higher than his eminence in the legal profession, his is the eternal job of mediating between the pressures from the official structure, of which he forms an integral part, or, as the case may be, the unofficial substructure of the government, and the requirements of the law. The medium between the legal and the political workings of the government, he also serves as a buffer. In the eyes of the legal profession, he clothes the political decisions of the cabinet with respectability while bringing home to his brethren in the cabinet how far he might engage his and his office's reputation in the pursuit of their projects.[31] Legal requirements are tendered to him in the form of the professional advice by his staff, based on thorough study and knowledge of the particularities of the individual case, including possible variations and uncertainties of legal interpretation.

The degree of centralization of services, as between the attorney general's or the minister of justice's office and the line prosecutors attached to the various court organizations, differs from case to case. Some countries, such as the Federal Republic of Germany, Great Britain, or Switzerland, have separate central prosecution offices. Such

[31] To put in a nutshell the difference between a constitutional and a totalitarian minister of justice: while the constitutional minister of justice tells his cabinet how much of what they plan is legally feasible, his totalitarian colleague tries to argue with his boss, to tell him that what he needs for speedy disposal of any foes can be handled almost as efficiently by his judiciary as by mere practitioners of violence. See the material published by Martin Broszat, "Pervertierte Strafjustiz im 3. Reich," *Vierteljahreshefte für Zeitgeschichte*, Vol. 6 (1959), pp. 390-443, esp. p. 408, for Guertner's jurisdictional complaint about the killing of people on the order of the leader without any semblance of judicial procedure.

organizations not only exercise the right of overseeing what cases should be carried to the highest court on appeal, but they are immersed in the business of indicting, *nol-pros*, and handling the trial stage of all major offenses, as in England, or at least all major political offenses. By their sheer professional and bureaucratic weight, and possibly, too, by the standing of their chief with government, public, and legal profession alike, they might enjoy considerable authority. But even there, the age of the telephone, which is at the same time the age of the enterprising reporter, eager to explore possible differences in the nuances of official communiqués and interviews, tends to strengthen the uninterrupted flow of communication between ministry or department and those in charge of the prosecution.

In Europe the members of the prosecution staff form a career service apart from the other branches of the civil services; they are in many ways assimilated to, though, to the chagrin of many of their members, not always a part of, the judicial establishment. There exists a possible option for them to transfer eventually into judicial ranks, and they are equipped with some guarantees against unjustified demotion or dismissal,[32] if not against exceedingly infrequent transfer to another prosecutor's office of equal rank in the interest of the service. Their *esprit de corps* and professional pride are fortified by a traditional, though sometimes overestimated, differentiation: between the necessary subservience to hierarchical orders down the line on the initiation of criminal action and other written submissions to the court and their freedom of appreciation during the trial. But not too much should be read into the ancient maxim, "La plume est serve, la parole est libre." It mainly reflects the need to protect the confidence that the man on the firing line will draw the correct conclusion from a rapidly evolving trial picture.

[32] In Dorly, *Sirey*, 1954, Vol. III, p. 3, the Conseil d'Etat had to decide on the complaint of a prosecutor disciplined for not having contradicted a petition for provisional release of a defendant arrested for strike-connected violence, though there existed a general circular by the Ministry of Justice asking the prosecutors to oppose petitions for release in such cases. The Conseil d'Etat, arguing from the fact that the prosecution forms part of the judicial services, refused to interfere with the functioning of such service. The formalistic and unsatisfactory decision has been criticized; see, for example, Georges Vedel, "Le contrôle jurisdictionel des mesures disciplinaires frappant les magistrats du Parquet," *Pouvoir Judiciaire*, October 1953, p. 3. Of course, the more elegant way to get rid of an obnoxious or politically unsympathetic prosecutor in a key job is to put him in a different and possibly more remunerative berth in another organization, or in a judicial job, a procedure sometimes followed in the Federal Republic of Germany.

The American lawyer in the service of the justice department, but particularly the federal district attorney, as a direct presidential appointee with a definite time limit to his service—not to mention the state or county attorney, completely politicized, at least at the top level of the office—is an animal of a somewhat different breed. Perforce he conforms somewhat less than the European lawyer to the image of a bureaucrat, responsible to his conscience, his superiors, and his chances for intraservice advance. The latter depends as much if not more on regularity and reliability of round-the-clock performance than on the record of some particularly remarkable and possibly well-publicized performance. The frequently temporary character of his office in the United States—at times a lawyer might even be hired as special prosecutor for a single job—forces him to make some sort of wider reputation, thus helping him to move on. But the self-promotion aspect, with the consequent tendency to overplay the prosecution in which he has landed a major role, has its rewarding as well as grotesque features. For the exceptional fool who might go to the extreme to misguide the grand jury into a baseless indictment so that he can lay the net for a well-advertised political prize catch—as in the 1953 Lorwin case[33] —and then must pay the penalty of dismissal when he cannot produce the promised evidence, there are likely to be at any time a few former prosecutors who have fallen out with their superiors over alleged mishandling of some prosecution with political overtones. Having opened shop on their own account, they are only too eager to tell all, influencing, as it were, the evolution of departmental policies from the sideline. No such safety valves exist for their continental colleague. Having invested heavily in a lifetime career, from which they cannot withdraw or resign without loss of pension rights, they cannot easily force the hands of possibly recalcitrant superiors by resort to publicity.

But that does not mean that the professional prosecutor is defenseless in the face of political pressure and that his services need revalorization, as is sometimes suggested,[34] by the mirage of a complete depolitization of the ministry of justice, or by opening up some way for the prosecutor to lay his intraservice difficulties officially before a higher court. Neither procedure would change the eternal, creative, and necessary conflict

[33] House of Representatives, 84th Congress, 1st Session. Hearings before the Subcommittee of the Committee on Appropriations, Department of Justice, Washington, 1955, pp. 85-96.

[34] From the continuing German discussion on this theme, we mention only Eberhard Schmidt, "Probleme der Struktur des Strafverfahrens unter Rechtsstaatlichen Gesichtspunkten," *Deutsche Richterzeitung*, Vol. 37 (1959), p. 16, and K. S. Bader, "Staatsanwalt und Rechtspflege," *Juristenzeitung*, Vol. 34 (1956), p. 4.

between political goals and the values embodied in the constitutional and legal structure of the community. It would only shunt it to another location. In practice, relations vary from country to country and from period to period. More than once the needed balance has been upset.

But it may be upset by either side. France of the Third Republic remains the classic example of the preponderance of the political apparatus. Here the parliamentary lawyer acts either on his own or in conjunction with the minister of justice, interfering with the prosecutor's job for his clients, often by granting strategically important action delays.[35] Weimar Germany offers the opposite and equally pernicious spectacle of the rapid growth of a quasi-independent federal ministry of justice apparatus, closely linked with the office of the chief federal prosecutor and the Supreme Court bench. Favored by the mere figurehead character of an everchanging incumbent in the position of the federal minister of justice, and by the absence of any effective parliamentary control, the professionals under the guise of strict neutrality and freedom from outside interference developed decidedly partisan criteria of their own in the conduct of their office.[36] Both cases mark extreme positions.

[35] Part of the rich material has now been collected, though without reference to contemporary sources of the period, in Maurice Garçon, *op.cit.* (Ch. 2, n. 25). Recently the West Berlin Senator of Justice has been heavily attacked for his interference with the local prosecutor's proceedings in a number of cases of bribery and influence peddling, which involved administrative officials or other politically well-connected persons. See Dettmar Cramer, "Die Staatsanwaelte und die Bestechungsfaelle," *Frankfurter Allgemeine Zeitung,* December 17, 1960, p. 2.

[36] The present Chief Federal Attorney Max Güde ("Das Weisungsrecht des frueheren deutschen Reichsjustizministers gegenueber dem frueheren Reichsanwalt," *Deutsche Richterzeitung,* Vol. 36 [1958], p. 4) puts the Weimar record on its head when he tries to show that in Weimar the permanent officialdom has energetically rejected any political interference. For that purpose he quotes a mild suggestion made in 1931 by the then-chairman of the Reichstag legal committee (as part of a Communist-right wing amnesty deal [see Ch. VIII, Sec. 5]), asking the ministry to have the chief federal attorney apply in his practice a narrower interpretation of the concept "undertaking of treason." The chairman's view was shared by most members of the legal committee and, as he assumed, was likely to be translated into a legal enactment in the foreseeable future.

This example shows the different meaning of "independence from politics" in different circumstances. In his official rejection of the suggestion, the Secretary of State in the Federal Ministry of Justice, Kurt Joel, main strategist of the partisan political jurisprudence of the federal authorities, was, as usual, hiding behind "professional neutrality" in order to safeguard the political line of the federal judicial apparatus. Güde himself, faced a quarter of a century later with a strong political establishment rather than with an impotent Reichstag committee, utilizes this example in order to increase the limited freedom of movement of the professional in the face of energetic and persistent political superiors.

But even under more favorable circumstances, in a society with a better equilibrium between political opinion, the authority of political personnel, and the weight of professional integrity, the decisions surrounding politically tinged prosecutions may at best be full of booby traps and unforeseeable consequences; at worst they are a heavy mortgage on the conscience and record of the regime. If the offensive behavior constitutes something of a clearly delineated action—pressed by the prosecution into such forms as tax evasion, embezzlement, receiving of bribes, influence peddling, sexual perversion, and charge of espionage committed by communication of classified information to agents of foreign nations,[37] or appearing in the derivative form of perjury or libel action relating to such behavior—rather than a complex touching on political deviation, the government of the day may, if it wants or can afford to, follow a strict hands-off policy. It may allow the law to "take its course," that is, leave the prosecutor without instruction and guidance, face to face with his professional conscience or routine.

Yet more often than not, the professional is all too eager to shift the burden of responsibility to stronger shoulders. Also, the fingers of some of the more enterprising members or subordinates of the government might itch; or it might be a case of saving the government some embarrassment if one of its own crew, a trusted subordinate or friend, is involved. Because of the reinsurance features of professional politics, the government rarely has the opportunity to enlarge on the real or imaginary private misfortunes of one of its more intimate enemies; occasionally, though, there might be an opportunity to catch a real or imaginary enemy of the state in the act of behaving like any other mortal law breaker. Once proceedings have begun, direct government interference might involve nothing more than its refusing to allow one of its members or subordinates to testify on some matter within his official knowledge; or there might be a statement by an official person either backing up or attacking the record and reputation of one of those under indictment. But what matters most of all we have said is not a government's occasional overeagerness, clumsiness, elusiveness, or rashness in fields where tradition, opinion, and a steady court practice have marked out more or less definite boundaries between permissible and illicit behavior. Before long, though possibly after some

---

[37] Espionage may have a double nature. It may involve engaging in a strictly prohibited type of operation for commercial profit. But it may also partake, and be the expression, of a high degree of intellectual and political alienation from the national community, thus involving a most accentuated form of political deviation.

costly detours, the common practice, re-emphasized by the professional in his daily, less controversial cases, will reassert itself.

However, in the whole complex of political deviation the usual relation between routine professional and political directive becomes reversed. Where in the traditional fields of law enforcement the administration's moving into the case is the exception, here it becomes a rule. Whether sanctioned only by administrative regulation, or, as in Switzerland, by explicit legislative enactment,[38] it is the politically responsible government, not the line prosecutor, who gives the go-ahead signal and charts the course for the prosecution in this field. Due to the previously discussed indefinite character of terminology used in the realm of state protection, there exists wide leeway for government policy. It is in this realm of political deviation that governments, and legal technicians who are more eager than conscientious, may use much ingenuity to stack the cards against the defendants; to this realm belongs the fine art of whom and what to include in or omit from the confines of an indictment.[39] For perfectionists with an eye on political effect, there is the crowning device known already during the French Revolution as the "amalgam": defendants with a background of common crime are associated in a single indictment with only remotely connected defendants charged for some offense of political deviation.[40] In such cases legal and political considerations constantly intertwine and the outcome of official deliberations depends as much on the political goals of the incumbent administration as on the feasibility consideration of its legal technicians.[41] Of course in an exceptional

[38] Art. 105 of the Swiss Code of Criminal Procedure.

[39] To speak only of the past: in the 1888 proceedings against the supporters of Boulanger, quite a number of his most important and distinguished backers were omitted from the indictment. See Maurice Garçon, *op.cit.*, Vol. 1, pp. 171-73.

[40] One of the most famous pre-Bolshevik "amalgams" occurred in the 1894 Paris trial of the 30 members of a so-called "association of criminals." Anarchists writers like Jean Grave and Paul Réclus were indicted, along with members of the "bande Ortiz," common criminals who had taken to explaining their exploits by resorting to anarchist lingo. The trick did not work, as the assizes acquitted the "theoretical anarchists" (Maurice Garçon, Vol. 1, pp. 238-39, and Jean Maîtron, *op.cit.*, p. 233).

[41] To quote Cockburn again (*op.cit.*, Vol. 1, p. 69): "It is difficult to read the state trials without feeling that if it had not been for the purpose of getting rid of a political adversary, or to promote a party object, rarely one out of ten of the political accusations with which that record is loaded would have been preferred. The only way to prevent this sympathy with crime is to be sure that it is guilt and for its own sake that it is prosecuted and that it is properly tried. And it is not enough that guilt be real. It ought also be great. Even a conviction in a weak case does no good. The confines of sedition are so easily and so unconsciously got into, that a good deal of the crime must be winked at." Of course Cockburn is writing against the background of an upper and upper middle

case, as presently in the Federal Republic, the government might tie its own hands by provoking the banning of a revolutionary organization via a Constitutional Court judgment, thus quasi-automatically generating an endless stream of criminal prosecutions.[42] But this was a deliberate political choice of developing set and long-range patterns rather than making decisions on combating enemies of the present state organization—decisions that are dependent on everchanging tactical considerations.

In prosecuting political deviation, governments take a number of risks. Lowest in ascending order of importance, courts might refuse to follow the government's lead. Such defeats may be neither clearcut nor final and are likely to be more in the nature of a seesaw. Generally, this risk might be overcompensated for by the proclivity of many courts—despite the United States v. Yates[43]—and juries to follow the line of the government as a presumed expert in the field of subversion,[44] or even to outbid the government as a custodian of state protection.[45]

The second risk is a straight political one. It concerns the likelihood that the "loyal" opposition will fasten on any inconsistency in the government action, if for no other reason than to embarrass the government in a field where the complicated ways of politics, forever harnessing legal formulas and devices into their service, are expected to be well concealed behind a show of immaculate rectitude and high principle. Thus while it is legally admissible to abandon a political prosecution that is already underway, it is at best a politically risky affair. In 1924 it even furnished the occasion for the resignation of Ramsey MacDonald's first minority government. John Ross Campbell, the acting editor of *Workers' Weekly*, had been prosecuted under an incitement to mutiny charge. When the case moved up for a hearing on August 13, 1924, the treasury counsel announced that he would not proceed with the prosecution on the grounds that representations had

---

class government which, as it turned out, had its period of unnecessary fright before the onrush of Chartism and the concomitant judicial repression safely behind it.

[42] See Ch. IV, Sec. 3.

[43] 356 U.S. 363 (1957).

[44] Cf. the typical remark of Justice Holmes on the propriety and wisdom of the Eugene Debs prosecution, with its two-edged tolerance for both the radical fool and the zealot upholders of the constituted order (*Holmes-Laski Letters*, Harvard University Press, 1953, Vol. I, pp. 203-04).

[45] For the remarks of an expert—who in recent years has often been in conflict with overzealous judges—see Federal Attorney Güde in *Probleme des politischen Strafrechts*, p. 24, to the effect that lawyers when in an official position only rarely deny the state the exercise of a privilege which seems due to it.

been made that the article did not have the suggested meaning. In the long drawn-out debate in the House of Commons on September 30 and October 8, 1924, the Conservative opposition, skillfully supported by John Simon, the Liberal member, tried to develop inferences to the effect that the decision to withdraw made by Sir Patrick Hastings, the attorney general, had not been made on his own initiative, but under heavy pressure, possibly exercised by the cabinet and prominent ministers but originating from the left wing of the Labor Party. At the same time, the opposition connected the withdrawal with government strategy concerned with the fortunes of the then-pending Soviet-British commercial treaty negotiations.[46] The attorney general's assertion, backed up by documentary evidence that political prosecutions had in the past been subject to both cabinet discussion and direction, was not refuted by any of the opposition speakers. They conceded the point either explicitly or by inference and went on to distinguish the permissible political discretion in starting a prosecution and the special safeguards which should surround its withdrawal.[47] As the government was not willing to accept the setting up of a commission of inquiry, proposed by Sir John Simon and adopted by the House with a 364-198 majority, it resigned. The Conservative election campaign used the Campbell incident to show the danger of irresponsible labor backbenchers' interfering with the administration of justice. However, the so-called Sinovjev note, a patent falsification, and its poor handling by MacDonald probably overshadowed the impact of any other single element in the election campaign.[48]

But the greatest and the most intangible risk for a constitutional government does not lie in the everpresent possibility that a prosecution

[46] House of Commons. Parliamentary Debates, Vol. 177, September 30, 1924, pp. 9-17; October 8, 1924, pp. 582-694. See also Robert Bechhofer, *Sir John Simon*, London, 1938, pp. 184-207.

[47] Parliamentary Debates, pp. 598-99, 615, 622-23. For a balanced account of the episode by a participant observer, together with a most reasonable presentation of the case for a high degree of discretion in political prosecutions, see Sidney Webb's recently published memo, "The First Labor Government," *Political Quarterly*, Vol. 32 (1961), pp. 6, 28-31.

[48] A record of MacDonald's embarrassed attempt to cover up his tergiversations in the Campbell affair may be found in his letter to Lord Stamfordham, the king's secretary, reproduced in Harold Nicholson, *King George V, Life and Reign*, London, 1953, p. 398. Hastings's reaction to MacDonald's tactics may be found in H. Montgomery Hyde, *Sir Patrick Hastings*, London, 1960, pp. 141-61. Stephen R. Graubard, *British Labor and the Russian Revolution*, Harvard University Press, 1956, Ch. 13, contains a criticism of the tactics of the MacDonald government and its willingness to enter the election campaign on the basis of the Campbell incident rather than the Russian treaty issue.

might presently backfire and bring its promoters a measure of legal and political discomfiture. Its greatest risk might be called the historical risk. Future generations, judging with the help of more precise knowledge of the motivations, expectations, risks, and dangers of all the participants, may not be very charitable when assessing the motivations of those ordering political prosecutions. The judgment of history might concern isolated instances of futility or blend into a judgment concerning wider policies as a whole. For each we wish to give an example.

The prosecution of the Minneapolis Trotskyites was instituted by an administration otherwise little given to prosecutions in the field of political deviation. It draws its interest not only from the choice of the object, but from the curious circumstances under which it was undertaken. It originated in an intra-union conflict between the Teamsters Union, represented by Messrs. Tobin and Dave Beck, and the Dunne brothers, who combined control of local Minneapolis trucking with a fervent adherence to the Trotskyite faith. When Dave Beck was unable to reclaim by normal blackguard methods the lost souls who had shifted their allegiance to the CIO, Tobin, who in contrast to the CIO's John Lewis was one of the mainstays of the administration, sought and received the latter's succor.[49] The fact that the Dunne group kept loyalty to and contact with Leo Trotsky, had previously organized long disbanded union defense guards against "Silvershirt" aggressiveness, had theorized about its possibly becoming a nucleus for future workers' control, distributed Marxist tracts, and kept organizational contact with and gave rather cautious advice to those members serving in the armed forces—all was projected into a criminal prosecution, based on the newly-enacted Smith Act and incorporating "incitement to subordination" concepts.[50] The prosecution leading to a month trial (October 30 to November 30, 1941) before the U.S. District Court in Minneapolis was carried through to victory against the major defendants amid sideline cheers of the Communist Party. The shade-less nebulous incitement to subordination charge relied, as usual in such proceedings, on the testimony of interested witnesses, former Dunne adherents who now held office under and drew pay from a newly-established AFL local.[51] The conviction survived scrutiny by the appeal court and the defendants lost out—in spite of the novelty of the Smith

[49] "Civil Liberties in Minneapolis," *New Republic*, July 28, 1941, p. 103.

[50] 18 U.S.C. 2387, 62 Stat. 811 (1948).

[51] See abstract from the record of the proceedings: Docket No. 12195, U.S. Court of Appeals, 8th District (April 1, 1942). Witnesses Bartlett, 277-79, Brennan, 685, 686, William, 741, 742.

Act charge—in the lottery for Supreme Court scrutiny.[52] It forms one of the few blots on the record of Attorney General Francis Biddle.

The second episode concerns the refusal of the German chief federal prosecutor to indict in 1931 the authors of the so-called Boxheim manifesto, an outline—quite a realistic outline, as the future showed—of the various steps to be taken by the NS Party for seizing power and organizing the suppression of its enemies. We need not dwell here on the official rationalization of the refusal to prosecute: the assertion, always forthcoming under such circumstances, was that the project was conceived only as an outline for countermeasures in case the Communists tried to start a *coup d'état*. This could not be refuted.[53] A government which prosecutes only the functionaries of a momentarily weaker revolutionary group, while closing its eyes to the presently much more dangerous activities of other hostile organizations of the opposite color, shows that it has started on the road to surrender to its foes.

The prosecution of a bewildering variety of political deviation is thus marked by two outer limits: the political strength of an almost universally upheld regime, which easily gives to the prosecution of small bands of political enemies the appearance of a paltry, trivial play; and the weakness of a regime which in the face of manifest and feverish attempts at its overthrow proves too weak to convert the legal armor of the statute book into one of the facets of concerted defensive action.

If we are speaking of concerted defensive action, we want to see clearly that legal action is only one facet—a conspicuous one, but not necessarily the most vital one—in the battle against the foes of an established order. From the vantage point of the law, interested in the intermeshing of various forms of state activities under a constitutional regime, the police

[52] Dunne v. U.S. (138 Fed 2d 137, 8th C.C.A. [1943]) certiorari denied 320 U.S. 790 (1943). The most provocative, if thoroughly partisan, discussion of motivations for starting an "amalgam" sedition trial, with ample speculation on the impact of special pressures on trial preparation and conduct, may be found in a book written by a lawyer and a defendant in the abortive 1944 right wing sedition trial before the D.C. District Court. Due to the death of the trial judge, it terminated after seven and a half months with a mistrial. See John St. George and Lawrence Dennis, *A Trial on Trial, The Great Sedition Trial of 1944*, New York, 1946. No retrial occurred. The indictment was later dismissed for failure to prosecute; United States v. McWilliams, 163 Fed 2d 695, D.C. Cir. (1947).

[53] Wolfgang Heine, "Staatsgerichtshof, Reichsgericht und Hessenmanifest," *Die Justiz*, Vol. 7 (1931-1932), pp. 154-66; and Gustav Radbruch, "Der Boxheimer Hochverrat," *ibid.*, pp. 195-197. Among the more modern literature, Merry and Serge Bromberger's *Les 13 complots du 13 Mai*, Paris, 1959, contains a number of astonishing parallels used by the organizational trailblazers of the Fifth Republic when the authorities of the Fourth Republic made some futile attempts to question them about their not-too-clandestine preparations for a revolt.

are nothing but an auxiliary of the prosecutor, which collects and prepares material under his supervision and for his use. In practice, however, the police in a modern state are a vast administrative bureaucracy,
following their own methods and pursuing their own goals.[54] It makes
relatively little difference whether the prosecution and the police are
working under different authorities, as in the continental countries,
where they are integrated into the ministry of justice and ministry of
the interior respectively, or whether, as in the United States, they are
formally under the common authority of an attorney general. Continental codes of criminal procedure might spell out the theory that the
police, whenever concerned with criminal investigation, act as judicial
police, that is, under the guidance, direction, and responsibility of the
prosecutor or the examining judge who is instructing the case.

But in spite of repeated attempts to enforce a clearcut hierarchical
subordination of the police under the prosecution, and in spite of the
reiteration of this claim in the legal texts,[55] their relation is characterized

[54] See the informative, though cautious, article by I. Engster, "Rechtsstellung und
Befugnisse des Bundesanwalt," *Neue Züricher Zeitung*, No. 1,459, May 19, 1957.

[55] The police's tendency to push the prosecution out of the preliminary investigation
and reduce its jurisdiction to preparing the act of accusation is criticized, with a plea
for at least adequate information of the prosecution by the police, in a recent speech
by a high level practitioner: Federal Attorney Harlan, in "Die Rechtstellung des
Staatsanwalt," *Kriminalpolitische Gegenwartsfragen*, ed. Bundeskriminalamt, Wiesbaden,
1959, pp. 121-25. For the recent German discussion, see E. Schmidt, "Probleme der
Struktur der Strafverfolgung unter rechtsstaatlichen Gesichtspunkten," *Deutsche Richterzeitung*, Vol. 37 (1959), p. 16. See also Heinrich Henkel, *Strafverfolgungsrecht*, Stuttgart, 1953, pp. 197ff.

French third degree police practices, by no means limited to political cases, are discussed in detail in Alec Mellor, *Les Grands Problèmes Contemporains de l'Instruction
Criminelle*, Paris, 1952.

According to the new version of the French Code of Criminal Procedure of December 31, 1957, there is now a strict separation between administrative and judicial
police, with the latter coming under the disciplinary power of the judiciary. Antonin
Bessin, Procureur General à la Cour de Cassation, "L'origine, l'esprit et la portée du
code de procédure pénale," *Revue de Science criminelle et de droit pénal comparé*,
Vol. 14 (1959), pp. 270-89, tries hard to convince a public—which is rather skeptic,
in view of the countless recent manifestations of police freewheeling—that these changes
signify more than pure window-dressing. The whole subject of the relations between
police and judiciary in France has been brilliantly and realistically treated in Ch. 4
of Casamayor's *Le Bras Séculier Justice et Police*, Paris, 1960. This essay, together with
Casamayor's *Les Juges*, Paris, 1957, is especially recommended to interested readers.
Recent French police brutalities in political cases—abetted by the extension of the time
limit, by decree, during which a prisoner may be held before being formally booked
with the judicial authorities—have recently led to open conflict and deadlock between
judiciary and police administration in metropolitan France. See "Le Juge et le Commis-
saire," *L'Express*, March 10, 1960. There is no need to go into the matter of Algerian
practices of the French security authorities; they are public knowledge.

The English practice—to give a wide area of initiative and freedom to the police,

by sometimes friendly, sometimes antagonistic cooperation. This is due not only to normal bureaucratic competition over closely related fields of activity, but also to the fact that the focuses of those responsible for the internal security of the country and of those handling professionally the business of criminal prosecution are quite different. The political police's attention centers on the surveillance of the adversaries of the present regime and, if need be, on foiling their plans at subverting it. The prosecutor is concerned with drawing the boundary line between licit and prohibited political behavior and, in this process, publicly establishing the criminal responsibility of those who have transgressed the often shadowy boundary line. The function of political police and prosecution bisect, but are not identical. The police under any constitutional regime consider that the administration of justice both limits and supports their action. It limits it to a varying degree by opening avenues of complaint and legal remedies to individuals whose liberty and privacy are threatened by overt and some form of covert police invasion. Yet it supports the police by allowing them, upon proper showing of cause, to invade these spheres legitimately by arrest, search, and seizure procedures. To what extent the police will make use of such support depends both on their facility in dispensing with a support which always leads to limitation and supervision of their own action and on the government's overall strategy against its foes. Aiming at knowledge and control of all shades of political deviation does not necessarily imply trying to circumscribe or root it out with the help of criminal prosecution.

First, the area of opinions and actions kept under watch by the police of any modern state includes far more than what constitutional governments could and would want to take up with the courts. Second, control through police channels covers a wide range of means, including infiltration, intimidation, and corruption. They might be infinitely more effective as instruments of control than resort to criminal prosecution; and they narrow down the necessity or desirability and, to a much smaller extent, the chances, of successful criminal prosecution.[56] Third, to the extent that prosecution presupposes unveiling some part,

---

who are working under the guidance of some general "judges' rules" and under the interstitial control of the committing magistrate and especially the trial judge—is described with some measure of circumspection and hesitation in Sir Patrick Devlin, *The Criminal Prosecution in England*, New Haven, 1958.

[56] Richard C. Donnelly, "Judicial Control of Informants, Spies, Stoolpigeons, and Agents Provocateurs," *Yale Law Journal*, Vol. 60 (1951), pp. 1091-131.

however small, of the knowledge of the police in regard to the plans and organization of its foes, it might, at least temporarily, counteract their successful control.

The government, acting on the basis of information proffered by its security organs, must make the final decision on which cases should and could stand the more rigorous tests of criminal prosecution. Relations between the political police and a constitutional government rest officially on strict hierarchical subordination of the "neutral" police to the government.[57] Again, however, it is different in practice. The head of the political police, whether under civil service or considered a political officeholder, whether restricted to political supervision jobs or, as in the United States, master of the whole federal police establishment, may outlast many a government.[58] His could be an independent and strategic position in the government, because of his intimate knowledge of the personal background of the political personnel, as well as by the prestige which his organization might have built up with the public at large as the chosen custodian of national security. While he officially only advises the government on a certain course of action, disregard of his advice is liable to cast aspersion on the good judgment of the government and may easily be used to impeach the government's patriotic loyalty should its decision in an individual instance become a matter of public controversy. The 1953 debate on President Truman's personnel action in the Harry Dexter White case, highlighted by J. Edgar Hoover's testimony, reveals the overtones and implications of the notion "advice" tendered to a government by its political police in security matters.[59] The temporary ostracism which many French politicians were able to decree against two of their political competitors, Messrs. Mitterand and Mendès-France, on the basis of some security organs' unsubstantiated suspicions of the record of these politicians (in the episode which later led to the so-called "procès des fuites," concerning the handing over of the minutes of some national defense council meetings to Communist

[57] The semi-official *FBI Story* by Don Whitehead (New York, 1956) strictly maintains the neutrality line as part of the organization's mission to execute the law. However, the judiciously chosen morsels of official documents cannot totally hide the fact that "executing the law" means different things to different people at different times.

[58] However, he might not outlast a change of regime. One of the first acts of the de Gaulle administration in 1958 was the replacement of Monsieur Wybott, the head of the external security organization. But it should not be assumed that his dismissal was in any way connected with the violent brushes, leading to the intervention of the Judicial Council, which Wybott had with the examining judges at the Tribunal de la Seine.

[59] Hoover testimony, *New York Times*, November 18, 1953, p. 23.

headquarters) demonstrates the constant intermeshing of seemingly purely objective and neutral security considerations with party politics.[60]

Present-day constitutional regimes may escape one of the more typical situations arising under totalitarian regimes. There the heads of the security services, thanks to their foreign contacts, and their knowledge of and familiarity with the ways of subversives, prove a constant source of potential disloyalty, or at least antagonism, to the regime. Under a constitutional regime, where the political police's action is limited by normal life satisfactions, public opinion, and access to the courts for the government's foes, and by the reciprocal need for the police to resort to court intervention for the more drastic ways of disposing of the regime's enemies, the police keep some measure of similarity with a normal governmental bureaucracy. They fight jurisdictional battles with mushrooming security competitors and spend considerable thought and ingenuity in converting secrecy into a built-in device which will heighten rather than detract from their popularity. And due to their function as well as to their built-up halo, the police have one great advantage over other government services. During the total lifetime of the regime they are foolproof against any investigation into their methods, assumptions, and efficiency. A seeming paradox, one might nearly be tempted to define a revolution by the willingness of a regime to open the archives of its predecessor's political police. Measured by this yardstick, few revolutions have taken place in modern history.[61]

3. The Meaning of Impartiality

Strategies and calculations of private parties and governmental organizations may explain the vital conditions under which courts become active. But now the question arises, why do courts decide as they do? Before searching for the elements entering into their decision, we should say a word about how judges arrive at their opinions. It is by now almost common knowledge—one of the few gifts bestowed by all shades of legal realism to legal theory which have found wide acceptance—

[60] Jacques Fauvet, "Le Procès Continue," *Le Monde Hebdomadaire*, May 17, and 23, 1956, and Jean-Mare Theollayre, *Le Procès des Fuites*, Paris, 1956.

[61] While Whitehead's book (*op.cit.*) is an exceedingly well done panegyric, Max Loewenthal, *The Federal Bureau of Investigation*, New York, 1950, while a diligent collection of every bit of unfavorable information, suffers somewhat from its limited horizon. Neither the spotless image of self-effacing patriotism nor the traditional watchdog concern over the main threat against civil liberties fits the very complicated reality of present-day political police organizations. Admittedly, it is difficult to scrutinize an organization from either the information with which it is willing to part, or from those effects of its activities which by sheer accident become a matter of public knowledge.

that only the law student will start his case by searching for applicable texts and authorities to guide him. The judge would rather rely on his hunches, which show him the desirable decision under the particular circumstances of the case. To the extent that he has become a routinist both averse to straining his mind and experienced in the ways of cases, he may soon abandon the possibly tedious business of following up his hunches and whipping them into the shape of a presentable solution; instead, he may rush straight to an accepted cubbyhole and put his case into it. If he does, no further problem arises, except that he must in his official reasoning cover up the lacunae left by the regrettable fact that yesterday's formulas might not quite fit the problem of today. If he avoids this shortcut and feels the persistent urge to solve the problem before him in the light of his initial perception, he must convert the perception into a defensible and reasoned position.

Thus the process of rationalizing and testing the hunches against precedents and norms will have to set in. Norms and precedents are part of the experienced, worked-out community reaction patterns of domesticating the influx of social reality that must be faced, absorbed, and shaped. It may happen—very rarely, though—that the hunch may not be strong enough to withstand the test of experience. Most frequently, the hunch may have led to the judge's grouping the facts in the case in a way that leaves the projected decision squarely within the recognized and affirmed rule. However, if need be, a precedent may be circumvented by (a) reducing the import of its *ratio decidendi*, thus establishing that it does not cover the present case; (b) distinguishing the facts of the present case from those which gave rise to the precedent, thus denying the latter's applicability.[62] In neither case is the precedent challenged. Only in the rarest of all occurrences may the hunch have been strong enough to provoke a frontal attack on the rule; a substitute rule, construed for the case under advisement, will be offered to the community for consideration and, through the parties interested in its survival, to a higher court for endorsement and formal "enthronization."[63]

[62] In his interesting discussion of how much the lower federal courts follow Supreme Court rulings, Paul H. Sanders (*The Warren Court and Lower Federal Courts*, paper delivered before the 1959 Political Science Association Convention) shows the frequency with which lower courts deny, bypass, and give no effect to the controlling authority of a Supreme Court ruling. In the field of political deviation, the authority of Yates v. U.S. seems not to have been questioned. But this may be due as much to changed "atmospheric" conditions as to the persuasive opinion of Justice Harlan, which left room for upholding convictions if arrived at on the basis of sufficient evidence (see Ch. IV, n. 47).

[63] Of the many modern discussions of the subject, only two particularly useful ones shall be mentioned: Alf Ross, *On Law and Justice* (n. 27 above), p. 84, and P. Cala-

Hunches will be the points of departure in those cases where the judge, feeling his way through radically contradictory party assertions about the actual course of past events, must concentrate on recon-structing a particular historical occurrence as prerequisite of its evaluation. Since we have lost the certainty of a former generation, which believed perfect reconstruction of an historical event was some-thing that could be objectively achieved as a matter of course,[64] the im-portance of the judge's unreflected reaction becomes quite evident. Many a political trial, such as a murder, espionage, or some artifact perjury case, turns on the judge's or the jury's reconstruction. Policy questions enter official consideration only when the question of the applicable norm and the shape of the sentence come under discussion. Of course, there might be from the outset a subterraneous, subconscious, though probably rarely unconscious, channel between the judge's original hunch —which shapes the Gestalt of the case, with the witnesses' tale falling in line with or being attached to the judge's vision—and the total socio-political complex from which the case arose.

If the question is not primarily whom to believe in the reconstruction of the facts, but how to judge and evaluate the meaning of the facts, then hunches, pristine images, and feelings of right and wrong that indicate a path through disputed fact situations recede in importance. In a sedition case many a minor detail may remain controversial and be seized upon by all participants to give more credence to their own interpretations of the meaning and permissibility of certain political activity. Yet the pattern of activity and propaganda of a political or-ganization and the utterances of the leaders themselves are most likely widely known. One might endlessly interpret and reinterpret the mean-ings and possible variations of their fine points of doctrine without necessarily getting involved in a wrangle about the facts of the situation. Whether propaganda against the continuation of the French military effort in Indochina constituted an attempt to demoralize the French army;[65] whether German Communist demonstrators parading before the court house where Communists were on trial, calling for their re-

---

mandrei, *Procedure and Democracy* (n. 18 above), pp. 23ff. Of course, precedents do not have binding force everywhere, and courts might, at their own peril, disregard them. But in practice, lower courts will rarely trouble to take up what is at best an uncertain fight for the sake of a result which could probably be reached less arduously.

[64] This touching faith is clearly revealed in the writings of one of the masters of the classical school of penal law, Karl Binding, *Strafrechtliche und Strafprozessuale Ab-handlungen* (written 1878, rev. 1914), 1915, Vol. 2, p. 188.

[65] Tribunal Correctionel, Château-Thierry, June 21, 1950, and Montpelier, March 28, 1950, in *Gazette du Palais*, 1 (1950), 370.

lease, are trying to influence the public authorities enough so that we may construe their activities as "an undermining of the constitutional order"[66]—these questions belong to the area of political evaluation, in which the judge along with other authorities consciously develops public policy. One might well maintain that the French courts just cited could have taken a more severe view of the concerted propaganda efforts of the French Communists against the Indochinese war, applying in Indochina the harsh terms of Article 76.3 of the Penal Code; on the other hand, the very harshness of its terms might easily have been the main reason for the courts' reluctance to convict. Reversely, German judges, acting long before the banning of the Communist Party, might have brought the mild manifestation of the Communists under the free speech guarantee, despite the facts that the shouts of the demonstrators were perceptible in the prosecutor's office and could therefore, if one tried hard enough, be construed as a case of intimidation. What made these courts decide such issues quite differently was the variance in their concept of state authority, their political experience, including the shape and structure of the community they were living in.

But can we say no more about the source of the judges' attitudes toward the political problems of their society than to refer back to a photographically truthful picture of the current state of mind of their society? Is it enough to learn that the judge might be prone to look at the people's attitudes in arriving at his verdict? Is the relationship between the two constructs, the people's consciousness and the legal consciousness of a given period, so easy and direct? Of course not. Even if we take the case of a relatively homogeneous political community like the United States, its attitude toward a particular problem might be, as Jerome Frank called it, "an unknowable, a slithery shadow."[67] The attempt to shift from the judge's consciousness to its source, the consciousness of the community, might therefore not always be revealing or rewarding. The relationship between popular and legal consciousness is not tantamount to a creation which simply reflects its creator; rather, it has the hallmarks of a continuing reciprocal process of making conscious and formulating the community's response to contemporary challenges. Slogans such as "the stream of law can not habitually rise above its source"[68] might underestimate this reciprocity, thus minimiz-

---

[66] Decision of the Bundesgerichtshof of July 3, 1953, in *Juristenzeitung*, 1954, p. 198.

[67] U.S. v. Rosenberg, 195 Fed 2d 583 at 608, 2d C.C.A. (1952).

[68] Wallace Mendelson, "Mr. Justice Frankfurter, Law and Choice," *Vanderbilt University Law Review*, Vol. 10 (1957), pp. 335-41. For a strong statement in the direction outlined here, see H. P. Laswell and Richard P. Donnelly, "The Continuing Debate over Responsibility: An Introduction to Isolating the Condemnation Sanction,"

ing the judge's legitimate role in the transformation of the community's inchoate concepts into its legal consciousness.

Businessmen, for example, attempt ceaselessly to create goodwill among officials with whom they must maintain professional contact. These endeavors consist perhaps in nothing more than making available to the officials and their families the temporary use of such worldly goods as an expensive car, a luxury hotel suite, an exquisite meal. These, at the taxpayers' ultimate expense, form in our day and age the normal surroundings of the business executive, but without his touching thoughtfulness they would scarcely be within the official's reach. In many cases, especially if no loans or expensive gifts were also tendered to the official, there might be little evidence that the official's attitude or action had been influenced by the businessman's temporary interest in his well-being. Opinion trends might sharply differ on the propriety of both the giving and receiving, while in the "best" opinion of lawyers, highbrow journalists, and of course the business community, such favors are nothing more than an "usance" mirroring the normal style of business relations today. Judges who take exception to these "usances," and style as "passive corruption" the behavior of the official at the receiving end, as recently happened in the Federal Republic,[69] do more than set up the old-fashioned standards of correctness as the official standards. The refusal to grant standing to these "usances" elevates from the world of private opinion to that of official policy the nondescript mixture of envy, animosity, skepticism, and mistrust of the man in the street toward the operations of business tycoons and procurement officials. Such an element is no less important in the formation of legal consciousness for its being in contradiction with prevailing upper class morality, including the thought patterns of the more regular formulators of public policy.[70]

Yale Law Journal, Vol. 68 (1959), p. 869 at 876. "An enlightened decision maker must choose his own goals. In this way he is able to act deliberately as an ally of one set or another of past practices which he then protects or extends. . . ."

[69] This happened in the so-called "car-borrowers" (Leihwagen) trials before the Bonn District Court. They involved officials of ministries and of the Bundestagadministration; executive officers of major business enterprises acted either as codefendants or as somewhat recalcitrant witnesses. Still pending is the hilarious case of the Stuttgart Lord Mayor's oriental rug, received as a fiftieth birthday gift from the biggest local enterprise. A preliminary nol pros of the Stuttgart District Court, which has since been reversed on appeal, had been grounded *inter alia* on the observation that many members of the business community had marched in the procession of gift-laden well-wishers, which helped to remove from the municipal official any consciousness of wrongdoing.

[70] See, for example, the articles of Hermann Schreiber, "Das Allgemeinübliche,"

The freedom of appreciation for the judge may not always be as wide. The community may have unmistakably formulated a legal position which the judge, whatever his personal notions, will have to respect and enforce. If the social order of the time has clearly excluded consideration and recognition of a factor, the judge, as the Finnish author Otto Brusiin has aptly shown,[71] would act illegally if he recognized such a claim. This duty of the judge to bow to explicit commands of the social order might involve heavy moral and intellectual sacrifices. Thus given the actual state of South African law, a judge, if asked to set aside an administrative order that prohibits a person from residing in a specific area because the administrative authority is satisfied that his continued residence would stir feelings of hostility between various races, would have to reject the petition of the aggrieved party for want of jurisdiction.[72] Were he to act otherwise, accepting jurisdiction on the basis of general considerations, he would intervene in one of the many fields of personal freedom from which the South African legislator has withdrawn any judicial protection.

This example leads to a related problem. We have been assuming the existence of a fairly homogeneous community where the judge has by common consensus become an authoritative formulator and inter-

---

Stuttgarter Zeitung, July 25, 1959 and Fabian v. Schlabrendorff, "Fiat Justitia," *Frankfurter Allgemeine Zeitung*, July 21, 1959. The latter goes so far as to call the court's giving in to everyday pressure on them "bias in its most naked form." See also Dettmar Cramer, "Verwirrung über den Bestechungstatbestand," *Frankfurter Allgemeine Zeitung*, November 24, 1960; and Heinrich Henkel, "Die Bestechlichkeit von Ermessensbeamten," *Juristenzeitung*, 1960, p. 507.

On the other hand, the Federal Court, in a decision of October 27, 1959 (5 StR 411/59, *Neue Juristische Wochenschrift*, Vol. 13 [1960], p. 830.), tried to show that penalizing the acceptance of gifts, irrespective of whether the official action of the defendant civil servant was in that instance influenced by such tenderings, is in line with long-established judicial practice. An increasing professional literature has been devoted to the subject, without, however, advancing our knowledge of the underlying social conflict situation of the so-called "falsification of the will of the state": the attempts by part of the judicial bureaucracy to exercise a control on the professional morality of the business community and their administrative counterparts—a stricter control than business community, administrator, or their numerous political allies are willing to accept.

United States criminal practice has concerned itself only with cases where gifts and loans have been clearly made to influence specific decisions, rather than with behavior directed toward generating unspecified good-will toward the private business partner. And even then the prosecution, as the first Mack-Whiteside trial has shown, may run into trouble with the jury.

[71] *Über Die Objektivität der Rechtsprechung*, Helsinki, 1949, p. 33.

[72] Section 3(5) of the Riotous Assemblies Act, No. 17 of 1956. See also E. H. Brookes and J. B. Macaulay, *op.cit.*, Ch. IV, p. 68.

preter of the present stage of the public consciousness. But what is the role of the judge in a large sociopolitical area where there exists little or no common ground? We might think again of the Union of South Africa, where a fairly, if not completely, united racial minority dominates the lives of presently subjugated racial groups that form the majority of the population. The structure of the law mirrors this power relation. Starting from the traditional common law premise of equality before the law, the South African body of statutory law is continually changed to reflect in every detail the abyss between dominant and servile class. Over such an abyss, the judge's discretion can only be limited.

However, the actual power structure and the fact of his belonging inextricably to the dominant minority is only one facet of the problem. As a judge he is not only constantly faced with the aspects of domination, but also, as we have seen in Chapter III, 1, he must make the system work with a minimum of friction, a task which is often in conflict with the backwash of petty iniquities and human misery which are such a system's inevitable result. Under such circumstances he might fashion the instrument of legal positivism both to protect his professional dignity and conscience and to create for himself some leeway, however small, to mitigate the harshness of official policies. The traditions of the constitutional system have limited his power to challenge parliament directly. Whatever power of this kind could be read into both the constitutional settlement and the elementary, self-explanatory rules of what constitutes the essence of a court seems to have been exhausted in the fight over the so-called entrenched clauses of the South Africa Act.[73] But his is still the power of statutory interpretation. In the admittedly diminishing number of cases where there are ambiguities in the statutory body,[74] the judge may still occasionally interpret laws in

[73] The first two stages of the battle are discussed in D. V. Cowen, "The Entrenched Sections of the South Africa Act: Two Great Legal Battles," *South African Law Journal*, Vol. 70 (1953), pp. 238-65.

The three stages of the fight are: (*1*) invalidating the abrogation of voting privileges guaranteed in Art. 152 of the 1909 South Africa Act without the majorities provided therein (Harris v. Minister of Interior, 2 S.A. 428 A.D. [1952]); (2) denying the High Court of Parliament, instituted in 1952 to cashier final judgments, the character of a court, for it was created only to circumvent the majority requirements prescribed for the change of Art. 152 (Minister of Interior v. Harris, 4 S.A. 769 A.D. [1952]); (3) the court's bowing to explicit statutory change carried through with the required majorities (Collins v. Minister of Interior, 1 S.A. 552 A.D. [1957]).

[74] For example, the law concerning squatting, codified on a federal basis in 1951, is now interpreted to include not only persons who unlawfully enter an area but also those who remain without permission in an area where they have always dwelt:

favor of the victims of the system.[75] In doing so he will carefully avoid taking issue with the purposes of the legislators.[76] Positivism, keeping to an exegesis of the meaning of the texts and harmonizing them among each other, may in this instance serve as a means to take an occasional stab at the widening gap between the legal consciousness of the majority and the dominant minority.[77]

In contrast to South Africa's dominant minority-suppressed majority pattern which the judiciary has had to accept, sometimes reluctantly, the judiciary in Germany's Weimar Republic (1919-1932) became from the outset an active element in the rise of new power constellations. Liberal in the middle of the nineteenth century and a champion of strict constitutionalism, the judiciary, along with the rest of the professional classes, had become cautious and minimized its political engagement in the later Bismarck days. The rude shock of the 1918 defeat, of the political rise of the working class, and especially of the middle classes' impoverishment through rapid inflation in the beginning of the twenties, had alienated the judiciary from the official political establishment. Thus, in what at first appeared a fluid power structure, the judicial apparatus set out to grant respectability and protection—at least initially against the wishes of and sometimes in open conflict with the au-

---

R. v. Zulu, 1 S.A. 263 A.D. (1959). But see the verdict under the previous set of provincial legal enactments: Tsose v. Minister of Justice and others, 3 S.A. 10 A.D. (1951).

[75] R. v. Mpekwa and others, 1 S.A. 10 Tn.D. (1958); a native who allowed his reference book to be taken by another was found not guilty of contravention against passport laws.

[76] If a decision concerns the financial consequences of apartheid on the white concessionary of a busline, rather than a complaint by native or colored elements, it may even invoke the unreasonableness of a specific act of apartheid; this happened in Moritzburg City Council v. Road Transportation Board, 3 S.A. 758, 774-75 N.D. (1959).

[77] In an appraisal of the retiring Chief Justice A. Van de Centlivres, we read: ". . . Centlivres again and again stressed the great care with which courts scrutinize statutes granting executive powers to invade liberties of subjects, and struck down unauthorized discrimination to a substantial degree between classes and races . . . but always he insisted that once it was clear that Parliament wanted to grant autocratic powers to the executive, the court had to give effect to the will of Parliament. . . ." The article also speaks of Centlivres as "a model of positivistic analysis that has hitherto—and wisely so, it is believed in a racially divided country—characterized judgments in constitutional matters" (*South African Law Journal*, Vol. 73 [1957], pp. 3-4). Centlivres himself, who since retirement from the bench and acceptance of high academic office has become an outspoken critic of the policies of the South African government, speaks of a "strict and complete legalism"; "Constitution and Law in South Africa," *Government Under Law*, ed. Arthur E. Sutherland, Harvard University Press, 1956, pp. 423-27. See also his opinion in R. v. Sachs, 1 S.A. 392, 399, 400 A.D. (1953). For application of a purely positivistic approach in a much more limited field, as a means of maintaining the confidence of all participants in federal-state struggles in Australia, see Ch. IV, Sec. 3c.

thorities of the day—to lawless behavior by people identified with patriotic goals.

Patriotism in this context meant anything directed toward expunging the instruments and the consequences of the 1918 defeat and the resurrection of a strong state authority. This inclination brought the judiciary into the spiritual neighborhood of the political right. At the same time it furthered the widespread inclination to devaluate the existing political structure, to measure it against the yardstick of assertedly higher values —faint echoes of a completely secularized natural law in which fond memories of an idealized past blended with indistinct images of a better future.[78] All the same, judicial attitudes toward positive law remained profoundly ambivalent: they mistrusted it, since it had become the plaything of uncontrollable social forces which were yet unable to solve society's most urgent problems; yet they saw it as a strong line of retreat and justification when the record of the judiciary came under fire for its partisan excesses. Only in areas where popular acclaim was secure, as, for example, when the judiciary rebelled against the fiction that a worthless mark is the legal equivalent of the prewar mark, did they venture to expressly formulate policy—thus forcing to the fore the issue of indemnification for the victims of inflation—rather than

[78] To what extent do legal theories actually influence judicial practice? Lon L. Fuller in his controversy with Professor Hart ("Fidelity to the Law," *Harvard Law Review*, Vol. 71 [1958], pp. 630-72) opines that the German pre-Hitler legal profession may have proved helpful to Hitler's assumption of power through their espousal of positivist doctrine. If the statement implies merely that the emphasis on legality played a certain role in the smoothness of the February 1933 establishment of the Hitler regime, and in the general willingness of bureaucracy and judiciary to go along with Hitler, it is unobjectionable. If it is meant to imply a more specific reproach, to wit, the unwillingness of the German judiciary to concern themselves with what Fuller calls "the inner morality of the law," the reverse is nearer the truth in the Weimar Republic. For specific sociopolitical reasons, discussed above, positivism had increasingly lost favor. Marschall von Bieberstein, *Vom Kampfe des Rechts gegen die Gesetze*, Stuttgart, 1927, even put this widespread sentiment of German judicial officialdom and their academic backers into verse. Certainly the successful campaign against the Mark equals Mark-fiction and the judiciary's at least ambiguous attitude toward the concept of extra-legal necessity in criminal law were anything but expressions of confidence in the wisdom of the legislature. If judicial attitude toward enactments became less critical during the first Hitler years, this was due as much to the large amount of consensus regarding policy as to the risks involved in expressing deviating sentiments in those restricted areas where judicial criticism was common. In the later years it became simply a matter of personal courage. The consideration that Hitler's regime was initially established in due legal form, with his legislative machine always referring back on the heading of a new order or decree to properly quoted enabling acts, certainly played no role in the attitude of the individual office holder in the later years of the regime. In short, legal theories may dimly reflect community attitudes, and serve as welcome rationalizations, but they are scarcely primary determinants of judicial action.

keep to shaping policy in the guise of routine application and interpretation of the texts.[79] Otherwise, along with the other professional groups, they remained bewildered and disoriented in the larger social and economic problem areas. Only in the political field the record remained painfully unequivocal. Exploiting the notion of judicial independence for all its worth, the majority of the judicial corps acted with some consistency as the benevolent protectors of the so-called patriotic forces of society.[80] In this way they helped to tip the balance in favor of these forces and in preparing their expensive total victory over those groups who were considered the abettors and profiteers of the 1918 defeat.

Having been able to transfer its corps, including prosecutors and the professional personnel of the various ministries of justice, without loss in numbers or authority, to the newly-founded Republic, the judiciary was immediately confronted with a novel situation. Grown up in the balmy days when official authority was disputed and criticized but never frontally challenged, it now confronted a society whose wide-open dissension had been intensified by the war and the, at best inconclusive, revolution. Its makeshift governments were too weak to integrate the various social and political strata and to produce authoritative decisions which had a chance of acceptance by all the major components of the population. Facing ceaseless rebellion against constituted authority on both its right and left flanks, and constant, almost exclusively rightist, resort to individual murder as a political weapon, a government steeped in constitutional tradition had to call uninterruptedly on the administration of justice to uphold and vindicate the public order.

From the outset the majority among the judiciary went overboard in supporting the government against its enemies on the left, but established a consistent pattern of refusal to tackle political law breakers on the right. During the critical initial years of the Republic (1919-1923) this consisted mainly of systematic unwillingness to take cognizance of rightist sedition and preparations for reversing the government by force; if caught redhanded, the judiciary let the perpetrators off, either completely or with ridiculous sentences, granting them pensions to boot,

[79] See Entscheidungen des Reichsgerichts in Zivilsachen, Vol. 104 (1923), p. 78. The commentary to the Civil Code published by the members of the Supreme Court—*Das Buergerliche Gesetzbuch*, Berlin, 1925, Vol. 1, p. 370—is rather more outspoken than the decision itself. "The legislator failed completely in face of this task. . . . Thus, it became incumbent on the judiciary, especially on the Highest Court, to perform the difficult task, without transgressing the boundaries drawn to it, of preventing that law become injustice."

[80] Hermann Kantorowicz had already condemned in the twenties the loathsome marriage between nationalism and the practices of political jurisprudence. "Landesverrat im deutschen Strafrecht," *Die Justiz*, Vol. 2 (1926-1927), pp. 92ff.

covering up the traces of rightist murderers, and whitewashing them.[81] During the period of stabilization (1925-1929) if the focus shifted somewhat, the tendency remained the same. At that time the foremost question was which part of the public establishment should be granted or refused protection. It was to be handsomely granted to the Reichswehr's clandestine rearmament, by application of the treason concept (invoked for divulging military secrets) to pacifists opposing such policies; it was withheld from both the symbols of the Republic and from those who were identified with it who could be libelled with impunity ad infinitum.

Needless to say that during the closing years of the Republic (1930-1932), when the balance of power was rapidly shifting to the right, the judiciary found no cause to change its political jurisprudence. Yet while this policy cast the judiciary into the role of a partisan, in the eyes of a good part of the population, the highest judicial dignitaries jealously watched over what had by now become the sheer myth of its political impartiality. In the defamation suit by Mr. Jorns, a member of the federal prosecution staff at the Leipzig Supreme Court, two lower Berlin courts had found, after an exhaustive scrutiny of the record, that Jorns, when in 1919 instructing the case against the murderers of Karl Liebknecht and Rosa Luxemburg, had actually given assistance to the murderers.[82] On a second appeal, the Supreme Court had to send the case back to a different, lower court, with detailed instructions on how to proceed in order to obtain the outlined whitewash of their colleague.[83] Exonerated, after such painful efforts, Jorns thereafter was appropriately appointed to be the first president of Hitler's People's Court.

[81] The history of criminal administration under the Weimar Republic has not yet been written, and German historians and jurists show no interest in probing into such a "controversial" subject. But there is a rich and often distorted partisan literature, both by participants and contemporary journalists as well as by recent East German academicians, who weaken their point by dogmatism and exaggerations. But the record itself has been preserved in the invaluable books by E. I. Gumbel: *4 Jahre Politischer Mord*, Berlin, 1922, and *Verraeter Verfallen der Feme*, Berlin, 1928; see also Philipp Löwenfeld, *Das Strafrecht als Politische Waffe*, Berlin, 1933. For the later years the record appears clearly from the volumes of *Die Justiz*, the periodical of the Republikanische Richterbund, 7 volumes, appearing from 1925-1933. The book by the former Bavarian Minister President Wilhelm Hoegner, *Die Verratene Republik*, Muenchen, 1958 (but written in 1934), contains, pp. 261-88, a small selection from the political jurisprudence under the Weimar Republic.

[82] The defendant's lawyer characterized Jorns as an examining magistrate "who does not give chase like a dog, but who has to be carried to the hunt." Paul Levi, *Der Jorns Prozess*, Berlin, 1929, p. 54.

[83] Entscheidungen des Reichsgerichts in Strafsachen, Vol. 64 (1930), p. 284; see also Josef Bornstein, *Der Fall Jorns und das Reichsgericht*, Berlin, 1930 and the same "Abschied von Jorns" in *Das Tagebuch*, February 7, and June 6, 1931, p. 884.

The meaning of legal consciousness in a heterogeneous society thus offers special problems. If no informal consensus exists on fundamental community issues, the judges cannot play their traditional role in realizing the community value structure and pointing it up in relation to specific issues. That does not mean that the judges then might not exercise an important enough function in society. But whether, as in South Africa, they serve to mitigate even to a small degree the harshness of an iniquitous social system directed against the majority of the population, or whether, as in the Weimar Republic, they throw in their lot— with some consistency, at least in the political field—with one of the contending power blocs, their role takes on a different color. In neither case do they fulfill the traditional function of translating the inchoate data of the people's consciousness into the molded form of legal consciousness. Or, to put it differently, under such circumstances the notion of impartiality which we attach to the exercise of judicial office will have no substance. Impartiality presupposes a commonly accepted starting proposition. If as his point of departure the judge uses propositions which are emphatically rejected by substantial elements in the community, he will not be able to rely on the presumption of obedience owed to his office, even if he can show that he has adhered with some consistency to his initial proposition. Judges will commonly be regarded as partisan if they sentence the members of one group to long terms of penal servitude or prison, while letting off the members of another, equally if not more dangerous, group, with whose goals they are more in sympathy. (In the latter case, the verdict may be only a light prison sentence, *custodia honesta*, or, as with the French military magistrates in March 1961, total acquittal.) No questions will be raised, of course, if the vast majority of the community share from the outset the judge's inclination to look at the first batch as enemies of the social order and the second as at best misguided patriots who made mistakes in the choice of their friends or weapons. In the absence of such a consensus, the element of force, always present in the judicial job but mostly dimmed and pushed into the background by the degree of universal recognition given to the judge's utterances, comes again to the fore; thus it deprives the community of the very benefit which it had tried to bestow on itself when it allowed the judge to become the keeper of its conscience. Whether such shortcomings reflect the judiciary's objective situation within a given social system or result from the judiciary's own political inclinations and sentiments, they gravely affect the judiciary's impartiality.

In a milder, less concentrated, more personalized form, a similar problem is bound to appear under any conceivable social and political system. Through the psychological deviant of legal realism we have become conscious of all the numerous factors in the judge's personality structure which might become determinative factors of judicial action. Not always constant and often not even conscious, they might make a shambles of the business of forecasting judicial attitudes and give rise to whimsical suggestions of psychiatric voyages of self-exploration for the judges.[84] In contrast to the infinite variety of personalized stimuli, large sociopolitical determinants might be easier to spot and identify, even if by no means easier to do away with. We will be more inclined to label them as bias, showing a lesser degree of toleration toward them. For example, as long as United States politics are still influenced by national group and denominational considerations, neither a judge of Jewish descent nor a practicing Catholic might appear to many as the most felicitous choice for trying a Jew arrested for having communicated vital national defense documents to agents of a foreign power with whose beliefs he is assertedly more in sympathy than with those of his own nation. The Jewish judge might somehow not be able to resist the opportunity to prove the baselessness of the identification of Jewry and radicalism, still extant in the minds of many citizens. His Catholic colleague might simply never get out of his mind the iniquities suffered by his fellow believers from the hands of the political friends of the defendants. Or, to quote a somewhat more farcical case, if a judge has in private life written books expounding the evils of speculation, would he form the most inspiring choice for trying a financier accused of fraud?[85] Only a political system already in its death agony, however, could admit doubts of the judge's impartiality, disqualify a judge for his belonging to a party, organization, or adhering to a certain belief system,[86] and abandon the assumption that whatever the judge's background and personal experience, all these factors would

[84] Such a recommendation constituted one of the pet themes of Jerome Frank until his very last publication, "Some Reflections on Judge Learned Hand," *Chicago Law Review*, Vol. 24 (1957), p. 666 at 676.

[85] Rex v. Milne and Erleigh, 1 S.A. 1 A.D. (1951), and comment, in *South African Law Journal*, Vol. 68 (1951), p. 151.

[86] See the decision of the District Court of Chemnitz, reported in *Die Justiz*, Vol. 7 (1931-1932), p. 259. In that case National Socialist defendants were successful in their attempt to obtain the disqualification of two judges who had been active on behalf of the Democratic Party and Jewish organizations, respectively. Once one court was willing to accept the National Socialist argument, National Socialist attempts to disqualify judges because of their political opinions or standing became a general practice.

recede behind his rectitude and self-control. The admissible element in the notion of bias thus remains a strictly and narrowly personal one: a particular relation to the party or the party's lawyer.[87] How realistic is the expectation that a judge can and will divest himself of his background and experience when he dons the robe of formulator of legal consciousness? This is quite another story. A perspicacious defense lawyer or a wise senior judge or a conference of senior judges distributing the court's case load might, within the very limited range of their possibilities, try to avoid testing this assumption. But from the viewpoint of the judicial system as a whole, the working assumption must remain that the prevalence of universally shared community values, the discipline of the profession, and the self-discipline required from each member of the bench will minimize whatever impediments arise from the judge's personal equation.[88]

From a different point of view, of course, it is meaningless to differentiate between the inherent limitations which the working of the social system might set on notions of impartiality, and the momentary deflection the system suffers through the personal equation of the individual judge. If we begin with a universe of antagonistic class relations, notions of impartiality or bias become equally meaningless. But the assumption of an all-pervasive class justice might be too general to be useful as a tool for analyzing what may be a somewhat more complex social reality. As already discussed, it is quite correct, though incomplete, to say that no judge may with impunity transcend the sum total of the social and political institutions of his time or, on his own initiative, jump too far ahead or slide too far behind them.

When Karl Liebknecht appeared in 1907 before the judges of the Leipzig Supreme Tribunal under an incitement to mutiny charge, the presiding judge asked him the meaning of class justice. He answered

[87] The U.S. judicial code 28 U.S.C. par. 144 (1958) explicitly restricts affidavits on bias to "personal bias and prejudice." Inferences of "subconscious prejudice" to be brought out by psychiatric evidence (as proposed by Lois G. Forer, "Psychiatric Evidence in the Recusation of Judges," *Harvard Law Review*, Vol. 73 [1960], pp. 1,325-31) might open the door to a more generalized bias concept; for this reason such suggestions are not likely to be regarded with favor by those entrusted with keeping the judicial business moving.

[88] A member of the German Federal Republic's highest court puts the requirements—not without a sideglance to a recent Bonn case involving a former aide of Chancellor Adenauer—in the following way: "The administration of justice must avoid in the case load distribution the slightest suspicion of any intention to remove a case from the jurisdiction of the competent judge, even if the rule continues to hold sway that judge B has the duty of deciding the case as objectively as judge A." Ernst Friesenhahn, "Richterliche Objectivitaet," *Object und Objectivitaet in der Wissenschaft* (Mainzer Universitaetsgespraeche 1959-1960, Mainz, 1960).

that as judicial office was held only by members of the ruling class, the judge would be in no position to judge objectively. Questioning him further, the judge asked whether the same reproach could not be made to judges belonging to a Social Democratic Party in power. Liebknecht replied that this group would be as little inclined toward objectivity as the present judge.[89] The defendant, caught somewhat off guard, forgot to add an argument which has been developed *ad nauseam* since: inasmuch as history marches inexorably toward higher forms, the notion of class justice, participating in and profiting from this progress, becomes purified and ennobled by its association with the objective laws of societal development. But unlike Rubashov and the modern Chinese, victims of class justice may not yet be attuned to this theory. Because they recognize the inevitability and correctness of their foes' actions, their spontaneous first reaction against being victimized is obliterated in their joyful acceptance of its objective necessity and progressiveness. What happens if they continue to have the same subjective feelings of hatred as their predecessors felt or still feel when ensnarled in the legal apparatus of the bourgoisie? If this is so, class justice will offer the melancholy picture of the "ewige Wiederkehr des Gleichen"—in sum, a universe of repression in which only the jailers and their victims are periodically made to exchange places. Who would deny that our contemporary period offers altogether too many opportunities to test this thesis?

But if the judge's role consisted only in his carrying through with preciseness, care, and as much haste as outward decorum allows the incumbent regime's orders, both he and the regime would soon be caught in a severe contradiction. The short-term needs of the regime, its urge to enforce obedience, might hinder its long-term needs, its desire for legitimacy and respectability. Yet this desire is somehow connected with allowing the judge to develop his own yardsticks for determining the outer limits of community tolerance. To continue for a moment the instructive Leipzig story of 1907: though the Empire's Attorney asked for a term of two years of penal servitude, the very judges whom Karl Liebknecht had apostrophied as standard-bearers of class justice inflicted on him one and a half years of *custodia honesta*, thus explicitly acknowledging the purity of his motives. Of course, the zealots of the class justice thesis might have a ready-made answer on hand: the mildness of the sentence, as compared with the ferocity of the sentences which the same judges' successors inflicted on defendants in the twenties, only goes to show that class antagonism in the first

[89] *Der Hochverratsprozess gegen Karl Liebknecht 1907 vor dem Reichsgericht, Verhandlungsbericht*, East Berlin, 1957, p. 67.

decades of the century had not reached the intensity of the post-World War I period. Be that as it may, such assertions may again overestimate a little the quasi-automatic element in the judge's response to the challenges of his time and society. If there is something like a judicial space within which the judge partakes creatively in the formulation of the community consciousness, the 1907 conduct of the Leipzig judges might be susceptible of a slightly different interpretation.

In acting as they did, they used the texts to recognize the claims of constituted authority while at the same time expressing the opinion, shared by many citizens, that the defendants' actions, if regrettable and nonpermissible, were at least understandable in the circumstances. Within the framework of their time and office, they were trying to weigh the established and pressing claims of the present against dimly visualized future claims that were just appearing on the horizon. Calling their behavior class justice tends to overemphasize the undeniable element of stand-pattism. It underestimates the fact that the judge, while bound by the ways of the past embodied in the structure of official society and its law,[90] might, if he wishes, make allowance for the inevitable imperfections and injustices inherent in any official political structure; but he must do so gently and unobtrusively, without any direct challenge to constituted authority. The ways of judges have a habit of freezing only if caught by panic and deadly fear: when the political structure becomes either so oppressive and monolithic or—which might be the same—so weak that it may burst wide open at any moment. If justice, as Simone Weil put it, is eternally in transit from the camp of the victor to that of the vanquished,[91] the judge, its handy man in an imperfect world, might keep the door for the flight slightly ajar, even if his function as a custodian of an established order never actually allows him to cross the threshold.

4. The Impact of the Jury

To what extent do juries increase the complexity of the judicial job and vitiate a system that is built to keep uncontrollable influence from affecting the labors of the bench? The point is still of considerable interest for the Anglo-American system, where the jury has retained some of its importance—the practice of waiver notwithstanding. In contrast, the continental assizes have in two ways withered away in the last half century: through their transformation into courts where

[90] Gerhart Husserl, *Recht und Zeit*, Frankfurt, 1955, pp. 57ff.
[91] *La Pesanteur et la Grâce*, Paris, 1948, p. 195.

a small band of professional judges are associated with a greater number of lay members in all stages of the trial proceedings; and by jurisdiction being shifted from even these emaciated substitutes which keep nothing from the original assizes but the name. Given the increasing apathy of people toward subjects outside their immediate life experience, it is hard to judge whether the passing of this landmark of early nineteenth century continental constitutionalism has evoked more than occasional regrets.[92]

Even before the turn of the century, professional European opinion had uttered doubts about an institution which limited the action of what it considered the conscientious, knowledgeable, and impartial professional in favor of the amateur, inefficient and easily swayed by the most contradictory emotions of the moment. Jhering, never one to miss coining a phrase, compared the choice to one between militia and professional army.[93] There is little doubt that a chief of staff, given a choice, will always prefer a battalion of army regulars to a battalion of national guardsmen for front line duty. But his judgment would not necessarily be controlling if the question were whether a state should organize its armed forces exclusively according to professional patterns or whether it should prefer a mixture of professional and civilians in uniform. Other considerations of a broader nature might be equally important. At the beginning of the nineteenth century, constitutionalism's recourse to the assizes was an integral part of the middle class drive to gain some measure of indirect check over the executive and to forestall resurgence of political oppression.[94]

[92] See the "sondage" on which R. Chadefaux reports in *Pouvoir Judiciaire* of May 1955, "Contribution a l'étude de la réforme de la Cour d'Assises." 81 questionnaires had been sent to jurors who served during the June 1948 session of the Cour d'Assises de la Seine. 52 (11 have since died) handed in answers to the following questions: 1) Did the presiding judge show partiality for or against the defendant during the trial? Did he try to bring out the truth? 2) Could you express your opinion freely and without any form of compulsion? Did the presiding officer or the other two professional judges bring pressure on you to arrive at a conviction or acquittal not in conformity with the wishes of the majority of the jurors? 3) Would you prefer the present method to jurors handing in a verdict without participation of professional magistrates? On all points—except for the last, where a minority of seven appeared dissatisfied with the present system—there was almost unanimous satisfaction. It is hard to speculate what a more sophisticated, less loaded questionnaire would have obtained, especially considering that the questionnaire's covering letter contained hints on recent campaigns against the French administration of justice.

[93] Jhering, *Zweck im Recht*, Vol. 1, p. 321, and Binding, *op.cit.*, pp. 62ff. But see the opposite statements by the Austrian authority on criminal procedure and later Minister of Justice, Julius Glaser, *Schwurgerichtliche Erörterungen*, 2nd ed.; Vienna, 1875, pp. 76ff.

[94] Erich Schwinge, *Der Kampf um die Schwurgerichte bis zur Frankfurter National-versammlung*, Breslau, 1926.

The arrival of mass democracy left the institution in a somewhat more ambiguous state. Both the judge's appointment and promotion, and especially control over prosecutions, now came under the control of a politically responsible government. The assizes become more of an educational enterprise than a means for political control: they appear to have been one of the various means to extend the sphere of direct popular participation in public affairs. Now they are often considered a kind of inevitable ransom to be paid to the reigning ideology of popular sovereignty and a necessary cover-up for the judges in the pursuit of their tasks. The relation between judge and jury seems comparable to that between executive and legislature, certainly not a flattering compliment in a society where the belief in the role and competence of the legislature is rapidly dwindling.[95] One gains the impression of some sort of sacred cow, possibly with excellent historical titles but presently at best a cumbersome relic. If properly treated, however, it may not cause too much harm and may even be turned to good purpose;[96] at worst it may be a definite hindrance to the proper functioning of the administration of justice.[97]

One may call this attitude the majority current in professional opinion that pays lip service, at most, to the institution. Against this stands a smaller but important band who fervently believe that the institution, if only made representative of the citizenry at large, constitutes a continuing democratic working device whose importance is far more than symbolic. The different shades of attitudes and expectations have come out most clearly during the various United States court debates over defense objections against both the New York blue ribbon juries and the preponderance of government officials on Washington juries.[98]

[95] Sir Patrick Devlin, *Trial by Jury*, London, 1956, p. 163. For the older French assizes, see the recollections of Pierre Bouchardon, *Mes Souvenirs*, pp. 182, 198.

[96] Compare Lord Goddard's inimitable charge in the Laski libel case: "The law of England is, a man may say, what a jury thinks is expedient. He may not say what a jury thinks inexpedient to say, provided that they have been properly charged as to when a thing may become expedient or when it may become inexpedient." Laski v. *Newark Advertizer*, London, 1947, p. 396.

[97] Glanville Williams, *Proof of Guilt*, 2nd ed.; London, 1958. See also the instructive comments by a trial lawyer, Benton L. Oppenheimer, in the symposium "Trial by Jury," *University of Cincinnati Law Review*, Vol. 11 (1937), pp. 142, 148; but see the interesting opinion of a juror (*ibid.*, p. 162), emphasizing the lawyer's treatment of the evidence as a reason for the jury's poor performance.

[98] Fay v. New York, 332 U.S. 261 (1947); Moore v. New York, 333 U.S. 565 (1948); Frazier v. U.S., 335 U.S. 497 (1948); Dennis v. United States, 339 U.S. 162 (1950). Recently the latter viewpoint has been exalted in a number of Justice Black's opinions; to combat the present practice of political deviation being handled by contempt proceedings, in the absence of a jury, Black utilizes the traditional image of the jury

Blue ribbon juries, with their conscious attempts to establish selection lists of educationally and intellectually specially qualified jurors (a practice abolished in England in 1949), are as clearly at variance with the idea of representative cross-section[99] as was the elimination of working men from the continental assizes of a former period, assertedly undertaken to spare the burden of public service from those who could afford it least.[100] Would a more representative cross-section be at the same time a more politically balanced cross-section? Though evidence on this point is scant, we may well assume that a European metropolitan jury of the beginning of the century, in which the laboring classes would have been represented according to their proportionate strength in the population, would have put obstacles in the way of the government's case as often as did some of their middle class predecessors with politically tinged prosecutions of the continental executives in the nineteenth century. Hence the persistent policy of many continental European administrations, continuing right up to the demise of the assizes proper, to withdraw as many political cases as possible (libel through publication included) from the jurisdiction of such courts. But does the same assumption hold true in our time and age? Is there any scintilla of evidence that a higher proportion of working class people on the Dennis jury would have brought in a different verdict? The Dennis defense lawyers, spending a good part of their initial effort in proving the unrepresentative character of the blue ribbon method of selection,[101] must have kept their tongues in their cheeks. They knew full well that with the popular mind being presently formed by the prevailing degree of material welfare, and attuned to and willingly resounding the fare offered by the mass communication media, a more representative jury composition would not have materially helped the defendants' case.

What does that mean for the impact of juries on the style of the administration of criminal justice? If we leave aside the important question of the jury's racial composition in cases involving the pos-

as bastion against oppression (see, e.g., Green v. United States, 356 U.S. 165, 193, 215 diss. op. [1958]). It is a problematic argument in the service of a worthy cause.

[99] See Justice Murphy's dissenting opinion in Fay v. New York, quoted above at 296, 300, and in Moore v. New York, quoted above at 569.

[100] Der Ledebour Prozess, Berlin, 1919, p. 18, with both the presiding judge and defendant discussing this point. Interesting data have been collected in R. Hermann, Die Schoeffen in den Strafgerichten des Kapitalistischen Deutschland, East Berlin, 1957.

[101] Judge Learned Hand deals with the point in U.S. v. Dennis, 183 Fed 2d 201, 216, 2 C.C.A. (1950).

sibility of racial prejudice,[102] even the most equitable composition of an American jury is not likely to heighten the chances of those who allow themselves the luxury of pointed dissent from prevailing opinion trends. Whether the full participation of all shades of the population in the jury work would give unpopular causes an even smaller chance is entirely a matter of conjecture. The assumption that a Washington, D.C. jury, sitting with a great number of government employees, might be more prone to fears that a vote not consonant with the government's wishes might be detrimental to their personal prospects, and that such a jury might therefore be potentially more disadvantageous for a defendant than a jury with fewer government employees, misjudges the nature of pressures in our society.[103] The urge toward spontaneous conformity arises from the sum total of our institutional patterns, rather than from the dread of a particular unfavorable reaction of a vengeful and zealous government investigator. While the latter fear might not be misplaced,[104] overemphasis of it only serves to hide a much weightier point.

Juries, to quote again Cockburn, the nineteenth century Scottish judge,[105] have the color of the case tinged by the color of their mind. This may lead to occasional unfairness, but is otherwise a useful correction where the public has intelligence, independence, and candor, supposed constituents of the proper jury mind. The dissenting Supreme Court opinions in the blue ribbon jury and the Washington federal employees' cases do not negate these premises on which any rational defense of the jury as an institution must be built; rather, they imply that the jury based on a faithful cross-section of the population would best fulfill these premises. Perhaps the nineteenth century jury representing the well-bred or property-owning strata, or the blue ribbon jury of the twentieth century answering to a similar description, might have met such requirements. But even there the capacity for rational judgment might not withstand the pressure for distortion if the juror

---

[102] Proper racial representation on a jury, in a society otherwise still ripe with race discrimination, might, as the recent Hoffa acquittal by a preponderantly Negro jury in the District of Columbia has shown, create its own dilemmas. Just as the United States government's prosecution can evoke a jury response to the image of the Communist danger, so E. B. Williams, the defendant's lawyer, by staging a show of solidarity between Joe Louis and Mr. Hoffa, was able to work a transfer of race solidarity to the benefit of his client.

[103] Dissenting opinion of Justice Jackson in Frazier v. U.S. (n. 97 above), 514.

[104] Gold v. U.S., 237 Fed 2d 764 D.C. Cir. (1956), 352 U.S. 985 (1957). See also the full discussion of the point in Dennis v. United States (n. 97 above), esp. the dissenting opinions of Black (181) and Frankfurter (183).

[105] Op.cit., p. 65.

rightly or wrongly perceives his or his group's status or interests to be involved in the outcome of the trial. Of course, the same may be said of the judge himself. In either case, however, one might argue that the ability to submit a confused complex of sentiments, actions, and projected goals to the rational dissection of its constituent parts may already be called an achievement that speaks well for the ability to resist the onslaught of distorting impulses.[106] To what extent the members of an ordinary cross-section of the citizenry selected to mirror the average intellectual and professional qualifications have equal mental facilities is another question.[107] Much will depend on whether the panel happens to include individuals who have had enough opportunities to compare the judgment and presuppositions impressed on them by their environment, including the mass media, with some radically different life situations, expectations, and evaluations.

In many respects the present-day jury has the quality of an echo, throwing back the most forceful sounds it receives. Sometimes the conditions of reception are unpropitious, and the sound comes back distorted or grotesquely magnified. But if the surroundings are carefully chosen, it throws back a faithful replica. It does not, however, register less perceptible sounds. To register them adequately, society would have to make a more conscientious and considered and less haphazard effort to form its human raw material. So far, society has had the greatest trouble in obtaining at least passable results in selecting persons, including the judges, to handle affairs where situations are not repetitious enough to allow for relatively simple, echo-like responses.

[106] R. M. A. Jackson, *op.cit.*, pp. 250-51, has a very informative treatment of British jury attitudes in political cases, which rests on the supposition that jury responses are mainly determined by a very realistic appreciation of the possibly shifting requirements of local self-interest. But such discernment evidently presupposes a certain level of sophistication.

[107] Rita James, "Status and Competence of Jurors," *American Journal of Sociology*, Vol. 54 (1959), pp. 563-70, reporting on some segments of the Chicago jury project, marks some more or less substantial differences between the various educational levels. What seem especially marked are the differences in capacity to follow the judge's instructions. However, as the author herself admits, the choice of the experimental case, trial for housebreaking with an insanity plea, probably does not permit far-reaching conclusions.

CHAPTER VI

THE DEFENDANT, HIS LAWYER,
AND THE COURT

+++

Jede dumpfe Umkehr der Welt hat solche Enterbte, denen das
Frühere nicht und noch nicht das Nächste gehört.

—RAINER MARIA RILKE, *Duineser Elegien*, 7. Elegie*

+++

1. The Goals of the Founders

IN what terms does the defendant representing a cause visualize his
relations with the court? Where does the fundamental difference
arise between a normal defense and one whose order of priority is
directed by considerations beyond obtaining a favorable court decision? A glance at the defendant's demeanor in the two most momentous trials of history might help to clarify the point.

Among the many reproaches cast upon the Sanhedrin's proceedings
against Jesus, none has been more deadly than the assertion that most
of its members, were from the outset, looking for a means to convict
Jesus for a capital offense. In elucidation rather than rebuttal, it might
be pointed out that whatever the frame of mind with which this body
approached its task, it was Jesus himself who gave them the cue for
their subsequent action: Are you Christ, the Son of the Lord? "I am;
and you will see the Son of man sitting at the right hand of Power
and coming with the clouds of heaven" (Mark 14:62).

From this assertion the members of the Sanhedrin could conceive
the utterances of Jesus as an at least implicit affirmation of his Messianic
quality, thus compounding both their tribal suspicions and the professional jealousy of those in charge of traditional teaching. Endless con-
jectures on how the Sanhedrin could have interpreted these answers
to bring them under the prohibition of their law have little meaning.
The accounts of the Evangelists are too fragmentary to inform us
about the true nature of the proceedings; not even the relation between
the role of the Sanhedrin and that of the Roman officials becomes clear.

* "Each sluggish turn of the world has such disinherited children, to whom the past
belongs no more than the future."

225

But what makes the accounts of absorbing interest is that they give some notion of how the Evangelists have visualized Jesus' own role.[1]

The central concern is what Ernest Renan called "la grande équivoque," the fact that Jesus' answers were couched in terms which not only could not satisfy the Sanhedrin, but also would not provide Pilate, "the local commander of the military government of a foreign occupation power"[2] with that degree of certainty which would make the most spineless bureaucrat willing to withstand indigenous pressure and risk having to justify himself before his superiors for having preferred a local brawl to a judicial murder.

On the theological level, of course, this question need not be answered. Here the actions of all the dramatis personae are preordained, necessary happenings in the history of Passion and Salvation. But Jesus' attitude before the two sets of authorities may also be explained by his contemporary role. He could not allow any misunderstanding to arise as to the character of his mission. He could avoid an answer when confronted with an asserted (however decisively modified, Matt. 24:2) formulation of his own: "At last two came forward and said: 'This fellow said, I am able to destroy the temple of God and to build it in three days'" (Matt. 26:61). Interpreted too literally, this statement smacks of an open revolt against constituted authority. As the testimony on this point was contradictory (Mark 14:59), Jesus could refer to the sum total of his public teachings, which would contradict any asserted intention of violence. "I have spoken openly to the world; I have always taught in synagogues and temples, wherever all Jews come together. I have said nothing secretly. Why do you ask me? Ask those who heard what I said; see, they will know what I said" (John 18:20-21). But when directly challenged to explain his calling, he could not, even in the face of a manifestly hostile crowd, allow any doubt to arise. "But he said to them, if I tell you, you will not believe and if I ask you, you will not answer. But from now on the Son of man shall be seated at the right hand of the Power of God. And they all said, are you the Son of God? And he said to them, you say that I am"

[1] See the comparative tabulations and characterizations from Greek and Roman history, and the history of Christ as narrated in the Gospel, in A. Toynbee, *Study of History*, New York, 1939, Vol. 6, p. 377. However, though his Socrates analogy is close in external happenings, it remains dubious in essentials. Jesus, visualized as a leader of an "internal proletariat," and Socrates, the intellectual critic befriended by the scions of the upper crust, exude different types of certainties. The man serene in possession of the ultimate truth and the patron saint of inquisitive intellectual pursuit agree in nothing but the consequentialness of their claims; *ibid.*, pp. 486-95.

[2] Karl Barth, *Dogmatik im Grundriss*, München, 1947, p. 125.

(Matt. 26:64 and Luke 22:69-70). It was an answer couched in terms that would show the difference between his enemies' imputation of the hostile character of his mission and his own more complex understanding. But it was not made to soothe the feelings of the custodians of traditional practices. Prophesy clothed in projection tends to solidify the adherents of its authority and infuriate those who see their own authority challenged by resort to sources which escape their control. Taking its departure from dissatisfaction with existing conditions, it might easily be interpreted by malevolents as a concealed call to action, even if such intention is presently absent from the mind of the defendant. Yet in the face of a hostile crowd and an unfriendly authority, unwilling to follow Jesus' own understanding of his preachings (Luke 22:71), it made no sense to expound in more detail his mission and actions; it would suffice to refer to the evidence and to stake the major claim. A more detailed exposition of the claim must await the more favorable and more decisive opportunity: Jesus' appearance before Pilate.

If Jesus had persevered in mutism, or if he had confirmed the Sanhedrin's version of his previous answer in the same apodictic and monosyllabic fashion, would Pilate have gone back to face the Jews with the statement that he found no fault with him (Mark 15:2-5)? Pilate's initial rejection of the Sanhedrin's interpretations must be understood not only as the result of his wife's intercession (Matt. 27:19), but also as his acceptance of Jesus' own interpretation of his mission. "My kingdom is not of this world; if my kingship were of this world, my servants would fight, that I might not be handed over to the Jews; but my kingship is not from the world" (John 18:36). In the face of an officer of the occupation power whose experience, horizon, and interests were different from those of the subordinate indigenous authorities, Jesus had a chance to urge an interpretation of his dominion as the kingdom of truth which, if all-embracing, did not—at least not yet—clash with Roman claims. Jesus could do no more than reveal the nature of his kingdom and give an authentic interpretation of his contested claims. Pilate would have no aptitude or inclination to measure the traditional Jewish concept of the role of Messiah against either the practices of Jesus' small band and Jesus' own assertions, or against the accusations of the Sanhedrin, which were intentionally couched for Pilate's benefit in terms of Roman sovereignty attacked and defended (Luke 23:2). When Kaiphas persevered to urge Jesus' death on the recalcitrant Pilate (Mark 15:3-5), the latter could not elicit any additional answer from

Jesus. As he had already explained the nature of his mission in the privacy of Pilate's office, any additional statement could do nothing but upset the always delicate balance between the affirmation of a spiritual claim and the defense against its misinterpretation.[3]

Socrates' story has come down to us not only in fragmentary form, but in the full report of an outstanding eyewitness, Plato, and by a secondary source, Xenophon. As in the case of Jesus, it gives in essence only the side of the defense. But it is fuller, not only because of the qualities of the reporters, but through the nature of the defense and the defendant. "This sublimation of a free personality" (Jacob Burckhardt) had no everlasting truth to assert, but was concerned with his particular universe of discourse and his system of unsystematic free inquiry. His demon, of which Meletus complained, was, as Pareto put it, "a cousin of reason and a brother of what liberal Protestants would call conscience."[4] Close reasoning is evident in the logically well-ordered first part of his defense; here he hammers at the weakest and inconsistent enough part of the accusation, atheism, but glides rather skillfully over the implications of the charge of introducing novel religious practices. But when he continues to give his own version of his worth, it becomes clear that his method of free inquiry is subject to the dialectic of confirmation. Unable to offer last certainties, he somehow overcompensates by an exaggerated emphasis on the uniqueness of his personality. But seen closer, both the aggressiveness and exaggerations in self-evaluation appear integral to the no-compromise line with which he surrounds his self-styled life pursuit: the examination of his own and others' actions, including the blocking of injustice whenever an official rank gives him such opportunity.[5] He would never invoke his war service record as a basis of appeal to the court's sentiment. Yet he alludes to it in order to explain the terms in which he visualizes the dangers threatening him now, when he feels duty-bound to continue in his mission. His general way of behaving and his demeanor in court cannot be separated. Socrates did not aspire to martyrdom,

---

[3] The various interpretations have been collected and commented upon again recently in Josef Blinzler, *Der Prozess Jesu*, Regensburg, 1955. The interpretations, varying between making Pilate the instrument of the Jews and putting the whole responsibility on the Romans, cancel each other out.

[4] V. Parefo, *Traité de Sociologie*, Paris-Lausanne, 1919, Vol. 2, par. 2,348. For changes in the concept of conviction, from the objective certitude granted by God to the various degrees of subjective assumptions elaborated since Kant, see the sensitive pages in Ernst Rudolf Huben, *Deutsche Verfassungsgeschichte seit 1789*, Stuttgart, 1957, Vol. 1, pp. 711-17.

[5] *Apology* (Jowett trans.), 28.

certainly not before his conviction and probably not even afterwards. But when "history marched towards him" (Jacob Burckhardt), he persevered without special effort to handle himself in a way most consonant with his own image of himself. Socrates actually faced a triple problem of which only the first two parts were of a tactical nature: first, how to modulate his defense so as to best deny the assertions of his adversaries; second, how to uphold the claim to continuation of free inquiry without concessions; third, after sentence was rendered, he gave the most significant and the most difficult service to his community: when given the chance to escape, he reaffirmed the foundations of the commonwealth by recognizing, with the sacrifice of his life, the validity of what was to him an unjust but formally unexceptional judgment.[6]

Jacob Burckhardt once spoke of the advantage granted to those who received the opportunity to appear great in suffering. And he added "But they [the hierarchs of the church] must make use of this advantage; because if they get into danger and try to escape it without martyrdom, they make a bad impression."[7] Burckhardt is thinking of a conscious and determined effort to add to the treasure of merits of an established belief system. In contrast, what stands out in the cases of both Jesus and Socrates is the seemingly effortless consistency with which the trials merge into the total image of what has come down to us as the essence of their historical personalities. The certainty which allowed Jesus and Socrates to face the court and use it as a vehicle to state their doctrines was an inner certitude. With Jesus it rested on the consciousness of objective participation in God, with Socrates on a subjective evaluation—on the basis of what he considered sufficient objective reasons—of the relevance of his methods of inquiry. Whatever their radically different foundations, religious experience or the unceasing quest for enlarging the fundament of reason (and these differences affected their ways of arguing), both showed the same certainty in defining and upholding their essential positions, which have left a lasting impression on disciples and posterity alike.

2. *In Quest of Group Identification*

What is self-evident and needs no further discussion in the personality *hors cadre*, the historical individual, becomes the probing and testing ground, the field of contention, between defendant and court in the

[6] *Crito* (Jowett), 50.
[7] *Weltgeschichtliche Betrachtungen* V.

majority of political trials. The certainty of the average political defendant derives from possible doctrine and loyalty group. Doctrine,
existing outside the person, must be appropriated by a process of learning and imitation. Whether one conceives a new loyalty group or
joins an existing one, the nature and intensity of intragroup relations
will determine the degree to which group loyalty will survive outside
attacks. From the viewpoint of the defendant, therefore, a political
trial might constitute primarily an attempt to smash and destroy loyalty
to his doctrine and group.

The relative significance of doctrine and group may change from
case to case. Among a fiercely intensive loyalty group such as revolutionary nationalists, the share of doctrine is probably quite small. Self-
evident facts of suppression by an overlord of different national or
racial complexion set goals quasi-automatically. Intensive persecution
seems, at least since the middle of the nineteenth century, but a prelude
to an inevitable climax in which revolutionaries win honor and glory.
Motivation, action, and loyalty patterns are clearcut. An example is
the recent case of the Arab members of the FLN who tried to assassinate
Jacques Soustelle, who, in the eyes of the organization, symbolized
French repression in the Maghreb. Not only those who directly participated in the attempt, but also others who had related assignments in
the operation, proudly claimed their share in the responsibility. All
the participants knew that no French military tribunal would recognize
their claim that membership in the FLN (on whose orders and
authority they acted) entitled them to be treated as prisoners of war.
They knew that they would be convicted and sentenced for attempted
homicide. However, neither this knowledge, nor the antecedent police
brutalities, nor the intense hostility of the audience, kept them from
merging their identity completely with that of an organization reviled
by official France.[8]

Compared with the certainties of revolutionary nationalism, where
relatively simple and clearcut goals narrow down the area of potential
dissension to the making of often excruciating, but in essence tactical,
choices, the revolutionary group bent on changing the whole social
fabric of society runs into greater difficulties. What appear to be tactical

[8] Said the defendant Ouraghi (*Le Monde*, February 6, 1959): "As soldier of the Army
of National Liberation, I have obeyed my officers without compulsion. The order was
given to liquidate a war criminal responsible for the death of thousands of my country-
men. I regret nothing, I would be only too glad if I had succeeded." For the practices
of identification at the recent FLN trial at Rennes (February 27-March 13, 1961), see
Marcel Pépi, "Un Procès Paradoxal," *Les Temps Modernes*, April 1961, pp. 1,437-44.

differences usually hide deeper conflicts. As long as the group is small and engaged in and fully agreed upon immediate action programs, strong personal bonds are created by the joint risks run by the participants. One thinks of the Russian social revolutionaries of the 1870's, the beginning of the eighties, and the first decade of this century. As Vera Figner put it: "I had always required logical and harmonious agreement of word and action from others and, of course, for myself; and it seemed to me that if I admitted theoretically that only through violence could we accomplish anything, I was in duty bound to take an active part in whatever program of violence might be undertaken by the organization which I had joined. I could not with quiet conscience urge others to take part in violence if I myself did not do so."[9] In such a situation, insight into the necessary way of action connotes a simultaneous moral obligation to act.

By contrast, when political programs extend over a total, yet vague, vista of future social developments, there is much greater likelihood that differences in interpretation and intensity of feeling among the members will cause doctrinal conflicts. Under such circumstances the group member might provoke a simultaneous conflict with the official authorities and his own group. When in 1917 Friedrich Adler (1879-1959) assassinated Count Stürgkh, the Austrian Minister President, his action connoted a double protest against both the official policies of the Austrian government and those of his own party executive. The latter, in his opinion, had become much too close to the government and too lukewarm both in the defense of workers' interest and in the energetic pursuit of peace. As his party had always rejected individual terror, he had to partially rehabilitate terrorism. Using the example of his sacrifice, he intended to shame his own associates into a better understanding of their duties in regard to collective action.[10] In order to reach this goal, his defense had to be directed to frustrate any possible attempt by the official authorities—and possibly also by a defense lawyer, though for quite different reasons—to raise the issue of diminished responsibility. From the viewpoint of the defendant, his amount of guilt was not different from that of the officer who during the war gave his soldiers an order to shoot. Adler fashioned his insight into the necessity of action: irresistible coercion akin to the absence of choice under a direct military command relation.

Disposal by the courts of a case involving revolutionary activity does not necessarily affect the future of the movement in a decisive way.

[9] *Memoirs of a Revolutionist*, New York, 1927, p. 168.
[10] Friedrich Adler, *Vor dem Ausnahmegericht*, Jena, 1923, esp. p. 81.

The trial may be just a skirmish in a continuing battle, or a flourish after decisive action has been taken elsewhere. On the other hand, it may be one of those rare occasions when the often diffuse conflict between the established authorities and their foes seems to come into sharper focus. Both sides will sort out their material and arguments with a view to public presentation, trying to put themselves into the most advantageous position before their respective publics. That public might be substantially different for each side. In a South African treason trial, for example, the defendants and the government will appeal to a quite different constituency; but never will the defense abandon hope that it can manipulate traditional symbols in a way that will widen its audience. In recent times the Communist Party has for that purpose tried very hard to develop almost scientific techniques to exploit trials of both Communist and non-Communist defendants; it has tried to take over these trials regardless of the desire of the defense.[11]

Yet whatever the possible impact on the audience at large, the defense's first and foremost concern remains the loyalty group itself. It must seek to show such abnegation, sacrifice, and complete identification of the defendants with their chosen cause that whatever the outcome of the trial, the consequences will include a maximum affirmation of loyalty by the members to the goals of the organization. Indeed, the group judges the defendant's performance primarily according to how well he contributes to this consequence. It is the organization's current interests as perceived by its leaders, not the personal interest of the individual accused, which determine the attitude of the defense.[12] Perhaps the organization is seeking to alter prevailing images of itself and another competing group. If so, it may desire the most dramatic possible court fight. It may want the defendant to hurl open defiance at the court, decline to recognize its jurisdiction, or tear off the judge's

[11] Johannes Zelt, *Proletarischer Internationalismus im Kampf um Sacco und Vanzetti*, East Berlin, 1958, used the case's handling by the Communist Party as a sort of vade mecum to show how to turn "a relatively minor occurrence" (p. 305) into a full-fledged political campaign.

[12] Felix Halle, *Wie verteidigt sich der Proletarier in Politischen Strafsachen bei Polizei, Staatsanwaltschaft und Gericht*, Berlin, 1929. Marcel Willard, *op.cit.* (Ch. III, 6), brings together accounts of famous Communist defendants whose behavior in court fully measured up to these expectations. In the most recent edition of the book, some heroes have fallen by the wayside and others have been substituted. This is not because flaws have been discovered in the trial conduct of those omitted, but because of disenchantment with those who meanwhile had become deviators and heretics.

mask of impartiality. This is more easily possible when the applicable procedural rules allow the defendant to make a coherent statement, if not during his interrogation, at least in his concluding remarks. This is possible in continental countries. Under Anglo-American procedure, where the defendant is usually reduced to the role of a "voluntary" witness answering specific questions put to him, the performance needs to be more subtle; its potentialities can, however, be enlarged if the defendant acts as his own counsel. Thus the organization may succeed in presenting a show of militancy, casting discredit on a regime for prosecuting a group merely for holding and seeking to spread their opinions; this was the case—albeit with the help of the judge—with the American Communist Party during the New York Smith Act trial of 1949. Yet gradually the party found it had underestimated the limitations on the drawing power of liberal values when these are appealed to by a group which has constantly derided such liberal premises in its own practices. The trial became increasingly a contest between the Communist Party's dwindling ability to organize opinion support against the prosecution and the judge's dexterity in convincing both himself and the community at large that he, rather than the defendants, was the victim of the proceedings.[13]

The trial showed how small the judge's margin of intellectual independence from momentarily prevailing opinion trends may be. Unable to afford what constitutes the most awesome as well as the most creative part of the judicial experience, the entertaining of a small but persistent grain of doubt in the purposes of his own society, he becomes merely the legal technician shuffling formulas to fit the purpose of the day. Yet the sacrifices made to elicit this painful demonstration were not balanced by proportional advantages to the defendant's organization. Once the trial had reached its end, with heavy sacrifice of energy, personnel, and prestige for the defendant group, their tactics had changed. In numerous follow-up trials the defendants and their lawyers

[13] Judge Harold Medina's *The Anatomy of Freedom*, New York, 1959, a slender volume of inconsequential speeches, reprints a 1955 address, showing that the judge still looks at his excursion into political trial practice as a successful popularity contest where a lonely and badly terrorized freedom fighter gets the better of the evil incarnate. The rejoinder of John Gates, an ex-Communist defendant in this trial, is in order: "One would think from the fuss raised by the judge that he was the victim and that he rather than we served 5 year sentences." *The Story of an American Communist*, New York, 1958, p. 124. For the whole range of the defendant's viewpoints and activities Laswell and Donnelly have coined the felicitous expression "counter-condemnation"; *op.cit.* (Ch. V, n. 56 above).

behaved in a businesslike manner. Though exploiting all the procedural avenues open to them and never once abandoning the strict canon of loyalty to and identification with their organization, they tried to protect their ranks from exposure to more suffering than was necessary.

3. The Informer: Enemy from Within

As loyalty to the group is the predominant forte of the political defendant, everything depends on his being able to protect himself from the feeling of loneliness brought on by separation from his comrades, and from the inevitable doubts which arise when he scrutinizes his and his group's purposes and performances in the light of his present predicament. It is at this juncture that the powers-that-be may be able to exercise pressure on the defendant by proposing a "deal" which will alienate him from his organization. The problem of informers is usually discussed from the viewpoint of the government's moral right to have recourse to their services. The informer is granted a special status, freedom from prosecution, or at least special consideration in the post-conviction state. This is often supplemented by other inducements made to both the genuinely repentant enemy with a useful memory as a professional witness and to the patriotic or professional infiltrator. These practices serve as a sharp reminder that while a trial centers around establishing the truth of a particular contention of the prosecution, the latter is free to put up the scaffolding, so to speak, from which to build its edifice. How it manages to put together the individual stages of the scaffolding remains its own concern, except for the rare instances when the whole structure comes crashing down, burying the builders under its ruins. On the practice itself, arguments and positions have not changed since the days when François Guizot, not yet advanced from the star of the opposition to Louis Philippe's minister, called informing a vile métier;[14] and when Frederick William IV of Prussia urged his minister, von Manteuffel, to follow through on what he himself characterized as the "not too honorable thought"[15] of putting a certain Stieber on the payroll in order to organize conspiracies which would enable the Prussian public "to enjoy the longed for spectacle of seeing a conspiracy uncovered and punished." We have elsewhere alluded to the infinite number of shades between straightforward informing on actual political activity

[14] *Dès Conspirateurs*, Ch. II, p. 12.
[15] The letter is reprinted in Karl Bittel, *Der Kommunistenprozess zu Köln 1852 im Spiegel der zeitgenössischen Presse*, East Berlin, 1955, p. 17.

and the fabrication of subversion, tailor-made to the political needs of those in power.[16]

In society as a whole, the range of activities connected with informing remains a problem of deciding priorities: against the need for political stability must be weighed, first, the chance that the political process can find its own level without constant official steering and managing of its marginal areas and, second, the degree of credibility of its judicial process.[17] To the political defendant the problem of informing constitutes a dangerous threat to his organization. In this threat, the attack on the belief system itself might easily outweigh the more tangible disadvantages of hamstringing or destroying useful means of legal defense. The more intimate the contact among the members of the group, the greater their mutual dependence in carrying out difficult and dangerous tasks. The more intensive the spiritual bond, the greater the blow when a trusted member turns out to have abandoned the cause or to have been a "plant" from the outset. To quote again Vera Figner, the Russian social revolutionary, when she found out in prison that her trust in Degajev had been misplaced: "To survive such as act of treason was a misfortune. It took away the moral beauty of mankind, the beauty of the revolution and of life itself. From the ideal heights

---

[16] See Ch. III, Sec. 6. During the Dennis trial the defense made a motion to strike from the record the testimony of the witness Philbrick, an FBI infiltrator, as such action curtailed the defendant's right to political activity (U.S. Supreme Court Record, Vol. 349, 494-532, Part 6, p. 4,501). In support, the motion quotes the memorable, but atypical, decision of Judge Anderson in Colyet v. Skeffington, 265 Fed 17, Distr. Ct. Mass. (1920). As Communism has made informing a routine practice and a duty for functionaries, the Communist Party is in a bad tactical position to invoke protection against it. But despite the authority of Judge Learned Hand (U.S. v. Dennis, 183 Fed 2d 201, 224 [1950]), the argument merits consideration in societies interested in maintaining the substance, not merely the outward forms, of free institutions; see Donnelly (cited Ch. V, n.56), p. 1,129. Already in the balmy post-World War I days, the U.S. authorities had taken to the job of steering the policy of their marginal foes in directions seemed "desirable" from the police's view point: see the story related in Theodore Draper, *The Roots of Communism*, New York, 1957, p. 373, where a police agent casts the decisive convention vote for a "radical" political program.

[17] It is almost needless to emphasize that though a twentieth century American jury may easily be found to convict on the basis of the evidence of professional witnesses, this does not reinforce the judicial process. One might be tempted to refer to the Parable of the Blind, as painted by Peter Brueghel (to be found in the National Museum of Naples). For the typical argument legitimizing the use of informers by the acceptance of their tales by juries, see Asst. Att. Gen. William F. Tompkins, "The Informant System Has Paid 'Rich Dividends,'" in *U.S. News and World Report*, October 14, 1957, p. 107. The various problematic aspects of "trading law enforcement for information" have only recently become the object of serious study in the thought-provoking, pioneering effort of Joseph Goldstein: "Police Discretion not to Invoke the Criminal Process: Low Visibility Decisions in the Administration of Justice," *Yale Law Journal*, Vol. 69 (1960), pp. 543-604.

I was hurled into the lowest slough."[18] The impact of disloyalty on a small band of secretive revolutionary terrorists increases the more their style of action keeps them from contact with the population and throws them among themselves. As popular response to their action must remain at best spotty and inconclusive, the need for permanent mutual confirmation of the meaningfulness of their activity remains prerequisite for maintaining their morale. It is this basis for self-confirmation which is at stake when the authorities succeed in winning over a member of their group.

If the wrecking of the dissident organization is an aim often achieved in the political trial, the reverse situation, the "conversion" of the public authority to the defendant's cause, can also occur. When, for example, Cesare Orsini undertook in 1858 the assassination of Napoleon III as a protest against the French policy on Italian unification, Orsini during the trial willingly admitted responsibility for the attempt, involving, as it did, heavy loss of life. Actually, the official trial as conducted by prosecutor and court served only as a kind of setting to register the impact of Orsini's deed on the emperor. Napoleon explicitly permitted Jules Favre, Orsini's lawyer, to read in open court the letter addressed to him by "a prisoner on the steps of the guillotine, adjuring Napoleon to give Italy its independence which its children lost in 1849 by the fault of France." The reading of the letter indicated that the prisoner was gaining his major objective, the change of France's policy of nonintervention in Italian affairs. If the emperor was not strong enough to save Orsini from the guillotine against both bureaucratic and popular opposition, the Italian revolutionary died with the satisfaction of having fulfilled his mission, having been instrumental in converting the emperor to changing the course of French policy.[19]

---

[18] *Op.cit.*, p. 154. A government might falsely assert that a person is an informer, in order to affect the morale of the hostile group and to reduce the member to the role of an impostor in a foreign country where he has sought asylum. This is what the Czarist government did to L. Hartmann, who had taken part in the assassination of Alexander II; P. Yarmolinsky, *Road to Revolution*, London, 1957, p. 298. Acceptance of the norm of the conspiring community as binding and exclusive presupposes total substitution for the existing authorities; the Russian conspirators of the first half of the nineteenth century, in contrast to their successors of the seventies, had not yet reached that stage and quite a number of them therefore felt free to inform on their co-conspirators once they were apprehended by the police; W. G. Korolenko, *Die Geschichte meines Zeitgenossen*, East Berlin, 1953, Vol. 2, p. 342; but see Bakunin's reservations in his *Confessions* (cited Ch. X, n. 7).

[19] The letter is reprinted as part of the author's summing up in Jules Favre, *Discours du Bâtonat*, Paris, 1867, p. 165. For the influence of Orsini's act on Napoleon, see Michael St. John Packe, *The Bombs of Orsini*, London, 1957, pp. 151-70.

Informing will be a somewhat smaller threat to larger movements, which neither need nor want to consider violence a necessary or exclusive means of undermining the foundations of an existing regime, but are intent and able to concentrate their efforts on a broader front. Due to the wider nature of their appeal, they are more immune to turncoats and infiltrators. Whether their strength rests on doctrine, on a secure popular basis, or both, penetration may perhaps cause tactical setbacks but will scarcely affect their long-run chances, which rest on many kinds of factors. The czarist police at one point even succeeded in infiltrating the small band of Duma members of the Bolshevist Party, a fact only reluctantly acknowledged by Lenin when he was faced with the evidence after the revolution. Here infiltration may be regarded as an unavoidable risk. It may even be exploited in moral terms against the enemy—with Karl Marx himself a past master in this type of moral vituperation—and utilized to separate the chaff from the wheat.

4. The Hostile Island: Aspects of Nonconformity

The attempt to force political adversaries into divulging the names of their political friends and associates has become a contemporary American specialty. To achieve this, the adversaries are threatened with contempt proceedings, when appearing as compulsory witnesses before legislative committees or voluntary witnesses when testifying on their own behalf before law courts. We are not discussing the moral dubiousness of such practices, clearly apparent in the undertone of displeasure which Supreme Court justices, among them the most security-minded, expressed when faced with a particularly shocking attempt to use contempt for such purpose.[20] What is interesting from our viewpoint is the underlying rationale of official attitudes. The pressure on weak

[20] Yates v. U.S., 355 U.S. 66 (1957). Justice Clark's majority opinion (p. 75) speaks of "petitioners' understandable reluctance" to be informers, although they are legally unable to explain their refusal. Douglas, for the minority, calls the district court's and the prosecution's multiplication of criminal contempts for each refusal to answer a query for names of individual members a "shocking instance of the abuse of judicial authority" (p. 76), and curtly speaks of Mrs. Yates's "not wanting to be an informer." The appeal court opinion on the case had assimilated the refusal to inform on political friends to the refusal to answer queries on the identity of an associate with whom one had jointly committed a murder. 227 Fed 2d, 825, 855 (9 Cir. 1955). It thus conformed religiously to the rule of denying any difference between a political and an ordinary criminal trial. But see the opinion of the court in NAACP v. Alabama, 357 U.S. 449, 462 (1958) (protection of membership lists of associations where there is no allegation of criminal behavior), and most recently, Douglas dissenting in Uphaus v. Wyman, 364 U.S. 388, 401 (1960).

and vacillating people to come forth with new information is obvious. But once the case is in court, this element recedes in importance. Only those who have not satisfactorily responded to pressure at a previous stage are exposed to new pressure. Far from submitting to pressure, they will utilize the opportunity to confirm anew loyalty to their cause; such line of questioning can only inflict on the defendants additional hardships and punishment, thinly disguised under another name. But beyond that purpose, through which the legal form is so often used to render the momentarily desirable political end, lies a less obvious consideration.

The politics of an industrial society have often become a rational interplay of interest organizations whose outward form is a gigantic and permanent popularity contest. Members of the legal profession functioning as custodians of the political game must themselves conform to its rules and precepts. Why, then, should anyone else be privileged to reject the prevailing political framework and insist on recreating politics in the image of a community resting on loyalty to group or cause rather than on rational, civilized, if uninspiring, calculation of profit and loss? The psychoanalytical theory expresses the answer pointedly: "Though gratifying the demand for expiation, we win a victory over evil within us and are grateful to the criminal who paid for what we subconsciously wished ourselves to do."[21] Whoever refuses to play ball, rejecting the standard political patterns of mass society, should be made to pay as heavy a penalty as anybody else who shuns mass-produced goods. This is not so much the product of fear of harmful results, but the price for being allowed to indulge in a display of nonconformity, especially if this nonconformity connotes access to modes of life, community of shared values,[22] purposefulness

[21] Fritz Alexander and Hugo Staub, *The Criminal, The Judge, and The Public*, New York, 1956, p. 216 (first published in Germany, 1929).

[22] The evidence on the nature of personal contacts and friendships in revolutionary organizations is at best conflicting, with the biographical accounts varying according to the infinite variety of human types involved. But closeness of personal contact was certainly important in pre-World War I social revolutionary and anarchist circles. In the higher and middle ranks of revolutionary mass movements, it had, even before Stalinism, played a considerable part among those members who had been brought into close contact by a special political bond; more often than not, this bond was opposition to the reigning party hierarchy. To this day it continues to be important among the low-level militant and sympathizer, for whom the common pride of belonging is not overshadowed by problems of discipline and competition. Any further assertions are difficult, because the quality of personal closeness, brought about and kept intact by shared political goals, is something quite different from friendship in the image of a Hermann Hesse novel. The statistical material and consequent discussions of G. Al-

outside the sphere of personal success; these conditions are becoming rare in a society that manages to solve its social problems but does not necessarily give its members desired psychological satisfactions.

There exist outside the sphere of patriotic and humanitarian sacrifice only a few traditional islands, mainly in the field of religious experience, where society makes allowance for such patterns of rejection. Even here, though, allowance is not always made gracefully: witness attitudes toward Jehovah's Witnesses. But the degree of tolerance granted the religious is seldom granted the political militant. Politics, too dangerous to be made available to the public in anything but conveniently pre-packaged form, may not be trifled with. In the language of the United States district court judge, who recently refused the application of a pacifist defendant to leave the court's jurisdiction pending an appeal against a two-year prison sentence for having sailed without authorization into the Eniwetok Atomic Proving Grounds: "If one is going to be a crusader and martyr, then, of course, he embarks upon those rather hazardous enterprises with the knowledge that somewhere along the line, if he is going to be a successful martyr, he must endure hardship."[23]

Reversely, the repentant enemy as ally of the superego, the one returned from the island of sacrifice and revolt, stands a better chance in American society. While totalitarian regimes will appreciate the gesture of the return to the fold at the last possible moment, they do not put much store in its effectiveness either on the public at large or on the future course of the individual who has returned. They prefer the mechanical certainty of destruction. Under American conditions, the Chinese decapitation tale, as related by Alexander and Staub,[24] holds more interest: "Among those sentenced to die lots are drawn. The one thus selected, should he succeed in decapitating his confederates in one stroke, wins his life. If he fails he lies down with the rest, and the next in line tries his chance." Definite disavowal of solidarity with one's erstwhile associates serves as kingpin of repression and keeps potential joiners in line.

Thus American industrial society may consider politics a friendly game played for the purpose of allocating preferences in status and

mond, *The Appeals of Communism*, Princeton, 1954, Part 2, should be read with this qualification in mind.

[23] Cited in the opinion of Justice Douglas granting the application: Reynolds v. U.S., 4 L ed 2d 46 (1959).

[24] *Op.cit.*, p. 217. Medieval sources know the practice of obtaining pardon by executing co-convicts; see *Survey of Release Procedures*, pub. by the Office of the Attorney General, Washington, 1939, Vol. 3, Pardon, p. 431.

consumer goods. If such games develop something like self-evident norms, a negligible minority's refusal to play will be considered not only impudent, but some kind of sacrilege. Yet historical antecedents and other factors peculiar to a special industrial society, such as Germany, may obstruct acceptance of this view of the character of politics. Seen against the recent background of German society, total change, though considered undesirable, may still not be looked at as a kind of monstrosity and sacrilege. Regarding the attitude of those beholden to counterimages and alternative solutions as affrontery and sacrilege, to be treated with universal exorcization rites, would scarcely serve the psychological needs of a society thirsting for certainties rather than crusades. It would prefer to avoid extreme attitudes.

How, then, would such a society treat its domestic political foes? It would want to avoid having threats to established institutions blown up to monstrous size. Yet it would not reconcile itself to accepting the ambiguities inherent in Lombroso's end-of-the-century naturalist approach to the political offender. It would not accept the doctrine that political offense is just a question of lag between official and revolutionary views on the tempo at which society should evolve.

If the political offender were someone who had merely miscalculated, or who had exaggerated notions of the speed of historical progress, only success or failure could measure right and wrong.[25] But who would be willing to accept such a tenuous basis for a legitimacy claim? In unison all existing regimes will assert that the outcome of political and military fortunes represents the fulfillment of deeply felt needs, or, as the case may be, the culmination of the historical process; the assertion of an ingrained moral right thus bolsters the legal claim of the beati possidentes. Judges of existing regimes will not only uphold the moral superiority of their own order over its detractors and competitors—which means the foes' claims are immoral—but may also profess a belief that any person of good will could not but come to the same conclusion.[26]

[25] C. Lombroso and R. Laschi, *Il Delitto Politico e le Revoluzioni* (Torino, 1890) has therefore been severely taken to task in G. Tarde, *Etudes Pénales et Sociales,* Paris, 1892, p. 106. Defending the right of a determinist to exercise moral judgment, Tarde upholds the search for motivations and fights against the predominance of the mere utility viewpoint, calling the subject matter of political crime the "penultimate refuge of utilitarianism in penal law" (p. 110).

[26] Cf. the characteristic assertion of the German Federal Court in its judgment of July 28, 1955, against the leading functionaries of the Society for German-Soviet Friendship (reprinted in Hochverrat und Staatsgefährdung, Vol. 1, pp. 241, 280). It rejects the opinion that the moral value of an act and an estimable conviction will

Attempts were made during the second half of the nineteenth century—in continental European societies with split and guilt-stricken political consciences more than in the robust and self-consciously righteous climates of Anglo-American societies[27]—to allow the courts to chivalrously recognize, in the sentencing stage, the honorable motivations of political foes. This practice foundered for practical reasons. What had begun as a means to enforce public order while making desirable moral differentiations turned against this order itself. The very group singled out for preferential treatment used the possibility for special consideration for political offenders as a further means of massive pressure against the state apparatus. But ideological considerations are as decisive. It is difficult to prosecute a heretic while explicitly recognizing the purity of motivation which triggered his action. Not only must he be shown to hold the wrong belief and action patterns, but these patterns must be demonstrated to reflect his own moral and intellectual corruption. The procedure applied might well be intentionally circular, never permitting analysis of the true origin of alienation. But then, despite all attempts to the contrary, the concept of a heretic has not taken on softer and more intelligible contours since having become secularized.

Still, a society may have so many potential deviators that it will prosecute only those acts which border on open rebellion; this is the case in some Western European countries. Or the supply of deviators may be artificially manipulated from territory outside the society's control, as in the case of the Federal Republic of Germany. The Federal Republic's police and prosecution organs, tracking down their Communist foes, isolating them from potential sympathizers, stopping whenever feasible the influx of agents from the DDR, have become operators of a highly professionalized game. But so have their opposite numbers, operating out of East Berlin, who specialize in keeping up the flow of subversive agents and modifying their assignments according to the changing tactical requirements of the situation. Both sides know that large-scale action would necessitate changes in the sum total of the

---

indicate a lesser amount of guilt, arguing that such train of thought has no justification "where the conviction is not in harmony with the moral law and the offender is in a position to recognize such."

[27] In 1921, at the height of the discussion on Eugene V. Debs's pardon (see Ch. X), Attorney General Daugherty read a well-prepared statement before the American Bar Association, in which he opined that none of the "excuses" for the concept of political offense as it may exist in the old world would apply where "the sovereign will of the people can express itself and where the ballot box is available." "Respect for Law," *American Bar Association Journal*, Vol. 7 (1921), pp. 505, 508-09.

political configuration. Meanwhile, constant probing and harassing operations are in order.

Political conviction or just the accident of professional chance may have been at the origin of a career in the subversive field. But whatever the point of departure, special training, ideological and practical, has supplanted any inclination to spontaneity or self-styled action among the German groups. A steady exhaustion of a ready supply of local militants with community roots determines the bureaucratic and highly specialized character of job assignment and of standardized performance tests in the profession of subversion.

Despite the sustained attempt of the Communists to arouse political interest in West German trials, the interest remains low and disposal of the cases therefore follows a slow bureaucratic routine. In minor cases periods of preventive detention, ranging not infrequently between half a year and a year or even more, might take up a sizeable part of the eventual sentence against which they are usually counted. Both the everpresent background of National Socialist atrocities and Communist repression in Eastern Germany and the possibility of a sudden new reversal of political fortunes serve to diminish the distance between prosecutors and prosecuted and generally act as a self-imposed control mechanism substituting for a barely noticeable public opinion. The professional character of the agent and fairly strict controls over his behavior explain the relative infrequency of the "converting" witness who lends color to political trials in those countries where political hostility to the established regime has not become bureaucratized.

5. *Stages of Identification of Client and Lawyer*

From Juvenal[28] to Lenin, the lawyer has often evoked less than friendly feelings. His constant need to propagandize himself and his client, his putting his talents out for hire to an everchanging clientele, and the aleatory character of his success have brought him along with admiration much criticism and contempt. The profession's spokesmen have always tried to vindicate his record by pointing to the narrow and well-defined purpose of his calling: to represent and advise his client in the concrete job with which he has been entrusted. If his job requires some measure of identification with his client, it remains on the professional level. He hires out talent to his client without embracing his cause.

But this answer has not always been deemed satisfactory. Thus Boswell: "But, Sir, does not affecting warmth when you have no warmth

[28] *Satires*, VII, 105-40.

and appearing to be clearly of one opinion when you are in reality of another opinion, does not such dissimulation impair one's honesty? Is there not some danger that a lawyer may put on the same mask in common life, in the intercourse with his friends?" This shaft goes more deeply into the problem than does the commonsense answer of Johnson: "Why, no, Sir, everybody knows that you are paid to affect warmth for your client, and it is therefore properly speaking no dissimulation. The moment you come from the bar, you assume your usual behavior."[29] The fact that the lawyer may fulfill a necessary social function does not eliminate the cleavage between his social role and his quality as a human being. Writing a century later, Dostoyevsky, in his bitter annotations to the Kronenberg case, called the fact that counsel is actually never able to act according to his conscience a nonsensical paradox, the more serious as it connotes "an abnormal state of life"; he was led to the conclusion that the bar is a "sad institution."[30]

What is at the center of the complaint is the degree of identification with a particular interest required for successful exercise of the profession. In a society where performance has been mechanized and standardized, where the individual more often than not sees the end product of his labor as a foreign object, the lawyer may still be among those who make a substantial individual contribution to the final disposal of his case or problem. There is an element of creative ingenuity involved in whipping diffuse elements of a given situation into convincing enough shape to obtain a favorable reaction for his client. But in this creative process of reconstituting fact situations and recommending to the court certain ways of evaluating them, the line between purely professional identification and a closer partnership relation is sometimes difficult to draw. The legal order has consequently developed formulas and rules to define the borderline between counsel's admissibly presenting debatable interpretations and inadmissibly lending his help to unjust action; between construing what the clients offer in the most favorable light and taking a forbidden hand in creating the useful facts which will produce a favorable court action.[31]

[29] James Boswell, op.cit., Vol. 2, p. 47.

[30] Diary of a Writer, New York, 1954, entries for February 1876, pp. 215, 237.

[31] Lord Shawcross, for example, the well-known British lawyer and former politician, does not doubt the possibility of a clear distinction between these two situations. Actually, under a legal system which considers it quite normal that the lawyers have direct contact with witnesses before the trial stage, the difference, clearcut in theory and spelled out in the canons of bar associations, may be more difficult in practice; "The Functions and Responsibilities of an Advocate," The Record of the Association of the Bar of New York, Vol. 13 (1958), pp. 483-509, at 491. For a more realistic view

But such rules, and attendant attempts to put into an easy formula the position of the lawyer in the legal process, can determine only the outer limits of allowable identification with the client. The means with which a lawyer defends his client may be entirely approved and yet not answer the problem of how the interests which he defends relate to the purpose of society at large. What are the criteria according to which the lawyer determines whether to take a case? To the extent that and as long as society remains a society of antagonistic interests, the answer can only be subjective. It is the answer of the individual lawyer, to be decided in the privacy of his own conscience and according to his own image of society. Only a society which claims to have solved its inner contradictions may feel competent to differentiate between objectively justified interests and those which do not accord with its purpose.[32] But even a totalitarian society, fulfilling its hypostatized function of interpreting authoritatively the objective interest of society, deprives the legal profession of its traditional role more by indirection and a variety of pressures. It may not, as pre- and semi-constitutional systems used to do,[33] exclude lawyers altogether from access to certain areas in the field of offenses against the state. Therefore, various contemporary paraphrases of the dictum of Boswell's oracle, that everybody is entitled to the service of a lawyer and that the justice or injustice of a case is the business of the judge and not the lawyer,[34] solve only the external problems of the lawyer. They help him to fence off adverse pressure, once he has made up his mind to accept a case. His clientele, the interest which he is willing to take on, are part of the often complicated equation between the requirements or, as the case may be, the chances of the existing social structure and his personal predilections,

---

of a nineteenth century American lawyer, see Joseph B. Warner, "The Responsibilities of the Lawyer," American Bar Association Report, Vol. 19 (1896), pp. 319-42.

[32] An interesting description can be found in a speech by a functionary of the official Czech Lawyers' Organization: "If the lawyer wants to keep to the principle that he has to preserve the interest of his clients in conformity with the interests of society and the principle of objective truth, he has to analyze clearly every case. He has to obtain clarity whether or not the interests, the protection of which his client desires, conform to the objective truth and the interests of society. For this reason we use the term 'justified interest of the client,' and only those interests may be taken care of by the lawyer." Konrad Galtz, "Aus der Arbeit der Advokatur in der CSR," Über Rechtsanwaelte in der Volksdemokratie, Ministry of Justice of the DDR, East Berlin, 1956, pp. 25, 26-27.

[33] See, for example, the practice of Czarist Russia as described in S. Kucherow, *Courts, Lawyers and Trials Under the Last Three Czars*, New York, 1953, pp. 200-12.

[34] Boswell, *op.cit.*, Vol. 5, pp. 26, 27. For a contemporary discussion that includes an ingenious formula, see Dahs, "Stellung und Grundauffassung des Strafverteidigers, *Neue Juristische Wochenschrift*, Vol. XII (1959), pp. 1158-62.

including his own views of society's existing and desirable shape. Unlike the physician, he does not serve all comers he can accommodate,[35] nor does he serve at all times the highest bidder for his skill.

Thus the lawyer's relation to his function is doubly different from that of the average job holder in industrial society. On the one hand, a decent job performance will require a high degree of intellectual involvement and purposiveness in the service of his client. The compensatory features rest on some freedom of choice about the kind of situation in which he will want to get involved.

One might assume, therefore, that nowhere would there be greater congruence between official role and personal choice than when a lawyer is willing to represent a client in his fight against authorities acting as defenders of the realm. Yet reality is somewhat more blurred and complicated, and it may perhaps be first approached through a vehement criticism. In January 1905 Lenin received a query from some incarcerated comrades asking him for advice about how to handle their defense. In answering, Lenin, after showing how other considerations should be subordinated to pressing on court and public the program and purposes of the party, came to discuss the role of the defense attorney. His remarks are imbued with the most acute mistrust of the "reactionary" profession; he viewed the group as a hotbed of unprincipled political opportunism, always prone to put forward in court distorted tales of the character of the political organization whose members they are defending. That these tales are fabricated in the interest of the client had no meaning for Lenin, inasmuch as the supreme rule of a political defense is propagation of the doctrine rather than the fate of the individual defendant. Therefore, Lenin proposed "to put the lawyers under a state of siege." He insisted on a vigorous bifurcation of court roles, with the lawyer restricted to handling the witnesses of the prosecution and the assertions of the prosecutor, trying to make them appear "ridiculous"—evaluating the evidence, as we would say. But the sources of the defendant's political convictions, the exposition of his political program and belief would be entirely outside the lawyer's province and reserved to comments by the defendant himself.[36]

---

[35] The British exception to the rule (re-emphasized by Shawcross, *op.cit.*, p. 498) is more apparent than real; cf. the discussion on the barrister in Jackson, *March of Justice in England*, pp. 209-13.

[36] *Sochineniya*, Vol. 8, p. 49. Marcel Willard, *op.cit.*, Preface, takes pains to stress that Lenin's strictures would not apply to the militant party lawyer who has broken with middle class habits and professional deformation.

At the opposite end of the spectrum is the attitude of a conscientious and punctilious member of the bar who looks at his job through shriveled up professional spectacles. One case is like another, in the sense that his job always remains the same: to create maximal conditions for a favorable outcome for his client. Hence his insistence that neither the client himself and still less an outside body would be entitled to interfere with his system of defense; he alone would carry the responsibility, with the defendant contracting, so to speak, to conform to a line determined by him.[37]

6. Types of Political Lawyers

In the unravelling of the individual's fate, a defense can efface the individual behind the cause, or it can tone down the cause into some faint background material. Between these two lines of defense there are infinite combinations. We shall try to sketch only the most important types of defense in political cases, keeping in mind, however, that in no field are there more transitions, particular circumstances, and special arrangements defying any attempt at categorization.

A political organization's complete control over the conduct of a trial and, what is important, its uninhibited access to the defendant in the pretrial stage—if he happens to be detained—is best guaranteed through closely affiliated lawyers. In regard to familiarity with and regard for shifting technical requirements, the modern party organization might be more demanding than that of the nineteenth century. For the brothers Freytag, August Bebel's and Wilhelm Liebknecht's lawyers, or for Francesco Merlino, lawyer, theoretician, and militant fighter for the cause of Italian anarchism,[38] their clients' absolute trust in their integrity, feel for the situation, and identification with the cause they represented was enough. Political allegiance has since lost this charming simplicity and modesty. The contemporary lawyer who is at the same time a sympathizer with or formal member of the political organization under attack has in principle the status of a skilled technician. He may advise the party management on the possible results of a

[37] A lawyer's characteristic business proposition is reprinted with obvious relish in Steve Nelson, *The Thirteenth Juror*, New York, 1955, p. 121. For the corresponding attitude of a well-known British lawyer, see Henry Slesser, *Judgment Reversed*, London, 1941, p. 175. The grievance of a political defendant for having agreed to such an arrangement is voiced in John McNair and John Maxton, *Beloved Rebel*, London, 1955, p. 63.

[38] Francesco S. Merlino (1856-1930) has narrated part of his experience with courts in *Politica e Magistratura del 1860 ad oggi in Italia*, Rome, 1925. For his biography, see the introduction of his *Questa è l'Italia*, Milano, 1953.

line of action. But the advice might be rejected as that of any other specialist—as seems to have happened, for example, in the Dennis trial[39]—if it does not fit in with major political requirements in the wake of the rule that the "difference between a juridical and a political concept of the trial is nothing but an empty slogan."[40] At any rate, it would belong within the province of the party authorities or special bodies entrusted with the tasks of selecting priorities among a variety of tactics, formulating the goals of the party for trial purposes so as to keep them ambiguous enough to stand the test of constitutionality, but at the same time avoid causing confusion among present and prospective adherents. Also within their province are the ways of attacking and handling the policies and witnesses of the prosecution, bowing to the traditional image of the impartial judge or attacking him as part of the official apparatus, discounting the judgment from the outset, and fitting its result in advance into their own propaganda line.

But to what extent this theory of the primacy of party decisions for trial tactics may control actual practices depends on the circumstances. The party executive, if hamstrung by internal party splits or external threats to its operations, may operate too leisurely or too dogmatically. Or it may be too decentralized for such work. In this case, the initiative for tactical conduct might pass into the lawyer's hands who, according to temperament, his own political involvement, and evaluation of the needs of the situation, might decide on an "aggressive defense" or might fulfill the party mandate without enthusiasm, trying his best to avoid antagonizing the court.[41]

The party lawyer has his maximum utility within the context of a well-organized group whose doctrine he espouses and whose members

[39] John Gates, op.cit., p. 126.

[40] The sentence appears in an August 15, 1914 memo written by Paul Levi, then a young socialist lawyer in Frankfurt (later, after he left the ledership of the Communist Party, the most brilliant German political lawyer of the 1920's), and submitted to a member of the Social Democratic Party executive. The latter had raised doubts about the propriety of Levi's tactics to ventilate, in popular meetings throughout Germany, Rosa Luxemburg's then-pending trial for defamation of the German army. (Paul Levi's papers are now in the possession of Joseph Buttinger in New York, and I am grateful to him for permission to inspect the trial file.)

For a parallel American case of the fifties, pertaining to the propriety of the trial lawyer's publicly discussing and attacking the conduct of a pending trial, see re Sawyer, 360 U.S. 322 (1958).

[41] See the 1952 material of the West German Communist Party, as excerpted in the judgment of the Federal Court of May 20, 1958, against leading functionaries of the "Central Council for the Protection of Democratic Rights and for the Defense of German Patriots"; in Hochverrat un Staatsgefährdung, Vol. 2, pp. 253, 270.

he represents in close contact with the organization. But the group might have reasons of its own—shades of the early stages of the Rosenberg case—to want not to disclose the group connections of the defendant; or it may simply find it more politic to resort to the services of an outside lawyer. Unless he is a well-known politician in his own right, the party lawyer might not enjoy much prestige; his efforts might be discounted from the outset by court and opinion alike as a corporate product of some party office. But almost as often the defendant no longer belongs to such an organized group. He may have acted alone or with a few close associates, or the organization in which he served might not have survived the debacle which brought him before his judges. This, then, is the field cut out for a slightly different kind of lawyer. Without obligation to the political organization, or not in agreement with the political action pattern of the defendant, he might be sympathetic enough to his individual plight and have enough affinity or at least respect for his cause to take on the defense. Rather frequently in the nineteenth century under conditions of an absolute regime or a constitutional monarchy, and somewhat less today, this lawyer himself might have been active in or at least sympathetic to some shade of politics more moderate than that of the defendant but still in opposition to the powers-that-be: a Whig or Liberal constitutionalist appearing for a "radical" of the old or new style; an Erskine appearing in 1794 for Thomas Hardy; or, a century later, a Grusenberg appearing in 1905 for Leon Trotsky. At times career expectations and political sentiment might be difficult to disentangle. For Jules Favre, French opposition politician from the forties to the end of the sixties and Thiers's foreign minister in 1871, entry into the political arena was staged by his assuming the defense of those Lyons participants in the 1834 uprising who defied the explicit desire of the majority of the defendants and took part in the trial before the Pairs.[42]

A lawyer's initial relations with a certain clientele might well determine the future pattern of his practice. This happened, for example, in the first and second decade of this century with G. F. Vanderveer (1875-1942), noted West Coast lawyer for the IWW.[43] In conformity

---

[42] After the Pairs turned down their demand to be defended by political spokesmen, even if they did not happen to be members of the bar, the majority refused to participate in the trial. Favre has been severely taken to task by his contemporaries for having broken the united front of the defendants by assuming this defense. See Louis Blanc, *Histoire des dix ans*, Paris, 1883, Vol. 4, p. 370. The defense by Favre's biographer Maurice Réclus (*Jules Favre, 1809-1880*, Paris, 1913) does not sound too convincing.

[43] *Counsel for the Damned*, biography of G. F. Vanderveer, by L. B. Hawley and R. B. Potts, New York, 1953.

with the changing political fortunes of his clients, such a lawyer might have to shift his arguments rather drastically. Such was the case of Friedrich Grimm (1888-1959), lifelong German lawyer for rightist causes. He started out as the defender of German industrialists and officials embroiled with French occupation authorities during the Rhineland occupation after World War I, and in the twenties became interested in the cases of the few nationalist murderers who had been prosecuted by the authorities of the Weimar Republic for having killed what they believed were informers who had served together with them in clandestine military formations. During the first National Socialist years, in order to shield former Weimar officials from corruption charges, he cashed in on his friends who had meanwhile become the authorities of the day. Then, starting with the days of the Reichstags Fire trial, he became negotiator, spokesman, and legal repesentative of the National Socialist regime's interests in criminal proceedings taking place in foreign countries. As in the murder of Gustloff, the German National Socialist agent for Switzerland, this assignment meant that Grimm had to make a curious switch from furnishing legal theorems justifying political murder to condemning it most sharply.[44] His career ended in postwar Germany in a thoroughly logical way: he again became the mouthpiece of those insisting on speedy and general amnesty for all National Socialist crimes.[45]

Grimm personifies the lawyer who has hitched his star to a specific cause, a cause which in this case has been embodied through two decades in a variety of men and organizations: German nationalism. He followed its various manifestations and mutations, serving them with whatever arguments were convenient for the specification of victory or defeat. Probably as frequent, at least in American practice, is the lawyer with whom political compassion for a cause takes the watered-down form of espousing a constitutional principle. The appearance of an organization devoted to the legal espousal of civil liberties as an abstract proposition pushes this form of action to its logical conclusion. Trying to separate the specific political circumstances in an individual case from the constitutional principle involved, the American Civil Liberties Union will intervene by brief, trial lawyer, as *amicus curiae*, or in public statement to uphold or enlarge the field of application of a constitutional principle. Whatever the political meaning of this separation, as a technique of defense it has some advantage, however limited.

[44] F. Grimm, *Politischer Mord und Heldenverehrung*, Berlin, 1938.

[45] F. Grimm, *Politische Justiz, Die Krankheit unserer Zeit*, Bonn, 1953. The book gives a thoroughly ex parte account of his career; see also Ch. III, Sec. 5, above.

Without identifying himself with the cause that is possibly detested by many members of the community, a lawyer might become associated with the political defense by pleading the case's implications in terms of the constitutional order. Opinion might be rallied for the principle and symbol involved rather than, or even in spite of, the cause. This procedure will allow lawyers from a variety of walks of life and with a widely varying clientele, including even erstwhile presidential candidates, to come forward in the defense of some aspects of the activity of a foe of the existing regime.

Often, however, much more will be necessary than standing on some libertarian interpretation of the constitutional order. If the case concerns violence rather than opinions, the bond between lawyer and client will have to be firmer. The lawyer's belief in his client's innocence, or, alternatively, in the justifiability of his action, will have to be stronger for him to be willing to undertake surmounting the difficulties inherent in such a situation.[46] Otherwise, there remains the professional looking at the political case as if it were "une affaire correctionelle." But the difference might be more in the mind of the client than in clearly observable patterns of conduct of the lawyer. In some situations the cause may have ceased to exist and nothing remains but an individual in need of urgent protection—possibly perilous for the lawyer who grants it—against momentarily strong opinion currents in population and court.[47] But it might not always be easy to find a competent nonpolitical lawyer willing to engage in the struggle for a political client, even if the client is willing to completely follow the lawyer's advice and instruction. Whatever the lawyer's cautionary devices to draw the line between his strictly professional services and the cause of the defendant, the public might nevertheless identify both.[48] Weighing the advantages

[46] Compare the well-known career of Clarence Darrow; even in such a case there may be some mistrust about whether the lawyer immersed in the job to win the case really "understands" the meaning of a political trial. See, for example, the typical remark by a Wobbly journalist on Vanderveer's strategy in his first IWW murder trial: "It was only with evident effort that attorney Vanderveer kept on the unfamiliar ground of the class struggle, his natural tendency being to try the case of a pure and simple murder charge." *Counsel for the Damned*, p. 213.

[47] See the vivid description of the lawyers' role in French purge trials by one of the defendants: Phillippe St. Germain, *Article 75*, Paris, 1951, esp. p. 65; for the moral impact of a helpful lawyer in such a situation, see p. 70.

[48] In a questionnaire sent out by Pittsburgh Law School students, 92 per cent of the law students questioned thought that the public associates lawyers with the guilt of the client in political cases; nearly half of those questioned said they would not take such cases, and 80 per cent of this group declared that their reason was fear of unfavorable public opinion. J. H. Olender, "The Right to Counsel in the Unpopular Cause," symposium, *University of Pittsburgh Law Review*, Vol. 20 (1959), pp. 727, 751.

of any publicity, even the most adverse, against the disadvantages of becoming publicly associated with the current image of the enemy of the realm, the lawyer might grow reluctant to take the possible risks of this business prospect. Tendencies run strongly in this direction. Leadership and authority in the profession now go to the specialist rather than to yesteryear's universalist who frequently shuffled back and forth between law and politics. In its relations both with other groups and with the authorities, in court and, more important, out of court, the specialist, or very often a group of specialists, represents the interest of a narrowly circumscribed clientele. This interest, to which in many a country he is tied by semipermanent arrangement, would not expect him to engage in controversial public pursuits unconnected with his specialized work. His public interests will therefore tend to become colored and circumscribed by such associations. In contrast, his weaker brother, the general practitioner, seeks everybody's business, but for these very reasons becomes vitally interested in staying within the safe margins of generally accepted opinions. He is an inveterate joiner, but only up to the point where joining will establish him in the mind of the community as a man who can serve either their particular needs or generally agreed community objects, rather than as proponent or defender of controversial currents and policies.[49]

If no lawyer is available on the basis of private arrangement, the bâtonnier or the bar association might try providing counsel. In cases where defense is mandatory, the court will make the assignment. Like Dimitrov in the 1934 Leipzig Reichstag Fire trial, the defendant might reject the tender of such services offhand. Or he may take exception to a specific line of defense by his lawyer, which may happen when the family provides counsel to their straying member. The Powers case, tried in Moscow in August 1960, graphically illustrates the difference between a political defendant and a defendant who by mischance becomes involved in a political trial. Whatever the immediate consequences in terms of the court's disposition toward him, the political defendant would have dissociated himself, in his final plea at the latest, from an ex officio defense lawyer who was serving his client while plugging for the propaganda interest of the authorities. Powers deferred such a step until it would no longer affect the outcome of the trial but only

[49] For the average lawyer's attitude toward a Smith Act defense, as reflected in the mind of the judge, see Judge Pope in re Sawyer, 260 Fed 2d 189, 214 (9 Cir. 1958), Pope speaks of the defendant as a lawyer who "is going so far as to appear for Smith Act defendants."

his eventual reception back home.[50] Assigned lawyers as well as privately arranged business counsels are unwilling to associate themselves with the politically motivated tactics of their clients. This feature recommends them to the authorities,[51] but makes it difficult for the political defendants to have recourse to their services. Even if they serve the defendant exclusively, as in the West, they will not permit themselves to be drawn into any attempt to try the case simultaneously before a public audience of the defendant's choice. They might also try their best to keep the defendant from doing likewise, or from introducing issues which, from their more limited viewpoint, might look extraneous.

7. *The Political Lawyer and the Court*

The latent conflict between the political lawyer and the courts and the legal profession at large rests on their necessarily different approaches to the lawyer's job. It is a conflict that has been handled in different ways. There is, first, what one might call the *laissez faire* approach. Traditional French indulgence toward the lawyers and their courtroom performance, reinforced by the judges' comfortable knowledge that theirs is, after all, the final word, has discouraged any search into problems of lawyers' allegiance. Courtroom discipline is dealt with on an *ad hoc* basis. Cases tried under floodlights and with political emotions raised to the highest pitch might lead to a lawyer's ejection or suspension from the trial, or to a reprimand. This happened in the trial of the Ustaschi murderers of King Alexander and Foreign Minister Louis Barthou before the Aix assizes in 1935; during the 1959 Paris military tribunal trial of the FLN attackers of Jacques Soustelle;[52] and in 1960, when members of the Jeanson group were tried for having given assistance to FLN members. But otherwise, a political lawyer, whether he is active in behalf of the left, or more frequently these days of the right, or in the affairs of Algerian nationalists, has been free to put his often considerable political talents and energies in

[50] See the post-trial statement of the defendant to his wife, as contrasted with his final plea: *New York Times*, August 20, 1960, p. 1.

[51] See the remarks of Judge Goodrich of the Third Circuit Court, when praising the so-called Philadelphia Plan, an internal bar association arrangement for assigning counsel to political defendants; "The Right to Counsel in the Unpopular Cause," *op.cit.*, p. 733.

[52] See *Le Monde*, February 4, 1959. The counsel was said to have violated his professional duties when insinuating that the prosecution had stalled in the Kovacs case. The court inflicted on counsel an *avertissement*, the mildest form of disciplinary sanction provided in Art. 32 of the decree of April 10, 1954 (*Journal Officiel*, p. 3,494); the decree provides for disciplinary powers for both the conseil de l'ordre (Art. 31) and the trial court (Art. 41).

and out of the courtroom to the service of whatever cause he sees fit. He might come to grief, as have a growing number of lawyers acting for the Algerian revolutionary cause. They did so for reasons of their own involvement in revolutionary politics, and also when they tried professionally to safeguard the rights of Algerian defendants.[53] The action of the security organs against such lawyers might not originate in or be related to the disciplinary function of court or bar. However, in October 1960, as a result of some courtroom clashes during the Jeanson group trial, the disciplinary powers of courts have been reinforced and the position of the defense in the present wave of political trials curtailed by an *ad hoc* ordinance.[54]

A sterner course is taken not only when the lawyer's courtroom performance is measured with less lenience, but when attempts are made to weed out or refuse admission to potential political troublemakers among the legal fraternity. The German Federal Republic has recently adopted some legislation in the latter direction.[55] The United States in recent years has seen a number of cases where lawyers were trying to wrest admission to the bar from recalcitrant admission committees challenging their moral fitness on political grounds.[56] In admission

[53] A number of lawyers have been forcibly excluded from defending Algerian defendants. Others have been detained and prosecutions against some lawyers have been started on the basis of utterances made while they were serving as defense counsel; the text of the memo submitted to the International Red Cross on the expulsion of the lawyers from Algiers may be found in *Les Temps Modernes*, Vol. 15 (1960), pp. 1,208-11. See also Gisèle Halimi, "La Défense hors la Loi," *ibid.*, pp. 1,185-94. There has been a recent proposal to create a special type of immunity for lawyers for their trial conduct; it would correspond to parliamentary immunity, but would not take away the disciplinary powers of the trial court and the conseil de l'ordre; Gonzalez de Gaspard, "L'immunité de la Défense," *Le Monde*, February 28, 1960.

[54] In the wake of incidents during the Jeanson trial, an ordinance of October 7, 1960 (*Journal Officiel*, p. 9,108) has worsened considerably the position of the defense in political trials. This has happened in three ways: 1) by changes of the rules applicable to all criminal proceedings, such as prohibiting general policy statements by witnesses for the defense (Art. 1); 2) by special rules applicable before military tribunals, e.g. incidental motions to be handled by the trial court in one en bloc decision (Art. 5); 3) by special rules applicable only to criminal trials relating to the Algerian rebellion; disciplinary measures taken by the trial court against the defense lawyer (ejection from trial) are immediately executory, without regard to a later appeal (Art. 9).

For the reaction of the bar, see the statement of Bâtoñnier André Toulouse in *Le Monde*, October 8, p. 3, who called the ordinance a "too rapid reaction to a particular situation"—a typical temptation of a regime under which legislative power has largely passed into the hands of a semi-independent executive.

[55] Par. 7,6 of the Federal Lawyer's Statute of October 1, 1959 (BGBL, 1, 565) refuses admission to the bar to any candidate "who fights the libertarian order in a *criminally punishable way*."

[56] Konigsberg v. State Bar of California, 353 U.S. 252 (1957); Schware v. Board of

policy as well as in courtroom discipline,[57] the rationalization by which various official bodies uphold broadly interpreted admission discipline and disbarment controls rests on the necessity of adherence to constitutional principle, the need for responsible professional standards, and safeguards against obstructive trial tactics—all offensive to the dignity of both the court and the profession. The counterargument focuses less on narrowing down the area of choice left to the actual or prospective political defendant than on the asserted violation of specific constitutional and procedural guarantees involved in such practices of exclusion and discipline.

Whatever the rationalizations in terms of the constitutional and legal system, the yardstick with which the courts measure such conflicts between political lawyers and their foes in bar associations, ministries of justice, attorney generals' offices, or, via contempt proceedings, on the bench itself, must rest on some concept of a possible equilibrium between the guaranteed functioning of the court system and the limits within which the political lawyer may pursue his obligations to his specialized clientele. Given a politically suspect lawyer, it might be slightly more difficult to keep him from being admitted to the bar by drawing inferences from some knowledge of or official research into his present or past political beliefs than to support disciplinary action on the basis of his actual past behavior in court. The first method belongs in the prudential area of planning total political security for an incumbent political system—always a problematic affair; the other is a control measure against specific abuses in the exercise of the lawyer's function.[58] The 1958 West German Lawyer's Statute in its final form

---

Bar Examiners, 353 U.S. 232 (1957); Sheiner v. Florda, 82 SO 2d 657 (1955). Anastaplo v. Illinois, 171 NE 2d 826 (1954), certiorari denied 348 U.S. 946 (1955). See also the 1959 majority and minority reports of the bar committee of the First Appellate Court District of Illinois on the character and fitness of George Anastaplo (11 against, 6 for nonadmission), reprinted in *Lawyer's Guild Review*, Vol. 19 (1959), p. 65.

[57] Sacher v. United States, 343 U.S. 1 (1951); re disbarment of Abraham J. Jssermann, 345 U.S. 286 (1953); but note the dissenting opinion of Jackson, *ibid.*, 289, indicating that in nineteenth century American practice, contempt of court citations were by no means followed by disbarment. Thus the Vinson court fell back on devices used against Peter Zenger's lawyers in 1735.

[58] In 1956 the Karlsruhe federal court excluded the lawyer of a Communist front organization functionary from further participation in the proceedings, because he had transmitted a DDR protest resolution against the proceedings to the court (Entscheidungen des Bundesgerichtshofs in Strafsachen, Vol. 9 [1956], pp. 20-23). The decision, invoking the omnibus doctrine of the lawyer as organ of the judicial process, construed the lawyer's action as an inadmissible attempt to exercise pressure on the

has avoided making admission to the bar dependent on political conduct be a prerequisite for refusal to admit or for disbarment.

The American decisions are not very favorable either to the politically minded lawyer seeking admission, or to his colleague demanding relief from contempt of court or disciplinary sanctions.[59] Yet in either case an element of chance—such as a change in the personnel of the higher courts reviewing these sanctions—might net the political lawyer some windfall.[60] But by and large his prospects are presently as poor in the field of disciplinary sanctions as in the admission field. Control over discipline involves policing the relations of lawyers on the lower benches with trial lawyers. This is a somewhat far-reaching demand to address to members of a profession among whom *esprit de corps* plays an eminent role; it is especially demanding if it is made by marginal professional elements persistently under attack for their irregular behavior and associations. In this way courts are prone to put the disciplinary problem and the "lawyer as an officer of the court" theorem in the foreground, overlooking a special feature, absent in this form from other

court. For a scathing criticism, see Arndt in *Juristenzeitung*, 1956, p. 376. A curious but justified exclusion of a lawyer from the proceedings may be found in Entscheidungen, Vol. 8 (1955), pp. 194-200. The case concerned the top political lawyer of the DDR, Kaul, who, admitted to practice before West Berlin courts, may also practice before West German criminal courts; but the particular case concerned espionage proceedings in which Kaul could not be expected to observe the duty of keeping from his political friends specific secret information obtained in the trial.

Recently the same court went much further: making no reference to the specific circumstances of the case, it totally barred this lawyer from participation in a proceeding (3 ST R 52,60 of March 2, 1961, *Neue Juristische Wochenschrift*, Vol. 14 [1961], p. 614). This decision was based on the lawyer's particular situation (the fact that he conducts his business on behalf of and in conformity with DDR policies). But the court also tried to develop some general theorems pertaining to independence, which would prohibit abusive tactics hostile to the state power. While the decision did not discuss the possibility of the defendant's disagreeing with a party line of defence, it gratuitously implied this situation. Altogether the reasoning comes uncomfortably close to the differentiation between those interests which "objectively" harmonize with prevailing trends, and those conflicting, inadmissible interests which the defendant pursues and, aided by a like-minded lawyer, is illicitly bent on upholding in court. (See n. 32 above, and Ch. VII, 4.)

[59] On admission, see the Konigsberg and Anastaplo decisions of the Supreme Court of April 24, 1961 (5:4), both unfavorable to the petitioners. For disciplinary proceedings, see n. 57.

[60] Sacher v. Association of Bar of City of New York, 347 U.S. 388 (1954), re Sawyer, 360 U.S. 322 (1958). For the diverse disciplinary practices of various bar associations in political cases, see B. Dreyfus and D. B. Walker, "Ground for Procedure for Discipline of Attorneys," *Lawyer's Guild Review*, Vol. 18 (1958), pp. 66-78.

trials: their own emotional and political involvement, the fact that the credibility of the trial, their own credibility, and that of the state organization they serve are for better or worse inseparably linked.

8. *Internationalization of the Political Trial*

Consciousness of this unavoidable link has become more important the more the role and impact of the political trial have shifted in the last fifty years. The political trial of the nineteenth century had been a national affair. This was true even if the figures involved a Blanqui, a Malatesta, a Vera Sassulitch, a Bebel, or a Kropotkin—all figures of political international stature. Even if all of them fervently hoped or calculated that oppressive governmental action against them would in the not-too-remote future abound to the definite advantage of their organization, their friends were not sanguine about the immediate echo of their behavior in court. The fruits of victory would come, but it would be in vain to try relating their momentary attitudes and gestures to immediate changes in political and social conditions. The individual acts of heroism carried out by the Russian revolutionaries of the seventies and eighties might weaken the czarist system and deeply influence the patterns of thinking of the Russian intelligentsia at a later period; August Bebel and Wilhelm Liebknecht's speeches to the Leipzig assizes in 1872 might furnish them a welcome opportunity to explain their views of the intermeshing of social change and political revolution, and might lay the seeds for their party's stupendous electoral victories—two decades later. In short, the political trial was an inevitable concomitant to a period of germination whose fruits would ripen later.

The political trial of the twentieth century takes place within a framework of drastically reduced periods of political germination and on an international basis. The road from apprenticeship in court and prison to leadership of the nation—De Valera, Gandhi, Nehru, Trotsky, Rakosi, and the crop of recent colonial leaders—has become a normal means of access to political office. The shrinking of the world, the development of its communication systems, the emergence of a national opposition of principle with supporting casts in foreign government, and the many times enlarged role of intelligence organizations have made the political trial a focal point of political strategy, not only for the trial participants but for many organizations around the world. Until the beginning of the 1930's, the Communists had possessed the near-monopoly in exploiting political trials for the production of effective political counterimages. The Reichstag Fire trial, due to the unique role of Dimitrov, possibly marked the culmination of their ascendancy in this field. To the extent that the Communist system has since assumed a more pronouncedly repressive character, the technique has been turned against them. In the 1920's they initiated the pattern of international jurisdical organizations, sending their delegates to political trials all over the world, assertedly to check up on the regularity of trial procedure.[61] Today the widely adopted technique serves the

[61] This is not the place to trace in detail the development of para-professional organizations concerned with the business of political justice. There are, generally speaking, three types of such organizations:

1) The partisan organization fighting in the service of specific causes. This cause may be as vague as the general left-wing spirit of the Ligue des Droits de l'Homme, which has long outlived its days of glory, falling victim to the irreparable split between Communists and non-Communists. (See Jean et Monica Charlot, "La Ligue des Droits de l'Homme," *Revue Française de Science Politique*, Vol. 9 [1959], pp. 995-1,028, which does not, however, enter into the details of its role in trial campaigns.) Or it may be just the offshoot of a specific political organization, functioning as its auxiliary in the legal field. This is the case with the Communist International Juridical Association of the twenties and thirties, which fought and propagandized the trials of Communists and sometimes, for tactical reasons, non-Communists all over the world. Its successor, the International Association of Democratic Lawyers, suffers from the incongruence of its task: defending Communists from oppression while at the same time upholding the often worse record of suppression under Communist rule. The painstaking research job of V. Kabes and A. Sergot, *Blueprint of Deception, Character and Record of the International Association of Democratic Lawyers*, The Hague, 1957, somehow underestimates the difficulties of their foes in keeping in line their not-totally-committed sympathizers, and in compromising and adjusting the viewpoints of farflung satellite jurists—viewpoints that mirror different stages of societal development and legal institutions.

2) The *ad hoc* partisan organization set up on a national or international basis to support, financially, morally, and legally, the action of a specific group of defendants (as in the South African treason trial).

3) The organization that embraces a specific principle—implementation of civil rights, or maintenance of the rule of law as such—both propagandizing its stages of implementation and giving legal help and advice in cases that involve the application of the principle. However, the organization would avoid entering into the concrete political disputes from which the case arose. This is the policy of the present board of the American Civil Liberties Union. The same applies in some ways to the more recent International Commission of Jurists. Founded in 1957 by Western jurists, it attempts to build as wide a network of members and sympathizers all over the world as that of its Communist competitors. It tries to enter cases as an observer, to influence governments and mold opinion through meetings, memos, questionnaires, and research reports. Unlike its Communist brethren, it wants to build up a reputation of fairness by inquiring into and sometimes commenting upon problems in Western judicial and police behavior. While it has recently branched out into the African area, the main concern of its leaders still seems to be to track down and publicize Communist violations of human rights, and of the rule of law, committed in and out of court.

The main Communist difficulty is the lack of credibility of a para-legal organization which espouses the case of "progressive" defendants against their government, but

Communists as well as their foes, or for that matter any movement opposed to some official policies anywhere on the globe. The sending of such observers and the reports they produce not only serve to create a counterimage of the trial but become an integral part of the policy of mobilizing foreign opinion support against repressive governmental policies.

The resultant internationalization of political trials, leading to a greater diffusion of counterimages, does not necessarily diminish the usefulness of the political trial for enlarging the domestic political stage. But it may diminish the total profit to be expected from the operation. It also sets a premium on a businesslike handling of the trial and on avoiding the eruption of conflicts useful for the production of counterimages. No regime can change the sum total of political and social conditions that surround a particular trial. By judicious selection of the material to be put in evidence, a regime may try to steer the trial away from dangerous or revealing subjects.

Can it really? Is it not the peculiarity of a political trial that even the most picayune happening may assume political color and significance and that the actual trial, however carefully staged, if allowed to follow its own course, may bring surprises?[62]

---

embraces the cause of the "progressive" government in an identical fact situation. The Western organizations try to avoid related difficulties by espousing abstract legal or constitutional principles rather than concrete historical causes; they suffer every time this separation proves artificial.

[62] Elevating a completely nonpolitical case into the political sphere might, if the goal is beyond their reach, discredit the party laboring to perform such transformation. A drunken brawl in a West German inn, ending in the homicide of a completely nonpolitical East German laborer, would need a pliant court or well-indoctrinated witnesses for it to emerge as the persecution of a valiant toiler of the DDR by West German fiends. In the absence of such a setting, even the DDR's most brilliant political lawyer cannot effect such a transformation. See "Herrn Kaul's Plädoyer und ploetzliche Abreise," *Frankfurter Allgemeine Zeitung*, March 30, 1960.

CHAPTER VII

"DEMOCRATIC CENTRALISM" AND POLITICAL INTEGRATION OF THE JUDICIARY

++

Mit wem sässe der Rechtliche nicht zusammen
Dem Recht zuhelfen?
Welche Niedrigkeit begingest Du nicht, um
Die Niedrigkeit auszutilgen?
Könntest Du die Welt endlich verändern, wofür
Wärest du dir zu gut?
Wer bist du?
Versinke in Schmutz
Umarme den Schlächter, aber
Ändere die Welt: sie braucht es!

    —BERTOLT BRECHT, *Die Massnahme*, 1930*

++

THE problem of the judge operating under the conditions of Western society has been discussed here mainly from the following standpoints: the types of situations in which he becomes active; the impact of his professional formation; his relation to other organs of the state; and the reciprocal relations which tie his activity to the presuppositions of society at large.

The balance between community and judge has emerged as a dynamic one. It changes with the sociopolitical structure of the particular society and has a variable margin in which the pressures of the day and the inchoate data of public consciousness are translated into judgments on individual situations submitted for examination. Under such conditions there are unavoidable differences between executive policies and the judge's interpretation of the general rule merging with

* "With whom would the friend of justice be unwilling to consort
To advance the cause of justice?
What baseness would you be unwilling to commit
To eradicate baseness forever?
If you could really change the world
Would you not roll up your sleeves and do it?
Who are you?
Be prepared to wade in filth,
Embrace the butcher, but
Change this world—it cries out for it!"

his understanding of the concrete situation. While they are not the rule, these differences flow logically from the arrangements of a society which visualizes the resultant friction as an active contribution to the well-being of its members. Some sphere of not-officially-controlled individual activity, if by no means safely guaranteed, is at least facilitated as long as some gaps are likely between the political executive's and the judiciary's understanding of the situation.

It is a characteristic of the judicial office within the sphere of Soviet-modeled institutions that it be organized to avoid as far as possible, contradictory interpretations of individual situations by the political authorities and by what is correctly known as the judicial functionary. The goal is the maximal harmonization of judicial activity with official policies, with every case "ideally" decided in the light of the contribution the decision will render to the fulfillment of the momentary program. The following pages will discuss how such a policy is carried through by formal and, more interesting, informal arrangements; how such a policy affects the relations of the judicial functionary with the rest of the official establishment, as well as with the population at large; how, in the absence of judicial participation in such work, the society decides conflicts in the rank order of its social priorities.

Most of the material regarding the working of such judiciaries is drawn from the experience of East Germany (Deutsche Demokratische Republik, abbr. DDR). This regime recommends itself for such purposes through the absence of totalitarian extremism. No continuous sequence of bloody purges in the ranks of the ruling party, after the pattern of the USSR and some of her satellites, has cramped the DDR's style; intraparty fighting over policy or repercussions of party shifts in the USSR have not played havoc with the style of the regime. Nevertheless, dealing with a population somewhat less submissive than in some neighboring countries, the DDR rulers have at times felt less secure and have acted more carefully than their colleagues abroad. Whenever the screws are tightened, there is a great deal more hesitation about loosening them; this leads to an aversion to liberalizing experiments. When the effects of both inordinately severe and lenient tendencies are lacking, the typical stands out in bold relief.

The discussion will take its point of departure from a 1954 case, bringing out the intermeshing pressures and considerations faced in its adjudication.

1. The Stray Dog and the Political Watchman

A pathetic story of vile persecution of an alltime party faithful was told at the 1954 national convention of the Socialist Unity Party (East German pseudonym for the Communist Party; abbr. SED) by party chief Walter Ulbricht.[1] The victim was a pre-1933 and post-1945 Communist from Mühlhausen, Thuringia. "M" had served on the local denazification board in the early postwar years and later was made SED representative of the plant protection unit in a government-owned industrial establishment. As he had made many enemies through over-zealous performance of his duties, his coworkers had long awaited an opportunity to get even with M. The payoff came on an unexpected occasion.

One night in October 1953, the vigilant chief of the plant guards discovered on the premises a tagless dog, which lunged at him. M grabbed a piece of timber and set off on a chase, issuing orders to watchmen under his command and juvenile workers within reach to help bring in the trespasser. Circumspectly led by M, the posse of dogcatchers succeeded in surrounding the enemy.

Still armed with the piece of timber, and unaware of victory, M repeatedly struck the dog, and, believing it to be seriously wounded, tried to kill it—out of humane considerations, as he later insisted. Inimical witnesses later testified that M in rage and fury had savagely beaten the defenseless cur. Assuming the dog to be dead, M ordered the carcass thrown into the furnace. But the order was not carried out. Back on duty the next morning, M detected on a wheelbarrow what the night before he had diagnosed as a lifeless corpse. He seized the object and hurled it into an ashpit where embers smoldered under the ashes. A hostile witness later claimed to have retrieved the dog's body, which still showed signs of life, insisting that death had not occurred until later, when he, the witness, interred the martyred dog.

Events then took a nightmarish turn. M's version of the nocturnal battle was sneered at by all and sundry as a tissue of lies. Overnight he had become a sadistic villain, a public menace. The populace was in an uproar. Numerous letters reached the local newspaper, and some were printed, wherein M was exposed as a savage torturer of animals. A petition was circulated in the plant and signed by many, demanding

[1] Protokoll der Verhandlungen des IV. Parteitages der Sozialistischen Einheitspartei Deutschlands, 30. März bis 6. April 1954, in der Werner Seelenbinderhalle in Berlin, East Berlin, 1954, p. 180; see p. 559 for a discussion by the speaker Kiefert.

M's instant removal. Crowds gathered in front of the courthouse where M was on trial, clamoring for severe punishment; some screamed for the hangman.

The immediate consequences were frightening. M was fired from his job, expelled from the party, and sentenced by a local court to one year in jail and damages—for "unlawful destruction of property in conjunction with an intentional act of cruelty to animals." On appeal, the district court confirmed the verdict, however, converting the prison term into a rather mild fine.

The story might have ended there had it not been for M's appeal to the highest party authorities, which lent a willing ear to his complaints. Less than six months after the dog-killing incident, the party's national convention was told about the plot that almost destroyed a valiant fighter. The local party machine was denounced for complicity. Its officials, Ulbricht said, had made themselves the tools of reactionary forces, failing to realize the class enemy's deeds and aims, and grossly violating the rules of intraparty democracy.

A week later, acceding to the extraordinary appeal of the Attorney General, the DDR High Court quashed the previous judgment. Acquitting the accused, the court stated that he had followed the call of duty in protecting plant property and safety endangered by the trespassing quadruped. The explanation the accused had offered for the alleged mistreatment of the dog and the time of the latter's demise the court accepted as manifestly sincere, thus disposing of the charge of willful cruelty. It went on to say that the affair had been staged by enemies of the new order, and that there had been a transparent pattern in the collection of signatures in the plant, the letters to the newspapers, and the courthouse rioting. It castigated the local prosecutor and magistrates for having fallen down on their job, which was to protect the citizen and the state from enemy attacks; they were guilty, the High Court said, of having misjudged the accused and his background, and for aiding and abetting hostile attacks on a proven fighter for peace and national unity.[2]

What the High Court did not say was that the local party machine had joined in what turned out to be an assault on the established order.

---

[2] High Court judgment of March 29, 1954. *Neue Justiz* (henceforth abbr. *N.J.*), Vol. 8 (1954), p. 242. The story of the "dog of Mühlhausen" has entered the legal hagiography of Eastern Germany as the Fourth Party Congress' legacy to the legal fraternity, "the living example of the dialectical unity of legality and Parteilichkeit." See Hilde Benjamin (Minister of Justice), "Vom IV. zum V. Parteitag der sozialistischen Einheitspartei Deutschlands," *N.J.*, Vol. 12 (1958), p. 437.

Without the party's nod there would have been neither newspaper stories nor rioting, nor the first exemplary sentence. What had brought this on? Clearly, local feeling had run high against M. Apparently, too, the local party bosses at one time or another had made up their minds to string along, whatever their true motives. How could the local court have guessed that the facts of the case would, at some later date, be seen in a different light by the highest party body?

What a strange predicament! Under conditions generally prevailing in the DDR, party and government authorities usually exert pressure on the courts in two directions. They see to it that the courts guarantee enforcement of official policy; and they urge the judges to keep an ear to the ground and do their utmost to prevent or deflect the people from distrusting judicial authority. Both jobs are tough, even under favorable conditions. Eager to implement official policy, the courts will be hard put to give popular sentiment more than perfunctory attention. The M case must have seemed a rare windfall to the Mühlhausen court: for once, party interests were in line with the popular mood. What disillusionment to find out that the stamp of judicial approval had been given to the character assassination of a proven fighter for the cause.

The fable is not without a moral. It stands out clearly that no local organization should be trusted to judge independently whether or not this or that individual act fits in with the general pattern of actions desirable for the maintenance and consolidation of the political order. When the popular foundations of the regime are shaky, there is always danger that government officials and enforcement agents will become entangled in hostile machinations, or become slack in enforcing central policies in the face of contrary local sentiment.[3] The greater the danger, the more imperative it is to put up safeguards which will insure that actions at all levels meet the requirements of official policy. What do such safeguards look like in the administration of justice?

2. Aspects of Judicial Organization

How much does the formal organization of the apparatus of justice reflect the changed function of the court system, the endeavor to bring the court's work as closely as possible in line with executive policies? The usual ministry of justice found in continental democracies assumes the tasks of selecting judges and prosecutors, instructing the prosecution

[3] For some recent occurrences in the latter direction, see G. Jahn (Vice President of the High Court), "Zu einigen Fragen der Durchsetzung der neuen Konzeption fuer die Arbeit der Justizorgane aus der Sicht des Obersten Gerichts," *N.J.*, Vol. 14 (1960), pp. 152, 154.

staff, doing part of the housekeeping job for the courts, and functioning as drafting office for nonspecialized legislation. In contrast, the DDR's two principal administrative agencies in the field of administration of justice, the Ministry of Justice and the Office of the Attorney General, have much wider tasks. They are responsible for the satisfactory functioning of the judicial order and are guarantors of the intellectual content of the judiciary's output. They insure that the courts will deliver judgments in harmony with the goals of the administration. From the principle of "democratic centralism," which permeates the whole state organization, the 1959 version of the statute on court organization formulates the logical conclusion in the following way: "The activities of local and district courts will be directed and controlled by the Ministry of Justice. The direction and control will have to guarantee the fulfillment of the judicial task as well as of the political work among the toilers."[4]

In explaining the organization of the various tribunals and in delineating their hierarchical relationship, we must constantly keep in mind this role of the Ministry of Justice. The judicial hierarchy of the DDR ends only in a very formal sense in its highest tribunal, the High Court. In practice, it extends beyond it and culminates in the two coordinated administrative organs, the Ministry of Justice and the Office of the Attorney General, which have both formal and informal means at their disposal to influence the disposition of individual cases and direct the course of future legal decisions. Rather than having the last word on the decision of individual cases, the High Court becomes a

---

[4] Par. 15(1,2) of the Amendment to the Statute on the Administration of Justice, October 1, 1959 (GBL. DDR, I, 753), as well as the very clearcut comments to the amended statute by H. Benjamin in "10 Jahre Justiz im Arbeiter und Bauernstaat, Rückblick und Ausblick," *N.J.*, Vol. 13 (1959), pp. 656, 661. See also Benjamin, "Vom IV. zum V. Parteitag" (cited above, n. 2), p. 438. In her evaluation of the tasks set by the SED Fifth Party Congress, she re-emphasizes the need for central direction of the courts' work. At any rate, the recent discussion in Russia of the locus and extent of court supervision, and the ensuing reformulation of Article 10 of the Principles of Criminal Procedure, though initially reported in *Rechtswissenschaftlicher Informationsdienst*, 6 (1957), p. 341, has so far found no receptive ear in Eastern Germany. For an English version of this discussion, see "Judicial vs. Executive Supervision Over the Courts," *The Current Digest of the Soviet Press*, Vol. 10, No. 20 (1958), p. 6. Minister of Justice Benjamin and other members of her ministry, citing the Czech example, have insisted on the need for continued direction of the courts by the Ministry of Justice, which is conditioned by the concrete economic and political situation of East Germany, whose circumstances are deemed at variance with those in the Soviet Union. Benjamin, "Aktuelle Fragen der Gerichtsorganisation," *Staat und Recht im Lichte des Grossen*, October, 1957, p. 189; H. Ostmann, "Ueber die Organisation der Justizverwaltung," *N.J.*, Vol. 11 (1957), p. 357.

kind of agent which transmits to the lower court the message of the administrative agencies of justice. A given message may concern the introduction of a totally new program or the rectification of some isolated but symptomatic mistake spotted by the Ministry or the Attorney General's Office. In this role the High Court neither advances governmental policy nor lags far behind it. Loyally following official gyrations, the court tries to keep in line with changing requirements. As democratic centralism requires all subordinate decisions to be made on the basis of the premises established by the political authorities, the ministries, in daily contact with both the political echelons above them and—through the network of inspectors, still to be discussed—with the regional courts below, have a better chance than the High Court "to recognise the points of concentration of societal development."[5]

The High Court thus functions as an adjunct of the administration rather than as an independent center of authority. As a technical means for carrying through the harmonization of government policy and judicial work, the DDR, borrowing both from Soviet system and the criminal procedure of the National Socialist state, has instituted an extraordinary appeal. Both the attorney general and the president of the High Court may bring any civil or criminal case before a plenary meeting of the court[6] within a year from the date final judgment has been issued, whether by a lower court or by a three-judge division of the High Court itself.[7] Such an extraordinary appeal, called "cassation," may be based on a simple error of law or on an allegation that the attacked decision is "fundamentally incorrect so far as the sentencing is concerned."[8] From the viewpoint of the government, the extraordinary appeal has a major advantage. By preserving the immutability of final judgments, the legal system of the DDR theoretically allows discrete problems to be settled in a manner which might not conform to the always shifting policies that characterize Communist regimes.

[5] K. Schumann (until spring 1960 President of the High Court), "Das Oberste Gericht am 10. Jahrestag der DDR und seine künftigen Aufgaben," *N.J.*, Vol. 13 (1959), pp. 673, 674.

[6] In the USSR, until the recent reform, the extraordinary appeal has not been dependent on observation of a time limit; hence, in contrast to DDR decisions, Soviet judgments have lacked the character of finality. For a description of the USSR practice, see *Government, Law and Courts in the Soviet Union and in Eastern Europe*, ed. V. Gsovski and K. Grzybowski, New York, 1959, p. 539 and Appendix.

[7] Statute on Court Organization (Gerichtsverfassungsgesetz, abbr. GVG) of October 2, 1952, GBL. DDR, 983, Par. 55 (1), 3, 56. (The 1959 revision of the statute has not changed these provisions.)

[8] Code of Criminal Procedure (CCP) of October 2, 1952, GBL. DDR, 996, Par. 301 (2 a, b).

The extraordinary appeal reduces the inconvenience that might arise from such a situation. No decision of any consequence can ever be established as a precedent unless it conforms to the official policy of the day. As the High Court follows as a rule the policy directives of the Attorney General, that court is readily seen as the principal means of transmitting policy decisions from the government to the judiciary.[9] While the court system is thus at the disposal of the authorities, care is taken at the same time that it cannot be employed as a weapon against the government. Damage suits against any governmental agencies or against any official cannot be pursued in any court.[10]

The 207 county courts, 14 district courts, the High Court, and the prosecutor's staff operate with a corps of judicial officers which has been almost completely changed since 1945.[11] Virtually all judges and prosecutors in office at the end of the Second World War were displaced at an early date by new personnel. The barring of NS and related categories from office accounted for 80 per cent of the incumbents. Of those who remained, many were presumed to have steered clear of the NS Party mainly because of its plebeian complexion. This group did not satisfy the new rulers. Furthermore, the Communists sought a radical change in social structure and property relations; for inexperienced personnel to handle the administration of justice in this situation was not as risky and costly as it might have been had superficial political change alone been intended.

The new dispensers of justice, called "people's judges" and "people's attorneys," first took office in the summer of 1945. At first the mandatory qualifications were simply graduation from primary school and recommendation by the local political group enjoying the confidence of the occupation authorities. Somewhat later, the completion of a four to six month training course became a further requirement. By

[9] While the "cassation" in criminal cases is completely dominated by the government, in civil cases a practice still prevails, much complained of by the authorities, by which the lawyers of the parties concerned try to use this device as a further appeal; Jahn, *op.cit.*, p. 152.

[10] GVG, Par. 9. Access to the courts has also been closed in lawsuits between "people's" enterprises; these lawsuits belong before the State Contract Commission (Decrees of December 6, 1951, GBL. DDR, 1,143, and June 11, 1953, GBL. DDR, 854). Some administrations grant a certain amount of indemnity for damages, based on considerations of individual need. For a limited program of reopening access to the courts, see G. Schreier, "Gedanken zu einer gesetzlichen Regelung der Staatshaftung," *N.J.*, Vol. 12 (1958), pp. 195-98.

[11] For the initiation of the new judiciary, with local variations as remembered by participants, see "Aus der Ersten Zeit Unserer Justiz," *N.J.*, Vol. 9 (1955), p. 267.

April 1953, 91 per cent of all judges and over 98 per cent of all prosecutors were of the new, people's variety. Eighty-five per cent of the judges and 98 per cent of the prosecutors were members of the SED. The old legal profession was out except for some Weimar survivors and victims of NS persecution who were devoted to the SED, and a handful of undaunted and adaptable careerists. Eventually the term of the lawyers' cram courses was made approximately as long as traditional university training. The curriculum centered on political indoctrination. "On-the-job training" was conducted in courts and prosecutors' offices which, in turn, underwent far-reaching structural change. Zeal in pursuing the government's objectives ranked much higher than familiarity with obsolete legal doctrine or technical skill in settling legal claims. The old law itself withered, although in most fields it was not formally abrogated.[12] By 1960 all members of the judiciary who do not have an academic background must pass a qualifying examination; they will be assisted by three- to five-year correspondence courses with the Walter Ulbricht German Academy for Political and Legal Sciences, the fountainhead of official wisdom. Entry conditions to the judicial career for the younger generation have developed in line with a practice which aims at radical change in the social antecedents of judicial and administrative personnel, as compared with those that still prevail in Western Europe and are pronounced in Western Germany. Both the admission policy to the universities and the continued possibility for lateral entry into the judicial career for whomever qualifies as "production worker"[13] serve that purpose.

Hitherto the Ministry of Justice has appointed lower court judges for three-year terms, while the judges of the High Court have been elected for five-year terms by the People's Assembly. According to recent decisions, this system of election by assembly was, as of fall 1960, extended to the lower courts whose members will be elected by the district and local assemblies and, in the more distant future, by the people. This extension will not bring any material changes in actual selection practices. The Ministry of Justice still exercises control; it submits to the electoral bodies the list of candidates made up in the ministry from those who have successfully terminated their eighteen-month prep-

---

[12] For a survey of developments in DDR judicial administration by its principal architects, see H. Benjamin and E. Melsheimer (Attorney General until his death in 1960), "Zehn Jahre demokratische Justiz in Deutschland," *N.J.*, Vol. 9 (1955), p. 259.

[13] Intensive search for the right kind of production worker, and enticing him to enter the judicial career, are described and exemplified in E. Horeni, "Auf neue Art zu neuen Kadern," *N.J.*, Vol. 14 (1960), p. 124.

aration and, as before, appoints among those elected the judges for all higher positions at all the courts.[14]

Any judge may be removed by the appointing agency on account of a criminal record, for "violation of the constitution and other laws," and for "manifest violation of [his] duty as judge"[15]—an elastic concept. Removal grounded on inefficiency or unreliability arising from policy disputes, possibly engineered by the party cell of the court itself, is a regular if not frequent occurrence.[16] A judge may also be removed for reasons of "political optics." Thus in April 1960 the president of the High Court asked "to be relieved of his office."[17] At the moment when the DDR authorities were carrying on a campaign to drive West German judges with a background of reprehensible service under a National Socialist repressive agency out of office, a former National Socialist Party member became unsuitable as High Court president.

Uncertain tenure, use of the extraordinary appeal, and the fact that as a last resort a rubber-stamp legislature can dexterously remove the long-range consequences of an unsatisfactory judgment serve to diminish the import of the judicial function. Unshakable validity over a substantial span of time is what lifts the legal judgment out of the stream of administrative orders that change rapidly under new impulses or an appraisal of political conditions. This validity is not a characteristic of a judgment arrived at under the East German system.

But one might argue that an East German judge, following the provisions of the DDR constitution,[18] is still free to decide individual cases

[14] See the explanations given by H. Benjamin, when she introduced the new law on judicial elections in the *Volkskammer*, October 1, 1959 (*N.J.*, Vol. 13 [1959], p. 689); the text of the statute may be found in GBL. DDR, 1, 751; see also Par. 13 of the "Praktikantenordnung" of August 1, 1959, reprinted in GVG (looseleaf edition of laws and decrees), East Berlin, 1960 no. 15.

[15] GVG, par. 16 (1a-b).

[16] Cases of removal have been reported in *N.J.*, Vol. 12 (1958), pp. 369, 623. Disciplinary transfers may be considered common practice.

[17] *N.J.*, Vol. 14 (1960), p. 289.

[18] Art. 127 of the Constitution, reiterated in GVG, Par. 5, reads as follows: "The judges are independent in their judicial function and only subject to the constitution and the laws." However, the provision should be read in the context of Section 1 of the 1959 Amendment to the Statute of the Administration of Justice, cited above, n. 4: "In his person and activity a judge must give guarantees that he exercises his office in accordance with the principles of the constitution, stands without reservation for the victory of socialism in the DDR, and is loyal to the workers and peasants state." The "functionary of justice," as he is called officially and correctly, has recently been apostrophized "an organizer of the masses in the societal process of the formation and realization of law," rather than an "umpire between contending parties." H. Strohbach, "Sorgfältiges Studium der Parteibeschlüsse verhindert Dogmatismus und Formalismus,"

according to pre-established rules and on the basis of evidence submitted to his court. His decisions may not be upset unless by certain fixed procedures. Thus he is unlike other officials, who may see their decisions unceremoniously discarded or ignored by their respective hierarchical superiors. This line of argument cannot be accepted.

3. The Informal Structure of Authority

The legal system of the DDR knows a number of informal devices which exert enormous influence on the final effect of a judicial decision. In East Germany's legal universe, private commentaries are as rare as privately sponsored law journals. A monopoly of legal interpretations rests with the official legal authorities. If a judge finds himself in need of elucidation on a point of law which the reports or the official textbooks do not provide, he may turn to the equally official law journal. But this law journal is as much an educational as an interpretative enterprise. Although controversy may be artificially stirred up for didactic purposes, the journal is primarily concerned with the "correct" indoctrination of court and prosecution personnel and carries only such articles and reports on judicial decisions as fit the purpose. Real controversy does arise if the most recent party directives and resolutions are susceptible to a variety of interpretations. But once the authoritative gloss on the interpretation is provided, and possibly calculated ambiguities are clarified, everybody falls in line.[19]

The absence of private commentaries is not accidental.[20] Nor is it

---

N.J., Vol. 12 (1958), pp. 689, 693. "The judicial organs are a part of the unified state apparatus of the Peoples Democracy"; W. Krutzsch and H. Richter, "Erste Schlussfolgerungen aus den Parteiaktivtagungen in den Bezirken," N.J., Vol. 13 (1959), p. 756.

[19] In this context it must be emphasized that political doubts which have an immediate impact on the legal interpretation of certain concepts, such as "danger to society," often remain for long without solution. A final solution may be reached only by a formal decision of the "Politburo"; see the cogent observations of Ernst Richert, *Macht Ohne Mandat*, Cologne, 1959, p. 137, n. 606.

[20] A few years ago the official law journal permitted a judge to ask why the DDR published no law commentaries by outstanding jurists; E. Volkland, "Ueber das Verhaeltnis zwischen Rechtwissenschaft und Justiapraxis," N.J., Vol. 8 (1954), pp. 227, 229. The answer was supplied by the highest ranking official of the Ministry of Justice, who is now the president of the High Court. Recommending to the readers an edition of legislative texts, he disposed of the subject by saying that "brief" commentaries were notoriously "insufficient and worthless." H. Toeplitz, "Zum Erscheinen der neuen Textausgaben," N.J., vol. 8 (1954), pp. 292, 293. The circumlocution made it abundantly clear that the very subject of comprehensive commentaries was taboo; the same phenomenon in Soviet Russia is described in R. David and J. Hazard, *Le Droit Soviétique*, Paris, 1954, Vol. 1, p. 220.

due to the kind of "phonograph" theory of law that inspired the great legal enactments of the era of Enlightenment, such as Prussia's Allgemeines Landrecht or the codes of the French Revolution. DDR doctrine certainly does not regard law as a closed system in which the judge has nothing to do but draw logical conclusions from rigidly fixed premises. The ban on private interpretation is deliberate and political; it serves to prevent the emergence of a rival center of legal doctrine which uncontrollable minds could use to disseminate independent opinion. Nothing could come of such independence of juridical thought but the obstruction of the government's effort to train the judge to make apply unquestioningly the frequently changing policy to the case on the docket.

Despite its stress on the judge's continuing "education," despite exhortations and cajolery, not even the DDR can force him to absorb all the official wisdom it is so eager to purvey. Where the call to study fails, more accentuated pressure appears. Under any legal system cases arise which, when scrutinized by higher courts, reveal delays below and insufficient attention to one or more phases in the proceedings; nevertheless, appellate courts are often unwilling to conclude that these factors constitute reversible error. While upholding a decision, a higher court may mention such shortcomings in passing. Especially under the East German system, which only knows *per curiam* opinions, the judgment on appeal will necessarily concentrate on the reasons for upholding the lower court's decision, thus it will touch only slightly on more problematic points. Consequently, the lower court ordinarily need not be exercised unduly over the appellate opinion, even though it may be critical in part. The institutionalization of judicial criticism, as introduced in paragraph four of the East German Code of Criminal Procedure, is designed to fill this gap. Whenever a case comes up on appeal, perhaps to as low a tribunal as a district court, the appellate bench may take action even when there exists no sufficient ground to modify or set aside the judgment of the lower court. For example, in the event of delays in arraigning prisoners, undue adjournments or procedural mistakes of some kind, the appellate court may expose shortcomings at the lower level by publishing a piece of educational criticism. This criticism does not affect the validity of the judgment. But reprinted in the official law journal, it is supposed to induce the court in question and other courts facing similar problems to discontinue the condemned practices. It is also within the authority of the higher courts to keep score on lower level colleagues in a kind of index file which records typical mistakes, both political and legal, and serves as a vade mecum for self-improvement.[21]

Both institutionalized criticism and an occasional index file of typical mistakes focus only on the segment of cases which come to the higher court's knowledge by way of ordinary or extraordinary appeals or protests. In actual practice, only a fraction of lower court cases attract the attention of the courts above. Review of the lower court proceedings at the request of the prosecutor general or by order of the High Court president takes place as a rule only when this or that segment of the SED especially interested in upsetting a specific judgment exerts sufficient pressure.[22]

Seen from the authorities' viewpoint, these institutionalized checks—appeals, extraordinary appeals, judicial criticism, helped along by some measure of law periodical comments—have one essential shortcoming. They do not specify how often and how quickly the lower courts will be able to produce decisions in conformity with announced official policies. Consequently, a network of political and moral pressures influencing and determining the attitudes of the judiciary has been built up to complement both the educational processes and the institutionalized checks on the judges' individual decisions. The call to self-improvement is the central theme of these additional controls.

Self-improvement does not come automatically. A double-pronged machinery sets it in motion: on the upper level, the Ministry of Justice and, for the prosecutors, the Attorney General's Office; on the lower level, the all-important administrative offices, instituted at the district courts and the individual court's party units. The administrative offices, beyond their housekeeping functions, have been given the specific job of analyzing and directing the work of the local courts and, since 1958, the district courts themselves; in this function they supervise both legality and quality, in line with the needs and suggestions of the Ministry of Justice.[23] The party unit comprises all party members, from the presiding judge to the charwoman. Often, the court's administrative officers,

[21] See the proclamation of the Leipzig Administration of Justice, reprinted in *N.J.*, Vol. 7 (1953), p. 725; J. Gras, R. Trautzsch, and G. Stiller, "Die Selbstverpflichtungen des Bezirksgerichts Leipzig zum Jahr der grossen Initiative," *N.J.*, Vol. 7 (1953), p. 759.

[22] In a reply to critics, such operational breaks were cited by the then-High Court Deputy President Walter Ziegler as a chief reason for the highest tribunal's shortcomings in implementing governmental policy. "Zur Kritik am Obersten Gericht," *N.J.*, Vol. 10 (1956), pp. 715, 717.

[23] The directing influence of the administrative section of the district court, on the work of both district and local courts, has been laid down in administrative decrees issued piecemeal, between 1954 and 1959, by the Ministry of Justice and now collected in the looseleaf ed. of the GVG.

who make the assignments and supervise the docket, enjoy a higher party rank and corresponding influence on the cell's resolutions than does the judicial personnel. It is before this body that the judge, as any other party worker, undergoes the ritual of "self-commitment." The "self-commitment" pledge specifies areas of mandatory improvement, either along the lines of previous criticism by superiors or party officials, or else simply in dutiful observance of recent policy pronouncements. In addition, each court holds frequent judicial conferences. Every judge is expected to submit a progress report; the individual members' weak spots are discussed, and the more advanced ones straighten out those who fail. When necessary, the party "plant unit" deals with obstinately repeated "mistakes."

How effective is self-improvement guidance by higher courts and party pressure? Much though it may upset the government, the answer always depends on the individual judge's zeal and application—another uncertain factor. Strong emphasis is therefore placed on continuing supervision by "instructors" who are expected to give to the everyday activity of the judiciary a steadier direction than the higher courts could. In the person of the instructor, the job of functional and political supervision merge; he studies, compares, evaluates, and criticizes the judge's performance from both professional and political viewpoints. Instructors operating out of the Ministry of Justice and the Office of the Attorney General reach down to the level of district courts and district prosecutors; in turn, instructors from the administrative office at the district level are assigned to the local courts. In addition, a whole brigade of inspectors, namely, all the district instructors, some district court judges, and personnel officers accompanied by the executive officer of the local court under review administer an annual evaluation of each court's performance.[24] The court's executive officer is then of particular value, both by his familiarity with the judges' records and by his standing in the party organization, which casts him in the role of the court's permanent political supervisor.[25]

[24] Inspection reports are frequently discussed and suggestions for improvement offered in print. See F. Boehme and G. Krueger, "Die Arbeit der Instrukteurbrigaden bei Revisionen verbessern," *N.J.*, Vol. 10 (1956), p. 11; H. Ostmann, "Ueber die Justizverwaltung," *N.J.*, Vol. 8 (1954), p. 37; J. Streit, "Aus den Erfahrungen einer Brigade im Bezirk Potsdam," *N.J.*, Vol. 12 (1958), p. 620; G. Windisch, "Die Veraenderung der Instrukteurtaetigkeit in der Staatsanwaltschaft," *N.J.*, Vol. 12 (1958), p. 839.

[25] Separate inspection teams within one jurisdiction, assigned to the court, the prosecutor's office, and the police department, actually proceed with a degree of coordination—though not necessarily in complete agreement with one another—to bring into the open interdepartmental friction and rivalry and to obtain uniform corrective results. G. Eberhardt, "Ueber die Durchfuehrung von Revisionen," *N.J.*, Vol. 10 (1956), p. 600.

One story tells of an overeager chief instructor who, feeling misgivings about a specific decision, went out to interview local people. When he had assembled the facts, he discovered that the court indeed had been at fault and he found the reasons for the error.[26] Was this his real mission? Not according to prevailing opinion in the mid-1950's. Most comments have expressed the view that it is not the instructor's function to retry individual cases.[27] The emphasis is on improving the quality of the court's work rather than on securing justice in particular instances. Cultural and political problems are to be investigated. Judges are to be counselled on the political and social imperatives and why judgments based on proper fact-finding and sound legal reasoning may be utterly wrong when the social and political implications of both the incriminating act and the judicial decision are left unheeded. Within this framework, judicial opinions are thoroughly studied. The performance of the individual judge and the political effect of his overall judicial record are evaluated by instructors and discussed with him. Beyond this, the annual inspection is to ascertain the extent to which each court's collective effort has contributed to the fulfillment of the judiciary's political and ideological obligations. As the political situation changes, however, so may that of the inspection brigade. The greater the pressure on functionaries of the judicial apparatus for active political participation, the more pronounced is the inspector's tendency to reinvestigate cases, to expose their class contents, the roles of the parties, and the judge's "formalistic" neglect of these factors.[28]

Prominent among the various techniques to make the judge concentrate on doing a political job for the government is the combination of everyday supervision and counselling by instructors and annual roundups. This combination is pervasive and has become symbolic of the courts' role and position. Whether a judge is good or bad is measured on a scale which registers his ability to grasp and assimilate, at any given moment and without delay, the executive view of the political and social situation. "First and foremost in the instructor's work," as one of the architects of the system put it, "is immediate transmission from the top to the bottom . . . he is a helper and political advisor."[29]

[26] M. Becker, "Eine praktische Methode der Revision," *N.J.*, Vol. 10 (1956), p. 359.

[27] Böhme and Krüger, *op.cit.*, pp. 11, 13.

[28] The experiences of the inspection brigade in the Postdam district are described in Streit, *loc.cit.*, p. 621; recently there has been detailed criticism of some Potsdam judgments in L. von Ehrenwall and H. Bürger, "Uber einige Mängel in der Arbeitsweise des Bezirksgerichts Potsdam," *N.J.*, Vol. 13 (1959). p. 256.

[29] H. Benjamin, "Der Instructeur-Helfer und politischer Berater," *N.J.*, Vol. 8 (1954), pp. 285, 290. For more recent discussion, see H. Eildermann, "Einige Hinweise fuer die Revision der Kreisgerichte," *N.J.*, Vol. 11 (1957), p. 272.

But however faithful and eager the transmitting agents may be, the government's political program is bound to suffer in transmission. Even agents who know all the answers and can correct all conceivable mistakes will not be able to eliminate or prevent error, deviation, and lack of intuitive political adaptability. The true test of their achievement lies in the frequency and intensity of the judges' voluntary, spontaneous identification with the DDR's political leadership. Facilitating the identification is a tendency to visualize the judge no longer as a creator of individual decisions, but as a member of a social collective in which his own person and individual efforts submerge.[30] All societal differentiations would become submerged in universal identity, wherein the mind of the "judicial collective" unconsciously but unremittingly communicates with the all-pervasive mind of the government—totalitarian reality taking the form of ultrademocratic chimera.

4. The Judge and the Other Organs of State

It is doubtful whether in German trial practice an equilibrium ever existed between the defense lawyer and the prosecution. Somehow, in spite of his theoretical status as officer of the court, private counsel could never quite compete with the prestige of the prosecutor, representative of the most "objective office" in the world, as it was known in official parlance. But whatever the previously existing element of imbalance, it has increased many times over in the practice of the DDR. The lawyer has lost in status as a professional man and consequently in usefulness to his client. This is due as much to the fact that the DDR is too busy reforming the life habits of its members to care much about equipping them with efficient ways to defend their claims as to special measures that narrowed the prerogatives of the profession. The Code of Criminal Procedure is not overly concerned with the lawyer's prerogative. What has most limited his field of activity is the disregard for the code by prosecutor and judge and[31]—as important—the re-evaluation of the respective positions of defense and state authority, to which the system constantly draws the lawyer's attention. He is to represent the "justified" interests of his clients. This will entitle the lawyer to

[30] The judge as organ of the "always just" collective is emphasized by Streit (who now holds the key job of handling questions of state and law in the Central Committee of the SED), "Die Justizorgane sind wichtige Hebel der sozialistischen Umgestaltung," N.J., Vol. 13 (1959), pp. 789, 792.

[31] During the short-lived thaw of 1956, the president of the Berlin Lawyers' Cooperative drew up a kind of list of grievances. See the report on the meeting of the chairmen of lawyers' cooperatives, "Fragen des Strafverfahrens vom Standpunkt des Verteidigers," N.J., Vol. 10 (1956), p. 434.

work only for solutions of societal and human conflicts which will accord with social and economic developments at large.[32] Moreover, since 1953 the lawyer has been increasingly unable to exist as an independent professional entity conducting his business either alone or in free association. New lawyers can be admitted to practice only as members of the official lawyers' cooperative.[33] Disabilities for nonmembers and privileges for the joiner make continued independent practicing a hazardous affair; their net effect is to undermine the fundamental relationship of trust between lawyer and client. In turn, the cooperative's administration, which assigns cases and clients, has recently been the object of special attention and "ideological schooling" on the part of the Ministry of Justice.[34] Whether the deprofessionalizing influence of this new bureaucratic fetter is balanced by radical elimination of the lawyer's predominantly pecuniary motivation—on which official criticism of the capitalist lawyer lays such stress—is an interesting if debatable point.[35] At any rate, as the prestige of the profession is incommensurably lower than that of other law jobs, and as the style and condition of the new society allow for only limited use of the lawyers' intellectual equipment, its members scarcely do now, nor can they in the future, form any counterweight against the prosecutor in his present role. As in the West, though not always for the same reasons, the future of lawyers as a profession lies in the changeover from forensic to advisory activity.[36]

[32] H. Heidrich, "Uber die Funktion des Verteidigers in der Deutschen Demokratischen Republik," *N.J.*, Vol. 14 (1960), pp. 168, 169; see also Ch. VI, n. 32.

[33] The decree on the formation of lawyers' cooperatives dates from May 15, 1953. GBL. DDR, 1, 725. The "model statute" attached to the decree has been considerably changed through the introduction of tight official supervision of the cooperatives' activities, by decree of March 22, 1958, GBL. DDR, 1, 311.

[34] A list of grievances against the lawyers' cooperatives' lack of social consciousness, together with a recital of officially applied remedies, has been furnished by the ministry's specialist in charge of lawyers' affairs. R. Helm, "Fragen der Entwicklung einer sozialistischen Rechtsanwaltschaft," *N.J.*, Vol. 12 (1958), p. 298. Mixed control brigades with the participation of the Ministry of Justice, the SED, and the Association of Democratic Jurists, are now recommended for supplementing the feeble activities of the lawyers' cooperatives' own control commission, and also as a means of bringing the cooperatives up to required standards. See the official report reprinted in *N.J.*, Vol. 12 (1958), p. 665.

[35] Lawyers' cooperatives still try to keep membership down in order to maximize members' incomes (Helm, *op.cit.*, p. 300), but this may be part and parcel of the "unsatisfactory political and ideological condition" of the cooperative.

[36] F. Wolff (Chairman of the Cooperative of East Berlin Lawyers), "Der Weg zur Sozialistischen Rechtsanwaltschaft," *N.J.*, Vol. 13 (1959), p. 682. According to W. Rosenthal, R. Lange, and M. Blomeyer (*Die Justiz in der sowjetischen Besatzungszone Deutschlands*, 4th ed.; Bonn, 1959, p. 83), the number of lawyers admitted to the

Inasmuch as the Attorney General's and Minister of Justice's activities are coordinated by the incumbents' common zeal to transform into administrative practice the impulses and orders received from the highest party authorities and formalized by the Council of Ministers, the independent position of the attorney general's office may have more symbolic than actual importance in the DDR scheme of things. Nevertheless, its enhanced status has some impact on the style and method of DDR policy. Through its determination of the competent criminal court and its power over extraordinary appeals, the attorney general's office plays a fundamental role in blocking out penal policy.

The political importance of the case rather than the fine art of legal classification determines the conduct of the prosecution. Political guidance may take a variety of forms. The first job of the prosecution is to spot the possible political implication of a given situation. The more tightly the government controls opinion-molding, the more visibly will politics color every seemingly-private situation; divorce, libel, assault, the mistreatment of animals—all might acquire a political meaning. Slight sounds of misgivings, doubts, passive resistance, or more active insubordination may pass through devious channels before they appear in the trial itself as private quarrels or trifling brushes with the lower fringes of authority. The very frequency of such cases betrays cramped living in a climate where complaining and personal grudges take the place of self-expression and personal endeavor. In the eyes of the rulers, even the least significant and most ludicrous or banal run-in necessarily becomes more sinister. In every aimless individual reaction, the exponents of governmental powers are bound to look for traces of a repetitive, rebellious design.

With these situations the judge and prosecutor, without special signals from higher authorities, must deal, day in, day out, in the required political manner. They are on their own, at least at the trial stage; in a way, the individual setting of each trial is unpatterned and the development of the plot is watched attentively by participants and bystanders. Without genuine newspaper coverage, repercussions of scenes on the judicial stage are weak. It is the educational job of the office of the attorney general to train even the lowest local staff member to recognize incipient political situations and their implications on his own.

If a case has been referred to the Attorney General's Office by political authority, if it has the making of a *cause célèbre* or at least suggests that

---

bar is 863. By January 15, 1961, the total had declined to 703. Of these, 447 were "cooperative" and 256 "freelance" lawyers.

it could be widely used for propaganda purposes, the prosecutor may be under orders to tell the court unequivocally how he would like the case to be handled with regard both to penalty and applicable law. When it is considered the job of the apparatus of justice to "come out with the right type of judgment at the right moment and place,"[37] the main burden of the administration of justice must necessarily fall on those responsible for staging the mass political effects: the prosecutors. Thus the expected roles are reversed. In theory, under the DDR code no less than under most continental codes, it is up to the court to choose the legal formula to be applied in a given criminal situation. Deprived of this interpretive function, the court is hamstrung in its punitive role as well. With respect to the punishment to be imposed, the court, under a widely accepted doctrine, may disregard the authority of the government, as represented by the prosecutor, only if it holds a basically different view.[38]

In a case tried under floodlights, the burden on the judge might be eased, of course, by his administrative superiors. The official intervention of the prosecution's representative might go hand in hand with direct, though backstage, intervention from the higher echelons of the Ministry of Justice. In these instances, ranking officials of the Ministry would confer with the judge about the disposition of the case. This, however, is limited mostly to exceptional situations justifying spectacular legal or propaganda performances. Frequent repetition would expose too many fissures; show trials as an everyday affair might generate indifference and cynicism instead of that tremor which electrifies the faithful and makes the timid pledge active allegiance. The requisite minute preparation of the show to be staged and the public reaction to be evoked pays off only in cases of outstanding political importance. But while individualized high-level production design and stage direction are infrequent, the political approach to justice is never absent.

Older continental doctrine conceived of the prosecution as a mere counterbalance against the defense. With obvious justification, East German penal practitioners now deem this a rather unrealistic conception. Today, because of the political approach to justice, the prosecutor has a far stronger impact at the trial stage. He embodies the permanent state interest and is, at least in theory, cognizant of the actual needs

[37] Josef Streit, "Zur Vorbereitung der Arbeitstagungen der Richter und Staatsanwaelte in den Bezirken," *N.J.*, Vol. 13 (1959), pp. 439, 440.

[38] E. Melsheimer, "Sozialistische Gesetzlichkeit im Strafverfahren, *N.J.*, Vol. 10 (1956), pp. 289, 295.

of the political powers at each and any moment.[39] True, at the pretrial stage a preventive detention warrant must be signed by a judge. But here the judge's power ends; at least on paper, the prosecutor is in charge of everything else.[40]

In everyday practice the stature of the prosecutor's office, tremendously enhanced vis-à-vis defense and court alike, does not appear quite so large. The criminal procedure code's "investigative organs," the criminal police and the ubiquitous security services, tend to relegate the prosecutor to the role of manager or writ-signer. This much was officially admitted during the brief political thaw of 1956 when the prosecuting staff's position as second fiddle to the security police was deplored and remedial action suggested. Yet a possible misunderstanding should be immediately dispelled: this is a general tendency of bureaucracies attempting to enlarge their jurisdiction, as we have seen in the relations of all prosecutors' offices with their respective police organizations.[41] It is especially facilitated through the police's greater proximity to the case at hand. It becomes more serious if, as in the DDR, the ways open to the individual for effective counteraction are few and far between. In political terms, however, neither the People's Police nor the Security Police play an independent role. It is the Politburo of the Central Committee which centralizes all major decisions in its own hands;[42] the police remain a subordinate organ.

At any rate, the prosecutor's office retains a strategic position, especially since the DDR, following the Soviet example, has made the office the kingpin of what might be called an attempt to establish an intra-bureaucratic balance. Because the Communist regime's parliamentary bodies lack popular backing, and because the interests of their mem-

[39] However, the gap between theory and practice is considerable, and the "revision reports" are full of complaints about wrong political estimates and lack of political-ideological clarity and unified political line in the district and county prosecutors' offices, For a recent criticism on the basis of experience in the Magdeburg district, see M. Spranger and R. Wunsch, "Ueberwindung von Maengeln in der Arbeit der Justizorgane und der Staatsanwaltschaft in Bezirk Magdeburg," *N.J.*, Vol. 12 (1958), p. 267.

[40] Judicial pretrial investigation has been abolished, leaving pretrial proceedings concentrated in the hands of the prosecution or the "investigative organs." If necessary, the prosecutor orders search and seizure; CCP, Sec. 116. The "investigative organs" may do likewise. Their measures, like those of the prosecutors, are subject to judicial confirmation within 48 hours; CCP, Sec. 140. During the trial, the prosecutor may put direct questions to the defendant, while the defendant's lawyer may question only through the presiding officer of the court; CCP, Sec. 201(2-3). The prosecutor sets conditions on lawyers' visits with defendants during pretrial investigations; CCP, Sec. 80,3.

[41] Ch. V, Sec. 2.

[42] See Richert, *op.cit.*, pp. 126-30.

bers too closely intertwine with those of the executive to allow them to act as their brethren's keepers, those bodies cannot fulfill the job of watchdog and critic of the administration. Thus, in order to avoid entrusting complete control to hierarchical superiors, departmental duties must be parceled out to make one department supervise and criticize the activity of another. The premise is that, within one department branch, the higher echelons are too much involved in the quality and detail of that department's performance to be honestly and impartially critical. Consequently, criticism should be the function of an outside agency. This sums up at least part of the reasoning which made the DDR follow the Russian model in assigning to the prosecutor's office the task of watching over the legality of administrative performance across the entire range of governmental services.[43]

The flaw in this kind of reasoning is obvious. No matter how painstakingly the prosecutor's men may wade through collections of laws and ordinances, make their inspection trips, and investigate individual citizens' complaints, they will always be on the outside. Unfamiliar with the day-to-day techniques and shortcuts of the agencies under review, the best they can do is detect manifest violations of the law. The prosecutor's office may then enter a protest and, if it carries enough weight at the moment, compel change. But the change will not eradicate the evil rooted in a chain of command over which the prosecutor's office has no jurisdiction. This difficulty could be overcome only if the

[43] In 1957 the purely bureaucratic character of the prosecutor's functions as general watchdog of legality was established by the then-Deputy Attorney General B. Haid, "Einige Aktuelle Probleme der Staatsanswaltschaftlichen Arbeit," *N.J.*, Vol. 11 (1957), p. 796. His job was defined as one of following up complaint signals, not undertaking investigations on his own. But meanwhile, this ranking official had been found "to have buckled under the attacks of the imperialists and (in conjunction with the Wollweber group) to have taken a revisionist position." *Neues Deutschland*, June 13, 1958, p. 4. See also G. Bohm, "Verbesserung der Arbeit der obersten Staatsanwaltschaft," *N.J.*, Vol. 12 (1958), pp. 629, 630.

By summer 1958, therefore, we find the members of district attorneys' offices developing the "new style of work" prescribed by the SED Fifth Party Congress. It may even go so far as to include putting in a two-week stint with agricultural cooperatives (present day "points of concentration," see n. 81 below), in order to be always at hand when advice and support are needed. But in spite of this feverish activism it seems doubtful whether control includes systematic, around-the-clock and self-initiated inspection of legality. Even the introductory text accompanying the attorney general's new directives of July 23, 1958, starts with the admission that the prosecutor has a hard enough time taking care of his in-box. Attorney General Melsheimer, therefore, sticks to the ritual of recommending close cooperation with other power holders and of prescribing the special initiatives needed for taking care of present "points of concentration." E. Melsheimer, "Die Aufgaben der Staatsanwaltschaft nach dem V. Parteitag," *N.J.*, Vol. 12 (1958), p. 511.

prosecutor's legality control were enlarged by its merging with control by professionally trained, specialized officers. General intensification of programs would bring in its wake a renewed emphasis on developing the potentialities of the prosecutor's office beyond its present watchdog-of-legality function.[44] But in losing its "sporadic and aimless" character, the newfangled "complex-control" superimposes a new and poorly defined link on the existing chain of industrial and administrative command. It suffers from overextending itself to the point of either becoming ineffectual or losing its identity in tasks which have not been pre-ordained.[45]

In the mutual supervision schemes to maintain intrabureaucratic equilibrium, local and district courts are on both the giving and receiving ends. The institution of judicial criticism enables them, if pertinent facts should come to their attention, to expose administrative activity inconsonant with the law. So far they have not made extensive use of this privilege—out of laziness, some critics assert.[46] The courts themselves are obligated to report regularly to the local and district municipal bodies' committees on administrative and police affairs. In addition, since 1957 an obligatory annual report has been submitted to the local deliberative assemblies, whose critical objections must be answered within four weeks.[47]

Such intrabureaucratic criticism is no substitute for public reaction, but under certain circumstances it may provoke, channel, or, more often, simulate genuine public response. There is no way to predict

[44] The need to overcome the "discrepancy" between formal legality control and control activity directed toward having an impact on the whole of public affairs is propagated in J. Streit, "Zur Vorbereitung einer Zentralkonferenz der Justizfunktionaere," *N.J.*, Vol. 14 (1960), pp. 73, 74.

This activist viewpoint, however, is not in accord with the Soviet theory, which emphasizes the restriction to legality control and the absence of any right to more far-reaching administrative interference. This fact has recently been brought home to German audiences by D. A. Kerimow and L. A. Nikolajewa, "Die Allgemeine Aufsicht der Staatsanwaltschaft ueber die Gesetzlichkeit in der sowjetischen staatlichen Verwaltung," *N.J.*, Vol. 14 (1960), pp. 413, 414. For a recent analysis of the USSR practices of the procuracy, see Glenn G. Morgan, "The Proposal of the Soviet Procurator," *The International and Comparative Law Quarterly*, Vol. 9 (1960), pp. 191-207.

[45] A. Grevenrath, W. Schultz, and W. Seifart, "Neue Aufgaben der Gesetzlichkeitsaufsicht," *N.J.*, Vol. 14 (1960), p. 149.

[46] J. Streit, "Einige Hinweise zur Auswertung der 3. Parteikonferenz der SED," *N.J.*, Vol. 10 (1956), pp. 257, 258; W. Berg, "Zur Anwendung der Gerichtskritik," *N.J.*, Vol. 10 (1956), p. 307.

[47] See the Statute on the Local Organs of the State Power of January 18, 1957, GBL. DDR, 1, 72. See also par. 4 of the Law on Judicial Elections (cited above, n. 14) and par. 13 of the Amendment to the Statute on the Administration of Justice (quoted above, n. 4).

whether local power positions will suffer from being pitted against each other or whether they will merge into consolidated power blocs, all local machines uniting to form a single mutual-aid society. Preservation of the intrabureaucratic balance must never be taken for granted, even though hierarchic dependencies, performance reports, and deadlines are designed to ensure it in a mechanical way.

5. The Judge and the Community

Intrabureaucratic controls work haphazardly, at best. To supplement them, the people at large must be drawn into a role which the official institutions perform unsatisfactorily: that of the friendly critic who voluntarily and actively participates in the development of the country's institutions. But attainment of this goal depends on whether the judge succeeds in winning the trust of the population. Developing proficiency in performing just such a feat has been one of the regime's permanent and urgent concerns.[48]

How is the judge to prove worthy of trust? As he no longer freely arbitrates when the individual clashes with the government, what does his superior knowledge of established norms or his keen insight into the hardships and conflicts of daily living matter to the public? In fact, the judge can win acclaim only if he has a chance to apply a good law or help enforce a government program that makes sense to people. Apparently, Soviet jurists and their colleagues within the Soviet orbit recognize this problem; when the party, in the wake of the Twentieth Congress of the Communist Party of the Soviet Union, denounced them for inhuman, bureaucratic, and formalistic handling of the law, they retaliated in kind and publicly urged that the people be given good statutes, carefully drafted and easy to understand.

But then, what laws are "good" in the judgment of the people? Many norms the judges must observe are purely technical regulations or are unrelated to the actual distribution of power; they do not represent issues of contention to the average citizen. In other spheres, such as violence against persons, the system that can most unobtrusively ensure peace and quiet in interpersonal relations and prevent turbulent flare-ups will meet with the widest approval.

[48] Par. 5 of the Law on Judicial Elections formulates: "In the activity of the judge of the workers and peasants, state judicial activity and political work among the toilers form a unity. The judges are under an obligation to educate the population toward keeping the laws and toward actively cooperating in putting them into practice by regular instruction on the Socialist state and its law, especially by commenting on its statutes and enlightening them on specific proceedings appropriate for that purpose."

In any event, the government is always eager to use the judge's contacts with the citizenry to gain greater resonance. The men of the judiciary are saddled with heavy chores foreign to the judicial functions as conceived by the Western mind. Judges are called upon to take part in variegated election campaigns; sometimes this adds, ambiguously, to their political prestige. As part of the regular routine, they attend and address plant meetings, conventions of farm cooperatives, and other officially sponsored gatherings.[49] There they may either orate vaingloriously on general subjects or, talking about their workaday business, try to obtain a sympathetic hearing for the courts' problems and difficulties.

Many a campaign to bring the judiciary and the population closer together has been tested. For example, two have been launched, after careful preparation and a great deal of publicity, to mobilize public interest and cooperation in the election of lay judges.[50] Considerable effort has been exerted to make the individual citizen pay attention to and assume responsibility for the work of the courts. Special courses are set up to train lay assessors; those elected are organized in "collectives" and required to report to the plants and offices from which they were elected. In some places lay assessors attend, over and above their trial duties, court sessions focused on criticism of past judicial performance.

Shunned by the average citizen, the lay assessor's part-time office at first attracted the wrong people. Many elected assessors had to be eliminated as unfit. By stressing the educational aspects of judicial work, the government expects to obtain more willing participation on a wider range. The expectation may not be altogether baseless, since people in the DDR can hardly escape "honorific" public duties of one kind or another, and service as a lay judge may be tempting as a politically uncolored and uncompromising chore.

The duty of protecting adherents and functionaries of the regime against outbreaks of popular hostility keeps the judge from entering

[49] In quantitative terms, the turnout looks impressive. In 1957 courts conducted 11,280 popular meetings on administration of justice problems. These meetings were attended by 530,000 visitors. But the prosecutors did even better. Their 15,130 meetings drew 830,000 visitors. To these figures, 11,000 "judicial accounts" before popular meetings and 14,000 meetings preparing the election of lay assessors must be added. These statistics are given by Benjamin, "Die dialektische Einheit von Gesetzlichkeit und Parteilichkeit durchsetzen!" *N.J.*, Vol. 12 (1958), p. 365.

[50] Trial by jury was virtually abolished in Germany as early as 1923. Instead, lay assessors, selected from panels drawn by municipal bodies, were made voting tribunal members. After the collapse of NS rule, this Weimar setup was fully restored in East and West. The main innovation subsequently introduced in the DDR was election of lay assessors at places of employment, such as industrial plants, offices, and collective farms.

very far into the people's confidence. To an average citizen, the declared enemy of the regime, the spy, or the deviator within high party ranks remains a figure from another world. But the local hero of labor, the rural party potentate, or the meticulous police officer are familiar to everybody. During a drunken brawl many a pent-up hatred may take the form of an insult or, if inebriety progresses, an assault against these worthies. With an assist from local witnesses, the county court judge, given a chance, might try to reduce such rather frequent occurrences to their lowest legal denominator.[51] But the party functionary, the higher court judges, and the instructor from the Ministry of Justice will be on the watch to insure that these insults and affrays are not downgraded as harmless disturbances of the public order, and are correctly treated and punished as major threats against the security of the country.[52] The judge's friendly contact with the community must never advance to the point where he loses his complete identification with the powers-that-be.

The same need to protect loyal adherents of the regime lies at the bottom of the newfangled concept, "socially justified criticism." What is at stake under this rubric is not so much the judge's popularity with the community at large as the law court's duty to protect third-party interests. "Socially justified criticism" accords judicial protection to the criticism of individuals by other individuals, a process popularly called "denunciation" and rooted in the spontaneity of petty interest, envy, rivalry, and personal animosity. Carry a tale about X to the personnel director of the plant or make a derogatory comment about Y in every neighbor's hearing in the village square, and the DDR High Court will commend you for "socially justified criticism," so long as X's or Y's actions or their possible consequences may be construed as harmful to society. This atmosphere permits a woman party member in good standing who holds a grudge against a female neighbor to go to the personnel office of the plant where she works and mention male visitors entering or leaving the neighbor's apartment (even when the neighbor was not

[51] Complaints against lower judges' failure to sense the correct political implication of such insults and brawls are frequent in the official legal literature. For an example, see Spranger and Wunsch, *op.cit.*, p. 270; Streit, "Fuer einen neuen Arbeitsstil in der Justiz," *N.J.*, Vol. 12 (1958), p. 368; and Streit, "Aus den Erfahrungen einer Brigade im Bezirk Potsdam," *N.J.*, Vol. 12 (1958), p. 620.

[52] See, for example, the High Court judgment of February 11, 1958, confirming a district court judgment sentencing the drunken attacker of a "hero of labor" to 18 months penal servitude by applying Section 19(3) of the Penal Code Amendment Act of December 11, 1957, GBL. DDR, I, 645; for an aggravated case of state-endangering agitation, see *N.J.*, Vol. 12 (1958), p. 323. For a parallel case involving party-school students, see High Court judgment of April 25, 1958, in *N.J.*, Vol. 12 (1958), p. 391.

at home). Her "criticism" will be "socially justified," provided she does not forget at the start to mention a briefcase of papers that the suspect neighbor brings home every night.[53]

By the courtesy of the High Court, a new privilege has been born, one that does away with the search for truth or falsehood.[54] "Socially justified" allegations require no evidence. The "critic" need not bother to adduce proof of legitimate interest, despite the fact that a defendant in a libel suit may have to supply such proof even though the formally libelous statements are admittedly truthful. No "socially justified" informer has to hide his face in shame; he has done his duty as a patriot and the government will insist that the community honor him for undaunted civic devotion.[55]

To be sure, any government may use, encourage, and protect informers. But to hold them in so high esteem as to deny the aggrieved individual the right to legal relief from their abuses is an unusual procedure. Surely this brazen "social justification" may swell the ranks of informers. But it may also overrate the malleability of public sentiment. The public's verdict may continue to depend upon a popular and realistic evaluation of the "critic's" motives or of the cause he claims to serve.

Public response and civic activity are elusive and hard to come by under the DDR's unrelenting control. Even so, a shaky pedestal for the volunteer informer is a skimpy reward for the government's continuous effort to produce such popular participation in the new rule. This failure may be a measure of the fissure between party theory and public

[53] Lower court proceedings in Streit, "Über die Abrenzung von Kritik und Beleidigung," *N.J.*, Vol. 10 (1956), p. 176; High Court decision of March 2, 1956, *ibid.*, p. 217. For further comment, see *ibid.*, p. 230.

[54] Refusing to test the veracity of a defendant's allegation to the effect that the plaintiff had placed milk to be delivered to a dairy center in his toilet cabinet for overnight storage, the court said that it was the defendant's duty to criticize unhygienic conditions, for improved hygiene was an element of social progress. See High Court decision of September 1, 1955, *N.J.*, Vol. 9 (1955), p. 634. Actual presence of unhygienic conditions is obviously immaterial; the mere possibility of the occurrence is a threat to social progress and must be denounced. Similar Polish developments are described in Jerzy Sawicki, *Schutz der Ehre und Freiheit der Kritik* (transl. from Polish), East Berlin, 1960. While in Poland, according to the report, the distinction between socially justified criticism and private defamation is upheld, acceptance of the defamer's belief in the justifiability of his objectively untrue assertions leaves the floodgates still wide open for the spreading of personal malice; *ibid.*, pp. 112-20.

[55] The underlying policy and principle has been expressly reaffirmed by a plenary High Court decision of February 21, 1958, rendered in pursuance of an extraordinary appeal of the attorney general, "Entscheidungen des Obersten Gerichts," Vol. 4 (1960), p. 125. For a comment in a similar direction, see "Öffentlicher Vorwurf einer Anzeigeerstattung als Beleidigung," *N.J.*, Vol. 12 (1958), p. 315.

acceptance. Yet "socially justified" and extolled as a boon to society, the informer may at least add a more lively beat and genuine unpredictability to the prearranged motions of the intrabureaucratic pendulum.

6. "Socialist Legality": Doctrinal Gyrations[56]

Since de-Stalinization was officially inaugurated at the Twentieth Congress of the Communist Party of the Soviet Union, strict observance of "socialist legality" has been the theme of many party and government pronouncements in the DDR no less than in other countries of the Soviet bloc, and the protection of individual rights has been steadfastly emphasized.[57] This purportedly libertarian philosophy was part of the general reaction to the denounced "excesses" marking the close of the Stalinist era. Yet "socialist legality"[58] or "Soviet legality" (called "revolutionary" in earlier years) is not a recent innovation, nor is its essential meaning capsulated in guarantees of personal security. The concept goes far beyond anti-Stalin polemics.

In the early days of Soviet power, "revolutionary legality" was governed by the practical requirements of a factual situation. Communist

[56] The original Russian texts, accessible to the author only in translation, were selected by Dr. A. R. L. Gurland.

[57] Both points were stressed in the Central Committee's report to the Congress. Khrushchev, *Otchetnyi doklad TsK KPSS XX s'yezdu partii* (1956), p. 109. The resolution subsequently adopted by the Congress insisted on the "strengthening of Soviet legality" and urged that the rights of citizens guaranteed by the Soviet constitution be "rigorously respected."

[58] For a recent study of the legal system of Soviet Russia itself, see Harold J. Berman, "Soviet Law Reform—Dateline Moscow 1957," *Yale Law Journal*, Vol. 66 (1957), p. 1191. This article, especially valuable for its searching exploitation of colloquial statements by Soviet legal authorities, rests on the implied thesis that Soviet juridical performance may somehow be traced to a dichotomy between legality and force, and that their respective provinces are dependent on the pressures and circumstances of the moment. In the light of this thesis, the present period—with inevitable deviations and countercurrents—could be considered as one of expanding legality, a development made possible by the fact that "a totalitarian system of government which operates by despotic methods in politics can create a legal order which operated with considerable stability and independence in matters considered nonpolitical." *Ibid.*, p. 1212, n. 75.

But whether Professor Berman's dichotomy, applicable as it might be to other systems, is a meaningful point of departure for analyzing the Communist concept of legality and the functioning of its judicial machinery is not so clear. Legality (*zakonnost'*) in Communist parlance has a complementary or possibly a counterconcept: *partiinost'*. This untranslatable term denotes both the party-subservient quality of ideas and institutions and the party allegiance of men.

The legality-force or political-nonpolitical dichotomy relates to the presupposition underlying the interplay between legality and *partiinost'*. Understanding this relation is fundamental to understanding the Communist "rule of law."

teaching clearly stated that the working class had taken hold of governmental power and would use it to further its own interests. Subservience of the government machine to proletarian class interest was deliberately flaunted; to quite an extent were legal "formalities" considered unnecessary. The standard-bearers of the victorious revolution took pride in divesting power relationships of legal adornments. "Bourgeois legality" was exposed as a fraudulent maneuver to prevent the oppressed from recognizing the true balance of power. Law, then, was just another ideological mask of domination, and not necessarily the most important one.

It was not for abstract philosophical reasons alone that Lenin felt irked by the emphatic concern for the principles of justice and personal freedom which his short-term non-Communist People's Commissar of Justice displayed. The maker of the revolution avowedly had no patience with what to him was a matter of form without intrinsic value, even though considerations of expediency made occasional observance of the principle of legality advisable.[59] When he in turn insisted on strict adherence to revolutionary legality, he meant only that all action emanating from organs of the revolutionary government must follow the pattern outlined by the central authority and must keep within the rigid confines of its directives. In essence, the concept of legality was directed against decentralization of power, uncoordinated action, and spontaneous initiative beyond that specifically authorized by the party's governing body, or by agencies to which that organ had delegated power.[60]

[59] This short-term colleague of Lenin has narrated the following episode:
"We were discussing a harsh police measure with far-reaching terroristic potentialities. Lenin resented my opposition to it in the name of revolutionary justice. So I called out in exasperation, 'Then why do we bother with a Commissariat of Justice? Let's call it frankly the *Commissariat for Social Extermination* and be done with it!' Lenin's face suddenly brightened and he replied, 'Well put . . . that's exactly what it should be . . . but we can't say that.'" J. N. Steinberg, *The Workshop of the Revolution*, New York, 1953, p. 145.

[60] By this very token, "revolutionary legality" was to bar abuse of power by individual government or party officials. In his last active period Lenin repeatedly insisted on combatting abuse of power, a task he thought it best to entrust to the prosecutors' offices with the rigid proviso that all cases of violation be referred to the courts. See Lenin, "O 'dvoinom' podchi nenii i zakonnisti," *Sochineniya*, 4th ed.; Moscow, 1922, Vol. 33, pp. 326-30. Later, in Stalin's interpretation, things were to be simplified to the extreme. In Stalin's view, which until his death was the law of the land, the history of revolutionary legality was reduced to two major phases. In the NEP period, when private enterprise was deemed indispensable, legality was to prevent excessive levies and confiscation of private property, but after the completion of the "foundations of socialism," its function had become protection of public property. This Stalinist gospel was severely taken to task in the very first official comment released

In this view, legality is nothing but a technique of domination. The party alone decides whether law or another instrument of social control should be given precedence. Law serves the ruling class as a tool for modifying or shaping the development of society, and revolutionary legality stands for planned, coordinated, and disciplined exercise of class rule.[61]

Not substantially molded by the institutional set-up in which it appears, legality takes its contours from the class that imposes them. Law is oppressive, fraudulent, and reactionary when in the hands of a class doomed to defeat; it is an instrument of liberation and progress when serving a class destined to chart society's future course. Judged by its result rather than the modes of action it embodies, legality is like the twin but respectable brother of terror, to whom a more specific task is assigned: ensuring the regularity and predictability of behavior.[62]

According to the Leninist interpretation of the historical process, the principle of revolutionary legality takes on added validity as a guide to action from the historical function which it must perform. Seizure of the government machine by the proletarian vanguard is not just the fortuitous outcome of transitory factual elements. It is an historically necessary event which marks a specific stage in the evolution of human society. The revolutionary working class, the first class to gain scientific insight into the objective laws of social development, is given the unique chance of adapting its action to historical necessity. From the laws of history, the workers derive binding norms of conduct en-

---

after the Twentieth Congress. It was authoritatively stated that Stalin's version was neither "exact" nor "comprehensive." Soviet legality was defined as (1) "a precondition of and means to organize and develop societal relations"; (2) "the foundation of governmental discipline"; in addition, (3) "it safeguards the rights and legitimate interests of the Soviet citizens." M. S. Strogovich (corresponding member, USSR Academy of Sciences), "Teoreticheskiye voprosy sovetskoi zakonnosti," *Sovetskoye Gosudarstvo I Pravo*, No. 4, p. 15 (passed for publication on June 22, 1956).

[61] Rudolph Schlesinger, *Soviet Legal Theory*, New York, 1945, p. 43. For an unusually frank, unembellished comment from a DDR source, see H. Klenner, *Formen und Bedeutung der Gesetzlichkeit als einer Methode in der Fuehrung des Klassenkampfes*, East Berlin, 1953.

[62] As Lenin put it in "The Immediate Tasks of the Soviet Government," *Selected Works*, Moscow, 1947, Vol. 2, p. 332: "In proportion as the fundamental task of the government becomes not military suppression, but administration, the typical manifestation of suppression and coercion will be not shooting on the spot, but trial by court." See also Lenin's proposals for formulation of offenses against the state, contained in his letter of May 17, 1922, to the Peoples Commissary of Justice, D. J. Kurski, *Sochineniya*, Vol. 33, p. 321: "The court is not to abolish terror—to promise such course would be self-deception and fraud—but it should make it understandable and should elevate it to a legal rule, as a matter of principle, clearcut, without hypocrisy and without embellishments."

dowed with objective validity. Revolutionary legality sums up the set of such norms applicable after the conquest of power and enables the victorious working class to fulfill its historical mission. For those in charge of making the new system work, legality is more than any single one of many conflicting directives, more than a warning to those who may be exposed to the new government's coercive pressure. A manifestation of the objective historical process, socialist law sets an inescapable behavior pattern for a clearly defined historical period and prescribes norms of conduct hallowed by recognizable and recognized historical necessities.

Though Lenin did not elaborate the historical role of revolutionary legality, it is easily deduced from his doctrine of the proletarian revolution. An eminently pragmatic thinker, however, Lenin always took care not to detract from the sovereign role of the Communist Party, which to him was the only revolutionary instrument conceivable under the laws of history. The supremacy of the party as the sole fountain of "objectively correct" thought and action was not to be questioned. Whatever the function of socialist law emanating from the revolutionary government, no legal norm was ever to supersede party decisions.

True, requirements of central coordination and disciplined procedure necessitated upholding the validity of unacceptable legal norms not yet formally abrogated or revised. The legislative prerogative of governmental institutions was to be retained, at least in theory. But even in Lenin's lifetime, rigorous procedural simplifications of law-making to suit party needs made short shrift of the sanctity of law and reduced to naught any hesitant doctrinal attempts to place the law, once promulgated with the party's approval, above shifting party decisions.

Later, during the three decades of Stalin's increasingly one-man rule, the art of interpretative distortion and retroactive revision of expectedly authoritative pronouncements was developed to a high point. Based on Lenin's teachings about the role of the party in the revolutionary process, an elaborate body of doctrine was construed to establish the all-pervasive quality of the principle of *partiinost'*.[63] This principle comprehended the unassailable primacy of party decisions, the inalienable authority of the party as the supreme arbiter in conflicts of ideas, and the all-embracing nature of the adherent's commitment to the party.

Party supremacy permitted the Soviet government to turn the balance of social power upside down and, more than once, to revamp its basic economic structures. When the uprooting of millions of people gener-

[63] See n. 57 above.

ated social malaise—always a threat to production—and when time and again the Soviet government found itself on the lookout for stabilizing factors, then the authority of the law was reinforced and greater importance attached to the historical mission of, and the element of objective necessity in, socialist legality. Doctrinal disquisitions on the law's lasting normative validity mushroomed.

Just such a climate prevailed in Russia after the 1956 Twentieth Congress. "Mistakes" committed in the Stalin era were denounced and the sovereignty of law was emphatically espoused. Restoration of legality became a mandatory topic in the official journal of legal doctrine.[64] In the issue sent to press on May 4, 1956, the turn was signaled by Soviet Prosecutor General Rudenko in person. "In the light of the decision of the Twentieth Congress," legality was to become the focal point of all endeavor in the legal sphere.[65] More specifically, the chief prosecuting official indicated that still greater emphasis would be placed on the work of the prosecutors' offices, principal custodians of legality.[66] New legislation in the area of substantive criminal law would ease the prosecutors' job. In the future, laws should be made only by legislative bodies assigned this function by the Soviet constitution. While there was no reason to downgrade decisions of the USSR Supreme Court, it was essential to stress that the court was without power to enact new legal norms or directives as equivalent of statutes.[67]

Six weeks later, the (delayed) next issue of the journal carried a declaration of theoretical principles in which lack of legal security in everyday life was directly linked with Stalinism: "An important cause of violations of legality in the past was the cult of personality. Personality cult is incompatible with the consistently maintained legality, for it creates a climate which obstructs vigorous observance of the law and fosters the tendency of individual law-enforcers to place themselves above the law instead of obeying it without reservations as legality demands."[68]

[64] *Sovetskoye Gosudarstvo I Pravo*, published by the A. Ya. Viskinskii Law Institute of the USSR Academy of Sciences.

[65] R. A. Rudenko, "Zadachi dal 'neishego ukrepleniya sotsialisticheskoi zakonnosti v svete reshenii XX s'yezda KPSS," *Sovetskoye Gosudarstvo I Pravo*, 1956, No. 3, p. 15. Rudenko is a candidate member of the Central Committee of the CPSU and a member of the USSR Supreme Soviet.

[66] *Ibid.*, 17.

[67] *Ibid.*, 20. How this discussion affects the characterization of the *directives* issued by the USSR Supreme Court or by the High Court of the DDR cannot be followed here. See my discussion in "Legality in East Germany," *Yale Law Journal*, Vol. 68 (1959), pp. 705, 710, 711, and "Die Rechtspflege und der Begriff der Gesetzlichkeit in der DDR," *Archiv für Öffentliches Recht*, Vol. 5 (1960), esp. n. 33.

[68] Strogovich, *op.cit.*, No. 4, p. 16.

True devotion to legality was missing in Soviet life. Many even invoked Lenin's authority to justify making observance of the law dependent on considerations of usefulness and expediency. But such considerations "can only imply the useful application to a given case, in conformity with the law of a provision authorized by law; [they] cannot imply circumvention or violation of the law."[69]

Following the lead of the prosecutor general,[70] the journal blamed Soviet legal theory for having neglected problems of legality. In particular, it attacked the allegedly "dialectical" denial of the validity of legal norms by the top legal authority of the bygone Stalinist era, who had asserted that the "dialectical approach to law interpretation precludes stereotype interpretation and stereotype application of legal norms."[71] Not "flexibility" but "unbending rigidity" must be displayed in the enforcement of statutes. Participation in a 1954-1955 discussion was castigated because the discussion had defended "flexible" attitudes: "These [are] absolutely incompatible with actual implementation of legality [and] are sometimes offered on the pretext that it was necessary to combat formalism in the application of the law, or that the law had to be treated dialectically. Whenever it accepts this, the science of law, instead of fighting for the strengthening of legality, embarks on the dangerous venture of laying the theoretical foundations for permissible departure from the law."[72]

Many a reiteration followed. By the end of 1956 an editorial restatement of immediate objectives once more spelled out the implication of the Twentieth Congress's stand on legality. The editors urged the active defense of the rights of Soviet citizens, the correction of "the most flagrant violation of Soviet legality" that had grown out of the "cult of personality," improved legislation, the codification of existing law, better training of judicial personnel, and clear demarcation of overlapping jurisdiction.[73] Then the tide changed and the topic was abruptly dropped from the columns of the official law journal.

A different mood prevailed when the discussion flared up anew in March 1957. Violation of legality was no longer the subject of grave misgivings. What now disturbed the rulers' peace of mind was the apprehension that all legal norms might be held sacred by the uninitiated. Clarification was supplied in a signed editorial by the associate chief

[69] *Ibid.*, 17.   [70] Rudenko, *op.cit.*, 18.

[71] Denisov, *Teoriya Gosudarstva I Prava*, Moscow, 1948, p. 480.

[72] Strogovich, *op.cit.*, 20.

[73] "Dal'neisheye ukrepleniye sotsialisticheskoi zakonnosti" (editorial), *Sovetskoye Gosudarstvo I Pravo*, October 1956, No. 10, p. 3 (printing authorized December 11, 1956).

editor. "On the whole the Communist Party and the Soviet state express correctly (in legislative acts) the people's conscious thinking; but this does not imply that every normative act always automatically, as it were, provides an adequate solution for economic requirements that must be met, nor that every such act expresses exactly what the people think. . . . Legal studies, however, have been prone to lift on the shield any judicial decision, even many an incorrect one, and any legislative act, including such as had to be rescinded later because of their temporary, transient nature or because they had been erroneous; theoretical justifications have been construed to prove that such decisions and acts have been correct and in accordance with the interest and will of the people." Because this objectionable practice defied Lenin's teaching, its discontinuation was urged.[74]

Harping on the mistakes and excesses of the Stalinist era was abandoned, and the rights of the individual were no longer in the foreground. The party's stand on law and legal order was shifting once more. Another blackout followed. Then, as so often happens in the totalitarian realm, the atmospheric change came into plain view, in a peripheral piece of doctrinal polemics. Made up as a special feature, a critical broadside was hurled by a writer of little renown[75] at the very same scholar who the year before had been commissioned to expound the anti-Stalin theory of legality. This scholar's 1956 book on procedural law and the evaluation of evidence in criminal trials[76] was severely criticized for having undialectically drawn a line between the "material truth" of factual evidence and the relative validity of judicial evaluation. The dialectical approach, so recently and vigorously condemned, was in vogue again.

The last touch was applied, not very gently, in an editorial denouncing the "antiparty activity" of Kaganovich, Malenkov, and Molotov. "Strengthening of socialist legality" was no longer the focal theme. The headline slogan, once again fed into courtroom loudspeakers, clamored for "the strengthening of the Socialist Soviet State under the leadership of the Communist Party."[77] The party, hitherto unmentioned in dis-

[74] S. N. Bratus, "Uchit'sya u V. I. Lenina resheniyu teoreticheskikh i prakticheskikh voprosov prava" (editorial), *ibid.*, April 1957, No. 4, pp. 3, 6.

[75] A. L. Rivlin, "Zakonnost' i istinnost' sudebnogo prigovora," *ibid.*, July 1957, No. 7, p. 114.

[76] Strogovich, *Material'naia Istina I Sudebnoye Dokazatel'stvo V*, Sovetskom Ugolovnom Protsesse, 1956.

[77] "Pod rukovodstvom Kommunisticheskoi partii za dal 'neisheye ukrepleniye Sovetskogo sotsialisticheskogo gosudarstva (editorial), *Sovetskoye Gosudarstvo I Pravo*, August 1957, p. 3.

cussions of the doctrines inaugurated at the Twentieth Congress, re-emerged overnight as the sole architect and custodian of socialist legality.[78] On behalf of Soviet juridical science, the editors of the law journal took a solemn oath to obey the decisions of the Twentieth Congress and carry on unwaveringly the fight against the "luckily unmasked antiparty group." This, however, was not enough; the science of law "still owes the party a tremendous debt." Scholarly juridical literature has failed to expound elaborately the "directing of the Communist Party in the construction and functioning of the state, and . . . as the living foundation of Soviet legal and governmental institutions and processes." The jurists, continued the journal, must do their utmost to redeem this onerous debt.[79]

Thus the widely publicized stress on the role of legality had evaporated. Official recognition went once again to the party's role as the "living foundation" of law and government. Although the contents of the new rules might well continue to mark important departures from Stalinist practices—witness the new criminal code—the rank of the party as initiator, motor, and regulator of social processes and the legal order was emphatically reconfirmed.[80]

In the DDR these gyrations of Soviet doctrinal thought were widely but not precisely followed. What the consumer at the end of the line received was not necessarily a true copy of the original. Even in the DDR, a faithful adapter, stereotypes already discarded and replaced in Moscow were used simultaneously with brand new ones.

Percolating into DDR jurisprudence with little delay, the Soviet legality course with its apologia of the supremacy of law became the official doctrine by spring 1956. But only briefly, for the Soviet Union was to shelve it within less than a year. Still, some legality enthusiasts found enough time to virtually repudiate the principle of *partiinost'* (or its German party-slang equivalent, *Parteilichkeit*).

The most extreme of these views[81] implied that, inasmuch as so-

---

[78] *Ibid.*, pp. 8-11.   [79] *Ibid.*, p. 10.

[80] The official elaboration of the results of the Twenty-first Party Congress sets up a confusing number of tasks for jurisprudence. They include: preparation of constitutional changes needed for the building of Communism; further strengthening of the party; battle against revisionism, and, interestingly enough, rejection of attempts to take over uncritically from the bourgeois system categories and forms for the Soviet law, even though they do not correspond to the social contents of the Soviet law of the present period. *Sovetskoye Gosudarstvo I Pravo*, February 1959, No. 2, pp. 3-11.

In sum, one gains the impression of a huge construction project for which the Soviet jurisprudence is asked urgently to submit some safety and traffic rules.

[81] See W. Artzt (Director, DDR Institute of Civil Law), "Zu einigen Fragen der

cialist legality expressed objective requirements of the historical process, only legal ways and means were appropriate for attaining society's goals. Rules of action should be drawn from normative acts passed by the government's legislative bodies rather than from *ad hoc* decisions of party bodies. Correspondingly, judicial interpretation would not be identical with ensuring that law, or the rationale of its application, met party specifications in the individual case before the court. Under this theory, *partiinost'* could no longer override the law. It would have to be regarded as inherent in the legal norm, a quality imparted to the normative act in the lawmaking process by virtue of the fact that the legislators represented the party in translating the objective laws of social development into rules applicable to specific situations.

Clearly, this reasoning stripped the party of the power informally to cast overboard legal norms no longer to its liking. If a legal norm proved a dead weight because the legislators had misread history's "objective" requirements or had miscalculated the malleability of social reality, it was up to the legislative bodies to remove the discrepancy by changing the law.[82] Intended to curtail the arbitrariness of party interference, this interpretation disregarded possible arbitrariness on the part of the lawmaker. It is indeed conceivable that the lawmaker, concerned with his own prestige and position, would, though fully aware of the discrepancy between norm and reality, nevertheless fail to "put socialist law in step with life," intransigently use the unrealistic norm as a whip, and insist on norm-prescribed goals beyond the social energies already harnessed. Who, then, would correct the lawmaker?

For obvious reasons, enthusiasm for legality in this extreme form conflicted with the party's traditional philosophy, in that "historical necessity" here appeared "objectively" expressed by legal norms, not by party action. Essentially, however, the new doctrine, substituting the legislative for the party machine, merely exchanged one institutional agent of "historical necessity" for another. The agent, whatever

---

sozialistischen Gesetzlichkeit in der Deutschen Demokratischen Republik," *N.J.*, Vol. 10 (1956), p. 581. Here the principle of legality finds consistent affirmation from what may be termed an "objectivist" or "positivist" point of view. Artzt has meanwhile duly recanted his errors. He has admitted that his teachings of "a certain independence of the law" and its separation from the politics of the party are in contradiction with the Marxist-Leninist theories of state and law. *Staats und Rechtswissenschaftliche Konferenz in Babelsberg am 2. und 3. Mai 1958*, Berlin, 1958, p. 154.

[82] This removal job, however, has a merely formal character if one accepts D. A. Kerimov's view (*Fragen der Gesetzgebungstechnik*, Berlin, 1958, p. 81, trans. from *Zakonodatel naya deyatel most Sovetskogo gosudarstva*, Moscow, 1955) that norms which did not order social relations according to the demands of actual life "in reality are no more valid."

its designation, was still ascribed a mystical mission in the pursuit of an abstract society's presumed goals, which in turn were assigned an infinitely higher rank than the interests of individuals who make up the actual and immediate society.

Still, when legality, no longer seen as a mere shorthand code for class rule, stands for concrete programs of social and economic action, the individual is bound to slip in through the back door. When the law serves as the chosen instrument for realizing wide-range governmental plans, the activity of the individual must be planned as well; to fulfill plan objectives, the individual must have some latitude of action, at least within a sphere circumscribed by the plan. If he remains passive, actual achievement will fall short of plan objectives. Accordingly, the individual is theoretically granted certain prerogatives. But insofar as his area of freedom is directed wholly toward plan objectives, these prerogatives shrink in practice.

The struggle for the fulfillment of plan objectives, varying but never relaxing, holds an entrenched priority. The prime concern of the party and government is to overcome all conceivable resistance to the overall program, whether it originates in recalcitrant moods, individual entanglements, inadequate understanding of objectives, or any other retarding factor rooted in the given social situation. The legal order adapted to this central policy requirement does not emphasize protection of the individual against loss of freedom, judicial restraints on administrative action, legal buttressing of private positions, or guarantees for acquired rights.

Technological, organizational, and manpower bottlenecks constantly delay and endanger the attainment of objectives set by party and government decisions. Naturally, those in power are reluctant to multiply such impediments by lending support and privilege to private interests (with the exception, of course, of those interests disguised in terms of official authority and public title). To be sure, individuals may file complaints with hierarchic superiors, and the prosecutor's office will accept requests for the review of allegedly illegal administrative decisions.[83] But beyond these measures, there is no legal remedy to preserve the rights of the individual against the administrative machine. Legal norms to protect such rights will remain a dead letter so long as there are no organized social groups to compel enforcement. In pluralistic societies, norms become effective to the extent that they create subjective rights which individuals or groups find advantageous to invoke

[83] Deutsches Institut für Rechtswissenschaft, Das Verwaltungsrecht der Deutschen Demokratischen Republik, Allgemeiner Teil (1957), p. 197.

and, if necessary, to uphold in organized action. The interplay of individual, group, and governmental interests competitively determines what norms will be enforced. While the choice hinges on the relative strength of the interests affected, the function of interpreting disputed norms devolves on an independent arbiter. Presumably removed from the interests involved, the judge is expected to apply to the dispute standards free from unilateral change by a party.

Free competition of ideas and social forces is anathema in a society that outlaws voluntary organizations and substitutes centralized planning and direction. The individual has little chance actively to invoke the protection of the law, and only governmental authorities can decide which norm is to be operative. The abstract thesis that every norm, once enacted, must be enforced as part of the all-embracing plan of social improvement will not apply in the absence of organized pressure to protect also those rights that interfere with the government's monopoly of action. Only selected areas of norm enforcement are within the individual's reach, and those are mostly in interpersonal relations.

The government, whose attention remains fixed on plan objectives, determines the vigor and intensity with which any chosen legislative program is made to operate in everyday life. By so doing, the central administration avoids relegating a wide area of choice to individual departments or regional agencies, which, as a rule, are less conscientious and tend to neglect a number of central projects, especially those that add to their administrative and propaganda chores.[84]

As the prime emphasis, if not the very content, of the norm enforcement changes, the significance of "legality" becomes less evident. The fluctuations must then be rationalized in terms of legality's shifting content. In actual practice, varying clusters of norms are designated from time to time as "points of concentration" on which law enforcement must be stressed.[85] This is part and parcel of the legal setup as it affects both administrative implementation and judicial interpretation of the law, provinces that largely overlap in the framework of socialist legal-

---

[84] Official opinion contends, for example, that plans for setting up a giant corps of lay judges met widespread apathy at the lower level, that is, among municipal and union officials and local magistrates, and that only unrelenting perseverance by high judicial authorities made it possible to effect the plans. Benjamin, "Zu Fragen der Gesetzlichkeit und der Leitung innerhalb des Justizapparates," *N.J.*, Vol. 9 (1955), p. 387.

[85] 1958 points of concentration were, for example, increased labor productivity, protection of socialist property, and furtherance of the socialist transformation of agriculture. See Melsheimer (n. 43 above), 513. By 1960, judicial, like any other state, activity was clearly concentrating on supporting and implementing agricultural collectivization.

lower level office holder will be well advised to watch out constantly for reactions of the authorized primary interpreter. Administrative objectives may be indicated by indirection, as in the criticism of operational mistakes or the designation of new "points of concentration."

This elastic system, which more often than not is at cross-purposes with strict observance of legality, infuses a calculated element of specificity. It grants those in power the opportunity to single out for condemnation whichever specific approach they may deem inopportune. As instruments of command, the sovereign uses vituperation, criticism, and exhortation as much as he does clearcut orders or formalized laws that set forth generalized rules of conduct. The backfiring of individual decisions may always be blamed on lower authorities whose job it is to institutionalize and individualize policies laid down by a superior agency.

The formal law on the statute books is overgrown with numerous interpretative glosses of varying origin and age that are as authoritative as the law itself. The judge-administrator must follow the latest signals from above. Simultaneously, he is expected to accommodate possible reactions of an undefined grassroots public. He does this not in the traditional way of striking a balance between norm requirements and the divergent interests of affected parties, but as an errand boy ordered to deliver a letter and to bring back a receipt signed by the addressee. The receipt symbolizes the widely advertised "educational function" of the law. While there is no doubt that the government program will be carried out regardless of public volition, the official, wherever he stands in the chain of command, is obliged to transform the citizens' passive obedience or stubborn obtuseness into cheerful cooperation.

The essence of "socialist legality," then, is guaranteeing that orders and signals are unfailingly observed at all subordinate levels. A measure of obedience may be insured by establishing regular and permanent channels for implementation; this may even include procedures that permit the individuals to react freely within limits that suit the government's convenience and tally with its objectives. But it is the objectives which count, not any degree of harmony between what the government wants and what grows out of institutional or legal positions accorded individuals or groups. When policies and official interpretation change, legality attaches to the new task at hand. Under no condition is it called upon to mediate between today's objectives of the sovereign and yesterday's expectations of the subject. At the service of a fixed policy rather than as a purveyor of societal equilibrium, legality represents a marriage between law and efficiency drive. It stands for the avoidance of lost motions: it becomes the government's whip to secure the attainment of top-priority goals.

Under such circumstances, what can be the nature of the law? No doubt, the SED and DDR government are fully aware of the beneficial effect that guaranteed expectations have on all factors which make the individual most cooperative with his neighbors and the authorities. A great number of initiatives formalized in legal enactments might be adduced to show how laboriously the various DDR administrations have toiled to produce a maximum of such satisfactions.[92] If the judge had adequate standing in the community to progress from individualizing these isolated norm complexes to independently deciding upon their respective priorities, he might help to create a more lasting balance between the claims of the individuals and those of the state. At the present stage of the DDR society, however, the problem simply does not present itself in such terms. Either the regime assumes too many new ventures and faces simultaneously, or it intentionally conjures up too many problems to be able to allow anyone outside its political leadership to decide what elements should enter the momentary balance between the requirements of the regime and the allowable satisfactions of the citizenry. When the regime's major goals have been fulfilled and its spiritual and social dominion safely anchored, the eternal guard against individual slackening may be relaxed—and a referee allowed to mark points for both sides. Until that day, however, the judge remains a simple party servant, a "functionary of the apparatus of justice." Like his peers in other departments, he may became tired or too sympathetic with the stragglers in whom he recognizes his own image. Nevertheless, so long as the political front line is moving and the chow line forming at the rear, he falls in step. Thus the variables in the guessing game called interpretation of the law reduce themselves rather drastically to the shifting policies of the Communist regime.

8. Law Under the Swastika in Retrospect

Viewed in the late 1950's, the political philosophy of National Socialist law and the Third Reich's directed administration of justice take on the appearance of an oversimplified and overcrude draft model of the DDR pattern: jurisprudence molded by and subservient to political domination. However, a comparison of the two systems of dispensing justice also reveals characteristic differences. While a detailed discussion

[92] The quest for individual security was stressed in a recent attempt to bring some order into the rather chaotic business of norm creation. See J. Gentz, "Zu einigen Grundsaetzen der Rechtsetzung," *N.J.*, Vol. 12 (1958), pp. 225-30.

of the legal setup under National Socialism may be dispensed with, such similarities and dissimilarities are worth looking into.

Like that of the SED rulers of the DDR, the legal thinking of the National Socialist leadership revolved around the notion of the judges' automatic identification with the group wielding political power. What loomed on the horizon as the ideal solution, according to an astute terror practitioner and self-confessed mass killer, SS Brigade Leader Otto Ohlendorf, was a judiciary whose collective mind would spontaneously work in union with that of the political leadership.[93] In this respect the leaders of National Socialism were in a more favorable position than those who succeeded them in Central Germany. To attain their objective in the legal sphere, the National Socialist rulers did not have to turn the legal system upside down, or provide for wholesale replacement of judicial personnel.

In contrast to DDR Communist planners, the National Socialist leadership never had as their primary goal a basic change in property relationships and social stratification. They had no reason to throw out the major features of the inherited body of law. Elimination of "Romanism," which they said had been superimposed upon basically Germanic patterns, was talked about by ideologists, and even made an object of study in a special institute, but it did not affect everyday practice. Actually, both the National Socialist Party and the purportedly nonpolitical governmental officialdom obstinately upheld the version of the legality of the National Socialist revolution and insisted on the continuity of law. Against this background it was easy for the bulk of the judiciary to accept the new political order and overlook its revolutionary features and innate lawlessness. In turn, the new rulers were in no hurry to breed a new type of judge and prosecutor, namely, functionaries who would consider themselves auxiliaries of the state administration and tackle the law as a technical implement for executing political decisions.

This setup eased the initial task of the National Socialist rulers. They did not have to bother much about the law, the courts, and the judges. In the long run, however, this favorable condition entailed an obvious disadvantage. The regime had to cope with a judiciary which, while not unsympathetic to many an aspect of the new order, was governed by rigid caste concepts and dedicated to a philosophy of self-perpetuation through proper recruitment and training of replacements. Without the conceptual apparatus of "Marxism-Leninism," which readily in-

[93] See the memorandum by Otto Ohlendorf, "Rechtssicherheit und Richterliche Unabhängigkeit" (dated October 11, 1942), with comment by Peter Schneider, in *Vierteljahreshefte zur Zeitgeschichte*, Vol. 4 (1956), pp. 399-422.

vokes the laws of history to sanctify the supremacy of party rule, it was not a simple matter to rationalize the law's subjugation to political dictates; jurists trained in the tradition of discursive logic and deductive argumentation, and clinging to the continuity of the legal system, were generally not overwhelmed by a dogma which taught that the charisma-endowed Führer was the incarnation of the will and, more important, of the racial destiny of the people. By and large they felt that the law was their province and brooked no outside interference.[94]

This old-style judiciary was not easy to handle. Not even Franz Gürt-ner, the man who in 1924 had let Hitler out of jail and until his death in 1941 served National Socialism as Reich minister of justice, was a voiceless puppet. The judiciary's most accommodating members still dreamed of catapulting the profession into a paramount position, where they could better withstand the onslaught of competing centers of authority, which mushroomed under the new rulers. Set apart from the bulk of the officialdom, the judiciary would draw its authority from the Führer's confidence in its top men; the Führer in turn would use the judiciary's own hierarchic channels to help the trial judge arrive at individual decisions in the maze of new problems beyond his horizon.[95]

Judges so thoroughly convinced of their own importance did not bend as easily as they should have. But unpleasant though it was for the rulers, this caste rigidity gave the courts a semblance of independence and kept popular distrust of the administration of justice within tolerable limits. Save in matters of strictly political and "racial" nature, the courts did not from the outset appear as terror tools of the dictatorship. Furthermore, at least until the outbreak of the war, the National Socialists enjoyed an added advantage over the first decade of the latter-day DDR regime, inasmuch as visible improvement in economic con-

[94] No full analysis is available of the role of the judiciary under the Third Reich. Herbert Schorn, *Der Richter im Dritten Reich* (Frankfurt, 1959), is a part well-intended, part apologetic collection of relevant material. Pp. 1-143 enlarge on the often dubious record of various courts and individual office holders; pp. 144-728 report and document the heroic or martyr role of individual judges, without any attempt to analyze the functioning of the profession as a whole.

[95] A corresponding memorandum of May 11, 1942 by President Kurt Rothenberger of the Hamburg Court of Appeals, along with his efforts to adapt the outlook of the judiciary to the regime's needs, impressed Hitler enough to make him appoint the ambitious judge under secretary in the Reich Ministry of Justice. It took the Führer a year to discover that the new appointee held *esprit de corps* above loyalty to the party; he was then, of course, fired. For the text of the memorandum, see Trial of War Criminals before the Nuremberg Military Tribunals, Vol. III, The Justice Case, Washington, 1951, pp. 469-83. See also August Jaeger, *Der Richter*, Berlin, 1939, pp. 72ff.

ditions evoked widespread favorable response. Encountering active antagonism only on a reduced scale, the National Socialist government succeeded in wiping out real or imaginary foci of resistance without recourse to a radical reorganization of the legal system; it applied purely administrative coercion or, exploiting whatever remained of the erstwhile authority of the courts, assigned the law-perverting court chores to known Hitlerites or opportunists willing to do a special stint for promotion or better pay.[96]

This idyllic division of labor did not last forever, of course. As the judiciary had not been remade into a perfect transmission mechanism at the service of the political leadership, judicial reality was subjected to increasing outside pressure, both political and administrative. To achieve the desired result, the government resorted to a medley of procedures: establishment of special courts all through the country and a central People's Court for the more important political cases; more stringent penal legislation; pretrial briefing sessions where court presidents and presiding panel judges were brought together with officials of prosecuting staffs and security services; individualized pressure through court presidents or prosecutors; instructions circularized by the Ministry of Justice for the attention of the magistrates; special appeal procedures to set aside final judgments considered too lenient; and, as a last resort, transfer or dismissal of a judge.

A rather weird combination made up the top of the judicial pyramid. Next to the party-selected People's Court and the partly party-packed Ministry of Justice, there remained, though shorn of its jurisdiction over political cases, the more conservative, tradition-imbued Leipzig Supreme Court, highest tribunal of the land. So long as the men at the top level functioned to the regime's satisfaction, flaws in the policy alignment of judicial attitudes at the middle and lower levels caused but minor inconveniences. When these piled up, a less cumbersome machinery was set in motion. "In an increasing number of cases," it was stated in 1942, "the police had taken over the job of improving upon unsatisfactory criminal judgments."[97] A defendant now prayed, or even furtively suggested, that an understanding trial judge put him into prison rather than acquit him, if only to protect him from being shipped off to a concentration camp by the police au-

[96] As a result, two different systems coexisted in the legal realm: continuity and legal conservatism on the one hand, and lawlessness, violence, and arbitrary innovation on the other. So long as overlapping was confined to a narrow area, it was no major feat to blur this dualism behind all the paraphernalia of the legal order. Ernst Fraenkel, *The Dual State*, New York, 1941.

[97] Ohlendorf, *op.cit.*, 416.

thorities. Court trial was degraded more and more to a merely preliminary procedure. The corrective action by the police overhauled, if necessary, the work of the judge; in full accord with the Ministry of Justice, the police took over completely all cases involving individuals outside the pale of the national community, that is, Jews, Poles, Russians, and gypsies.

When war had cut short economic advance, and particularly when all available resources had been drained off because of the armed forces' failure to crush Soviet resistance within a few months, terror had to be stepped up in proportion to spreading hardships and the dwindling of popular sympathy. The government still asked for and welcomed the help of the judiciary, fuming about tergiversations of "reactionary" magistrates. But it was by no means stumped by the latter's hostility or resistance; it ignored the "old-fashioned crowd" and had the police or the People's Court take care of chores offensive to the court oldtimers' sense of propriety or professional queasiness.

National Socialism's Communist successors had no use for the luxury of dual standards, nor an interest in retaining pre-1945 judicial personnel. From the start, their basic objective was a radical reversal of the socioeconomic setup; sooner or later the establishment of new legal patterns would be inevitable. Continuity of law, preserved on paper for a time, did not matter much; it only served to delay the widening of the rift between the people and the law. By and large, the mass of the people under SED rule disliked and distrusted the new regime from the very beginning, for both material and ideological reasons. Backed by the occupying power, the SED rulers, however, felt strong enough to start reshaping the country's social and economic structure from top to bottom. To do the job they needed reliable courts and new kinds of judicial officials. The courts' corrective and oppressive functions had to be synchronized with the government's general policy.

This marks the difference. The Third Reich never felt compelled to strive for that judicious blend of persuasion and repression which today is applied in the courts of the DDR; the chance to use it for strengthening the home front in wartime did not present itself. Beyond education by terror and self-interest, educational instruments of domination were not in demand. If required at a later time, they would be designed according to specifications of victory or defeat.

CHAPTER VIII

TRIAL BY FIAT OF THE
SUCCESSOR REGIME

++

Unparteilichkeit im politischen Prozess steht ungefär auf einer Linie
mit der unbefleckten Empfängnis; man kann sie wünschen, aber
nicht sie schaffen.

—THEODOR MOMMSEN, *Römisches Strafrecht*, 4. Buch*

++

Introduction: Special Political
Jurisdictions

WHILE the logic of the Communist system leads to a revamping of the sum total of conditions under which
the judiciary operates, more traditional political orders
have reserved their special attention mostly to organizing
jurisdiction in politically tinged trials. Before plunging into discussion
of a particularly intensive type of political trial, the trial by fiat of the
successor regime, we shall analyze briefly the various types of special
jurisdiction established by a number of regimes to handle political cases
quickly and effectively.

When Charles I and Louis XVI met their fates, there was, as they and
their counsels spoke of amply, little doubt as to the complete irregularity
of both jurisdiction and procedure. Those who framed the indictment
and those who judged the case were practically indistinct from each
other. As their cases and their ultimate disposal were at the same time
the constitutive acts of a new era, the decisions on the cases and the
principles applied formed identical manifestations of the same political
will. But did the fifteenth, sixteenth, and seventeenth century sovereigns
act much differently when their own political interests were at stake?
The British king might not only order a command performance of his
judges, questioning the tenor of and reasons for their prospective
judgments, but he might also dismiss them should their opinions give
him sustained reason for displeasure. The French king would have

* "Impartiality in political trials is about on the level with Immaculate Conception:
one may wish for it, but one cannot produce it."

found it difficult to dismiss his judges, for it would have involved a costly refunding operation for the charges they had bought from the Crown. But from the days of Jacques Le Coeur to those of Cinq-Mars, Fouquet, and Mademoiselle de Montespan, the king might entrust instruction and judgment of his enemy's cases or any other delicate matter to specially appointed extraordinary commissions, in which learned friends of the king or cardinal and open enemies of the persons to be judged might find a strategic place. The eighteenth and the beginning of the nineteenth century saw the generalization of the judge's appointment "quamdiu se bene gesserint," and the prohibition against withdrawing cases from the judge to whom the law had assigned jurisdiction.

But these secular moves did not solve the problem of jurisdiction in political cases. As we mentioned previously, such prosecutions often take place at the strategic juncture when the old regime has been replaced and the incoming one prepares to sit in judgment over it. As a result of such change, the whole court system might well be reorganized; at the very least, the regime will fashion its own system of juridical defense against its political foes, manning strategic legal bastions with its own men of confidence. But even under a long established regime there might arise a number of special occasions, such as prolonged riots bordering on civil war, where the traditional court organization will not suffice. Constitutional lawyers interpreting constitutional documents that prohibit *ad hoc* jurisdictions might haggle endlessly over whether the ban on such jurisdictions only excludes resort to courts selected and manned for a specific case, or whether it also intends to protect against establishment of a new line of jurisdiction to meet situations of some duration. In one form or another—and there exist many subterfuges— the second practice, of setting up special courts for an indefinite time and for special, mostly political, offenses, has been a frequent practice in many countries.

Apart from the political needs of a new regime and of a government hard-pressed by its foes, there exists a long historical tradition of special political jurisdictions. Archbishop Laud, the Earl of Strafford, and Warren Hastings before the House of Lords, Justice Chase and President Johnson before the United States Senate, Polignac, the conspirators of 1843, Caillaux (treated more exhaustively in Chapter III), and Malvy before the Senate—all have become integral parts of their countries' historical lore. The present system of regular, that is, constitutionally or traditionally sanctioned, political jurisdictions operates with a great number of variations and combinations. But of the established forms of jurisdictions there are three distinct types.

There is first what one may call the political assembly, doubling in selected and rather infrequent instances as a political court: the House of Lords up to 1948 or the United States Senate sitting in cases of impeachment arising from the personal quality of the defendant, a British peer, a United States president, or a federal judge. Apposite, too, is the French Senate. Until the demise of the Third Republic, the Senate sat as High Court, both to judge a few categories of political offenses (ratione materiae) and to decide the responsibility for acts (ratione personae) committed by a cabinet member, relating to his tenure of office, and, in cases of high treason, by the president. France's last two constitutions have remodeled both the composition and jurisdiction of the High Court. In 1960 it was composed of 24 members elected in equal numbers from both assemblies. With one exception,[1] it has relinquished jurisdiction over everyone but the president and cabinet members. The ancient quarrel over the qualification of the reprehensible acts has been resolved—except for the president, whose high treason remains intentionally undefined—in favor of a narrow interpretation: the acts are defined and limited by the descriptions of the Criminal Code.[2]

Of ancient vintage, political jurisdiction by assembly formed a costly and cumbersome apparatus. Even before it was largely formally abolished, it became obsolete. This was due partly to the reduced political weight of some of the defendants, the peers, and partly to the fact that since Hannoverian and Benjamin Constant's days, other ways have

[1] A person may now be deferred to the High Court only in a security offense if he has acted in concert with a member of the government. In conformity with the anti-parliamentary tendency of the 1958 Constitution, the rules concerning the High Court have been carefully established with a view to preventing this jurisdiction from ever becoming a sort of auxiliary parliamentary weapon for combatting either president or government. Not only must the act of accusation emanate from both houses—an anomaly in constitutional theory and practice—but neither house of parliament has any influence on the conduct of pretrial proceedings. They are entirely in the hands of five judges selected every year by the Bureau de la Cour de Cassation; they may, if they so choose, either completely countermand or modify the action of the parliament. Constitution, Art. 68, and Ordiñance of January 2, 1959, esp. Arts. 18, 25, and 26.

[2] In contrast, the present Italian Constitution, in its Arts. 90, 96, and 134, and Par. 43-52 of the implementing law of March 11, 1953, have travelled the opposite road. They leave to the Constitutional Court, enlarged for that purpose with sixteen lay judges, the job of defining the "attempt at the Constitution" and "high treason"; in addition, they saddle the court with the discretionary determination of sanctions, criminal and civil, "adequate to the fact," and this both for presidential offenses and the crimes committed in the exercise of their functions by members of the government.

been found to enforce the political responsibility of a straying cabinet minister or possibly even a president before the inevitable, catastrophic change in political climate that leads to parliamentary impeachment.

In more serious political offenses by less exalted persons, the second type of jurisdiction seems to be a contemporary trend. Some countries (such as France or Italy, as cited in Ch. II) will leave it to established lower court jurisdiction to deal with political offenses, permitting themselves leeway to shift choice cases to military jurisdiction, there invoking intelligence with the enemy and demoralization aspects. Other countries, such as the German Federal Republic or Switzerland, will concentrate jurisdiction over political cases to some extent in their highest civil court. From the viewpoint of the defendant, the latter procedure has obviously the same disadvantage as historical upper house or high court proceedings. The federal court might become the final judge of both law and fact; the possible benefit of a change of political perspective is thus excluded in those types of cases where it may come strongest into play, not to mention the fact that the quota of reversible errors has never tended to decrease when proceedings are granted immunity from review.

The third type of jurisdiction, in vogue after the war, is the constitutional court, now existing in the German Federal Republic, in Austria, and in Italy. It functions mostly as a kind of arbiter between the highest organs of the state within the constitutional system, especially important in a federal structure, as a guarantor of individual rights embodied in the constitution, and as a general guarantor of the constitutionality of all legal and administrative enactments. But the court has also been entrusted with functions similar to those traditionally exercised by upper house jurisdictions. The president—in some countries the cabinet ministers, too—might be indicted by parliamentary majorities before the court for "intentional violation of the constitution," again a doctrinal and somewhat impractical echo of Benjamin Constant's preoccupations under a constitutional but preparliamentary system.[3] The German Constitutional Court, as discussed in Part Three, also exercises a quasi-repressive function, allowing the broad operation of political repression clothed as penal action. The government may, at its discretion, start proceedings before this court for banning a political party, the tendencies of which endanger the constitutional order.

Established as a self-evident matter with the inception of a new regime, or—as experience with regular American juries in this century

---

[3] See below, n. 10.

would suggest—as a possibly unnecessary precaution by an established regime, or simply as an historical and somewhat anachronistic survival, political jurisdictions function in many countries. Special jurisdictions have frequently been created for trials instituted by successor regimes against the personnel of their predecessors. Discussing this trial category, we shall dwell on the yardsticks used by successors for measuring the political responsibility of the predecessors' personnel. Which are the value structures that transcend the lifetime of a political regime against which acts of predecessors can be measured? Further, how is the attitude of the individual to be related to the sum total of the record of the regime he served? Is the concept of a *régime criminel* a useful tool for such an enterprise? Where is the more or less precise point at which action in the service of a political goal turns into criminal conduct? If the obstacles to a successor's justice are admittedly substantial, which of them are germane to the particular situation of this kind of trial and which should be counted among the general and unavoidable risks involved in any major trial?

1. The Quest for a Yardstick

The legal formulas under which trials by fiat of a successor regime take place might show a close resemblance to those of the run-of-the-mill criminal law categories. Nevertheless, from the viewpoint of both their instigators and their victims, such trials have a different significance from those that occur under the authority and rule of a long-established regime. They constitute more than just a link in a chain of tribulations and maneuvers through which a regime either achieves greater solidity or marches toward its final disintegration. Setting the new regime off from the old and sitting in judgment over the latter's policies and practices may belong to the constitutive acts of the new regime. In charting the course of action toward its predecessor, any successor regime, whether purporting to achieve moral and political regeneration, or intent, in addition, on consciously remodeling the whole social fabric, faces two contradictory sets of pressures.

Its staunchest adherents and those who might have suffered most from the oppressive hands of the old regime cry not only for revenge, but for the construction of a permanent, unmistakable wall between the new beginnings and the old tyranny. In the passionate language of St. Just asking the Convention to make short shrift of Louis XVI, they all seem to clamor: "Une loi est un rapport de justice: quel rapport de justice y-a-t-il donc entre l'humanité et les rois? Qu'y a-t-il de commun entre Louis et le peuple Français, pour le ménager après sa trahison?"[4]

On the other hand, there is pressure, probably somewhat less vehement but nonetheless persistent and likely to be more widespread, toward minimizing the insecurity from widespread prosecution and indiscriminate rejection of the record of the old regime. The length and the bloodiness of the battle, or reversely, the comparative ease with which the transition took place, might be reflected in the attitudes of the new masters. Some may accentuate repression, such as the Franco regime in Spain, after it won out in a three-year civil war; on a smaller scale, the French provisional government in 1944, liquidating the heritage of Pétain and collaboration; and in our own day Fidel Castro, dealing with the remnants of the Batista regime. In contrast, the incoming English and French Restoration regimes of 1660 and 1814, acting under conditions where large popular masses still remained unconcerned, or where they were prudent onlookers of the affray, found convincing enough reasons to try minimizing the rancor against the protagonists of the old order—not to mention the "Glorious Revolution" which, with Jeffreys removed by death, saw no need for prosecutions. More recently, the French shift from the Fourth to the Fifth Republic not only occurred in the outward forms prescribed for constitutional change, but was conceived so as to obliterate the categories of victors and vanquished, beneficiaries and victims, accusers and accused; it was to cover all under the image of a father lovingly embracing all his children.

Original political intent and social pressures may conform with each other: Charles II gave assurances not only to old and new friends, but also to the great mass of those who had been actively engaged in upholding or carrying through some aspect of Cromwell's administration (witness the declaration of Breda). With full assent and even under prodding of Parliament, he exempted from this show of benevolence only a selected few, who had been instrumental in the demise of his father's regime or directly involved in his death. Louis XVIII went even further and declared his willingness to accept the regicides into the national community. But in the harsher climate of the Second Restoration, a Royalist majority of a chamber—more royalist than the king—though unable to underpin the irregular white terror of the provinces by wholesale legal proscriptions had the last word on the regicides. Eventually three quarters of the still living regicides saw themselves exiled from France. Yet the fateful vote in January 1793

[4] From the speech before the Convention of November 13, 1792, concerning the judgment of Louis XVI.

trapped only those who had compounded the remote crime of having murdered the king with the imprudence of having rallied to Bonaparte's cause during the One Hundred Days.

The declared intentions of a new regime may not always determine the course of political repression. Original political intent may be deflected by supervening pressures. Modification in the structure of the new regime, reinforced by obstruction from the administrative and judicial corps, may wash out and redirect repressive policies. Italian repression of Fascism, as set out in the decree of July 27, 1944, seemed all-embracing on paper. The members of the Fascist government, the purveyors of violence, whoever had through his action contributed to keeping Fascism in power, as well as the collaborators with the German invaders—all fell under the spell of the wide, imprecise, and retroactive definitions of the ordinance. Yet a jurisprudence that was as narrow in its interpretation of the decree as it had been liberal regarding the 1946 amnesty, helped along by the maintenance of the judicial and administrative cadres of the Fascist regime, quickly ended any attempt to eradicate the political heritage of Fascism.[5]

If the practice of dealing with one's predecessors shows great variations, so do the formulas applied. Momentary needs and strategies, including anticipated defense mechanisms against the portents of the future, intertwine with *ad hoc* legal procedures. Rarest seems the open or even implied admission that the new regime is taking an unprecedented course. At times, though, this may be inevitable. The trial of Charles I rested on the juxtaposition of two radically different constitutional theories. Starting from the premise of traditional constitutional law, Charles' refusal to recognize the jurisdiction of the High Court is irrefutable: "No impeachment," he says, "lies against the King; they all go in his name."[6] But if he continues to ask his accusers to show him the basis of the new law, they have a readymade answer, implied in the very manner in which they drew up their charges and the verdict. Their detailed stories of his manifold hostile acts presuppose the existence of an authority, Parliament, fully empowered to make

---

[5] The legal and political elements in the failure of purge attempts are exhaustively narrated in Achille Batagllia, *Giustizia e Politica Nella Giurisprudenza* in Dieci Anni, cited above. Luigi Villari gives the Fascist version of this legislation (*The Liberation of Italy, 1943-1947*, Appleton, 1959, Ch. 25). But even in this thoroughly ex parte account, the author admits (p. 219) that what he calls injustices committed by the various governments succeeding one another after July 25, 1943, have been corrected either through the action of the judiciary or through changes of heart by some of the more influential members of the cabinet and officialdom.

[6] S. R. Gardiner, *The Constitutional Documents of the Puritan Revolution*, 3rd ed.; Oxford, 1951, p. 375.

the final decisions for the realm. But many of Cromwell's colleagues recoiled from carrying such an interpretation to the logical conclusion of calling the king's assumption of his traditional prerogative treason.

The Convention's case against Louis XVI was stronger, for the simple reason that Louis had accepted, albeit with mental reservations, the role of a constitutional king under the 1791 document. The Convention could therefore brush aside St. Just's perspective, calling the execution a "mésure," a necessary incident in the fight between the new and the old order. As against St. Just's general verdict on the king's record, "On ne peut régner innocement," the Convention preferred specific allegations against the constitutional king's acting systematically in defiance of his constitutional position and in collusion with foreign countries inimical to France. If there was no choice but to execute Louis—and, exactly as in the case of Charles I, many wanted to avoid such a conclusion—there was sustained interest in constructing at least as watertight a case as possible. The various constructs to get around the king's constitutionally sanctioned inviolability sound better to the ears of the historian, who knows the extent of Louis' foreign involvement, than to many a member of the Convention. But at least the findings in the famous "cachet," giving some indication of the nature of the king's foreign connections, would substitute proof of his intentions for what was missing in constitutional prerequisites for trying a king.

But regimes do not topple only after having lasted centuries, and then by great revolutionary convulsions, leaving the constitutive act of violence, the murder of a king or czar, the dispersion of a constituent assembly, standing out in stark nakedness, defying even half-hearted attempts at regularization and justification. Many regimes that are only uncertain way stations in the evolution of new societies come to their end after a relatively short span of life, opening for their successors alternative lines of conduct. On paper one might disregard one's predecessor entirely and treat the previous regime as if it had never existed. But this is a style of political play-acting rather than a policy. "The political acts of the preceding regime," writes a contemporary German author, "are attacked in their very legal existence, but only few ideological fools will try to carry such policy to its logical conclusion."[7]

Charles II and Louis XVIII dated their accession to the throne from the execution of their predecessors. As previously discussed, this did not keep them from giving their placet to most of the changes that had taken place since then. The August 9, 1944 ordinance of the provisional French government adopted this policy in regard to the Pétain

[7] Hans Dombois, *Politische Gerichtsbarkeit*, Gütersloh, 1949, p. 12.

regime, pronouncing its legal nonexistence. The same ordinance, however, then proceeded to lay down a complex network of rules determining the various degrees of validity or validity presumptions of its predecessor's enactments. By refusing any recognition to the Pétain constitutional settlement, however, the successor widened the choice of legal
formulas under which to attack those who had served under Pétain.

What is at stake, therefore, is the question of how to measure the
record of those who operated for the now-defunct regime. Here any
number of legal complications might result from the uncertainty or
novelty of the norms applicable to facts and events of the previous
regime—without such difficulties ever having become insurmountable
barriers for the courts of a resolute successor regime.

When Charles X was overthrown by the July Revolution of 1830,
Louis Philippe carried on under the revamped Charte of 1814. It was
therefore under the terms of the Charte, unchanged in this particular
point, that proceedings were instituted against the members of Charles'
cabinet who, under Polignac's leadership, had tried to refashion the
regime of the Charte in an absolutist direction. Part of what they had
done might be called an abuse of discretion granted to the king under
the terms of that document; other actions of theirs were in direct contravention of its explicit terms. As the Charte had survived the fall of
Charles X, Martignac, Polignac's predecessor who had become his
lawyer, could not convince the Pairs sitting in judgment that in de-
throning the king the revolution had terminated Polignac's responsibilities, leaving no case to try.[8] But other more serious legal difficulties
arose. Had they not been ministers, their punishability for an attempt
to endanger the internal security of France would have seemed beyond
dispute. However, the Charte established the ministers' criminal responsibility for "treason and concussion" without defining these terms;
nor was the promised implementing legislation ever issued. The Senate,
sitting as High Court, convicted them on the basis of some assimilated
articles of the Penal Code and sentenced them to some arbitrarily
fashioned punishment.[9]

But fifteen years before the Senate had forged the indeterminate
treason concept of the Charte into a weapon against Polignac's defeated
crew, the intellectual godfather of early French constitutionalism, Benjamin Constant, had tried his hand at fashioning a treason concept
that would be stripped of defamatory notions and would relate purely
to reproaches concerning inadmissible political conduct. In the short-

[8] *Procès des Ex-ministres*, 3rd ed.; Paris, Vol. 2, p. 353.
[9] *Ibid.*, Vol. 3, p. 266.

lived "Acte Additionel" he prepared for Bonaparte's use after his return from Elba, Constant had installed the Senate as a jurisdiction before which the lower house could try ministers and army chiefs for "having compromised the security and honor of the nation"; logically this also allowed the political jurisdiction to fix a discretionary punishment.[10] It is a political formula for formal elimination of a scapegoat or political enemy rather than a clearly incriminated fact situation.

In the terminal stage of the French monarchy, 1766, a similar formula was used by the Paris *parlement* to justify the conviction of General Lally-Tollendal, executed in the wake of his misfortunes in India. The Third Republic has seen—without benefit of a clear-cut text covering it—the 1918 conviction and banishment of former Minister of Interior Malvy by the Senate for "having violated the charges of his office." While the United States has never gone through a change of regime since the inception of the Republic, a similar question arose over the meaning of the phrase "high crime and misdemeanor" in Article 2, Section 4 of the Constitution. The opinions of the fathers, who viewed it as a "method of national inquest into the conduct of public men,"[11] and the fact that conviction results only in forfeiture of office might have suggested a wide interpretation. But if one abstracts from the provision's cumbersome use as a device to eliminate indelicate federal judges from lower courts, the limited practice—on Justice Chase, President Johnson,[12] and Secretary of War Belknap—suggests that the provision is a kind of shorthand allusion to specific offenses. In more recent times, the Vichy regime has tried its luck with impeaching the record of its predecessors by resort to a similar formula. On July 30, 1940 Pétain instituted a new Supreme Court of Justice, to which all former ministers and their immediate civil and military subordinates could be deferred not only for specific offenses, but also "for having acted treasonably in the exercise of their duties." But in contrast to the acts defined in the

---

[10] Benjamin Constant's *Cours de Politique Constitutionelle* (first pub. 1818-1820), Paris, 1861, p. 387, contains a somewhat facile attempt to differentiate between the political and the normal criminal responsibility of a dignitary; for Constant finance matters and matters politic were, at least in theory, easily distinguishable.

[11] Alexander Hamilton in *The Federalist*, No. 65.

[12] Johnson's counsel, former Justice Benjamin R. Curtis, emphasized a number of times that affirmation of the impeachment charges would presuppose a violation of existing law, such as "an intentional misconstruction of the Tenure of Office Act"; *Trial of Andrew Johnson*, published by order of the Senate, 1868, Vol. 1, pp. 147, 383, and 691. The opposite view is expressed in Willoughby, *On the Constitution of the United States*, 3rd ed.; N.Y., 1929, Par. 931. It invokes the authority of former President Taft, but the cases quoted by Taft refer to the situation of lower court judges for whom the "good behavior clause" suggests a wider interpretation.

Penal Code, this treason, in line with the treason of Article 51 of the Charte Constitutionelle of 1814, remains undefined. From the viewpoint of present powerholders it thus implies a judgment on erroneous and nefarious policies rather than commission of a definite criminal offense. The actions exposed to judicial scrutiny were to have a double aspect. From the viewpoint of the German authorities who took a sustained interest in the Riom proceedings, they were to serve the purpose of having official France sanction the thesis that the men of the defunct Third Republic were responsible for the outbreak of the war. For the Vichy regime, interest concentrated on the asserted negligence of those who had left France without adequate preparation to conduct military operations. Both the act of accusation and the accompanying propaganda were carefully planned to avoid discussion of military operations; they concentrated instead on all those elements which would show up the shortcomings and lack of judgment of the leaders of the Third Republic in the years immediately preceding the outbreak of the war.[13] Before inquiries had advanced enough to lead to the opening of the trial, however, Pétain, anxious for the condemnation of the leaders of the Third Republic, convoked an *ad hoc* Council of Justice in August 1941. By the very formula of the July 30 decree, the Council was to report on the sanctions to be taken. It promptly did so, with the result that four political and military leaders of the defunct Republic were put in a fortress without their having been questioned in the course of these administrative proceedings. With the subsequent trial thus prejudged—in spite of the contrary assertions of the president of the Supreme Court of Justice—public proceedings began in Riom on February 19, 1942. While the court accepted the treason definition of the July 30, 1940 enactment, it discarded the count relating to the German-inspired search for those responsible for having started the war. It retained proceedings only against those defendants who could be held responsible for gaps in the organization and equipment of the French military forces.

As usually happens with arguments of constitutionality and retro-action in the courts of the victors, the court rejected the procedural argument of the defense; their argument had rested on the lack of a constitutional basis for the proceedings and on the fact that the newly-

[13] Among the literature on the trial, probably the most revealing are Maurice Ribet (Daladier's lawyer), *Le Procès de Riom*, Paris, 1945, together with Léon Blum's own tale in *L'Oeuvre de Léon Blum*, Paris, 1955, Vol. 2, esp. pp. 220-30. Ribet also brings out the interesting orders given to the press (p. 38); they clearly indicate the regime's desired goals and what problems it tried to avoid both in court and certainly in public.

created offenses had not been in existence when the reproached act had been committed.[14] Thereupon the defense took to contesting the lack of proper war preparations, laying many of the shortcomings directly at the doorsteps of the pre-*Front Populaire* Minister of War, Marshal Pétain. Neither the Germans, who had been cheated out of the expected inquiry into the war guilt issue, nor the Pétain regime, whose authority was jeopardized by the course of the Riom debates, would evince any further interest in the enterprise. As the course of future French history was entirely open in spring 1942, Vichy propaganda had a difficult time opposing the interpretations of Blum and Daladier, the masters of the defunct regime. With convincing enough counterarguments they defended their own record by attacking the tactical mistakes and the spirit of defeatism exuding in the thirties from the circle of those now in power. German displeasure with the course of the trial was brought home to Vichy by a special visit of Dr. Friedrich Grimm, the Third Reich's foreign trial specialist. It became clear that the antecedents and the course of the Vichy regime were beset with too many question marks to serve as a propitious background for an open settling of accounts with Vichy's predecessors. The Riom debates were therefore suspended by government fiat on April 14, 1942, though as a matter of form the court was asked to complete pretrial investigations. The government thus abandoned its attempt to get judicial confirmation of the executive measures it had taken.

The political wheel turned in summer 1944. The new regime, General de Gaulle's Provisional Government, as well as the re-established constitutional governments of Belgium, Holland, and Norway, did not recognize the legal existence of the Pétain or Quisling predecessors. The clearer it was that members of such regimes were functioning as native auxiliaries of the enemy invader, the easier it became to apply such treatment; the regime could consider them as traitors, excluding debate on the feasibility and justifiability of their course of action, which would have necessitated discussion of their aims and programs. But even in such countries as Holland, Norway, and Belgium, the relative simplicity of the treason–foreign invader formula, while it took effective care of the problems of the ranking collaborators, left a considerable legacy of borderline cases. Where, for instance, is the line between merely keeping office in order to administer to the current needs of the population and action which implicitly involves recognition of the invader's title?[15] What is the form and style of obedience

[14] Ribet, *op.cit.*, pp. 41-50.
[15] Interesting examples of how to draw the dividing line may be found in Henry L.

which reflects acknowledgment of the power of coercion but avoids any move toward helping to transform naked power into authority? Many a contemporary would be happy to know the answer.

Under the impact of complete and voluntary submission to a foreign invader, which from the outset stamps as traitors those nationals who become full-fledged collaborators, the patriotic norm may serve as a guidepost. The problem—legal texts to the opposite notwithstanding— becomes more difficult and complex in France and Italy. In neither case would denial of the legal character of the predecessor regime and constructs of treasonable relations with the enemy work out too smoothly. We have already mentioned the debacle of the Italian legislative attempt to establish the criminal responsibility of the major figures and abettors of the Fascist regime after it had lasted over two decades. The attempt of the April 22, 1945 decree to establish the criminal responsibility of those who had collaborated with the Germans and held office under Mussolini's short-lived Social Republic of Saló, installed in northern Italy after his rescue, foundered equally as quickly in the courts. A number of poor devils held the bag, while the principals were able to show that they had worked both the Fascist and, clandestinely, the anti-Fascist racket—practitioners of *doppo gioco*, as the Italians called it.[16] In Italy collaboration with the Germans had been the policy of a government which had been in power for twenty years. Both the regime and its policies became increasingly unpopular from 1942 on. There might have been a national consensus in the crisis years 1942-1944, consisting in the attempts of many combined forces, old-line political personnel, Catholic Church, the independent and the Communist resistance, to guide Italy back toward independence from its German overlords. But this consensus, too fragile and narrow, and too uncertain in its ultimate effect, could not serve as a patriotic norm of such unquestionable strength that it would support criminal sanctions for reprehensible political action, unless aggravated by acts of special brutality.

In the Vichy regime foreign domination and a certain amount of home-grown initiative to replace the institutions of the Third Republic with a new authoritarian model became inextricably mixed. By some

Mason, *The Purge of Dutch Quislings*, The Hague, 1952, esp. pp. 85ff. The unenviable record of the Dutch High Court during the German occupation has been dealt with in detail, from the viewpoint of the destruction of the court's authority-building image, in Gerald I. Jordan, "The Impact of Crises on Judicial Behavior," paper read before the American Political Science Association meeting in New York, September 8-10, 1960.

[16] Details, especially the legislation's vain attempts to transform participation in the Saló enterprise into a nonrebuttable presumption of collaboration, are dealt with by G. Vasalli and G. Sabati in *Il Collaborazionismo e l'Amnistia Politica*, Rome, 1946.

avenue of correct legal transition the regime had been connected with the institutions of the Third Republic. The respective amounts of voluntariness and coercion in the 1940 change were certainly not much smaller than during the 1958 transition from the Fourth to the Fifth Republic. The threat of Massu's parachutists stood as much as godfather to the Fifth Republic of de Gaulle as the proximity of German tanks did to the ascent of Pétain. Thus if the acceptable origin of the Pétain regime and the smooth transition were doubtless generated by the pressure of circumstances, they were still confirmed by a substructure of willing, if passive, popular acceptance. Moreover, at least until the country's total occupation in November 1942, the regime retained a certain margin of freedom for maneuvering, a margin probably not much smaller than that held by many contemporary governments. However that may be, the refusal to concede legal existence to the Vichy regime would allow its leaders to be made responsible after-the-occasion for an attempt to scuttle the republican regime, endangering the internal security of the state; it would also open the way to prosecuting them for treason. Inasmuch as the armistice with Germany, even if its validity were recognized, would not end the war with Germany, relations with the Germans could be called "intelligence with the enemy." The 1939 decree modifying Article 75(4,5) of the Penal Code specifically incriminated "intelligence with a foreign nation," with a view to forwarding that nation's endeavors, as well as the support given in time of war to military personnel joining the services of a foreign nation.

Thus once one admits the correctness of the initial hypothesis, the legal nonexistence of the Vichy regime and the continuation of a state of war with Germany,[17] there exists a detailed enough body of treason law for building up a good case against the major Vichy leaders. The "intelligence with the enemy" construction was supplemented for the various categories of officials by ordinances establishing echelons of criminal and disciplinary responsibility according to the importance of the function and the degree of facility with which acceptance or maintenance of such function could have been avoided. The courts, with the help of the "intelligence with the enemy" concept, could measure the attitude of the defendant by a patriotic norm whose continuing validity was assumed even if the actions of those temporarily in power did not correspond to it. In this way, the problem of the genuine domestic basis of the Vichy regime and the various impulses it was

---

[17] The point has been elaborated in Emile Garçon, *Code Pénale* (cited above, Ch. II, n. 34), annotation 192 before Art. 75, following the decision in Suarez by the Cour de Cassation, *Sirey*, 1945.1.29.

obeying, which were not necessarily always determined by the German overlords, could be skirted, at least officially.

Due to the rapid change of political alignments, the "intelligence with the enemy" concept has been allowed to fall into oblivion since the beginning of the fifties. To put it differently, it has been reduced from an official tenet of policy to a piece of intellectual property of the extreme left. But during the immediate postwar period it fulfilled a psychological, political, and juridical function. No cognizance needed to be taken of the fact that among many strata of society the patriotic norm of the traditional state had been eroded. These assumptions, however fictitious they might have been, created a legal basis that allowed the courts to circumvent discussion of the nature and goals of the Vichy regime, measuring its performance instead by a narrower yardstick: its attitude toward the German enemy.

Of course, not even the "intelligence with the enemy" thesis, and even less the hypothesis of retrospective subverting of the constitutional government, could eliminate one fundamental ambiguity which leaves questions about some, though by no means all, of the trials against the Vichy personnel.[18] In conflict are two interpretations of history. One, made with the benefit of hindsight, rests on the knowledge that Vichy's policy of collaboration was doomed to eventual defeat and hence to the detriment of France. The other interpretation and its consequent choice of action were made at a time when the future course of history was a matter of conjecture. Even if we, like the court in Pétain's case, brush aside the defense argument of "double jeu,"[19] a carefully worked-out system to simulate adherence to the German cause while in substance trying to work itself free from German domination; even if we admit that Vichy had, at least since Laval's return to power in spring 1942, been set on the German card, can we determine whether this was a mistake or a crime?

Under two suppositions this policy may be called a crime. The first is interesting but need not detain us here. It leads back to the successor

[18] As usual, there exists an enormous body of partisan literature, written more often than not to justify the cause of the various defendants; despite its useful biographical information, I would classify José Agustin Martinez, *Les Procès Criminels de l'Après-Guerre*, Paris, 1958, in the same category.

[19] Trochu, former president of the Paris Municipal Council, testifying as a defense witness for Pétain, expressed himself in the following way: "Le double jeu, il y a beaucoup de gens qui l'invoquent; mais le double jeu d'un particulier est zéro, tandis qu'un chef d'état et un ministre des affaires etrangères ont quelque fois le dévoir de jouir le double jeu!" Haute Cour de Justice, *Procès du Maréchal Pétain*, Paris, 1945, p. 181; for the court's refusal to accept the argument, see the verdict, p. 386.

regime's judgment of the political worth of its predecessor. It is indeed possible to conclude from all the available evidence that German collaboration was not only sought to improve France's national position, but was in conformity with the desire to foreclose return to democratic institutions. The implications of the second supposition will detain us longer. At least since mid-1942 the Vichy authorities must have been aware that collaboration with Germany implied part acquiescence to, part active collaboration with, policies that far transcended a regime's traditional effort to keep itself in power: collaboration with German programs of forced labor and Jewish extermination.

2. *"L'État Criminel" and Individual Responsibility*

We are facing a question that transcends the successor's always problematic judgment on the qualities and policies of their predecessors. Beyond the evanescent yardsticks of successor regimes, with their conflicting principles of organization, belief systems, and interest configurations, we are searching for a fundamental notion to which all groups and nations must at least submit, if not always subscribe. Respect for human dignity and rejection of the degradation of human beings to mere objects comes to mind. To define such a notion is easier than to determine its meaning in the individual circumstance. There is a temptation to conceive an ideal normal state which, in its legal pronouncements and organizational devices, meets the minimum requirements of respect for human dignity and is opposed to the image of an *état criminel*. On the basis of its attitude toward and treatment of the human material under its domination, such a state could not ask that credence be given to its acts nor expect the actions of its servants to be clothed with the presumption of legality. But is there such a state, one that is somehow analogous to the criminal organization construct of the London War Crimes Statute?

During a somewhat less complicated period of history, one of the most intelligent scoundrels of all time, Prince Talleyrand, tried in his own inimitable way to conceive an answer, and it is one that is no less interesting for its being tailored to a specific situation. In 1823 Savary, Napoleon's Minister of Police, accused Talleyrand of having been instrumental—in 1804, while Napoleon's minister of foreign affairs—both in the seizure of the Duc d'Enghien, scion of the Bourbon family on the territory of the Grand Duke of Baden, and in d'Enghien's subsequent execution in the Vincennes fortress. In the aide-memoire which Talleyrand submitted to Louis XVIII, he argued—contrary to all evidence that has come down to us—that his part in the events was decidedly minor; he was sort of a diplomatic agent doing a routine job, strictly within the limits of his office, with all vital decisions emanating from Napoleon himself. But for good measure, Talleyrand added a more far-reaching argument:

"If a man, by the force of circumstances, is forced to live under an illegitimate regime, the decision of what to do when ordered to commit a crime should depend on the following circumstances: if the crime should draw the country into great danger, into social disorganization, contempt of law, he should not only resist the order, but do all in his power to do away with the enemy of the country. However, if the crime should remain an isolated one and have no other consequence than to stain the reputation of the individual who committed it, then one might be given to grievance over the admixture of greatness and weakness, of energy and perversity, yet the respective distribution of glory and the elements of infamy must be left to the justice of future ages. Anyhow, when the act only compromises the good name of the principal, with the law of nations, the general state of morality unaffected, the servant of the state has a right to continue in office. Were it otherwise, government jobs would be deserted by the more capable and more generous of men. Terrible results would derive if this principle were neglected. It should be adhered to as long as the defense of the social order and moral right are preserved intact."[20]

Talleyrand's theorem has been echoed in dozens of variations, often embellished in the immediate postwar period by the contention that the job was kept by the individual in question only to stave off worse tragedies.[21] It would be acceptable only if its logical presupposition, the distinction between an easily perceptible cleavage between the occasional operation of a normal state organization and the contemptible and inhuman doings of the criminal state—the dead-end street of an entirely vicious political setup—corresponded to reality. The argument does not improve by its being turned upside down. Professor Hermann Jahreiss, laying the theoretical foundation for the Nuremberg defense, readily admitted that Hitler, in contrast to Talleyrand's picture of a Napoleon who only occasionally deviated from the social norm,

---

[20] *Memoires of the Prince de Talleyrand*, New York, 1891, p. 216.

[21] When proferred by Franz Schlegelberger, acting minister of justice (Justice case transcript, 27 and 30 June 1947, pp. 4347 and 4384-87), the argument was rejected by the Military Tribunal No. 10 (Vol. 3, p. 1086). The rejection has been explicitly approved by Gustav Radbruch, "Des Reichsjustizministeriums Ruhm und Ende," *Süddeutsche Juristenzeitung*, Vol. 3 (1948), pp. 58, 63. Configurations where the "preventing worse evil" argument might find a foundation in a particular situation are discussed in H. Jeschek, *Die Verantwortlichkeit der Staatsorgane nach Völkerstrafrecht*, Bonn, 1952, p. 398.

was the evil incarnate. He thereupon used this admission to demonstrate that inasmuch as all decisions were concentrated in Hitler, all agents below his level, unable to affect his will, were devoid of responsibility.[22] Between the occasional aberration within the framework of the social order and the effortless affirmation of the existence of an evil incarnate, elevated to the rank of an abstract mechanism of imputation, the principle of personal responsibility evaporates.

No pure *état criminel* exists in practice. There is no criminal genius who would be able to cajole, seduce, or force a whole people into absolute obedience. As everywhere else in human society, the elements of freedom and coercion, of enthusiastic, matter-of-fact, resigned, or reluctant obedience, of underhanded obstruction and rebellion are inextricably mixed. A modern state organization cannot be run like a concentration camp with the overwhelming majority of the population as its inmates. In order to be workable, even a despotic state organization must serve the basic needs of a sizeable number of the population. Hence the necessity to organize a great number of "neutral" services closely corresponding to those of any other modern state.[23] But it is not only in their common pursuit of necessary societal functions that a normal and criminal state are indistinguishable. The very notion of their separability accounts for only part of our contemporary experience. It originates with the Third Reich, whose goals, the forcing into subservience of the people of the European continent, were as evil as the means of killing and enslaving millions of its real or fictitious, present or future enemies.

The goals need not be abhorrent or repulsive. Collectivization and accelerated industrialization within the administrative framework of the Soviet state are also, though by no means exclusively, motivated by the desire to eventually raise the living standard of the population. And in the last decade, within the framework of their policy to maintain France's predominant position, the French in Algeria have certainly worked toward raising the cultural and material standards of the in-

[22] *IMT*, Vol. 17 (1948), pp. 458-94. (The *IMT* abbreviation refers only to the trial before the International Tribunal, not the American Military Tribunals sitting in Nuremberg.) For a measured refutation of Jahreiss' argument, see H. Donnedieu de Vabres, "Le Procès de Nuremberg devant les principes modernes du droit pénal international," *Récueil des Cours de l'Academie Internationale de la Haye*, Vol. 70, No. 1 (1947), pp. 483, 570.

[23] The same point has recently been made in a judgment of the German Constitutional Court (2 BV.R 234/60, Entscheidungen des Bundesverfassungsgerichts, Vol. 11 [1961], p. 150: "Even an unjust system cannot but solve problems of daily community life in a way which, on the surface at least, comes close to the ways of the traditional legal order."

digenous population. In both cases the framework in which these policies have been carried through by those in power has involved untold
misery for large numbers among the population, including those who
have not dared to resist the official promptings. Yet official policies
may be subject to many oscillations and to varying degrees of implementation. Other segments of the population or of the official apparatus
might try not only to check or soften measures of implementation, but
to reorient the very goal structure. This might lead, as it has in France,
to the curious situation of two segments of society existing side by side:
the normal sector, following the traditional rules of a state, where
state-individual relations are organized within a legal framework, and
a military and police order, geared to maintain French domination over
Algeria and utilizing for this end any means from persuasion and indoctrination to open terror.

But this is only an extreme and especially vivid illustration. Each
society has such islands where the rule of law is at best uncertain, conjectural, and often nonexistent. These islands may connote identifiable
geographic areas or specific group relations; in other cases they may be
nothing more than predispositions of certain groups ready to enter
the field if the sociopolitical configuration changes and restraining influences remain weak. The decisive difference, in separating a normal
from a criminal state, involves the degree to which such islands are
kept under control and whether they are encroaching on wider and
wider fields of social activities.[24]

In the problematic enterprise of couching political responsibility in
legal terms, it may be considered futile to even begin to try and differentiate between political responsibility for a policy that failed and
political responsibility for a policy whose criminal character rests in
its inherent violation of the basic rules of human conduct. One might
argue, for example, that the means of destruction utilized in any future
war are so horrible, the consequences so disastrous, that whoever en-
gages in a major warlike enterprise must necessarily become a criminal,
regardless of his goals and motivations. Any power holders and their
major subordinates who would apply violence exceeding the amount
compatible with maintaining the present state of civilization would
automatically acquire the status of criminals.[24a] Such a course is alto-

---

[24] For a discussion, under a related heading, of the beginning years of the NS state,
see Ernst Fraenkel, *op.cit.*

[24a] As Guenter Lewy put it succinctly in his recent "The Dilemma of Military
Obedience in the Atomic Age," *American Political Science Review*, Vol. 55 (1961),
pp. 3, 21: The question awaiting answer is, where does legal warfare end and
humanity begin?

gether likely, even though the word "criminal," connoting an institutionalized type of handling, might be out of place; the action against the criminal would probably be closer to the way the Italian partisans disposed of Mussolini after his final capture. But still there might be violence in one country or in a region and with tacitly or openly agreed upon restrictions to conventional weapons. This might allow, or even make it advisable for, successor regimes to sort out the motivations, goals, and action patterns of those who saw their cause defeated.

At any rate, it might be useful for us to see how much the difference between responsibility for political failure and for inhuman conduct is more than a utopian construct or, worse, a hypocritical formula put up to enhance the prestige of a specific type of successor operation.

3. Nuremberg: The Prerequisites of a Trial

A. THE NATURE OF THE CHARGES

What does the Nuremberg war crimes trial before the International Military Tribunal, the most important "successor" trial in modern history, teach us about the relation between traditional political charges and those concerning the total destruction of human dignity and personality?[25] The trial differs in one important respect from other successor trials: instead of a domestic successor regime, a syndicate of four foreign powers handled the trial. Whatever the differences over legal formulas by which to construct this fact, these powers in 1945 became the provisional, yet firmly established successors of the Hitler regime.

The charges preferred in the Nuremberg indictment show throughout a hybrid character. The trial originated as an inquest of the victor-successors, charging the preceding National Socialist regime with its major policies; aggressive warfare aimed at subjugating the continent. Due both to the nature of the parties concerned with the prosecution, a victorious foreign power syndicate, and their declared aim, to stamp out aggression, the type of political charge changed: instead of an inquest into the reasons for losing the war, the men in the dock faced responsibility for having started it. From the outset this fact determined the entire trial configuration. Mismanagement of the nation's affairs and the history of subversion of the constitutional establishment, the usual fare of successor trials against the preceding regime's top-ranking personnel, receded behind the grievances of those who had suffered from National Socialist Germany's wanton aggression.

[25] Except when specifically referred to, the discussion does not pertain to the trial before the Far Eastern International Military Tribunal, nor to trials before United States military commissions operating in the Far East.

But this political charge was tied to other ones, directed toward making the defendants accountable for inhumane conduct in the pursuit of their political goals. To complicate the picture still further, part of the war crimes charge concerned not the acts of unprecedented cruelty, such as killing millions of Jews and prisoners of war, or enslaving the population of entire countries, but the uncertain and shifting boundary lines of the laws of warfare—practices in the taking and killing of hostages, for example, and similar problems in partisan and submarine warfare. Of course, the fact that these practices happened often at the explicit orders of a regime which had planned aggressive war and was committed to the physical destruction of nations and races blurred the picture to some extent. It was not always easy to differentiate between typical incidents, coming up under conditions of any modern war, and action which originated from and related to Hitler's preconceived campaign plans.

This kind of hybrid prosecution, which mixes political accountability for planning and initiation of aggressive war with criminal responsibility for inhumane conduct, has to our eyes a politically justified element. Full-fledged warfare in contemporary society must almost necessarily lead to inhumane results. Therefore, establishing a precedent for penalizing aggressive warfare could justifiably be regarded by Justice Jackson as the paramount political goal of the Nuremberg proceedings. Had the noble purpose of the crime against peace charge succeeded, had it helped to lay a foundation for a new world order, the uncertain juridical foundation of the charge would now be overlooked and the enterprise praised as the rock on which the withdrawal of the states' rights to conduct aggressive warfare came to rest. As the coalition pursuing the Nuremberg enterprise broke up before the ink on the Nuremberg judgment had time to dry, the dissensions among the wartime partners threw a shadow over the whole affair. Exceptions taken to the charge of crime against the peace—one of the trial's integral charges but legally the most problematic one—have often been used as strategy to discredit the enterprise as a whole.

Discussion of this new variant among successor trials might well admit both the difference in structure and legal conclusiveness between the crimes against peace and the legally unnecessary conspiracy charge,[26] closely coordinated with the former in the findings of the court, and the war crimes charges proper. The crime against peace charge was a political charge in a double sense: it incriminated a certain type of

[26] Donnedieu de Vabres, *Le Procès de Nuremberg* (Cours de doctorat), Paris, 1947, p. 254, calls it "la construction intéréssante mais un peu romancée de l'acte d'accusation."

political conduct, namely the National Socialist attempt to subjugate Europe by all available means, including the launching of aggression; and the degree of illegality of the incriminated course of action remained as conjectural as in some of the previously discussed proceedings.

While the outlawry of aggressive warfare had been enshrined on parchment in 1929 and duly ratified by the major states, it was not until the London War Crimes Charter, perfected six years after the Nuremberg trial had begun, August 8, 1945, that what had been a charge of international illegality was converted to the status of international punishability. In preparing the charter, both the French and to some degree also the USSR members of the London conference had anticipated the difficulties which this type of charge would raise.[27] However, together with their governments they bowed to the missionary zeal of the American representative Justice Jackson, who was eager to undertake the job of a "commission of codification."[28] In doing so he had to overlook that a codification commission must either confirm firmly implanted practices—which certainly did not exist in this field —or restrict itself to announcing rules for future behavior rather than maxims by which to judge past performances. Experience shows that every successor regime feels intensely that in condemnation of the predecessors' practices is the key to humanity's future. In spite of all justified scepticism against successors' evaluations of their predecessors' efforts, and because we know what we do of the likely shape of future wars, we must admit that Justice Jackson's position, though it has the inevitable share of hypocrisy, possesses an element of inherent logic: the need to create a precedent which can form a barrier, however weak, against future aggression.[29]

[27] The record of this conference, in many ways as interesting as the final judgment of the IMT, may be studied in *International Conference on Military Trials*, London, 1945 (Dept. of State Publication 3080, Washington, 1948), esp. 335, 378, 379, 385.

[28] *Ibid.*, p. 335. The objections to the (unnecessary) crime against peace counts were vigorously stated at the time by Erich Hula, "Punishment for War Crimes," *Social Research*, Vol. 13 (1946), p. 22.

[29] The one member of the IMT who had been a lifelong student of international criminal law, the Sorbonne professor Donnedieu de Vabres, though not hiding his reservation against the charge, has vigorously stressed the function of the judgment as an "incomparable precedent." *Op.cit.* (see n. 22 above), p. 577. The incomparable precedent would backfire, however, if it induced the leaders of a future war to fight to the bitter end rather than surrender and face the possible fate of war criminals.

See also the arguments of Robert K. Woetzel, *The Nuremberg Trials in International Law*, London/New York, 1960, pp. 170-71, 242, which rest on the charter's and judgment's confirmation by the international community. Given the after-history of the international community, a frank attempt to break the fetters of legal positivism,

If the crime against peace charge was a legal novelty, in that it created the offense of aggressive warfare,[30] it was also a typical successor regime concern, establishing the responsibility of the governing ranks of the predecessor for the policy course they had taken. With the war crimes charges and the related crimes against humanity charges we are directly concerned with the quality of human action regardless of the hierarchical level at which it occurred.[31] The newly coined "crimes against humanity" concept (Article 6c of the charter) corresponds to a deeply felt concern over the social realities of our age: the advent of policies intent on and leading to debasing or blotting out the existence of whole nations or races. But if the social and political mechanism employed in such cases is unfortunately very clear, the legal formulas to cover and repress such actions remain problematic. In the absence of a world authority to establish the boundary line between atrocity beyond the pale and legitimate policy reserved for the individual state, the French government and its Algerian foes, the South African government and the representatives of the downtrodden negro and colored population, not to mention the Hungarian regime and its adversaries and victims, might continue to have a very different viewpoint on the meaning of the concept. While the IMT, in the particular instances which it had to judge, might have had little doubt about the concrete meaning of the classification, it nevertheless appreciated both the looseness of some of the terminology of Article 6(c) and the novelty of the charge. It therefore preferred, whenever feasible, to convict the defendants on the basis of the war crimes charges, which embraced all the traditional common crimes, while underemphasizing as much as possible the charges of crimes against humanity. Only in two cases,

---

especially if the latter serves as "value-blind guarantees for any kind of status protection," seems preferable. Such an attempt is outlined by Helmut Ridder, "Nuernberger Prozesse," *Staatslexicon*, 6th ed.; Freiburg, 1961, Vol. 5, pp. 11, 131-135.

[30] But strictly speaking, legally, the charge that this "novelty" violated the *nulla poena sine lege* principle is not well taken. Although most advanced constitutional systems contain this protective rule, positive international law does not know it. Woetzel, pp. 111-17, shows the impracticability of the rule, for both the development of international law and the absence of injustice where violated obligations are recognizable.

[31] It may well be that policy and lower level action are closely connected. The reprehensible goal, the subjugation of Europe by aggressive war, and the criminal means, the inhuman treatment of the underlying populations, form part of one and the same pattern. But the evidence would suggest that it might have been possible to accept the premises of power politics, including wars of aggression, without originally perceiving how closely such policy was geared to inhuman means. See the characteristic testimony of Feldmarschall v. Paulus, *IMT*, Vol. 7, p. 284.

Julius Streicher and Baldur von Schirach, did the conviction rest exclusively on a crimes against humanity charge, though even in these cases the court made an effort to find related war crimes aspects.[32]

Thus the main weight of the conviction—for what the French prosecutor François de Menthon aptly characterized crimes against the human status, with this status an image of the constitutive elements of any civilized society[33]—must rest on the war crimes aspect. Even if they were accepted as a category, crimes against peace would have to rest on the concrete possibility that major policies were furthered; just like the older successor trials, therefore, trials based on crimes against peace would involve mostly top-ranking personnel. But the individual fact situation brought under war crimes charges might involve responsibility way below the top echelons.

There exists, as pointed out before, no pure *état criminel.* Even when the London charter tried much more mildly to have the court determine the criminal character of organizations to which various defendants belonged, the court's recommendations, which form an integral part of the judgment, closely circumscribed the possible results for the members of these organizations, if, indeed, they did not completely vitiate those results. There remains nothing but to search for individual responsibility for inhumane conduct. In this search for the commission of common crimes, undertaken in connection with totalitarian political programs by various war crimes tribunals and, in a more haphazard and incidental way, by indigenous German courts, some defense arguments retain more than technical interest. We want to consider four of these arguments.

B. FOUR REJOINDERS

I. The Sanction of the Legal Order. In the first argument, a judge or another official attempts to invoke the sanction of the existing legal order. The defendant may assert, as in the "Justice" case, for example, that the incriminated act was carried through in pursuance of legal enactments whose validity went unchallenged at the time of the trial. Such a plea raises a point of principle. Not every piece of legislation enacted by a government in conformity with its own rules acquires, by the mere fact of enactment, the quality of binding the lower echelons. If it shows on its face the character of inhumanity, as did the decree

[32] See de Vabres' critical evaluation of the crime against humanity charges, *op.cit.* (n. 22 above), pp. 243-46.

[33] *IMT*, Vol. 5, pp. 406-07. "It [the human status] signifies all those faculties the exercising and developing of which rightly constitute the meaning of human life."

concerning the administration of penal justice against Poles and Jews in the incorporated Eastern territories,[34] then reference to its valid enactment cannot be invoked as defense by those who applied it. In those patently exceptional cases the value of legal certainty is not strong enough against the principle that intentional violation of minimum standards deprives an enactment of the claim to legal validity.[35] Setting up machinery for the wanton destruction of human beings "selected out" on the basis of national or racial characteristics in the form of a general command rather than by specific order does not give such enactments the dignity of law. It is the negation of the purpose of law, which even in the form of the shoddiest enactment must still offer a password: the ordering of human relations. However, even under terroristic conditions, framers of legislation rarely couched their legislation in offensive terms. The need for legal certainty will make it awkward to contest the validity of a legal enactment on account of the illegitimacy of the regime or of the presumed policies which the originators of such legislation might pursue on the basis of the enactment.[36]

The presumed validity of an enactment does not necessarily exculpate those who might consider invocation of the statute a foolproof defense mechanism. An enactment in itself is a mere cipher, whose real import and weight, changing from situation to situation, are determined by those who fashioned it or learned to mold it in constant practice. The ease with which the rulers of the day might manipulate legislation is not a carte blanche for the last-line interpreter to exhaust all the possibilities which the enactment might open up to him. At best, the enactment is a credit card which tells nothing about whether judicial or administrative implementation was necessary, convenient, or abusive. Those who sit in judgment on the enforcers of such legislation will have to examine the circumstances of application in the individual case.

In one case, for example, the presiding judge of a German special

---

[34] The text of the decree of December 4, 1941, is reprinted in the Justice case volume, *op.cit.*, p. 632.

[35] See the formulations of Gustav Radbruch, *Rechtsphilosophie*, 5th ed.; Stuttgart, 1956, p. 353. Among the more recent discussions, see Lon L. Fuller, *op.cit.*

[36] Entscheidungen des Bundesverfassungsgerichts, Vol. 6 (1957), pp. 132, 198-200, discussing the validity of National Socialist civil service legislation. The decision differentiates between the setting up of manifestly unjust law, bare of any effect, and those parts of the National Socialist legislation which, while illegitimate in origin, enjoy "sociological validity." I take this expression to mean *inter alia*: a) that such rules do not create protected legal situations extending into the period following the demise of the regime; b) that they may be invoked as justification of action, unless the circumstances of the case established the bad faith of the actor.

court sentenced to death a Polish farm laborer who had had alterca-
tions with his employer and had also made advances to his employer's
wife. When the military tribunal in the "Justice" case asked how the
case of a "racial German" would have been treated if submitted to the
German Reichsgericht on the identical fact situation, the judge replied:
"This is a very interesting question, but I cannot even theoretically
visualize the case, as the decisive elements cannot be transferred to a
German."[37] The basic fact that the way he handled his job violated
the minimum standards of decency and equality before the law to
which all human beings are entitled did not occur to the judge. Should
he therefore escape punishment?[38]

II. Binding Orders and Necessity. The second argument draws its
strength from the concrete condition under which individuals below
the highest level exercise their function. The London charter, in Article
8, had somewhat sweepingly done away with the invocation of binding
orders except in mitigation of punishment. This problem, which comes
up time and again, is most frequently discussed in terms of military
hierarchical relationships. Authors of many nations, especially in the
wake of the Korean conflict where no side has been strong enough to
insist on the punishment of their adversaries' alleged war crimes, have
commented on the conflict of loyalties which the policy of the London
charter would create. They have denied that the rejection of binding
orders could ever be squared with the social reality of hierarchical com-

---

[37] Justice case transcript, December 4, 1947, p. 10625.

[38] The most persistent critic of the Nuremberg trials, especially those before the
American Military Tribunals, August von Knieriem (*The Nuremberg Trials*, Chicago,
1959), tried to exculpate those who framed the decree of December 4, 1941, with the
argument that referring the case to such a tribunal was preferable to the method
chosen thereafter: killing Poles and Jews without benefit of any trial (p. 279). This
is a somewhat specious application of the lesser evil argument. Does the fact that
others invented devices to kill speedily millions of people exculpate those who put a
somewhat less efficient machinery into motion, only killing hundreds? In Radbruch's
judgment of such arguments in the Schlegelberger case: "For the man of the law
seeing that a frontal attack against an evil situation appears impossible, the only way
is to acknowledge that in legal terms there remain no remedies except those with
which he would stain his own reputation" (*op.cit.*, p. 62).

While in Knieriem's mind the first argument serves those who framed the legislation, its application by a judge, constituting the putting into practice of "valid" law,
was no offense if the judge did not know that he acted wrongly (p. 284). Knieriem
overlooks that the Federal Court considers that the application of excessively severe
punishment in cases clearly not warranting such action is a crime, even though the
law under which the judge was operating would authorize such sentence. Bundesgerichtshof, Entscheidungen in Strafsachen, Vol. 3 (1952), pp. 110, 118; Vol. 10
(1958), pp. 295, 301.

mand relations.[39] The harsh judgment is not unwarranted. However, a differentiation imposes itself.

Military command relationships on the lower level, where strict discipline and complete subjection of the individual judgment to that of the commanding officers may be the price of survival, are quite different from the social reality of higher level command relations. Except for their outward forms, higher level military command relations are more like relations within what might be abbreviated a power elite, and should correspondingly be judged in these terms.[40] In contemporary bureaucratic establishments only the lower level, doing a more or less repetitive, partly mechanical job, finds both work routine and assignment externally determined, with a minimum of its own control over rhythm and conditions of work; for many jobs this involves difficulties even in asking for reassignment. In contrast, the executive groups, whether public or private, find their assignments rely much less on explicit, formal rules than on traditions and goals of their organization. The more important their place in the organization, the more intimate their knowledge of its ways, and the more strategic their role in the system of intra- and interorganizational coteries and alliances, the better their chance to evaluate the force and speed of outside demands on the organization and of the ways and means to cope with them. None of the higher executives could adequately perform his job or reach some measure of personal security if he did not try to become as conversant as possible with the action patterns of related and superior organizations which could harm his own setup. If the whole political regime changes, he might flatter himself for a time on his ability to safeguard the integrity of his own organization while outwardly going along with policies which he knows to be unacceptable by the standards of human decency. But in every case there will come a point when the illusion that one's own influence can arrest more general developments will be dis-

[39] See, for example, Pierre Boissier, *l'Epée et la Balance*, Geneva, 1952, esp. pp. 89, 140; Jean Pierre Maunoir, *La Répression des Crimes de Guerre devant les Tribunaux Français et Alliés*, Geneva, 1956, with interesting material on the possible effect of the 1949 Geneva Red Cross Convention on Korean war practices.

[40] There is an instructive German discussion in Beilage zu Des Parlament, July 17, 1957, on "The Criminal Order," dealing with the legal implications of and the attitudes toward the so-called "Commissar Befehl" by high level German officers; see esp. the comments of the prosecutor Hölper (p. 438), emphasizing the relation between command position and degree of knowledge, and of Freiherr von Gersdorf, which relates a commanding general's reaction when asked to participate in a common protest to Hitler against the illegality of the "Kommissar Befehl": "If I do that, Hitler will send you Himmler as commanding general" (p. 439). (He visualizes Hitler's retaliatory action in terms of his replacement, not his punishment!)

pelled. At this moment there arises the conflict of open resistance or silent withdrawal. No successor regime can legitimately judge the elite of its predecessor according to its willingness to engage in active resistance. Active resistance will always remain a highly personal decision. However justified resistance might be, to whatever degree constitutional settlements may make a show of recognizing the right to resist oppression, any existent regime will consider resistance a sacrilege. Its justifiability will only be vindicated in the courts and market places of a strong successor regime.

If active resistance to the oppressor is therefore an illusory yardstick, withdrawal from significant participation in public life of the defunct regime, industrial command posts included, is a legitimate yardstick. It could be otherwise only if the individual in question established proof that such withdrawal would have been tantamount to a serious threat to his life. A large body of experience teaches us that many men show a fatal proclivity toward pushing themselves, or allowing themselves to be pushed, into positions where they know in advance the honors and rewards will entail corresponding entanglement and responsibility.[41] But vague assertions to the contrary,[42] it is much less certain that incumbents who under some pretext did drop out incurred major risks. Only when a regime is nearing its final agony will last-minute deserters be uniformly treated without mercy by those whom they desert and those whom they seek out. Otherwise, terroristic regimes will discount the value of those who vacillate and will ridicule the scruples of those too weak to serve. Too irresolute either to resist or to serve, they may, from the viewpoint of the regime, just as well withdraw into obscurity.

[41] The recent book by Herbert Schorn, *Der Richter im Dritten Reich*, would confirm this position. Its comments on p. 114 demonstrate (a) that with enough perseverance it was possible for a judge to have a nomination to a "special court" withdrawn under some pretext; and (b) that there were enough judges available who thought it would enhance their career prospects to work on the bench of a "special court" that was handling cases in which the regime took a special interest. There is a conclusion that Schorn refrains from drawing: a silent strike of the profession, with its great majority refusing to serve on such courts, would have embarrassed the regime, lowering its prestige with the population at large.

[42] Knieriem, *op.cit.*, p. 263; but see Donnedieu de Vabres, *op.cit.* (n. 22 above), p. 570. The state of necessity pleas have been dealt with at various times in the decisions of American military tribunals in Nuremberg. The plea has been rejected —in somewhat extreme terms—in the Krupp judgment (German trial record, pp. 13,396-97); here as well as in others, among them the so-called Wilhelmstrasse judgment, the rejection of the plea rested on the absence of proof of an imminent danger to life and limb; Wilhelmstrasse trial record, p. 27,468. In contrast, the court in the Flick case (trial record, p. 10,736), without going into any details, has accepted the plea in regard to three of the defendants.

But for exactly the same reason—a modicum of danger to their personal security—willingness to disappear into oblivion is a standard which may be rightfully imposed by those sitting in judgment over the elite personnel of a regime which, during its course, gave rise to many practices constituting crimes against the human condition.[43]

III. The Prejudicial Court. The last two arguments are of a wider nature, and while they were utilized by the critics of Nuremberg for all they were worth, they could be leveled with equal force against all political trials, and especially against all trials by successor regimes. The third argument concerns the partisan quality of the court. It has been asserted very often that the judges in Nuremberg were the judges of the victors. It is alleged that the defendants should have been tried either before a tribunal composed from the ranks of victor, neutral, and German judges or, still better, before an exclusively German tribunal. The latter, it is said, would have guaranteed the application of familiar German substantive and especially procedural rules, rather than the hodgepodge of retroactively applied foreign *ad hoc* substantive law and the mostly Anglo-American procedure to which the defendants and their German lawyers saw themselves exposed.

As to the court of the victor argument, the rebuttal is simple and unavoidable. It goes straight to the very nature of political trials. In all political trials conducted by the judges of the successor regime, the judges are in a certain sense the victor's judges. Whether their jurisdictions have been newly formed, or whether they have been confirmed, with whatever modifications, by the victors, they will be working on the basis and within the framework of the legal organization created by the political system of the victor. In a somewhat wider sense, all judges, not only those of a successor regime, are working under the conditions of the existing legal and political system which they are dutybound to uphold. Could John Lilburne decline the judges of Charles I or of the Long Parliament; could Gracchus Babeuf make his rejection of the Haute Cour of the Directoire stick; General Mallet refuse to have truck with Napoleon's military commission; or did Daladier and Léon Blum and three years later Pétain have more luck with their attempts to contest the jurisdiction of the various high courts installed by the respective regimes of the day?[44]

---

[43] See also Appendix B. Guillaume du Vair: The Case of a Successful Loyalty Shift.

[44] A recent incident sharply illuminates the extent to which jurisdictional complaints are now considered a necessary property of any major political trial. At the very opening stage, when public attention is greatest, these complaints give the trial an air of legal finesse and propriety without ever putting the regime that is staging the

In the London discussion on organizational form, law, and procedure of the future International Military Tribunal, there were apparently two theses on the function of the judges and the character of the future trials. With a realistic appreciation of the historical role of the forthcoming trial, but with a lack of subtlety quite understandable against the background of the political trial formulas of the Stalin period, General Nikitschenko, the USSR representative, emphasized that the speedy procedure he wanted adopted should guarantee the execution of the decisions regarding the chief war criminals; these decisions, which he called "convictions," had been previously announced by the heads of the Allied establishments.[45] Justice Jackson thereupon took to underline the traditional Western position on the distinction between the executive power to set up a tribunal and organize the prosecution, and the independent role of the trial judges evaluating the evidence presented to them.[46] Both the cynical realism of the USSR representative and the apparent traditionalism of Justice Jackson overstate their respective cases.

---

trial in any untoward danger. The rejection of the jurisdictional objection is a foregone conclusion.

In April 1960, *in absentia* proceedings opened before the High Court of the DDR against the West German Minister of Expellee Affairs Theodor Oberländer, for his participation in war crimes. The DDR court provided two defense lawyers, including the chairman of the East Berlin Lawyers' Cooperative, and the defendant himself took no notice of the proceedings. The lawyers preferred written objections against the jurisdiction of the DDR court. These were rejected, with great learning, by a professorial member of the bench (*Neues Deutschland*, April 21, 1960). Thereafter, the prosecution began to produce experts and witnesses from the DDR and other eastern states, connecting Oberländer with the elaboration of war crimes policy. Local inhabitants, too, identified the defendant as having been personally present at and in command of the commission of atrocities. The trial reporting does not mention any attempt by the official lawyers to question the story of the identifying witnesses, even leaving a perfunctory "Are you certain?" kind of query to the president. (See the testimony of the witnesses Kuchar and Hübner in *Neues Deutschland*, April 23 and 24, 1960.)

Jurisdictional objections give the performance the atmosphere of a trial; otherwise, the scenario is arranged to cast as few doubts as possible on the perfection of the propaganda image to be produced by the trial. Analysis of the judgment, distributed as a supplement to *N.J.*, Vol. 14 (May 20, 1960), No. 10, would confirm this impression. An almost simultaneous preliminary investigation of the Bonn district attorney's office, based on the testimony of witnesses located in Western lands, led to a *nol pros* fully rehabilitating Oberländer in regard to his alleged participation in atrocities. In neither of the two proceedings was there an opportunity for the two sets of witnesses, from East and West, to confront each other. But the rulers of the DDR were at a tactical advantage: they had proposed a joint investigation which, as they knew beforehand, the Federal Republic would be unwilling to accept.

[45] *International Conference on Military Trials*, pp. 104-05.

[46] *Ibid.*, pp. 113, 115.

Occurring in the wake of a National Socialist defeat, the trial could not but take the defeat of National Socialist doctrine and practice as its starting point. But in the Western mind this self-evident fact did not exclude judicial freedom of appreciation of the role of the individual German leaders. This fact was expressed, among others, against the protest of the USSR member of the court, in the acquittal of three of the defendants in the proceedings before the IMT. The antithesis between *judicial tribunal* and *manifestation of power*, which pervades part of the war crimes discussion and also finds its way into some of the judicial opinion on the war crimes issue,[47] therefore misses the point. The appointment procedure and the nature and genesis of applicable texts do not in themselves decide the character of proceedings. When determining the type of credit and rating given to a successor trial, one must take equal account of the method of examining and evaluating submitted facts, for it reflects the tribunal's amount of independence from momentary outside pressures.

The IMT had been mandated to follow up the political eradication of National Socialism and the general revulsion from its inhumanity by a search into individual responsibility for National Socialist policy and action patterns. To this extent, the addition of judges from neutral nations, while psychologically possibly useful, would have created great inconvenience for Allies and neutrals alike. It would have forced these nations to underwrite the Allied policy on which the trial rested; and it would have made a semblance of unified conduct of the trial by prosecution and court, which was difficult enough, almost impossible. In essence it would have meant the anticipation of a world penal court which, despite all projects in this direction, has, in the absence of a unified world community, never been established. The proceedings before the Eastern War Crimes Tribunal have grown no less objectionable

---

[47] See the Indian judge Pal's dissenting opinion, which uses this point as one of his main arguments to brand the proceedings before the International Military Tribunal for the East as outside the province of genuine legal proceedings. *International Military Tribunal for the East*, dissident judgment of R. B. Pal, Calcutta, 1953. Justice Douglas, in his concurring opinion in Koki Hirota, Pet. v. General of the Army Douglas MacArthur et al., 330 U.S. 197, 205 (1948), turns the same argument into grounds for rejecting Supreme Court review of the proceedings of the Eastern IMT. "It took its law from its creator and did not act as a free and independent tribunal to adjudge the rights of petitioners under international law." Douglas compares the American president's political decision made in conjunction with America's allies on how to treat the enemy leaders with the 1815 decision to banish Napoleon to Elba. However, the fact that similar proceedings could have been applied to the Japanese leaders by executive fiat does not control what standard and criteria should apply once an irrevocable decision in favor of a trial has been made.

by the Indian judge Pal's being given the opportunity to pen to them his fulminant dissent of principle.[48] Whatever its legal shortcomings, the charter that established the function of the IMT expressed the objective necessities of a political situation which in this case—possibly a rare but salutary coincidence—happened to conform with the moral consciousness of humanity at large.

To say that a German court, dealing with the defendants under German law, would have been more appropriate is more than an argument to impugn the fairness of the trial in technical terms; it wants to convey the opinion that an indigenous German trial would have been able to provide a greater amount of "objectivity." The reverse would be nearer the truth. The victorious Allies could be nothing but inimical to the National Socialist system as a whole. However, the cases of the individual defendants were for the judges nothing but news items. They had little, if any, relation to the judge's own life experience, and this guaranteed a maximum of fairness in the weighing of the individual charges. Unlike the German proceedings against German officers indicted for war crimes after World War I, which took place before the unregenerated bench of the Leipzig Supreme Court, a German successor trial in the second half of the forties would have taken place before German judges and with German prosecutors from the ranks of those untainted by service under the National Socialist regime; it might also have included both domestic foes and victims of Nazism. It is quite possible that such a trial would have covered different territory and have led to a closer and more vivid understanding of the action patterns of the defendants. From the viewpoint of the defendants, this might not have been an advantage. Equipped with the weapons of continental criminal procedure, the court would have concentrated the conduct of the trial in its own hands, rather than presiding impartially over a time-consuming contest between a great variety of prosecutors and defense lawyers. Without need to engage in prolonged wrangling over the admissibility of evidence according to rules originating in the practice of jury trials, and without need of cumbersome translations, it would have judged the documentary evidence against the background of its own knowledge, understanding, and experience of National Socialist policies and procedure. A German court if left its freedom would naturally have shown less interest in one of the most problematic aspects of the various Nuremberg trials: the definition of the

---

[48] The manifold and quite substantial objections to the proceedings of the Eastern IMT are discussed in J. A. Appleman, *Military Tribunals and International Crime*, Indianapolis, 1954, Ch. 38.

boundary lines of the rules of warfare under actual combat conditions. Instead of discussing crimes against peace, it would have concentrated on some of the domestic aspects of the regime, specifically omitted from consideration by the IMT. Whether the judgments and sentences of German courts would have evoked a more positive response from the German citizenry and thus helped the population to come to a sharper and less opportunistic appreciation of their immediate past; whether it would have led to a more rational pattern of dealing with a great variety of offenders against the concept of the human condition, and avoided the spotty, lottery-type trials now taking place over much too long a period of time before the regular German courts—this is another question.[49] But the claim that the juridical liquidation of the National Socialist heritage by the foreign "victors-successors" was less dispassionate than corresponding proceedings before indigenous German jurisdictions would have been in 1946 and 1947 is, to put it mildly, hard to believe.

IV. Tu Quoque. Successor justice is both retrospective and prospective. In laying bare the roots of iniquity in the previous regime's conduct, it simultaneously seizes the opportunity to convert the trial into a cornerstone of the new order. Against the inherent assertion of moral superiority, of the radical difference between the contemptible doings of those in the dock and the visions, intentions, and record of the new master, the defendants will resort to *tu quoque* tactics.

This fourth and last argument raises the objection that the new regime is guilty of the same practices with which it now tries to besmirch its predecessor's record. It is advanced as an estoppel against the victor's attempt to call into question the lawfulness of acts by the defendants. It was anticipated in the discussions of the London War Crimes Commission,[50] and it formed a weapon which the Nuremberg defense frequently tried to use and to which later critics returned frequently and invariably when assailing the Soviet Union's participation in the Nuremberg proceedings.

[49] Only in 1958 did the various judicial administrations of individual German states agree to put up a joint office which is systematically collecting information on and coordinating investigations of people suspect of participation in various forms of atrocities. Yet from May 1960 on, prosecutions for anything but first-degree murder have been excluded through the operation of the statute of limitations. Parliamentary attempts to defer the statute's coming into effect have been justifiedly defeated. German authorities had a full decade to get busy, and, official assertions to the contrary, could have undertaken many more prosecutions than they managed to do. At best, uncertain shifts in public appreciation are not a good enough reason to withdraw from anybody the benefits of the statute of limitations.

[50] *International Conference*, pp. 102, 304-06.

In a wider sense, the *tu quoque* argument could be leveled against any type of terrestrial justice. Only the archangel descending on judgment day would be exempt from the reproach that blame and praise have not been distributed according to everyone's due desert. Only a dispenser of justice who is fortunate enough to preside over the ordering of property relations in a society which has solved its problems of economic organization and has satisfied the status and psychological problems of its members would be justified to hold court over offenses against property relations. In matters politic, only a state organization which never applied coercion and foul methods to keep itself in power could bring its foes to justice for unsuccessful attempts to gain power by the same methods. Seneca's query of how many prosecutors would escape conviction under the same law they are invoking expresses an elementary fact of life.[51] The *tu quoque* proposition in political trials, therefore, implies more an argument addressed to the public at large and the future historian than a legal defense.[52] In asserting that an accident of history rather than an inherent quality of those who govern determines who should sit in judgment and who should be the defendant, it tries from the outset to devaluate the meaning and import of the judgment.

But *tu quoque* can become a legally pertinent objection only if it is built up enough to indicate the lack of universally agreed norms. It cannot simply show what is usual, that the prosecution has not shown the same zeal against violators of a universally acknowledged norm in its own ranks.[53] Whether the legal claims of the new order will ever be converted into moral claims, with present power holders being able and willing to live up to their own new order concept, is a question only posterity will answer. A judge who is more than a technician translating prevailing trends into formal community evaluations will strive, at least in his sentencing practice, to weigh the known, presumed, and ex-

---

[51] *De Clementia*, i, 7.

[52] A recent attempt to invoke *tu quoque* occurred before a Paris military court, when the lawyers tried to relate the attempts of their NFL Algerian clients to assassinate Soustelle to French depredations in Algeria for which they made him responsible. *Le Monde*, February 7, 1959.

[53] It has been asserted that while the appeal to *tu quoque* has no place in municipal criminal law, the situation should be different in international criminal law. Under municipal law, it is argued, any person may register grievances to the authorities, which the latter are dutybound to follow up. Thus anyone could function as initiator of criminal proceedings. Such possibilities of redress would be lacking in international criminal law; see Jeschek, *op.cit.*, p. 277. This argument would be valid only if the legality principle were everywhere observed; moreover, it shows a somewhat mechanical faith in the operation of the administration of justice.

pected sins of commission and omission of his own side against the depredation of those whom the course of events has brought before him. But it would be foolish for a defendant to rely on what might at the very best be an unusual coincidence, the presence of a sensitive and fearless judge.

As to *tu quoque* in the trial before the Nuremberg IMT: both in its acquittals and gradation of punishment—which were by no means only mechanically related to the number of counts under which the defendants were found guilty—the court made an attempt to differentiate between the various incriminating fact situations. Of those misdeeds which we call offenses against the human condition, no comparable practices of any state of the world, whether represented on the bench or not, could serve in exculpation or mitigation, even if the court had allowed greater latitude in introducing proof of such misdeeds by victor nations. In cases where the *tu quoque* argument was salient and strong enough to raise doubts about the existence of a well-established body of law, as happened in regard to unlimited submarine warfare, the court disregarded the respective incriminations.[54] But in cases concerning the participation of the USSR in acts of aggression or their utilization of prisoners of war in danger zones, the court rejected the argument at hand. Obviously, the more nearly identical the asserted practices were with those which the court was asked to judge, the less moral ground the court's rejection had.[55]

C. THE QUALITY OF A COURT

The Nuremberg trial had its own peculiar dialectics. It constituted an attempt to enforce on a multinational basis criminal responsibility for political action whose implementation involved crimes against the human condition. The criminal action may have been planned from the outset as integral to the political planning, as in the liquidation of Jewry. Or it may have been improvised as the most efficient or least burdensome way to carry through the military and political program, as in the murdering and starving to death of millions of PWs. As the case was unprecedented, so was the pattern of the four-state prosecution, the criminal procedure, and the criminal law fashioned for the purpose by the statute elaborated at the London International Conference and by the Nuremberg court. Therefore, when compared with any homegrown

---

[54] See, for example, the motivation of the Doenitz sentence, *IMT*, Vol. 22, pp. 556, 559, and the Raeder sentence, Vol. 22, p. 561.

[55] A sweeping statement of the court rejecting the *tu quoque* argument may be found in *IMT*, Vol. 13, p. 521.

variety of law and procedure, the case will show any number of anomalies. If these anomalies are stated cumulatively, the proceedings might give the impression of gross irregularity, allowing the trial itself to be put on trial. What would then remain but a kind of morality play which, being refuted immediately thereafter by the course of history, would have nothing to teach? What is the answer?

Recent experience has familiarized us with enough proceedings which do not merit the name of trial to establish the difference between a trial—even though it may have the particular features of a political trial—and an action which for propaganda purposes is called a trial but partakes more of the nature of a spectacle with prearranged results. A trial presupposes an element of irreducible risk for those involved. It derives from the judge's or jury's freedom and their preparedness to evaluate the unfolding of both the official and the defendant's story in the light of a conduct norm. Of this norm the defendants are by and large aware. The judge who mortgages his freedom in advance, whether out of fear or out of subservience, does not, as both German and French courts had occasion to insist, want to act as judge. "Who does not want to render justice cannot invoke the fact that he has observed the trappings of the law, because his fundamental attitude makes it evident that this was only an act of simulation."[56] A judge who is willing to assume the function of a presiding judge—after having assured the minister of justice pushing the proceedings that he can count on him—and sentences defendants to death on the basis of retroactively raised punishment (which the authorizing decree inserted into the law gazette in such a way as to mask its retroactive character) does not partake in the administration of justice.[57] As another example: a court-martial, composed of members handpicked for the case by the secretary general in charge of public order and meeting in the prison director's office, which, in the absence of any defense lawyers, sentences to death 28 defendants within four hours for participation in a prison riot "cannot be considered to have rendered a judicial decision."[58]

Even in the administration of injustice, however, there are gradations. In the courts-martial of the Vichy militia and the people's tribunals of the first liberation days, enemies, whose fate had been settled in advance, were butchered. The liberation type of cour de justice, with all its

[56] Bundesgerichtshof, Entscheidungen in Strafsachen, Vol. 10 (1957), pp. 295, 301.

[57] This incident of summer 1941 is narrated in detail in Robert Aron, *Histoire de Vichy*, Paris, 1954, p. 416. For a feeble attempt by one of the main participants to explain away his role in the case, see *France Under the German Occupation*, Stanford, 1959, Vol. 2, p. 595.

[58] *Cour de Cassation*, 1948, No. 133, p. 199.

prejudices, allowed for some primitive rights of defense.[59] Finally, there is the marginal case of an elaborate military commission set up by the United States for the trial of Japanese foes. The commission held months of formal hearings; the lingering doubts pertained mainly to the ways of handling evidence and to the question of the commission's *de facto* independence of the commander in chief.[60] In each case the tribunal sought the mechanical certainty of the result while trying to partake—illegitimately—in the creative suspense of a result which can legitimately originate only in the unfolding of the trial itself.

Viewed in this light, the Nuremberg trial before the IMT was not a simulated trial. If there was some measure of retroactive law applied, not only were the defendants, while acting, fully aware of the possible consequences of their action, but, as pointed out previously, their sentences could be explained without resort to the retroactive features. The jurisdictional problems of the trial, if compounded by the multinational character of the prosecution, were not particular to this trial. They are, as shown, common to political trials and inevitably connected with trials by successor regimes. As in all such trials, the general frame, though not the decisions reached for the individual defendants, was set by the political and military context in which the trial took place: to confirm the defeat of Hitlerism. Whatever pressure there was, was of the situation rather than of an organized group determined to have its way. It was no organized Montagne asking for the head of the king, no clamor of the street, as in Polignac's case. It was the language of the charnel houses, the millions who had lost their families, husbands, or homes. If isolation against this language was possible or even desirable for the calm of the judicial process, such calm was better guaranteed in the chambers of the Nuremberg Allied and American Temporary War Crimes bureaucracy than in the disoriented minds and bare courtrooms of the 1946 and 1947 Germans.

It has been shown how difficult it will be in the future to have recourse to violent political change on a state-transcending level without at the same time creating situations that lead to the very negation of

[59] For these gradations, see Robert Aron, *Histoire de la Libération de la France*, Paris, 1959, pp. 532ff.

[60] See the dissenting opinion of Justice Rutledge re Yamashita, 327 U.S. 48, 56 (1945), and Frank Reel, *The Case of General Yamashita*, Chicago, 1949, p. 162. In fairness to the commission, it must be pointed out that its judgment rested essentially on the defendant's responsibility for omitting supervision of the military forces under his command. The defense tried to show either that atrocities committed did not occur under the defendant's jurisdiction, or that he had had no power to prevent them. However, he submitted scarcely any affirmative proof that he had positively tried to prevent such occurrences.

the "human condition." And in wading through the evidence on mass annihilation and mass enslavement, those fact situations which we have since come to describe as genocide have established signs, imprecise as they might be, that the most atrocious offenses against the human condition lie beyond the pale of what may be considered contingent and fortuitous political action, judgment on which may change from regime to regime. The concrete condition under which the Nuremberg litigation arose and the too inclusive scope of the indictment may make it difficult for us to separate the circumstantial elements which it shares with all other successor trials[61] from its own lasting contribution: that it defined where the realm of politics ends or, rather, is transformed into the concerns of the human condition, the survival of mankind in both its universality and diversity. In spite of the Nuremberg trial's infirmities, the feeble beginning of transnational control of the crime against the human condition raises the Nuremberg judgment a notch above the level of political justice by fiat of a successor regime.

4. Trial Technique: Eternal Quest for Improvement

Of all the shortcomings of the Nuremberg proceedings, none has been more consistently attacked than the inequality which existed between prosecution and defense. This inequality was grounded in the procedural law applied. In the absence of a court—it was established only after the indictment—the whole trial preparation was left to a prosecution working in conformity with Anglo-American rather than continental practices. Continental prosecution, at least in theory, means that a state organ sifts impartially all available evidence. The Nuremberg prosecution aimed at convicting the defendants. Beyond this, it was impossible for the defendants to resort to counsel in the pretrial stage.

[61] Not only successor trials. Because of the division of Germany, the judges of one regime, the Federal Republic, may be sitting in judgment over the (fugitive) judges of the courts of the DDR. See the decision of the Bundesgerichtshof of January 28, 1959, reported in *Recht in Ost und West*, Vol. 2 (1958), p. 204. The fugitive DDR judge who presided over a trial of five Jehovah's Witnesses was prosecuted and convicted of having deflected the law to the disadvantage of a party (par. 336, Penal Code). The conviction was quashed, with emphasis resting on the question of whether the judge, while acting as he did, was convinced that the law he applied was binding. However, the court must have realized that this argument might open up more questions than it was then prepared to tackle. (The same argument could obviously have been used, and was used, to defend the record of NS judges; Max Güde, *Justiz im Schatten von Gestern* [cited above, Ch. I, n. 4].) Thus the argument adds a number of more concrete grievances against the lower court judgment, including the compulsion under which the judge may have acted.

The second disadvantage was a great factual inequality between prosecution and defense. Powerful, if not highly organized, the prosecution could roam around freely, collecting its material and marshaling its witnesses. The defense had meager resources and, due to prevailing conditions, restricted freedom of movement outside the courtroom. Though always in evidence, however, this inequality affected the outcome of the trial less than it might have. The prosecution's case rested less on oral testimony than on the production of documentary evidence taken from original German files. Thus there was little of the uphill battle of a defense exposed to partisan witnesses of the victorious side and unable to marshal effective enough testimony in rebuttal. The defense's problem was an intellectual one: to explain why the responsibility for whatever had happened did and could not rest with their clients. Despite multiple handicaps, the defense was equipped to handle the problem.

All this is well known. What is less well known is the extent to which these disadvantages contain risk elements inherent in all criminal trials, not only in this specific trial. The following pages, therefore, will try to show that a) the risk deriving from factual inequality in trial representation is one of the most doubtful features in Anglo-American trial practice, and that b) the European trial procedure, recommended by many of the critics of the Nuremberg trial, has, for quite different reasons, as strong a built-in aleatory element as the Anglo-American practice.

How does trial organization affect the outcome of the political trial? Anglo-American and continental trial organization rest on two radically different assumptions. The Anglo-American trial remains essentially at the disposal of the parties, while the continental trial revolves around the judge's own responsibility to search for the truth. Anglo-American adversary procedure organizes the trial as a battle of wits between the prosecution and defense, with the judge acting as their referee, constantly deciding what line of questioning and what material should be allowed to enter the minds of the jury. Yet the judge's authority in this respect may be more official than real: a skillful lawyer will be able to make his point before his adversary can open his mouth to object. The resulting wrangling on admissibility and the judge's ritual exhortation in summing up what points to disregard—for example, the political loyalties of the defendant in an espionage trial—only make the forbidden fruit more tempting to the jury than all the rest.[62]

[62] Judge Jerome Frank refers to such warnings as "an empty ritual," and infers that the only remedy is to waive a jury trial. United States v. Rosenberg, 195 F 2d (CCA 2d) 582, 596.

Anglo-American procedure takes this chance as part of a deep-seated conviction that from the endless flow and counterflow of argument, centering on the prosecution's attempt to make the indictment stick, with both defense and prosecution mercilessly searching into and exposing the weaknesses and inconsistencies of each other's position, the truth or falsity of the indictment will finally emerge. This method is at its best when a revealing flash illuminates the whole situation. Even if it languishes under the seemingly uncoordinated chaos of themes and materials, now picked up, now discarded, according to the whims and hunches of the lawyers, a jury might not miss such a flash, especially as the lawyers will endlessly amplify it and drive its impact home relentlessly while summing up. If neither party is blessed with such luck, the lawyers will have to rely on thumbing methodically through the material—an ungrateful job under the circumstances of adversary procedure—and either put together isolated parts into a composite picture or tear them asunder before they are firmly joined.

To yield satisfactory results, adversary procedure rests on the implied premise of a strictly maintained legal equality between the parties, on their parity in research, resources, and preparations, and above all on forensic skill and general level of intelligence. If the defense lawyer lacks these prerequisites, may parity be restored by the judge's intervention? Many authorities will answer unhesitatingly in the affirmative, upholding the judicial practice not only to put to the witness additional questions that are liable to clarify an issue, but also to call additional witnesses, even expert witnesses, if need be; the latter the judge may do on his own.[63] The proposition sounds excellent on paper, but how would it fit into the system of adversary proceedings?

To take a concrete example from recent political trial practice: in the Rosenberg trial the only witness to the open act, David Greenglass, contended that he had delivered drawings made from memory to Julius Rosenberg. The circumstances under which copies of such drawings were made by Greenglass, while under detention, became therefore

---

[63] This position is held most strongly by Wigmore, *On Evidence*, 3rd ed.; 1940, Vol. 3, par. 151, and Vol. 9, par. 2484. See also the opinion of Justice Frankfurter, dissenting in Johnson v. United States, 333 U.S. 46, 54 (1948): "Federal judges are not referees at prize fights but functionaries of justice"; and the note, "The Trial Judge's Views of his Power to Call Witnesses—an aid to adversary presentation," *Northwestern University Law Review*, Vol. 51 (1957), pp. 761-74. There is a particularly instructive discussion by Judge Charles Wyzanski, "Freedom of the Trial Judge," *Harvard Law Review*, Vol. 65 (1952), pp. 1281-1304. However, it should be especially noted that Judge Wyzanski gives two telling examples from his own trial practice (p. 1284), showing that in political libel cases "the judge is not the commander but merely the umpire."

vital for the evaluation of Greenglass's testimony. Mr. E. H. Bloch, Jr., the defendant's principal lawyer, did not call the prison officials to learn in somewhat greater detail how the copies of these blueprints originated. Did he just forget about the possibility? Not very likely. Or, given his pattern of submissiveness and exaggerated deference to the judge, only hiding with difficulty his marked feelings of insecurity, did he take a cue from the judge's remark that the charge related to the transfer of secret material rather than to its accuracy in detail?[64] In this case an insecure lawyer might well have become doubtful about the importance of the question. Or did he simply follow the instruction of his clients who did not expect to benefit from such testimony? The same would hold true for what might have been the equally vital testimony of an expert witness who had probed into how a person with David Greenglass's mediocre school record could develop the ability to produce such sketches from memory. Again, did Bloch never think of such a possibility? Did he or his clients have no resources for hiring such experts, or did his clients, again for good reasons of their own, not want to pursue this line?[65] Conceivably, the judge might have made good some of these omissions—if they were omissions, which obviously we do not know. But the judge in his own mind might have been quite satisfied with the degree of preciseness with which the FBI witness testified on the origin of the copy blueprints, and with the answers given by Greenglass when Bloch tried his hand in probing into his amount of technical knowledge.[66] Moreover, if, in this deeply politically tinged case, supplementary witnesses had provided further support for the allegation of the prosecution, it would have appeared as if the judge had taken it upon himself to tip the scales against Bloch's clients.[67]

[64] Transcript of record, Vol. 1, p. 613 (reprint by Sobell committee).

[65] John Wexley's ex parte work, *The Judgment of Julius and Ethel Rosenberg*, New York, 1955, reproaches Judge Kaufmann for preventing Bloch from asking the witness Derry the "all important" question (p. 430) relating to Greenglass's capacity to prepare a copy unaided. However, Bloch's question was rightly excluded, as the answer was not in the witness's province. But Wexley fails to enlighten his readers on why Bloch did not present his own expert probing into Greenglass's intellectual capacity, as, for example, the Hiss defense did in regard to the mental state of Chambers. Wexley states (p. 432) that "there was no time given the defense during trial to elicit expert opinion on the question." He adds as a footnote that it is highly doubtful that any American scientist would have risked his career in challenging the very essence of the government's case. The trial record shows no attempt by the defense either to call such an expert to the witness stand or to secure a recess to procure such an important witness after the defense must have recognized the importance of the issue from Greenglass's testimony.

[66] Transcript, Vol. 1, pp. 610, 611.

[67] See the comment of Judge Wyzanski, *op.cit.* (n. 63 above), and Bernard Botein,

The American judge's interference with the arrangement of testi-mony—at best an exception in proceedings at the disposal of and under the responsibility of the parties—is necessarily limited. Unlike British proceedings, the frame within which federal judges and most state judges may comment on the evidence in their summing up is rather narrow.[68] Thus if one follows the activist school, the judge would be able to take a decisive part in the trial but be unable to evaluate the meaning of his interference: a somewhat contradictory situation. More-over, one of the most fateful trial decisions, whether to put the de-fendant on the stand or not, must remain entirely outside his province. Judicial activism and adversary principle are not easily compatible. But the Rosenberg case, where a smoothly functioning prosecution, abundantly equipped with resources, manpower, intelligence, and self-confidence, confronted a struggling lawyer who had little confidence in his own ability, vividly illustrates the inherent limitations of the trial by combat principle. Just because the case as built up by the prosecution was logically consistent and might well have reflected rather clearly the actual sequence of happenings, at least as far as the Rosenbergs were concerned, the absence of a more powerfully presented defense was felt all the more.[69]

But what about the continental procedure? While under Anglo-American procedure the prosecution tries to establish proof of the con-tentions made in the indictment, with the defense trying to refute same, in continental European practice the act of accusation only offers the court a preliminary version of the historical happenings. It is the job of the court to find that reconstruction of the historical incident which will serve as an adequate basis for the verdict. In this job of reconstruc-tion the judge is not bound by the assertions and offerings of either party; rather, both prosecution and defense, although given a number of procedural prerogatives, among them to call witnesses and experts, remain auxiliaries of the court.[70] The court, sitting mostly with some lay

---

Trial Judge, New York, 1952, p. 104, who quotes the telling remark on the troubles of a judge taking over the questioning of a witness when confronted with an inexperienced lawyer: "Judge, I don't mind your trying the case for me, but for God's sake, don't lose it."

[68] The rules were laid down in Querica v. United States, 286 U.S. 466 (1933).

[69] For an incisive comment on the potential consequences of inequality in representa-tion, see Joseph B. Warner, "The Responsibilities of the Lawyer" (*op.cit.*, Ch. VI, n. 31), p. 326. For an example of the dominating influence of an insufficient defense, see G. Louis Joughin and Edmund M. Morgan, *The Legacy of Sacco and Vanzetti*, New York, 1948, Ch. III.

[70] See the discussion in Ursula Westhoff, *Über die Grundlagen des Strafprozesses*

assessors, does not have to face the problem of keeping a jury both instructed and protected against possible prejudicial knowledge. Consequently, it will be both willing and able to admit almost any evidence liable to throw light on the incident under discussion. But it is the court which will direct the taking of the evidence toward as coherent a picture as possible. Proceedings will first concentrate on interrogation of the defendant who, as he does not testify as a witness, may answer as he sees fit. The witnesses, too, will be questioned by the judge, with the parties as a rule expected to ask them questions through him. It goes without saying that in proceedings dominated by the judge, he can call supplementary witnesses and appoint experts of his own in pursuance of his search for the objective truth.

But this concentration of power in the hands of the judge, somehow uniting in his person the functions of prosecutor, defense lawyer, and truthfinder, has a built-in shortcoming. To be able to direct the proceedings with authority and efficiency and to concentrate the hearings from the outset on the relevant points, rather than to listen to whatever the parties see fit to submit, the judge will have to be fully informed about all that has transpired at the pretrial stage. Unless a pretrial motion has by chance come his way, the Anglo-American judge enters the courtroom with his mind a *tabula rasa*. The continental judge, though, will have made a painstaking study of the whole file of the case transmitted to him by the prosecutor. It will contain everything which has transpired so far, including police reports, pretrial depositions of defendants and witnesses, and defense motions to the criminal record of the defendant. As he has perforce formed some opinion on the case, his is the temptation to make reality conform to the file.[71] Unlike his Anglo-American colleague, he might well go on questioning and calling witnesses until he arrives at what seems to him the most meaningful reconstruction of reality. But he may in point of fact be satisfied with much less: with the facile confirmation of what his blue and red pencils have previously underlined in the file as his understanding of the

---

mit besonderer Berücksichtigung des Beweisrechts, Berlin, 1955, esp. pp. 62 and 173; see also Binding, *Strafrechtliche und Strafprozessuale Abhandlungen*, pp. 190-201. Art. 166, II, of the new French Code of Criminal Procedure, establishes the rule that if, in the opinion of the court, an expert opinion becomes necessary, two experts should be immediately appointed by the bench. They would be asked to furnish a joint report or, if necessary, to discuss explicitly the reasons why they have arrived at different conclusions from one another.

[71] See F. Hartung (former judge of the Leipzig Supreme Court), "Einführung des Amerikanischen Strafverfahrensrechts in Deutschland?" in *Festschrift fur Rosenfeld*, Berlin, 1949; and Maurice Garcon, *op.cit.*, Vol. III, p. 26.

relevant facts. Again, this is an extreme. Witnesses, defense counsel, and prosecutor will have the opportunity to mark their points, possibly counteracting the judge's first hypothesis. Both the judge-official who enters the trial with strong preconceptions about the "Gestalt" of his case and the judge-arbitrator who settles for making a go of what parties, often unevenly represented, may have to offer[72] face an equally stiff uphill fight, if they want to arrive at the best possible result.

[72] Hermine M. Meyer, "German Criminal Procedure," *American Bar Association Journal*, Vol. 41 (1955), pp. 592-94, emphasizes the precarious position of the American defendant who depends on the skill of his lawyers. The author also shows the much stronger legal position of the lawyer in European pretrial investigations. The inferior position of the defendant in the American pretrial stage has only recently become the subject of systematic and searching study: A. S. Goldstein, "The State and the Accused: Balance of Advantage in Criminal Procedure," *Yale Law Journal*, Vol. 69 (1960), pp. 1149-99; pp. 1163 and 1182-83 are especially relevant to our discussion.

PART THREE

Political Justice Modified:
Asylum and Clemency

After an analysis of the action patterns of political justice, a discussion of devices for their frustration is in order. The more problematic the character of political justice, the more intensive the interest in institutionalized ways of escaping and mitigating its impact. Both asylum and clemency countermand the course of political justice. The asylum seeker takes himself out of a presumably hostile zone of jurisdiction; he seeks admission into an area where the political rulers' disposition to him is, until further notice, conjectural. It is the accident of diversity, the various interest constellations of the asylum state, which may frustrate the course of political justice. Clemency rests either on the political operator's insight into the character of his own past action, or on his expectation of the possible future benefits of modifying that action.

Often we can only guess what the cause-effect relation is between asylum or clemency grant or refusal and the attitudes of rulers and public in third countries; we can only guess about the future behavior of beneficiaries and more general aspects of domestic policy. Further, there are the unconscious, semi-conscious, and conscious urges for reinsurance in the face of many future uncertainties whose weight might be difficult to assess. And, too, there is the famous sense of justice: the ability of power holders to detach themselves from the pressures and necessities of the moment and look at human affairs with greater serenity. This sense may hover more distinctly over the whole complex than our search for rational determinants of action might let us admit.

Even so, the search for rational elements in the asylum and clemency practice may not be fruitless. Some amount of successful juridification, especially in the extradition field, has not changed much in the basic and intimate relation of asylum and clemency to the political objectives of power holders. Recent rapid shifts in political constellations and usages are therefore bound to be rather quickly translated into corresponding modifications of asylum and clemency patterns. What do such changes mean for the approaches of the decision makers and for the fate of those on whom the decisions are operating? How do these changes intermesh with time-honored practices and traditional principles? And how do they relate to the irreducible remainder beyond rational determination? These questions will now be taken up.

CHAPTER IX

ASYLUM

++

1. Mass Influx of Fugitives

AFTER the conquest of Sardes, Cyrus placed Pactyas, a native, in a position of trust in the occupied city. No sooner was Cyrus gone than Pactyas organized a revolt against the new regime. When he learned that Cyrus' troops were on the march to quell the insurrection, he fled in terror to Cyme. Cyrus' military governor demanded the rebel's surrender by penalty of the city's destruction. The oracle of the Branchidae, where the Cymeans sought to learn the will of the gods, advised extradition, and the city made ready to abide by the decision. But one Aristodicus, a citizen of distinction, balked, successfully; a second mission was dispatched to seek out the oracle. The oracle stood pat. Thereupon Aristodicus, who was one of the envoys, circled the temple, removing all birds' nests within reach. The oracle's voice interceded for the birds, bidding Aristodicus to state his case. Are you in haste, he asked, to protect suppliants while you command the Cymeans to give one up? Said the voice: "Verily, I did so order the Cymeans that they may perish the sooner for their impiety nor ever return to seek my oracle's counsel on the surrender of suppliants." So informed, the Cymeans dared to face neither the ire of the gods nor a siege by the Medes. They chose, in fact, to evade the issue and sent Pactyas to the men of Mytilene. The latter, however, took up negotiations with the Medes to discuss extradition. To avoid the threat, the Cymeans then took Pactyas to Lesbos. But the Lesbians sold him to his enemies for a strip of land on the Asian coast, dragged him out of the temple of Minerva where he had sought refuge, and turned him over to the pursuers. And yet for a long while they dared not use the crops from the new colony for sacrificial or other religious purposes.[1]

Since Herodotus narrated this tale from Asia Minor, political asylum has remained a perplexing subject. The menace created by the right course of action may not always be as tangible; present-day instances add fuel without necessarily striking the match. Yet to pursue the right course in the din of propaganda and ideological clashes may be as difficult today as it was then. The oracle of our day, the legal formula,

[1] From Herodotus, *History* Book One, secs. 153-60.

351

needs molding by the dictates of the conscience of a rare Aristodicus no less than did that of the servitors of Apollo.

Situated at the crossroads of national and international law, compassion and self-interest, *raison d'état* and human capacity for shame, the institution of asylum has gained importance with the shrinking of global distances. Governments and movements steeped in violence, or at least susceptible to it, have multiplied. They tend more and more to shape their political and social systems with a minimum of interference from the human material with which they deal. Resolutions passed by international lawyers' meetings,[2] codification proposals, and, most recently, bills of rights on the national and international levels,[3] even when supplemented by a few international agreements,[4] have a lesser bearing on the asylum problem than attitudes of political regimes and the change, due to power shifts, in composition of the body of supplicants.

The prototype of the asylum seeker in the twentieth century differs from that of the nineteenth century. The exile then was a rebel: a Mazzini or a Marx, a Herzen or a Bakunin. Whenever exiles appeared in larger numbers, they were survivors of revolutionary battles, like the men of 1848 or the participants of the Paris Commune. With the pen, the revolver, or in armed campaigns, all had dared to defy the established powers. Assurances to the contrary notwithstanding, many, especially those who failed to reach the shores of the Americas, never stopped fighting their respective home governments.[5]

---

[2] See, for example, the wide-range legal discussion at the Bath session of the Institute of International Law; account in Annuaire de l'Institut de Droit International, Vol. 43 (1950), Part II, pp. 198-255.

[3] See Article 14 of the Universal Declaration of Human Rights. Circumspect reference is made to "the right to seek and enjoy in other countries asylum from persecution."

[4] The Geneva Convention of July 25, 1951 (see below, p. 363) may serve as an example. Cf. comment by P. Weiss, "Legal Aspects of the Convention of July 25, 1951, Relating to the Status of Refugees," *British Year-Book of International Law*, Vol. 30 (1953), pp. 478ff.

The multinational European Convention on Extradition, signed by eleven members of the Council of Europe on December 13, 1957, and in force, as of 1960, among Norway, Ireland, and Turkey, tries to define both political offenses excluded from its scope and those that fall under its purview. But the convention is purely permissive in defining the conditions under which a state may, but need not, refuse extradition for a political offense. For a criticism of the convention, see F. Honig, "Extradition by Multilateral Convention," *International and Comparative Law Quarterly*, Vol. 5 (1956), pp. 549, 557.

[5] It is sometimes said that abstention from political activity by the asylum seeker is a prerequisite of the asylum grant. This has recently been restated by Prime Minister Nehru in regard to the Dalai Lama. Nehru remarked that the Dalai Lama, while in exile in India, would be free to carry on his "legitimate religious activities";

A steady trickle of such rebels continues down to the present day. On the building that sheltered Lenin in Zurich, a plaque commemorates the exile's sojourn. But in our day his associate Trotsky had ample reason to speak of a "planet without a visa,"[6] when describing his last search for an asylum outside the range of his country's rulers. The politically persecuted still roam the globe, and escapees from Fascist countries sometimes rub shoulders with non-Communist fugitives from totalitarian Communism, with Communists escaping anti-Communist persecution campaigns in countries of traditional freedom, and, more rarely in the 1950's, with totalitarian rulers à la Peron fleeing prosecution by less totalitarian successors.

But while political opponents must still seek refuge abroad from persecution by many governments, the fate of political exiles proper is frequently determined against a background much different from the one predominating in the nineteenth century. The global extent of World War I, with the ensuing radical redrawing of the political map and the far-reaching social upheavals in subsequent decades, gave rise to both chaotic flight and deliberate exodus of entire social or ethnic groups; the numbers of fugitives—men, women, children—soared up to six and seven digit figures.[7] While this collective escape was undoubtedly caused by political events, only a small number of the asylum seekers were individuals involved in political activity and dedicated to unending political battle against the regimes they fled. This confronted the countries of asylum with major social and administrative problems and complicated the pertinent issues of legality and justice. The Armenian survivor of Turkish massacres, the Russian "bourgeois" of the 1920's, the conscript soldier of the anti-Soviet "White" armies, the Eu-

---

but "political activities are not carried on from one country to another." See *Washington Post and Times-Herald*, April 21, 1959, p. A4. Aside from the fact that it might not always be easy to differentiate between "legitimate" religous and "illegitimate" political activity, the extent to which the asylum country might want to enforce such a policy by threat of expulsion depends on its own interest configuration, which shifts from country to country and from period to period. To the extent that the United States in the late forties and fifties only admitted asylum seekers who were not inimical to major United States policies, as distinct from being opposed to some facet of periodical tactical shifts toward Caribbean or South American regimes, the problem does not presently emerge in an acute form. (See also below, p. 360.)

[6] Leon Trotsky, *My Life*, New York, 1930, Ch. 45.

[7] Jacques Vernant, *The Refugee in the Post-War World*, London, 1953. And, more recently, H. Rogge, "Das Flüchtlingsproblem als internationale Rechtsfrage," *Internationales Recht und Diplomatie*, Vol. 1 (1958), pp. 28, 109, 236, attempting a typology of recent mass migrations.

ropean Jew in Hitler's Europe, the Spanish conscript who fought on the loyalist side in the civil war, the member of an ethnic minority proscribed in the USSR in World War II—all these exiles ran from the threat of being penalized for what they were, not for what they had done, were doing, or intended to do. Their appearance gave the word asylum a new connotation and led the authorities of the countries of refuge to put a different construction upon it.

The nineteenth century rebel's demand for asylum raised political problems. The attitude of the country of origin had first to be considered. Would it make trouble? Was it safer to reject the supplicant's demand, deport, or even surrender him to his enemies? Would it be too costly to affirm the right of asylum? Or would standing on the principle not only enhance the host country's domestic or international authority but also give it better leverage in dealing with the country that demanded the rebel's removal? Weighing and reconciling these elements was a matter of politics. At the lower level it was a police problem necessitating surveillance or special devices to check the fugitives' "harmful" influence on domestic groups. There was no administrative or social problem. Once admitted, the seeker of asylum was on his own so long as he did not run afoul of the police or established national policy rules.

The position of the ordinary refugee is different in our day. He is not usually an individual who has made a mark by his ideas or deeds and evoked personalized hostile reaction from the government of his country of origin. He is just one of hundreds of thousands or millions threatened by a policy directed against a social stratum or an ethnic group. While his escape has not as a rule been furthered by the regime he flees, the regime might not have severely hindered it. Having been reduced to a servile social status, the victimized group may be held for exploitation or extermination. But they may also be regarded as a disturbing alien matter, or an unnecessary cost element to be shoved across the border rather than "liquidated" in a manner bringing disrepute upon the liquidators. In this respect the modern refugee is less troublesome than the old-style rebel, who, a rather rare and interesting specimen, could attract considerable attention and gain influence on the policies of the host country; in the last analysis only his demise could ensure the peace of mind of actual and potential rivals at home.

As a mass phenomenon, the nonactive fugitive from group discrimination need not become a strategic liability to his home government. In exporting the undesirables or permitting them to spend their last resources on the permission to leave, the country of origin saddles the country of destination not only with individuals but also with burdensome problems. The roles, correspondingly, become reversed. The country of exit will not protest the admission of the rebel and define it as a hostile act. But when the new political refugees appear en masse, it is the country on which they are unloaded that will protest their ejection, or the introduction of policies resulting in the exodus, as an unfriendly act by the country of origin and a threat to the safety and interests of the recipient.

Mass influx of fugitives dislocates the labor market, overtaxes the facilities of the recipient countries' welfare agencies, creates acute housing, health, school, and retraining problems, kindles and exacerbates animosities between racial and religious groups; the menace of unemployment pressure brings about ambiguous, contradictory, and sometimes hostile attitudes of labor unions, which feel ill at ease with conflicting dicta of principle and group interest. Reminiscent of forefathers who long ago granted sanctuary to Huguenots or Jews from Spain fleeing from disastrous homeland policy shifts, government leaders in countries exposed to the new influx may sometimes be willing to extend asylum terms to newcomers. But how is one to distinguish the "political" refugee —and especially his most endangered subspecies, the politically persecuted,[8] who, as a member of a specific group, faces collective persecu-

[8] The term politically persecuted should encompass actual and potential victims of racial, national, religious, or political persecution, along with active fighters. In turn, the term political refugee should apply to any person having left his or her country of habitual residence for political or ideological reasons without necessarily having incurred or being exposed to persecution. Though distinctive criteria may not be easy to establish, the difference would matter if preferential treatment were granted to the persecuted by legislation or international agreement; see Heinrich Grützner, "Auslieferungsverbot und Asylrecht," in Franz L. Neumann, Hans Carl Nipperdey, and Ulrich Scheuner, eds., *Die Grundrechte. Handbuch der Theorie und Praxis der Grundrechte*, Berlin, 1955, Vol. II, pp. 585-604, esp. p. 601; and Hermann von Mangoldt and Friedrich Klein, *Das Bonner Grundgesetz*, 2nd ed.; Berlin, 1957, Vol. I, Art. 16, V (c-e).

However, apart from small groups certified by the country of asylum as having previously been in politics, official recognition would be an innovation with respect to most categories of the politically persecuted. Swiss policy is a case in point. From 1933 through 1948 a total of only 2,124 persons previously granted asylum asked Swiss authorities for recognition as "political persecutees." Of these, only 746 obtained recognition. Refugees for "merely [sic!] racial reasons" were never granted such privileges by the Swiss government in the late 1930's and early 1940's; cf. documents compiled by Professor Carl Ludwig of Basel for Swiss executive departments: *Die Flüchtlingspolitik der Schweiz seit 1933 bis zur Gegenwart, Bericht an den Bundesrat zu Händen der Eidgenössischen Räte*, Bern, 1957, p. 208. Save for individual instances of imminent personal danger, Swiss authorities not only refused special privileges but asylum itself to Free French followers of de Gaulle, German Social Democrats, and French nationals escaping deportation for slave labor (*ibid.*, p. 230).

tion, ostracism, or at the very least social and economic degradation—from a "social" refugee escaping "merely" the general conditions of hopelessness and repression and the drabness and dreariness of everyday life, or evading presumable future discrimination or persecution? It is of this would-be expatriate that Hugo Grotius wrote when he remarked that society would come to an end if the right to emigrate were given to every man.[9]

In the twentieth century this would amount to saying that social refugees should be refused recognition as politically persecuted. How difficult it is to draw the line may be seen from the Austrian dilemma. The constant addition of refugees from Yugoslavia and the temporary inrush from Hungary confront the Austrian government with problems it cannot possibly solve. In countries flooded with refugees of both categories, the issue of political asylum evokes not merely a political but also a sharp administrative reaction, which is bound to be negative. Even where the government may favor upholding the tradition of political asylum, the added dimensions of the problem inevitably will be reflected in its handling.

2. A Noble Service or a Troublesome Burden?

A typology of prevailing attitudes will have to account for this change in dimension. An impressive array of postwar constitutions on both sides of the ideological curtain as well as the United Nations' Declaration of Human Rights, a rather vague testimonial of praiseworthy intentions, acknowledge the right of political asylum. But except for exceptional cases, this does not indicate willingness to undertake a binding commitment. As a rule, the principle is retained that asylum is a privilege freely granted or refused, not a matter of right.[10] At close view a curious twist becomes apparent.

[9] Hugo Grotius, *De iure belli ac pacis* (1625) liber II, 5, *xxiv*. An illustration may be added. During the Brussels World's Fair of 1958, some 300 visitors from totalitarian lands asked the Belgian authorities for political asylum. It may be taken for granted that the wish to live outside the totalitarian realm and enjoy the high Belgian living standards, rather than an imminent danger of persecution, motivated the requests in most instances.

[10] See Oppenheim and Lauterpacht, *International Law*, 8th ed.; London, 1955, par. 316, for the prevailing opinion that the right-of-asylum commitment is not presently part of the law. According to M. D. Raestaed's paper at Bath (*Annuaire*, p. 135), this clause is generally taken to imply the individual nation's right to grant asylum. Richard Lange, *Grundfragen des Auslieferungs- und Asylrechts*, Karlsruhe, 1953, p. 20, is right in stating that the generous provisions of the Bonn Basic Law go beyond the established practice of international law.

A recent discussion (March 23-March 25, 1959) in the Commission of Human

The liberal affirmation of political asylum had been aimed at protecting all those who suffered or were threatened because of political convictions; the specific nature of these convictions did not matter. In contrast, postwar documents must be read in the light of present-day ideological battles. To some extent they are polemical assertions. The Italian constitution, for example, promises protection to those barred from the "enjoyment of democratic liberty." And the preamble to the 1946 French constitution guarantees political asylum to those persecuted for "action in support of freedom."[11] Enacted with strong Communist support, both documents refrain from defining liberty or freedom; identification of freedom fighters entitled to asylum remains subject to differential interpretation.

Constitutions within the Communist orbit are, as a propaganda device, more specific in naming the intended beneficiaries. The USSR constitution now in force, omitting victims of religious persecution who were promised refuge in an earlier enactment, offers sanctuary to those in jeopardy for having defended the interests of the toilers, exercised scholarly activity, or participated in struggles for national liberation. Constitutions belonging to the same spiritual family modify their promises in detail only.[12]

Implementation of constitutional promises is determined by the basic ideological conflicts and the political situations of the day, with a multitude of national variations. Small- and medium-sized countries most exposed geographically to the influx of asylum seekers must watch out for the slightest policy reaction of stronger powers. In reacting to changing conditions, they are more given to empiricism than the super- and maritime-powers; the latter are farther from the points of ingress and

---

Rights of the United Nation's Economic and Social Council, geared toward eventually producing a UN draft of asylum principles, bears evidence that even as ambiguous a formula as *"Every person whose life, physical integrity or liberty is threatened, in violation of the principles of the Universal Declaration of Human Rights, shall be regarded as entitled to seek asylum"* can encounter resistance. Therefore, Article 1 of the revised French preliminary draft, accepted by 15 votes with 2 abstentions for discussion in other interested agencies, restates the right of asylum in the traditional way, *"as the right of every state to grant asylum."* (United Nations Economic and Social Council, Commission on Human Rights, Fifteenth Session, agenda item 13; E/CN. 4/L/534/Add.3; 3 April 1959.)

[11] Italian Constitution of December 27, 1949, Art. 19(3); French Constitution of October 27, 1946, Preamble. The present constitution omits a detailed preamble.

[12] USSR Constitution of January 21, 1937, Art. 133. According to the more recent Constitution of the People's Republic of China (September 20, 1954, Art. 99), asylum is assured to all aliens persecuted for having defended a just cause or participated in the fight for freedom, or for scholarly activity.

have a better chance to develop programs in line with both domestic requirements and outside pressure.

In the Soviet Union and the countries within the Soviet orbit, traditional nineteenth century notions of political asylum as a noble service to be granted to the politically persecuted clash most strikingly with actual practice. A comparison with Czarist Russia would seem appropriate. Constitutional affirmations emphatically publicized at Communist-sponsored asylum conferences in the mid-thirties are one thing, and the granting of asylum another. Far from benefiting all persecuted toilers, admission of exiles has been determined solely by the political and economic needs of the Soviet government. A limited number of refugees, mostly victims of racial persecution, may have owed the entry permit to special technical skills. Full-fledged Communists and proven sympathizers escaping from the homeland or from their country of first refuge were welcome only on a strictly selective basis. Even those facing certain death outside were not admitted to the Soviet Union without express authorization by USSR party authorities acting in accord with the respective national sections of the Communist International.[13]

Not the degree of his safety, but how serviceable an individual was to the party machine, was the decisive question for his chances. In some instances the politically persecuted who were not Communists were granted USSR transit visas enabling them to escape from Nazi-dominated areas. Aside from this, political asylum in the Soviet orbit was a matter of party job assignment; it was handled by the party machine in accordance with its personnel needs and political plans for the future. Security and loyalty were primary criteria; the personal situation of the persecuted did not count. But for the possible recruitment of highly qualified technicians, the granting of asylum to organizational outsiders on the merit of their persecution status is completely alien to Soviet thinking.[14]

Asylum grants by the other super-power, the United States, still show some vestiges of the hallowed tradition of America as a haven to all comers, much though three decades of restrictive immigration policies have narrowed the scope of asylum chances accessible to the persecuted.

[13] A characteristic circular letter by the executive board of Rote Hilfe, the German Communist Party's auxiliary for relief and assistance, dated Moscow, May 26, 1936, may be consulted in Schweizer Bundesblatt, Vol. 2 (1946), p. 227.

[14] Years ago the USSR's purely service-centered approach to the rescue of persecuted European Communists was exposed in minute detail by a prominent Spanish exile: Jesus Hernandez, *La Grande Trahison*, Paris, 1953. In the years that followed, many lurid accounts were added in a fast-growing array of memoir publications and historical studies.

National quotas and subsistence requirements have been kept rigid, however grave and imminent the threat of persecution. For a long time immediate emergency refuge was only to be found under visitor entry provisions, which in turn made admission conditional upon the applicant's social and financial status and denied him chances reserved for those immigrants admitted as permanent residents. Effective implementation of asylum promises required special legislation not easily enacted and virtually unattainable without severe discriminatory restrictions. Such a departure from the existing national origins quota provisions in favor of more liberal admission of persons displaced by war and revolution began with the Displaced Persons Act of 1948. The latest manifestation of this policy appears in the "parole immigration" instituted in 1956 for participants in the Hungarian anti-Soviet uprising.

While liberalized emergency programs undoubtedly brought improvements, even the new admission criteria for the persecuted were still derived from domestic policy considerations and ideological desiderata, rather than from the degree of danger threatening the aspirants or the worthiness of their claim to asylum. The 1952 dispensation from the cumbersome quota system for a small number of admissions was clearly predicated on American national interest. Conversely, those who became enmeshed in the net of "undesirable" categories were excluded regardless of their status as political refugees in dire need of sanctuary.

Although admission is limited by national quota barriers to keep out groups deemed undesirable, and to a lesser degree to assure the immigrants' adaptability, and although the refugee's need for a sanctuary is merely incidental to national policy determining acceptability, the United States' system has made possible the ingress of many and varied categories of political refugees. It contrasts clearly with the Soviet system of selection. The United States' legal admission criteria do not limit social acceptability to restricted groups of highly skilled technicians; and the political criteria, largely negative, are aimed at barring the entry of specific groups deemed potential risks and liabilities. Only very little do the positive criteria of serviceableness influence admission practices.[15]

[15] The interrelationship between immigration and refugee problems is touched upon in Richard Robbins, "The Refugee Status. Challenge and Response," *Law and Contemporary Problems,* Vol. 21 (1956), pp. 316-33. The same issue also contains some contributions dealing with the effects of the 1952 McCarran-Walter Act. Under the thick overlay of recent American provisions aimed at excluding political undesirables, the general body of immigration law still contains some isolated relics giving positive privileges to the politically persecuted. Purely political offenses are not deemed to

The United States also faces the problem of individuals intent on actively pursuing in the country of refuge their original political aims. Those whose stand on the Communist issue or whose past activity in relation to it is open to doubt will find no admission under a policy prevailing in the present decade. This does not necessarily apply to the same extent to active politicians from South and Central America and the Caribbean regimes, who seek temporary refuge with the intention of making the United States a base of operations against the home government. Though they may be expected to "make trouble" and cause embarrassment to the United States government, they are not invariably barred. Those sponsored by influential groups or by individuals in the United States will be able to overcome diplomatic obstacles. Sometimes their very presence might provide the government with greater leverage in dealing with the rulers of their home country; or it may, as in 1961, provide instruments for a policy of scarcely-disguised intervention in the destiny of their home state.

The United States' asylum policy is both dogmatic and pragmatic. Foreign policy objectives, interest group pressures and counterpressures, and the traditional imagery of a haven for the oppressed and humiliated —all intertwine and clash in a jungle of contradictory practices. These practices the lucky winners extol and the losers vilipend.

More steadfastly than any other country, Great Britain continues to uphold the liberal tradition of political asylum. Her fortunate location, limiting access to sea and air lanes, has made highminded policy easier. To reach the British Isles mass migrations had to fight their way through continental countries. This was enough to permit selectivity and programming. Though it may be questioned whether England still measures up to the high standards of hospitality and political shelter set in the nineteenth century,[16] the tradition which refused to make the

---

involve moral turpitude barring admission per se. 8 U.S.C. 1182(a) (9, 10). Illiterate immigrants are exempt from the exclusionist rule of 8 U.S.C. 1182(a) (25) if they happen to be victims of religious persecution; 8 U.S.C. 1182(b) (2).

Recent American practices of exclusion for security reasons have been described in a study carried through with the support of the various official US agencies and their officers: A. T. Bouscaren, *The Security Aspect of Immigration Work*, Milwaukee, 1959. According to a table on p. 91, the number of those excluded from entry to the US because they fell under the "subversive" or "anarchistic" category has increased from around 3 per cent of the total exclusions in 1950 to 33 per cent in 1957. Under the Refugee Relief Act of 1953, 7 per cent of the visa refusals were for political reasons (p. 66).

[16] For realistic comment, see *The Economist*, April 14, 1956, p. 121.

grant of asylum dependent on the victim's politics has not been extinguished.[17]

Among the continental countries, the Federal Republic of Germany merits special mention. With the memory of Hitler's merciless persecution of political adversaries still vivid, the Bonn constitution makers inserted political asylum into their 1949 Basic Law in a way that made the principle immediately operative. A legally enforceable right to asylum came to benefit all those who might claim the status of the politically persecuted. Administrative machinery under court control has been established to implement the constitutional mandate, and the interpretations of various federal courts have tended to bolster the asylum claim by liberally interpreting the categories of persons and attitudes coming under its protection.[18] Whoever had been left stranded in Western Germany in the wake of the war and the occupation and could not return to his home country without meeting politically inspired persecution enjoys unrestricted asylum privileges. Of the more recent situations, the most important one seems to be the case of the 4,000 Algerians who have drifted into Germany. So far, the German authorities, exposed to conflicting pressures, have resorted to the expedient of giving the Algerians temporary permission to stay, and so have avoided making a hard and fast decision on the personal status of those among them—probably a majority—who have not yet attracted the special attention of the French authorities.

[17] Overall analysis of British admission policies will be found in Felice Morgenstern, "The Right of Asylum," *British Year-Book of International Law*, Vol. 26 (1949), pp. 327-52. In 1929 Trotsky had asked J. Ramsay MacDonald's Labour government for an entry permit. The application was denied by Home Secretary John Robert Clynes. Earlier, Clynes's fellow cabinet member, Foreign Secretary Arthur Henderson, had complained about the bluntness with which his subordinates reduced the issue to one of benefit or damage to British interest. The episode has been narrated by Hugh Dalton, *Call Back Yesterday*, London, 1953, p. 219.

Stranded in an English port after his escape from American penal action, Gerhart Eisler, well-known German Communist official, was not extradited by the British authorities. Without touching on the political issue, the British magistrate's court refused to entertain the action—on the grounds that the offense for which the extradition had been requested by the United States (perjury) was defined differently in British law. Having refused to extradite Eisler, Great Britain was prepared to grant him asylum; Eisler, however, did not avail himself of the offer. Obviously the American government, given the whole background of the Eisler case, must have realized full well that putting extradition proceedings into motion could be for no other reason than to satisfy prevailing opinion trends. Philip E. Jacob, "International Extradition. Implications of the Eisler Case," *Yale Law Journal*, Vol. 59 (1950), pp. 622-34.

[18] Cf. Lange, *op.cit.*, and Grützner, *op.cit.* For the German extradition practice, see below, notes 48, 54.

It is possible, then, barring sudden and overwhelming influx, to bring political refugees under the protection of the law. The Geneva Convention of July 28, 1951 gives this possibility wider recognition. Though prudently refraining in its operative part from touching more than very slightly on the crucial point, the admission of refugees,[19] it clarifies and limits the meaning of the term refugee, sets up procedures to determine his status under a regime of prescribed cooperation between the UN high commissioner and the national authorities, and settles in some fashion the rights and the personal status of the persons concerned in the country of asylum. From the viewpoint of this study, its most important result is that Articles 32 and 33 codify and thus vaguely limit the reasons why and the specific conditions under which a refugee may be expelled. Experiences of some European nations which date back to the 1930's and 1940's, however, suggest that countries adjacent to areas of cataclysmic social and political upheavals will not guarantee refuge or even as much as temporary asylum to huge numbers of escapees from revolutionary turmoil. To call the roll of countries neglectful of asylum principles would be insidious. And which authorities should take most of the blame? The Swiss,[20] for having egged on the Nazi government to institute procedures by which passports carried by German nationals of Jewish descent were marked, to enable Swiss frontier guards to spot and turn back Jews in quest of asylum without

---

[19] At first sight Art. 32, with its catch-all permissive clause allowing expulsion "on grounds of national security and public order," looks rather meaningless. However, its importance lies in the adoption of some international standards of procedural due process, including the right to present evidence, to be represented by counsel, to appeal an unfavorable ruling and—as a last resort—within some "reasonable period" to seek admission elsewhere. Only "compelling reasons of public security," in other words, much more than intonation of a formula by some administrator, may serve as an excuse for dispensing with due process. It should be noted, however, that the number of persons protected by the Convention has been limited; its Art. 2 carries a cut-off date of January 1, 1951.

[20] Ludwig, *Die Flüchtlingspolitik*, carries many documents outlining Swiss official policy, whose harshness was first documented in US Department of State, Documents on German Foreign Policy, 1918-1945, Series D, Washington, D.C., 1952, Vol. 5, nos. 642-644, pp. 895ff. The Swiss—there is no doubt about it—actively sought to stop the influx of German Jews and interceded to this effect with the Nazi government; it matters little that the choice of procedures—the marking of passports, for example—was left to German discretion, as related in Ludwig, p. 148. True, in one instance the Swiss firmly opposed discriminatory measures: they bluntly refused to order the marking of passports carried by Swiss Jews, as had been suggested by the Germans. The suggestion had apparently been made for bargaining purposes; to the Nazis it served to underscore the fact that the German government had done the Swiss a special favor in giving them a chance to bar the entry of Jews from across the border at a time when what Germany wanted most was to dump her Jews on neighboring countries.

interfering with Switzerland's welcome to "Aryan" Germans as cash-carrying tourists?[21] The Swedes of 1944-1945, who, fearing the ire of the Russian victors, refused asylum to members of the German armed forces who had fled the Baltic states, even if their persecution from the new Russian rulers was a certainty?[22] The French, for making a steady practice of ordering the deportation of persons without a country—bliss-fully mitigated, though, by administrative laxity and delays? For deny-ing them the travel papers indispensable for admission to another country, and having the courts impose jail sentences on violators of deportation orders? (The sentences increased in severity with the con-strued occurrence of a continuous offense which the offender had no power to stop committing.)[23] And again the French, for opening the frontier to Spanish Republicans pursued by Franco's armies in 1938-1939, and then confining them in camps devoid of facilities for orderly human living?[24]

Whatever their moral obtuseness—target of searching criticism at home—the Swiss authorities, at least, have not tried to make anyone believe that future emergency situations would find them dedicated to uncompromising protection of asylum privileges. In negotiations preceding the 1951 Geneva Convention, the Swiss insisted on, and ob-tained, a drastically restrictive interpretation. In the event of mass

[21] The contemporary Swiss record is in stark contrast to past performance. Both in the 1830's and again in 1848 and 1849, German and Italian fugitive revolutionaries streamed across the Swiss frontiers in great numbers (15,000 in 1849) and found a sympathetic reception among the population. Popular sympathies did not even totally wane after Mazzini's and Garibaldi's attempts to use Swiss territory as bases for carrying on their fight against Austria, which created countless difficulties for those in charge of Swiss foreign policy. J. Langhard, *Die Politische Polizei der Schweizer Eidgenossenschaft*, Bern, 1909, p. 159; and E. Bonjour, in H. Nabholz, L. von Muralt, R. Feller, E. Bonjour, *Geschichte der Schweiz*, Zurich, 1938, Vol. 2, No. 79.

[22] See the December 1959 legal opinion of Dr. Hellmuth Hecker of the Institute of International Law, the University of Hamburg: "Die Rechtmässigkeit der Auslieferung aus Kurland nach Schweden geflüchteter Deutscher Soldaten an die Sowjet Union Ende 1945" (mimeographed).

[23] Such practices have been banned by Art. 31 of the Convention of July 25, 1951. Under its terms, the country of asylum shall not impose penalties on the asylum seeker for illegal entry or unauthorized residence—provided only that the offender present himself without delay to the competent authority. Section 20 of the USSR statute on crimes against the state, December 26, 1958 (translated in *Highlights of Current Legis-lation and Activities in Mid-Europe*, Vol. 7, No. 1, January 1959), contains a similar provision in favor of asylum seekers, in the form of an exemption from the penalties for illegal frontier crossing. Taken at face value, this provision would show that under any social structure, administrative routine may sometimes be enough at cross-purposes with political goals as to evoke explicit new general rulings.

[24] Glimpses and criticisms of these French practices appear in A. Gleisberg, *A la recherche d'une patrie*, Paris, 1946, pp. 109-55.

migrations, the convention would not exact from the contracting parties the undertaking never to return a refugee to a country where his life or liberty were endangered because of his race, religion, nationality, participation in a specific group, or political opinion.[25] A friendlier attitude may well be taken by countries more removed from the turmoil of sudden mass treks; it is likely to materialize when the host government is in sympathy with the political cause of the exiles seeking admission, as was the case of the Mexican government vis-à-vis Loyalist Spain.

All this was patchwork. In European practice the hoped-for general rule for meeting mass exodus emergencies never came to be established. Neither a legal claim nor an informal promise ensuring admission to migrant masses ejected on political grounds from neighboring countries was ever agreed upon by Europe's democratic powers. Not even temporary asylum pending more far-reaching international arrangements was ever subscribed to as a generally binding principle.

Nor has the position of the politically active individual in search of asylum become more secure. Principle may count to some extent, especially when supported by powerful groups. Political affinities may count more, even in countries where principle has been thrown overboard. Political expediency, regardless of ideological affinities, has always counted most. There may be hope of reaping rewards, as displayed in the French government's refusal of asylum to "nihilist *emigrés*" to please czarist Russia.[26] There may be fear of reprisals and aversion to disturbances. In the late 1930's both contributed toward banishing Leon Trotsky's unruly political genius from all countries but Mexico. As Belgium was not powerful enough to retaliate, Franco Spain could well

[25] Weiss, *op.cit.*, p. 482. This point was also strongly emphasized in the Swiss government's message to parliament, in which approval of the convention was recommended; see *Feuille Fédérale*, Vol. 2, No. 28 (July 15, 1954), pp. 49ff., esp. p. 62. In theory, this marked anti-asylum stand has been abandoned, according to Ludwig, *op.cit.*, p. 404. The new doctrine expressly rejects the view that, in time of increasing international tension or war, admission of refugees above a fixed low ceiling (originally set at 7,000, *ibid.*, p. 214) is contrary to the interests of national defense. It is now held that the right to asylum "is one of the facts which national defense must take into consideration." Asylum must be granted unless this interferes with military requirements. A restrictive clause, however, reneges upon the liberal promise. No admissions would be permitted during the "period of mobilization," which is so broadly defined that it includes partial call to arms and special inductions for the reinforcement of frontier defenses. Nor is there any indication of what would terminate each "period of mobilization" and make operative the newly-promised admission of the persecuted.

[26] Maurice Paléologue, *An Intimate Journal of the Dreyfus Case*, New York, 1957, p. 84, carries, for example, a letter by the Russian ambassador, in which the "collaboration" of the Paris police prefect is gratefully acknowledged.

afford the luxury of sheltering the Belgian Fascist Leon Degrelle. But however cordial previous relations may have been between Spanish Foreign Minister Lequerica and Pierre Laval, the latter was taken back to territory under Allied occupation by the same airplane which had flown him to Spain. Who can rationalize the difference between asylum as a benefit for those who suffer undeservedly, and denial of asylum to persons accused of acts injurious to humanity? Grotius, himself a political refugee, makes such a distinction; he is familiar indeed with the part expediency plays in setting legal mantraps.[27] It is easy enough to stand up and protect a man who fled his enemies and had the good luck (or wisdom) to escape to a country in sympathy with his ideas and politics. The true test comes with the marginal case, when asylum is sought by a man who not only has made enemies at home but also sticks to ideas and actions utterly out of fashion everywhere and evokes universal reprobation.

3. The Menace of Informal Extradition

It takes revolutionary change to reverse the roles of oppressors and oppressed within a nation. The defeat of the Kaiser's Reich and its army opened the gates of the penitentiary to Karl Liebknecht. Pétain and Laval must fall to set free Daladier and Blum; Laval's lawyer then will implore Blum to appeal to Charles de Gaulle to help save his client's life. But let there be a frontier post between the oppressed and his former oppressor, and things will be different. Having escaped his government's wrath, the expatriate "coexists" abroad with the home regime he combats. To that regime such coexistence may well be intolerable, and it will try its utmost to get hold of the enemy and detractor. Success will depend on the attitude, official and otherwise, of the country of refuge. Things will be arranged informally, and the twentieth century's Pactyas will be surrendered without further ado if the asylum country is a dependency or a satellite of the pursuer state, or if it has other reasons to oblige. The government insisting on the surrender of the rebel will be spared the unpleasantness of constructing a foolproof extradition case out of minor criminal charges or fabricating charges out of whole cloth.

Interstate amity that harms asylum rights need not be based on ideological affinity. It may be simply that token of esteem by which one totalitarian regime wishes to smooth its relations with another totalitarian regime of different complexion. Pursuant to a protocol attached

[27] Grotius, *op.cit.*, II, 21, *v.*

to the German-Soviet treaty of August 1939,[28] Stalin's Russia repatriated a considerable number of German citizens, mostly technicians. She profited from this occasion by carrying through the deportation, between September 1939 and spring 1940, of a certain number of German Communists and radicals who had been residing in the USSR but whose reliability no longer met the Communist Party's requirements. Some were given the chance to become experts in comparative studies of totalitarian prison and concentration camp systems.[29]

Between a major totalitarian power and its satellites, or among such satellite states, regulation of asylum issues has always been informal. The Soviet Union, for example, never even bothered to enact a model extradition law that was widely discussed in 1924. Not until recently did she proceed to sign wide-range legal aid agreements, settling extradition issues as well, with states within her orbit. A number of similar agreements have come into being between such states. Treaties entered into by the German Democratic Republic may illustrate prevailing practices. Under their terms, extradition is guaranteed for all offenses with a penalty exceeding a one-year term; political offenses have not been exempted.[30]

Of course, outside the Soviet orbit, too, relations between nations of greatly unequal strength may be highly informal, to the benefit of the stronger power. Such was the case of weak Vichy France vis-à-vis powerful Hitler Germany, partly as a consequence of the armistice treaty of 1940. When Vichy France let Spain take and execute Louis Companys, erstwhile head of the Catalan government, she was hardly

---

[28] The text of the protocol, dated September 29, 1939, is carried in US Department of State, Documents (cited above, n.20), Vol. 8, no. 158, p. 165.

[29] F. Beck and W. Godin, *Russian Purge and Extraction of Confessions*, London, 1951, p. 106; Margarete Buber-Neumann, *Von Potsdam nach Moskau. Stationen eines Irrweges*, Stuttgart, 1957, p. 174.

[30] Signed on November 20, 1957, the DDR-USSR treaty became effective on June 12, 1958; Gesetzblatt der Deutschen Demokratischen Republik, 1958, Part I, pp. 241, 509. Similar agreements with Czechoslovakia, Poland, Bulgaria, Rumania, and Hungary came into force in 1957 and 1958; Helmut Ostmann, "Die Rechtshilfevertraege der DDR," *Neue Justiz*, Vol. 12 (1958), pp. 545-50. No corresponding arrangement seems ever to have been made with Yugoslavia. The Czech-Polish convention of January 2, 1949 (UN Treaty Series, Vol. 31, 1950, p. 300), which excludes in its Art. 60(b) the extradition for political crimes, has to be regarded as a remnant from a former period, when institutional coordination of international law devices did not yet fully function; Art. 59 of the DDR-Czech convention of September 11, 1956. (Gesetzblatt, 1956, Part I, pp. 1201ff., enumerating the cases where extradition does not apply, is conspicuously silent on that point.) The purely administrative character of extradition practices between Ireland and England, which exclude any discretion for refusing surrender of alleged political offenders, is dealt with by Paul O'Higgins, "Irish Extradition Law and Practice," *British Year-Book for International Law*, Vol. 34 (1958), pp. 274, 304-05.

in a position to claim the status of a helpless satellite. In Mexico, protection of the asylum grant is dependent on the relative strength and
persistence of effort by the government interested in recapturing its
political foes. While the position of the asylum seeker from Central
and South America, guarded by an attentive public opinion, is relatively secure, the same is not always true in the select cases in which
Big Brother beyond the Rio Grande exhibits a more than routine
interest.[31]

Violations of asylum claims also occurred in the aftermath of World
War II, as a result of specific postwar conditions not likely to crop up
again. At the end of the war Allied commanders in Germany, for example, let Swiss authorities seize informally a small number of Swiss and
German citizens who had served as wartime Nazi agents in Switzerland. As a rule, though, Great Britain and the United States have been
clinging to a legal order which, as now interpreted, bans the informal
surrender of beneficiaries of asylum.[32] This does not erase the fact that
neither Great Britain nor the United States disdained taking and prosecuting nationals of their own who had been delivered without due
process by countries to which they had fled to escape politically motivated criminal prosecution at home.

Generally, those countries that take advantage of informal surrender
of exiles may be considered in a comfortable, though not unassailable,
legal position. The underlying doctrine was recently restated by Judge
Irving Kaufman in one of his Sobell case opinions.[33] It rests on the
thesis that only a government, not the apprehended individual himself,
may insist on strict observance of protective clauses incorporated in
extradition treaties (which usually bar extradition for political offenses);
in surrendering the exile, the country of asylum obviously waives all
claims it may have invoked to avoid extradition.[34] The opposite doc-

---

[31] For a characteristic evaluation of the same incidents from the viewpoint of the
participating US authorities, see the "authorized" *FBI Story* by Don Whitehead, pp.
297, 318.

[32] Chief Justice Hughes in Valentine v. U.S., ex rel. Neidecker, 299 U.S. 5 (1936).

[33] 12 F Supp. 515 (1956). See also Chandler v. U.S., 171 F 2d 921 (1948); Ker v.
Ill., 119 U.S. 437, 443 (1886). For the identical attitude in German jurisprudence, see
Entscheidungen des Reichsgerichts in Strafsachen, Vol. 70 (1936), p. 286, where per-
sons subject to extradition are referred to as "extradition objects" [*Gegenstände der
Auslieferung*]. "Objects," of course, may not derive asylum claims or contest the legal-
ity of extradition.

[34] Similar rules seem to apply to cases of exiles kidnapped on asylum territory.
The kidnapped individual's fate would seem to depend on whether or not the government of the asylum country took steps to obtain his return. In this sense, the remarks
of Mario Amadeo, the Argentine representative at the Security Council discussion of
the Eichmann case (reported in the *New York Times*, June 23, 1960, p. 4) were entirely

trine, applied in two minor cases without much political background,[35] holds that an exile handed over to his country of origin without due observance of extradition agreements and thereupon prosecuted in a national court may contest court jurisdiction on the ground of the irregularity of his seizure.

The latter interpretation is undoubtedly more in harmony with the dictates of human decency. It may well be argued that an extradition treaty is made the law of the land through the process of incorporation, and that therefore an exile sheltered by a country signatory to such a treaty should be within his rights in expecting not to be deprived of asylum in a manner other than that prescribed by the treaty. Still, the argument lacks in realism. In the absence of a viable international jurisdiction to turn to, the exile in danger of being deported to the home country will hardly find a national tribunal willing to let him go free in the face of the government's contention that this would cause grave injury to national interest.

If there is a remedy at all against informal "rendition" to the home state by way of deportation, it is in the wide acceptance of the principle set forth in Article 33 of the Geneva Convention. Under this rule, no refugee shall be deported to, or returned to the frontier of, a territory

---

correct. The alleged consent of Eichmann to his forcible transfer to Israel could not extinguish Argentina's claim to "appropriate reparation" for the violation of its sovereignty through Eichmann's abduction. However, since Argentina did not care to insist on repatriation, the Israeli court acted in conformity with prevailing practice: it rejected Eichmann's jurisdictional complaint based on the illegality of Israel's establishing custody over his person.

For Swiss protests in the Berthold Jacob abduction case, see *American Journal of International Law*, Vol. 24 (1935), pp. 502-07. Legal evaluation of surrender effected through overzealousness or corruption of the asylum country's lower-level officials is controversial. Dealing with the abduction from Mexican territory of a fugitive United States national sought for narcotics offenses, the Federal district court in ex parte Lopez, 6 F Supp. 342 (1934), denied the abducted man's habeas corpus petition on the ground that whatever had occurred under the sovereignty of the Mexican government was outside the court's jurisdiction and should be taken up with the United States Department of State.

[35] See discussion in Manuel R. Garcia-Mora, "Criminal Jurisdiction of a State over Fugitives Brought from a Foreign Country by Force or Fraud. A Comparative Study," *Indiana Law Journal*, Vol. 32 (1957), pp. 427-49. Of the two cases, one (tribunal correctionnel d'Avesnes in *Recueil Sirey*, Vol. II [1934], pp. 105ff.) referred to a Belgian suspect of larceny who had been abducted from Belgian territory by French officials. The French court ordered the prisoner released as seizure on Belgian territory constituted grounds of absolute nullity of the proceedings. In the other case (part of a damage suit before the US-Panama Claims Commission, related in *Annual Digest of Public International Law Cases*, 1933-1934, Case No. 96, pp. 250-51), a similar act of abduction on foreign territory was likewise held illegal.

in which his life or freedom may be endangered because of race, religion, nationality, membership in a social group, or political opinion. In one form or another, many nations have made this rule part of accepted practice. Even though in the United States the present wording of provision 243(h) of the 1952 national security legislation widens the attorney general's discretionary power to stop or not to stop deportation to a country in which the deportee will face physical persecution, the principle itself has found well-nigh unanimous recognition.[36] The same goes for many European countries.[37] While it is conceivable that constitutional governments of the major powers will continue to condone and reap the fruit of violations committed by weaker nations to please them, it is likely that they will not be tempted to encroach on their own upon the Geneva rule. It may well be that such self-restraint will last long enough to let the principle of nondeportation to hostile territory become a customary rule of international law in the community of nontotalitarian states.

4. Political and Diplomatic Protection

Where informal procedure is of no avail, the country that seeks the surrender of an escaped national may make an extradition request. To make the request effective, the government must formally prefer criminal charges based on an offense not exempt by extradition agreements. From the 1830's on, however, political offenses, for which extradition had been granted most easily down to the early nineteenth century, were repeatedly declared nonextraditable. What, then, is a political offense? The multiplicity of theories may be ranged into three categories:

(a) Emphasis on the objective structure of the committed act, such as the Franco-Belgian differentiation between purely political crime, mixed offense, and common offense connected with political elements;

(b) The more indistinct Anglo-American "political character" approach; and

(c) The subjectivist Swiss doctrine of predominant motivation.

[36] 8 U.S.C. 1253(h), *United States Statutes*, Vol. 66, p. 212 (1952). For the administrative and court practice, see my article on asylum in *American Political Science Review*, Vol. 53 (1959), pp. 987, 1,000, n.33.

[37] Recent rulings of the German Federal Republic's highest administrative tribunal approved in principle the deportation of aliens convicted of crimes or misdemeanors. But it explicitly prohibited deportation to a country where the deported would face prosecution for political reasons; Entscheidungen des Bundesverwaltungsgerichts, Vol. 4 (1957), pp. 235, 238.

All three are just positions from which to begin the search for the decision deemed desirable in the individual case and political situation.[38] Under such circumstances, the motives behind the decisions of the administrative agencies and the judiciary—wherever the latter should be involved—require further elucidation.

Most extradition requests point to individuals whose role in the home country has been marginal. Major changes in the prevailing political setup would not have been expected to ensue from their political activity or from the specific incriminated action for which extradition is sought. But a number of instances of a different nature affect persons and actions that are of great relevance to the government seeking extradition. Two characteristic instances deserve mention: the case of the last Kaiser, who found shelter in Holland at the end of World War I, and that of the Croatian Fascist Ante Pavelic, who escaped to Italy after the 1934 assassination on French soil of King Alexander of Yugoslavia.

In refusing to surrender Wilhelm II to the Entente for trial, on charges of having gravely violated international morality and the sanctity of treaties, the Dutch government followed a road practically free of obstacles. Whatever David Lloyd George may have promised the British voters, it did not seem likely that the Entente powers, beset with major troubles on all sides, would back up the extradition demand with major sanctions. But there was all the reason in the world to believe that compliance on the part of the Netherlands, causing bitter resentment in many a quarter in neighboring Germany, would inflict lasting damage on Dutch interests; and Germany was bound to remain Holland's most powerful and most important neighbor. Moreover, refusal to extradite was safely grounded in accepted legal doctrine. To a large extent, professional opinion in the Entente countries concurred with that of German jurists in holding that the incriminated actions had been of a strictly political nature; that under no code had these actions

---

[38] See the comment in Pierre A. Papadatos, *Le Délit Politique*, Geneva, 1955, p. 71. An attempt by a Harvard research group to define offenses of a political nature— *American Journal of International Law*, Vol. 29 (1935), Supplement, pp. 107-19—was not overly successful. The authors thoroughly examined definitions in statutes and extradition treaties as well as the exceptions appended, and came up with the statement that nonextraditable offenses included treason, sedition, and espionage, regardless of whether the incriminated acts were committed by one or several persons. They added acts connected with organized groups' offenses against the safety of the governmental system in the country requesting extradition, and they did not brush aside other criminal acts aimed at political objectives. Instead of a definition, the study thus elicited an inventory of possible, though not exclusive, categories of cases.

as charged been punishable when committed; and that the ex post facto legal construct was too vague to serve the cause of justice.[39]

Legal precedent was perhaps not as easy to adduce in the Pavelic case; the political motivations dictating Italy's attitude were as obvious. The Marseille shooting, triggered by Pavelic and a close associate, both Yugoslav nationals, had caused the death of the Yugoslav king and of his host, France's Foreign Minister Louis Barthou, and severely injured a general of Barthou's retinue. And yet to extradite the man responsible for the shooting would have been incompatible with what Mussolini's government considered vital national interest. There was no love lost between Italy and Yugoslavia. Italy's Balkan strategy aimed constantly at the disbandment of the South-Slav Federation; in fact, Pavelic himself was to become the chief architect of the "independent" Croat state set up under Fascist auspices in the course of the Nazi-engineered dismemberment of occupied Yugoslavia. In rejecting the extradition request, Italy no doubt unleashed fury and indignation in France. In view of the power shift brought about by the German rearmament speedup, however, this mattered less than preserving intact the operational center of the anti-Yugoslav conspiracy.

The French extradition request, accordingly, was denied by the Court of Appeals of Turino. The court said that political crimes were excluded from the purview of the Franco-Italian extradition treaty, and that the definition of political crime in Article 8 of the Italian Penal Code was broad enough to cover the case.[40] The ruling was strongly criticized in France.[41] Indeed, the court's opinion failed to take into consideration

---

[39] How soon considerations of political expediency may triumph over emphatically stated moral convictions has been shown by Lord Curzon's change of mind in regard to criminal proceedings against Wilhelm II. On November 13, 1918, Lord Curzon, in a talk with Lloyd George, his political superior, mapped out elaborate plans for trying the Kaiser in England. And on July 3, 1919, he penned a letter in which he emphatically insisted on a trial in Holland, arguing that if the exiled monarch were to be convicted on British soil, Britain would forever lose Germany's friendship, but that Britain would be exposed to ridicule if he were tried in England and acquitted. The story has been preserved for posterity by Lord Beaverbrook, *Men and Power, 1917-1918*, New York, 1956, App. IV, pp. 385ff.

[40] Appeal Court of Turino, November 23, 1934, in Foro Italiano, 1935, Vol. II, col. 20. More recently, Pavelic's extradition for murders committed under his authority as head of the Ustashi regime in Croatia was demanded from Argentina by Yugoslavia. The Perón regime allowed him to disappear. He left Argentina following Perón's downfall, after his identity became accidentally divulged, and died in Spain in 1959. (For a parallel American case, see below, n.68.)

[41] Henri Rousseau, note to decision cited above, n.40, in *Révue Critique de Droit International*, Vol. 30 (1935), pp. 766-68. Legal distinctions between the assassination of the Yugoslav king and that of Barthou were discussed by Maximilien Philonenko, "Le refus d'extradition des terroristes Croates," *Journal de Droit International*, Vol. 61 (1934), pp. 1157-69.

or to refute many of the current narrower definitions of political crime. It also ignored the fact that the Croat terrorists did not have sufficient political reasons to kill a French statesman and wound a French general. However, the French critics' position neglected essential features of the political setup. After all, France had through the years been the most loyal ally of King Alexander's unitary state, distasteful to Croat nationalists, and French interests undoubtedly were at stake in Yugoslavia's domestic imbroglio.

As an essential factor in extradition cases, the governmental machine's striving for self-preservation and survival may not be as tangible as considerations of foreign policy strategy. In countries with unstable governmental system given to frequent revolutionary removal of rulers, physical survival often hinges on strong asylum safeguards reinforced by an iron-clad rule of nonextradition for political offenses. Reciprocal recognition of such protective services, which saves lives in revolutions, junta uprisings, and other instances of government selection through bloodshed have established a kind of supranational cartel of the ruling elite. The tacit understanding that unites South America's regimes is an illustration.

Nonextradition for political offenses is supplemented by "diplomatic" asylum. Instead of escaping across the border, endangered individuals seek refuge behind the walls of a foreign embassy, extraterritorial on the national territory, and the regime from which they escape respects the sanctity of such refuge and even provides safe-conduct provisions for those willing to leave the protection of diplomatic immunity in the homeland and go abroad. Too frequent use of this device has been vehemently attacked. It obviously handicaps the ferreting out of political offenders, as it ensures their safety too close to the locale of their rebellious activities.

Diplomatic asylum was overworked, for example, during the Spanish Civil War, when some 12,000 enemies of the loyalist regime were sheltered by foreign, mostly South American, legations. The loyalist government acquiesced in order to avert South American political obstruction of its efforts in the League of Nations.[42] The sanctuary provided in 1948 by the Colombian embassy in Lima for the Peruvian Aprista leader Haya de la Torre offers another characteristic instance. Its legitimacy was contested by Peru. The legal battle resulted in a series of rather diffuse judgments by the International Court in The Hague.

[42] R. B. Greenbaum, "Recent Developments in the Law of Diplomatic Asylum," *Transactions of the Grotius Society*, Vol. 41 (1956), pp. 103ff.; Norman Padelford, *International Law and Diplomacy in the Spanish Civil War*, New York, 1939, p. 157.

The court sought to confine legitimate diplomatic asylum to cases involving immediate danger of life, and denied the right of the asylum country unilaterally to pass on the merits of the asylum claim. It failed to evolve a realistic assessment of the standards and guarantees that should be required to prevail in a nation's administration of justice if asylum is denied to its nationals by foreign powers. Nor did it rule on the issue when both parties to the dispute expressly asked for a judicial decision; it merely suggested that direct negotiations would be the best way to terminate Haya de la Torre's residence on Colombian extraterritorial premises in the Peruvian capital.[43] It might well be that the more future South and Central American upheavals deviate from the pattern of narrow changes in political and military elites and become the expression of social revolutionary or counterrevolutionary movements, the more the still-prevailing practices of diplomatic asylum will become controversial. The larger the number of people actively engaged in the overthrow of the previous regime, the more likely that the new political elites' rational interest in their future security will recede behind the irresistible urge to eradicate the remnants of the old regime, a pattern which must involve a drastic curtailment of the usages of diplomatic asylum.

Thus far, legal formulation and limitation of diplomatic asylum have not materialized, except to some varying extent among the South and Central American states (on the basis of the 1928 Pan American Asylum Convention of Havana and its modifications and elaborations through the Montevideo Convention of 1933 and the Tenth Interamerican Conference of Caracas in 1954). In the changing international balance of power, diplomatic asylum, though in the long run it may be growing more problematic in South and Central America, has become more attractive to the great world powers. Even the United States has shown a change of heart. Hitherto American opinion has frowned upon diplomatic asylum as a device fit at best for areas and governments that lack political maturity and stability. The opinion prevailed that diplomatic shelter should be granted only to potential victims of mob violence and never be used to sidetrack law enforcement by legitimate agents of the local government.[44] The grant of diplomatic asylum to Cardinal Mindszenty, sheltered since the end of 1956 on the premises of

---

[43] For the International Court of Justice, see ICJ Reports, Vol. 5 (1951), p. 81f.; cf. Alona Evans, "The Colombian-Peruvian Asylum Case: Termination of the Judicial Phase," *American Journal of International Law*, Vol. 45 (1951), pp. 755-62.

[44] For the traditional Big Power view, see G. H. Hackworth, *Digest of International Law*, Vol. 2 (1941), pp. 623, 770; cf. a characteristic quotation in Padelford, *op.cit.*, p. 162.

of the United States embassy in Budapest, indicates a departure from traditional Big Power doctrine and practice.[45]

While the South and Central American cartel protests national ruling groups by means of a broadened concept of political asylum and rather consistent refusal to extradite for political offenses, the opposite tendency has been on the rise in the more moderate political climates, where the established political setup is in no danger of being overthrown and the groups in power do not live in fear of death by violence. Under such stable conditions, it is easier for the national political and administrative elites to guarantee each other safety from insurrectionist activities by narrowing the scope of offenses whose political nature would protect the offender from being extradited at the request of the home government. Common interest in whittling down asylum protection has never been a leitmotiv. At most it has been a constant among many variables that determine governmental attitudes. Often, though, this constant has been weighty enough to tip the scales.

5. *The Changing Scope of Nonextraditable Offenses*

Through the second half of the nineteenth century, increasingly restrictive interpretation of political offenses was furthered by both legislative enactments and judicial interpretation. As early as 1856 a restrictive clause, the so-called *Attentat* provision, was inserted into the Belgian extradition law, following an abortive attempt by one Celestin Jacquin to blow up a train that carried Napoleon III. Similar provisions, excluding murderous assault upon the person of a foreign sovereign, were subsequently incorporated into numerous extradition treaties. Other restrictive practices followed.

There was considerable effort to separate acts committed during the preparation or attempted implementation of revolts and revolutions—acts viewed as political—from individual acts of violence not conceivably conducive to a change in the political order and therefore refused recog-

[45] Hungary's failure to take action against the Cardinal's being sheltered by the United States embassy indicated tactical choice rather than recognition of the principle of diplomatic asylum. In the analogous case of the unfortunate members of the Nagy government who had taken refuge in the Yugoslav embassy, the Hungarian government (and its Soviet protectors) obtained the fugitives' surrender by the express promise of nonprosecution and safe conduct, which was immediately broken. In notes addressed on November 24, 1956, to both Hungary and the USSR, the Yugoslav government filed a strong protest and requested information on the whereabouts of the victims. The Hungarians' reply of December 1, 1956, insisted on the strictly domestic nature of the action taken; this was once more protested by the Yugoslavs on December 6. Another protest was entered on June 23, 1958, after the execution of Nagy had been officially announced.

nition as political offenses.[46] At first sight the logic of this distinction is not conclusive. It protects established regimes from individual acts of terror which, whatever their long-range effect, rarely if ever menace the regime's preservation. But it extends its blessings to participants in revolutionary action which, had it succeeded, would have been deadly.

This strikingly spurious logic made political sense to the ruling groups of pre-1918 Europe. Of these, hardly a single one had to face the threat of major uprisings, once the 1871 Commune insurrection in Paris was suppressed. Conversely, acts of individual violence were plentiful. Particularly around the turn of the century many a European government was repeatedly vexed, if not badly tormented, by terrorist acts of Western anarchists and various kinds of Russian revolutionists. Hence the wide-range attempts to debar from protection accorded two categories of political offenders: (1) anarchists who were alleged enemies of any social order, not just of a specific political regime; and (2) perpetrators of particularly brutal and atrocious acts.

Obviously, enemies of any social order is a vague enough category to permit broadened interpretations at any time to match the fashion of the day. A recent suggestion, for example, envisaged its application to those termed "subversive" in the American political jargon in vogue in the 1950's.[47] Once applied, the doctrine becomes entangled in the most fantastic difficulties and contradictions. Examples galore may be found in Swiss juridical annals, for Switzerland, by virtue of geographical location, had been saddled with a larger proportion of extradition cases than most other countries. Swiss court practice in the 1900's showed the doctrine in operation, after a different start, in extradition proceedings involving adherents of Russia's Socialist Revolutionary Party (SR) whom the czarist government charged with acts of violence and murder. Again and again judicial effort was directed at granting a recognition of sorts to revolutionary violence that might have succeeded in bringing about political change; no such consideration was shown toward the forbidden fruit of individual violence. According to this doctrine, individual violence flows out of vengeance or protest; it carries its end in itself and has no effect on political reality. (Additional juridical elaboration was contributed in the 1880's and 1890's by British judicial utterings, an echo of the legislative endeavors of John Stuart Mill

[46] Two British cases set the precedent: Castioni, *Q.B.*, Vol. 1 (1891), pp. 149ff., and Meunier, *Q.B.*, Vol. 2 (1894), pp. 415ff.

[47] Manuel R. Garcia-Mora, *International Law and Asylum as a Legal Right*, Washington, D.C., 1956, p. 71. Reviewers have been skeptical on this point; see, for example, Quincy Wright, *University of Chicago Law Review*, Vol. 24 (1956), p. 202.

and the refinement of James Stephen, Britain's most eminent criminal lawyer in the late nineteenth century.)

Here, violence was viewed, as it were, through the eyes of an efficiency expert. Nonextradition was handed out as an award for the hypothetical success of the desired goal, the overthrow of the government. The SR's acts of violence obviously had not measured up to efficiency standards expected in Switzerland, Europe's most orderly country. Had the chosen means been in keeping with the SR's idealistic goals, the Swiss Federal Court asked in the case of an exile who had carried out party orders to "execute" the czarist chief of police in Penza, Russia? The party's "verdict" had "convicted" the police official of savage brutality against peaceful marchers in a political parade at the height of the revolutionary wave, October 1905. Answering the question in the negative, the court conceded extradition.[48] But in the case of two

[48] Wasilieff, Entscheidungen der Schweizerischen Bundesgerichts, Vol. 34 (1908), Part I, p. 557. The legal basis of the Swiss practice, Art. 10 of the law of January 2, 1892, rests on the so-called "predominant element" theory. It is conveniently vague enough to allow for unlimited judicial discretion. See Papadatos, op.cit., p. 80, and Hans Schultz, Das Schweizer Auslieferungsrecht, Basel, 1953. The 1922 Fort-Concepcion case—terminated by simple administrative procedure in the absence of judicial hearing, which was not introduced in Germany until 1929—bears close similarity to the above case, in regard both to facts involved and ultimate disposal. It concerns the Spanish extradiction demand for two members of an anarchistic group who had participated in the murder of Dato, president of the council of ministers. The murder had been an act of reprisal against Dato's oppressive measures. The defense of the decision to extradite fell upon Federal Minister of Justice Gustav Radbruch, venerable and famous as philosopher of law and reformer of criminal law, and inexperienced and naive as a politician and administrator. Radbruch spoke of an "inflexible law" that defined the meaning of offenses connected with a political act. This law would lead to a "legally and humanly disagreeable result": the granting of extradition would become a necessary part of German loyalty to its treaty obligations. This attitude was all the more necessary as it would set a precedent facilitating the expeditious granting of Germany's pending extradition demand for the murderers of Mathias Erzberger by Horthy Hungary—a grant that was promptly refused. Deutscher Reichstag, I. Wahlperiode, Stenographischer Bericht, session of February 23, 1922, p. 6042.

A more recent German decision—Skzantos, Bundesgerichtshof, Entscheidungen in Strafsachen, Vol. 8 (1955), pp. 59-66—ordering the extradition of a member of Elas, sentenced to death in absentia for participation in murder, follows the same line. (The Greek government had, however, declared its preparedness to renounce the execution of a death sentence.) The decision, which is not in accord with the two German cases cited below, n. 54, affirms the continuing applicability of Art. 3(3) of the 1929 extradition statute, exempting murder from the rule of nonextradition in political cases. The reasoning concentrates on the act committed by the asylum seeker rather than on the political coloring of prosecutions in the home state. Rejecting the interpretation that Art. 3(3) of the 1929 extradition law has been superseded by Art. 16, 2(2) of the Basic Law, it speaks in rather general terms of an "accentuated tendency toward combatting

Georgian revolutionists who had robbed a treasury office in Tiflis, the same court refused to extradite.[49] Was robbery considered a technique more appropriate to the overthrow of the czarist regime than the punitive killing of a trigger-happy police commander? Which was more likely to sap the foundation of an established political order, the holdup of a government agency by men of the revolution, or an act that showed organizers of the revolution capable of countering government violence with the quasi-judicial "execution" of the responsible official? Or, reading between the lines, was it simply that law-abiding jurists in a civilized community were shocked by the spectacle of a clandestine party group's pronouncing a "death sentence" and executing the "delinquent"? Had the participants in the armed robbery, scions of well-to-do families and alumni of Swiss universities, made a more civilized impression upon a perplexed court?

What makes a strike political? Smooth procedure and absence of violence? In a German city on the Swiss border, a large-scale strike aiming at the improvement of working conditions had caused the authorities to institute martial law and have troops take possession. To make the troops withdraw, the strikers had taken hostages; they also had manhandled a businessman they hated. Reprisals followed. Of the strikers, a few escaped to Switzerland. Did the court deny extradition? It did not, for the objectives of the strike, it said, were not political.[50]

What about the killing of *agents provocateurs*? An agent of the Fascisti, said to have been dispatched to France under orders to lure Italian exiles into terrorist acts which would make the French police take action against them, had been killed in Paris by an Italian anti-Fascist. The killer had succeeded in escaping to Switzerland. Was his a political act that precluded extradition? The Swiss court said no.[51] The killing, the

---

political offenses directed against life"; *ibid.* p. 65. But see n. 62 below for an implicit refutation of this argument.

A recent German decision by the Appeal Court in Stuttgart, December 15, 1960, neatly avoids these interpretative difficulties when refusing extradition. It was made in the cases of Belkai and Hammou, two Algerians who had killed a compatriot suspected of French sympathies, whose extradition the French were demanding. According to the decision, France, by refusing to give legal aid to Germany for apprehending persons who had murdered an Algerian on German territory—alleging the political character of the offense involved—had failed to observe the reciprocity which would form the necessary prerequisite of any extradition (Par. 4, 1 of the German extradition law).

[49] Keresselidse, Entscheidungen, Vol. 33 (1907), Part 1, p. 169.

[50] Vogt, *ibid.*, Vol. 50 (1924), Part 1, p. 249; cf. the Kaphengst case, *ibid.*, Vol. 56 (1930), Part 1, p. 547.

[51] Paven, *ibid.*, Vol. 54 (1928), Part 1, p. 207.

magistrates held, could not have affected the political setup in Italy, nor could it have been necessary to help the cause of Italian exiles in France; things had been kept well under control by the French police. Besides, the court argued, nonextradition could be interpreted as encouraging political terrorist acts by exiles on the territory of a third country (meaning Switzerland).

What were the motives behind such judicial reasoning? Was it, in the first case, sympathy with legally established German authorities, reinforced by fear of German radicals who, once encouraged by a Swiss court, would carry their nefarious influence into neighboring Basel, Swiss center of labor unrest? Was it, in the second case, the desire to keep Italian domestic struggles from overflowing onto Swiss soil, a consideration perhaps more pertinent than theorizing about the proper relation of means and ends in political warfare tinged by violence?

As early as the 1920's, when a string of cases involving Italian anti-Fascists had come up for adjudication, the criterion of efficiency for establishing the nonextraditable nature of offenses serving a remote goal had lost much of its attraction for the judicial mind. In the course of election battles, homicides, even though they had occurred when the Fascist regime could not possibly have been jeopardized by individual acts of violence, were found to have been political, and their perpetrators were exempted from extradition.[52] Had the Fascist regime's contempt for accepted standards of legal procedure so thoroughly upset the Swiss judiciary?

At least one of the court decisions entered during this period may be termed unconditionally outspoken. The Italian government had requested extradition of a refugee for the slaying of a Fascist. The request denied the accused the benefit of the royal decree of December 22, 1922, which had proffered amnesty for all acts of violence committed for the sake of the national good, regardless of whether the crime had matched provocation or motivation. The Swiss court could not help realizing the obvious. The Fascist government applied the amnesty provisions to exonerate perpetrators of violence which had paved Fascism's road to power; their acts were excused or lauded as having served the national interest. Contrariwise, analogous acts imputable to Fascism's vanquished foes were dealt with as reprehensible crimes. The violation of the principle of equality before the law was self-evident. The Swiss court did not mince words in turning down the extradition request.[53]

[52] Camporini, *ibid.*, Vol. 50 (1924), Part I, p. 299.
[53] Ragni, *ibid.*, Vol. 49 (1923), Part I, p. 266. Similar acts were sometimes seen as

Radical departures from the concept of means efficaciously fitting a political end came in Switzerland, somewhat sooner than in Britain, with a decision of the Federal Court involving escapees from totalitarianism. The Yugoslav government had demanded extradition of an aircraft crew guilty of a successful escape flight in a government airplane, in the course of which unwilling passengers had been forcibly detained. The extradition request charged acts of violence, endangering the passengers' safety and lives, and misappropriation. As the men had acted for the sole purpose of escaping homeland conditions they considered oppressive, there was no way of construing their actions as means, appropriate or not, to bring about a fundamental change in the established political order. Emphatically pointing to changing historical and political conditions as an element of judicial factfinding, the court incisively reversed itself and abandoned the traditionally restrictive doctrine. It recognized the political nature of common offenses committed for the sake of escaping a political regime that denied opposition and struggle for power.[54]

---

political disputes, such as the killing of a Nazi by a member of a democratic German combat group; Ockert, *ibid.*, Vol. 59 (1933), Part I, p. 136.

Roger Corbaz, *Le Délit politique d'après le Tribunal Fédéral Suisse*, thesis, Lausanne, 1927, p. 57, notes that the efficiency-of-means test had a different meaning in 1923 as compared to 1907. Yet it was restored to its original meaning, at least temporarily, after Fascism lost its paramount importance. Cf. the following cases: Peruzzo, Entscheidungen, Vol. 77 (1951), Part I, p. 50; Nappi, *ibid.*, Vol. 78 (1952), Part I, p. 123. But in Picorelli (*ibid.*, Vol. 77 [1951], Part I, p. 57), the court denied the extradition of a member of a neo-Fascist division who, in December 1944, had carried out the execution of a traitor. The court held that at the time there had still been armed conflict involving both foreign and domestic enemies, that the defendant had had no personal motive for committing murder, and that all members of his unit faced identical penalties if returned to Italy.

[54] Ravic and associates, *ibid.*, Vol. 78 (1952), Part I, p. 39. A similar British case (ex parte Kolczynski, All English Law Reports, Vol. I [1955], p. 31) was commented upon by E. Denny, "An Affair of a Political Character," *Modern Law Review*, Vol. 18 (1955), p. 380. In this case the court brought out the inadequacy of the earlier formula under which nonextradition had been confined to incidents involving political disturbances.

A German decision (Lestrel, Bundesgerichtshof, Entscheidungen in Strafsachen, Vol. 3 [1953], p. 392) denied the extradition of a fugitive sought by Ecuador for larceny, on the presumption that prosecution was politically inspired; for criticism, see Lange, *op.cit.*, p. 19. More recently, the Federal Constitutional Court has confirmed and extended the policy of the Lestrel case. After first affirming the admissibility of a preliminary injunction in a constitutional complaint based on violation of Art. 16, 2(2), Entscheidungen des Bundesverfassungsgerichts, Vol. 6 (1957), p. 443, the court recently reversed the appeal court decision that had granted the extradition of a Yugoslav citizen demanded by his home state for embezzling charges deriving from his activity as director of a state enterprise; *ibid.*, Vol. 9 (1959), p. 175. The court's far-reaching decision established three principles: (1) Assurances by the demanding state that the defendant will be accountable only for the specific charges covered in the extradition

Extradition doctrine began by protecting only the political contestant who had, at least in conjecture, a realistic chance to succeed. In the 1950's it extends a helping hand to the potential victim, albeit an innocent bystander, still exposed to the fangs of iniquitous political power after he has fled beyond their immediate reach. More and more it is being considered a noble service to shield nonpolitical fugitives whom totalitarianism threatens with a politically motivated prosecution. The concept of political asylum thus takes on new contours. Yet it still remains uncertain whether protection against extradition extends to perpetrators of political homicide stemming from the fight against their home government or, more recently, deriving from national liberation struggles.[54a] We may have meant to take two steps, but stopped after one.

Moreover, there is no denying apparent tendencies to the contrary, which are closely connected with after effects of World War II. The international dragnet for perpetrators of war crime offenses[55] need not be discussed here. Yet repercussions of such punitive efforts have to a

---

demand do not provide a sufficient guarantee that political goals might not influence the punishment, if the totality of life situations has come under political control in the demanding state. (2) The protection against extradition is not excluded by the fact that the defendant's political activity against his home state—accession to a royalist emigré organization—has begun only after the defendant reached the asylum country, provided the accession has been undertaken in good faith and not simply to establish "persecutee" status. (3) Court protection against a politically-tinged extradition demand does not depend on recognition of the "political persecutee" status of the defendant by the administrative authorities of the asylum state. With the help of this construct, which recognizes political activity postdating the flight from the home country, the German court reached the same results as the Swiss and British courts. But see Government of India and Mubarak Ali Ahmed, All E.L.R., Vol. 1 (1952), p. 1,060.

[54a] In the recent case Mazai (*Neue Zuricher Zeiting* Nr. 190 of July 13, 1961, page 17) concerning the killing of a FLN member suspected of treachery by his supervisors, the Swiss Federal Court, in granting extradition, returned to the seemingly discarded efficient means doctrine.

[55] See Robert G. Neumann, "Neutral States and Extradition of War Criminals," *American Journal of International Law*, Vol. 45 (1951), pp. 495-508. In the course of its first session the UN General Assembly turned down a USSR proposal to deny UN protection to "Quislings and traitors" among displaced persons; Journal of the First General Assembly of the United Nations, First Session 1946, pp. 544-64. The resolution of the UN General Assembly of October 31, 1947, which recommends the extradition of war criminals, throws together war criminals and traitors (defined as national subjects who are accused by their home country of having committed treason or active collaboration with the enemy). United Nations Yearbook 1947-1948, New York, 1949, p. 222. However, as the resolution contained a provision that made extradition dependent on existence of a prima facie case, it was adopted by only 42 votes, with 7 against (Soviet bloc), and 6 abstentions. The very necessary delineation between political crimes and crimes against humanity is treated—and its difficulties somewhat underestimated—in M. R. Garcia-Mora, "The Present State of Political Offenses in the Law of Extradition and Asylum," *University of Pittsburgh Law Review*, Vol. 17 (1953), pp. 371-96.

lesser extent affected national jurisdiction, imposing restrictive checks upon the customary rules of political asylum. Two specific instances stand out: (1) Under a peace treaty provision Italy has undertaken to extradite nationals of Allied powers charged with acts of treason or collaboration punishable under the respective national statutes.[56] (2) Similar, if more far-reaching, commitments were subscribed to in a reciprocity declaration between France, on the one hand, and Luxemburg and Belgium, on the other.

Imposed by the victorious Allies, the first-mentioned undertaking has been observed by Italy as a matter of necessity,[57] though more recently in a rather restricted interpretation.[58] As for the agreement between France and her neighbors, which had grown out of common postwar experience, there were soon considerable differences of opinion among French magistrates. Most French courts dealing with extradition cases have shown a pronounced tendency to disregard the reciprocity declaration and refuse extradition under its terms; they have held that the purely administrative agreement unlawfully usurped treaty-making prerogatives and had no power to derogate from the principle of non-extradition of political offenders.[59]

Although the precedent has not been encouraging, further interference with nonextradition guarantees might conceivably evolve from the common pursuit of national security interests within the framework of the North Atlantic Treaty Organization. Cooperation of NATO powers has resulted so far in new provisions in several national codes; under these provisions the safety of Allied, that is, NATO, powers is given the same protection as the external security of the legislating country itself.[60] This entails extension of national jurisdiction to offenses committed against the external security of any other member country of NATO. While established extradition provisions have not yet been

[56] To what extent other peace treaty provisions have remained a dead letter because of the involved countries' affiliation with different power blocs is discussed by Edward Hambro, "New Trends in the Law of Asylum and Extradition," *Western Political Quarterly*, Vol. 5 (1952), pp. 1ff.

[57] In re Court, in Foro Italiano, Vol. 11 (1952), p. 113.

[58] In re Serclaes, in *Annual Digest* (cited above, n.35), 1952, p. 366. Such peace treaty provisions may well be termed "retrogressive steps," as has been suggested by Oppenheim and Lauterpacht, *op.cit.*, par. 338-40.

[59] Van Bellinghen, Paris Court of Appeals, November 28, 1950, in *Recueil Dalloz*, 1951, p. 440. Court opinion has not been uniform. For criticism, see Emile Garçon, *Code Pénal Annoté*, Art. 84, no. 43.

[60] For France, see Penal Code, Art. 86(3) [Art. 103 since June 1960]; and decree of July 11, 1952, Art. 1. The Soviet Union's state security concepts render similar results. Section 10 of the law on state crimes, December 26, 1958 (cited above, n.23), makes part of the state security legislation applicable to "especially dangerous acts against the state," committed against "another state of the toilers."

affected, attempts in this direction have come to light. Intensification of common effort in the field of military, economic, administrative, intelligence, and police matters could one day elicit so streamlined a concept of external security as to take away the political-offense shield from any act deemed detrimental to the security of one or several of the NATO powers; all such acts would then become extraditable. Steps to this end would certainly meet with strong opposition, for they would indicate far-reaching subjection of national policies to external pressures, possibly even to pressures emanating from a hegemonic power. And few governments would care to admit openly that this was the state of affairs. In any case, the objective, protection of allied nations' external security, is well within reach of those governments that have amended national legislation for the purpose of warding off attacks on their allies.[61]

To be sure, even closely associated powers only occasionally draw together to the point where they renounce independence of action; this remains the exception, whereas diversity of political regimes is still the rule.[62] In recent years diversity within the two major power coalitions has been on the increase. Deviations in regard to principles of government in both camps is more accentuated than it was a decade ago. As a result, extradition for political offenses is bound to encounter serious opposition. In addition, the menace which once caused many nations to reduce the scope of nonextraditable offenses, so that they could better protect political and administrative elites from individual acts of violence, is on its way out. There are hardly any traces left of violence committed by anarchists or other minor groups. This "individual terror" has been replaced by systematic violence by specific states (and state-connected "movements" taking orders from such states) which are either strong enough to apply organized violence or else

[61] Accordingly, as stated in Annual Report of the Attorney General of the United States for 1957, Washington, D.C., 1958, p. 52, France did not agree to extradite one Zlavotsky and his wife indicted in the United States for intelligence activity on behalf of the USSR. A different decision, however, obtained in a recent case involving sale of technical information on weapons, in which Italy had been requested by the Federal Republic of Germany to extradite one Keitel; the extradition was granted.

[62] Under the impact of the assassination of King Alexander of Yugoslavia, a convention to make terrorism and penetration for terrorist acts extraditable offenses was signed by 23 states on November 16, 1937, under the League of Nations' auspices. A supplementary agreement to establish an international criminal court was signed by 10 powers. The court was to have jurisdiction over acts of terrorism committed by persons sheltered and guaranteed nonextradition by one of the signatory powers. For the vast literature on the still-born project, impossible of realization in a world of antagonistic power groups, see Oppenheim and Lauterpacht, *op.cit.*, par. 127a.

primarily concerned with reducing violence directed against themselves. No letting down of asylum guarantees is likely to influence their decisions one way or another.

6. *The Asylum Principle Restated*

Writing in the mid-1880's, Heinrich Lammasch, Imperial Austria's last Prime Minister, sought to derive the principle of nonextradition for political offenses from that of nonintervention in other nations' domestic affairs. A national government prosecuting its enemy, he observed, could not possibly assume even a hypothetical legitimacy of the incriminated action. But faced with the decision whether or not to extradite a foreign national accused of unlawful political acts against his government, the country of refuge would first have to ask whether or not the fugitive's actions had been legitimate. It would then have to discuss and evaluate all the political practices prevailing in the exile's home country, thus inevitably intervening in the affairs of a foreign state; to avoid this, the country of refuge must generally refrain from extraditing political offenders.[63] The point is interesting, but the emphasis seems differently weighted today, when every country, by propaganda, public criticism, or the granting and withholding of military and economic aid, continuously intervenes to the hilt in the affairs of all other countries.

To state the argument differently might be helpful. Instead of basing nonextradition of political offenders on the jaded principle of nonintervention, one should try to see it as a device to prevent the government that seeks extradition from projecting its domestic entanglements on the country of asylum. National states are imperfect entities. Their predominant interests are subject at all times to continuous criticism by friend and foe within and without; and their political systems produce enough administrative malpractice and miscarriage of justice. Coupled with nonextradition for political offenses, the right to political asylum permits the shortcomings and imperfections of one country or system to stay at home, as it were, and spares the people of other countries ineffectual but onerous involvement.

Moreover, strict observance of the unqualified principle of nonextradition of political offenders does more than merely protect the country of asylum from the injection of foreign standards into its political system. If, despite all urgings and entreaties a country sticks to the principle, it lets both the supplicant and his home government uphold

[63] Heinrich Lammasch, *Das Recht der Auslieferung*, Vienna, 1884, p. 51.

their respective causes. Rather than suppress one side of the argument, it gives both parties a chance to adjourn their dispute to a more propitious day. Lammasch's argument is valid if the country of asylum takes no stand on the political positions involved. Only inasmuch as it requires knowledge of the outer contours of the political complex at stake does the country have to inquire into the circumstances of the case. It notes that the supplicant may someday have as good a chance as his pursuers to be recognized as the true representative of his homeland. In preserving the chance for both parties to restate their case in the future—unequal though the chance may be—the country that offers sanctuary to the persecuted will have defended before the tribunal of history its own reputation and the good name of the exile's nation, which in the eyes of generations to come may have been compromised by its rulers.

What standards and what quality of justice should be guaranteed at home to the exile returned to his country's authorities for trial has been discussed time and again. National statutes and specific conditions stipulated in extradition judgments—more recently, for example, the International Court's first ruling in the Peruvian-Colombian dispute, with its politely futile suggestions—have insisted on the prohibition of courts-martial, military or special courts, and so on.[64] While showing legitimate concern for standards of justice, such discussions and recommendations bypass the essential. As long as there is no world community, the standards they envisage will inevitably vary from one country to another. The fact that national courts enforce different standards need not as such be disquieting, provided that deviations are confined to the fields of property, trade, and, possibly, family relations. It is disquieting when such deviations express different political vistas of the administration of justice even under seemingly "normal" conditions.

When political standards are close enough to each other, the differences do not seem to matter in regard to the judicial system. But molded by the political atmosphere of the day rather than by procedural guarantees, judicial standards actually applied may be at variance even within countries of the same political culture. The more so when an unbridgeable abyss separates the individual countries' political systems. It seems a comfort at times to prevent foreign standards from being projected or superimposed on our own—witness the cases of escapers from totalitarianism, discussed above. In other situations, when

[64] ICJ Reports, Vol. 4 (1950), p. 284.

the oppressor turns victim, our sense of duty may conflict with our sympathies.[65]

Whatever the case may be, strict enforcement of the rule of non-extradition of political offenders will always shield the courts from overwhelming outside pressure. In the dealings of Vichy France with Franco Spain, for example, the observance of this practice turned out to be a precious asset at the hands of courts willing to put the asset to proper use.[66] Certainly the courts in weak countries have to tread warily, so as not to place the national government in an unnecessarily difficult position. In powerful countries such as the United States, the courts have long been in the habit of adequately fulfilling their protective mission. They may have shown condescension to the poor devils and strange customers who come from an incomprehensible, perilous, and topsy-turvy world;[67] and they may have provoked the resentment of these less fortunate ones. But they did their job. Now that the United States has a stake in maintaining many existing foreign governments of whatever questionable domestic record, the true test of the American courts' asylum doctrine is yet to come.[68]

[65] Cf. Brazil's refusal to extradite a Danish "collaborationist," *Annual Digest*, 1947, p. 146. Kindred souls attract one another. This is why Franco's Spain, Perón's Argentina, Trujillo's Dominican Republic, Stroessner's Paraguay, and Nasser's Egypt have become post-war havens for totalitarian asylum seekers. But it should be noted that these governments do not rejoice in getting embroiled in disputes over the boundarylines between political offenses and crimes against humanity. They may deny knowledge of the whereabouts of their "guests," urge them to move on, or, if a clearcut decision becomes unavoidable, rationalize the desired result—nonextradition—without reaching the question of the political character of the offense charged by the demanding state. When Egypt recently rejected the German demand for the extradition of "concentration camp doctor" Eisele, it grounded its refusal in differences between the applicable Egyptian and German statutes of limitations; *Frankfurter Allgemeine Zeitung*, October 17, 1958. See also n.69.

[66] See Joseph Magnol on the judgments of the courts of appeal of Aix (May 12, 1941), Toulouse (June 6, 1941), and Algiers (October 10, 1941), in *La Semaine Juridique*, Vol. 11 (1942), p. 1795.

[67] See, for example, the Ezeta case, 62 F 972 (1894), Northern District of California, and the Rudewitz case, reprinted in Hackworth, *op.cit.*, Vol. 4, p. 49.

[68] Three recent cases should be mentioned here. The first concerns five sailors from the Spanish Navy who deserted while on shore leave on the West Coast and fled to Mexico. Seized by Mexican officials, they were transported back to the US frontier under the coaxing of both US and Spanish Navy officers, and, as the appeal court put it, "rather unvoluntarily" brought back on American soil to be handed back to the Spanish authorities. In its somewhat tortured conclusions, the appeal court for the Ninth District avoided any reference to the political asylum problem and chided the appellant's lawyers for ever having raised the question. It based its findings, favorable to the sailors, on the inapplicability of Article 24 (surrender of deserters) of the Spanish-American treaty of 1902. For this purpose the court construed the act of desertion as having occurred only at the moment when the sailors went to Mexico. As they had

What, then, do present-day conditions hold in store for the asylum seeker? As the composition of the body of supplicants has changed in the course of decades, so have accepted attitudes. To those in power the political exile characteristic of the nineteenth century presented at most a tactical problem in politics. To governments today which must deal with huge masses of the politically persecuted, asylum is an economic, public welfare, and administrative headache of quite a different magnitude. The way the problem is solved depends on a multitude of considerations of national policy and political expediency. As infinitely more exiles are sheltered than ever before, the individual's prospects for finding refuge have deteriorated enormously.

Once the supplicant is admitted, however, most governments outside the totalitarian orbit tend to protect him from being handed over, in

---

been brought to the United States against their will, they would have to be put back on Mexican soil, a feasible solution inasmuch as the Mexican government had meanwhile disavowed the attitude taken by its local officials and granted the sailors permission to stay. Medina v. Hartman, 260 F 2d 569 (1958).

The second case concerns the attempts of the Yugoslav government to effect the rendition of Andrijga Artucovic, former minister of the interior in Ante Pavelic's Ustashi government. The same appeal court accepted the political character of the murders, which were alleged to have been committed on Artucovic's orders and labelled war crimes by the Yugoslav government. Rejecting the Yugoslav demand, the court concluded that the UN resolutions of 1946 and 1947 "have not sufficient force of law to modify long-standing judicial interpretation of similar treaty provisions." Karadzole v. Artucovic, 247 F 2d 198 at 205 (1957). The Supreme Court, Justices Black and Douglas dissenting, sent the case back to the district court for a hearing on the material submitted by the Yugoslav authorities; 335 U.S. 393 (1958). However, the district court confirmed the conclusions of the court of appeals.

Gallina v. Fraser, 177 F Supp 856 (D.C. Conn.), aff'd 287 F 2d 77, 2 Cir. (1960), certiorari denied 5 L 2d 74 (1960), grants extradition of a so-called Sicilian bandit (convicted *in absentia*) to Italy, rejecting his contention that he had acted as a member of a separatist group. In the face of conflicting statements, the lower court opinion (*ibid.*, p. 868) rests on the testimony of a former OSS agent, produced by the Italian government, regarding Gallina's bandit qualifications—a somewhat problematic procedure.

Presently pending on appeal is the case of ex-dictator Marcos Perez Jimenez, whose extradition to Venezuela had been granted after long-drawn-out hearings in the U.S. District Court of Southern California.

The more strategic the differentiation between political offense and crime against the human condition, the more important it becomes to avoid basing extradition demands on opinion offenses, even if these opinions should bear evidence of an advanced degree of moral degradation. The German authorities misjudged this difference when they asked Italy for the extradition of the former high school professor Zind, convicted for extreme anti-Semitic utterances, a request which was quite justifiedly turned down both by the Appeal Court in Naples and by the Court of Cassation in 1961. The Federal Ministry of Justice did not, however, make such a request to the Israel government in the Eichmann case, when such course would have been amply justified on moral and equally defensible legal grounds.

an informal way, to foreign authorities that threaten his life or freedom. There are exceptions, though, in politically dependent countries.

The handling of formal extradition demands long attracted legal rigmarole. Elaborate legal formulas defining nonextraditable categories of political offenders often served to disguise expediency and interest in combinations varying from one country to another, and from one political regime to the next. As asylum-granting governments need no longer fear isolated individual violence on the part of exiles, and as the totalitarian regimes' contempt for the rights of political captives has become a matter of common knowledge, the recent tendency has been toward judicial reinforcement of safeguards against extradition. While the opposite tendency found some nourishment in political conditions of the early postwar period, it was not strong enough to overcome the courts' reluctance to weaken the protection granted; nor has there been a noticeable inclination to depart from the new, broader definition of the group exempt from extradition as political offenders. Moreover, the fact that decisions on the prerequisites of extradition have generally passed into the hands of courts diminishes both the pressure potential of the country seeking extradition and the susceptibility to pressure of the country whose courts decide such requests.

Asylum—Herodotus already knew it—has its flaws. It is likely to remain mostly inoperative unless safely anchored in man's propensity for shame. The danger today is not that the institution be valued too little. It is in mistaking transitory considerations of expediency for the institution's intrinsic limitations. To be sure, recognition of satisfactory protection against extradition as an integral part of political asylum raises a number of difficult problems of delimitation. Even in a period where so many people are sucked against their will into the maelstrom of politics, the political background of personal activity may, in an individual case, appear too slight to rate protection against extradition. Moreover, there is the urgent problem of drawing the line at the odium generis humani, the crime against the human condition.[69]

[69] Laxness of controls, the hallmark of younger countries without a fully experienced bureaucratic apparatus, facilitates ingress of the persecuted with or without appropriate documents. The availability of such countries is one of the most effective safeguards for individuals facing political repression. But it also has the effect of creating sanctuaries for offenders who cannot justifiedly be brought under the political category, a fact which became quite clear from the remarks of the Argentine representative at the Security Council meeting on the Eichmann case (cited above, n.34). "It has not always been easy to separate the ore from the pure metal." Under such circumstances, extradition demands may not only meet preliminary legal difficulties in regard to the proof of the nonpolitical quality, but may founder on the dexterity of the individual whose

Here the difficulty lies not only in elaborating somewhat larger or narrower groups of responsible agents, but in the much more fundamental fact that in the age of the hydrogen bomb, means-ends categories are rapidly losing their meaning. The application of asylum criteria may now seem hopelessly inappropriate and unrealistic.

But this is taking a needlessly pessimistic attitude, foreshadowing the certainty of a war in which international law would perish together with everything else. The very greatness of the danger illuminates the continuing positive function of political asylum. Free political competition on an international level is a weapon, however small, in the fight against the coming of universal barbarity. This may also be the real reason why, after each new deluge, which seemingly swept away political asylum, it staged a comeback. A necessary institution in a deeply divided world, political asylum sets limits—imperfect, broken, movable, but nevertheless tangible limits—to any regime's power.

---

extradition is sought in making good use of the facilities, personal and spatial, offered by such a country, even in the absence of any official complicity. See, for example, the case of the concentration camp Doctor Mengele, as reported in *Frankfurter Allgemeine Zeitung*, July 4, 1960.

CHAPTER X

THE QUALITY OF MERCY

✦✦✦

1. The Role of Clemency in the
Apparatus of Justice

IN IMPOSING sentence on a convicted prisoner, a court must somehow tie together the requirements of society—as expressed in codes and rules regarding expected behavior, and behind these in official and unofficial pressures—with the experience it has had with the man in the dock. The court may gauge society's requirements incorrectly, and it may misinterpret the record chalked up against the defendant, but it cannot just shove aside either of them. In granting clemency, however, the power holder is not necessarily subject to these considerations. He may indeed be influenced by the requirements of society, but clemency, unlike a judicial procedure, is not intrinsically an instrument for serving the public interest. And while his decision may be affected by actions of the prisoner, it also may be wholly unrelated to the affairs of the prospective beneficiary. Moreover, the prisoner, once the offense is entered into the books against him, finds his chance of self-determination considerably lessened, his physical movements and outside contacts almost completely subject to the control of others; he may still retain some means of influencing those who hold sway over him, but the efficacy of these means is uncertain and their price may be prohibitive. In short, clemency, unlike judicial procedures, contains elements of both arbitrariness and purposefulness.

What role does this aspect of power perform in the apparatus of justice? Does it, despite its place outside the established instruments of control, serve a function in the social order? In particular, what is its role in the area of political offenses against the very authority that has the power of decision? I propose to approach these questions first by way of illustration.

The history of clemency probably knows few rencontres so ironic and symbolic as one that occurred in the spring of 1921, bringing together Henry Daugherty, who was President Harding's attorney general, political mentor, and man Friday, and Eugene Debs, symbol of the last homegrown variety of American socialism. At that moment Debs was serving a ten-year sentence in Atlanta Federal Penitentiary for having sustained in his Canton, Ohio, speech of June 18, 1918, the cause of those who were deemed to have obstructed recruiting for the World War I effort. His conviction had been upheld by a unanimous Supreme Court opinion,[1] rendered by Justice Holmes. Somehow that opinion failed to go beyond putting Debs's demeanor and remarks into the framework of the incitement-to-insubordination provision of the June 1917 Espionage Act; it refrained from testing the facts of the case against Holmes's own "clear and present danger" doctrine, enunciated a few months earlier.[2]

Holmes's private correspondence suggests that he had some doubts about the case.[3] He considered the decision justifiable, regarding both the constitutionality of this provision of the Espionage Act and the circumstances of wartime society. But he questioned the wisdom of the prosecution, and gave an impression that Oliver Wendell Holmes as juror might have reached different conclusions from those of Mr. Justice Holmes. To his mind—somewhat disturbed by a series of political prosecutions carried on after the business of war, to which they were related, had come to an end—the results of the conviction, though it had passed both the sieve of a wartime jury and the patriotic reflexes of the higher courts, were not compatible with the changed requirements of the postwar situation. In fact, he felt that the discrepancy called for a presidential pardon "for a lot of poor devils that it was my misfortune to have to write opinions condemning."

But fulfillment of this desire, shared by small but vocal minorities[4] and by many outstanding individuals not necessarily in sympathy with Debs's cause, found no favor with Woodrow Wilson, the incumbent President. Doubly removed from the calculus of political benefit and loss, by ingrained stubbornness and by the approaching end of his political career, he would not even retrospectively forgive the sins of those who had resisted his policies. Thus the decision on what to do with the Atlanta prisoner and Socialist presidential candidate—whose million votes at the 1920 election had betokened him as a faint beacon or, according to others, a picayune nuisance, but scarcely a danger to the

---

[1] Debs v. United States, 249 U.S. 211 (1919).

[2] Schenck v. United States, 249 U.S. 47 (1919).

[3] See Mark de Wolfe Howe, ed., *Holmes-Pollock Letters*, Cambridge, Mass., 1941, Vol. 2, pp. 7, 11, 15; and *Holmes-Laski Letters*, Cambridge, Mass., 1953, pp. 190, 203.

[4] As for the majority, "the great mass of plain people in all such melodramatic affairs are almost unanimously on the side of the prosecution." H. L. Mencken, in *A Carnival of Buncombe*, ed. Malcolm Moss, Baltimore, 1956, entry for October 18, 1920, p. 26.

realm—devolved on the incoming president and, at his behest, on his confidant, Henry Daugherty.

The tale of the personal rencontre of the attorney general and the prisoner of Atlanta hailed into his office was twice told by Daugherty himself:[5] once in his report to the president, recommending Debs's release by commutation of his sentence, as of December 31, 1921; and once in his memoirs. The first and contemporary version, even if probably not entirely Daugherty's brainchild, has a greater ring of authenticity than the mentored autobiography of a decade later. There, the note of condescending and at the same time chivalrous benevolence for the valiant but errant soul was overplayed to reflect a kind of posthumous credit on Attorney General Daugherty, otherwise known to his contemporaries only through the disrepute he brought to his office.

At the time of their meeting, April 19, 1921, Daugherty and his chief, Harding, had already publicly taken the position that there could be no distinction between political and genuine crime,[6] a theorem that Daugherty reiterated in his report to the president. However ironical this position must look when taken by a Daugherty, when it was propounded it aggravated the job of searching for a rationale under which to release Debs. The latter did little to help Daugherty toward formulating favorable conclusions resting on the customary basis that the prisoner understood and sincerely repented his previous wrongdoing. Few political prisoners have the imagination and intelligence of Michael Bakunin, who put his 1851 "confession" for Nicholas I in terms that allowed the czar to dwell on the indubitably common ground between them—Slav patriotism and contempt of things German; thus he not only contrived a stratagem for advancing his own case, but maintained even in abject submission some semblance of a political position.[7] In contrast, Debs's exposition of his doctrine and basis of political action drove Daugherty, who was highly impressed by the prisoner's dignified demeanor, to the exasperated conclusion, revealing the honest incomprehension of a total stranger to the world of ideas and convictions, that, "So far as he thinks correctly he might be conscientious, but he

[5] Letter from the attorney general to the president, "Application for Pardon of Eugene V. Debs," Senate Document No. 113, 67th Congress, 2nd Session, 1922; and Harry M. Daugherty, in collaboration with Thomas Dixon, *The Inside Story of the Harding Tragedy*, New York, 1932, pp. 115, 121. Debs himself, who made a promise of silence to the prison warden, has not left an account of his conversation with Daugherty; see McAllister Coleman, *Eugene Debs, A Man Unafraid*, New York, 1930, p. 324.

[6] H. M. Daugherty, "Respect for the Law," *American Bar Association Journal*, Vol. 7 (1921), pp. 505, 508-09.

[7] See Bakunin, *Confessions*, transl. Paulette Brupbacher, Paris, 1932.

does not think correctly and apparently cannot do so on the questions involved in his case."

What then to do with a man who thinks incorrectly and on whose "principles no thinking man would set up a government"? Gathering together the reasons why a commutation of sentence (not a full pardon restoring civil rights) should be granted, Daugherty enumerated the obvious: Debs's apparently selfless personality, his exemplary conduct in prison, the repeal of the section under which he had been convicted, his advanced age and weakened health, and the excessiveness of the sentence in terms of his life expectancy. Yet there remained one insuperable obstacle. An act of clemency will not restore the recipient to what he has never been: a good citizen and patriot. Nevertheless, the conviction that neither imprisonment nor clemency could reform Debs seemed in the final analysis less important to Daugherty than the fact that many others thought his punishment unjustifiable. Thus from the admittedly scant effect of imprisonment on the prisoner the scene shifts to its possible adverse effects on others. Daugherty's accurate perception of the degree of momentary pressures in favor of Eugene Debs's release can be rationalized as what theorists would call a kind of application-in-reverse of the doctrine of criminal law's general preventive function; in other words, as a belief that enforcement would fail to have beneficial effects on potential offenders.

Of course, the Debs film could be, and in other less publicized instances has been, played backward. Rather than emphasizing the failure to convince others, an enemy of clemency could invoke the need to overawe potential enemies in the face of threatening political situations as an argument to justify the opposite course, a refusal or delaying of pardon.[8] One can see in the rencontre between Daugherty and Debs just one of the endless absurdities of history, or one can savor the deeper irony: a Daugherty given a chance to be remembered himself, because for the better part of a day he constituted a sort of captive and somehow also captivated audience for Eugene Debs. Afterwards he took care of the matter with the politician's knack, releasing Debs in a manner nicely calculated to balance the expectations of Debs's specialized constituency against the requirements of the official credo.

To further illustrate the ways of clemency I turn next to Shakespeare's *Measure for Measure*. Isabella comes to Angelo, deputy of the absent Duke, to plead mercy for her brother Claudio, who has been sentenced

---

[8] See the discussion and material in William Preston, "The Ideology and Technique of Repression, 1903-1933," *American Radicals*, ed. Harvey Goldberg, New York, 1957.

to die for fornication, an offense punishable under an enactment that has long gone unenforced. To Angelo's statement that her brother is "a forfeit of the law," she replies: "Why, all the souls that were were forfeit once; and He that might the vantage best have took found out the remedy. How would you be if He, which is the top of judgment, should but judge you as you are? O, think on that; and mercy then will breathe within your lips, like man new-made" (II, 2).

Angelo is known as a man of probity. As the Duke said earlier of him: "Lord Angelo is precise; stands at a guard with envy; scarce confesses that his blood flows, or that his appetite is more to bread than stone" (I, 4). But he falls victim to Isabella's beauty and eventually comes round to asking her: "Which had you rather,—that the most just law now took your brother's life; or, to redeem him give up your body to such sweet uncleanness as she that he hath stain'd" (II, 4).

For Angelo, clemency to Claudio is a mere means for satisfying his lust; he will refrain from exercising lawful authority if in exchange Isabella grants her favor. But Isabella has a different, more highminded, understanding of clemency: "Ignominy in ransom and free pardon are of two houses; lawful mercy is nothing akin to foul redemption" (II, 4). Of what nature is the clemency ultimately extended by the Duke in his triple grant of mercy?

As for the ruffian Barnardine, even his availability as an object of clemency is "an accident that Heaven provides." His head, to have been lost for a cause "most manifest, and not denied by himself," was going to be used for a necessary project, but in the last minute is replaced by a more suitable one, which has became available through natural causes. In this instance, clemency is a product of fortuity, derived from the same roots as the mediaeval practice of rescinding capital punishment if an attempt to carry through an execution has miscarried.[9] Another element in the decision is the Duke's pronouncement: "Thou'rt condemn'd: But, for those earthly faults, I quit them all, and pray thee take this mercy to provide for better times to come" (v, 1). This is an affirmation of the sovereign's right to grant clemency without furnishing an explanation of why it has been exercised in the particular instance.

The Duke's determination to effect Claudio's release from Antonio's harsh sentence is fully motivated. Isabella, when pleading with Angelo for Claudio's life, put it in the following vein: "Who is it that hath

[9] See the historical account in the Attorney General's *Survey of Release Procedures,* Washington, 1939, Vol. 3 on Pardon, pp. 16, 42. Modern American usage does not honor this custom, though it could well be rationalized by reference to the Eighth Amendment's provision against cruel and unusual punishment. See Francis v. Resweber, 329 U.S. 459 (1947).

died for this offence? There's many have committed it" (ii, 2). It is a dubious argument for forestalling conviction; yet, conforming to what natural law theory called "intrinsic"[10] cause for clemency, it carries cogency in any clemency proceedings.

There remains the most problematic case, clemency for Angelo, of whom the Duke himself says: "Being criminal, in double violation of sacred chastity and of promise-breach thereon dependent, for your brother's life,—the very mercy of the law cries out most audible, even from his proper tongue, an Angelo for Claudio, death for death" (v, 1). Nevertheless, and even though she believes her brother dead, Isabella asks clemency for Angelo. She tries to cloak his proposed clemency-chastity deal, fulfilled not by herself but by Mariana, in a legal formula: "His act did not o'ertake his bad intent, and must be buried but as an intent that perish'd by the way: thoughts are no subjects; intents but merely thoughts" (v, 1). But this construction, which ignores Angelo's intent to renege on the deal and have Claudio killed despite it, does not exculpate Angelo for his abuse of office, and it is waved away by the Duke with a curt "Your suit's unprofitable."

Is the Duke moved, then, by the loyalty of Mariana, once affianced to Angelo and now wed to him on the Duke's orders? Or does he find reason for clemency in Angelo's remorse: "I am sorry that such sorrow I procure: and so deep sticks it in my penitent heart that I crave death more willingly than mercy; 'tis my deserving, and I do entreat it" (v, 1)? The two latter grounds for clemency, hope and repentance, may be both probable and intrinsic causes in natural law doctrine,[11] but they remain slender reeds to build on. Finally, is the Duke's reasoning based on the degree of apparent, but only apparent, symmetry between Angelo's case and that of Claudio?

What looks like a plethora of possible explanations is in reality much closer to the opposite. Clemency to Bernardine may be styled merely the caprice of the prince, which in confirming the outcome of an accidental constellation gives a new lease on life to the riotous underdog. But clemency to Angelo corresponds to what Hegel called "die grundlose Gnade."[12] It is a clemency untouched by any bond to the particular circumstances of either benefactor or beneficiary. It appears as a humble recognition of the universality of human abjectness and the infinite pos-

---

[10] "Instrinseca cum si non injusta dura tamen est poena ad factum comparata." Grotius, *De jure belli*, note 8, bk. ii, ch. *XX*, 25.

[11] *Ibid.*, bk. ii, ch. *XX*, 24 and 26.

[12] Hegel, *Philosophy of Law*, addendum 173 to par. 282.

sibilities for redemption. Unrelated to ulterior motives, it proceeds from the Duke's all-embracing, all-forgiving mercy.

In this respect, the clemency granted Angelo is in line with Portia's admonition, "the quality of mercy is not strain'd; it droppeth as the gentle rain from heaven." Yet in *The Merchant of Venice* the focus of clemency is somewhat different. Clemency appears here as a remedy for imperfections of the legal system itself. As Portia says to Shylock: "Of a strange nature is the suit you follow: yet in such rule, that the Venetian law cannot impugn you as you do proceed" (IV, I). If performance of the bond is impossible, no alternative legal remedy or substitution is at hand. Therefore, clemency would serve as a safety valve for justice, correcting structural inadequacies of the judicial process, or unjust individual results that it might lead to.[13]

What are the implications of these examples for our central problem, the function of clemency in a social order? What is the use of chalking up good against evil, establishing a balance sheet, and shuffling around accounts until a small positive balance appears? Is clemency to be regarded merely as an antidote to the meaninglessness of earthly existence in general? In implying as much, Shakespeare stands on the shoulders of St. Augustine, with his concept of grace. To St. Augustine, God's freedom signifies a choice to select for salvation whomever He deems fit, and the Christian's belief in salvation, in *gratia cooperans*, thus constitutes no more than a precondition for his receiving it.

Whether or not we accept this interpretation of clemency, it must be granted that the power holder's position in the process of extending clemency is problematic. Who is the guarantor of his disinterestedness, and where lie the limits of his justifiable interest? Josef Kohler, child of the benign second half of the nineteenth century, pays his respects to Hegel in viewing clemency as the intellectual feat through which the power holder ennobles the highest aims of culture.[14] Still, he knows quite well that this premise holds true only if the regent is able to avoid the temptations of private interest and concentrate on "the holiest concern of law and social order."

[13] That the safety-valve and corrective function of mercy—as stressed, for example by Jhering, in *Zweck im Recht*, 3rd ed.; Vol. I (1916) p. 333—is only one component of clemency is emphasized by Radbruch, who has produced by far the best and most succinct discussion of the issue; see his *Rechtsphilosophie*, 5th ed.; Stuttgart, 1956, pp. 276 and 337.

[14] Josef Kohler, *Shakespeare von dem Forum der Jurisprudenz*, 2nd ed.; Berlin, 1919, p. 178.

Over the stretches of history, clemency has taken many forms and served many purposes. The philanthropy exercised by the Hellenic ruler and the well-advertised *clementia* of the Roman emperor were products of civilizations that made for a rapid alternation of cruelty and civility, of calculating schemes and boundless liberality. It differed from the practices of earlier Greek and Roman periods, when the course of the legal order was allowed to suffer few interruptions, and then only, as a rule, for weighty political reasons. In many periods, however, there has been an undercurrent of magical, religious, or even social usages, existing outside the plans and schemes of major power holders. These usages sometimes functioned without a mediator, as when the criminal's ostentatiously chance encounter with a vestal virgin or a cardinal was sufficient to cause his release. In other instances they entailed active intercession: a condemned man might be saved through the good offices of a virgin who was willing to marry him, or, in a somewhat less active form of intervention, through the word of an ecclesiastical dignitary or a nobleman, whose office or family had inherited a privilege of interceding with the local authorities for the release of convicted criminals. Thus many a poor and hungry vagrant, but also some more dangerous, more politically-tinged malefactors, escaped the hangman. This *bon plaisir* of those who had but small control over man or mind, but were still able to play providence, served as an antidote to a brutal and haphazard exercise of power; as a rule it disappeared when power became centralized.[15]

Does the transition from the deified personality of antiquity's ruler to the Christian prince, styled to be dependent on the grace and benevolence of God, connote a new departure in the exercise and usages of clemency?[16] The point is at best arguable. Francis Bacon tried hard to find a principle of statecraft in Henry VII's lottery-like alternation of pardons and executions; but even for him, Henry's practice remained at best in the nature of an *arcanum imperii*. When Henry chose clemency it was always calculated to turn to his own advantage, be it through the ostentatious showing of his feeling of security, the filling of his exchequer, or, as with his last, general pardon, the expectation of "a securer coronation in a better kingdom."[17]

[15] See the account in Heinrich Gwinner, *Der Einfluss des Standes im gemeinen Strafrecht*, Breslau, 1934, pp. 150-58, 247-59.

[16] See the interesting though inconclusive discussion in Wilhelm Grewe, *Gnade und Recht*, Hamburg, 1936, pp. 81-96.

[17] See Bacon's *History of the Reign of Henry VII*, in *Works*, ed. Spedding, Ellis, and Heath, Vol. 11, pp. 274-75, 347; also Howard B. White, "The English Solomon: Francis Bacon on Henry VII," in *Social Research*, Vol. 24, No. 4 (Winter 1957), pp. 457-81.

Theological and constitutional reactions against the Augustinian-Jansenist concept of grace and the corresponding unchecked privilege of the sovereign in granting clemency are but expressions one and the same phenomenon: a middle-class quest for certainty. In the eighteenth century this quest was characterized by the rationalism of the Enlightenment. A clemency prerogative construed after the Jansenist concept—with God as the free dispenser of grace, owed to nobody and distributed with sovereign independence—became inadmissible. In contrast, Jesuit doctrine in the eighteenth century construed God's grace as a calculable reward owed by God. Under the criticism of Filangieri, Beccaria, and Kant, clemency became outmoded. What Montesquieu still regarded as the "most beautiful attribute" of the prince's sovereignty became with Kant, half a century later, the "most slippery of all rights of sovereignty."[18] For the dangers of the sovereign's benevolence the certainty of a good and wise law was to be substituted. In Beccaria's choice between the "noble prerogative" and the perfect legislation, with its "mild punishments and regular and expeditious proceedings," victory easily went to the omniscient law.[19] The French Criminal Code of 1791 did away with the practice of clemency.[20]

But the rationalist illusion that an omniscient legislator could instruct and enlighten the judge enough to avoid any need for further consideration of the case did not survive the emergence of Napoleon. Since then it has been agreed that a procedure for the granting of clemency is necessary. And even at that time, it might be added, Jeremy Bentham, while sharing the illusions of his age and calling clemency a "veritable betrayal of trust," regarded pardon in the marginal political field—our main interest here—as a necessary part of the legal system.[21]

To be sure, there has been intermittent struggle over the ultimate location of the pardoning power, with the results of the conflict mirrored in changing constitutional allocations. Some European countries assign to the legislature the business of general amnesties for whole categories of crimes or defendants; for the granting of individual pardons they oscillate between a number of solutions, ranging from assigning this power as a prerogative of the head of state, to be exercised in

---

[18] Montesquieu, *De l'esprit des lois*, bk. VI, 5; Kant, *Metaphysische Anfangsgruende der Rechtslehre*, II, I, II.

[19] Beccaria, *Dei delitti e delle pene*, ch. 26.

[20] Part I, Title VII, Art. 7. The argument in the Constituent Assembly, which was mainly concerned with curtailing the king's prerogatives, rested on clemency's character as an individual dispensation outside the general law; see *Archives Parlementaires*, Vol. 36, pp. 736-38.

[21] Bentham, *Theory of Legislation*, London, 1914, Vol. 2, p. 171.

the constitutionally prescribed form, to putting it at the disposal of parliamentary majorities. A dubious intermediate solution is to put the right of pardon exclusively at the disposal of the judiciary, thereby equipping with a political prerogative the members of an organization outside the circuit of any political responsibility.[22] Anglo-American usage, while its history has not been free of jealousies and disputes between king or president and parliament—witness Andrew Johnson's bout with Congress—has now settled both individual and general pardons in the hands of the executive. But whatever the changing allocation principles, the need for an instrument with which to correct the actions of courts has never been doubted since the rationalist intermezzo of the Enlightenment.

Usually society makes the premature release of its prisoners dependent on their contrition, involving both good conduct while under detention and insight into the illicit character of the act. In a mass society like ours, however, conditional release has often become a general and fairly standardized procedure, both for economizing official efforts and, more important, for preserving some means of effective postrelease control over the prisoner's activities. (Conditional release as used here differs from the release provided by "good-conduct laws," which give the prisoner a statutory right to have a certain part of his sentence set aside for good conduct while serving it, irrespective of his beliefs and probable future extramural activities.) This practice serves to give clemency the qualitatively different aspect of a generalized legislative policy, making it a built-in part of the sentencing system and somehow akin to the mediaeval judging by mercy. Correspondingly, contrition, too, becomes formalized—reduced to an absence of troublemaking while serving the sentence, with the sum total of postrelease expectations calculated from a parole chart.

The granting of clemency to political prisoners is especially caught up in cross-currents. The parole chart may show the prisoner as one of the best overall risks for cooperative existence; yet in the one point the

[22] An example of the most destructive exercise of such a judicial fiat was the 1924 release of Adolf Hitler after he had spent six months of his five-year sentence; see Karl Schwend, *Bayern zwischen Monarchie und Diktatur*, Munich, 1954, pp. 292-302. The French Fourth Republic associated the president with the Council of the Judiciary in the exercise of clemency. In spite of the difficulties that arose in regard to the ministerial countersignature and the share of the Ministry of Justice, this practice amounted to a balancing of judicial and political influence. The Fifth Republic (see Article 65 of the Constitution) returns the prerogative to the president, leaving the Council of the Judiciary only the right to be heard.

state is most vitally interested in—his willingness to refrain from opposing the present political system and from working in the direction of its destruction—the authorities are not likely to get much cooperation. It may even be that the prisoner himself is not willing, except at best under the strongest mental reservations, to sign the official papers and petitions needed to put clemency proceedings into motion.[23] Thus in 1856 Napoleon III offered repatriation to the left-wing republicans-in-exile on the condition that they petition the government and recognize the established regime; his 1859 amnesty omitted even the need for an application, excluding only Ledru-Rollin, styled a common criminal. Nevertheless, some of the outstanding political figures, among them Louis Blanc and Victor Hugo, refused to avail themselves of the offer, instead waiting another decade for the fall of the regime. In short, the regime's foes may want to avoid anything that could even remotely be interpreted as recognition of the present power holders' title for proceeding against them. In the minds of such prisoners, capture and consequent imprisonment or exile connote purely physical events, without any greater dignity or justification. As Barbès put it when appearing before the French Senate after the unsuccessful revolt of 1839: "If the Indian is vanquished, if the accident of war delivers him into the hands of his enemies, he will not venture to defend himself with empty words, but offer his head to be scalped."[24]

Those in power, if unable to obtain their foes' submission, may well tend to exhaust all the punitive possibilities opened up by the judicial sentence.[25] For such tendencies there are many and possibly contradictory motivations, including moral indignation, a feeling of overwhelming strength, and even a desire to compensate for weakness. Equally often, however, the state authorities have scaled down or even relinquished their claim. They can more easily bring themselves to do this if a formula is available that seems to uphold their freedom. When

[23] See the exhaustive discussion and material on a 1933 German case in Richard Scheringer, *Das grosse Los unter Soldaten, Bauern und Rebellen*, Hamburg, 1959, pp. 279-85, esp. the letter of General von Reichenau to Scheringer, suggesting a petition for mercy; see also Ralph Chapin, *The Wobbly*, Chicago, 1947, p. 322. More than a century earlier, Prince Polignac had had similar troubles when deciding whether to accept clemency from the hands of Louis Philippe; see Pierre Robin-Harmel, *Le Prince Jules de Polignac*, Avignon, 1950, p. 192.

[24] See Louis Blanc, *Histoire des dix ans*, Vol. 5, p. 182.

[25] See, for example, the experience of John Gates, *The Story of An American Communist*, p. 139. For recent United States policies in this direction see the Letter to the Editor, "To Free Gold and Sobell," in the *New York Times*, February 16, 1960, p. 36; for a similar Swiss case, see the story of Pierre Nicolle as seen from the viewpoint of the Swiss authorities, in *Bundesblatt*, Vol. 2 (1952), p. 331.

Barbès had been sentenced to death for his part in the uprising, there was a considerable amount of pressure on Louis Philippe's government to commute the sentence. Victor Hugo, in a poem dedicated to the memory of the Princess d'Orléans, the king's daughter, tried to put the call for clemency toward Barbès into the conventional framework that had long marked the sovereign's complete discretion in granting clemency, by evoking two major events in the king's family—death and birth:[26]

> Pour votre ange envolée ainsi qu'une colombe
> Pour ce royal enfant, doux et frôle roseau
> Grâce encore une fois, grâce au nom de la tombe
> Grâce au nom du berceau.

By evoking both the plenary power of the king and basic reasons for general human compassion, Hugo put in the foreground motivations that could efface any impression that the king was yielding to the clamor of the street.

A ruler may, of course, be beyond caring what impression his action will make. Though Nicholas II of Russia would grant clemency, even full pardons, to members of the Black Hundred, to murderers of Jews or of moderate politicians, in the case of social-revolutionary attackers of military men he saw no cause to arrest the course of the law. And Nicholas' Bolshevist successors, in their early days, had such a small margin of security and cared so little for the meaning of legal forms that they looked on the imposition of a death penalty as a normal object for horse-trading: they were willing to remit the sentence in exchange for pledges of good behavior by the political organization to which the convicted person belonged.[27]

In cases involving political offense, this use of the clemency prerogative as an opportunity for making a deal is not infrequent, though the connection between the pardon and its calculated effect may be a bit less crude than it was in the hands of the Bolshevists. De Valera and his Sinn Fein colleagues were beneficiaries of political strategies rather than partners to a deal. After that bloody Easter Sunday in Dublin in 1916, they owed their lives to the fact that the British had found it politic to take into account American political susceptibilities and the considerable number of Irish sympathizers in the United States. And the withholding of clemency can be subject to devious political con-

[26] See Georges Weill, *Histoire du parti républicain en France*, Paris, 1900, p. 175.
[27] See, for example, the text reprinted in Edward Hallett Carr, *The Bolshevik Revolution*, London, 1950, Vol. I, p. 183.

siderations. In the Haymarket Affair it appears that the governor's final determination, whereby he rejected clemency for five out of seven defendants (among the five one who had signed an attenuated repentance declaration in regard to his group's propaganda pattern), had relatively little to do with either the defendants' repentance or the governor's conviction of their guilt. It was rather a normal political compromise—in a field, though, where the category of compromise has little meaning.[28]

But political purpose is not always or exclusively the controlling factor in extending clemency. While Lincoln never lost sight of the need to re-establish the Union in the hearts of his foes, this consideration alone does not explain the pattern of his clemency practice, either toward those sentenced by the civil courts on treason charges or toward those in the clutches of courts-martial. From the viewpoint of the proximate effect on military operations, Sherman's quip that forty or fifty executions now would save thousands of lives in the next twelve months may have had an element of reasonableness, however conjectural. Yet Lincoln lived in a world in which clemency was not yet a matter of channels, triple-space memos, and stereotype briefings by pardon attorneys and staffers mouthing the conventional phrases. For him it was a very personal decision, under the burden of which he suffered considerable anguish. He handled it according to his own deep-seated feelings of the value of human life, with a consciousness of both the contingent nature of all political decisions and the duty he owed to his office and the nation.[29]

The decision on the granting of clemency, however lonely it may ultimately be, is subject to manifold pressures. And the more the clemency-

[28] See Henry David, *The History of the Haymarket Affair*, 2nd ed.; New York, 1958, esp. p. 457.

[29] See J. T. Dorris, "President Lincoln's Clemency," *Journal of the Illinois State Historical Society*, Vol. 20 (1927-1928) pp. 547-68; also Carl Sandburg, *Abraham Lincoln: The War Years*, New York, 1939, Vol. 4, p. 132. Especially relevant in this connection is Lincoln's handling of the 313 Minnesota Indians convicted to death by court-martial (*ibid.*, Vol. 1, p. 614); he personally reviewed the case history of every individual concerned, reprieving all but 38. For a judicial echo from the days when major office holders examined on their own the files pertaining to life and liberty, see Frankfurter dissenting in Jay v. Boyd, 351 U.S. 345, 370 (1956). For an inkling of contemporary practices, see Frank Reel, *The Case of General Yamashita*, Ch. 35; even if Mr. Reel's literary gifts are fully taken into consideration, the comparison remains painful. Criticizing the present Home Office practice of refusing to answer parliamentary questions in regard to the exercise of the prerogative of mercy, Geoffrey Marshall, in "Parliament and the prerogative of Mercy," *Public Law*, Spring 1961, pp. 8-25, gives some evidence of the part played by political pressures in the Home Secretary's decision. However, the article treats the problem from the viewpoint of ministerial responsibility toward Parliament, rather than of how, within a given social system, the most "just" decision may be reached.

dispenser is in the thick of the political fight, the greater the pressure he may be exposed to in regard to the exercise of this prerogative. In August 1932 the bestial National Socialist murderers of Potempa beat to death a helpless political foe of theirs—a curtain-raiser for things to come—and were sentenced to death for their deed. Chancellor von Papen, acting in his capacity as Reich Commissioner for Prussia, may have had a number of strong moral, legal, and political reasons against having the sentences carried out; but in commuting them into life terms after Hitler had chosen the disposition of this case as a battleground between himself and the authorities, Papen created the impression of having yielded to the most insolent type of pressure.[30]

Often, however, the pressure on public authorities can be expected to work in reverse. Especially when it is exerted by an organized propaganda machine, many governments will refuse to exercise the right to grant clemency, as did President Vincent Auriol, for example, on the occasion of the campaign for the release of the Communist naval officer Henri Martin, convicted to long-term penal servitude for incitement to sabotage on a man-of-war.[31] In such cases it is quite immaterial to the propagandists whether clemency is granted. If the offender is released, this action, irrespective of its circumstances, is ascribed to irresistible popular action; if clemency is refused, the very refusal is made the pivotal point of a continuing and stepped-up campaign. Whatever the power holder's reaction to such pressure, whether he yields or resists, he has fallen victim to a trial of strength between the state authority and its foes. An interesting case of this kind occurred in April 1957, when the West German authorities, after having refused to accede to a demand for a general political amnesty, released the Communist Youth functionary Jupp Angerforth, then serving a five-year penal-servitude sentence—a punishment that was out of line with both the type of penalties and the length of sentences usually meted out to Communist functionaries in the Federal Republic. Communist propaganda represented the release as an important victory, though in reality it was a well calculated measure, motivated by a desire to underscore the continuing reasonableness and humanity of the government's policy in political prosecutions.

A government itself may exert pressure in regard to clemency, offering this boon as a reward for service rendered. The convicted person,

[30] See Paul Kluke, "Der Fall Potempa," *Vierteljahrshefte für Zeitgeschichte*, Vol. 5 (1957) pp. 278-97, and, more recently, Gerhard Schulz, in Bracher, Sauer, and Schulz, *Die Nationalsozialistische Machtergreifung*, Cologne, 1960, p. 522, n. 29.

[31] *L'Affaire Henri Martin*, p. 220.

especially if sentenced to death, may in extremes be willing to turn informer, even though he refused to do so before. The manifest danger of his service lies in the possibility that in his anxiety to please he may make assertions whose interest for the government does not equal their accuracy.[32] The judgment of contemporaries and that of posterity may vary in regard to the prisoner's helpfulness. Yet power holders, whose vital interests may be at stake, cannot be blamed if they take advantage of such a situation, especially if they only respond to the prisoner's initiative rather than eliciting the information by advances of their own.[33]

There is, however, an inherent limitation to the proper exercise of the clemency prerogative. If it is one of the functions of clemency to correct and efface shortcomings of the judicial process, the reverse procedure, that of using the expectation of clemency as lure for a postconviction confession that would shore up a problematic judgment, contradicts the very essence of both clemency and justice. Postconviction confession is not a proper prerequisite for the commutation of a death sentence.

It was made one, however, in the Rosenberg case. The widely publicized fact that a wire from the White House to the death cells was kept open at all times was formally an invitation to inform on accomplices, but it logically implied an invitation to confession on the part of defendants who had so far been completely recalcitrant. It reflected the official desire to strengthen by a confession a conviction that rested essentially on circumstantial evidence and on testimony by a highly interested accomplice witness. While the state had a legitimate interest in finding out about accomplices, this interest, given the particular circumstances of the case, should have yielded to the necessity to defend the integrity of the judicial process.

If the administration shared the disquiet of the few who believed that the basis of the conviction itself was debatable, either in law or in fact, or of the many who entertained serious doubts about the decisive assumptions that entered the sentencing process (the factual basis of which was known, even when sentence was passed, to be purely conjectural),

[32] See the story of the Preston pardon by William III in 1691, as narrated by Macaulay in his *History of England*, Vol. 4, Ch. 17.

[33] Caillaux (see Ch. III, Sec. 3a) offers some material which he thinks would allow the inference that the French authorities tried to elicit from Bolo, sentenced to death for treason, information against Caillaux suggesting the possibility of a pardon for Bolo. However, the material is not conclusive, especially the extremely prudent letter of transmittal with which Poincaré sent back the rejection of a pardon to Clemenceau; Caillaux, *Mes Mémoires*, Vol. 3, pp. 204-06; the text of Poincaré's letter is on p. 381.

then a commutation of the sentence was indicated.[34] Such a course would have been indicated even though the extent of the pro-Rosenberg campaign and the resultant countercampaigns made dispassionate consideration of the case especially difficult. On the other hand, if the administration neither shared these doubts as to judgment or sentence, nor believed clemency to be an indicated policy toward those who had forsaken national allegiance, it might have proceeded without obfuscation, on the basis of the jury's and the judge's action. But one course emphatically should not have been taken: suggesting to the defendants that as a condition *sine qua non* for commutation of the sentence they confirm the assumption on which the verdict rested. Not only was this a tactical mistake, which settled once and for all the stature of the Rosenbergs as authentic martyrs, but it devaluated the finality of the judicial process, by turning the possibility of clemency into a device for obtaining confirmation of what by definition should neither need nor—except as specified by the law itself—accede to further confirmation: the final verdict of the jury and the sentence of the judge.

This case also illustrates once more clemency's unavoidable dialectics. Clemency is deeply immersed in the substructure of politics, its campaigns and strategies, its assumptions and symbols. But at the same time it provides the possibility of transcending the configurations of the day and introducing a touch of subjectivity into the rational rule by which we attempt to govern human relations. Such an element of subjectivity, distasteful as it may be to theorists, is considered necessary by many who are left unconvinced by the present performance of humanity. The American presidency, in the limited but highly significant area where such a question would come under its purview, could perform such a function, acting under the authority of its democratic basis and within the frame of its vast potentialities for functioning both above and within the political arena. At one of its most trying moments, the presidency, as Lincoln demonstrated, found an officer equal to the task.

2. *Types of Political Amnesty*

What men in power do to individuals, be it benign, stern, or odious, can always be explained by the particular circumstances of the case, the merits or demerits of the "candidate" in the eyes of those who will make the decision. General considerations may hover uncertainly over

[34] For a concise review of the most important problems, see the book review by William H. Mann in *Yale Law Review*, Vol. 67 (1958), p. 528.

the decision, not specifically discarded, but just crowded out by what is more immediate and pressing.[35]

Yet, to regulate the circumstances of the many by way of a positive policy will necessarily be a more orderly, thought-out procedure than to administer the fate of a single individual. An individual pardon is inevitably a mixture of caprice, coincidence, and calculation. Amnesty must rest on a more coherent view of the desirable or necessary objectives; a power holder cannot simply issue an order giving himself or a trusted subordinate a blank check to release whomever he pleases.

A generalized policy of clemency may spring from a variety of motives: finding some novel, untapped ways to line one's pockets;[36] expecting political consolidation as a result of building bridges to reach political foes; the desire of those in power to communicate, to even the most wretched subjects, the new feeling of security and relief from a happy event—be it the birth of a long-desired successor to the throne, or, as in the Soviet amnesty of March 1953, the death of a tyrant. Whatever the labels and reasons, amnesty will invariably transform diffuse motives into general rules, serving the lower authorities and potential beneficiaries as a kind of vade mecum for their actions, plans, and expectations.

The legal ritual of a political amnesty is fairly routine. Whether he has already exercised his prerogative to punish a political foe or is still at the stage of brandishing his claim and intentions before his prospective victim, a power holder might renounce his claim. He may do so with or without strings attached. For example, both Lincoln, in December 1863, and Johnson, in his proclamation of a pardon on May 29, 1865, and September 7, 1867, made their offer to certain categories of secessionists contingent on the taking of a loyalty oath. The pardon offered in the amnesty may be a plenary one, erasing all consequences of penal action, including confiscatory measures and loss of civil rights; or it may

[35] Yet at times there may be a method in refusing to accede to demands for a general rule and in keeping things on the level of individual decisions. The French Chamber in 1875 and the *Sénat* in 1876, for example, refused to entertain a move for an amnesty for the 10,000 Communards of 1871. Accepting the government's reasoning that all the rewarding cases had already been taken care of by individual pardons, this attitude implied provisional victory for a general policy to avoid both a fullfledged jail delivery as well as the problem of restoring civil rights to the minority of those already released. The whole issue is treated in great detail and thoroughness in Jean T. Joughin, *The Paris Commune in French Politics, 1871-1880*, Baltimore, 1955.

[36] The merger of political purpose and financial gain is by no means a novelty in amnesties or pardons; see, for example, R. Davidson, *Geschichte von Florenz*, Berlin, 1912, Vol. 3, p. 592.

involve only commutation or remittance of sentences or fines. In most cases it will have to involve a minimum of executive or, according to the choice of the amnesty law, judicial action to determine whether the individual case falls under the amnesty. Or, as in the French practice of the "grâce amnestiante," the amnesty may explicitly give to some authority broad discretion on whether to apply the law in the individual case. The amnesty may be worded so as to apply only to specific offenses; it may embrace them all or it may specifically exempt certain modes of committing them or certain motivations discernible in their commission, deemed especially reprehensible by the legislator. While phrased in the language of general rules, offenses amnestied as well as exemptions might have been made with some specific persons in mind.[37] The first French postwar amnesty of 1947 was mainly concerned with granting amnesty to persons who had made a special contribution to, or had suffered particularly during, World War II.

According to the constitutional and administrative patterns of the country, the amnesty is to be issued by either executive fiat—the Anglo-Saxon general pardon—or legislative act. But the form is not necessarily decisive for the political import of the act. This depends on the political situation and distribution of political forces. In this regard we might eliminate amnesty offers made by a government that is engaged in an all-out struggle for survival, and offers made on the condition that those who want to benefit must surrender or withdraw to the sidelines. Such tactics have often been tried, with varying success, since the day when the Roman Senate offered such terms to Marc Antony's soldiers.[38] Napoleon made the same offer after his return from Elba. So, as we saw, did Lincoln in 1863. But his offer was not

---

[37] An example is the German amnesty of October 24, 1930 (Reichsgesetzblatt, I, 467). When amnestying crimes against life committed in political fights, it explicitly exempted murders of members of the federal government. Thus it kept open the possibility of punishing the fugitive murderers of the Minister of Finance Erzberger (1921); one of them was caught and sentenced as late as 1947.

On December 15, 1959, the German Constitutional Court (Entscheidungen, Vol. 10 [1960], p. 234) decided an interesting case in which it tried to draw a fine dividing line between a possibly objectionable amnesty norm pertaining only to an individual case and a general norm, with a clearly restricted field of applicability. The case arose over the interpretation of par. 8 of the amnesty law of 1954 (BGBL, I, 203) granting full amnesty for unauthorized communication and procurement of official material before January 1, 1952. The court found *inter alia* that the legislator might well have had certain persons in mind when framing the act. This alone did not give it the possibly objectionable character of a hidden dispensation for the benefit of an individual or small group, if the subject matter lent itself to application to an indeterminate number of people who were not identifiable in advance.

[38] Cicero, *Phil.* v, 12, 34; VIII, 11, 33.

only conditional on an explicit loyalty oath; it was tailored to exclude the legal, military, and civilian elite of his foes.[39] Thus it was more an attempt to split the masses from their leaders. It necessarily remained without much effect as long as the decision which the pardon tried to discount was still beyond Lincoln's reach.

Amnesties that result from political or military consolidation may amount to a legalized form of self-restraint. The victorious party abandons some legal claim to deal with the defeated party, as if it had committed acts of treason or sedition. As touched on previously, President Johnson issued a somewhat less than complete amnesty in September 1867 which, like Lincoln's, was coupled with a loyalty oath; and it still left around 200 people in the exempted categories.[40] Yet on December 25, 1868, he decided to let bygones be bygones and avoid the embarrassment of having to carry through criminal proceedings against Jefferson Davis, who still stood indicted. He granted a full pardon for treason and adhering to the enemy, restoring all privileges and property titles, except, of course, the most important property title in slaves, and except for the political disabilities resulting from the third section of the Fourteenth Amendment, which, however, had been remedied by various acts of Congress.[41] Johnson's pardon mirrors a situation in which a victorious government, in the interest of speedy pacification, renounces any claim to treat the defeated party as rebels.

Thiers' government in 1871 took exactly the opposite course in regard to the fighters of the Paris Commune. He refused to grant the rebels any belligerent privileges. A total of 20,000 individuals were shot on the spot, or on the order of the so-called Cours Prévôtales—the greatest fully premeditated bloodbath in modern French history before the days of occupation and liberation. Thereafter, military commissions went to work: they convicted 10,137; most of these were shipped to the South Sea Islands, 270 were sentenced to death, and only 2,443 were acquitted.

As Thiers did not intend to abolish universal suffrage and the parliamentary regime, he left his successors a thorny legacy. The agitation for a full amnesty became a prominent feature of the French political scene in the seventies. For a small minority it was a personal concern

[39] U.S. Stat., Vol. 13, p. 737.
[40] U.S. Stat., Vol. 15, p. 700; the figure is from J. T. Dorris, "Pardoning the Leaders of the Confederacy," *Mississippi Valley Historical Review*, Vol. 15 (1928), pp. 1-21.
[41] Jefferson Davis did not have his civil rights re-established, for he refused to apply for a pardon. "It has been said that I should apply to the US for a pardon, but repentance must precede the right of pardon and I have not repented. If I were to do over again I would again do it." Dorris, p. 21.

and deep seated conviction; for many others it became a convenient political rallying point. The democratic survivors of an earlier revolutionary period in 1848, the Victor Hugos and Louis Blancs, the new middle class left around Clemenceau, as well as the Socialists reorganizing their ranks after the shattering defeat—all collaborated on the amnesty issue. They especially joined forces when a Communard in exile or prison was put up as a symbolic candidate at election time. For the bulk of the Republican politicians amnesty was a question of tactics, to be treated gingerly according to the needs and pressures of the situation. As long as President MacMahon and the Monarchists still threatened the survival of the Republic, and as long as the latter could play on widespread fears raised by the image of the return of the Communards —a name which to many had become synonymous with Communists —official policies remained resolutely hostile to any amnesty and were satisfied with examining individual files.

This policy still basically dominated the partial amnesty of March 1879. Utilizing the device of the grâce amnestiante, it left all the basic decisions still in the hands of the government. But after the 1879 senatorial electoral victory, which showed the Republic fully established and accepted, amnesty was no longer treated as a measure which could not possibly be carried out. Suddenly, under the leadership of the same Léon Gambetta who had so far avoided a clear-cut position, amnesty became a measure which had to be enacted.[42] By July 1880, the Chamber, with a 312-136 majority, accepted a full amnesty. Only slightly narrowed down by the Senate it allowed the overwhelming majority of the Communards to re-enter the country and its political system. After nine years the left had won its incessant battle and at the same time lost its most effective and concrete political rallying cry.

In matters of amnesty, what does a political victory hold in store for the victors? It depends on their needs and on the type of victory. The victory might be just a small change on the parliamentary checkerboard, as in the victory of the French Cartel des Gauches in the spring of 1924. It was good for a sort of symbolic reparation, allowing two political men, Caillaux and Malvy, to re-enter the political scene from which they had been forcibly eliminated at the end of the war. From the discussion in the Senate it would be difficult to conclude that the majority of the members realized that they themselves or their predecessors had acted wrongly four or six years before. Approximately the same majority that had previously believed itself justified in convicting the two men, in the interest of the country, now thought it appropriate,

---

[42] I follow here the conclusion of J. T. Joughin, *op.cit.*, p. 493.

as the president of the council Edouard Herriot put it to them, "to efface and forget earlier struggles and divisions."[43] Disregarding the advice of one of their rightist colleagues who quipped, "What you are up to is not amnesty, forgiveness, but amnesia, the sickness of senility,"[44] they decided on a text which, inserted into an omnibus amnesty bill, amounted to a full pardon.[45]

The amnesty of totalitarian victors may be nothing but the technical form for shielding the new regime's followers from criminal prosecution, the state's stamp of forgiveness on all the misdeeds and brutalities carried out during totalitarianism's march to victory. After their accession to power both Mussolini and Hitler issued several amnesties. In most instances they granted a full pardon for all offenses and types of punishment if the offense had been directly or indirectly "in the service of the national goal," or, as the German text has it, "in the battle or preparation for the national revolution or in the battle for the German peasantry" [dynamiting and rioting to prevent forced sales].[46] Stretching the service of the national revolution concept somewhat beyond its limits, Hermann Goering used it as a pretext to remit penalties and, more important, to cancel proceedings in cases of major tax defraudants. The tax delinquent was given the opportunity to show his gratitude to the Prussian minister president in a way more akin to the practices of Henry VII (Tudor), James II, and Jeffries than to those of the modern era.[47] In contrast to the magnanimity covering the worst atrocities committed by adherents of the regime, the defeated foes of Fascism and National Socialism received at best some crumbs—amnesty for minor offenses, carefully hedged with restrictions and exceptions to insure their continued legal harassment.

But amnesty need not connote some degree of magnanimity, the victor's desire for speedy pacification, or his attempt to secure and fully

[43] Senate Debates, Vol. 101, session of November 18, 1924, p. 62. [44] *Ibid.*, p. 64.
[45] Amnesty law of January 3, 1925, Art. 2, Récueil des lois, 1925, p. 3.
[46] The various Fascist amnesties, starting with the amnesties of December 22, 1922, may be consulted in G. Biagni, *Amnestie Condoni e Indulti,* 1948. The German amnesties of the Third Reich have been collected in Wolfgang Menschell, *Gnadenrecht,* 5th ed.; Berlin, 1943. The record starts with the amnesty of March 21, 1933.
[47] The memorable document of July 28, 1933, which glorifies tax frauds done to "escape the Bolshevist method of taxation of the Weimar Republic," is reprinted in Menschell, p. 255. The study of its application will go a long way to explain the origin of Goering's fortunes and the concept of morality of the German business class and the National Socialist administration in the early thirties. Actually, Goering was in such a hurry to arrogate to himself amnesty powers in regard to tax frauds completely outside Prussian jurisdiction that his assumption of powers belonging to the federal authorities had to be especially legalized by federal enactment.

exploit the moral and material fruits of victory. Amnesty may simply express a universal need for a general protective device by which to orderly terminate an era of disputed sovereignty; this was the character of Henry VII's (Tudor) *de facto* act of 1495.[48] But beyond eradicating the possibly disastrous consequences of a wrong political choice, amnesty may contain a compromise, expressing the present relation of forces between the parties concerned. This compromise might be embedded in a more inclusive peace or armistice, which not only grants all parties of a civil war oblivion of the past, but establishes guarantees that some sort of equilibrium will be maintained in the future.

The most famous case in history concerns Henry IV's Edict of Nantes of April 1598, which opens with the following sweeping provision: "The memory of all things which took place on the one or other side since March 1585 until our accession to the throne and during the troubles and on the occasions which preceded them remains extinct as if they never happened. Neither our procurator nor any other individual in their private or public capacity at any time or occasion may refer to them or start prosecution against anybody in relation to them in whatever jurisdiction."[49] Enforcement did not rest on the king's and his officers' good will alone, but on the religious minority's representation in offices and courts and the special securities granted to them. As with all compromises, observance depended on changing situations and interest constellations. During Henry's reign it was the Jesuits, intellectual mainstays of the Ligue, rather than his former comrades-in-arms, the Huguenots, who had reason to complain about persecutions carried through in violation of the Edict.

An attenuated form of this compromise character may be found in the amnesty strategies of governments trying to uphold a certain proportionality in benefits granted to political foes. But such proportionality is by no means a foregone conclusion. In 1924, after several rightists, including Hitler, had been prematurely released from Bavarian prisons, the left called in vain for "compensations."[50] It was simply too weak to obtain them at the time. In April 1960 the Kadar government in Hungary found it politic to introduce an element of compensation into its amnesty practices, releasing some noted victims of the 1956 revolu-

[48] Statutes of the Realm, Vol. 2, p. 568. See also the comments of Ernst H. Kantorowicz, *The King's Two Bodies*, Princeton, 1957, p. 371.

[49] For the text, see Art. 1 of the ordinance in Isambert, *Récueil général des anciennes lois françaises*, Paris, 1829, Vol. 15, p. 170. See also Arts. 58 and 59, which invalidate all judgments and proceedings against "ceux de ladite réligion prétendue réformée."

[50] See *Vorwärts*, December 20, 1924, which, incidentally, declared at the occasion of Hitler's release that he did not constitute a political danger.

tion, including Tibor Deri, as well as some high ranking security agents of the Rakosi period.[51] In the next section we shall see how thoughts of compensation affect the course of parliamentary amnesty debates.

3. A Contemporary Amnesty Record

Present-day amnesty legislation has become a kind of thermometer by which to measure the changing temperature of the fight between the state power and its various foes. Totalitarian remission of penalties and renunciation of criminal proceedings, which have been both un-limited and unilateral, indicate that a democratic constitutional regime has ceased to exist. But as long as such regimes continue to struggle along, there will always be forces at work trying to establish a balance between the claims of the public order for support in its fight to keep political foes in check, and the frequent desire to forego oppressive meth-ods, preventing courts, prisons, meetinghouses, and editorial offices from overflowing with the grievances and protests of the oppressed and hunted. If the aggrieved and their friends are strongly represented in parliamentary assemblies, they will bear down on the debate and pos-sibly also on the final outcome of the amnesty deliberations. In recent times a combination of both domestic tranquillity and the handling of the total subject matter of clemency by the executive has kept such debates from Anglo-American parliaments.[52] But they have often in-vaded and occupied continental assemblies.

A bird's-eye view of the German experience in the interwar years and of the German and French experience after the war might give a clue to the nature and scope of the problem involved. In the initial proclamation of the People's Commissars, the German revolution of 1918 issued a general amnesty for all political offenders. The Weimar Republic's first parliamentary amnesty reads like a lineup of all the characteristic difficulties which were to beset the Republic. The am-nesty followed the failure of the rightist *coup d'état* by Kapp in March 1920 and of regional leftist attempts to turn the defense against the *coup* into a change of the regime's political and social structure. In both cases government representatives had made specific promises of leniency.

[51] Decree law of April 1, 1960 on the implementation of partial amnesty and cessa-tion of internal security detention, in Magyar Koclony, No. 27, esp. §1, permitting release of persons sentenced to periods of less than six years before May 1, 1957.

[52] Except insofar as immunity aspects are involved, where the forgiveness element merely allows smaller fish to escape so that bigger ones may be caught. Cf. Brown v. Walker, 161 U.S. 591 (1896), and, more recently, Ullman v. United States, 350 U.S. 422 (1956); see also the discussion in W. H. Humbert, *The Pardoning Power of the President*, Washington, 1941, Ch. 2,

With the leftists these promises had been formalized in an agreement; with the rightists they had amounted only to personal and oral promises by a member of the cabinet, later disowned to some extent by his colleagues.[53]

The majority of criminal trials were handled by state tribunals, and some of the states, such as Bavaria, refused to recognize the plenary jurisdiction of the federal government over amnesties. In order to avoid sabotage by recalcitrant state governments, amnesties needed the two thirds majority prescribed for constitutional amendments. Therefore, as many political interests as possible on both the right and the left had to be taken into account to garner the necessary majority. But there was a further problem, quasi-built into the whole judicial system, which made agreement on terms and formulations of amnesties especially difficult. It was by then well known that prosecuting agencies and courts contained many partisans who measured left and right with different yardsticks. It was certain in advance that leftists brought to book for homicide and qualified assault committed in open battle with army and police would be convicted. It was also known that few of the rightist ring leaders of the *coup d'état*, though explicitly excluded from the terms of the amnesty, would ever be caught or, if caught, convicted.[54] But the left had at least obtained an extension of the amnesty that covered the year 1919. As a need for pacification was generally felt, the amnesty bill passed.[55] Yet a pessimistic feeling prevailed. Everybody realized that the amnesty amounted to an armistice rather than oblivion of the past and an overture to a new and better future.

Not counting state amnesties or amnesties proclaimed in the pursuance of international obligations, three major amnesties were issued in the twenties.[56] The last of the three, July 1928, was the first to touch on the problem of political assassination. Rightists campaigned for a full amnesty that would bring release to those few members of clandestine paramilitary formations who had been brought to justice for having assassinated comrades of their own whom they had considered

[53] The report of the parliamentary debate may be found in Stenographische Berichte Deutscher Reichstag, 1. Legislaturperiode, Vol. 344, 16. Sitzung, August 2, 1920, pp. 522-52.

[54] Some of the material, among it the *nol pros* in the case of General Ludendorff and the account of a trial against a rightist leader, may be found in *Hochverrat und Verfassungsgrundlagen*, ed. Karl Brammer, Berlin, 1922.

[55] Reichsgesetzblatt, 1920, I, p. 1,487.

[56] The Weimar amnesties may be followed in Ulrich Kuss, *Die materielle Problematik der Politischen Reichsamnestie*, Breslau, 1934, a diligent collection of the relevant material with the usual degeneration of comment on everything concerning the period after 1932.

potential traitors. The Communists, on the other hand, were interested in regularizing the status of those of their members who were either threatened with, or had fled the country to escape, high treason charges. In the final compromise, pending and prospective proceedings for murder were not amnestied, but life sentences in political cases were scaled down to seven and a half years imprisonment.[57]

It needed the entry of the National Socialists into the Reichstag in full force in 1930 to achieve a full-fledged amnesty for such murders.[58] The bill had had hard sledding in the previous Reichstag, opposed by both the Social Democratic Party and among the state administrations, and pushed by middle-class and right-wing groups as a concession to the spirit of nationalism. They had yielded to the propaganda, widespread in both political and legal circles, that believing oneself to have acted in the national interest, if it does not justify assassination, at least exculpates it. These groups were the first to regret bitterly that they ever allowed themselves to embrace a thesis whose logical extension led a few years later to the generalized murder of inconvenient political adversaries under the National Socialist regime.

By mid-1932 the Reichstag, due to the presence of a National Socialist-Communist majority, was unable to function. Yet at the last session it ever held, on December 5, 1932, its last law was, symbolically enough, an amnesty law. To get a two-thirds majority, though, the extremist parties had had to enter compromises. Political sentences of less than five years were remitted or higher sentences scaled down correspondingly. Life sentences were omitted from the law's benefits, which excluded the murderers of Potempa from its scope. They had to wait another three months until Hitler released them with his own brew of amnesties.[59] Also exempted were attempts to undermine the loyalty of the army.[60]

In contrast, the Bundestag of the postwar period has been almost as reluctant to touch the amnesty issue as the Reichstag of the Weimar Republic was eager to deal with it fairly frequently. Politics have returned to normalcy, and violence, yesterday's daily dish, becomes a faint memory. Correspondingly there is a change of yardsticks. However, there remains the difficult inheritance of the Nazi regime, awakening

[57] Reichsgesetzblatt, 1928, I, p. 195.

[58] *Ibid.*, 1930, I, p. 467.

[59] Stenographische Berichte, 7. Legislaturperiode, Vol. 455, pp. 90-105.

[60] See Scheringer's account, *op.cit.*, pp. 275-76. He thinks that the nonapplication of the 1932 amnesty on his case, prolonging his stay as a prisoner, gave him a chance to survive, saving him from the hands of the National Socialists who were furious that he switched over from their side to the Communists.

so many memories, hatreds, and passions. The first of the two amnesties issued in the whole decade since the inception of the Federal Republic almost passed over the issue in complete silence. In the amnesty of December 31, 1949,[61] the problem of National Socialism and war criminals was touched on only to the extent that persons registered under wrong names were offered amnesty for falsification of their records, if they declared themselves to the authorities by a certain cut-off date—a sort of small reward for facilitating clean-up operations, interesting only for the small-fry. In contrast, the second and last amnesty of July 17, 1954,[62] cautiously enters the war crimes field. Rejecting Socialist advice to go slowly and, at least at the parliamentary level, weak rightist pressure to go further, it offers amnesty for acts of violence committed by those who believed themselves authorized by an official position to such lawless action, and by those unable to perceive its illegality. But the offer is restricted in time: it applies to acts between October 1, 1944, and July 31, 1945. Further, it applies only to punishments up to three years and to proceedings foreseeably leading to no higher punishment. Since then, the Bundestag has withstood manifold pressures to enlarge on this amnesty for war criminals under German jurisdiction. If they happen to be apprehended, concentration camp personnel and officers who have ordered unjustified shootings of subordinates, but also German prisoners-of-war in Russia who helped to mistreat their comrades, might be tried, at least until the statute of limitation—twenty years for murder—has run its course. In the first years of the new establishment amnesty remained a battle cry of former rightists and former National Socialists. If their grievances concerned disabilities visited on them for political behavior in the NS period, rather than for homicide and related acts, these were largely settled—after the total fiasco of allied and especially American denazification policies—under almost universal agreement by the various state and federal acts terminating denazification proceedings.

A panoply of new and inclusive legislation for state protection brought to the fore a new crop of amnesty interests, all more or less centered on the Communist Party. Not represented in the Bundestag since 1953, the Communists in their amnesty drive have been able to muster support in non-Communist circles. First there was their small but perceptible disquiet over the resumption of political prosecutions made on the basis of a jurisprudence which interpreted vague enough state protection in an expansive way. More audible was their discomfiture over the interpreta-

[61] BGBL, 1 (1950), 37.
[62] BGBL, 1, 203.

tions of the federal attorney and federal court, which allowed proceedings against all those Communist functionaries who had carried through routine organizational and propaganda jobs before the party was banned by the Constitutional Court on August 16, 1956.[63] Such policy, they protested, would lead to a flood of criminal proceedings, or at least to an avalanche of unnecessary paperwork designed to short-cut such proceedings or to minimize its effects on hundreds of camp followers. This was a consequence which the explanation of the federal minister of justice could minimize but not dispel.[64]

All these considerations, however, were completely dwarfed by one major concern: many Germans hoped that a policy of clemency by the authorities of the Federal Republic would make it difficult for the government of the DDR not to reply in kind and not to relinquish their hold over at least some of their political prisoners. But the government of the Federal Republic—some of whose political friends had, at a 1956 debate on the fate of the population of the DDR, been quite willing to relent on West German Communists in order to create a better climate for the release of their own friends in East German jails[65]—remained adamant and rejected all suggestions for a new political amnesty. Was it the rational argument, often reiterated by the majority's speakers in the debate, that the disproportionality between the number of political offenders held by the Federal Republic and the DDR, a figure of three digits as against one with five, was too great to allow hope for any political effect of such a West German move? Did the rejection point to the resumption of the Weimar practice in which the federal government and the government of the USSR had exchanged prisoners of their respective nationalities after convictions had been obtained? Was it part of the overall governmental policy toward the DDR? Or was it just another manifestation of a conservative public order concept, unlike

[63] Entscheidungen des Bundesgerichtshofs in Strafsachen, Vol. 11 (1958), p. 233; Entscheidungen des Bundesverfassungsgerichts, Vol. 9 (1959), p. 162.

[64] Bundestag, 2. Wahlperiode, Vol. 36 session of April 4, 1957, pp. 11,421-61, at 11,430-32. On January 1, 1957, 2,358 preliminary investigations were pending at the prosecutor's level, of which only 900, with total of 1,400 defendants, went to the courts (*ibid.*, 11,430). The criminal statistics for 1957 show only a total of 141 persons tried for high treason and state endangering activities. (This figure pertains to purely political activity, excluding espionage and similar activities.) See also Ch. III, n. 74. Only recently (decision of March 21, 1961, Juristenzeitung 1961, page 321, has the Constitutional Court annulled Art. 90 (a,3) of the penal code; this was long after this questionable practice had ceased to furnish a strategic weapon for repression of political foes. Until this decision intervened wrong guesses about the likelihood of one's organization being banned had been punished under this article.

[65] Bundestag, 2. Wahlperiode, Vol. 36, Sitzung of May 30, 1956, pp. 7,699-737, esp. Lemmer, p. 7,726.

amnesty policies of the past? Whatever the reasons, the official amnesty debate has not been resumed since, and the slow pace of public life has not allowed suspicious fringe interests to generate much commotion around the issue.

In France the four major postwar amnesties in the last twelve years show a similar preoccupation: collaborationists and Communists. Both in the time sequence—the near-omission of the burning theme of collaboration in the first amnesty—and in the growing determination to narrow down the satisfactions granted to the Communists, the changing political climate and the shift in parliamentary majorities become readily apparent. But there remains an important point of difference between the political climate in the Federal Republic and in France. Emotionally and morally, the West German regime has had to build from scratch, so to speak. There was no way to fall back on a common and universally accepted interpretation of the immediate past that would point to binding norms of conduct for the individual. In France, despite the rapid fading out of the resistance myth and the full reintegration of Vichyites into the national community, the patriotic norm of the resistance, which includes the performance of the Communist Party, remains some sort of yardstick of evaluation to which the various amnesty laws will invariably refer.

In the first postwar amnesty of 1947—written mainly to grant amnesty benefits for the heroes and victims of war—the only real skirmish (and it began as a political skirmish) was due to the amnesty grant for the false denunciation of collaborators, written into the law with the votes of the right against the Communists and Socialists.[66] The amnesty of January 1951, issued under the auspices of the first legislature elected in 1946, shows a certain equilibrium. It eases up on collaborators but does not yet go whole hog. The symbolic cases handled by the Haute Cour are refused consideration altogether. Those convicted by other jurisdictions will get consideration for penalties up to three years; but the prosecutors examining the cases are ordered to exclude those who exposed their victims to cruelty or deportation, or who assisted police or espionage agents. At the other end of the political spectrum there is now an automatic amnesty for every type of offense committed between June 1940 and January 1946 "in the interest of the cause of liberation." This will cover almost any act of violence in the preliberation and liberation period, even if the perpetrator did not always keep a proper balance

[66] Assemblée Nationale, 1st Legislature, session of August 1, 1947, Vol. VII, pp. 3,840-49.

between his particular Communist Party interest and those of the liberation in general.

By mid-1953 a turning point is definitely reached. The Communist weight has been diminished by the working of the electoral law, and the new right-wing government will take steps to enlarge considerably the amnesty for collaborators, even though the worst cases still remain excluded. The parliamentarians who voted for plenary powers for Pétain and were therefore declared ineligible will again be able to present themselves before the electorate. More important, in daily practice the pension benefits of collaborationist officials, even if not again integrated into the service, will now be re-established. The parliamentary majority would not insist—as previously planned—on tying this operation to the elaboration of a satisfactory plan for alleviating the financial situation of war victims. Communist interests receive little satisfaction. The majority would refuse to enlarge on the now-traditional provision amnestying riots regarding labor conflicts. It would not accept Communist amendments allowing amnesties for participants in riots which took place *on the occasion of*, rather than *relating* to, labor conflicts; nor will it amnesty those who provoked the military to disobedience—a rather frequent occurrence at the time of the Indochinese war.[67] It must have given the Communists some satisfaction that they could in some way show their own brand of patriotism, even though it was probably not always fully appreciated by their voters. They helped to vote down a Socialist proposal to re-examine the files of conscientious objectors with the view to granting them a pardon, bringing to a close the infernal circle which sent objectors from the arrest barracks stumbling back to the recruiting depot and from there right back to the military tribunal and the arrest barracks.

The Fifth Republic saw its first amnesty law adopted in July 1959. As usual with amnesties of a new regime, the law takes care of those who have committed illegalities in the regime's germination period—May 1 to September 28, 1958. But the formula "infraction in direct relation with the political events which have taken place in this period" (Art. 7) is broad enough to cover not only the friends of the uprising but also those few who have actively shown their displeasure. Communist attempts to include in the amnesty any action deriving from opposition to the military policy of the government are rejected by parliamentary majority and government in the name of "morality and

[67] Assemblée Nationale, 2nd Legislature, session of June 24, 1953, Vol. XVII, pp. 3,908-47.

patriotism."[68] Yet the government's attitude is not entirely unresponsive. Wanting to avoid the impression of a "one-way" amnesty, it will, within a six-month period, give individual consideration to the cases of military and resistance personnel who might have committed treasonous actions in the Algerian conflict. Thus the new regime tries carefully to keep some balance between opposing trends and forces. Does it realize that today's friends will be tomorrow's enemies, and vice versa? Whatever the government's motivations, its rightist supporters, even when arguing against the Communists, have already had a distinct feeling that amnesties are a good thing to look forward to. John-Baptiste Biaggi, a rightist speaker soon to get himself into trouble with the authorities, put it providentially: "One should never malign amnesty laws, because sooner or later in these troubled times in which we are living anyone may benefit from them."[69]

Mr. Biaggi's remarks seem to sum up the virtues and discomfitures of political amnesties. As a technical device they might serve anybody's interests: those in power or on the margin of power, those ejected from power, those preparing to attack present power holders, and those presently planning a strategic retreat. Amnesties are baptized acts of oblivion. But that is just the calling card by which they are introduced or smuggled in by anyone making a special plea for a particular group of potential beneficiaries. They are intended to efface the memory and possible consequences of past acts. The process of effacement becomes most effective if the situation to which the act is related has changed beyond recognition. Then and only then does amnesty conclude a chapter and ease a new beginning. To the extent that such a transformation has not taken place, political amnesty connotes neither oblivion nor effacement, but respite and armistice. It might foreshadow realignment, but just as likely it means resurgence and continued strife, with the old battle formations kept intact. It may well be that the first goal is intended and only the second one obtained. The reverse process, the armistice which converts into true oblivion, might be more enjoyable, but it is also more rare.

[68] Assemblée Nationale, 1st Legislature, session of July 7, 1959, pp. 1,330-70, 1,350-51.
[69] *Ibid.*, p. 1,332.

CHAPTER XI

SUMMING UP

✦✦✦

La justice est sujette à disputes: la force est très reconnaissable, et sans dispute. Ainsi on n'a pu donner la force à la justice, parce que la force a contredit la justice et a dit qu'elle était injuste, et a dit que c'était elle qui était juste. Et ainsi, ne pouvant faire ce qui est juste fût fort, on a fait ce qui est fort fût juste.

—BLAISE PASCAL, *Pensèes*, Brunschwicg, no. 298*

✦✦✦

1. The Strategy of Political Justice:
Necessity, Choice, and Convenience

THE aim of political justice is to enlarge the area of political action by enlisting the services of courts in behalf of political goals. It is characterized by the submission to court scrutiny of group and individual action. Those instrumental in such submission seek to strengthen their own position and weaken that of their political foes.

In each case resort to the courts may be a matter of necessity, choice, or mere convenience. 1) If, for instance, an important political dignitary has been assassinated, but the government structure as a whole remains intact and continues to function within a legal framework, the authorities will usually find it *necessary* to try the assassin. 2) If the regime is confronted with an "opposition of principle," it has a number of choices, running the gamut from genuine toleration to total suppression. The decision against toleration and the legal implementation of a variety of repressive measures are a matter of *choice*. 3) A regime may want to gain, stabilize, or destroy political positions by manipulating opinion through the medium of a political trial. Resorting to political justice for that purpose is a matter of *convenience*, one of many channels in interpersonal and intergroup political warfare.

* "Justice is subject to dispute; might is easily recognized and is not disputable. So we cannot give might to justice, because might has gainsaid justice, and has declared that it is she herself who is just. And thus unable to make what is just strong, we have made what is strong just."

In actual practice, as we have seen, these considerations may overlap, and governmental action will frequently embrace elements of all.[1] But as a guide through the maze of political justice, they do retain a measure of usefulness.

Under a constitutional regime power holders have a large arsenal of weapons, ranging from partial control of employment and public opinion to police pressure for harassing and closely supervising their political foes. But if the foes should try to destroy the existing regime, the authority may conclude that it has no choice but to eliminate them. This necessarily involves recourse to the courts. In such circumstances the court proceedings will play a number of roles. First, they will serve as a forum for publicizing the vileness of the challengers. Second, they will confirm and legitimize the power holders' proposals for disposing of their opponents. And finally, they might keep the power holders from giving in to the temptation to utilize the occasion for a wholesale elimination of all their political foes, even those unconnected with the group constituting the direct threat.

Knottier and more involved problems arise from power holders' attitudes toward the handling of large parties or popular organizations whose leaders, members, or sympathizers are scarcely integrated into the political structure and whose loyalty at any given time is at best conjectural. Nineteenth century English Chartists and German Social Democrats, pre-1933 German National Socialists, present-day French or Italian Communists—such groups oscillate between integration into the official structure, displacing the present power holders, and sheer decomposition. Their ultimate destiny depends on many circumstances. Leadership and internal organization as well as the opportunities and pressures of the surrounding social structure—including the behavior of the regime itself—are independent variables. Therefore, the question of how to deal with such mass movements remains essentially a problem of choice.

Among the elements that continuously enter both the motivation and rationalization processes of power holders, there is a fairly constant one.

---

[1] As an example of the relation between necessity, convenience, and choice: When a governmental leader has been assassinated, a well-functioning governmental system operating within a legal framework will find it *necessary* to try the assassin. It is a question of strategy, that is, *convenience*, whether an attempt will be made to use the trial of the murderer to show that the group with which the murderer was affiliated has the character of a gang of assassins. At the same time, the act of assassination may be a decisive element in the government's exercising a *choice* of total repression of the hostile organization. On the connection between a necessary and a convenient operation, see also p. 423 below.

That is the situation arising from the conjunction of an alienated domestic opposition with an external foe. From Pausanias and Alcibiades, to the sixteenth century French religious wars, the days of the younger Pitt, Thomas Hardy, and Thomas Paine, and the various Socialist and Communist Internationals, this conjunction has plagued and exasperated the power holders and their followers and swelled the expectations of their domestic foes. Its modern impact might be easily overestimated by friend and foe alike. In contrast to the world before the French Revolution, the modern national state has been able to develop a higher degree of cohesion among its citizenry. Even in extremis, as the careful study of De Jong has shown,[2] the fifth column contribution has been of rather secondary importance to the success of a foreign invader. Despite sometimes considerable domestic opposition to their course, countries since 1945 have, with few exceptions, stayed within the orbit of the governmental and alliance system toward which they had gravitated in 1944-1945. What remains are certain ideological affinities and sympathies and organizational devices, all keyed toward, though not necessarily securing, the mutual reinforcement of the position of the domestic opponent and potential external foe. Whether these parallelisms of attitudes and sympathies, existing in many countries in more or less organized or inchoate form, will ever amount to anything more than fleeting aspects of the political landscape, one more element in the political actors' calculations, depends entirely on future contingencies.

What motivates the representatives of the state power to decide for or against repression of the opposition of principle is one thing. What justifies their decision, in terms of the existing legal order, is another. There will always be plenty of rationalizations available for justifying either course; action programs, utterances of leaders, the excesses and revelations of followers provide enough material for any official decision. If, however, repression is decided on as a matter of choice under a constitutional system, the carrying out of such a choice rests on the full participation of the legislative, administrative, and judicial agencies. Judicial cooperation of some kind might be needed first to legitimize the repressive scheme in terms of the constitutional settlement. Once that hurdle is passed—and it may be a difficult one—the judiciary's sanction will be needed in each specific case where an individual has persevered in political activity which has been declared illicit or where the boundaries between licit and illicit activity are difficult to establish. What develops then are those paradoxical characteristics which are the saving

[2] Louis De Jong, *The German Fifth Column in the Second World War*, Chicago, 1956.

grace of political repression under constitutional systems. These fashion a kind of race between the administration and its foes. The very character and procedural hurdles of the judicial system, together with the limits to the power holders' ability to exercise total control by informal devices, often make the actual administration of a policy of repression fall short of the original blueprint.

Beyond necessity and choice lies the area of convenience. Here we are dealing neither with the necessary defense against the violent onslaught of a foe seizing the reins of government, nor with the often excruciating problem of how to handle the alienated segment of the community. What characterizes the case of convenience is the fact that the actual restraint of foes is very much less important than the psychological effect on the public at large and on potential or actual competing parties loyal to the regime. Both constitutional and totalitarian systems have resorted to the courts in this kind of operation. In either case the prosecuting regime, party, or individual chooses a past action of its foe as a convenient battleground on which to influence the shape of future political action. If the foe has already been eliminated from political competition, the prosecution will try to surround the fact of his defeat with a wider frame of historical and moral justification. The technique may be to seriously limit the area of proof, producing a telling snapshot of the adversary. Or it may be to try and elaborate a full-fledged historical thesis in the image of the initiators of the trial. In any case, past events are reconstructed in court in order to shape desired images of persons or groups.

Courts are not the only agencies in which such identifications and projections for political purposes take place. Every group of power holders or power aspirants will try ceaselessly to make such identifications and projections—favorable to their own activities and plans, and unfavorable to their foes and competitors—with the help of all propagandistic facilities within their grasp. But ex parte identifications and projections suffer a handicap. They must proceed on the strength of purely prima facie impressions created by the choice of a fortunate and telling image plus the beneficial effect of its endless repetition. Counterimages and, more important, the endless stream of new impressions may play havoc and deprive the original political image of a lasting effect. In this respect the image-creating effect of a trial is vastly superior. The trial seems to elevate the image from the realm of private happenings and partisan constructions into an official, authoritative, and quasi-neutral sphere. The public is given a unique chance to participate in the re-creation of history for the purpose of shaping the future. It matters little that the segment offered in proof may be too limited, the witnesses from whose tales the story is reconstructed too close to or too remote from the historical events. The trial's reduction of history into either/or propositions fits a simplified understanding of history. Besides, it enlivens the show.

The yardstick of measurement is the effectiveness, not the meaningfulness, of the image. But while an element of successful photomontage stuns, and secures immediate effect, only completeness of the image can stand the test of time. Thus the convenience type of trial frequently appears as a skirmish, one of a multitude of interconnected elements which may influence the eventual course of history and often, though in a quite different way, contribute to history's final verdict. Yet while the trial may enter history, only rarely will it become part of history's own verdict. In an exceptional case, such as the Nuremberg trial, the record of the defunct regime may be so clear-cut that the image produced in court could not but appear a reasonably truthful replica of reality. While the methods, the preoccupations, and the competency of prosecution and court may be endlessly taken to task, the criticism will neither efface nor materially rectify the permanency of the image. But while it retained many overtones of the convenience type of trial, did the Nuremberg trial, with all the hypocrisy and grotesqueness deriving from its very subject, not belong very profoundly in the category of a morally and historically necessary operation?

2. Planned Justice and Judicial Space

The resort to court might thus be merely a technical device for disposing of a vanquished rebel. It may signify a more or less concerted effort to rid the community of its stock of political foes, or it may be directed toward creating effective political images. In nearly all such cases the judge will regard his involvement with mixed feelings. As long as the regime counts more friends than enemies, he might not be averse to being hoisted from comparative routine tasks to the center of things. But he is also aware of the risks inherent in the situation which will require him to take a position in a complex of political claims, some of which must, by necessity, come off second-best in the proceedings.

The judge, or for that matter the jury, officiates within a given social and political structure. Like the prosecutor or policeman, he is an instrument of a concrete political system established at a particular time and place. If community-wide agreement on methods and objectives exist, if the public order has been so long established that it is taken for granted by all strata, the judge may be listened to as the spokesman of a God-given and just order. But the degree of group satisfaction may vary considerably, and systems and power holders may change in rapid succession. Under such circumstances, the judge's ability to officiate as the incarnation of the authority of the group, dispensing justice to the individual even while adjudicating attacks on the regime, will suffer correspondingly. It will become more difficult for him to perform the feat for which the community selected him: to give a just decision to the individual case thrust upon him. "Just" in this case would mean a decision not merely serving the needs and pressures of the moment, but capable of finding a wider and less transient adherence; a skillfully rationalized decision able to withstand a dispassionate scrutiny of its motivations.

To a considerable degree the judge may fulfill community expectations by confining his role to the application of generally accepted rules and standards of procedure to the political case at hand. In this attempt he may encounter complications, some much more difficult to deal with than others. Special provisions may have been enacted, curtailing procedural guarantees (time granted for preparing the defense, mode of citation of witnesses, abolition of remedies) in order to speed up proceedings and, indirectly, to diminish the obstacles facing the authorities. He may also be subject to unofficial promptings by the authorities, urging him to make haste and suggesting the desirable outcome. On the other hand, the difficulty may come from a defense more interested in propagandizing the iniquities of the official system, including the court, than in taking advantage of the available means to conduct an effective defense. The judge's firmness and resolve may overcome the unofficial hurdles; intelligent use of even an abbreviated procedure may at least mitigate the impact of special legislation. In fortunate jurisdictions, judges may even be able to police indirectly the preliminary investigations; they may, for example, set aside abusive pretrial investigations, thus avoiding damage to the credibility of the trial as a whole.

Procedural guarantees operate to some extent as self-enforcing devices that carry with them their own sanction. Since the violation of procedural guarantees is visible to all, the image-creating purposes of the proceedings are jeopardized. Yet the defendant might want to extend the mandate of justice to the quality of substantive law and, even further, to the character of the society and the regime which invokes the law. Rarely will he succeed with such a frontal attack, even where the constitutional settlement has given him some opening for questioning the policy of the enactment which happens somewhat more frequently these days. He will certainly be unable to utilize such a weapon where it would be most appropriate: in the courts of totalitarian states.

But experience with regimes that cross the dividing line between a harsh but debatable policy and humanly inadmissible endeavors should have made one point clear to judges, who did not sense it previously. Like every other office holder, the judge carries the burden of the regime; when the regime tumbles, he must be able to stand on the actions he took in the concrete situation, rather than on the broken shield of a possibly iniquitous enactment.

Such exceptions aside, the policy of the law and the ultimate goals of those pushing the case, if only within the terms of the law, will remain more often than not outside the judge's province and official scrutiny. Yet if he wants, he might be able to devise other means, more subtle and less ostentatious, of playing a more active role. The conceptual tools allowing him to mediate between the pressures of society and his own insight into the rank order of priorities and values are called interpretations of the law, or, as the case may be, analysis of the law as relating to the evidence and finally the policy of sentencing. The political authority may produce new enactments, lay down rules in fields left previously to judicial interpretation, or, if the opportunity arises, appoint new judges with whom it hopes to obtain a more attentive hearing for its purposes. But as long as the institution persists, the "judicial space," though it may be reduced, cannot be completely abolished.

The elimination of the "judicial space," the conversion of the judge into a functionary of the apparatus of justice, is supposed to produce the certainty of result which power holders everywhere seek, but which only an administration of justice fully integrated into and responsive to the political apparatus achieves. But is it worth the price?

The totalitarian judicial functionary tries to guess what would be the safest, that is, immediately most desirable, interpretation from the viewpoint of the authorities. This is in line with the assumptions of the system that it is better to share mistakes and carry through or copy any policy change right down the line than to let society find its own equilibrium by sharing authority among its various organs. For that purpose, the individual is kept from invoking the authority of the courts before a line of conduct has been officially laid down. Thus the system is safeguarded against sudden surprise.

Keeping the machinery of justice from ever deliberately interfering with policy lines is one thing. Putting it to maximum productive use by integrating it into the official planning effort is another. Can one plan

justice as one plans production schedules or propaganda campaigns?
The answer is doubtful at best. Offenses against the state cannot be
produced artificially, according to a preconceived plan, without reviving
Stalinist practices of prefabrication. But one can orient the apparatus of
justice in advance to specific social programs. Courts can be keyed to
stand in ideological and organizational readiness to deal, for example,
with expected resistance to enforced collectivization. Specific cases of
obstruction can be selected for referral to the courts for their adaptation
into a combined program of education and intimidation. The stage can
be set in such a way as to cut trial risks to a minimum and allow the
propaganda aspect of a case to be deployed in full.

Nevertheless, political justice without risks remains a contradiction
in terms. It is the totalitarian corollary of the figment of total political
security. Just as the latter manages to produce only a languishing political establishment, the political trial with predetermined results misses
a preeminent goal; the images it creates are worth neither more nor less
than the authority that ordered them. In this sense the trial planned with
a view toward establishing a priority program becomes just another
avenue to communicate to the population at large the official message.
This is because the desired third-party effect of a trial rests less on the
message of the verdict than on the tension generated by the public
sense of participation in an unfolding drama, the outcome of which remains doubtful until the very last moment. Planned justice can scarcely
communicate this experience.

The existence of a "judicial space," connoting an element of uncertainty and risk, separates the trial from the administrative act in disguise, the pseudo-judicial propaganda play. How extensive is the space
for judicial action in societies that eschew both mechanical and ideological coordination between their political and judicial bodies? The
answer depends on the type of political action involved. In the face of
an actual rather than a construed attempt to overthrow constituted
authorities, the judge's office will be invoked as a kind of ceremonial
requirement, rendering legitimacy to the official story; the speed or
minuteness of verification will depend largely on the propagandistic and
strategic needs of the power holders. Whatever the judge's personal sympathies, which evolve in line with the record of the regime, the outcome of the proceedings is preordained. Once the authority of the
existing regime has been frontally assailed, the judge must be its vin-
dicator. Before making the defendant pay the penalty of defeat, he may
allow him facilities to measure his credo a last time against the assertions of the official world. (These facilities were more readily granted

by the more sceptical or cynical judge of the nineteenth century's constitutional or half absolutist regimes than by his present-day successors, whose performance is keyed to a wider audience.) But whether the defendant's actions can be interpreted as such a frontal attack may be within the province of judicial interpretation. Whenever the situation is ambiguous and allows for a multiplicity of interpretations, the judicial space widens. It seems greater if the judge applies some indeterminate legal concept—"danger-to-security" type of phraseology—to a given political situation than if the prosecution is able to corral the behavior of the defendant into the possibly deceptive framework of a true-false dichotomy. But even then, the state of mind of the defendant, his own understanding of the meaning and significance of his acts, opens another interpretive area.

Because of both the infirmities and the protective devices which surround his office, the judge can act on problems only in the shape and under the particular circumstances in which they are submitted to him. Confined by the restrictions of his office to dealing with a certain segment of reality, the judge may often long for the freedom to reorganize the whole subject matter according to his own predilections. But he may just as often be relieved that others have already switched on the power and that his only responsibility is to sort out the various elements of a situation that he did not initiate.

This separation from the actual world of political and administrative action may turn out to be an unavoidable handicap for his job of transforming the inchoate data of the popular consciousness into the finished product of the legal formula. Even if he wanted to withstand the onslaught of legislative and executive considerations, highlighting the dangers resulting from a refusal to sanction their policies, he might be hard pressed or without the intellectual resources to do so. But while such deference to authority is widespread, it is not the hard and fast rule. No sociological thesis of diversity of judicial reaction according to the homogeneous or heterogeneous character of societies can sufficiently explain differences in judicial approach. Moreover, pressures and vistas may change rapidly with the unfolding of new situations.

In countries where the opinions of judges are the product of individual effort, rather than the collective result of intrabureaucratic compromise that follows more clearly the rule of the lowest common denominator, one might be able to discern the range of preoccupations which enter into the individual judge's image of justice.[3] Reaction to

[3] Greater facility for interpreting judicial behavior is a welcome byproduct of the practice to publish separate opinions as part of the court record. Whether this practice

official power holders' promptings may be a patriotic identification with their goals, accommodating to their views at almost any price; it may mean a recalcitrant and limited assent to their propositions, emphasizing other agencies' primary responsibility; or it may be a frosty reception and an attempt to independently assay or analyze the underlying factors in a given situation. Motives may be just as diversified. There is Justice Frankfurter's solicitude for the survival of embattled authority in mass society, and Justice Harlan's pronounced upper middle-class sentiment of the limited debt which society owes to the various classes of its citizens. Justice Clark appears as a stand-in for J. Edgar Hoover's "big brother" image of state power, while Justice Douglas' conscious role is auxiliary dynamo for the attainment of a better society.

There is a correspondingly wide range of rationalizations. Elaborate dogmatic and historical structures may shakily hide basic clashes between a concern for the suffering individuals and all the comfortable and time-honored devices upholding the promptings of official authority. There may be subtle interpretations of texts and almost imperceptible shifts in identical formulas to reach goals that deviate sharply from formerly sanctioned practices, minimizing the element of a new departure. Occasionally, more often in dissenting opinions, there is some willingness to tear away the veil of rationalizations, moving toward open

---

is advisable in the interest of the administration of justice is another matter. Decision on this point would depend among other things on (a) whether the business of separate and dissenting opinions strengthens or, more likely, weakens the official court opinion's chance for acceptance; (b) whether the practice of publishing only the agreed upon version, the opinion of the court, prohibiting even private circulation of the judge's memoranda, excludes the minority from exercising an influence on the formation of the opinion; or whether the need to get through with the business at hand, yet keep a tolerable amount of intracourt amity, would favor intracourt compromises and affect the nature of such compromises; (c) last but not least, whether the tonic effect of having possibly unpopular dissenting opinions come forward, if not with the seal at least from the seat of authority, is substantial enough to justify the practice of separate opinions.

From the rich literature on the subject, see esp. Justice Jackson's conclusion: "Each dissenting opinion is a confession of failure to convince the writers' colleagues, and the true test of a judge is his influence in leading, not in opposing, his court"; *The Supreme Court in the American System of Government*, Harvard University Press, 1955, p. 19. The practices of various nations in this field are discussed in Kurt H. Nadelmann, "The Judicial Dissent," *American Journal of Comparative Law*, Vol. 4 (1959), pp. 415-32. The author, favorable to dissents, does not consider their effect on the internal structure of the courts. From the German discussion, see J. Kaiser, "Erfüllung völkerrechtlicher Verträge des Bundes durch die Laender," *Zeitschrift für auslaendisches öffentliches Recht und Völkerrecht*, Vol. 18 (1958), pp. 526, 556, recommending introduction of dissenting opinions for the Federal Constitutional Court.

juxtaposition of the opposing claims of constituted authority and the willingness to assume the risk of political freedom.

Thus the Western judge's policy directive, unlike that of his totalitarian colleague, does not come from explicit or intuitive communion with a party hierarchy. It emerges from his own reading of the community needs, where lies its justification as well as its limitation. At best, his reading may certify that *rebus sic stantibus*, the community needs require the proposed solution. But politics is a volatile subject. There are fundamental minimum requirements of human decency which are valid for all regimes and all proposed solutions and cannot be waived either in advance or retrospectively; but changes in political requirements and perspectives are nonetheless in the nature of things.

It is the irony of political justice that while its mandate remains perforce ambiguous and time-bound, its practitioners must insist that their procedure and results have been not only formally correct, but necessary to both authority and justice. The detour via the road of justice, taken to reach politically desirable goals, is necessitated as much by desire to give political action greater dignity and wider acceptance as by the formal requirements of the constitutional order. Justice in political matters is the most ephemeral of all divisions of justice; a turn of history may undo its work. For this very reason it must work the concept of judicial authority for all its worth. Old Chancellier Pasquier, chameleon of law and politics, was successively councilor in the pre-revolutionary Paris *parlement*, Napoleon's prefect of police, Louis XVIII's minister of justice, and Louis Philippe's president of the *Chamber des Pairs*, directing all the major political trials of the latter regime. In 1850 Pasquier expostulated: "Je suis l'homme de France qui a le plus connu les diverses gouvernements qui se succèdent; je leur ai fait à tous leurs procès."[4] Did he really try them all? Or did he just verify the fact that in a specific moment of history group A had the better of group B? Whatever the case may be, the practitioners of political justice must assert not only that they certify winners, but that they select them by their intrinsic merits.

3. The Political Trial as Detour: in Quest of Justice

Having denigrated political justice, we should now state its benefits: 1) Its alternative, political arbitrariness without benefit of access to courts, is appalling; 2) As long as political justice puts the stamp of official confirmation on the results of a prior defeat, it is neither more

---

[4] Thureau-Dangin, *Histoire de la Monarchie* (cited Ch. IV, n. 14), Vol. 2, p. 300.

nor less painful than the defeat itself. On the contrary, most people, if they have to be hanged, enjoy being able to protest against it. 3) If used to produce new images rather than confirm previous political or military results, it is one of the more civilized of political games. Possibly it gives the masses a more intimate sense of participation in the world of politics than present-day parliamentary performances will allow. Its rules are intricate. Its immediate results may be quite spectacular. Its illusions are sufficiently hidden from the onlooker not to disturb his sense of drama and aesthetic enjoyment. Moreover, they do not detract from the immediate results, especially the trial's image-creating capacity.

Its illusions concern the assumptions of the whole concept of political justice—the enlarging of the radius of political action by resort to the courts. Political claims eventually stand or fall on their own strength. A political trial might bring out and focus attention on areas of weakness or strength of a political organization or a cause. Yet the authority of the trial neither adds nor detracts from the fundamental justification of such political claims, namely, the justness of the cause.

To that extent political justice is bound to remain an eternal detour, necessary and grotesque, beneficial and monstrous, but a detour all the same. It is necessary and beneficial because without the intercession of the judicial apparatus the fight for political power would continue as relentlessly, but it would be less orderly. Thus what Pascal calls the "grimaces," all the external marks of distinction by which the judges establish their title and dignity, are beneficial.

But what is beneficial is invariably grotesque and monstrous, too, because whoever metes out political justice has to assume that the cause in whose name he acts is a just one. Could he otherwise face a defendant whose action and existence are predicated on the righteousness of his cause and the future claims he is staking on this assumption? Could the judge otherwise meet him face to face, maintaining that his claims must be disallowed in the name of the continued happiness of the present generation, baptized legal certainty and security? Must not the judge equally assert that the defendant's alternative solution constitutes a danger to the highest values of society? Or would he be satisfied to tell the defendant flatly that his claims have been duly examined under the existing rules and found wanting, and that all future talk about justice is nothing but an illusion which excites his emotions by stimulating his suprarenal glands?[5] I doubt that either judge or defendant could

[5] Alf Ross, *On Law and Justice* (cited above, Ch. V, n. 25), p. 275.

play his role, whether self-styled or appointed, without continuing to assume that the justice they both invoke is more meaningful and inclusive than that. If delusion it be, it is a necessary delusion in an antagonistically organized society.

Clio in her compassion may hide from both defendant and judge what and whose titles will eventually be disproven. In the end, it might be the judge who would have to confess that he served an unworthy system; or the defendant who would have to concede how far short of its promises his cause has fallen in realization. Whose tragedy would be the greater? And may not Clio refuse a clear-cut answer, marking them both as fools whose efforts were neither necessary nor salutary for whomever they were appointed to serve? Meanwhile, may we pray for both potential brethren in error?

> Liber scriptus proferetur
> in quo totum continetur
> unde mundus judicetur
>
> Judex ergo cum censebit
> Quidquid latet, apparebit
> Nil inultum remanebit
>
> Lacrimosa dies illa
> Qua resurgit ex favilla
> Judicandus homo reus
> Huic ergo parce, Deus?[6]

[6] From Thomas of Celano, *In Commemoratione Omnium Animarum*, beginning of thirteenth century; last stanza added later.

> All books are opened
> And all judgments surveyed
> As they have been passed here beneath.
>
> When the world's judge will summon the court,
> All that has been hidden will come to the light of day.
> Nothing will remain without its due reward.
>
> Constantly tears will flow
> When the guilty rise from the ashes to the judgment throne.
> God, we beg, be kind to them.

APPENDIX A

THE ROMAN EMPIRE AND THE CHRISTIANS

Relations between the Roman Empire and the Christians from the latter part of the second century to the beginning of the fourth show how the leader-follower differentiation can be the basis of a policy of prosecutions. In conformity with Emperor Trajan's ruling, transmitted to Pliny in partial answer to a series of queries, those suspected of Christian leanings were asked to sacrifice to the gods.[1] This ceremony served as a general loyalty oath. In theory, the Roman procedure allowed a suspicion of Christian leanings, if they were not officially repudiated in the prescribed way, to be converted into a charge of treason and sacrilege, visited, at the discretion of the Roman official in charge, with various forms of the death penalty.[2] The same ruling, however, united the concern for the proprieties of official obedience with a marked reluctance to risk producing a surplus of martyrs. By establishing a policy of waiting for personally signed accusations rather than endorsing the self-initiation of official inquiries, Trajan from the outset limited the number of potential proceedings. After all, though they flouted the official style of life and its symbols and rites, the Christians at that junction of history were not intent on openly challenging the social or political system. If the official truth held no meaning for them, they did not immediately endanger the existing institutions except by their obstinacy in banding together and refusing to conform to official usage. From the viewpoint of the authorities they were obstreperous, strange, and contemptible rather than actively hostile.

Once established, the pattern was not easily cast aside. The persecutions of the third century—whether unsystematic and spotty like those of Maximinian Thrax (235), or more systematic like Valerian's topping (257) and Domitian's grand finale (302)—were directed mainly against what we would call the spiritual and social leaders.[3] On

---

[1] Pliny, *Letters* No. 97.

[2] Rudolf Sohm, *Kirchengeschichte im Grundriss*, 2nd ed.; Leipzig, 1888, p. 12. "The accused Christian was suspect of a *laesae majestatis* offense. The proceedings were conducted in such a way that he had to be found guilty of the offense in case he persevered in his Christian beliefs." Karl J. Neumann, *Der Römische Staat und die Allgemeine Kirche*, Leipzig, 1890, p. 239, emphasizes the Roman magistrate's interest in Christians' obeisance and formal reconversion to official customs rather than in their punishment and martyrdom.

[3] As Mommsen formulates it: "Where apostasy becomes a mass crime, punishment, insofar comparable to the case of rebellion, hits by preference, though not exclusively,

the other hand, Decius' attempt to turn the whole vast empire into closely regulated military barracks (250) remained an isolated instance not easily repeated. The mass of followers were visited less with mass prosecutions than with a number of legal disabilities (such as loss of the right to sue and of the capacity to make a will). A pattern was set; when the tables were turned and Christianity became the official belief system, both the members of heterodox sects and those who refused to embrace Christianity were treated the same way.[4]

APPENDIX B

GUILLAUME DU VAIR:

THE CASE OF THE SUCCESSFUL LOYALTY SHIFT

In the literature dealing with loyalty conflicts there is a volume especially valuable, because it was written by a high official at a time when he was himself deeply engaged in such a situation: Guillaume du Vair's *Traîté de la constance et consolation eux calamitéz publiques*, probably written in 1590, first published in 1594, and often reprinted during the first half of the seventeenth century.[1] Du Vair, counselor at the Paris *parlement*, used the third part of his book to explain his own attitudes and those of his brethren when in February 1589 they refused to follow the previous king's order to leave the capital, then in revolt, and transfer themselves to Tours. They remained in a Paris that was politically dominated by the Council of Sixteen, the unruly local political arm of the king's foes, the League, and militarily in the hands of the Duke of Mayenne, the League's shield in its dispute with Henry of Navarre for possession of the kingdom.

Du Vair narrated the story of the monkey who had seized a child and carried it with him to the roof. The terrified parents thought that run-

---

the leaders." *Römisches Strafrecht*, p. 577. See also E. Caspar, *Geschichte des Papsttums*, Tübingen, 1930, Vol. I, esp. p. 71. The discussion in Neumann, *op.cit.*, p. 23, criticizes the halfhearted character of the Roman policy.

[4] In contrast, medieval prosecutions of heretic sects by the church authorities, who sought more unconditional obedience, often led to the slaying of all foes regardless of their individual importance to the policy of resistance. Jean Guiraud's *Histoire de l'inquisition au moyen âge* (Paris, 1938), precisely because it is as biased toward the Catholics as Lea's classic *History of the Inquisition in the Middle Ages* is anti-Catholic, is a witness beyond suspicion. This story with the supporting documents would show a pattern of mass execution of recusants, without reference to their role either in the defense of city or fortress or in the organization of religious services. An example is the conquest of Montségur in March 1244; Guiraud, Vol. II, pp. 136-45.

---

[1] I am using the J. Flach and F. Funck-Brentano edition, Paris, 1915.

ning after the monkey or otherwise making noise might cause the monkey to drop the child; they sweated it out and by the grace of God the monkey climbed down.[2] Thinking of himself and his brethren caught between the irate city mobs, worked up by the "prédicateurs" against an officialdom suspected of not having had enough zeal for the cause of the League, and needing to justify their attitude should Henry of Navarre win out, Du Vair added: "Honest people might well behave this way, standing close to the precipice."

Yet he realized that this was not enough of a defense for an important servant of the realm. In addition to personal and family reasons—having charge of an old and helpless father, and being threatened with the loss of his possessions, which would be confiscated if he left the city—he added some considerations more fitting to his station in life: "If things have come to such a point that violence overthrows the law and brute force carries the day over justice, we never should look at our particular interest and hold it against the public interest, because whoever, for fear of some particular evil with which he is threatened, becomes the author or supporter of public calamity has no reason for excuse. One must judge with prudence whether the greater evil which we fear can not be avoided any other way; if there is no way but to give in to such pressure then only in the manner of a master of a ship threatened by a storm; he may throw overboard part of the consignment so as to save the remainder."[3] To this variant of the lesser evil theory Du Vair added a note suggesting a more active role: "Whoever by necessity or by an honest design to help his country has gotten himself into an illegitimate enterprise might try to observe closely all available possibilities so as to work gradual changes in the minds of his cocitizens in order that they will understand what is needed and will want to behave correspondingly."

These propositions serve to some extent as an outline of Du Vair's actual demeanor in the early 1590's. His organization, in whose affairs he came to play an important role, acquiesced in the *de facto* authority of the Duke of Mayenne as long as this was their only device for keeping some semblance of public order in Paris. But at least since 1592, and probably in a less active form even earlier, he worked toward recognition of Henry IV. This culminated in his exploit, admired by his contemporaries, of June 28, 1593. On that date he managed to have his colleagues put their signature to an "arrêt," prepared in advance by

[2] *Ibid.*, p. 204. Adds Du Vair's by no means unfriendly biographer: "But the history of the League shows that meanwhile the monkey had done quite some damage." Réné Radouant, *Guillaume du Vair*, 1556-1596, Paris, 1907, p. 205.

[3] *Op.cit.*, p. 207.

himself and a few others, which confirmed the argument of his previous speech in which attempts to circumvent the *lex salica* and the fundamental laws of the kingdom were declared void.[4] This maneuver involved a decisive rebuff of current plans ventilated in the Estates-General to settle the crown on a Spanish princess and a husband to be chosen by the Estates.

But that is only one side of the story. In the last years of Henry III's reign Du Vair had, if not formally joined, at least strongly favored, the king's enemy, the League. He had made funeral speeches for both the Duc de Guise and for Mary Stuart, one the murdered chief and the other a revered martyr of the League. And if he disobeyed the order of Henry III to leave the city, it was not only for the reasons he gave. It may be explained in good part both by his political attitude at the time and, probably even more, by his hope and calculations that the central role which the Paris *parlement* was likely to play in the years to come would serve him better than the weak and impecunious Valois King Henry III as a launching pad for his personal ambitions.

Neither the princes supporting the League nor Henry III or IV thought or acted in totalitarian terms; they fought for power with the weapons and methods of their time and age. What was troublesome, dangerous, and incalculable was the intrusion of the ideologically-tinged reaction of the Paris populace and their spiritual leaders in the political and military game, applying violence to both the bodies and souls of the official classes.[5] They were the "precipice" over which some of Du Vair's colleagues were shoved and lost their lives. Hence Du Vair's need to bow to the necessities of the day, but also to take a calculated risk in working for the recognition of Henry IV.

At a relatively early stage Du Vair switched to a cause that eventually won out. What gives his case more than antiquarian interest, however, is the fact that once he solved his loyalty problem in his own mind, he took risks befitting his station in life and considerably transcending counsels of prudence which he advanced in the literary defense and projection of his career.[6]

[4] Text of the arrêt in Isambert, *Récueil général des anciennes lois Françaises*, Vol. 15, p. 71. I follow the narrative of E. Mangin, *Histoire du Parlement de Paris*, Paris, 1914, Vol. 2, pp. 109-21.

[5] The best description is still Charles Labitte, *De la democratie chez les prédicateurs*, 2nd ed.; Paris, 1866.

[6] See also the recent interesting discussion by Roman Schnur, "Französische Juristen im Konfessionellen Bürgerkrieg," *Festschrift für Carl Schmitt*, Berlin, 1959, pp. 179-219. However, the attitude of the *parlement* of Paris is less a "neutralisation grossen Stils" than a constant adjustment to a rapidly shifting situation, involving some extra premium for those who have corralled the main group in the desirable direction.

INDEX

TABLE OF U.S. COURT CASES

INDEX OF NAMES

SUBJECT INDEX

TABLE OF U.S. COURT CASES

INDEX OF NAMES

SUBJECT INDEX

accommodation, between German Federal Republic and DDR in Germany, 90
Action Française, 71; in Caillaux case, 68
active resistance, 331
ad hoc legislation, dual nature of, 158
administrative action, validation by court, 116
administrative decision, 179-80
administrative fiat, discrimination by, 168
administrative procedures, relation to judicial disposal, 96-97
African National Congress, 122
agent, distinction between independent, political operator, 91
agents provocateurs, 377
Aix assizes, 252
Algerian conflict, 418
Algerian nationalists, 252-53
Algerians, in Germany, 361, 377n
Alien and Sedition Law, 137
allegiance, of masses, 7
allegiance, patriotic, 37
Allgemeines Landrecht, 270
"amalgam," 196, 196n, 200n; in Stepinac case, 99
ambiguity, in Stepinac case, 100
amnesties, 8n
American Civil Liberties Union, 249, 257n
American Federation of Labor, 199
American occupation authorities, 8n
amicus curiae, 249
amnesty, ending Ebert defamation suit, 83; grâce amnestiante, 406, 408; legislation, 411; loyalty oath, 405, 406; from political, military consolidations, 407; in totalitarian regimes, 409; types, 405-11; war crimes, 414
amnesty record, French, 416-18; German, 411-16
anarchism, 15n
anarchist group, 376n
anarchists, 238n, 382; writers, 196
Anglo-American selectivity, 189-90
antisocialist legislation of 1878, 128-29
antisubversive federal legislation in U.S., 138
arcanum imperii, 396
Armageddon, 15
Arnold, case of, 89
assistance to enemy, allegation in Caillaux case, 73
asylum, 20, 351-88; bill of rights, national, international levels, 352; codification proposals, 352; contemporary refugees, 354-55; current practices, 386; flaws, 388-89; in Europe, 364-65; international lawyers' meetings, 352; Mexico, 364, 367, 385-86n; 19th

century refugee, 354; policy in Great Britain, 360-61; principles, 383-86; supplicants, 352; Swiss policies, 362-63, 362n; violation of claims in World War II, 367
Athens, *Aeropag*, 11; ancient doctrine, 10n; assembly *Helia*, 11
attentat, 39
Australian Dissolution Act, 156
authentication, 6, 7; exercise of authority, 11

Bantu, 122
bar association, provision of counsel, 251
bill of attainder, in case of Strafford and Laud, 12
Bolshevist Party, Duma members, 237
Bolshevist Revolution, 40
Bolshevists, 400
Bonn Basic Law, 136, 142, 143, 146, 147, 154, 356; political asylum, 361
Bonn District Court, 208n
Bonnet Rouge, 69
Bourbons, of Kentucky, 54, 55
Boxheim manifesto, 200
Brest-Litovsk, German-Russian negotiations, 78
British Commonwealth, 168
British rule in India, 125
Bundestag, 413, 414, 415n

Caillaux case, 154n. *See also* Caillaux, Joseph
Cartell des Gauches, 184n, 408
"Cassation," 265
Catholic Church, 38n; in Italy, 316; in Stepinac trial, 99
Catholics, 434
Centuriate Assembly, Roman, 12
Chamber of Deputies, French, in Caillaux case, 71
charisma, 11
Charte of 1814, 312
Chartist propaganda, 34, 34n
Chartist riots, 127
Chartists, English, 9, 420
Christians, 433-34
church, 12; and heterodox beliefs, 29; jurisdiction of, 25
civil liberty organizations, viii
civilized nations, 5, 47
clemency, 20, 389-418; Anglo-American, 398; Augustinian-Jansenist concept, 391; conditional release, 398; dialectics, 404; in Goebel murder, 60; historic, 396-97; "intrinsic" cause for, 394; political prisoners, 398-400; in mass society, 398; political deals, 400-401; pressures, 401-03
coercion, 15; apparatus, 5

444

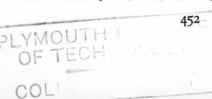